DATE DUE

NO 2 8 '94		
MY 5 '95		
JE 15 '95		
MR 8 '96		
MY 3 '96		
DE 20 '96		
FE 12 '98		
MR 21 '98		
OC 12 00		
NO 1 1 '00		
DE 7 '00		
DE 20 '00		
JE 6 02		
FE 12 '09		

DEMCO 38-296

WORLD CLASS BUSINESS

R

PHILIP MATTERA

WORLD CLASS BUSINESS

A GUIDE TO THE 100 MOST POWERFUL GLOBAL CORPORATIONS

A HENRY HOLT REFERENCE BOOK

HENRY HOLT AND COMPANY · NEW YORK

Copyright © 1992 by Philip Mattera
All rights reserved, including the right to reproduce
this book or portions thereof in any form.
A Henry Holt Reference Book
Published by Henry Holt and Company, Inc.,
115 West 18th Street, New York, New York 10011.
Published in Canada by Fitzhenry & Whiteside Limited,
91 Granton Drive, Richmond Hill, Ontario L4B 2N5.

Library of Congress Cataloging-in-Publication Data
Mattera, Philip.
World class business : a guide to the 100 most powerful global
corporations / Philip Mattera.—1st ed.
    p.   cm.—(A Henry Holt reference book)
Includes bibliographical references and index.
1. International business enterprises—Handbooks, manuals, etc.
I. Title.   II. Series
HD2755.5.M384   1992   91-45585
338.8′8′025—dc20   CIP
ISBN 0-8050-1681-3

Henry Holt Reference Books are available at special discounts
for bulk purchases for sales promotions, premiums,
fund-raising, or educational use. Special editions
or book excerpts can also be created to specification.
For details contact: Special Sales Director,
Henry Holt and Company, Inc., 115 West 18th Street,
New York, New York 10011.

First Edition—1992

Designed by Victoria Hartman

Printed in the United States of America
Recognizing the importance of preserving the written word,
Henry Holt and Company, Inc., by policy, prints all of its
first editions on acid-free paper. ∞
10 9 8 7 6 5 4 3 2 1

CONTENTS

ACKNOWLEDGMENTS

Writing *World Class Business* involved a rather overwhelming task of information gathering. To carry it out I depended on a wide range of written sources and human assistance.

I derived a great deal of data from annual reports and other company documents, which I could not have obtained without the assistance of scores of public relations and investor relations officials at the firms. While there is no room to list all of these people, I should mention a few who made special efforts on my behalf: Angelica DiSilvestri of Fiat, Arne Heinich of Hoechst, Eliane Lapeyrade of Alcatel Alsthom, and Paul Whitelaw and Janet Sparre of Hill and Knowlton (representing Daewoo).

For general information on various companies and industries I received help from the Asia Monitor Resource Center; Paul Dysenchuk of the United Nations Centre on Transnational Corporations; Sue Hagen of the Newcomen Society; Roger Kerson of the Midwest Center for Labor Research; Robert Meerwaldt and Sjef Stoop of the Dutch research center SOMO; Roger Moody of PARTiZANS; Bill Ridgers of Team Video Productions; Lenny Siegel of the Pacific Studies Center; the Transnationals Information Exchange; and the Washington Office of the International Labour Organisation.

For help in researching the sections on labor relations I am indebted to Mary McGinn of Labor Notes; Paul Garver and Joy Anne Grune of the International Union of Food and Allied Workers Associations; David Cockcroft of the International Transport Workers Federation; Aidan White of the International Federation of Journalists; the International Metalworkers Federation; Ron Blackwell of the Amalgamated Clothing and Textile Workers Union; Richard Leonard and Rod Rogers of the Oil, Chemical and Atomic Workers International Union; Raymond Scannell of the Bakery, Confectionery and Tobacco Workers International Union; Greg Villanova of the International Chemical Workers Union; Kate Pfordresher of the New York Labor Committee Against Apartheid; Julie Kushner of District 65 of the United Automobile Workers; Elaine Harger of the Empire State College Library; and Scotty McGary, retired from United Steelworkers of America.

In compiling the environmental records of companies I received invaluable assistance from Bill Walsh, Melinda Lawrence, and Kenny Bruno of Greenpeace USA; Jonathan Schorsch; Martin Gelfand; the Council on Economic Priorities; the Citizens Clearinghouse for Hazardous Wastes; Robin Zeff of the Environmental Research Foundation; and the Citizens Fund, whose report *Manufacturing Pollution: A Survey of the Nation's Toxic Polluters* was of enormous help.

Since every book builds on those that have preceded it in the field, I should also mention the works I consulted most frequently: the *International Directory of Company Histories* (St. James Press); *Everybody's Business,* 1980 edition (Harper & Row) and 1990 edition (Doubleday); *Hoover's Handbook* (Reference Press); *The Global Marketplace,* by Milton Moskowitz (Macmillan); and the Council on Economic Priorities' *The Better World Investment Guide* (Prentice Hall).

Special thanks to Dick Staron, formerly of Henry Holt, for making this project happen, to my agent Edythea Ginis Selman, and to Ken Wright, Paula Kakalecik, and Sabrina Soares of Holt. I am grateful to Ray Rogers and everyone else at CCI, who were once again patient during my book-writing interlude. Thanks also to Bob Perry for sharing his out-of-town newspapers and to my letter carriers, who cheerfully put up with the enormous volume of incoming mail generated by this project.

Deep appreciation goes to my family members (especially my father), who continue to be understanding about the demands of the writing profession. This book could not have been completed without the support of my wife Donna Demac and our young son Thomas. My debt to Donna is boundless; her encouragement, her tolerance of my endless hours at the keyboard, her editing and research help, her strength—these are what got me through this long and difficult process.

—Philip Mattera
May 6, 1992

INTRODUCTION

"The Multinational Corporation. The sun never sets on it." So began an advertisement a large commercial bank was running a few years back to promote its financial services for globetrotting companies. These days the level of internationalization is even more advanced: in 1990 *Business Week* published a cover story on "stateless corporations"—which, the article says, "are effectively making decisions with little regard to national boundaries."

The globalization of business has given a new prominence to the leading multinational companies. They, rather than governments, increasingly are the primary players in the world economy. The privatization of government-owned industries in Europe and the third world, along with the emergence of private enterprise in Eastern Europe and the former Soviet Union, makes the process all the more dramatic.

This new orientation of business is creating the need for a new approach to business information. The national focus of most existing reference materials is no longer adequate. Any compilation of information on leading corporations must follow those companies across borders. This is what *World Class Business* seeks to accomplish.

World Class Business takes as its universe the world's one hundred most important enterprises. These are the companies that are controlling the destiny of the global economy. Many of them are household names, while others exercise their power with a lower profile. *World Class Business* tries to bring to life both the well-known companies and the unfamiliar but powerful ones.

The one hundred companies were selected according to a variety of criteria. One of the most important was size. Most of the list consists of the very largest corporations in the world. The biggest firms also tend to be the most important and influential ones. In aggregate the one hundred companies have annual revenues of some $2.9 trillion and a net income of $78 billion. Together they employ more than twelve million people.

The second major consideration was the extent of a company's international activity. The ones chosen are the companies that are virtually ubiquitous around the globe. They have manufacturing operations in a variety of countries and sell their products almost everywhere. They are often in joint ventures with one another. If a firm was large but was essentially a domestic enterprise, then it was excluded. This tended to rule out, for example, public utilities and insurance companies.

There was also an attempt to present a diversified list in terms of industry and geography. This means that some firms made it onto the list by virtue of being a dominant player from a particular country or in a particular field of activity. In turn, some fairly important companies in "crowded" industries—Volvo in the auto business, for instance—got left out, even though they may be more significant generally than some companies in fields with fewer big names. The principles of diversification employed were not entirely egalitarian. Fields, such as telecommunications and electronics, that are destined to become even more crucial to the world economy were given larger "quotas."

The geographical cut also took into account the relative strength of the various nations and regions of the world. Thus the single country with the largest number of companies was, unavoidably, the United States, with forty-three. Though Japan was second, with sixteen companies, the European countries combined fielded thirty-two firms. This suggests that economic integration in that continent may make Europe an even more formidable contender than Japan for the leading position in the world economy.

Given the talk of the emergence of third world multinationals, an attempt was made to find companies in Asia, Africa, and Latin America to include on the list. Yet with the exception of South Korea, the countries in these parts of the world have simply not produced companies that are leading players in the global arena. Many of the largest companies in the third world are subsidiaries of corporations based in the wealthier countries.

A final consideration was the need to include some companies that are not yet at the top tier of international business but are clearly on their way there. These up and comers include Apple Computer and Waste Managment from the United States, and Fanuc and Kyocera from Japan.

It was not a requirement that a company be free from financial difficulties. This book was written during a recession in much of the world, and even some of the most powerful companies have been affected. Many of the companies profiled have also been experiencing intense competitive challenges that have undermined positions of dominance. In some cases companies have dealt with their troubles by selling off large parts of their operations. If this is taken too far, the company can lose its status as a major player. This is what had happened at Maxwell Communications, for example, which was originally to be included in this book but was eliminated after it began shedding some of its most important businesses and was further dismantled after the death of its founder in late 1991.

To be one of the one hundred most powerful companies in the world does not mean being invulnerable. An attempt has been made to look beyond the short- and even medium-term problems to find those companies that will be major influences on the international economy for many decades to come.

For instance, as of this writing, IBM is struggling with a variety of problems, but no one can doubt that "Big Blue" will remain an overwhelming presence in the computer industry.

The reason why there are only ninety-four chapters rather than one hundred is that the seven so-called Baby Bell telephone companies in the United States are grouped together in a single chapter. This was necessary because of their common origin and their similar development since becoming independent. But these seven firms are definitely autonomous companies.

On the other hand, there are several instances in which single chapters cover more than one firm but are counted only once. These are the Japanese *keiretsu* conglomerates and the Korean *chaebol* conglomerates.

The *keiretsu*, included under the names Mitsubishi Group and Sumitomo Group, have common histories and are closely allied enough to be analyzed together. Yet they do report separate financial results, so in theory they, too, should be counted as separate firms. The problem is that there are dozens of companies in the *keiretsu*, so it was not practical to list all of them. The Mitsubishi and Sumitomo chapters focus on the key affiliates in varying degrees of detail. Rather than pick an arbitrary number of firms, these groups were treated as single companies for numerical purposes. A similar approach was taken with the South Korean *chaebol* conglomerates. The companies in these groups (Daewoo, Hyundai, Lucky-Goldstar, and Samsung) are more closely tied to one another than those in the Japanese groups, yet only Daewoo discloses full consolidated results for the group.

The profiles have been written with the general reader in mind. Unnecessary business jargon and detailed financial analysis have been avoided. The aim is to provide an overall understanding of each company's background, its main areas of operation, its current competitive position, and its labor and environmental records, while also providing some basic information on each firm.

Profiles of several thousand words cannot provide an exhaustive account of the history and current activities of companies as complex as the ones included in *World Class Business*. The following pages do, however, seek to present, for each company, the major developments of the past and the key realities of the present. Reading these profiles will put into context the endless flow of information being presented by the business media about these companies and their competitors.

The profiles have been written with emphasis on the events that have shaped the structure of these companies, especially the major mergers and acquisitions. As for recent developments, there are two aspects that receive special attention.

The first is the dramatic trend among major companies to form a variety of joint ventures, technology-sharing agreements, marketing pacts, research consortia, and all other manner of alliances. Despite all the talk of the triumph of free enterprise and competition, modern capitalism increasingly takes the form of cooperation between ostensibly rival enterprises. Whether this represents a retreat from risk taking or simply the old practice of hedging one's bets, it is a key component of how business is done today. *World Class Business* takes pains to identify these alliances and put them in the context of a company's other activities.

The second major trend is the move by U.S. and European companies to invest in Eastern Europe and, to a lesser extent, the former Soviet Union. The collapse of the state-controlled economies in these countries has been dramatic, and the new governing groups have embarked on a rapid transition to private ownership. In many cases this means foreign investment. *World Class Business* pays close attention to these developments and seeks to provide a thorough account of the activities of the one hundred companies in this new gold rush.

World Class Business also addresses what has become one of the hottest issues with regard to corporate social responsibility: the environment. Over the past few years companies in the United States—and increasingly in other countries—have jumped on the environmental bandwagon. Manufacturers are hastening to alter their products and their packaging to meet "green" criteria.

World Class Business seeks to view these current reforms in the larger context of a company's environmental record. Drawing on information from a wide range of sources, the book outlines both past problems and, where significant, the remedial measures being employed. It is only with such information that one can decide whether a company's expressions of environmental concern represent real progress or merely hucksterism.

Overall *World Class Business* attempts to outline all of the essential information one needs to know in beginning to understand the companies that are shaping contemporary global commerce. The author hopes that readers will find the book both a useful resource and compelling reading.

A GUIDE TO
WORLD CLASS BUSINESS

World Class Business is a road map for the vast network of operations that make up the most powerful corporations on Earth. This section provides a guide to using that map by describing what is included in each section of the company profiles.

BASIC DATA

Each profile begins with basic information on the company or group of companies being examined. This includes the formal name of the company and the address and main telephone number of its headquarters. Next are figures in U.S. dollars for the revenues and net income in the company's most recent fiscal year (available as of early May 1992); when the fiscal year does not coincide with the calendar year, the ending day of the fiscal year is indicated. For financial institutions, figures for total assets are also included.

The data are, in all but a handful of cases (which are noted), consolidated numbers taken from annual reports and other official company documents, especially the 10-K reports filed by U.S. public companies and the 20-F reports that foreign corporations whose securities trade in the United States are required to provide to the U.S. Securities and Exchange Commission.

Revenue figures for oil and alcoholic beverage companies are given net of excise taxes. The term *revenues* is used to cover what some firms call sales, net sales, or turnover.

Next is an indication of whether the company's shares trade on stock exchanges or whether the firm is privately held or government owned. A company is considered publicly traded even if only a portion of its shares are traded.

This is followed by a figure for the company's total number of employees, according to the companies' annual reports. Sometimes the numbers are as of the end of the fiscal year and sometimes they are averages for the year. Most companies do not indicate whether the numbers include both full- and part-time workers or full timers alone.

The final piece of basic information is the year of founding. The dates given refer to the founding (not necessarily the incorporation) of the company itself or, if there have been major mergers, of a significant portion or direct descendant of the company.

The information in these items forms the basis of the rankings and lists provided in the appendixes.

OVERVIEW

A short overview provides a quick account of what the company does, how it developed, its current reputation, and its future prospects.

HISTORY

A lengthier section provides a relatively detailed description of the origins of the company, with emphasis on the conditions of its founding and the emergence of its major lines of business. The subsequent historical account focuses on mergers, new products, triumphs, failures, and the evolution of the company's competitive position. The story is brought right up to the present. For recent years there is special emphasis on describing the company's strategic alliances and its expansion into new markets, such as Eastern Europe.

OPERATIONS

A description of the company's major business activities is then provided. The operations are divided up according to the way the company itself reports its business segments, and for each segment there is a figure on its share of the company's total revenues in the most recent fiscal year. The descriptions include lists of products and services and indicate well-known brand names.

TOP EXECUTIVES

Included in this segment are the names and titles of the leading members of the company's management team. The names are listed in rough hierarchical order, beginning with the most powerful executives. The number of executives listed varies from company to company, but in each case an attempt was made to pick out the core group among the highest-ranking corporate officers.

OUTSIDE DIRECTORS

Outside directors are then listed. These are the members of the company's board of directors who are not "insiders"—that is, those who are not full-time executives of the company. In some countries these are known as non-executive directors; in others, such as Japan, many companies do not have such directors, so no names are listed for those firms.

Also included are the primary affiliations of these directors outside the company being profiled. In most cases this information is provided by the company's annual report or proxy statement. In some countries, such as Switzerland, that information is not divulged. In those cases the author made an attempt to identify the affiliations from other sources.

FINANCIAL DATA

A section on financial data provides basic information on the company in its primary currency. Data on revenues, net income, and, in the case of financial institutions, total assets are given. In most cases there are five years' worth of information, but in some instances fewer years are given because a merger or a major change in accounting procedures makes earlier years impossible to compare. Where the fiscal year is not identical to the calendar year, the ending date is given.

GEOGRAPHICAL BREAKDOWN

To give an idea of the range of a company's global activities, a geographical breakdown indicating revenues and income by major portions of the world is provided. The extent and form of the data depend on the information divulged by the company in its financial reports. Some companies give geographical information only on revenues (or net sales or turnover), some also provide such data on net income, others do it on the basis of operating income, and some provide no breakdown at all.

There are also variations on the way in which the world is divided up. Some companies simply separate domestic and foreign results, while others give more detailed breakdowns. Where the number of areas reported by a company was more than three, they have been combined into larger groupings. The breakdowns are given apart from adjustments and eliminations.

LABOR RELATIONS

The main focus in the segments on labor relations is on how the company has dealt with organized labor, though occasionally there are comments on general personnel policies. The accounts vary considerably in length according to the extent to which the company has had to deal with trade unions. Where there is extensive history in this area, the account begins with the advent of collective bargaining at the company and then looks at the general tenor of labor relations by recounting the evolution of contract negotiations and the existence of any major strikes or other confrontations.

In some countries, such as Germany, Sweden, and Japan, labor relations are highly formalized and almost ritualized, so there is often little to say about negotiations or strikes, which may be largely nonexistent. For companies based in these countries, as well as for the other firms, accounts are also given of any major labor problems in their foreign operations.

ENVIRONMENTAL RECORD

Major issues relating to the impact of the company's operations on the physical environment are then examined. Because of the absence of systematic environmental reporting practices, the information in this section—drawn from many diverse and specialized sources—tends to focus on scandals and controversies regarding the company's practices. Where appropriate and available, information also is given on the positive steps companies have taken to lessen the detrimental environmental impact of their activities.

Environmental information has not been included for a number of service companies—such as banks, telecommunications carriers, and information providers—whose products are abstract or intangible and thus have little direct impact on the physical world.

In some cases this section is called "Environmental and Health Record" or "Environmental and Safety Record." These designations are used where the environmental record of the company is closely tied to its direct impact on people (as in the case of a drug maker) or to the safety of its product (such as an auto manufacturer).

Many of the sections on the environment refer to data from the U.S. Environmental Protection Agency (EPA). These come from the Toxic Release Inventory (TRI), a remarkable source of information on the extent to which companies release hazardous substances into the environment. The TRI was created by the Emergency Planning and Community Right-to-Know Act of 1986, which requires all manufacturers in the United States to file annual reports (form R) with the EPA estimating the volume of the toxic releases of each of their facilities that meet certain threshold criteria.

The reporting covers releases of some three hundred substances into the air, waterways, or the ground. Although the TRI shows rather startling levels of toxic emissions, many critics have charged that it understates the problem because of the many substances it does not cover.

BIBLIOGRAPHY

The bibliography at the end of each chapter is limited to books and major reports, since the inclusion of articles would have taken up too much space. The works listed, which are largely limited to those in English, are ones that deal exclusively with the company, a major figure in its history, or the primary industry in which the company operates. For the most part, the works listed are ones consulted by the author, though some that were not available to the author are included in the interest of completeness.

WORLD CLASS BUSINESS

ABB ASEA BROWN BOVERI, LTD.

P.O. Box 8131
CH-8050 Zurich
Switzerland
(1) 317 71 11

1991 revenues: $28.9 billion
1991 net income: $609 million
Publicly traded company (ASEA and Brown Boveri shares are
    traded separately)
Employees: 214,399
Founded: 1988 (ASEA was founded in 1883, Brown Boveri in
    1891)

OVERVIEW

ABB ASEA Brown Boveri is in effect a permanent joint venture between
Sweden's ASEA and Switzerland's Brown Boveri, both leaders in the electrical equipment industry. A result of a 1988 marriage that was the largest
cross-border merger ever to occur in Europe, ABB has taken a collection of
old-line industrial operations and turned them into one of the world's most
dynamic companies.

ABB fancies itself a new breed of corporation. It flaunts cosmopolitanism
by conducting all of its activities in English and doing its accounting in dollars.
Although encompassing some thirteen hundred companies around the world,
ABB calls itself a "multidomestic" enterprise, encouraging each of its subsidiaries to act like native companies in their home countries.

The success of ABB has been based in part on its breathtaking acquisitions
spree in the late 1980s, which in the United States included the purchase of
Combustion Engineering and major Westinghouse electrical equipment operations. The company has plunged into new areas as well, most notably

robotics, a field it now leads in Europe. It also has developed some of the most extensive operations of any Western company in Eastern Europe.

HISTORY

The ASEA portion of the company dates back to 1883, when Elektriska AB was formed in Stockholm to produce dynamos based on the innovative designs of the young engineer Jonas Wenstrom. The company was a success, and after several years its founder, Ludwig Fredholm, expanded operations by merging with a company run by Wenstrom's brother Goran.

The combined firm, Allmänna Sevensak Elektriska AB, or ASEA, was established in 1890 to manufacture a variety of electrical generating and transmission equipment. ASEA, with Goran Wenstrom serving as president after the death of Fredholm, was a pioneer in the electrification of industry. The company's installation of electric power at a rolling mill in the Swedish town of Hofors resulted in what has been called the world's first electric industrial facility.

In the late 1890s the leading Swedish industrialist Gustaf de Laval took over the company after buying a 50-percent interest. Laval mismanaged the firm, prompting a move by the management of ASEA, aided by Enskilda Banken, to regain control. J. Sigfrid Edstrom, the former manager of the Gothenburg Tramways Company, was installed as president. Under his direction ASEA recovered and expanded its operations to England, Spain, Denmark, Finland, and Russia.

ASEA was hit hard by the closing of markets during World War I and by the Swedish postwar recession. Yet Edstrom's prudential financial policies allowed the company to survive. By the late 1920s the picture was improving, with ASEA providing the first electric locomotives for the Stockholm-Göteborg railroad line. During the 1930s the company entered into a market-sharing arrangement with its rival, L. M. Ericsson, enabling ASEA to diversify and expand more easily. It purchased a Swedish company specializing in airfreight-handling technology and a Polish firm that made electric motors.

Although Sweden once again remained neutral in World War II, ASEA suffered from the curtailment of its operations in many parts of Europe. After the war the company enjoyed a rapidly rising demand for its products but faced material shortages and labor unrest. In 1947 ASEA first entered the U.S. market through a licensing agreement that permitted Ohio Brass Company to produce surge arrestors.

During the 1950s the company supplied equipment for numerous major electric generating and transmission facilities, including the Tennessee Valley Authority in the United States. At home the company built new high-voltage transmission systems to carry power from hydroelectric facilities in the north to the population centers in the south of Sweden. It also claims to have produced the world's first synthetic diamonds. At the same time, ASEA maintained its dominance in the Swedish market for electric locomotives.

By the 1960s ASEA had made the move into electronics and was chosen

ABB • *3*

to build Sweden's first full-scale nuclear power station, though a national referendum later called for the phasing out of nuclear power in the country. In the mid-1960s ASEA purchased a major stake in the Swedish appliance giant Electrolux, which, like ASEA, was controlled by the Wallenberg family.

Like many other makers of electrical equipment, ASEA stagnated during the 1970s. Under the direction of Percy Barnevik, who took over as managing director in 1980, the company gained new life by moving into high-tech electronics and such growing fields as robotics. Barnevik, who cut costs and jobs ruthlessly, also moved to exploit the growing interest in pollution-control equipment. To improve ASEA's (and later ABB's) position in electrical equipment, Barnevik has bought up dozens of state-owned or -subsidized companies in power and related industries throughout Europe.

The company's new, dynamic image was tarnished in 1985 when a former executive was charged with illegally diverting sophisticated U.S. computers to the Soviet Union. ASEA ended up paying a fine of $440,000 to the U.S. government.

BBC Brown Boveri was founded in Switzerland in 1891 Charles Brown and Walter Boveri to produce electrical components. Like ASEA, it became involved in equipment for electric railways and power generation. Through a 1919 licensing agreement with the English firm Vickers, the company's products spread throughout the British Empire and Europe. The Vickers arrangement expired in 1927, but by that time Brown Boveri had successful operating subsidiaries in Italy, Germany, Austria, and several other countries. In fact, some of these subsidiaries, which tended to operate with a great deal of autonomy, grew larger than the parent company.

While this state of affairs sometimes caused logistical problems, Brown Boveri prospered after World War II, especially in the construction of nuclear power plants and electrification projects in the third world. The company went through various restructurings in the 1970s and 1980s and was frustrated in its attempts to gain a greater presence in the United States.

In 1987 Brown Boveri and ASEA announced plans to overcome their individual problems by pooling most—but not all—assets and forming a new company called ABB ASEA Brown Boveri. The joint venture, which took effect at the beginning of 1988, immediately became number one in the power equipment business—ahead of Siemens, Hitachi, and General Electric. ASEA's strong position in Scandinavia and northern Europe complemented Brown Boveri's position in Austria, Italy, and Switzerland. The arrangement allowed the two companies to cut costs by combining such activities as research and development. In stock market terms the two companies remained separate, with each firm's shares continuing to trade on their own.

The new company formed a joint venture in 1989 with Westinghouse, providing the North American foothold that Brown Boveri had been seeking. Before long, ABB exercised its option to buy out Westinghouse's share in the venture and thus ended up with the American company's electrical distribution and transmission operation. (At the insistence of U.S. antitrust regulators, the power generation part of the business had been excluded from the original deal.)

Also in 1989, ABB formed a joint venture with Italy's state-owned Finmeccanica and signed a five-year marketing agreement by which Matsushita Electric Industrial was to sell ABB's robots in the Japanese market.

Even more dramatic was ABB's decision later that same year to spend $1.6 billion to acquire the U.S. company Combustion Engineering. This propelled ABB into a variety of U.S. power-related fields, including nuclear reactors and municipal incinerators.

Barnevik's whirlwind activities continued in 1990, when he purchased the robotics business of Cincinnati Milacron, the last major American maker of heavy robots. ABB also began moving into Eastern Europe, by taking a majority position in the Polish turbine maker Zamech and forming an alliance with Bergmann-Borsig, a leading electrical equipment supplier in eastern Germany. In 1991 ABB arranged to take over AAC, another electrical manufacturing firm in what used to be the German Democratic Republic.

ASEA announced in 1991 that for stock market purposes it would divide into two companies. One company, which was to continue trading under the ASEA name, would consist of ASEA's 50-percent share of ABB as well as its shares in the shipping company Brostrom. The other, given the name Nybroviken, was to consist of ASEA's Swedish industrial operations that were not merged with Brown Boveri, along with investments such as the 49-percent interest in Electrolux. At the same time, Barnevik indicated that ABB would end its shopping spree and focus on consolidation.

OPERATIONS

Power Plants (17 percent of 1991 revenues). This segment consists of various kinds of power generation systems supplied to utilities and industrial customers. These include plants based on steam, gas, oil, coal (pressurized fluidized bed combustion), and nuclear reactors. Among the recent major contracts are a combined-cycle plant ordered by National Power, the largest utility in the United Kingdom; two gas-fired combined-cycle plants ordered by Korea Electric Power; and an order for a combined-cycle plant for the smelter operations of Aluminum Company Bahrain.

The reach of ABB's power generation business has been expanded by the acquisition of Combustion Engineering and by recently formed joint ventures in Poland, Hungary, and Yugoslavia.

Power Transmission (17 percent of revenues). ABB produces a complete range of transmission equipment, including cables, capacitors, and transformers. In 1990 the company received contracts for a new undersea cable link between Sweden and Denmark and for equipment to protect the transmission system along the Pacific coast in the United States.

ABB · 5

Power Distribution (10 percent of revenues). ABB produces various kinds of low- and medium-voltage systems for local delivery of electricity to users. Now the leader in this field in northern Europe, the company is looking for significant growth in Eastern Europe (based in part on a joint venture that has been formed in Czechoslovakia) and the Far East.

Industry (13 percent of revenues). This varied segment consists of motors and drives for industrial systems, automation systems, electrical and control products for oil and gas drilling, industrial instruments, metallurgical systems, and semiconductors (high-powered discrete devices).

Transportation (6 percent of revenues). ABB is a leading supplier of railway cars, mass transit vehicles, and other transport products. The company is especially strong in electric locomotives, seventy-five of which were ordered by the Swiss Federal Railways in 1990. ABB supplies high-speed trains that run on conventional tracks. The X2000 system, put into operation on the Stockholm-Göteborg line in 1990, cut travel time between the two cities by nearly 25 percent.

Environmental Control (12 percent of revenues). ABB was one of the first companies to recognize the market opportunities in the growing concern about the environment. Its ABB Fläkt subsidiary produces equipment for air pollution control, waste-water treatment, and resource recovery. In 1990 it received a contract to provide a ventilation system for the rail transportation component of the tunnel being built under the English Channel. The segment also includes indoor climate systems for industrial, commercial, and public facilities as well as process equipment for various industries.

Financial Services (3 percent of revenues). This segment consists mainly of systems that manage ABB's financial transactions and provide asset-based financing to customers.

Miscellaneous Activities (23 percent of revenues). This rather large catch-all segment includes general contracting on power plant construction, railway electrification, and other projects; superchargers for diesel engines; broadcasting equipment; telecommunications equipment; heating systems; and robotics. The most highly publicized part of this segment has been robotics, especially after the acquisition of Cincinnati Milacron. Thanks in large part to ASEA and ABB's efforts, Sweden is now the most automated country in Europe. In 1991 ABB introduced a new robot called the IRB 6000, which the company claims opened up "a new dimension of flexible cost-efficient automation."

TOP EXECUTIVES

- David de Pury, cochairman
- Peter Wallenberg, cochairman

- Percy Barnevik, president and chief executive
- Thomas Gasser, deputy chief executive

OUTSIDE DIRECTORS

- Donald H. Rumsfeld, chief executive of General Instrument
- Stephan Schmidheiny, chairman of Leica
- Bjørn Svedberg, chairman of Ericsson
- Gaston Thorn, former president of the European Commission
- Heinrich Weiss, president of the Federation of German Industries

FINANCIAL DATA

Revenues (in millions of U.S. dollars)

1991	28,883
1990	26,688
1989	20,560

Net Income (in millions of U.S. dollars)

1991	609
1990	590
1989	589

GEOGRAPHICAL BREAKDOWN

Revenues (in millions of dollars)

Year	Western Europe		North America		Elsewhere	
1991	17,340	(60%)	5,265	(18%)	6,278	(22%)
1990	15,231	(57%)	5,483	(21%)	5,974	(22%)
1989	12,942	(63%)	3,273	(16%)	4,345	(21%)

LABOR RELATIONS

Barnevik's ruthless cost cutting and layoffs at ASEA and at ABB have made him a bête noire of unions. ABB was one of several dozen companies hit by a three-week strike of Swedish white-collar and technical workers in 1988.

In 1990 ABB launched a program to encourage its workers to become shareholders. The plan involves employee purchase of special bonds that give the holders warrants to buy shares in ASEA and Brown Boveri.

ABB · 7

ENVIRONMENTAL RECORD

In its annual report ABB calls itself "a clean technology company." The company is indeed involved in hydroelectric power, but it also produces generating plants that use fossil fuels and nuclear reactors.

In 1991 an ABB subsidiary in the United States was fined in $197,230 by the Environmental Protection Agency for violating regulations relating to the shipment of waste acid.

BIBLIOGRAPHY

ASEA Brown Boveri: Anatomy of a Merger. Geneva: International Metalworkers Federation, 1988.

ALCATEL ALSTHOM

54, rue La Boétie
75008 Paris
France
(1) 40-76-1010

1991 revenues: $30.9 billion
1991 net income: $1.2 billion
Publicly traded company
Employees: 205,500
Founded: 1898

OVERVIEW

Alcatel Alsthom is the name chosen in 1991 by one of France's largest industrial firms to replace the rather generic Compagnie Générale d'Électricité appellation it had for the previous nine decades. The change, which followed by several years the privatization of the company, puts emphasis on its two major subsidiaries. Alcatel N.V., built with the former overseas telecommunications equipment business of the U.S. company ITT, is the second-largest player in that field. The Alsthom name reflects the electrical and transportation equipment operations now residing in a joint venture (GEC-Alsthom) with Britain's General Electric Company.

Alcatel Alsthom is keenly aware of the need for cooperation in order to survive the rigors of the largely mature industrial markets in which it operates. Toward this end it formed a wide-ranging alliance with Italy's Fiat in 1990, an arrangement that already has resulted in mergers of various operations of the two companies.

HISTORY

Alcatel Alsthom's roots go back to 1898, when a power generating company controlled by Pierre Azaria merged with several electrical equipment firms. Compagnie Générale d'Électricité (CGE) initially served as a holding company for electric utilities and other electrical manufacturers, such as Société Française des Cables Electriques Bertrand-Borel, that were acquired.

CGE was initially capitalized with private money, but it soon began to receive financial support from the French government and thus began to experience some of the same political pressures faced by a government-owned operation. In the 1920s it formed a light bulb company called Compagnie des Lampes, a joint venture with Thomson, France's other major electrical equipment maker.

In the 1930s CGE purchased construction and civil engineering companies while adding batteries to its electrical line. As war became imminent, the French government nationalized CGE as part of an attempt to mobilize resources to defend the country against a Nazi onslaught. That proved unsuccessful, and during the German occupation CGE was run by Nazi functionaries. Consequently, the company's factories and generating facilities were frequent targets for Allied bombs.

After the war CGE returned to private control and played a key role in the redevelopment of the French economy, expanding into such fields as home appliances, telephone equipment, electronics, and military products. The company ended up with more than two hundred subsidiaries and a fair amount of bureaucratic inertia.

During the 1960s the company went through an internal restructuring, forming half a dozen major business groups, including power generation, engineering, telecommunications, cable and wire, raw materials, and other products. CGE also got pulled into a restructuring of the French electrical equipment industry by the government. As a result of that plan, the Alsthom subsidiary of Thomson was joined to CGE. Alsthom manufactured power generation equipment and built power plants. In 1976 Alsthom merged with the shipbuilder Chantiers de l'Atlantique.

CGE, meanwhile, experienced additional reorganizations and other interference from the state. After the Mitterand government assumed power, this process was taken a step further: in 1982 CGE was nationalized once again, though many of its nonconsolidated subsidiaries remained in private hands. The company went on to expand its foreign activities while acquiring the electrical equipment operations of Sprecher & Schuh and the railroad equipment business of Jeumont-Schneide. In 1983 the telecommunications operations of Thomson were transferred to CGE.

The most important development in CGE's modern history came in 1986, when CGE paid $1.1 billion to purchase a majority share in the foreign telephone equipment operations of the U.S. company ITT. Its operations— which included the trouble-ridden System 12 digital switch ITT had spent some $1 billion to develop—were combined with those of CGE to form Alcatel N.V., a company registered in Holland with headquarters in Brussels. Its ownership consisted of a 55.6-percent share for CGE, 37 percent for ITT, and the rest held by the Belgian company Société Générale and the French bank Crédit Lyonnais. (CGE later took over those smaller interests and in 1992 bought out ITT's share.)

From its birth Alcatel N.V. was the second-largest telecommunications equipment company in the world, behind AT&T and its Western Electric subsidiary. The ITT operations put into Alcatel were, in fact, ones that originally were built by AT&T early in this century and then sold under government pressure to ITT (then International Telephone & Telegraph) in 1925.

By the mid-1980s, with the conservative Jacques Chirac in the prime minister's job, nationalization was out of fashion in France. So in 1987 CGE was returned to private-sector control in one of the largest stock offerings in French history. The spearhead of CGE's strategy as a privatized company was Alcatel N.V., which chief executive Pierre Suard set out to make a fully Europeanized operation. At the same time, Suard used his new freedom from government mandates to drop unsuccessful operations in areas like televisions and personal computers. He also joined with Britain's General Electric Company in 1989 to form the GEC-Alsthom power and transportation systems company.

CGE agreed in 1990 to sell a 6-percent stake in itself to Fiat and formed a strategic alliance with the Italian company. The agreement involved coordination of manufacturing operations through a series of mergers and other cooperative endeavors. Those mergers were to involve such fields as auto parts, railroad equipment, and telecommunications systems. For example, Fiat took over CGE's auto battery business, while CGE gained control of Fiat's Telettra subsidiary. The overall CGE-Fiat deal caused some concern in the European Commission, which, using its recently adopted powers to review cross-border business alliances, set certain conditions on the transactions between the two companies.

In 1991 the French firm—which as of the beginning of the year changed its name to Alcatel Alsthom—overhauled its complex financial structure by absorbing three of its subsidiaries: Générale Occidentale, the former holding company of raider Sir James Goldsmith; Saft, an industrial battery producer; and Locatel, a television rental company.

Meanwhile, Alcatel N.V. is moving ahead with its ambitious goals. Alcatel Alsthom's deal with Fiat gave it greater access to southern Europe, and in 1991 it gained an important foothold in the U.S. market by purchasing the transmission equipment division of Rockwell International. The move put it in second place in the U.S. transmission equipment market with a share of 15 percent, though this was far less than the 58 percent held by market leader AT&T. In 1991 Alcatel N.V. also agreed to purchase the cable business of Daimler-Benz subsidiary AEG.

OPERATIONS

Network Systems (25 percent of 1990 revenues). Through Alcatel N.V., Alcatel Alsthom is now one of the leading producers of sophisticated switching equipment for telephone companies. Its E10 and System 12 products are used around the world; by the end of 1990 they were handling a total of 47 million phone lines. The company is making a special effort to participate in the modernization of the telecommunications infrastructure in Eastern Europe and China. Alcatel is also the largest European supplier of line transmission systems.

Radio Communications, Space, and Defense (6 percent of revenues). Alcatel makes radiotelephone systems for public and private networks, ground-to-air telephone links, truck localization and messaging systems, microwave transmitters, and satellite earth stations. The company has formed alliances with France's Aérospatiale, Italy's Alenia, and Loral of the United States for the construction of satellites.

Business Systems (10 percent of revenues). This segment consists of private branch exchange (PBX) systems for companies and other institutions, digital terminals, and associated data networks. Alcatel ranks first in the European PBX market. Also included here are such consumer products as telephone handsets, cellular phones, and facsimile machines.

Cables (18 percent of revenues). Alcatel Alsthom is the world's leading producer of electrical and telecommunications cables. The business is operated by Alcatel Câble along with the cable divisions of other European units, such as Alcatel STK and Alcatel Standard Electrica. Recent projects include an underground power distribution network in Qatar, underwater telephone links between Australia and New Zealand, and a fiber-optic cable transmission system for the 1992 Winter Olympics in the French Alps. In 1991 Alcatel N.V. agreed to purchase a majority interest in the cable business of the AEG subsidiary of Daimler-Benz.

Other Communications Products (6 percent of revenues). Included here are railway signaling systems, vacuum technologies, and various other engineering and network installation activities.

Energy and Transportation (15 percent of revenues). This segment consists of GEC-Alsthom, the joint venture operated with General Electric Company of Britain. Among the wide range of products of this company, which is 47-percent owned by Alcatel Alsthom, are power plants, turbines, boilers, incinerators, power transmission equipment, locomotives, high-speed trains, subway and streetcar systems, factory automation equipment, industrial cooling systems, tankers, container ships, and other marine equipment. Recent power plant projects, for example, have been undertaken in China, Thailand, South Korea, India, Mexico, and Morocco. Perhaps the most famous products of this segment are the TGV high-speed trains used in France. The company has been asked by officials in Texas to plan a two-hundred-mile-per-hour rail system linking major cities in the state.

Electrical Engineering (10 percent of revenues). This segment includes the activities of the subsidiary Cegelec in such fields as control systems for power plants, power transmission equipment, and equipment for heating, ventilation, and air-conditioning systems.

Batteries (4 percent of revenues). Alcatel Alsthom is a leading producer of heavy-duty batteries for transportation, telecommunications, and general industrial applications; automobile batteries; portable batteries for use in home appliances, cellular telephones, laptop computers, and other consumer products; advanced-technology thermal and lithium-cell batteries; and emergency lighting systems.

Other Activities (7 percent of revenues). Included here are the operations of Générale Occidentale, including the Groupe de la Cité book publishing company and *L'Express* magazine; Framatome, a builder of nuclear power plants; Sogelerg, which provides engineering consulting services in such areas as energy, transportation, hydraulics, and urban planning; and Locatel, which rents television sets and provides pay-TV systems for hotels and hospitals.

TOP EXECUTIVES

- Pierre Suard, chairman and chief executive
- François de Laage de Meux, president and chief operating officer
- Philippe Dargenton, executive vice president
- André Wettstein, executive vice president and chief financial officer
- Bernard Pierre, executive vice president ·

OUTSIDE DIRECTORS

- Rand Araskog, chief executive of ITT
- Guy Dejouany, chief executive of Compagnie Générale des Eaux
- Frank M. Drendel, chairman of COMM/SCOPE Inc.
- René Lamy, honorary governor of Société Générale de Belgique
- Jean-Paul Parayre, vice chairman of Lyonnaise des Eaux-Dumez
- Jean Peyrelevade, chief executive of Union des Assurances de Paris
- Cesare Romiti, managing director of Fiat
- Ambroise Roux, chairman of the Association of French Private Companies
- Guy Verdeil, chief executive of Athéna
- Marc Vienot, chief executive of Société Générale

FINANCIAL DATA

Revenues *(in millions of French francs)*

1991	160,100
1990	144,053
1989	143,897
1988	127,958
1987	127,461
1986	80,903

Net Income *(in millions of French francs)*

1991	6,180
1990	5,035
1989	3,904
1988	2,158
1987	1,832
1986	1,159

GEOGRAPHICAL BREAKDOWN

Revenues (in millions of French francs)

Year	France		Rest of Europe		Elsewhere	
1990	70,040	(49%)	61,980	(43%)	12,033	(8%)
1989	74,706	(52%)	55,386	(38%)	13,805	(10%)

LABOR RELATIONS

Alcatel Alsthom's heavily unionized work force has become increasingly restless in recent years, as the company has eliminated jobs. In early 1992 for instance, there were strikes at facilities in Laval and in Brussels. Four years earlier there was a five-week walkout at the company's shipbuilding subsidiary, Chantiers de L'Atlantique.

AMERICAN TELEPHONE AND TELEGRAPH COMPANY

550 Madison Avenue
New York, N.Y. 10022
(212) 605-5500

1991 revenues: $63.1 billion
1991 net income: $522 million
Publicly traded company
Employees: 317,100
Founded: 1877

OVERVIEW

Until it was divested of its local phone companies in 1984, the American Telephone and Telegraph Company (AT&T) was the owner of nearly all of the telephone business in the United States. Since the breakup it has concentrated on learning how to operate in competitive markets. This has required restructuring the remaining corporate divisions, trimming its massive bureaucracy, and, most important, exploring new unregulated businesses.

Nearly a decade into its postdivestiture reality, AT&T is finally beginning to have some serious success in the global arena. Returning to international equipment markets, the company has won some major contracts on its own (in Indonesia and Kazakhstan, for example) and has formed manufacturing joint ventures in such countries as Italy, South Korea, and Thailand.

In the provision of telephone service overseas, Ma Bell has helped U.S. companies in Europe evade the high costs imposed by the state telecommunications monopolies in those countries. AT&T also is seeking to expand foreign calls from the United States by spending heavily on new transoceanic fiber-optic cables.

Although AT&T's UNIX computer operating system has become increasingly popular, Ma Bell had little success during the 1980s as a hardware producer, even in partnership with Olivetti. In 1991 the company gave itself a major new opportunity in the computer business by winning a $7.5 billion takeover crusade for NCR Corporation. AT&T also has sought to improve its semiconductor operations by forming alliances with Japanese companies like NEC and Mitsubishi Electric.

HISTORY

After the Civil War, various researchers began exploring the possibility of transmitting voices in the same way that the telegraph conveyed electric currents. One of the most successful of these inventors was a speech therapist named Alexander Graham Bell. Assisted by Thomas Watson (no relation to the IBM Watson), Bell hit on a promising technique in 1876, and one of his wealthy backers rushed a description of it to the U.S. Patent Office on February 14.

Later that day, rival inventor Elisha Gray of Chicago, hoping to be first, filed a notice with the Patent Office that he was working on a speaking telephone. Those few hours, and some notes scribbled in the margin of Bell's application, would prove to be decisive. The truth was that neither Bell nor Gray had actually succeeded in transmitting a human voice. That came on March 10, when Bell succeeded in sending the message "Mr. Watson, come here; I want you." However, Bell's filing was first. Equally important, even though it did not mention the telephone, it did mention the crucial element— the variable-resistance transmitter—that made voice transmission possible.

Early on there was considerable skepticism about the practical applications of the new device, and when one of Bell's backers offered all rights to the telephone to the president of Western Union for $100,000, he was turned down. Yet once the Bell Telephone Company initiated commercial service, in 1877, attitudes changed. Western Union, realizing that it had missed a big opportunity, made a deal with Elisha Gray and formed the American Speaking Telephone Company. A promising young inventor named Thomas Edison was commissioned to build an improved transmitting device. With this Western Union (the first truly national corporation) plunged into developing its own nationwide telephone business.

Led by Theodore Vail, a former telegraph operator, the Bell Company launched a legal counterattack, accusing Western Union of patent violation. The telegraph company was limited in its ability to fight AT&T's charges, since it was the target of a takeover effort by financier Jay Gould. In 1879 it consented to a settlement in which Western Union agreed to get out of the telephone business entirely, in exchange for 20 percent of Bell Company's phone rental receipts over the seventeen years of its patents.

After this the Bell Company secured its legal rights through hundreds of other patent suits. However, Bell had difficulty financing the expansion of the system and resorted to licensing others to build telephone operations in various places. In 1899 the company's headquarters were moved from Boston to New York and the name American Telephone and Telegraph was adopted.

As the twentieth century began, AT&T had a monopoly on long-distance service and equipment manufacturing. In 1881 the company purchased a controlling interest in (later expanded to full ownership of) the Western Electric Company and made it the system's sole supplier.

But it was not long before the Bell monolith began to encounter resistance and new sources of competition. Public discontent over Bell's rates (fifteen cents a call) escalated and states began considering regulation of the business. In the 1890s, as Bell's original patents began to expire, hundreds of independent phone companies were established.

In 1907 AT&T was the target of a takeover battle that ended with victory for a group of bankers led by J. P. Morgan. Theodore Vail, who had left the company in 1887, returned to rebuild the sagging monopoly. He regarded telecommunications as a natural monopoly and devoted his energies to eliminating all competition. With Vail at the helm, AT&T took over many of the independent phone companies, refused to connect Bell's long-distance lines to other phone companies, and, in 1909, even managed to win control over Western Union. At the same time, Vail's endorsement of government regulation and of the phone company's public service obligations mitigated the impact of Bell's monopolistic tendencies.

Naturally, the rest of the industry objected to AT&T's dominance and lobbied the Justice Department to investigate whether AT&T was violating the antitrust laws. AT&T decided to compromise rather than fight and in 1913 agreed to divest itself of its Western Union holdings, purchase no more independents without the consent of the Interstate Commerce Commission, and connect with other phone networks. Although Vail's dream of a comprehensive national monopoly was dashed, AT&T still enjoyed many local monopolies as well as control over the long-distance business.

In 1918 a move in Congress to nationalize the phone company was reversed after a year. After that, AT&T felt free to dabble in new areas, such as radio broadcasting (which it abandoned in 1926) and the development of sound systems for motion pictures.

The 1930s presented a challenge to the phone industry in the form of more extensive federal regulation. Congress enacted the Communications Act of 1934, the country's primary communications law, which established the Federal Communications Commission (FCC) to regulate both broadcasting and common carriers. The latter consisted of services, such as telephone and telegraph, that were obliged to provide access to anyone on a first-come, first-served basis. Over the next half century the nation's telephone policy called on AT&T to provide the widest possible service, on a nondiscriminatory basis, at affordable rates.

After World War II telephone usage soared, helped by the fact that most of the Bell system had been converted to direct dialing. AT&T also moved to improve transatlantic cable service, which had been initiated in 1927, by installing sophisticated repeater devices that made voices more audible and less prone to interference. After these improvements were made, cable service was launched in 1956.

Yet AT&T's successes were once again hampered by a Justice Department antitrust suit. This time the government sought divestiture of Western Electric. After seven years of legal maneuvering AT&T signed a consent decree in 1956 that allowed it to hold on to Western Electric but limited the subsidiary to manufacturing equipment for the Bell system (except for military work). The agreement also prohibited AT&T from entering any business other than common-carrier communications.

The consent decree restriction on entering new businesses turned out to be a severe limitation on AT&T's ability to compete in the new, rapidly emerging telecommunications industry.

AT&T's battle in that new marketplace began with the issue of customer equipment. In the 1950s a device called Hush-a-Phone, which allowed someone speaking into a phone to avoid being overheard by others in a room, was approved by the FCC and put on the market. Ma Bell was horrified. For decades Bell's right to supply all equipment used in its network had been Bell gospel and was viewed by the company as an essential part of maintaining a reliable network.

Legal action by AT&T convinced a federal appeals court to overrule the FCC on Hush-a-Phone. However, this was just the opening salvo in a series of skirmishes that saw various retailers insisting on their right to enter what was soon known as the interconnect industry. Ma Bell fought these incursions, both in court and by finally introducing new models. But it was too late. In 1968 the FCC opened up the equipment business to a variety of new competitors.

The 1960s also saw the beginning of a challenge to Ma Bell's dominance in the long-distance business. A venture called Microwave Communications Inc. (MCI) applied to the FCC in 1963 for permission to furnish private-line service via microwave between Chicago and St. Louis. While MCI's application was being fought by AT&T, another proposal was submitted by the Texas entrepreneur Sam Wyly, who wanted to offer a digital data transmission service through a company called Datran. In 1970 the FCC decided to authorize the fledgling carriers. AT&T responded by developing its own digital service.

Worsening AT&T's situation, in 1974 the Justice Department once again filed an antitrust suit that sought to break up the Bell system. The suit was based on charges that since the 1956 consent decree, Ma Bell had deliberately blocked the interconnection of competing equipment and had sought to prevent the establishment of specialized carriers.

AT&T executives now believed that the company was under siege. Assailed by antitrust charges in its core business and restricted by the 1956 decree from entering new ones, Ma Bell had the disadvantage of being regulated as a monopoly while also suffering from the absence of immunity from antitrust prosecution and competition that legitimate monopolies could expect.

Moreover, subject to provisions of the 1956 consent decree and other restrictions imposed by the FCC, AT&T was unable to compete in the new businesses that were emerging to service the expanding computer operations of American industry. Since the 1960s the FCC had been examining the thorny issue of where data processing left off and communications began. These proceedings, known as "computer inquiries," stretched over a decade and never fully resolved the key issue. Yet the commission was firm in its restrictions on AT&T and its determination to prevent the Bell system from gaining an unfair advantage by using revenues from monopoly businesses to subsidize unregulated ones.

Pressure from AT&T finally caused the FCC to abandon its position in 1980. The commission decided that, starting in 1983, Ma Bell could enter some unregulated businesses, so long as it did so through an "arm's-length," unsubsidized subsidiary—which the business press immediately dubbed Baby Bell.

Neither the Justice Department nor AT&T's competitors were happy with this arrangement, and they sought to block it in court. Charles L. Brown, then chairman of AT&T, decided that the mess could not be straightened out until the cloud of the antitrust suit was lifted. He and the rest of Bell management began to accept the idea that the only way to do this would be to agree to the severing of the twenty-two Bell operating companies that provided local service around the country.

This option became more likely once the Reagan administration took office in 1981. By the end of the year an agreement was reached, and on January 8, 1982, the Justice Department announced that the suit would be dropped, with AT&T agreeing to divest itself of the operating companies by January 1, 1984.

Under the terms of the divestiture, drawn up and implemented under the supervision of federal judge Harold Greene, AT&T was allowed to hold on to Western Electric, the long-distance business, and Bell Laboratories, and was given the right to enter unregulated businesses.

The operating companies were reorganized into seven regional holding companies that remained as regulated monopolies and were supposed to focus on providing local service. Judge Greene allowed them to retain the profitable Yellow Pages business and the exclusive use of the Bell name and logo in the United States. He also barred AT&T from entering electronic publishing.

The Bell divestiture was the largest corporate breakup in U.S. history. Implementation of the new arrangements involved dividing up some $150 billion in assets and nearly a million employees among AT&T and the seven regional holding companies. While in terms of management this came off rather smoothly, customers experienced disruptions in service and delays in the installation of residential equipment.

Local phone rates began a steady climb upward as a result of the abandonment of the Bell practice of keeping long-distance rates artificially high to subsidize local service. Under the new arrangement the charge for each call was to be determined by the cost of providing it.

Since divestiture AT&T has focused on expanding its international operations. New cable routes have been installed in the Pacific and the Caribbean, and work has begun on expanded links to Australia, New Zealand, and China. In 1990 Hungary became the fiftieth country—and the first in Eastern Europe—to be connected to International 800 Service, which allows callers free access to U.S. businesses. AT&T also has expanded to one hundred countries its USADirect Service, which allows traveling Americans to reach an AT&T operator when calling home. Electronic mail and high-speed facsimile transmission services have been widened, especially in the United Kingdom and Japan.

AT&T purchased 20 percent of Società Italiana Telecommunicazioni (ItalTel) and formed a joint venture for selling phone systems in Italy and, later, elsewhere in Europe. AT&T is also in a joint venture with ItalTel's parent company, STET (a telecommunications holding company controlled by the Italian government), and Compañía Telefónica Nacional de España to develop and market sophisticated switching and transmission equipment in Europe and elsewhere. AT&T has similar joint ventures with the Taiwanese government and the Lucky-Goldstar Group in South Korea. In 1989 AT&T ended its partnership with Olivetti in the production of personal computers, but it has signed semiconductor technology-sharing agreements with NEC and Mitsubishi.

In late 1990 AT&T moved to overcome its traditionally lackluster computer business by making a bid to acquire NCR Corporation, the descendant of the once-powerful National Cash Register Company. The management of NCR, which remained in the shadow of IBM for decades but survived through its strong connections with retailers and banks, strongly resisted the hostile bid but in May 1991 surrendered to AT&T's sweetened offer of $7.5 billion.

OPERATIONS

Telecommunications Services (62 percent of 1991 revenues). Since the divestiture plan was implemented, AT&T has been working hard to see that its long-distance business, now its main revenue producer, remains dominant. At the beginning AT&T was particularly worried about what would happen after the introduction in September 1986 of "equal access," the elimination of the extra digits that users of competing long-distance providers had needed to dial.

Long-distance prices declined steadily during the late 1980s as AT&T sought to retain its command of the market and the upstarts acted to sustain their price advantage (which has become narrower). AT&T's profitability was bolstered in 1989 when the FCC shifted from a system of regulating the company's profit margin to one that controlled rates. This allowed AT&T to increase earnings, rather than simply lowering rates, as a result of improved operating efficiency.

AT&T's lead over competing long-distance carriers remains quite large, even though the company's share has declined to two-thirds of the market. This may change before long, depending on whether the prohibition imposed by Judge Greene against the regional holding companies entering the long-distance market is retained.

The image of efficiency and technical superiority cultivated by AT&T was tarnished on January 15, 1990, when a malfunction shut down the company's long-distance system for nine hours. A similar incident in September 1991 disrupted airline traffic in New York City and caused delays around the country because air traffic controllers in different areas were unable to communicate with one another.

AT&T's telecommunications activities, other than its long-distance service, include such business products as wide-area telecommunications services (WATS) and toll-free 800 services. The company also provides electronic mail and telex services, which were acquired from Western Union in 1990. The following year AT&T announced that it was considering getting into the cellular phone service business outside the United States.

Sales of Products and Systems (25 percent of revenues). AT&T equipment is sold to governments, businesses, and other institutions as well as to individuals. Since the 1950s, as federal regulators and the courts have stepped in to limit Ma Bell's attempts to be the sole source of the hardware that was linked to its system, AT&T has faced increasing competition in this area.

Once subscribers were able to purchase their own phones, which was not possible until the 1970s, an astounding range of products flooded the market. Many of these were electronic "smart phones," which could store frequently called numbers, dial them automatically, and perform other feats. Despite this diversity, it turned out that most subscribers were satisfied buying the phone they had been leasing from AT&T. More recently AT&T has moved into the lead in sales of yet another device: the answering machine, an area in which its market share stands at about 25 percent.

Once companies did not have to accept a standardized service from AT&T, they became interested in sophisticated private branch exchanges (PBXs—that is, switchboards), which are more closely tailored to the user's requirements. AT&T had been facing competition in this market since 1977, when Canada's Northern Telecom introduced the first electronic digital PBX. The company countered with its own Dimension switchboard, but many customers found it lacking and turned to the competition. By the early 1980s AT&T had lost a majority of the PBX market, allowing Northern Telecom to rise to first place. Yet in the following years AT&T rebounded, pushing the Canadian company back to second place.

This segment of the company's operations also includes a subsidiary that develops and markets UNIX software, which was created by AT&T and is now widely used, in numerous variations, for sophisticated computer systems. Also involved are minicomputers and personal computers—including a laptop computer called Safari introduced in 1991—as well as microelectronic products, such as integrated circuits. The company owns semiconductor facilities in Singapore and Thailand and plants in Mexico that produce computers, microelectronic products, and answering machines.

AT&T's computer operations expanded tremendously with the acquisition of NCR in 1991. NCR was a natural choice for AT&T, since several years earlier the company had adopted Ma Bell's UNIX operating system for a new line of microcomputer networks. In 1990, shortly before AT&T announced its bid, the company introduced a full range of computers employing an open systems approach rather than the more common practice of adopting proprietary hardware and software. AT&T's 19-percent holding in Sun Microsystems, a leading producer of computer workstations, was sold after the NCR deal was set.

Rentals and Other Services (11 percent of revenues). This segment of AT&T's operations covers the rental of communications and computer products to both residential and business customers. Because of the preference of most customers to own their own equipment, this business continues to decline.

Financial Service and Leasing (2 percent of revenues). This segment consists of AT&T Capital Corporation, a leasing operation, as well as AT&T Universal Card, a general-purpose credit and calling card introduced in 1990. The card was a big hit, attracting 4.5 million accounts in its first nine months of operation and shaking up Citicorp and other established players in the field.

TOP EXECUTIVES

- Robert E. Allen, chairman and chief executive
- Randall L. Tobias, vice chairman of the board
- Richard S. Bodman, senior vice president, corporate strategy
- W. Frank Blunt, group executive, communications products
- Robert M. Kavner, group executive, communications products
- William B. Marx, Jr., group executive, network systems
- Victor A. Pelson, group executive, communications services
- Sam R. Willcoxon, group executive, international
- Gilbert P. Williamson, chief executive officer of NCR

OUTSIDE DIRECTORS

- M. Kathryn Eickhoff, president of Eickhoff Economics, a consulting company
- Walter Y. Elisha, chief executive of Springs Industries
- Louis V. Gerstner, Jr., chief executive of RJR Nabisco
- Philip M. Hawley, chief executive of Carter Hawley Hale Stores
- Belton K. Johnson, owner of Chaparrosa Ranch
- Drew Lewis, chief executive of Union Pacific
- Donald F. McHenry, professor of diplomacy at Georgetown University
- Donald S. Perkins, retired chief executive of Jewel Companies
- Henry B. Schacht, chief executive of Cummins Engine
- Michael I. Sovern, president of Columbia University
- Franklin A. Thomas, president of the Ford Foundation

- Joseph D. Williams, chief executive of Warner-Lambert
- Thomas H. Wyman, chairman of United Biscuits (Holdings) U.S. and former chairman of CBS

FINANCIAL DATA

Revenues (in millions of dollars)

1991	63,089
1990	62,191
1989	61,100
1988	61,756
1987	60,530

Net Income (in millions of dollars)

1991	552
1990	3,104
1989	3,109
1988	− 1,231 (loss)
1987	2,440

LABOR RELATIONS

Telephone workers have tended to fall into two categories: electrical crafts-people and less-skilled phone operators. The first telephone operators were teenage boys. However, they proved difficult to supervise and were replaced by adult women. The job remained a pink-collar ghetto until the 1970s.

Organizing attempts started slowly but accelerated after the founding of the International Brotherhood of Electrical Workers in 1891. The IBEW, a male-dominated union, ignored the large number of female operators until a wave of militancy began in Boston around 1912. In response the union reluctantly offered to take these workers into the organization, but only in a separate, second-class department.

The IBEW had some success after World War I, but telephone management moved to create company unions, which remained in place until the early 1930s. Even the fact that AT&T cut many jobs during the early years of the depression while keeping the dividend intact did not lead to serious unrest. It was the passage of the Wagner Act that revived independent unionism in the industry, and in 1939 the National Federation of Telephone Workers (NFTW) was formed.

For years the IBEW remained highly decentralized and rather weak. As a result, pay for telephone workers fell behind other industries. Eventually, in the midst of postwar labor militancy in 1946, the NFTW threatened a strike and got AT&T and the operating companies to bargain on a national level for the first time.

The following year the NFTW sought another big raise, but the company declined to resume national bargaining. This time a strike did take place. More than three hundred thousand workers around the country walked out in what was the most widespread strike in U.S. history. The NFTW had not prepared adequately for the action, and after several weeks the strike began to crumble. Local unions began settling with individual operating companies for small wage increases. Later that same year the NFTW decided to reorganize itself into a more centralized body and to change its name to the Communications Workers of America.

In the 1950s the Communications Workers of America (CWA) conducted a number of regional strikes, including a seventy-two-day walkout at Southern Bell in 1955. In the 1960s the union had to fight off raids from the Teamsters and contend with the expanding automation of the system.

In the 1970s the threats to the CWA were from an organizing offensive by the IBEW, especially in the interconnect industry. There was also uncertainty concerning what would happen if and when the Bell system was broken up. The union engaged in a week-long national strike in 1971 and won a substantial wage increase. Three years later AT&T agreed to national bargaining.

After divestiture was announced in the early 1980s the union set out to minimize the impact on AT&T's workers. There were signs that the newly empowered regional holding companies would resist national bargaining and that a less regulated AT&T would be harder to deal with. The latter proved true in 1983, when AT&T sought to hold the line and the CWA ended up calling a national strike. The walkout lasted about three weeks and ended with an 8.5-percent wage increase over three years.

The CWA has worked hard to adapt to the new environment created by deregulation. In the great long-distance wars of the 1980s the CWA spent several million dollars promoting AT&T because it continued to use human telephone operators. In contrast, the newer carriers were almost entirely automated. Yet this cooperative approach did not stop AT&T from announcing in 1985 that it planned to eliminate twenty-four thousand jobs in its Information Systems Unit. A strike over the action was narrowly averted when the CWA and AT&T reached an agreement limiting the layoffs and restricting the use of subcontracting.

In the 1989 contract negotiations a strike was averted at AT&T when the company agreed to a settlement package that included innovative improvements in family benefits. At the same time, the cost of living adjustment was eliminated.

Perhaps setting itself on a future course, AT&T has been shifting work from a unionized electronic components plant in Virginia to a *maquiladora* facility in Mexico that pays its workers less than a dollar an hour. The company also has antagonized the CWA by resisting unionization of the employees at Paradyne Corporation, a modem manufacturer acquired by AT&T in 1989.

Labor relations took a turn for the worse when AT&T began its takeover campaign against NCR. The CWA protested what it saw as an attempt by the company to expand its nonunion operations, and in 1991 the union adopted what it called a Mobilization Action Plan, which involved continual demonstrations at AT&T facilities. The CWA also vowed to organize workers at the company's new subsidiaries, such as the credit card operation.

This atmosphere of tension was exacerbated in September 1991, when the company initially blamed union workers for a major breakdown in long-distance service. When the CWA protested, AT&T backed down, admitting that equipment problems and procedural mistakes by managers were mainly at fault. The confrontation escalated in March 1992 when AT&T, on the eve of new contract talks with the CWA, announced plans for eliminating the jobs of up to one-third of its 18,000 operators.

In 1991 AT&T agreed to pay $66 million to settle a suit that had been brought by the Equal Employment Opportunity Commission charging the company with discrimination against pregnant employees.

ENVIRONMENTAL AND HEALTH RECORD

In 1987, when a study conducted by Digital Equipment found that women working with acids and gases in the fabrication of semiconductors had an elevated rate of miscarriages, AT&T encouraged pregnant women working on its chip production lines in the United States to transfer to other jobs. In its electronics plant in Mexico, however, the company reportedly has paid little attention to the health problems of the workers and is believed to engage in many of the questionable environmental practices common among *maquiladora* facilities.

AT&T has been an avid proponent of recycling office paper and has been cited for its efforts by the New Jersey Department of Environmental Protection and the Council on Economic Priorities. The council also has commended AT&T for its plan to end the use of ozone-depleting chlorofluorocarbons (CFCs) in its electronics manufacturing.

Less than appealing to environmentalists is AT&T's role in managing Sandia Laboratories, which specialize in nuclear energy and nuclear weapons research, for the Defense Department.

According to a study of Environmental Protection Agency data by the Citizens Fund, AT&T was responsible for releasing the thirty-ninth-largest volume of known or suspected carcinogens (1.9 million pounds) among U.S. manufacturing companies in 1989 (the latest data available).

BIBLIOGRAPHY

Barbash, Jack. *Unions and Telephones: The Story of the Communications Workers of America.* New York: Harper Brothers, 1952.

Brooks, John. *Telephone: The First Hundred Years.* New York: Harper & Row, 1976.

Brooks, Thomas R. *The Communications Workers of America.* New York: Mason/ Charter, 1977.

Coll, Steve. *The Deal of the Century: The Breakup of AT&T*. New York: Atheneum, 1987.

Goulden, Joseph C. *Monopoly*. New York: G. P. Putnam's Sons, 1968.

Kleinfield, Sonny. *The Biggest Company on Earth: A Profile of AT&T*. New York: Holt, Rinehart & Winston, 1981.

Norwood, Stephen H. *Labor's Flaming Youth: Telephone Operators and Worker Militancy*. Urbana: University of Illinois Press, 1990.

Schacht, John N. *The Making of Telephone Unionism, 1920–1947*. New Brunswick, N.J.: Rutgers University Press, 1985.

Tunstall, W. Brooke. *Disconnecting Parties: Managing the Bell System Breakup— An Inside View*. New York: McGraw-Hill, 1985.

AMR CORPORATION

4333 Amon Carter Boulevard
Fort Worth, Texas 76155
(817) 967-1234

1991 revenues: $12.9 billion
1991 net income: − $240 million (loss)
Publicly traded company
Employees: 116,300
Founded: 1930

OVERVIEW

AMR Corporation is a holding company formed in 1982 to serve as the financial parent of American Airlines. American, the world's largest air carrier (in terms of revenue) flies to nearly 200 destinations on five continents. Founded during the rough-and-tumble early days of U.S. commercial aviation, the company has taken an aggressive posture during this era of deregulation, ruthlessly cutting its costs, especially by taking a hard line with its labor unions.

American has expanded rapidly since the late 1980s and has dramatically increased its foreign presence, especially in Europe and Asia. Foreign routes now account for more than 20 percent of its revenues. Despite the financial troubles of the early 1990s relating to the recession and the Persian Gulf war (which resulted in net losses for 1990 and 1991), American stands poised to remain one of the world's leading airlines.

HISTORY

After the pioneering flights of the Wright brothers, commercial aviation was slow in getting off the ground in the United States. The first regularly scheduled passenger line was established in 1914 to fly between St. Petersburg and Tampa, Florida, but the venture did not last long. Although passenger lines were being established across Europe, aviation in America centered on the delivery of mail.

In 1925 Congress passed the Kelly Act, which compelled the Post Office Department to open up all but transcontinental routes to private contractors. This prompted a number of barnstormers to become entrepreneurs and encouraged the growth of commercial aviation. The business became all the more glamorous after Charles Lindbergh's historic solo flight from New York to Paris in 1927; both Main Street and Wall Street became enamored of flying.

The late 1920s saw the emergence of a slew of companies bidding for the potentially lucrative postal contracts. Before long these small firms coalesced into the predecessors of what would become the major carriers, including United Aircraft and Transport, Eastern Air Transport, and American Airways. The mail carriers also began offering passenger service.

In the case of American the main predecessor was the Aviation Company, or Avco, which was formed in 1929 by Fairchild Airplane Manufacturing as a holding company for various aviation enterprises. Avco took over a number of large and small air service companies and soon had some eighty subsidiaries. Chief among these were Colonial Airways (which had the airmail contract for the New York–Boston route); Embry-Riddle (which flew between Cincinnati and Chicago); Interstate Air Lines (Atlanta-Chicago); Southern Air Transport (a merger of Texas Air Transport and St. Tammany Gulf Coast Airways); and Universal Air Lines system (which started out flying between Cleveland and Louisville and then acquired other carriers). In 1930 this motley collection of operations started to be restructured under the umbrella of a new entity called American Airways.

After Walter Folger Brown was appointed postmaster by the Hoover administration in 1929, he developed a plan to restructure and stabilize the airmail industry. He successfully lobbied for legislation (the Watres Act) that created a system under which airline companies were compensated by the volume of space available for mail rather than by the actual weight of the mail they carried, thus encouraging the use of larger planes. Bonuses were paid for using the most-advanced equipment.

Brown's plan took on the appearance of a sinister conspiracy during congressional hearings called by Senator Hugo Black after the Roosevelt administration took office. Brown and the leading carriers were accused of carving up the airmail business in an improper manner, and the resulting public outcry prompted the president to put airmail in the hands of the army air corps. The army pilots were not used to flying at night or in poor weather, however, and after a series of crashes Roosevelt relented and turned airmail service back to the more experienced private sector. The major carriers were supposed to be excluded from the new system, but the post office restored their contracts after they made slight changes in their names and replaced some executives.

American (now American Airlines), Eastern Air Lines, Trans World Airlines (TWA), and United Airlines (the carrier was known as United Air Lines until the 1970s) were firmly established as the big four of the domestic air transport business. The determination of fares and the allocation of routes in that business were placed in the hands of a federal regulatory agency called the Civil Aeronautics Board.

American's ascent was overseen by C. R. (Cyrus Rowlett) Smith, an accountant by training, who took over the presidency of the carrier in 1934 and remained in charge for decades. During his early years on the job Smith championed the development of larger and more comfortable planes, most notably Douglas Aircraft's DC-3, which opened the door to large-scale air transport. By the end of the 1930s American was the leading domestic carrier, a position it would hold until United and Capital merged in 1961 and then regain in 1985.

During World War II much of the commercial fleet was turned over to the government for military purposes, but after the war the airline industry grew rapidly as planes became more sophisticated. By 1949 American had the only fleet that consisted exclusively of up-to-date, pressurized planes. Four years later American pioneered nonstop transcontinental service using the DC-7. By this time American had surpassed the Pennsylvania Railroad as the world's largest single carrier in terms of passenger revenue. The next milestone came in January 1959, when the first scheduled transcontinental flight of a jet plane in the United States took place with an American Airlines Boeing 707.

That same year American and IBM announced the joint development of the first computerized reservations system for an airline—called Semi-Automatic Business Reservations Environment, or SABRE. The system cut down the amount of time required to process a reservation from forty-five minutes to three seconds. In 1976 American began making the system available to travel agents.

American continued to promote the development of new aircraft, often taking the lead in placing orders with the leading manufacturers, McDonnell Douglas and Boeing. The flamboyance of the carrier's management diminished somewhat when C. R. Smith left in 1968 to become secretary of commerce. But Smith was called back in 1973 after his successor, George Spater, ran into difficulties, including the revelation of his illegal contributions to the Nixon reelection campaign in 1972.

American was primarily a domestic carrier in its early years, though a transatlantic division called American Overseas Airlines was in operation from 1945 to 1950, when it was sold to Pan American. In 1970 American again became an intercontinental airline as flights were started from the U.S. mainland to Hawaii, American Samoa, the Fiji Islands, New Zealand, and Australia. These routes were suspended several years later, but American began flying to Puerto Rico, Haiti, and other destinations in the Caribbean.

In the era of deregulation the company fared well. Robert Crandall, who became president in 1980 and chief executive in 1985, used a street fighter's approach to hold on to lucrative markets and resist pressure from upstart carriers like People Express. Crandall got himself in legal hot water, however, when he made a price-fixing proposal to the head of Braniff during a telephone conversation in 1982.

After deregulation took effect in 1979, American moved into a number of new U.S. cities and in 1982 returned to Europe after thirty-two years when it was chosen to replace bankrupt Braniff for Dallas-London nonstop service. European service was expanded in 1985 with flights to Paris and Frankfurt, and in 1987 service to Tokyo was initiated.

During the 1980s the airline also opened new domestic hubs in Nashville and Raleigh-Durham. Additional cities were served through the American Eagle network of regional carriers that was created in 1984. American's presence on the West Coast expanded dramatically with the 1987 purchase of AirCal.

In 1989 Crandall rebuffed a takeover bid by Donald Trump and purchased the Central and South American routes of ailing Eastern for $349 million as well as a Chicago-London route and other assets from TWA. American also purchased a Seattle-Tokyo route from bankrupt Continental, and after a battle with regulators the carrier was able to purchase a group of lucrative London routes from TWA.

By the beginning of the 1990s Crandall was moving to make American the premier airline in the world. United Airlines was proving itself a substantial challenge, but American's prospects were quite promising. As *Business Week* put it, the aim was to turn the carrier into "the globe-girdling powerhouse that Pan American World Airways was supposed to be but never really was."

OPERATIONS

American Airlines serves 119 airports in forty mainland states and the District of Columbia. The carrier also flies to seventy-one destinations outside the continental United States, including Alaska and Hawaii; Puerto Rico and numerous other places in the Caribbean, Central America, and South America; Japan, Hong Kong, Australia, and New Zealand in the Asia-Pacific region; and Brussels, Budapest, Düsseldorf, Frankfurt, Glasgow, London, Madrid, Manchester, Milan, Munich, Paris, Stockholm, and Zurich in Europe. A number of these destinations are made possible by code-sharing arrangements with three foreign carriers: Malev of Hungary, Cathay Pacific of Hong Kong, and Qantas of Australia.

American has two megahubs in Dallas–Fort Worth and Chicago and five additional hubs in Miami; Nashville; Raleigh-Durham; San Juan, Puerto Rico; and San Jose, California.

In 1991 American had more than 854,000 departures, more than 70 million passenger boardings, and 82 billion revenue passenger miles. At the end of 1991 its fleet included 622 jet aircraft, 275 of them owned and 347 leased. Most of the planes were McDonnell Douglas MD-80s and Boeing 727s. The carrier had 156 jet aircraft on order, including 62 Fokker 100s, 42 Boeing 757s, and 10 McDonnell Douglas MD-80s.

In addition to American's own fleet, there are six regional carriers that feed passengers to American flights and operate under the American Eagle name. These are Command Airways, Executive Air, Metroflight, Nashville

Eagle, Simmons Airlines, and Wings West. These carriers serve 143 points in the United States and 21 in the Caribbean and the Bahamas.

American's SABRE computerized reservations system is the largest in the world. The system, which is used by travel agents as well, allows users to book flights on more than 300 carriers as well as reservations with more than 22,000 hotels and other lodging facilities, 60 car rental companies, and 37 tour wholesalers. There are more than 123,000 SABRE terminals in operation in 19,000 locations. In 1990 SABRE and Reed Electronic Publishing launched SABREvision, an enhancement of the system that allows travel agents to view color pictures, maps, and other detailed information on the same screens they use to make reservations.

TOP EXECUTIVES

- Robert L. Crandall, chairman, president, and chief executive
- Robert W. Baker, executive vice president
- Donald J. Carty, executive vice president and chief financial officer
- Michael J. Durham, senior vice president and treasurer
- Max D. Hopper, senior vice president
- Anne H. McNamara, senior vice president and general counsel
- P. Jackson Bell, senior vice president
- Michael W. Gunn, senior vice president

OUTSIDE DIRECTORS

- Howard P. Allen, chairman of the executive committee of Southern California Edison
- Edward A. Brennan, chief executive of Sears Roebuck
- Christopher F. Edley, retired chief executive of the United Negro College Fund
- Antonio Luis Ferré, president and publisher of the newspaper *El Nuevo Dia*, San Juan, Puerto Rico
- Charles T. Fisher III, chairman of NBD Bancorp
- Dee J. Kelly, partner in Kelly Hart & Hallman, a Ft. Worth law firm
- John D. Leitch, chairman of Upper Lakes Group, Toronto
- William Lyon, chief executive of the real estate development firm William Lyon Company, Newport Beach, California
- Ann D. McLaughlin, visiting fellow at the Urban Institute
- Charles H. Pistor, Jr., former chairman of First RepublicBank
- Joe M. Rodgers, chairman of JMR Investments Group, Nashville
- Maurice Segall, retired chief executive of Zayre Corporation
- Edward O. Vetter, president of the management consulting firm Edward O. Vetter & Associates, Dallas
- Eugene F. Williams, Jr., retired chairman of Centerre Trust Company

FINANCIAL DATA

Revenues (in millions of dollars)

1991	12,887
1990	11,720
1989	10,480
1988	8,824
1987	7,198

Net Income (in millions of dollars)

1991	−240 (loss)
1990	−40 (loss)
1989	455
1988	477
1987	198

LABOR RELATIONS

Sixty percent of American Airlines employees are represented by labor unions. The pilots and flight attendants are members of unaffiliated unions: the Allied Pilots Association and the Association of Professional Flight Attendants. Mechanics and other ground personnel are represented by the International Association of Machinists and the Transport Workers Union.

Since taking office, Robert Crandall has made the reduction of labor costs a personal crusade. Arguing that the advent of deregulation required much tighter control of expenses, Crandall pressured the unions in 1983 into accepting one of the first two-tier wage systems in the United States. The arrangement, which allows management to pay less to new workers, ends up causing tension between employees doing the same job at very different pay scales. Although he never became as despised as the now-deposed head of Texas Air and Eastern Air Lines, Crandall probably has done more to erode the power of unions in the airline industry than Frank Lorenzo.

By 1987 the pilots and flight attendants were far less willing to make sacrifices. Their unions demanded an end to the two-tier system, and when Crandall refused, the pilots began talking strike and the flight attendants embarked on a corporate campaign to pressure the company. In the end, compromises were reached, with each of the unions modifying (but not abolishing) the two-tier system.

In the following years the flight attendants union got involved in a long legal battle with the carrier over company weight requirements. The union charged that the rules constituted sex and age discrimination because they did not provide for the fact that women tend to gain weight as they grow older. A suit brought by the union and the Equal Employment Opportunity Commission was settled in 1991 when the company agreed to modify its regulations to account for age differences.

Tensions with the pilots intensified again in 1990 and 1991, with the company accusing the union of organizing an illegal sick-out of its members. The two sides narrowly averted a strike by reaching a settlement that further eased the two-tier system and raised salary levels.

ENVIRONMENTAL RECORD

American reports that its fleet complies with noise abatement regulations established in 1977 by the Department of Transportation and the Federal Aviation Administration (FAA). The company also states that the engines on its aircraft meet emissions standards set by the EPA.

In the area of toxic wastes, American has been named as a potentially responsible party at three Superfund sites: the Hardage disposal site in Criner, Oklahoma; the Operating Industries, Inc. site in Monterey Park, California; and the Sand Springs site in Sand Springs, Oklahoma. In each case American is a member of a joint defense committee of potentially responsible parties, though the company insists that its potential liability in each case is minimal.

The company also has launched programs to recycle soft drink cans and other packaging used in meals served on planes as well as paper used in AMR's offices.

BIBLIOGRAPHY

Allen, Oliver E. *The Airline Builders*. Alexandria, Va.: Time-Life Books, 1981.
Sampson, Anthony. *Empires in the Sky*. New York: Random House, 1984.
Serling, Robert J. *Eagle: The Story of American Airlines*. New York: St. Martin's Press, 1985.
Smith, C. R. *A.A.: American Airlines Since 1926*. New York: Newcomen Society, 1954.
Solberg, Carl. *Conquest of the Skies: A History of Commercial Aviation in America*. Boston: Little, Brown, 1979.

ANGLO AMERICAN CORPORATION OF SOUTH AFRICA, LTD.

44 Main Street
Johannesburg 2001
South Africa
(011) 638-9111

1991 revenues: Anglo American does not disclose its revenues
1991 net income: $512.9 million (year ending March 31)
Publicly traded company
Employees: 300,000 (est.)
Founded: 1917

OVERVIEW

To a great extent Anglo American is synonymous with the economy of South Africa. It has been estimated that its activities account for some 10 percent of the entire gross national product of the country, and its publicly traded affiliates represent nearly half of the market value of the Johannesburg Stock Exchange. As the *Los Angeles Times* once put it, "in South Africa, one can scarcely buy a book, a car, a beer, a bottle of wine, an egg, a pair of shoes or a sofa, take out an insurance policy or open a bank account, heat the home, read a local newspaper, rent an office or erect a skyscraper without in some way enriching this secretive conglomerate of 600 companies."

The Anglo empire was founded in 1917 by the Oppenheimer family, which still controls it through its private company E. Oppenheimer & Son. Yet the ownership structure of Anglo and its subsidiaries and affiliates is an incredibly complicated network of cross-holdings. Founder Ernest Oppenheimer and then his son Harry directly ran the company until the latter's retirement in 1982. Harry's son Nicholas now serves as a deputy chairman as he prepares to ascend to the top spot.

Anglo is best known as one of the world's leading producers of gold and diamonds, the demand for which it stimulates through heavy spending on

33

advertising—with such messages as "a diamond is forever"—around the world.

Those businesses, in particular, have been built on cheap black labor, yet the Oppenheimers have expressed opposition to the apartheid system in their country. In 1985 Harry Oppenheimer's successor as chairman, Gavin Relly, defied his government and met with exiled leaders of the African National Congress. The company also has been more willing than most other large companies to accept unionization of black workers—though this did not prevent Anglo from coming down hard on mine workers during a 1987 strike.

The company's relatively enlightened position on race and labor relations may be sincere or it may simply be based on the realization that the days of white domination in the country are limited. In any event, Anglo is determined to remain a major factor in South Africa once the system of apartheid is completely dismantled.

HISTORY

The mining industry in South Africa got started in a serious way in 1867, when a diamond deposit was discovered in Hopetown. Within a few years the area known as Kimberley was the site of the most extensive diamond mining operations in the world. At first the digging was done by individuals and small entities. By the mid-1880s the industry began to come under the control of larger, joint-stock companies, the largest of which was De Beers Diamond Mining Company.

In 1888 De Beers, whose chairman was Cecil Rhodes, took over one of its largest rivals, Kimberley Company, and changed its name to De Beers Consolidated Mines Ltd. By the beginning of the new century De Beers had complete control over the mines in Kimberley. The output of De Beers and producers in other parts of the country was marketed through a series of syndicates that acted to manipulate prices by controlling the supply of stones made available for sale.

De Beers found itself with a new rival in 1902, when a diamond discovery near Pretoria led to the creation of the Premier (Transvaal) Diamond Mining Company. De Beers attempted to establish a marketing agreement with Premier and with South West Africa Company, which operated in what was then German Southwest Africa (now Namibia).

Diamonds were not the only valuable substance being extracted from the earth during this period. Various gold deposits were discovered in the 1860s and 1870s, but it was late in the following decade that the discovery of large deposits of gold in the Witwatersrand ridge near Johannesburg launched large-scale mining of that precious metal. Several of the leading diamond magnates, including Rhodes, rushed into this new endeavor. In 1887 they registered in London a firm called Gold Fields of South Africa Ltd., which, along with a few other firms, quickly assumed the kind of control over gold production that De Beers had over diamonds.

By the mid-1910s, however, the fastest-growing part of the gold business was found not in the main Witwatersrand area but in a newly developed peripheral section known as the Far East Rand. The major company in the area was Consolidated Mines Selection Company, which was founded in 1897 and had come under control of diamond trading firm A. Dunkelsbuhler & Company in 1905.

The key figure in the Dunkelsbuhler firm was Ernest Oppenheimer, a cousin of the company's founder (Anton Dunkelsbuhler), who had gone to South Africa in 1902 to run Dunkelsbuhler's Kimberley office. In 1917 Oppenheimer decided to establish his own company to exploit the gold potential of the Far East Rand. The plan was to base the company in Johannesburg and raise capital in New York (from the likes of J. P. Morgan & Company) rather than in London. Oppenheimer originally wanted to call the firm African American Corporation, but his backers prevailed on him to change the name to Anglo American.

With Oppenheimer as chairman, Anglo American soon began taking over various gold mining operations. Then it moved into diamond mining in Namibia, merging eleven mining companies into Consolidated Diamond Mines of South West Africa. In 1922 Anglo formally took over Consolidated Mines Selection Company and moved into diamond production in Angola and the Congo. From that position Anglo challenged De Beers's leadership of the diamond industry, and in 1927 Anglo made a hostile takeover offer for that company. Despite the resistance of De Beers, Anglo finally achieved that goal in 1929.

That achievement might have seemed dubious in the 1930s as the diamond market plunged as a result of the depression. Yet during that same decade the gold side of Anglo's business charged ahead, spurred on by rising prices for the metal and by rapidly improving productivity in the mines. The company also gained control over many of the promising mines in the Orange Free State Province. As World War II ended, Anglo was in a commanding position in both gold and diamond mining. It was also a major producer of uranium, coal, and copper. Through a web of holding companies and investments it was becoming the dominant force in the entire South African economy.

Anglo's influence was not limited to mining. Through its takeovers and investments it gradually developed a portfolio of interests in various industrial sectors, including steel, explosives, fertilizers, and chemicals. In 1955 Anglo formed, with the support of Barclays Bank and Lazard Brothers in Britain, its own private merchant bank, Union Acceptances Ltd.

During the 1960s, amid a general economic boom in the country, there was a dramatic acceleration of Anglo's industrial diversification. The group, then headed by Ernest Oppenheimer's son Harry, formed Highveld Steel and Vanadium Corporation to produce high-quality steel and acquired a number of metalworking companies that used that steel. Other major investments were made in paper production, newspaper publishing, construction, and textiles. In the 1970s an Anglo subsidiary merged with Chrysler's South

African operation and another got involved in a major project to produce plastics from coal, thus reducing the country's dependence on imported petroleum products.

In addition, Rand Mines, which had come under Anglo's control in the early 1960s, merged with Thos. Barlow and Sons in 1971 to form the huge Barlow Rand mining-industrial group. Barlow was the third-largest industrial company in South Africa, with activities ranging from the manufacture of electrical equipment and railway cars to the marketing of heavy equipment, steel, timber, and motor vehicles.

There was consolidation in Anglo's financial activities as well. Its merchant bank, UAL Holdings, merged with Syfrets Trust Company, and the combined company joined itself to the Dutch-owned Nedbank Group. The result was one of the largest banks in the country. In 1974 Anglo subsidiary Rand Selection Corporation took over Schlesinger Insurance and Institutional Holdings, giving Anglo an important foothold in both life and property insurance.

Anglo's intricate web of holdings was not limited to southern Africa. During the 1970s, beginning with the proceeds from the nationalization of its Zambian copper holdings, Anglo used companies called Charter Consolidated and Minerals & Resources Corporation (Minorco) to spread its tentacles to Europe, North America, South America, and Australasia.

By the beginning of the 1980s Minorco, which focused on the Americas, had become one of the largest foreign investors in the United States. Through its holdings in the commodities trading company Phibro Corporation it ended up with a close tie to one of the leading American investment banking firms, Salomon Brothers, which Phibro acquired in 1981. Minorco also had significant holdings in the U.S. mining company Englehard Corporation and in the British-based firm Consolidated Gold Fields, which in turn was the largest shareholder in Newmont Mining, a leading U.S. copper producer. Minorco failed, however, in a takeover bid for all of Consolidated Gold Fields.

During the late 1980s, as the pressure for divestment prompted many foreign companies to sell their South African subsidiaries, Anglo bought up a number of these operations, including those of Barclays Bank. Anglo, which had long hoped to gain a foothold in resource-rich Australia, began a drive into that country in 1987 by taking a major position in a company called Normandy Poseidon.

Such further diversification was made more urgent by the financial squeeze that Anglo began to feel in its core businesses in this period. Gold profits plunged as a result of stagnant gold prices and rising South African inflation. By the beginning of the 1990s the diamond business was also in a slump as recessionary conditions in countries like the United States depressed demand. Anglo also had to contend with a challenge to the De Beers sales cartel from Botswana.

OPERATIONS

Gold and Uranium (11 percent of 1991 investment earnings). Anglo has a commanding position in the South African gold mining industry through its relationship with what it calls client companies (such as its subsidiary Anglo American Gold Investment), its direct investment in mining operations, and its indirect holdings. In fiscal year 1991 client companies milled 46 million tons of ore and produced nearly 252 tons of gold. Anglo indirectly owns interests in gold mines in such countries as Brazil, Chile, and Australia.

Diamonds (18 percent of investment earnings). Anglo's affiliate De Beers Consolidated Mines is one of the world's leading diamond producers, with a fiscal 1991 output of 8.2 million carats. In 1990 the foreign operations of De Beers were put under the control of a Swiss-registered company called De Beers Centenary. The most important of those functions is the Central Selling Organisation, the London-based cartel that controls the sale of some 80 percent of the world's diamonds.

Coal (5 percent of investment earnings). Through its Anglo American Coal Corporation subsidiary, Anglo is a major coal producer. In fiscal 1991 it sold forty-three million tons of coal, equal to about one-quarter of the total for South Africa.

Platinum, Base Metals, and Other Mining (20 percent of investment earnings). Through a variety of subsidiaries and affiliates, Anglo is involved in the mining of chrome, cobalt, copper, manganese, nickel, platinum, potash, soda ash, zinc, and other metals and minerals. In addition to its South African operations, this sector includes such foreign activities as copper mining in South America and a zinc, lead, and silver mine in Alaska.

Industry and Commerce (25 percent of investment earnings). Largely through its Anglo American Industrial Corporation Ltd. affiliates, Anglo has interests in a vast range of industrial activities. Among these are the production of iron and steel, pulp and paper, chemicals, explosives, motor vehicles, and electronic components.

Financial Services and Property (21 percent of investment earnings). Anglo has significant holdings in a major South African bank (First National Bank) and a leading insurance company (Southern Life Association). It also has a wholly owned subsidiary that engages in real estate development.

TOP EXECUTIVES

- Julian Ogilvie Thompson, chairman
- Nicholas F. Oppenheimer, deputy chairman
- W. Graham Boustred, deputy chairman

OUTSIDE DIRECTORS

- G. C. Fletcher, director of various companies
- E. P. Gush, director of various companies
- R. N. Hambro, managing director of J. O. Hambro & Company
- J. H. Steyn, chairman of the Independent Development Trust
- A. L. Vilakazi, professor emeritus of anthropology at the University of Zululand

The board also includes the following individuals associated with various parts of the Anglo American network:

- T. N. Chapman, chief executive of the Southern Life Association
- M. B. Hofmeyr, chairman of Argus Holdings
- Philip Oppenheimer, president of the Central Selling Organisation
- P. F. Retief, chairman of Johannesburg Consolidated Investment Company
- C. J. Saunders, chairman of the Tongaat-Hulett Group
- H. R. Slack, president of Minorco

FINANCIAL DATA

Market Value of Investments (in millions of South African rands)
(years ending March 31)

1991	34,703
1990	40,553
1989	30,195
1988	20,070
1987	25,336

Net Income After Distribution to Outside and Preferred Shareholders
(in millions of South African rands) (years ending March 31)

1991	1,401
1990	1,507
1989	1,254
1988	1,037
1987	1,031

LABOR RELATIONS

As the small-scale diamond mining of the 1870s gave way to corporate ownership in the following decade, the mining companies began to amass large work forces. Starting in the late 1880s those workers began to organize themselves, although this was done separately by white and black miners. The first strike by white miners took place in 1884 and the first by black workers five years later. Such action by the blacks was especially difficult in that they were forced to live in compounds and their activities were closely controlled.

In gold mining many of the white workers came from Europe and had experience in trade unions. By the mid-1910s they were organized well enough to carry out several industrywide strikes, which, despite their eventually being put down, succeeded in shaking up Consolidated Gold Fields and the other employers. In the years after World War I there was also rising militancy among black workers, culminating in a walkout by some seventy-one thousand black miners in 1920. That action, too, was defeated by the mine owners, but it signaled that what was called the native labor force could not be manipulated at will.

After that strike the gold mining companies intensified divisions between white and black workers by deciding to train some blacks for a number of positions that previously had been considered exclusively white. By putting lower-paid blacks in those jobs, the companies planned to lower their labor costs substantially. In 1922 white miners walked off the job and conducted a violent two-month strike in which 250 people were killed. A declaration of martial law ended the dispute, which became known as the Rand Revolt, in favor of the employers.

Unrest among black miners rose during World War II as their real wages declined. In 1946 the African Mine Workers Union called for a strike to demand a minimum wage, prompting a walkout of nearly a hundred thousand black workers throughout the mining industry. The employers and the state responded swiftly, sending in police officers to break up picketing and demonstrations and force the miners back to their jobs. Following the defeated strike, the government put in place additional regulations controlling the activities of black workers, including a ban on their membership in unions and their right to strike.

Those restrictions became more intense as the Afrikaners solidified their control of the country. Most black miners were migrants on short-term contracts who were housed in hostels on company property. In the 1970s the opposition to these conditions grew more intense and black unionism began to revive. The employers, including Anglo, responded by raising wage levels for blacks and making some effort to get blacks into higher-level jobs. Anglo was, however, the only major mining company to support black unionization— a position that might have been enlightened, in part, but it also was based on a desire for a more stable work force. Nonetheless, even at Anglo, no black supervised a white worker and blacks continued to be paid less than whites (though the differential had been reduced).

The black miners at Anglo's operations and elsewhere were not content with the improvements that had been made, and there were a series of militant strikes in the early 1980s. The National Union of Mineworkers (NUM) was formed in 1982 and quickly gained a large membership at Anglo facilities. Although the mining companies had tried to deal with smaller, less-threatening unions, Anglo accepted the NUM, thus opening the door to the first industrywide negotiations between the companies and the black unions. There is some question about how seriously the companies negotiated, but the wage increase enacted for black miners in 1983 was the first that (at least formally) came about through collective bargaining.

In 1985 the NUM managed to reach a wage agreement with Anglo (though some other companies were struck briefly), but two years later, negotiations broke down. More than 250,000 gold and coal miners walked off the job at Anglo and other companies. This time Anglo's response was not so enlightened: it dismissed forty thousand workers and joined with its fellow employers in refusing to budge on its last contract offer. The NUM stayed out for three weeks but then decided to go back to work without getting any improvement in the companies' offer.

The walkout apparently did shake up Anglo, however, for a few months later the company announced a plan to encourage loyalty among its employees, including blacks, by making them participants in a stock-ownership plan. Many of the dismissed miners were rehired and the NUM negotiated some compensation for those who were not. Even so, the NUM released a report in January 1989 accusing Anglo of intensifying repression of black miners since the strike.

Since then Anglo has continued to alternate between toughness and cooptation, the latter seen most recently in mid-1991, when the company got the NUM to agree to a profit-sharing plan for some workers.

ENVIRONMENTAL AND SAFETY RECORD

Many of Anglo's workers toil in jobs that are inherently unsafe, but sometimes company policy exacerbates the problem. In 1988 the NUM charged that a toxic polyurethane foam was to blame for a fire at an Anglo gold mine in which seven workers were killed. The miners died when the foam caught fire, spreading lethal fumes through the mines.

The union said that the foam should not have been in the mine, since the industry was supposed to have recognized that the same foam was responsible for an earlier mine fire in which 177 workers were killed.

In 1990 Anglo was one of about a dozen leading mining and metals companies from around the world that formed the International Council on Metals and the Environment to address health and safety and environmental issues in the industry.

BIBLIOGRAPHY

Friedman, Steven. *Building Tomorrow Today: African Workers in Trade Unions, 1970–1984*. Johannesburg: Ravan Press, 1987.
Gregory, Theodore. *Ernest Oppenheimer and the Economic Development of South Africa*. Oxford: Oxford University Press, 1962.

Innes, Duncan. *Anglo American and the Rise of Modern South Africa*. New York: Monthly Review Press, 1984.

Jessup, Edward. *Ernest Oppenheimer: A Study in Power*. London: Rex Collings, 1979.

Sampson, Anthony. *Black and Gold*. New York: Pantheon Books, 1987.

Wheatcroft, Geoffrey. *The Randlords*. London: Weidenfeld & Nicholson, 1985.

APPLE COMPUTER, INC.

20525 Mariani Avenue
Cupertino, California 95014
(408) 996-1010

1991 revenues: $6.3 billion (year ending September 27)
1991 net income: $309.8 million
Publicly traded company
Employees: 14,432
Founded: 1976

OVERVIEW

Apple Computer did not invent the personal computer, but it was the company that transformed it from a novelty for electronics hobbyists to something that revolutionized work, play, and education for a much wider population.

In its early years Apple still bore the marks of its origins: a couple of young men tinkering in a garage. The company's unorthodox style began to change, especially after the giant of the traditional data-processing industry, IBM, charged into the personal computer business and seized a large part of the market. For a number of years Apple remained an ardent opponent of IBM, depicting it in a famous television advertisement as an Orwellian Big Brother. While IBM and its clones came to dominate the office market, Apple defended its stronghold in the educational world. The company gave away large numbers of its machines to schools, which, aside from the good publicity, served to cultivate future customers at a young age.

Yet the professional managers who took over Apple decided that that was not enough. They began positioning Apple's lead product, the Macintosh, as a device that was not out of place in a corporate setting. This approach had limited effect, so in 1991 Apple's managers did the unthinkable: they forged an alliance with IBM to develop a new operating system and to make IBM and Apple machines more compatible. Whether the decision is seen as a betrayal of Apple's traditions or a shrewd strategic move, it assured Apple of a leading role in the future of the personal computer business.

HISTORY

The first machine to be presented as a personal computer was named after a destination of the USS *Enterprise* in the original "Star Trek" television series. The Altair, announced on the cover of *Popular Electronics* in 1975, was built by an engineer and entrepreneur named Ed Roberts, who ran a tiny company called Micro Instrumentation Telemetry Systems (MITS) he had formed in 1968 with other electronic buffs while serving in the air force. Altair was primitive in comparison with what was soon to follow. It had no keyboard or display screen, and after the circuit board was assembled, programming could be introduced only through a series of switches. Nevertheless, hobbyists of that time were excited by the fact that Altair, with its Intel 8080 microprocessor chip, was indeed a computer.

The excitement generated by Altair encouraged other small companies to enter the field. All of these, including IMSAI, Processor Technology, and North Star, were started by young "hackers" in the San Francisco and Silicon Valley computing scene. These pioneers were committed to making computers accessible to a wide range of users and mistrusted those who attempted to make a business out of micros.

Others seeking uses for the computer had explicitly political objectives and talked of "computer lib" as a new and potent tool for changing society. Lee Felsenstein started the Community Memory project to provide free computerized information services to the public, but he ran into enormous financial obstacles. Eventually both the politicos and the techies came together with the budding entrepreneurs in a group called the Homebrew Computer Club.

Among the participants in the Homebrew meetings were Steven Jobs and Stephen Wozniak. Each had been involved in electronics since their teens and were drawn into "phone phreaking"—that is, creating devices called blue boxes that allowed one to make long-distance phone calls for free.

Before long Jobs ended up working for Nolan Bushnell at Atari. Bushnell, who invented the first video game, an electronic version of table tennis called Pong, was already a Silicon Valley success story. Yet Jobs was more interested in computers than in games, and after Bushnell turned down his proposal for a micro he persuaded his friend Wozniak to build one independently.

What came to be known as Apples were built first in Jobs's parents' house and then in the proverbial garage. After fifty copies of the primitive Apple I were well received, Jobs and Wozniak persuaded Mike Markkula, a former marketing manager at Intel who was comfortably retired in his mid-thirties, to help Apple Computer, as they named their company, get off the ground. About the same time, leading Silicon Valley publicist Regis McKenna agreed to take on the firm as a client.

Jobs had insisted that the Apple II have an inviting design and be as easy as possible to use. His instincts paid off. Sales of the new machine soared. More than any other product, it helped to bring computers out of the hobbyist world and into the homes of a wide range of the general population. Partly responsible for Apple II's success was the availability of VisiCalc, the first financial analysis program for micros.

Apple Computer experienced rapid growth. Its operating revenues soared from $8 million in 1978 to $117 million in 1980. This progress was launched with the help of $517,000 in venture capital from Venrock Associates (the venture capital arm of the Rockefeller interests), Don Valentine, and Arthur Rock. When Apple subsequently went public in December 1980, that $517,000 was suddenly worth about $200 million, and the shares owned by Jobs, Wozniak, and Markkula made them centimillionaires. Many other Apple employees prospered from this, too, thanks to the company's generous stock options.

Meanwhile, planners at computer behemoth IBM were closely monitoring the growth of the micro market. Although Big Blue traditionally had focused on selling large systems and had been reluctant to enter even the minicomputer field, IBM was confronting the 1980s in a more aggressive manner. An operation was set up in Boca Raton, Florida, to develop a small IBM computer to compete with the micros produced by the entrepreneurs who had not even been born when Big Blue got into the computer business in the early 1950s.

Introduced in August 1981, the IBM Personal Computer (PC) took the world by storm. While it was not a great technological leap forward—the components were standard ones from outside vendors—the machine did have the IBM name. Big Blue also was shrewd in giving the PC an open software system, which encouraged the creation of many compatible programs by independent software firms.

Another factor was that IBM's machine was announced at a time when the Apple III was suffering from technical problems (which led to major recalls) and poor marketing. IBM was able to make great strides in the office and professional segment, matching Apple's market share within a year. In 1983 Big Blue gained more ground as Apple's new entry for the business market, the $10,000 Lisa, failed to win widespread acceptance because of its limited software and inability to communicate with other computers, especially IBM mainframes.

In 1984 Apple launched its counterattack, led by John Sculley, a marketing specialist who had been lured from PepsiCo to serve as president. Apple brought out a new version of Lisa and a less expensive but impressive system called Macintosh. Sculley and Jobs hoped to pitch the Mac—which offered a more-powerful (32-bit) processor, excellent graphics, and a mouse input device—to smaller companies and university students.

Before long, however, Apple abandoned its hope of routing IBM from the personal computer market, realizing that it was more realistic to develop ways of making Macintoshes compatible with IBM office systems. With Sculley completely in charge after Jobs was forced out in late 1985, Apple improved its profit rates but continued to slip in market share.

Apple's slide was in part the result of a new force in the micro market that was challenging Big Blue as well: producers of IBM-compatible PCs. Just as happened in the mainframe and peripheral markets, a group of producers saw an opportunity in making micros that worked on the same software as the IBM PC but were better or cheaper than the machines put out by IBM itself.

Among the clone producers the most successful was Compaq Computer, which was the first to come out with a PC based on the advanced Intel 80386 processor. Known as the 386, the chip started to revolutionize desktop computing. PCs were now often able to replace mainframes and minicomputers. Yet not long after the 386 entered the scene, IBM introduced a series of PCs (called Personal System/2) that used the new OS/2 operating system developed by Microsoft and employed a graphical interface that resembled that of Apple's Macintosh. (Apple responded to the introduction of that software, known as Windows, by bringing a multi-billion-dollar copyright infringement suit against Microsoft.) In fact, as Apple revamped the Macintosh to make it more appealing to corporate customers, the products of IBM and Apple began to converge in many respects.

Apple began to make some progress in that effort, but by the beginning of the 1990s it was confronting a slowdown in revenue growth and slippage in the company's market share in the United States. This was counterbalanced by a long-overdue surge in Japan and other foreign markets. In fiscal 1989 Apple began to get a majority of its operating income from outside the United States.

Sculley responded to the domestic problem by shaking up his top management, bringing Michael Spindler, who had led Apple's successful drive into Europe, back home as chief operating officer. Spindler's plan involved a strict plan to cut costs—at a company that for years had given its top managers luxury cars like Jaguars—and a drive to win back market share with a new line of Macs.

In late 1990 those new machines appeared on the market. They included a low-priced Mac Classic aimed at first-time buyers and a more affordable system with a color monitor. Apple also announced a high-end model, the Mac IIsi, which used a chip comparable to the 386. The Mac Classic part of the plan, in particular, was a great success, so much so that the company had trouble keeping up with the demand. Encouraged by the turnaround, Sculley announced in March 1991 that he would focus his efforts on developing breakthrough products.

A sign of Apple's success was that it finally had to confront a challenge that IBM has been facing for twenty years: cloning. A small company named Nutek Computers Inc. announced that it was developing a machine that would be Macintosh-compatible. While Nutek was attempting to create a clone through reverse engineering, Sculley revealed that Apple was considered competing with Microsoft in the software arena by selling its operating system for use on machines made by others.

An even more dramatic change in Apple occurred in mid-1991, when it was revealed that the company was involved in wide-ranging discussions with its old rival IBM on the sharing of technology. The two leaders of the personal computer industry soon announced that they would form a joint venture to develop an advanced operating system that each would employ in its own machines and license to others. The operating system would be used with an IBM-designed microprocessor that in Apple's case would be supplied by Motorola. They also agreed to develop products to make it easier for IBM-based machines and Macs to share information. The plan presented a direct challenge both to Microsoft, whose operating systems had dominated the industry, and to Intel, which had a near monopoly in the market for microprocessors for IBM-compatible machines.

The companies were slow in providing full details of their plans, but there was no question that the IBM-Apple alliance would be the proverbial five-hundred–pound gorilla in the personal computer industry, able to do virtually anything it wanted.

Soon after the IBM deal was announced, Apple made its long-awaited move in the notebook style market with three laptop Macintoshes, including one manufactured for it by Sony. This was the first time Apple had put its name on a machine made by another company, and there were indications that it might be only the first in a series of products made for Apple by the Japanese company better known for televisions and other entertainment devices. The cooperation with Sony is part of Apple's strategy to move into consumer electronics and multimedia systems that combine video, sound, graphics, and text. Apple has joined forces with Japan's Sharp Corp. to develop a new class of pocket-sized information devices.

OPERATIONS

Apple operates in a single segment: the business of designing, manufacturing, and marketing microprocessor-based personal computers and related peripheral devices, such as printers, scanners, CD-ROM players, modems, and both monochrome and color monitors. The personal computers include the Apple II line and, more important, the Macintosh line. Apple's wholly owned subsidiary Claris Corporation develops and markets software for Macintosh systems. Apple's manufacturing facilities are located in Fremont, California; Cork, Ireland; and Singapore.

TOP EXECUTIVES

- John Sculley, chairman and chief executive
- Michael H. Spindler, president and chief operating officer

- Joseph A. Graziano, executive vice president and chief financial officer
- Albert A. Eisenstat, executive vice president
- A. C. Markkula, Jr., vice chairman and former chief executive of Apple; chairman of ACM Aviation Inc.

OUTSIDE DIRECTORS

- Peter O. Crisp, general partner of Venrock Associates
- Bernard Goldstein, partner in the investment firm Broadview Associates
- Arthur Rock, principal of Arthur Rock & Company
- John A. Rollwagen, chief executive of Cray Research

FINANCIAL DATA

Revenues (in millions of dollars)
(years ending in late September)

1991	6,309
1990	5,558
1989	5,284
1988	4,071
1987	2,661

Net Income (in millions of dollars) (years ending in late September)

1991	310
1990	475
1989	454
1988	400
1987	217

GEOGRAPHICAL BREAKDOWN

Net Sales to Unaffiliated Customers (in millions of dollars)

Year*	United States		Europe		Elsewhere	
1991	3,485	(55%)	1,285	(29%)	1,000	(16%)
1990	3,241	(58%)	1,545	(28%)	772	(14%)
1989	3,401	(64%)	1,209	(23%)	673	(13%)
1988	2,766	(68%)	858	(21%)	447	(11%)

*Fiscal year ends in late September.

Operating Income (in millions of dollars)

Year*	United States		Europe		Elsewhere	
1991	9	(2%)	223	(48%)	228	(50%)
1990	229	(33%)	367	(52%)	104	(15%)
1989	305	(46%)	250	(38%)	101	(15%)
1988	332	(54%)	206	(33%)	77	(13%)

*Fiscal year ends in late September.

LABOR RELATIONS

For most of its history Apple was one of those freewheeling young companies that were said to treat their employees so well that a union would be superfluous. Indeed, Apple attracted a young, creative, highly motivated work force and provided a stimulating and informal environment. Members of the team that developed the Macintosh liked to wear T-shirts emblazoned with the message: WORKING 90 HOURS A WEEK AND LOVING EVERY MINUTE OF IT.

Boring and repetitive work in production was reduced through the use of advanced technology. It was reported that the facilities built for producing the Macintosh were so automated that direct labor costs amounted to less than 1 percent of the total expenses of producing the machine.

This is not to say that everyone employed by Apple enjoyed an ideal situation on the job. The company laid off twelve hundred people in 1985, and many of those hired since then have been temporaries, with limited or no job security. A group of fifteen black employees filed a race discrimination complaint with the U.S. Department of Labor; Apple paid $437,000 in 1991 to settle the case.

Yet employee loyalty remained fairly high until mid-1991, when the company announced that it would dismiss 10 percent of its work force, some fifteen hundred jobs, as part of an effort to cut costs. In the wake of that announcement a dissident organization called Employees for One Apple was formed, and there were reports that the group was considering launching a union-organizing drive at the company.

Apple also has been embroiled in a campaign by the janitors who clean the company's offices to get collective bargaining rights. Technically the janitors are employees of a subcontractor, but the workers and the Service Employees International Union have pressured chief executive Sculley to intervene. A group of the janitors protested at Apple's annual meeting in 1991 and later demonstrated outside Sculley's home.

In early 1992 Apple finally gave in and publicly called for a representation election. Soon after that the subcontractor recognized the union.

ENVIRONMENTAL RECORD

Like many other electronics companies, Apple has made extensive use of chlorofluorocarbons (CFCs) in the cleaning of circuit boards and other components. CFCs have been recognized as causing the destruction of the earth's ozone layer and thus raise the risk of skin cancer. In 1991, however, Apple announced that it had developed techniques to reduce the need for CFCs and expected to cease using the chemicals entirely by 1993.

BIBLIOGRAPHY

Butcher, Lee. *Accidental Millionaire: The Rise and Fall of Steve Jobs at Apple Computer*. New York: Paragon House, 1987.

Freiberger, Paul, and Michael Swaine. *Fire in the Valley: The Making of the Personal Computer*. New York: Osborne/McGraw-Hill, 1984.

Levering, Robert, Michael Katz, and Milton Moskowitz. *The Computer Entrepreneurs*. New York: New American Library, 1984.

Moritz, Michael. *The Little Kingdom: The Private Story of Apple Computer*. New York: William Morrow, 1984.

Rose, Frank. *West of Eden: The End of Innocence at Apple Computer*. New York: Viking, 1989.

Sculley, John, and John A. Bryne. *Odyssey: Pepsi to Apple*. New York: Harper & Row, 1987.

BABY BELLS

American Information Technologies Corporation
Bell Atlantic Corporation
BellSouth Corporation
NYNEX Corporation
Pacific Telesis Group
Southwestern Bell Corporation
US West Communications

American Information Technologies (Ameritech)
30 South Wacker Drive
Chicago, Illinois 60606
(312) 750-5000

1991 revenues: $10.8 billion
1991 net income: $1.2 billion
Publicly traded company
Employees: 73,967
Founded: 1984
Primary service areas: Illinois, Indiana, Michigan, Ohio, and
    Wisconsin

Bell Atlantic
1600 Market Street
Philadelphia, Pennsylvania 19103
(215) 963-6000

1991 revenues: $12.3 billion
1991 net income: −$222.7 million (loss)
Publicly traded company
Employees: 75,700
Founded: 1984

Primary service areas: Delaware, Maryland, New Jersey,
Pennsylvania, Virginia, West Virginia, and the District of
Columbia

BellSouth
1155 Peachtree Street NE
Atlanta, Georgia 30367
(404) 249-2000

1991 revenues: $14.4 billion
1991 net income: $1.5 billion
Publicly traded company
Employees: 96,084
Founded: 1984
Primary service areas: Alabama, Florida, Georgia, Kentucky,
Louisiana, Mississippi, North Carolina, South Carolina, and
Tennessee

NYNEX
335 Madison Avenue
New York, New York 10017
(212) 370-7400

1991 revenues: $13.2 billion
1991 net income: $601 million
Publicly traded company
Employees: 83,900
Founded: 1984
Primary service areas: Connecticut, Maine, Massachusetts, New
Hampshire, New York, Rhode Island, and Vermont

Pacific Telesis
130 Kearny Street
San Francisco, California 94108
(415) 394-3000

1991 revenues: $9.9 billion
1991 net income: $1 billion
Publicly traded company
Employees: 62,236
Founded: 1984
Primary service areas: California and Nevada

Southwestern Bell
One Bell Center
St. Louis, Missouri 63101
(314) 235-9800

1991 revenues: $9.3 billion
1991 net income: $1.1 billion
Publicly traded company
Employees: 61,200
Founded: 1984
Primary service areas: Arkansas, Kansas, Missouri, Oklahoma,
     and Texas

US West
7800 East Orchard Road
Englewood, Colorado 80111
(303) 793-6500

1991 revenues: $10.6 billion
1991 net income: $553 million
Publicly traded company
Employees: 65,829
Founded: 1984
Primary service areas: Arizona, Colorado, Idaho, Iowa,
     Minnesota, Montana, Nebraska, New Mexico, North Dakota,
     Oregon, South Dakota, Utah, Washington, and Wyoming

OVERVIEW

The seven telephone companies known informally as the Baby Bells were created as the result of the breakup of American Telephone and Telegraph (AT&T) in 1984. Since becoming independent these regional operating companies have fought to do much more than provide basic phone service. Eager to make use of their combined revenues of some $80 billion, they have pushed federal and state regulators and the federal judge who oversees their activities to allow them to expand into a variety of new fields.

Many of these new activities are taking place far from their primary service areas. In fact, the Baby Bells have become the most aggressive players in the international telecommunications industry. They have invaded Europe with projects involving cellular telephones, cable television, and paging systems. They have pursued business in Asia, South America, and Australasia. No project seems too ambitious or too risky—as seen, for example, in US West's controversial proposal to lay a fiber-optic cable across the former Soviet Union. The Baby Bells have even taken control of privatized telephone companies in such countries as New Zealand and Mexico.

While a number of the companies have found themselves in legal trouble because of questionable practices, the Baby Bells are situated to play an increasingly powerful role in world telecommunications.

HISTORY

Independence Day for the Baby Bells was January 1, 1984, the effective date of their separation from AT&T. Under the divestiture agreement, the local telephone companies took on new identities as seven regional holding companies. Yet, unlike the newly deregulated parent company, the regional holding companies were regulated monopolies. U.S. District Judge Harold Greene, who was overseeing the divestiture, allowed them to retain the profitable Yellow Pages business and the exclusive use of the Bell name and logo in the United States.

Confined to the unexciting business of providing local telephone service, the regional holding companies soon became restless. The very names that some of them adopted—Pacific Telesis and Ameritech, for example—reflected their high-tech ambitions.

For the first few years of their existence the Baby Bells engaged in strategic planning specifically aimed at convincing Judge Greene to lift the prohibitions on their entry into nontelephone ventures. They soon became involved, for example, in computer retailing, software, real estate, and financial services. By the end of 1986 these companies had spent an estimated $3.5 billion to purchase businesses as well as additional but undetermined amounts to start new ventures.

But Greene frowned on attempts by the Baby Bells to diversify their operations. In a series of decisions on the Bells' requests for relief, the judge ruled that these companies could engage in the new fields only if they got permission for each venture and the new activities accounted for no more than 10 percent of revenues. The companies submitted to these restrictions reluctantly and kept the pressure on Greene.

By 1986 the Baby Bells had begun to enter the long-distance business. Ameritech won permission to produce telecommunications equipment overseas. That same year a federal appeals court reversed one of Greene's decisions and allowed the Baby Bells to market specialized services outside their geographical areas.

It was clear that Greene would not be able to confine the Baby Bells much longer, much as he tried to remain firm in keeping them out of the long-distance and equipment manufacturing fields. He permitted them to enter the data-transmission business (particularly the providing of gateways to electronic data base services) and to expand their cellular telephone business outside their primary service areas. This loosening of the reins prompted some major deals, including Southwestern Bell's 1986 purchase of most of the cellular operations of Metromedia for $1.4 billion.

The next significant challenge to Greene's authority occurred in 1990, when an appeals court told him to reconsider his refusal to allow the operating companies to provide computer-based services. Sensing that the time had come to shift authority away from Greene, the Baby Bells soon launched an intensive "free the Bells" movement to get Congress to return oversight of the industry to the Federal Communications Commission (FCC). This campaign publicized their conviction that Greene's restrictions were a serious deterrent to the country's ability to compete, but not enough legislators were persuaded to act.

The Baby Bells' determination to expand into nontelephone endeavors led them to pursue opportunities overseas with foreign governments and companies. US West, for example, won a cable television franchise in Hong Kong, got a contract to set up a cellular telephone business in Hungary, and made a deal to lay a fiber-optic cable across the Soviet Union. However, the Soviet deal was blocked by the U.S. Commerce Department for national security reasons. Pacific Telesis developed the first private cellular operation in West Germany and invested in three cable television companies in Britain. Bell Atlantic won a contract to upgrade Spain's telephone network in preparation for the 1992 Summer Olympics in Barcelona.

The Baby Bells also moved to take advantage of spreading privatization of telecommunications overseas. Working together, Ameritech and Bell Atlantic paid more than $2 billion to acquire the state-owned telephone company of New Zealand; later their share will be reduced to just under 50 percent after a planned public stock offering. Southwestern Bell was part of a consortium that acquired 51 percent of the Mexican national telephone company in 1990.

Pursuing diversification at home, NYNEX announced plans in 1989 for an ambitious videotex information service. Pacific Telesis that same year became the first Baby Bell to enter the domestic cable TV business when it bought a majority stake in a Chicago cable franchise; it covered itself by arranging for the acquisition to be kept in the hands of an intermediary until Judge Greene ruled on the deal. In 1991 US West joined with AT&T and Tele-Communications Inc., the largest cable TV operator in the United States, in a test project to provide "video-on-demand." This service, which gave the phone companies a toehold in the world of visual entertainment, would transmit movies and other features via an upgraded cable TV system.

Such ventures were made more feasible in 1991, when Greene further liberalized his restrictions on the Baby Bells. He decided that they now could offer information and other computerized services, including electronic publishing, home banking, and on-line shopping. A few months later the FCC sought to free the Bells even more by proposing that they be permitted to package and transmit television programming.

Also in 1991, BellSouth and RAM Broadcasting Corporation agreed to form a joint venture to operate international mobile data communications networks. Focused primarily on bolstering both companies' holdings in the wireless data field, this deal also enabled BellSouth to acquire RAM's 26-percent interest in Honolulu Cellular Telephone Company, raising its stake in this company to 51 percent.

At the same time, Pacific Telesis announced that it would cooperate with McCaw Cellular Communications in providing service in a number of large U.S. cities, and Bell Atlantic said it would spend $2.5 billion to acquire Metro

Mobile, the eleventh-largest cellular telephone company. Ameritech announced that it would imitate AT&T and introduce its own combination credit card and calling card. And US West formed an alliance with France Telecom to introduce a version of that company's Minitel videotex service in the United States. BellSouth was part of a consortium that won the right to provide telephone services in Australia in competition with that country's state-owned telecommunications operation.

There is a tendency to look at the Baby Bells as a group, but their performances have been far from identical. BellSouth, which serves fast-growing states like Florida and Georgia, has in many ways emerged as the leader of the pack. The largest of the group in terms of revenues and profits, BellSouth is also the most technologically advanced. It has been especially aggressive in the cellular phone business. After acquiring the cellular phone and paging properties of Mobile Communications Corporation of America for $710 million in stock, it moved ahead of McCaw to take first place in the field (as measured by the number of subscribers).

In their zeal to grow, some of the Baby Bells have cut corners and gotten themselves in trouble with regulators and the courts. In 1990 Bell Atlantic was temporarily barred from receiving federal contracts because the company gave misleading information in a bid for a $100-million contract to modify the Treasury Department's phone system. US West was fined $10 million in 1991 for violations of the divestiture consent decree.

NYNEX suffered a series of embarrassments in 1990, beginning with the announcement that the FCC was fining the company $1.4 million and ordering a refund of $35 million to customers because of excessive markups on goods and services by the company's purchasing arm. The inflated costs were passed on to customers in the form of higher rates. Then a federal grand jury indicted NYNEX for criminal contempt, charging that the company had violated the divestiture consent decree by providing data-processing services through a small software subsidiary. Soon after that there were revelations that annual gatherings of company officials and representatives of suppliers were more like orgies than business meetings. The reputation of NYNEX sank so low that the New York State Public Service Commission seriously considered forcing the company to divest itself of its New York Telephone Company unit.

Courts and regulators are not the Baby Bells' only problems. In their basic telephone business they have been facing increased competition from companies that supply private telecommunications systems, involving microwave antennas and satellites, that bypass the traditional phone grid. The Baby Bells are both threatened by this spread of wireless systems and are using the fact to bolster their arguments concerning the need for further deregulation.

OPERATIONS

Each of the Baby Bells provides basic telephone service to residential and business customers in its service areas; each also publishes White Pages and

Yellow Pages directories. The companies are heavily involved in other communications services, such as cellular telephones and paging. To varying degrees they also are involved in untraditional areas like real estate, computer services, software, and leasing. They are still barred from providing long-distance telephone service and from manufacturing telephone equipment. Outside the United States the Baby Bells provide many of the same services they supply at home, while also engaging in activities, such as cable television, that have been forbidden to them in their domestic operations.

TOP EXECUTIVES

Ameritech
- William L. Weiss, chairman and chief executive
- William H. Springer, vice chairman
- Ormand J. Wade, vice chairman
- Robert L. Barnett, president of Ameritech Bell Group
- Louis J. Rutigliano, vice chairman

Bell Atlantic
- Raymond W. Smith, chairman and chief executive
- Anton J. Campanella, president
- Robert A. Levetown, vice chairman

BellSouth
- John L. Clendenin, chief executive
- Harvey R. Holding, vice chairman
- Walter H. Alford, executive vice president and general counsel
- Raymond L. McGuire, executive vice president for governmental affairs
- Roy B. Howard, senior vice president

NYNEX
- William G. Ferguson, chairman and chief executive
- Robert J. Eckenrode, vice chairman
- Frederic V. Salerno, vice chairman and president, worldwide services
- Ivan G. Seidenberg, vice chairman, telecommunications

Pacific Telesis
- Sam Ginn, chairman and chief executive
- John E. Hulse, vice chairman and chief financial officer
- C. Lee Cox, group president, PacTel companies
- Philip J. Quigley, group president, Bell operating companies

Southwestern Bell
- Edward E. Whitacre, Jr., chairman and chief executive
- Gerald D. Blatherwick, vice chairman

- Robert G. Pope, vice chairman and chief financial officer
- James R. Adams, president

US West
- Richard D. McCormick, chairman and chief executive
- Laurence W. DeMuth, Jr., executive vice president
- Charles M. Lillis, executive vice president

OUTSIDE DIRECTORS

Ameritech
- Weston R. Christopherson, retired chairman of Northern Trust
- Donald C. Clark, chief executive of Household International
- Robert C. Ernest, retired president of Kimberly-Clark
- Richard M. Gillett, retired chairman of Old Kent Financial
- Hanna Holborn Gray, president of the University of Chicago
- James A. Henderson, president of Cummins Engine
- Hal C. Kuehl, retired chairman of Firstar
- John B. McCoy, chief executive of Banc One
- John D. Ong, chief executive of BFGoodrich

Bell Atlantic
- Frank C. Carlucci, vice chairman of the Carlyle Group
- William G. Copeland, chairman of Continental American Life
- James H. Gilliam, Jr., executive vice president of Beneficial Corporation
- Gerald T. Halpin, chairman of the investment company West*Group
- Thomas H. Kean, president of Drew University
- John C. Marous, Jr., retired chairman of Westinghouse
- John F. Maypole, managing partner in Peach State Real Estate
- Thomas H. O'Brien, chief executive of PNC Financial
- Rozanne L. Ridgway, president of the Atlantic Council of the United States
- Shirley Young, vice president of General Motors

BellSouth
- Ivan Allen III, president of the office products firm Ivan Allen Company
- Andrew F. Brimmer, president of the economic consulting firm Brimmer & Company
- James B. Campbell, chairman of MISSCO Corporation
- Amando M. Codina, chief executive of the Codina Bush Group
- Marshall M. Criser, chairman of the law firm Mahoney Adams & Criser
- Gordon B. Davidson, chief executive of the law firm Wyatt Tarrant & Combs
- Phyllis Burke Davis, retired senior vice president of Avon Products
- John G. Medlin, Jr., chief executive of Wachovia Corporation
- C. Dixon Spangler, Jr., president of the University of North Carolina

- Ronald A. Terry, chief executive of First Tennessee National Corporation
- Thomas R. Williams, president of the investment firm the Wales Group
- J. Tylee Wilson, retired chairman and chief executive of RJR Nabisco

NYNEX

- John Brademas, former president of New York University
- Randolph W. Bromery, professor emeritus at the University of Massachusetts at Amherst
- John J. Creedon, retired chief executive of Metropolitan Life Insurance Company
- Stanley P. Goldstein, chief executive of Melville Corporation
- Helene L. Kaplan, counsel to the law firm Skadden Arps Slate Meagher & Flom
- Elizabeth T. Kennan, president of Mount Holyoke College
- David J. Mahoney, chief executive of David Mahoney Ventures
- Edward E. Phillips, chief executive of the New England Mutual Life Insurance Company
- Walter V. Shipley, president of Chemical Banking Corporation
- John R. Stafford, chief executive of American Home Products

Pacific Telesis

- Norman Barker, Jr., former chairman of First Interstate Bank
- William P. Clark, chief executive of the Clark Companies
- William K. Coblentz, senior partner in the law firm Coblentz Cahen McCabe & Breyer
- Myron Du Bain, former chairman of SRI International
- Herman E. Gallegos, chairman of Gallegos Institutional Investors
- James R. Harvey, chief executive of Transamerica Corporation
- Paul Hazen, president of Wells Fargo & Company
- Ivan J. Houston, chairman of Golden State Mutual Life
- Leslie L. Luttgens, civic and community leader
- Mary S. Metz, former president of Mills College
- Toni Rembe, partner in the law firm Pillsbury Madison & Sutro
- S. Donley Ritchey, former chief executive of Lucky Stores

Southwestern Bell

- Clarence C. Barksdale, vice chairman of Washington University
- James E. Barnes, chief executive of MAPCO Inc.
- Zane E. Barnes, chairman emeritus of Southwestern Bell
- Jack S. Blanton, chief executive of Eddy Refining Company
- August A. Busch III, chairman of Anheuser-Busch
- Ruben R. Cardenas, partner in the law firm Cardenas Whitis Stephen Corcoran & McLain

- Tom C. Frost, chairman of Cullen/Frost Bankers Inc.
- Jess T. Hay, chief executive of Lomas Financial Corporation
- Bobby R. Inman, former chief executive of the Microelectronics and Computer Technology Corporation and former deputy director of the Central Intelligence Agency
- Charles F. Knight, chief executive of Emerson Electric
- Sybil C. Mobley, dean of the business school at Florida A&M University
- Haskell M. Monroe, Jr., professor of history at the University of Missouri–Columbia

US West

- Remedios Diaz-Oliver, president and chief executive of All American Container, Inc.
- Grant A. Dove, chief executive of the Microelectronics and Computer Technology Corporation
- Pierson M. Grieve, chief executive of Ecolab, Inc.
- Shirley M. Hufstedler, partner in the law firm Hufstedler Kaus & Ettinger
- Allen F. Jacobson, former chief executive of Minnesota Mining & Manufacturing
- Glen L. Ryland, president of RYCO, Inc.
- Jack D. Sparks, former chief executive of Whirlpool
- Jerry O. Williams, managing director of Monotype Corporation
- Daniel Yankelovich, chairman of the research firm DYG, Inc.

FINANCIAL DATA

AMERITECH

Revenues (in millions of dollars)

1991	10,818
1990	10,663
1989	10,211
1988	9,903
1987	9,548

Net Income (in millions of dollars)

1991	1,166
1990	1,254
1989	1,238
1988	1,237
1987	1,188

BELL ATLANTIC

Revenues (in millions of dollars)

1991	12,280
1990	12,298
1989	11,449
1988	10,880
1987	10,747

Net Income (in millions of dollars)

1991	−223 (loss)*
1990	1,313
1989	1,075
1988	1,317
1987	1,240

*Reflects $1.6 billion after-tax accrual to adopt a new accounting standard for retiree benefits.

BELLSOUTH

Revenues (in millions of dollars)

1991	14,446
1990	14,354
1989	13,996
1988	13,597
1987	12,230

Net Income (in millions of dollars)

1991	1,472
1990	1,632
1989	1,741
1988	1,666
1987	1,665

NYNEX

Revenues (in millions of dollars)

1991	13,229
1990	13,582
1989	13,195
1988	12,650
1987	12,084

Net Income (in millions of dollars)

1991	601
1990	949
1989	808
1988	1,315
1987	1,277

PACIFIC TELESIS

Revenues (in millions of dollars)

1991	9,895
1990	9,716
1989	9,593
1988	9,483
1987	9,156

Net Income (in millions of dollars)

1991	1,015
1990	1,030
1989	1,242
1988	1,188
1987	950

SOUTHWESTERN BELL

Revenues (in millions of dollars)

1991	9,332
1990	9,113
1989	8,730
1988	8,453
1987	8,003

Net Income (in millions of dollars)

1991	1,076
1990	1,101
1989	1,093
1988	1,060
1987	1,047

US WEST

Revenues (in millions of dollars)

1991	10,577
1990	9,957
1989	9,691
1988	9,221
1987	8,697

Net Income (in millions of dollars)

1991	553
1990	1,199
1989	1,111
1988	1,132
1987	1,006

LABOR RELATIONS

The regulated operations of the local telephone companies have always been heavily unionized. In 1986, as the time came for the first postdivestiture contract negotiations, the Bells made it clear to the main union, the Communications Workers of America (CWA), that they would take a hard line.

Before talks with the local companies began, the CWA and AT&T reached an agreement, but only after an arduous fight. The CWA rejected AT&T's offer of an 8-percent wage increase over three years and initiated a national strike. AT&T stood fast and took its offer directly to workers through newspaper advertisements. The strike ended after twenty-six days and the two sides reached a settlement that included the same wage package but also had special provisions for job retraining. Only a few weeks later CWA talks with some of the Baby Bells broke down and some seventy thousand workers went on strike for about a week until settlements were reached.

A protracted fight at AT&T was averted in 1989 when the company agreed to a settlement that included innovative improvements in family benefits, though the cost-of-living adjustment for wages was eliminated. However, intense frustration by rank-and-file workers led to more-difficult contract negotiations at the Baby Bells. Workers at four of the seven companies walked out, objecting to management demands for reductions in health benefits. At one point some two hundred thousand people were on strike. While three of the Baby Bells settled within a few weeks—with the health-care issue being resolved by agreements to establish preferred-provider systems to keep down costs—the strike at NYNEX grew more bitter. The deadlock finally was ended after sixteen weeks when NYNEX agreed to drop its effort to shift health-care costs to workers and the unions agreed to a smaller wage package.

The CWA and NYNEX adopted a very different approach in 1991, when the two parties settled on a new contract eleven months before the expiration of the agreement. The agreement included no concessions by the union and a larger wage increase than the previous two contracts.

BIBLIOGRAPHY

Barbash, Jack. *Unions and Telephones: The Story of the Communications Workers of America*. New York: Harper Brothers, 1952.

Brooks, Thomas R. *The Communications Workers of America*. New York: Mason/Charter, 1977.

Coll, Steve. *The Deal of the Century: The Breakup of AT&T*. New York: Atheneum, 1987.

Holding the Line in '89: Lessons of the NYNEX Strike. Somerville, Mass.: Labor Resource Center, n.d.

Norwood, Stephen H. *Labor's Flaming Youth: Telephone Operators and Worker Militancy*. Urbana: University of Illinois Press, 1990.

Schacht, John N. *The Making of Telephone Unionism, 1920–1947*. New Brunswick, N.J.: Rutgers University Press, 1985.

Staley, Delbert. *NYNEX in a New Age*. Exton, Pa.: Newcomen Society, 1987.

Tunstall, W. Brooke. *Disconnecting Parties: Managing the Bell System Breakup—An Inside View*. New York: McGraw-Hill, 1985.

BASF AG

Carl-Bosch-Strasse 38
D-6700 Ludwigshafen am Rhein
Germany
(621) 600

1991 revenues: $30.8 billion
1991 net income: $685.8 million
Publicly traded company
Employees: 129,434
Founded: 1861

OVERVIEW

Starting out as a dye producer, BASF became part of the huge IG Farben combine that took over the German chemical industry in the 1920s and then was dismantled after World War II. BASF, again an independent company, made a rapid recovery and emerged as a world leader in such areas as plastics, fertilizers, and paints. Today it is at the top of the world chemical industry, just barely ahead of its former IG Farben partners Bayer and Hoechst.

From the late 1960s through the mid-1980s BASF made a major expansionary drive in the United States, but it found itself the target of a union-led corporate campaign that highlighted the company's environmental transgressions. In recent years BASF has turned eastward, developing new operations in the former German Democratic Republic and the former Soviet Union.

HISTORY

Badische Anilin- und Soda-Fabrik was founded in 1861 by a jeweler named Frederick Englehorn to exploit recent discoveries about the use of coal-tar derivatives in making synthetic dyes. It pioneered the production of the reddish orange dye alizarin and received the first German patent for a coal-tar dye for methylene blue in 1877. Toward the end of the century the company introduced a highly successful synthetic indigo.

While gaining fame as a producer of dyes, BASF began moving into other chemical markets. In 1888 it developed a process of making highly concentrated sulfuric acid, and in the early years of the twentieth century it created a process for synthesizing ammonia from nitrogen and hydrogen—a breakthrough that led to the production of nitrogenous fertilizers.

The dye industry in Germany (and other countries) had a strong propensity for anticompetitive practices. BASF went along with this by joining the Dreibund cartel with its rivals Bayer and Agfa, while Hoechst was part of another grouping, called Dreiverband. The cartels carved up the market among themselves and undermined the growth of the dye industry in countries like the United States. During World War I the German dye companies altered their formulas to produce mustard gas and explosives.

In 1916 the two dye cartels joined forces to create the *Interessengemeinschaft der deutschen Teerfarbenfabriken* (Community of Interests of the German Tar Dye Factories). Known later as the Little IG, this combine had complete control over the dye industry and soon acquired extensive coal mining operations to carry out a plan initiated by BASF to create liquid fuel through the hydrogenation of coal.

By the 1920s dye industry leaders, led by Carl Bosch of BASF and Carl Duisberg of Bayer, were pushing for a complete consolidation of the industry—that is, the merger of the dye makers into a single company. This is what happened in 1925 with the creation of the *Interessengemeinschaft Farbenindustrie AG* (Interest Community of the Dye Industry, Inc.), or IG Farben.

This huge corporation, which soon included related industries, such as explosives and fibers, was the biggest enterprise in all of Europe and the fourth-largest in the world, behind General Motors, United States Steel, and Standard Oil of New Jersey. With Standard Oil IG Farben entered into a noncompetition arrangement for oil and chemicals while agreeing to cooperate on the development of synthetic rubber (though Jersey Standard later came under fire because of evidence that the German company was impeding its progress in this crucial area). As part of the cartel BASF continued to innovate, developing new products like magnetic tape and polystyrene.

Although Carl Bosch, the head of IG Farben's managing board, opposed the anti-Semitism of the Nazis, the company gave financial support to Hitler and—without Bosch, who resigned in 1935—became indispensable to the German military effort during World War II. The company made use of slave labor, locating one of its synthetic rubber facilities in Auschwitz in order to be near the captive labor supply of the infamous concentration camp, for which it also produced the lethal gas used in exterminating inmates. For such practices a group of IG Farben executives were convicted of war crimes at the Nuremburg trials. Several years later, in 1952, the company was dismantled and redivided into several independent firms, including BASF, Bayer, and Hoechst.

BASF, now a much smaller operation, wasted no time rebuilding its facilities, which had been heavily bombed during the war. It returned to its nitrogen and ammonia products, especially fertilizers, as well as plastics. In 1953 the company formed a joint venture with Royal Dutch/Shell for making polystyrene and developed new dyes for the synthetic fibers that were taking over the textile industry. This was part of BASF's move away from coal-based products and into petrochemicals.

The company's growth was remarkable. By the 1960s it was once again a leading chemical producer and led the field in plastics, although its entrance into synthetic fiber production brought BASF the headaches associated with overcapacity in that industry. In 1969 BASF strengthened its petroleum position by acquiring the German oil and gas producer Wintershall, which also brought with it a major potash business.

The company also expanded its U.S. operations, founded in the mid-1950s, with the purchase of Wyandotte Chemicals in 1969 and the buyout of Dow Chemical's half interest in a joint venture the two companies had formed in 1958. Other BASF investments in the United States during the 1970s included the Chemetron Pigments Division of Allegheny Ludlum, a minority interest in the automotive coatings business of Cook Paint & Varnish, and the flavor and fragrance company Fritzsche, Dodge & Olcott (later sold). Yet a plan to build a dye and plastics plant in South Carolina was canceled because of local opposition.

During the 1980s BASF stepped up its involvement in the United States, in part to hedge against fluctuations in the exchange rate between the deutsche mark and the dollar. The new wave of investments included the Enka synthetic fiber operation of the Dutch company Akzo, the Inmont paint and auto-coatings producer owned by United Technologies, and other businesses bought from Celanese, Rohm & Haas, and American Cyanamid.

After a bloody labor battle in the United States (see the section on labor relations), BASF began to turn its expansionary sights elsewhere, namely to Eastern Europe. In 1990 it acquired Synthesewerk Schwarzheide, the first outside purchase of a major chemical business in what had been East Germany. BASF's Wintershall subsidiary set up a joint venture with a Soviet company to market natural gas by constructing a pipeline across Czechoslovakia and into Germany. Growing demand in Eastern Europe also has provided a boost to BASF's Comparex operation, which sells mainframe computers and peripheral equipment manufactured by Japan's Hitachi.

OPERATIONS

Oil and Gas (15 percent of 1991 revenues). BASF engages in the exploration, production, and refining of oil and natural gas through its Wintershall subsidiary. In fiscal 1990 its output was 4.2 million metric tons of crude oil and 2 billion cubic meters of natural gas. Oil activities are concentrated in Germany, the Dutch sector of the North Sea, North Africa, western Africa, and North America. In 1990 BASF concluded an agreement with the Soviet company Gazprom for building a natural gas pipeline to Western Europe. The company also has coal mining operations in Germany.

Chemicals (15 percent of revenues). BASF's chemical business includes industrial products, such as plasticizers, solvents, and laminating resins; and high-end items, such as vitamins, flavors, and fragrances. Chemical operations are located in Belgium, Brazil, Britain, Colombia, Germany, Spain, and the United States.

Agricultural Chemicals (11 percent of revenues). The company is a major producer of fertilizers and crop-protection products (fungicides, herbicides, and so on). Potash, magnesium salts, and rock salt are produced by its subsidiary Kali und Salz AG.

Plastics and Fibers (21 percent of revenues). BASF produces a comprehensive line of plastics, extending from commodity items like polyolefins, polystyrene, and polyvinyl chloride to specialty products like styrene copolymers, polyacetals, nylons, and polyurethanes. The company is especially strong in polystyrene-based foams used in packaging and as heat insulators.

Dyestuffs and Finishing Products (18 percent of revenues). Included in this segment are the company's original products, dyes, as well as chemicals used in the production of paints, inks, adhesives, coatings, lubricants, polishes, and textiles.

Consumer Products (20 percent of revenues). BASF is best known to consumers as a leading producer of audiocassettes and videocassettes. This segment also includes computer disks, automobile coatings, paints (a market in which BASF ranks fourth in the world), and inks. Other products include pharmaceuticals, including a calcium antagonist, an antiarrhythmic, a gastrointestinal drug, and several analgesics.

TOP EXECUTIVES

- Jürgen Strube, chairman of the board of executive directors
- Hans Albers, chairman of the supervisory board
- Wolfgang Jentzsch, deputy chairman of the board of executive directors
- Detlef Dibbern, executive director
- Albrecht Eckell, executive director
- Max Dietrich Kley, executive director
- Ingo Paetzke, executive director
- Hans-Jürgen Quadbeck-Seeger, executive director
- Hanns-Helge Stechl, executive director
- J. Dieter Stein, executive director
- Dietmar Werner, executive director
- Gerhard R. Wolf, executive director

OUTSIDE DIRECTORS

- Marcus Bierich, chairman of the board of executive directors of Robert Bosch GmbH
- Dieter Brand, general manager of the Ludwigshafen branch of the Chemical, Paper and Ceramics Industries Union
- Manfred Eigen, director of the Max Planck Institute for Biophysical Chemistry
- Johan M. Goudswaard, former deputy chairman of the administrative council of Unilever NV
- Kurt Hohenemser, member of the board of executive directors of the German Association for the Protection of Owners of Securities
- Robert Holzach, honorary president of Union Bank of Switzerland
- Hans Joachim Langmann, chairman of the partners' council of E. Merck
- Wolfgang Schieren, chairman of the board of executive directors of Allianz AG
- Klaus Südhofer, deputy chairman of the board of directors of the Mining and Energy Industries Union
- Jürgen Walter, member of the central board of executive directors of the Chemical, Paper and Ceramics Industries Union
- Ulrich Weiss, member of the board of executive directors of Deutsche Bank
- Herbert Willersinn, former member of the BASF executive board

The supervisory board also includes seven employee representatives.

FINANCIAL DATA

Revenues (in millions of deutsche marks)

1991	46,626
1990	46,623
1989	47,617
1988	43,868
1987	40,238

Net Income (in millions of deutsche marks)

1991	1,039
1990	1,111
1989	2,030
1988	1,432
1987	1,055

GEOGRAPHICAL BREAKDOWN

Revenues (in millions of deutsche marks)

Year	Germany		Rest of Europe		Elsewhere	
1991	16,283	(35%)	14,903	(32%)	15,440	(33%)
1990	15,964	(34%)	15,387	(33%)	15,273	(33%)
1989	15,211	(32%)	15,483	(33%)	16,923	(36%)

LABOR RELATIONS

Although BASF has a long history of fairly harmonious relations with its unions in Germany (which by law are represented on the company's supervisory board), the company took a hard line with labor in the companies it purchased in the United States. BASF managed to eliminate unions at several plants and force others to accept major contract concessions.

The biggest confrontation came in 1984, after negotiations between the management of the company's operation in Geismar, Louisiana (part of Wyandotte) and the Oil, Chemical and Atomic Workers International Union (OCAW) broke down over company demands for concessions. BASF then locked out four hundred union employees, supposedly to guard against sabotage, and brought in replacement workers.

The OCAW fought fire with fire. The union launched an aggressive campaign against BASF, charging, among other things, that health and safety conditions at the Geismar plant were so dangerous that there was a risk of a "Bhopal on the bayou." BASF was placed on the AFL-CIO boycott list, and the OCAW won support from the company's unions in Germany, which donated money to the Geismar workers and set up solidarity committees. The union's allegations of environmental hazards at the plant prompted a congressional inquiry into the matter.

In 1987 BASF announced the end of the lockout but refused to take back 110 maintenance workers whose jobs the company said would be contracted out. It also said that it would implement unilaterally the concessionary conditions it had been seeking in negotiations three years earlier. The union thus kept up its campaign until 1989, when BASF agreed to reinstate all of the locked-out workers and sign a new, nonconcessionary contract.

According to the OCAW, however, BASF is still attempting to undermine unions at its other U.S. facilities.

ENVIRONMENTAL RECORD

The environmental problems of BASF, especially in the United States, began to come to light in the course of the company's five-year battle in Geismar, Louisiana, with the OCAW. The union made the environment a cornerstone of its international campaign against the company, leading to some dramatic results.

The OCAW formed a coalition with the Sierra Club and local environmental groups that got state authorities in Louisiana to establish stricter rules governing a new plant BASF wanted to construct in Geismar. The coalition also helped bring about an investigation of toxic releases by the EPA that led to a $4.3-million fine being levied against the company.

The union charged that the replacement workers brought in by the company were responsible for a series of accidents and toxic leaks at the Geismar plant, including one that sent a cloud of phosgene gas into the surrounding area. An accidental release of sixteen thousand pounds of toxic toluene in 1986 led to a $66,000 fine by the Occupational Safety and Health Administration (OSHA).

A more-serious accident occurred in 1990 at the company's plant in Cincinnati, where an explosion and fire killed two workers, injured seventeen others, and resulted in extensive property damage to the surrounding neighborhood. A subsequent OSHA investigation led to citations for more than one hundred willful violations of safety rules, for which the agency levied a $1.1-million fine. A few weeks later there was another explosion at a BASF facility in Ohio.

Studies conducted by BASF on the health effects of dioxin have come under fire. In 1990 a German epidemiologist studying the impact of an accident at a BASF plant in 1953 reported that the company had supplied him with data in a way that disguised the incidence of cancer among workers exposed to dioxin in the accident. In 1990 the environmental group Greenpeace petitioned the EPA to reevaluate its rules regarding dioxin because of questions surrounding data relating to the BASF accident and another at a Monsanto plant in West Virginia in 1949.

BASF also has had recent problems at its facilities in Germany. In 1990 ten metric tons of dichloroethane were discharged into the Rhine, and five months later another two metric tons of weed killer leaked into the river.

The company claims to have stepped up its attention to environmental concerns by such actions as increasing the use of scrubbers to control air emissions and developing programs for the recycling of plastics. Still, according to a study of EPA data by the Citizens Fund, BASF's American operations were responsible for the eleventh-largest volume of toxic releases (more than seventy-six million pounds) among all U.S. industrial companies in 1989 (the latest figures available).

BIBLIOGRAPHY

Borkin, Joseph. *The Crime and Punishment of I. G. Farben*. New York: Free Press, 1978.

Grant, Wyn, William Paterson, and Colin Whitson. *Government and the Chemical Industry: A Comparative Study of Britain and West Germany*. Oxford: Oxford University Press, 1989.

Hayes, Peter. *Industry and Ideology: IG Farben in the Nazi Era*. Cambridge: Cambridge University Press, 1987.

BAYER AG

Bayerwerk
5090 Leverkusen
Germany
(214) 301

1991 revenues: $28.0 billion
1991 net income: $1.2 billion
Publicly traded company
Employees: 164,200
Founded: 1863

OVERVIEW

Bayer is known in the United States as a brand of aspirin, but the company bearing that name is one of the big three German chemical producers. Bayer AG was stripped of its rights relating to aspirin in the United States during World War I, though the company sells that analgesic throughout much of the rest of the world.

Bayer started out as a dye company and, on the basis of an outstanding research operation, soon became an important force in pharmaceuticals and chemicals. Its innovations included the first synthetic pesticide, synthetic rubber, and, of course, aspirin. From the mid-1920s through the end of World War II, Bayer was part of the huge IG Farben combine that controlled the German chemical industry and helped the Nazi war effort.

Bayer made a rapid recovery from the war and now, along with former IG Farben partners BASF and Hoechst, is one of the leading chemical companies in the world, with more than four hundred affiliated companies in seventy countries.

HISTORY

Bayer, founded in 1863 by Friedrich Bayer, was one of the companies that grew up with the development of manmade dyes in the second half of the nineteenth century. Its first major product was a synthetic magenta. Although Bayer remained a leading dye producer, it went on to become a major innovator in the larger fields of chemistry and pharmaceuticals.

Bayer created the first synthetic pesticide, Antinonin, and in 1899 the company introduced aspirin, which was destined to become one of the world's most famous drugs. Nine years later Bayer chemists produced a compound that initially was used for a reddish orange dye but then was found to be an effective drug against pneumonia, although Bayer did not release the sulfa drug for some time.

In 1915 the company began production of the first synthetic rubber. During World War I the U.S. government seized the American assets of Bayer (and other German companies) and later handed over the U.S. trademark for Bayer aspirin to Sterling Products, which (as Sterling Drug, now part of Eastman Kodak) has been selling the product ever since.

The dye industry in Germany (and elsewhere) had a strong propensity for anticompetitive practices. Bayer went along with this by joining the Dreibund cartel with its rival BASF, while Hoechst was part of another grouping, Dreiverband. The cartels carved up the market among themselves and undermined the growth of the dye industry in countries like the United States. During World War I the German dye companies altered their formulas to produce mustard gas and explosives.

In 1916 the two dye cartels joined forces to create the *Interessengemeinschaft der deutschen Teerfarbenfabriken* (Community of Interests of the German Tar Dye Factories), known later as the Little IG. This combine had complete control over the dye industry and soon acquired extensive coal mining operations to carry out a plan initiated by BASF to create liquid fuel through the hydrogenation of coal.

By the 1920s dye industry leaders, led by Carl Duisberg of Bayer and Carl Bosch of BASF, were pushing for the merger of the dye makers into a single company. This happened in 1925 with the creation of the *Interessengemeinschaft Farbenindustrie AG* (Interest Community of the Dye Industry, Inc.), or IG Farben.

This huge corporation, which soon included related industries, such as explosives and fibers, was the biggest enterprise in all of Europe and the fourth largest in the world, behind General Motors, United States Steel, and Standard Oil of New Jersey. With Standard Oil IG Farben entered into a noncompetition arrangement for oil and chemicals while agreeing to cooperate on the development of synthetic rubber (though Jersey Standard later came under fire because of evidence that the German company was impeding its progress in this crucial area).

Although Carl Bosch, the head of IG Farben's managing board, opposed the anti-Semitism of the Nazis, the company gave financial support to Hitler and (without Bosch, who resigned in 1935) became indispensable to the German military effort during World War II. The company made use of slave labor, locating one of its synthetic rubber facilities in Auschwitz in order to be near the captive labor supply of the infamous concentration camp. Lethal gas made by IG Farben was used in the death camps. For such practices a group of IG Farben executives were convicted of war crimes at the Nuremburg trials. Several years later, in 1952, the company was dismantled and redivided into several independent firms, including BASF, Bayer, and Hoechst.

Bayer ended up with the photographic supply company Agfa, but it lost Bayer of Canada and its half interest in the U.S. drug company Winthrop Laboratories. Like BASF, Bayer grew rapidly in the 1950s. The company introduced an antituberculosis drug in 1952 and two years later formed a joint venture with the U.S. firm Monsanto called Mobay Chemical Company, which introduced Bayer's polyurethane technology in the United States. Bayer also developed new insecticides and synthetic fibers. Starting in the late 1950s the company began expanding abroad.

In 1964 Bayer's subsidiary Agfa merged with its Belgian competitor, Gevaert Photo-Produkten, to form Agfa-Gevaert, in which Bayer had a 60-percent interest (this increased to 100 percent in 1981). Bayer focused more of its attention on the United States, where it bought dye maker Verona Chemical Company in 1957, initiated U.S. operations for its Haarman & Reimer flavor and fragrance subsidiary in 1962, bought out Monsanto's share in Mobay in 1967, and acquired Cutter Laboratories in 1974. Four years later Bayer made its most conspicuous U.S. purchase—Miles Laboratories, maker of Alka-Seltzer and One-A-Day vitamins. Bayer also has been active in the United States in the graphics business through its increasing investment in Compugraphic Corporation (which reached 100 percent in 1989).

Although the company is still barred from selling aspirin under its own name in the United States, it did work out a deal with Sterling Drug in 1986 to sell Bayer-brand industrial products in that country. Bayer has given Miles Labs a boost by having it market Cirpo, one of a new family of antibiotics that took off in the late 1980s because it was the only oral antibiotic effective against a broad range of infections. The purchase of the U.S. company Cooper Technicon helped push Miles, with which it was merged, to the top tier of the medical diagnostics business.

Like its competitor BASF, Bayer also has been looking east. In 1991 it announced investments in the Bitterfeld-Wolfen region, the traditional center of the chemical industry in the former East Germany. Bayer's Agfa subsidiary announced plans for a plant in the eastern German town of Gera to produce laboratory instruments.

OPERATIONS

Polymers (18 percent of 1991 revenues). Bayer is a leading producer of plastics used in electrical, electronic, and automotive products; synthetic rubber and raw materials for the rubber industry; and synthetic fibers. The Wolff Walsrode subsidiary makes cellulose products used in building materials, drugs, and cosmetics.

Organic Products (14 percent of revenues). Included here is a broad range of organic chemicals used in the production of plastics, coatings, photographic film, dyes, and drugs. Bayer also produces a variety of dyes and pigments for clothing, carpeting, plastics, paper, and other products. This segment also includes carbonless copying paper and the Haarmann & Reimer fragrance and flavor business.

Industrial Products (18 percent of revenues). This segment of Bayer's operations includes inorganic chemicals, such as silicones, fluorotensides used in chrome plating, and silica sols used in dental materials and as polishing agents in semiconductor production. Also included here are polyurethanes and inorganic pigments, enamels, and ceramics.

Health Care (21 percent of revenues). Bayer produces pharmaceuticals for cardiovascular problems, age-associated disorders, diabetes, hemophilia, and general infections. In the self-medication area the company sells analgesics, such as aspirin (which outside of the United States is a Bayer trademark) and ibuprofen, as well as Alka-Seltzer stomach and cold remedies. Bayer also has a strong position in the medical diagnostics business through its production of systems in such areas as diabetes, hematology, and urine chemistry.

Agrochemicals (13 percent of revenues). The company makes a variety of crop-production products, such as fungicides and insecticides, as well as consumer products, such as insect repellents, cleansers, air fresheners, skin-care lotions, and artificial sweeteners.

Imaging Technologies (16 percent of revenues). This segment includes the photographic products of Agfa, which ranks third in the industry, behind Eastman Kodak and Fuji Photo Film. Those products include film, developing paper and supplies, and darkroom equipment. Bayer also produces graphics products, such as pre-press systems, laser printers, and micrographic equipment.

TOP EXECUTIVES

- Manfred Schneider, chairman of the board of management
- Hermann J. Strenger, chairman of the supervisory board
- Hermann Wunderlich, vice chairman of the board of management
- Herbert Grünewald, chairman of the supervisory board
- Dieter Becher, member of the board of management
- Karl Heinz Büchel, member of the board of management
- Klaus Kleine-Weischede, member of the board of management
- Helmut Loehr, member of the board of management

OUTSIDE DIRECTORS

- Werner Bischoff, district manager of the union IG Chemie
- Heinz Gester, legal adviser to the German Trade Unions Federation
- Constantin Freiherr Heereman von Zuydtwyck, member of the Bundestag and president of the Deutscher Bauernverband
- Robert A. Jeker, president of the board of management of Credit Suisse
- Karlheinz Kaske, chairman of the board of management of Siemens
- Hilmar Kopper, member of the board of managing directors of Deutsche Bank
- Manfred Lennings, management consultant
- Hermann Rappe, member of the Bundestag and chairman of IG Chemie
- Walter Seipp, chairman of the board of management of Commerzbank
- Heinz A. Staab, president of the Max-Planck-Gesellschaft zur Förderung der Wissenschaften

The board also includes seven employee representatives; Gerhard Fritz, former member of the board of management; and André Leysen, chairman of the board of administration of the Bayer subsidiary Gevaert NV.

FINANCIAL DATA

Revenues (in millions of deutsche marks)

1991	42,401
1990	41,643
1989	43,299
1988	40,468
1987	37,143
1986	38,284

Net Income (in millions of deutsche marks)

1991	1,853
1990	1,903
1989	2,116
1988	1,909
1987	1,544
1986	1,354

GEOGRAPHICAL BREAKDOWN

Revenues (in millions of deutsche marks)

Year	Europe		North America		Elsewhere	
1991	27,662	(65%)	8,764	(21%)	5,975	(14%)
1990	28,080	(67%)	8,053	(19%)	5,510	(13%)
1989	28,630	(66%)	8,580	(20%)	6,089	(14%)

Operating income (in millions of deutsche marks)

Year	Europe		North America		Elsewhere	
1991	2,219	(70%)	416	(13%)	543	(17%)
1990	2,498	(70%)	597	(17%)	457	(13%)
1989	3,040	(71%)	699	(16%)	551	(13%)

LABOR RELATIONS

Bayer has a long tradition of paternalism in its dealings with workers in Germany. It was one of the first companies to offer paid holidays and has provided employees with subsidized housing, medical care, and cultural and recreational facilities.

The company's good relations with unions extends to the United States, where its Mobay subsidiary has contracts with the Oil, Chemical and Atomic Workers International Union and with the International Chemical Workers Union.

ENVIRONMENTAL RECORD

Bayer has been the subject of frequent criticism, especially by a group called Critical Bayer Shareholders, concerning its environmental practices in Europe. A major point of contention was the company's sale of the dangerous insecticide parathion, which Bayer finally took off the market in 1989, ostensibly for financial reasons.

Bayer's Mobay subsidiary was one of two chemical companies that refused in 1989 to sell the U.S. Army feedstock needed to produce nerve gas. The following year Mobay paid $72,000 to settle charges by the EPA relating to improper labeling of pesticides sold to foreign customers.

In 1991 Mobay was one of some two hundred companies that received a hazard alert from the EPA concerning a pair of chemicals—orthotoluidine and aniline—used in making dyes, drugs, rubber, and pesticides. This followed a study that showed a strong link between exposure to these substances and bladder cancer.

Also in 1991, Mobay was charged by the EPA with importing unapproved chemicals into the United States and with falsifying reports made to the agency about the shipments. The EPA levied a fine of $4.7 million against the company.

According to a study of EPA data by the Citizens Fund, Mobay's plant in Baytown, Texas, was among the fifty manufacturing facilities with the highest releases of known or suspected carcinogens in 1989 (the most recent figures available).

BIBLIOGRAPHY

Borkin, Joseph. *The Crime and Punishment of I. G. Farben*. New York: Free Press, 1978.

Grant, Wyn, William Paterson, and Colin Whitston. *Government and the Chemical Industry: A Comparative Study of Britain and West Germany*. Oxford: Oxford University Press, 1989.

Hayes, Peter. *Industry and Ideology: IG Farben in the Nazi Era*. Cambridge: Cambridge University Press, 1987.

Mann, Charles C., and Mark L. Plummer. *The Aspirin Wars: Money, Medicine, and 100 Years of Rampant Competition*. New York: Alfred A. Knopf, 1991.

BCE INC.

2000 McGill College Avenue
Montreal, Quebec H3A 3H7
Canada
(514) 499-7000

1991 revenues: $17.2 billion
1991 net income: $1.2 billion
Publicly traded company
Employees: 124,000
Founded: 1880

OVERVIEW

BCE, formerly known as Bell Canada Enterprises, is a holding company for the phone company Bell Canada, the telephone equipment company Northern Telecom (53-percent owned), other telecommunications operations, and various other businesses.

Since the breakup of AT&T in the United States in 1984, BCE has been the leading telecommunications operation with phone service, equipment manufacturing, and research and development all under one corporate roof. Its Northern Telecom subsidiary took the U.S. equipment market by storm in the early 1980s but later ceded first place back to the traditional leader, AT&T. It has since been expanding its presence in other equipment markets, especially Europe, where it acquired STC, the British producer of telecommunications equipment.

HISTORY

Canada played a role in the early development of the telephone because it was to there that Alexander Graham Bell and his family first emigrated from Britain for health reasons in 1870. The Bells—Alexander, his parents, and the widow of a brother who had died of tuberculosis—settled in the town of Brantford, located about eighty miles southwest of Toronto in the province of Ontario.

Bell ended up teaching speech at schools in Massachusetts and Connecticut, but it was while visiting his parents in Brantford in 1874 that he came upon the principle of the telephone. While Bell pursued the invention in the United States with the aid of some wealthy backers, he handed over the Canadian patent rights to his father, Melville Bell.

Bell senior at first limited his activities to licensing his son's technology to various local phone operations. Then the U.S. operating entity, the Bell Telephone Company, decided to expand north of the border. In 1880 it formed the Bell Telephone Company of Canada, under the leadership of Andrew Robertson and Charles F. Sise. Within a few months the company had some two thousand customers, with telephone exchanges or agents in thirty-two cities and towns across Canada.

Within a few years the company established long-distance service between major Canadian cities with links to U.S. cities, such as Detroit. Bell Canada also grew by purchasing local independent telephone companies, though in the early years of the twentieth century the operating entities in such provinces as Manitoba, Saskatchewan, and Alberta were taken over by local government authorities. Bell Canada, which also withdrew from the maritime provinces, ended up focusing its service on Quebec and Ontario. The Trans-Canada Telephone System was formed in 1932 to provide integrated national service for customers of the various phone companies.

In 1957 Bell Canada purchased 90 percent of Northern Electric, the Canadian division of the Western Electric manufacturing subsidiary of AT&T; the remainder was acquired several years later. Bell Canada's share in Northern Electric, renamed Northern Telecom in 1976, was later reduced in stages to just over 50 percent, with the rest sold to private investors. AT&T's holdings in Bell Canada itself declined over the years and eventually ended entirely.

While Bell Canada moved into areas like satellites and international telecommunications consulting, its most visible presence outside Canada was through Northern Telecom. During the 1960s it set up manufacturing subsidiaries in Turkey, Brazil, Ireland, and Malaysia. It then became a major player in the market for telecommunications equipment in the United States after AT&T failed in its effort to maintain its hardware monopoly.

Northern Telecom specialized in digital equipment, both switching systems purchased by Bell operating companies and sophisticated switchboards, known as private branch exchanges (PBXs), bought by companies. In 1977 it challenged AT&T by introducing the first electronic digital PBX. Ma Bell responded with its Dimension switchboard, but many customers found it lacking, and by the early 1980s Northern Telecom rose to first place in this important market.

In the middle of the decade technical problems with Northern Telecom's products and a rebound by AT&T pushed the Canadian company back to second place. Northern Telecom, however, expanded its international activities, forming subsidiaries in Europe and the Pacific and buying a 27-percent interest (later extended to 97 percent) in the British telecommunications equipment maker STC. It also made big sales to such customers as Japan's Nippon Telegraph and Telephone, and in the U.S. PBX market it stayed well ahead of rivals like Siemens, Mitel, and NEC.

Bell Canada Enterprises was established as a holding company in 1983 to separate the regulated local telephone operations of Bell Canada from its unregulated businesses, such as Northern Telecom. That same year BCE bought 42 percent (later increased to 47 percent) of TransCanada Pipelines, operator of one of the largest natural gas pipeline networks in the world. During the rest of the 1980s the company also got involved in a variety of other new businesses, including real estate development, commercial printing, and computer retailing and servicing. Through TransCanada it even made a brief attempt to take over Hiram Walker Resources, the big liquor and oil producer.

In 1991 Northern Telecom announced that as part of its plan to expand foreign operations, it was considering establishing new factories and research centers in Europe and forming alliances with companies in that part of the world. The company also formed a joint venture with Motorola to sell cellular telephone equipment throughout the western hemisphere.

OPERATIONS

Telecommunications Services (43 percent of 1991 revenues). BCE's wholly owned subsidiary Bell Canada is the country's largest telephone company, serving some seven million customers, mostly in Ontario and Quebec. The company provides both local and long-distance service to residential and commercial customers, including cellular and paging services. BCE's Tele-Direct subsidiary publishes telephone directories for Bell Canada and sells Yellow Pages advertising.

Telecommunications Equipment Manufacturing (47 percent of revenues). Northern Telecom's largest operations are the production of central office switching equipment and business communications systems, such as PBX switchboards, voice mail systems, and teleconferencing systems. It also makes telephone transmission equipment and cable products, both traditional and fiber optic.

Northern Telecom, with 1991 revenues of U.S. $8.2 billion, does the largest part of its business in North America, but it has expanded its presence in Europe through the purchase of 97 percent of the British company STC and its participation in the French joint venture NT Meridian SA. The company also uses direct sales, distributors, and licensees to sell in Western Europe, Africa, the Middle East, Asia, and Latin America. Recently it also has begun to sell systems to customers in Eastern Europe and the former Soviet Union. The company operates fifty-five manufacturing and repair facilities in Canada, the United States, Australia, Britain, China, France, Ireland, Malaysia, Mexico, and Thailand.

Financial Services (7 percent of revenues). BCE's financial activities stem from the 1989 purchase of Montreal Trustco, which provides a full range of banking services at some 155 branches and offices throughout Canada. It is a major real estate lender, and in Quebec it provides real estate brokerage services as well. The RoyNat subsidiary specializes in medium-term lending to small and medium-sized businesses.

Other Operations (2 percent of revenues). Included in this segment are the activities of Bell Canada International, which provides telecommunications consulting services in such countries as Japan, Australia, Morocco, Mexico, Hong Kong, and New Zealand. Other operations include minority interests in Videotron, a cable television operator in the United Kingdom; Trans-Canada Pipelines, which operates a natural gas delivery system between eastern and western Canada and the United States; and Encor, which engages in oil and gas exploration and production in Canada, Indonesia, Australia, and several other countries.

TOP EXECUTIVES

- J. V. Raymond Cyr, chairman
- Lynton R. Wilson, president and chief executive
- Jacques B. Bérubé, group vice president, telecom international
- Thomas J. Bourke, group vice president, directories

OUTSIDE DIRECTORS

- Peter A. Allen, chairman of LAC Minerals
- Ralph M. Barford, president of Valleydene Corporation Ltd.
- Laurent Beaudoin, chief executive of Bombardier Inc.
- Marcel Bélanger, president of the consulting firm Gagnon et Bélanger Inc.
- Warren Chippindale, former chief executive partner of Coopers & Lybrand (Canada)
- Charles W. Daniel, former chief executive of Shell Canada Ltd.
- John P. Gordon, former chief executive of Stelco Inc.
- Donald J. Johnston, legal counsel to the law firm Heenan Blaikie
- Edward N. McKelvey, legal counsel to the law firm Stewart McKelvey Stirling Scales
- James E. Newall, chief executive of Nova Corporation
- Alastair H. Ross, chief executive of Pacific Enterprises Oil (Canada)
- Charles R. Sharpe, chairman of Sears Canada Inc.
- Louise Brais Vaillancourt, director of various companies
- Jeannine Guillevin Wood, chief executive of Guillevin International Inc.

Also on board are Albert Jean de Grandpré, former chairman of BCE, and the following chief executives of BCE subsidiaries: Paul G. Stern of Northern Telecom, Gerald J. Maier of TransCanada Pipelines, and Jean Claude Monty of Bell Canada.

FINANCIAL DATA

Revenues (in millions of Canadian dollars)

1991	19,884
1990	18,373
1989	16,681
1988	14,445
1987	14,321

Net Income (in millions of Canadian dollars)

1991	1,329
1990	1,147
1989	761
1988	846
1987	1,076

GEOGRAPHICAL BREAKDOWN

Revenues (in millions of Canadian dollars)

Year	Canada		United States		Elsewhere	
1991	13,942	(65%)	5,637	(26%)	1,864	(9%)
1990	13,865	(71%)	5,168	(26%)	558	(3%)
1989	12,384	(70%)	4,807	(27%)	488	(3%)

LABOR RELATIONS

Most of Bell Canada's nonmanagement employees are represented by the Canadian Telephone Employees Association (clerical and sales) and the Communications and Electrical Workers of Canada (craft and service). The longest strike in the company's history came in 1988, when workers stayed off the job for seventeen weeks. The militant walkout ended with a settlement that included wage increases of about 5 percent a year and improvements in job security provisions.

Some 40 percent of Northern Telecom's employees are represented by unions, especially the Canadian Auto Workers and the Communications and Electrical Workers of Canada. There was a three-week strike at the company in 1988. The Communications Workers of America (CWA), which represents about six hundred Northern Telecom workers in the United States, staged a six-week strike in 1989 before winning a pay package totaling 10.7 percent over three years. The following year the CWA filed suit against the company for engaging in electronic surveillance of employees. The company announced in early 1992 that it would end secret monitoring of workers.

In 1991 representatives of Northern Telecom workers in eleven countries formed a solidarity coalition to help one another protect labor rights at company facilities around the world.

ENVIRONMENTAL RECORD

Northern Telecom was fined $20,000 by the U.S. EPA in 1988 for discharging some three thousand gallons of sodium hydroxide into the municipal sewer system at its circuit board plant in San Diego.

Northern Telecom also has been one of the heaviest users of CFCs in the United States, although in 1990 the company said it would phase out the substances, which contribute to the deterioration of the ozone layer. In 1991 the company said it would take the lead in eliminating CFCs from its operations in Mexico as well.

BIBLIOGRAPHY

Brooks, John. *Telephone: The First Hundred Years*. New York: Harper & Row, 1976

Eadie, T. W. *"Too Startling for Belief!": A Story of Telephone Development in Canada*. New York: Newcomen Society, 1955.

BERTELSMANN AG

Carl-Bertelsmann-Strasse 270
Postfach 55 55
D-4380 Gütersloh 100
Germany
(052) 41-80-0

1991 revenues: $8.0 billion (year ending June 30)
1991 net income: $298.1 million
Privately held company
Employees: 45,110
Founded: 1835

OVERVIEW

In the course of forty years Bertelsmann has grown from a war-ravaged family-owned religious publishing house into one of the world's most powerful media conglomerates. The company, which does two-thirds of its business outside Germany, is a leading publisher of books and magazines in Europe and the United States, the largest operator of book and record clubs (with an aggregate membership of more than twenty-two million members), and one of the top producers of recorded music.

Bertelsmann has taken advantage of German unification to expand its operations to the eastern part of the country and has plans for other areas of Eastern Europe as well. Although the company's U.S. operations have not met expectations in recent years, Bertelsmann remains a major competitor for the likes of Time Warner, Sony, and News Corporation.

HISTORY

In 1835 Carl Bertelsmann, the son of a Lutheran pastor, established a business to print hymnals and prayer books. Although one hymnal, "The Little Mission

Harp," ended up selling more than two million copies, for decades the firm remained a modest one, based in the rural northern German town of Gütersloh.

The company's rise to power came after World War II, when Reinhard Mohn, great-great-grandson of the founder, returned to Gütersloh. He had served as an officer in the army, surrendered in North Africa, and was interned as a prisoner of war in Kansas. Back home, his father persuaded him to revive the family business, which had been destroyed during the war.

Mohn shunned religious publishing in favor of selling books through the mail. In 1950 he founded Germany's first book club, Lesering, which had several million members by the end of the decade. He had similar success with record clubs, though there was some resistance from the record companies. To overcome that obstacle, Bertelsmann began pressing records itself, forming Ariola Records in 1958.

During the 1960s Bertelsmann expanded its clubs throughout Europe and Latin America, in both urban and rural areas. The company also purchased a major German television and film production company and 25 percent (later expanded to 75 percent) of Gruner & Jahr, publisher of the popular weekly *Stern* and other periodicals.

The company went on to enhance its status as a major media conglomerate with additional acquisitions: 51 percent of paperback publisher Bantam Books in 1977 (later this was increased to 100 percent), Arista Records in 1979, and RCA Records in 1986. The latter two purchases made Bertelsmann the third-largest record company in the world, but a bigger stir was caused by the takeover of Doubleday, one of the most famous names in American book publishing.

Doubleday was for many years the lumbering giant of the industry. Frank Doubleday, who founded the house in 1877 with S. S. McClure, developed close relationships with such writers as Rudyard Kipling and Joseph Conrad. His son Nelson, who took charge in the late 1920s, had no literary pretensions. In 1978 Nelson Doubleday, Jr., took over the company and, overcoming his reputation as a bon vivant, confronted the growing financial crisis of the publishing operation. After some severe cost cutting, including the shutting down of Dial Press in 1985, the business began to turn around. In 1986 the publishing operation, which included several book clubs, was sold to Bertelsmann for $475 million.

Bertelsmann has faced some disappointments in the United States—such as the performance of Doubleday's book clubs and an unsuccessful bid for *U.S. News and World Report* in 1984—but the company now enjoys nearly $2 billion in American revenues. Bertelsmann has been scouring the United States, as well as Europe and Asia, for additional acquisitions.

OPERATIONS

International Book and Record Clubs (14 percent of 1991 sales). This segment of Bertelsmann's operations consists of seventeen companies serving a total membership of fourteen million in seven countries, which along with its German operations makes Bertelsmann the largest book club operator in the world. Some 44 percent of sales were to French-language markets, 30 percent were in English, and 12 percent were in Spanish and Portuguese. Among the clubs are the France Loisirs Group, Book Club Associates (Britain), and Literary Guild and Doubleday Book Club (United States).

The U.S. clubs, faced with strong competition from Time Warner's Book-of-the-Month Club and other operations, have been among the least successful of the company's properties in this field. Blame for the heavy losses of the U.S. book clubs is placed by many observers on the attempt by Bertelsmann to apply its European practices to a very different American market.

In 1990 one of the companies in this segment, Société Générale d'Edition et de Diffusion (jointly owned with Groupe de la Cité), launched a ten-volume encyclopedia entitled "Our World in Word and Sound," which includes audiocassettes along with the books.

Book Germany, Austria, Switzerland (9 percent of sales). This segment includes the company's German-language book clubs and book publishing. Among the publishing imprints in Germany are Siedler, C. Bertelsmann, Albrecht Knaus, Blanvalet, and Goldmann. In addition to general-interest titles, this segment emphasizes cartography, how-to books, and reference volumes. Book clubs are operated in Germany, Austria, and Switzerland.

The company also has moved to take advantage of the changes in Eastern Europe. In the former German Democratic Republic Bertelsmann has set up a book club and purchased the leading textbook publisher, Graphischer Grossbetrieb Poessneck. The Donauland Book Club in Vienna is being used to expand operations in other parts of Eastern Europe.

Bertelsmann Publishing Group International (10 percent of sales). The largest portion of this segment is the company that combined Bertelsmann's U.S. publishing acquisitions: Bantam Doubleday Dell Publishing Group. According to the newsletter *BP Report*, this was the seventh-largest U.S. book publisher in 1990, with $820 million in revenues, and the second-largest publisher of general books, with $640 million in revenues in that field. In 1991 Jack Hoeft was named as chief executive of the operation.

The Bantam imprint, which in the 1980s expanded from just paperbacks to include blockbuster hardcovers, has prospered from the best-sellers of such authors as Stephen Hawking and Lee Iacocca. Paperback reprints of titles by Frederick Forsyth, Joseph Wambaugh, and Robert Ludlum also have been lucrative. In 1991 Bantam agreed to pay some $6 million for the world rights to General Norman Schwarzkopf's memoirs.

Doubleday was a troubled house before being taken over by Bertelsmann, and—despite big sellers by Bill Cosby—continued to ail under the new owner and the new president, Nancy Evans, they installed. In 1991 Bantam Doubleday Dell dismissed rumors that Doubleday would be folded. Doubleday would remain alive, the company said, but with a sharply reduced book list.

Dell was started in 1921 by George T. Delacorte as a publisher of magazines and comic books (it is still a leader in crossword puzzle magazines). It began publishing paperbacks in 1942 and became one of the leading mass-market houses. Dell's hardcover line, Delacorte, has had its greatest success with the popular novels of Danielle Steel, which are subsequently issued in paperback by Dell. In 1990 the company paid a staggering $12.3 million for two forthcoming books by Ken Follett.

This segment also includes Spanish publisher Plaza y Janés; Transworld Publishers, which operates in Britain, Australia, and New Zealand; and a slew of German scientific and technical publishers, business newsletters, medical magazines, and other information services.

Printing and Manufacturing (19 percent of sales). Bertelsmann owns printing houses for magazines and books in Germany, Italy, Austria, Spain, Portugal, Colombia, and the United States. This segment of Bertelsmann's operations also includes paper mills in Italy and Germany.

Bertelsmann Music Group (23 percent of sales). This segment, which operates in thirty countries, represents the fusion of three major forces in the record industry. RCA Records dates back to the Victor Talking Machine Company, formed in 1901 following the introduction of the gramophone. That company, purchased by the Radio Corporation of America in 1930, issued a wide variety of popular and classical recordings with the famous "His Master's Voice" symbol of a dog listening to a Victrola.

Arista Records, established by Columbia Pictures in 1974, has distributed the music of such varied pop artists as Barry Manilow, Whitney Houston, the Grateful Dead, and Patti Smith. In 1979 Bertelsmann bought the company, selling half of it to RCA four years later. After RCA was purchased by General Electric, Bertelsmann bought back its interest in Arista along with RCA Records. In 1991 Arista found itself the target of lawsuits brought by individuals who had purchased records by Milli Vanilli, who had admitted that the songs actually were sung by others.

These two companies, along with the Ariola Records label formed by Bertelsmann in the late 1950s, give Bertelsmann a significant presence in the $22-billion world music market. Among the leading performers whose work is sold by Bertelsmann Music Group are Stevie Wonder, Lionel Richie, Lisa Stanfield, the Eurythmics, and the European superstar Eros Ramazzotti. The biggest music market for Bertelsmann is North America, which accounted for 40 percent of sales in 1990; Germany, Austria, and Switzerland followed, with a combined share of 20 percent.

Despite its size, Bertelsmann's U.S. record business has not thrived in recent years. Many slower-selling artists have been cut and new blockbusters have been harder to find, especially in light of the reluctance of the German overseers to spend heavily to attract big names.

Electronic Media (4 percent of sales). This segment consists of investments in radio and television stations in Germany's growing private broadcasting system. It also includes pay-television services, such as Premiere, a joint venture with Canal Plus of France and the German Teleclub network. Other ventures include sports event syndication, TV and film production, and the production of videodiscs. The company is also said to be considering starting an all-news, CNN-type station for Germany, Switzerland, and Austria.

Gruner & Jahr (21 percent of sales). This subsidiary is one of the world's leading magazine companies, with sales of more than 550 million copies in 1990. Within the crowded German periodical business, the company's titles include the weekly *Stern*, the travel publication *Geo*, the business journal *Capital*, and a variety of women's magazines. The company suffered a great deal of embarrassment in 1984 when the Hitler diaries, published by *Stern* with great fanfare, turned out to be a hoax.

Foreign titles include *Femme Actuelle* and *Prima* in France, *Vera* in Italy, *best* in Britain, *Estar Viva* in Spain, and *Parents* in the United States. An American edition of *Geo*, launched in 1979, was an expensive failure.

Gruner & Jahr also publishes the daily *Hamburger Morgenpost* and in 1990 expanded its newspaper operations to eastern Germany. The company also owns the Gruner Druck printing plant in Germany and Brown Printing in the United States. The latter prints editions of *Time*, *Sports Illustrated*, *Business Week*, and other leading magazines.

TOP EXECUTIVES

- Mark Wössner, president and chief executive officer
- Gerd Schulte-Hillen, vice chairman

OUTSIDE DIRECTORS

- Gerd Bucerius, owner of Zeitverlag Publishing
- Horst Burgard, member of the executive board of Deutsche Bank
- Joachim C. Fest, publisher of *Frankfurter Allgemeine*
- Michael Hoffmann-Becking, attorney in Düsseldorf
- Karl Otto Pöhl, former president of Deutsche Bundesbank
- Friedrich Schiefer, managing director of Robert Bosch GmbH
- Jürgen Terrahe, member of executive board of Commerzbank
- Dieter Vogel, chairman of Thyssen Handelsunion AG
- Heinrich Weiss, president of Federation of German Industries
  Note: the board also includes former chairman Reinhard Mohn and four employee representatives

FINANCIAL DATA

Revenues (in millions of deutsche marks) (years ending June 30)

1991	14,483
1990	13,313
1989	12,483
1988	11,299
1987	9,160

Net Income (in millions of deutsche marks) (years ending June 30)

1991	540
1990	510
1989	402
1988	362
1987	207

GEOGRAPHICAL BREAKDOWN

Sales (in millions of deutsche marks)

Year*	Germany		Foreign	
1991	5,380	(37%)	9,120	(63%)
1990	4,355	(33%)	8,958	(67%)
1989	3,990	(32%)	8,493	(68%)
1988	3,690	(33%)	7,609	(67%)

*Fiscal year ends June 30.

LABOR RELATIONS

Bertelsmann has a tradition of paternalistic management, including extensive benefits and a generous profit-sharing plan. Several employee representatives are members of the company's supervisory board. Such a climate has not been conducive to union organizing.

BIBLIOGRAPHY

Tebbel, John. *A History of Book Publishing in the United States.* 4 vols. New York: R. R. Bowker, 1978–81.

BOEING COMPANY

7755 East Marginal Way South
Seattle, Washington 98108
(206) 655-2121

1991 revenues: $29.3 billion
1991 net income: $1.6 billion
Publicly traded company
Employees: 159,100
Founded: 1916

OVERVIEW

Boeing is the powerhouse of the commercial aircraft industry. Its planes, among the most widely known industrial products made in the United States, have helped make air travel available to the masses. Traditionally Boeing has been willing to make huge gambles on developing new generations of planes—seen most recently in the 777 series that will become available in the mid-1990s.

Boeing is also among the top dozen military contractors in the United States, but its defense business operations are much smaller and much less impressive than its commercial ones. The company's military position has, however, started to improve as it has joined with other manufacturers, such as Lockheed and Grumman, in forming teams to compete for the largest Pentagon contracts.

At the beginning of the 1990s Boeing, while continuing to face intense competition from Airbus Industrie and McDonnell Douglas, had so many orders that its main problem was speeding up production. Although many of its main customers—U.S. airlines—have been in crisis, Boeing is betting on a resurgence of air travel, both in the United States and abroad.

HISTORY

The Boeing Company was born of the fascination that the son of a wealthy timberman had with flying. William Boeing first experienced airplanes up close in San Diego in 1910, when a French stunt pilot named Louis Paulhan took him for a ride. After finishing his studies Boeing went to work for his father. While in Washington State to acquire some land, Boeing got another chance to go up in a plane.

By then he was hooked. Before long, Boeing learned to fly, and he purchased one of the first seaplanes made by aviation pioneer Glenn L. Martin to use on fishing trips. While living in Seattle he began tinkering with planes and gradually put together a group of people to produce other flying machines. In 1916 he incorporated the operation as Pacific Aero Products and sold his first plane to the government of New Zealand.

Boeing's firm trained flight instructors during World War I and was one of the few postwar survivors from among the slew of aircraft companies that sprang up to meet the enormous needs of the U.S. and Allied armed forces. The Coolidge administration moved to assist the development of the industry by setting long-term aircraft procurement plans for the army and navy and by encouraging the growth of private carriers through the awarding of lucrative airmail contracts. Among those carriers was Boeing, who won a contract to shuttle mail between Chicago and San Francisco under the name Boeing Air Transport Company.

The new climate brought with it a spate of mergers. Boeing joined in the fun, acquiring several small carriers, and in 1928 he formed a holding company called Boeing Aircraft and Transportation Company. The following year it became part of United Aircraft and Transportation, a larger holding company that also included various carriers, the Pratt & Whitney engine business, and other operations. Boeing, who was named chairman of this company, went on to grow wealthy by exchanging his stock with the holding company—a process that came under congressional scrutiny in 1933. An irate Boeing retired from the company and sold his holdings.

The consolidation of the industry that had been promoted by postmaster Walter Folger Brown came under attack after the Roosevelt administration took office. Senator Hugo Black led the charge, which resulted in the passage of the Air Mail Act of 1934. The law established both a ban (which turned out to be short-lived) on the private transport of airmail and the requirement that aircraft producers and air transport companies be separated from one another.

This resulted in United Aircraft and Transportation being split into three independent firms: United Air Lines, Boeing Aircraft (in the Northwest), and United Aircraft (East Coast based; renamed United Technologies in 1975), which included Pratt & Whitney and Sikorsky Aviation, a pioneer in helicopters.

The aircraft industry expanded during the 1930s, despite the Great Depression, thanks to the growth of the airlines. Boeing first took the lead with the development of its 247, sixty of which were ordered by United Air Lines. But then Douglas Aircraft, at the request of TWA, created the DC-1, the first of its highly successful DC (Douglas Commercial) series. Boeing, meanwhile, was one of the firms involved in producing the famous "flying boats," the huge planes commissioned by Juan Trippe of Pan American to fly across oceans and alight on water where there were no airfields.

When the wartime mobilization began, Boeing began producing hundreds of B-17 Flying Fortresses for the U.S. government. A later model, the B-29 Superfortress, was the type of plane used in the dropping of atomic bombs on Hiroshima and Nagasaki in 1945. The company's series of bombers also includes the renowned B-52.

After the war, Boeing set out to challenge the domination of the civilian aircraft market by Douglas. The result was the Boeing 707, introduced in 1954. That plane put Boeing in an intense contest with Douglas for the loyalties of the world's airlines. Douglas was prompted to develop the DC-8, but Boeing gained the lead in the new jet planes and solidified it with the introduction of the 727 in 1964.

The development of fan-jet engines, stimulated by the Pentagon's interest in building the huge C-5A cargo planes, made substantially larger commercial aircraft possible as well. Juan Trippe of Pan Am essentially decided to bet the company on the idea and enlisted Boeing to produce planes with 350 or more seats—the 747. A purchase agreement for twenty-five of the jumbo jets was signed in 1966.

The 747 eventually helped usher in a new era of mass airline travel. But the orders were slow in coming in, which put an enormous strain on Boeing's resources, coming as it did when the company also was involved in developing a supersonic transport (a project the company abandoned after Congress ended its financial support). Boeing survived the squeeze and went on to develop a new generation of planes that met the demand for aircraft that could carry up to about 250 passengers.

The market for these planes, designated as wide-body, was already being met by Lockheed with its L-1011s and the DC-10 from Douglas. A new player on the scene was Airbus Industrie, a consortium formed by British, French, German, and Spanish aerospace companies. Its first product, the A300, managed to seize one-fifth of the international commercial aircraft market by the end of the 1970s.

Once Boeing introduced its new narrow-body 757 and wide-body 767 in the early 1980s, the Seattle company once again took command of the market. As a result the teetering Lockheed, which in the 1970s had been rescued by a federal government bailout program, abandoned the commercial aircraft business in 1981.

This new climate was not without its drawbacks for Boeing. Having spent years and massive sums of money developing new, fuel-efficient technologies, aerospace companies were now finding that the reduction in oil prices was making airlines less concerned about fuel costs. This was a particular blow for Boeing, which (along with engine maker General Electric) was spending several billion dollars to develop a new type of engine to be used on its belated entry into the 150-seat market. The project, which Boeing called the 7J7, involved an unducted fan engine, a device that made use of external fan blades that looked suspiciously like propellers and that was designed to burn one-third to two-thirds less fuel than existing engines.

Boeing decided to share the risk and the development cost of the plane with a group of Japanese companies eager to gain access to U.S. aerospace technology. (Those companies have, since the late 1970s, been major suppliers for Boeing's 767.) Yet the slump in fuel prices and planning problems caused Boeing to delay the project indefinitely.

The Reagan administration's escalation of defense spending fattened the military side of Boeing's operations. In addition to getting more money to build its E-3 Airborne Warning and Control Systems (AWACS), the company began to get more involved in military electronics—though not as much as it had hoped when it made a $5-billion bid in 1985 for Hughes Aircraft. Hughes ended up with General Motors instead. Boeing's position as a military contractor was tarnished in 1989 when it pleaded guilty and paid a $5-million fine in connection with charges that it illegally obtained classified Pentagon planning documents.

McDonnell Douglas, the product of a 1967 merger of Douglas Aircraft and the military contractor McDonnell Aircraft, found itself facing intensified competition from Boeing and Airbus in the late 1980s. For customers wanting to replace aging DC-10s with a longer-range wide-body, McDonnell Douglas developed the MD-11, which fit between Boeing's 747 jumbo jets and its 200- to 250-seat 767. Boeing, however, responded by downsizing the 747 and stretching the 767.

During the same period, Airbus—which in 1986 began to receive serious acceptance from U.S. airlines for its A320 medium-range plane—brought out a long-range A340 to compete directly with the MD-11. Able to price aggressively because of its government subsidies, Airbus began to take market share from McDonnell Douglas while making Boeing uneasy. In early 1988 Boeing strengthened its position by introducing new versions of the 747 and the medium-range 737. These received an enthusiastic response from airlines, and the company's ten-year-old midsize 757s also began to catch on. By 1989 the main challenge for Boeing was keeping up with the flood of orders.

The company also was busy developing and promoting a new, long-distance, 350-seat plane called the 777. Yet the fact that the twin-engine plane would not be available until at least 1995 was causing some potential customers to turn to alternative products from McDonnell Douglas and Airbus. In October 1990, however, United Airlines showed its faith in Boeing by placing a whopping $22-billion order for sixty-eight of the 777s—the largest aircraft order ever made. Not willing to concede defeat, Airbus began talking with airlines about building the largest planes in the world, capable of holding six hundred passengers. Boeing, in turn, began to consider producing a "superjumbo" of its own.

Boeing's military business also began to surge again. In 1991 a team headed by Boeing and the Sikorsky Aircraft division of United Technologies was chosen to build a new generation of combat helicopters for the U.S. Army. The contract could be worth an eventual $34 billion. Boeing was also part of a team (with Lockheed and General Dynamics) chosen to supply 650 Advanced Tactical Fighters to the U.S. Air Force, a deal that could be worth $90 billion to the three companies. The Seattle company joined yet another team (including Grumman and Lockheed) to compete for the contract on the U.S. Navy's new A-X attack plane. In 1991 Boeing formed an alliance with the Thomson-CSF subsidiary of Thomson SA to pursue opportunities in global military markets.

OPERATIONS

Commercial Transportation Products and Services (78 percent of 1991 operating revenues). Boeing, the leader of the commercial aircraft industry, currently sells 737 and 757 standard-body models and the 747 and 767 widebody series. In 1990 the company began development of the twin-engine 777, which will fill a market segment between the 767-300 and 747-400 models.

The company's 1991 results in this segment also include sales of the Dash 8 turboprop commuter aircraft made by its de Havilland division, which Boeing purchased in 1985. In 1991 Boeing announced plans to sell de Havilland to Alenia SpA of Italy and Aérospatiale SA of France, but the plan ran into opposition by European Community antitrust officials. In 1992 Boeing found a new buyer: Canada's Bombardier, Inc.

Military Transportation Products and Related Systems (14 percent of operating revenues). The main activities in this segment are the production of the E-3 AWACS aircraft for the U.S. Air Force and foreign governments; modernization and support programs for the B-52 and KC-135 aircraft and CH-47 helicopters; and avionics systems for the B-1B bomber. The company also is involved in teams that have won contracts for new combat helicopters for the U.S. Navy and new fighters for the U.S. Air Force.

Missiles, Space, and Other Products (7 percent of operating revenues). Included here are design and development work on the ground basing for the MX intercontinental ballistic missile (ICBM); continued modernization and improvement of the Minuteman ICBM; production and launch support for the booster for the Titan missile; work on space shuttle payloads; and development of living and working quarters for NASA's planned space station. Other activities include computer services and operational support services.

TOP EXECUTIVES

- Frank Shrontz, chairman and chief executive
- Dean D. Thornton, executive vice president; president of Boeing Commercial Airplane Group

- B. Dan Pinick, executive vice president; president of Boeing Defense and Space Group
- B. E. Givan, senior vice president and chief financial officer
- D. P. Beighle, senior vice president

OUTSIDE DIRECTORS

- Robert Beck, chairman emeritus of Prudential Insurance
- John B. Fery, chief executive of Boise Cascade
- Paul E. Gray, chairman of MIT
- Harold J. Haynes, retired chief executive of Chevron
- Stanley Hiller, Jr., partner in Hiller Investment Company
- George M. Keller, retired chief executive of Chevron
- Donald E. Petersen, retired chief executive of Ford Motor Company
- Charles Pigott, chief executive of the transportation equipment company PACCAR Inc.
- Rozanne L. Ridgway, president of the Atlantic Council
- George P. Shultz, professor of international economics at the Stanford Graduate School of Business; former secretary of state
- George Weyerhaeuser, chairman of Weyerhaeuser Company
- T. A. Wilson, chairman emeritus of Boeing

FINANCIAL DATA

Revenues (in millions of dollars)

1991	29,314
1990	27,595
1989	20,276
1988	16,962
1987	15,505
1986	16,444

Net Income (in millions of dollars)

1991	1,567
1990	1,385
1989	675
1988	614
1987	480
1986	665

GEOGRAPHICAL BREAKDOWN

Revenues (in millions of dollars)

Year	United States		Europe		Elsewhere	
1991	11,458	(39%)	8,745	(30%)	9,111	(31%)
1990	11,502	(42%)	7,762	(28%)	8,331	(30%)
1989	9,255	(46%)	5,429	(27%)	5,592	(28%)

LABOR RELATIONS

Like all of the major aerospace companies, Boeing has been less than enthusiastic about the unionization of its employees. The International Association of Machinists and Aerospace Workers (IAM) did, however, eventually succeed in winning collective-bargaining rights for many of the company's production workers.

The bargaining power of the IAM has fluctuated with the erratic condition of the aircraft market. During the uncertainties of the early 1980s Boeing, along with competitors, got a lot tougher at the bargaining table. In 1983 the IAM signed a contract with Boeing that substituted lump-sum payments for wage increases and instituted a two-tier pay structure. The pact prompted other companies to demand concessions. The industry was booming in 1986, but Boeing again got the IAM to take lump sums instead of increases in base pay.

In 1989, while the company was flooded with orders and falling behind in filling them, the IAM went on strike to pressure the company to make up for the six years without an increase in base wage. The workers—many of whom welcomed the strike as a respite from exhausting amounts of mandatory overtime—stayed out for forty-eight days and then accepted a settlement that included both lump-sum payments and moderate increases in base pay.

ENVIRONMENTAL AND HEALTH RECORD

For decades Boeing has generated hazardous wastes at its production facilities in Washington State. In 1990 a federal jury found that the company had not knowingly dumped toxic material in waste sites in the 1950s and 1960s but that it had done so in the following decade. Boeing thus was found partially responsible for the cleanup of two heavily contaminated sites in Washington.

In 1990 the company settled a class action lawsuit brought on behalf of seven hundred people who allegedly had been hired by Boeing for jobs that involved exposure to electromagnetic pulse radiation and were monitored for health effects without their knowledge. The lead plaintiffs' counsel charged that the seven hundred individuals had been used as human research subjects without their consent. The settlement, in which Boeing admitted no wrongdoing, involved payment of $500,000 in cash and an annuity to the family of one employee who claimed that he had developed leukemia as a result of the exposure. The company also agreed to pay for regular medical examinations over ten years for the other class members, who reserved the right to bring claims for compensation if they develop adverse health effects.

In 1991 the EPA fined the company $620,475 for improper storage of hazardous wastes and deficiencies in its training practices regarding toxics. That same year, the company was sued by a group of employees who charged that Boeing had concealed the dangers of a substance (Ferro CPH2284P) they were exposed to on the job.

A study of EPA data by the Citizens Fund found that among all U.S. manufacturing companies in 1989 (the latest figures available), Boeing had the fortieth-largest volume (9.4 million pounds) of toxic releases into the air.

BIBLIOGRAPHY

Adams, Gordon. *The Iron Triangle: The Politics of Defense Contracting*. New York: Council on Economic Priorities, 1981.

Biddle, Wayne. *Barons of the Sky*. New York: Simon & Schuster, 1991.

Bluestone, Barry, Peter Jordan, and Mark Sullivan. *Aircraft Industry Dynamics: An Analysis of Competition, Capital and Labor*. Dover, Mass.: Auburn House, 1981.

Gansler, Jacques S. *The Defense Industry*. Cambridge, Mass.: MIT Press, 1980.

IMF Guide to World Aerospace Companies and Unions. Geneva: International Metalworkers Federation, 1987.

Newhouse, John. *The Sporty Game*. New York: Alfred A. Knopf, 1982.

Rae, John B. *Climb to Greatness: The American Aircraft Industry, 1920–1960*. Cambridge, Mass.: MIT Press, 1968.

Serling, Robert J. *Legend and Legacy: The Story of Boeing and Its People*. New York: St. Martin's Press, 1992.

Shaw, Linda, et al. *Stocking the Arsenal: A Guide to the Nation's Top Military Contractors*. Washington, D.C.: Investor Responsibility Research Center, 1985.

BRIDGESTONE CORPORATION

10-1, Kyobashi 1-chome
Chuo-ku, Tokyo 104
Japan
(03) 3567-0111

1991 revenues: $14.1 billion
1991 net income: $59.8 million
Publicly traded company
Employees: 95,276
Founded: 1931

OVERVIEW

Bridgestone, the Japanese tire company with the American-sounding name (it derives from a translation of the founder's name), rode the wave generated by the Japanese automakers to become one of the leaders in its industry. Then in the late 1980s it joined in the merger mania that swept the tire business, paying a hefty $2.6 billion to acquire the number-three producer in the United States, Firestone.

Bridgestone is now neck and neck with Goodyear for second place behind Michelin in worldwide market share. Yet size and market control have turned out to be less than a panacea. Bridgestone has been particularly hard hit by the overcapacity and ruthless competition that has characterized the tire industry in recent years. The biggest headache has been Firestone, which singlehandedly has pulled its parent company's net income nearly into the red.

To some U.S. observers, Bridgestone's problems with Firestone have served as a satisfying illustration that the Japanese are not infallible. The company, which also is known for its bicycles and sporting goods, may have its problems, but it will remain a leading player in an industry that will remain important as long as people travel in vehicles supported by hollow pieces of rubber.

HISTORY

Bridgestone had its origins in a family clothing business that Shojiro Ishibashi and his brother Tokujiro took over in 1906. Later they moved into the production of the traditional Japanese footwear known as *tabi*, to which they eventually added a rubber sole, allowing them to be worn outdoors. With this start in rubber, the Ishibashi brothers expanded into tire production in 1923, despite the fact that there were relatively few automobiles in the country at the time.

Bridgestone was established in 1931 and from the start put emphasis on foreign sales. The tire maker, taking advantage of the forcible opening of markets (that is, occupation) by the Japanese military during the 1930s, built factories in China, Manchuria, and Korea. During World War II the firm's anglicized name was changed to Nippon Tire (and was changed back in 1951).

The company lost all of its foreign facilities as a result of the war, but a factory that had been built at Kurume on the island of Kyushu (where the Ishibashis had begun their operation) did survive. Another plant at Asahi, which had been built during the war, was converted to bicycle production.

With the technical assistance of the American company Goodyear, Bridgestone modernized and expanded its operations in the 1950s. Goodyear took a small stake in the company, which it held until 1979. Following a boost from U.S. military orders during the Korean War, the company automated its cord production and began producing nylon tires. In the following decade Bridgestone began making radial tires and opened plants in Singapore and Thailand.

The company expanded its manufacturing to Indonesia in 1973 and formed a joint venture with the U.S. company Spalding for the production of golf balls, a business that Bridgestone originally had entered back in the 1930s. During the 1970s the company, sharing in the success of the Japanese automakers, saw its revenues grow sixfold, reaching $3 billion. This brought the company from seventh or eighth among the world's tire makers to the number-four spot.

It was not until the 1980s that Bridgestone began to get serious about selling abroad. In the case of the United States this was done first by producing in that country. Following the Japanese auto companies, Bridgestone took over a Firestone factory near Nashville, Tennessee, and began producing heavy-duty radial truck tires there in 1983. The company later began producing auto tires as well in the United States.

In 1984 Bridgestone introduced a new tire design system called Rolling Contour Optimization Theory, which made more effective use of air pressure to provide better road contact and shock absorption, reduce unnecessary movement, and achieve lower rolling resistance.

The Japanese company's boldest move came in 1988, when it first attempted to form a joint venture to manage Firestone's worldwide tire business. That $1.25-billion deal was sidetracked when Italy's Pirelli made a $1.85-billion bid for Firestone. Not about to lose its prize, Bridgestone topped Pirelli with a whopping $2.6-billion offer that won it all of Firestone.

Firestone, founded in Akron, Ohio, in 1900 by Harvey S. Firestone, rose to the top tier of U.S. tire makers through its association with Ford Motor Company. It began to falter when the industry moved from bias-ply to radial tires—a switch that shrank the replacement market. In the late 1970s the company was the subject of controversy because of defects in its Firestone 500 steel-belted radials. The company's reputation was further tainted by scandals involving illegal campaign contributions and tax violations. John J. Nevin, who was brought in to repair the damage, shut down plants, abandoned the plastics business, sold numerous foreign operations, and eliminated tens of thousands of jobs. He then delivered the company into the hands of Bridgestone.

Right after the takeover was approved, Firestone suffered a severe blow when General Motors announced that it would no longer purchase tires from the company, thus depriving Firestone of one of its largest customers. Bridgestone forged ahead. It agreed to spend more than $1 billion to revive Firestone but promised to allow the American company a high degree of autonomy. It turned out that the problems at Firestone were more serious than the Japanese company had expected. Consequently, a hiring freeze was instituted, additional jobs were eliminated, and more businesses were sold. Losses at the number-three U.S. tire maker drastically reduced Bridgestone's overall 1989 earnings. The following year a $350-million deficit at the Firestone unit nearly wiped out Bridgestone's profits altogether.

In 1991 Bridgestone replaced George Aucott, the American who was running Firestone, with one of Bridgestone's executive vice presidents, Yoichiro Kaizaki. The chief operating officer's post went to James McCann, an American executive from Bridgestone's side of the business. The Japanese company also decided to inject another $1.4 billion into the ailing American operation.

OPERATIONS

Tires (75 percent of 1991 revenues). The company manufactures more than eight thousand varieties of tires for passenger cars, trucks, buses, motorcycles, airplanes, subways, monorails, and off-road vehicles. The aircraft portion was expanded with the 1990 purchase of part of the Thompson Aircraft Tire operations of the U.S. company Banner Industries. Tire-manufacturing operations are located in Japan, Australia, France, Indonesia, Italy, Portugal, Taiwan, Thailand, Turkey, and the United States.

Nontire Products (25 percent of revenues). Included here are industrial rubber products, such as conveyor belts, roofing materials, marine hoses and fenders, and inflatable dams. The company also makes golf clubs, tennis rackets, and other sporting goods. Bridgestone is also one of the world's largest manufacturers of bicycles. Nontire products are manufactured in Japan, Australia, Malaysia, and the United States.

TOP EXECUTIVES

- Akira Yeiri, president
- Yoichiro Kaizaki, executive vice president
- Akihiro Ono, executive vice president
- Satoshi Tokoro, senior vice president
- Tadakazu Harada, senior vice president
- Akio Mino, senior vice president

FINANCIAL DATA

Revenues (in millions of yen)

1991	1,763,885
1990	1,784,104
1989	1,689,025
1988	1,191,229
1987	820,419

Net Income (in millions of yen)

1991	7,468
1990	4,502
1989	9,645
1988	39,960
1987	36,001

GEOGRAPHICAL BREAKDOWN

Revenues (in millions of yen)

Year	Japan		Foreign	
1991	819,397	(46%)	944,488	(54%)
1990	758,800	(43%)	1,025,300	(57%)

LABOR RELATIONS

Bridgestone has long practiced a generous form of paternalism toward its employees, providing such amenities as day care, low-cost housing, and vacation facilities. For many years Bridgestone prided itself on never dismissing workers.

Following its creation in 1935, the United Rubber Workers (URW) achieved its first major breakthrough in organizing the industry when Firestone recognized the union the following year. The recognition did not come quickly; it was only after a fifty-nine-day strike and a U.S. Supreme Court ruling on the issue of exclusive representation that the company gave in.

After several decades of relative prosperity at Firestone—though there was a 131-day strike in 1976—union members at the company responded to the dismal new reality of the company in 1981 by voting to accept a wage cut and other contract concessions. After Bridgestone bought the company, it voluntarily restored more than a dollar an hour in pay cuts as a goodwill gesture toward the union.

When the URW's contract came up for renewal in 1991, Bridgestone decided to continue with the carrot rather than the stick. The company agreed to a three-year contract that included a reasonable wage increase and no contract concessions.

ENVIRONMENTAL AND SAFETY RECORD

Bridgestone bought a company with a less-than-sterling safety record when it acquired Firestone in 1988. The U.S. company had been accused of concealing the fact that its Firestone 500 steel-belted radials had a tendency to blow out, causing the deaths of at least twenty-seven people. In response to federal government pressure, Firestone finally agreed in 1978 to recall ten million of the tires.

Along similar lines, Firestone was sued in the 1980s by the family of a mechanic who had suffered severe injuries when a tire he was mounting on a truck exploded. The mechanic, despondent over his condition, later committed suicide. His family sued Firestone, charging that the company had known of the potential danger. Firestone settled the case out of court for $4.9 million in 1991.

Another major court settlement occurred in 1990, when Firestone agreed to pay $11 million to the widow and two children of a worker who developed pancreatic cancer that, his family alleged, was the result of exposure to toxic chemicals on the job.

In 1991 two consumer groups singled out Firestone in the course of criticizing the tire industry for failing to take more significant steps to address a long-standing safety problem. The criticism related to the fact that owners of light trucks frequently put sixteen-inch tires on sixteen-and-a-half-inch rims, which can cause the tire to explode during inflation. The consumer groups—Public Citizen and the Institute for Injury Reduction—asked that Firestone and other companies recall sixteen-inch tires that did not include reinforcing beads. According to the two groups, Firestone knew of the danger in the early 1970s but only began reinforcing its tires in 1990.

BIBLIOGRAPHY

French, Michael J. *The U.S. Tire Industry: A History.* Boston: Twayne Publishers, 1991.
Lief, Alfred. *The Firestone Story: A History of the Firestone Tire and Rubber Company.* New York: Whittlesey House, 1951.
Roberts, Harold S. *The Rubber Workers: Labor Organization and Collective Bargaining in the Rubber Industry.* New York: Harper & Brothers, 1944.

BRISTOL-MYERS SQUIBB COMPANY

345 Park Avenue
New York, New York 10154
(212) 546-4000

1991 revenues: $11.2 billion
1991 net income: $2.1 billion
Publicly traded company
Employees: 53,500
Founded: 1989 (Squibb was founded in 1858, Bristol-Myers in
    1887)

OVERVIEW

The 1989 marriage of two second-tier pharmaceutical companies has produced a powerful global player that ranks near the top of the prescription drug industry. With manufacturing operations in seventeen countries, Bristol-Myers Squibb has products ranging from mundane items like toilet bowl cleaners to sophisticated medications for treating cardiovascular problems.

The record of drug development at both Bristol-Myers and Squibb was uneven, but there have been signs—including a new AIDS drug approved in 1991—that the joining of forces has put the combined company in a strong position to compete with industry leaders, such as Merck.

HISTORY

Squibb originated in the work of Dr. Edward Robinson Squibb, a Quaker who began a crusade for pure drugs while serving as a doctor in the U.S. Navy in the middle of the nineteenth century. He became particularly concerned about ether, a volatile substance that surgeons of the era were trying to use as an anesthetic. In 1854, while doing research at a naval laboratory in Brooklyn, New York, Squibb perfected a technique for producing pure ether. He also developed the first chloroform of uniform quality.

After quitting the navy, Squibb began to exploit his discoveries commercially in 1858 with the establishment of a manufacturing operation in Brooklyn. Soon after opening, however, the carelessness of an assistant caused a fire in which Squibb was seriously burned. He managed to get himself and his business back in working order before long.

The company's trade expanded dramatically as a result of government orders received during the Civil War. The growth continued in the following decades, despite Squibb's refusal to patent his innovations. Squibb put his sons in control of the company in 1890, though he continued to work in his laboratory until his death in 1900.

Control by the family ended in 1905 when Theodore Weicker, the German chemist who established the American branch of Merck, and his father-in-law, Lowell Palmer, a wealthy midwesterner, bought a majority interest in Squibb for $900,000. Under the new owners the company held to Squibb's ideals but also took a more aggressive business posture. There was a substantial investment in promotion, including extensive advertising in professional and lay magazines and sponsorship of radio and, later, television programs. The company also built a sales organization of some seven hundred detail men, one of the largest in the industry.

Squibb, which served as a major supplier of morphine and penicillin during World War II, merged with Mathieson Chemical Corporation in 1952. The following year the combined operation joined with Olin Industries to form the Olin Mathieson Chemical Corporation.

The Squibb operation languished within the conglomerate until it was spun off as an independent company once again in 1968. For several years Squibb tried diversifying its operations—buying Beech-Nut Life Saver candies and other nondrug properties—but during the 1970s it focused again on pharmaceuticals.

Squibb remained generally lackluster until the latter part of that decade, when the company's scientists developed a drug for hypertension based on an enzyme derived from the venom of an extremely poisonous Brazilian pit viper. Using new biochemical techniques, the researchers reproduced the enzyme. The result was Capoten, which was prescribed by doctors in great quantities during the 1980s. Its success was later diminished by the rise of a competing drug, Vasotec, sold by Merck.

Bristol-Myers began as the Clinton Pharmaceutical Company, founded in Clinton, New York, in 1887 by William McLaren Bristol and John Ripley Myers. This endeavor by the two recent Hamilton College graduates was an audacious one, since they knew nothing about the drug business. They managed to lure some people who did, and before long, the firm was building a modest trade selling a wide range of drugs to physicians and dentists.

The company, which took the name Bristol, Myers in 1898 (and replaced the comma with a hyphen shortly thereafter), moved into over-the-counter preparations in the early years of the new century. Its biggest successes were with Sal Hepatica, a laxative mineral salt known as the "poor man's spa," and Ipana toothpaste, the first dentifrice to include a disinfectant to protect against the effects of bleeding gums.

After World War I the company disposed of its pharmaceutical business and concentrated on those two big sellers plus a dozen or so toiletries, antiseptics, and cough syrups. It then changed its marketing orientation from doctors to the public. Bristol-Myers was one of the early radio advertisers, tying its two leading products together in the heavily promoted slogan "Ipana for the Smile of Beauty; Sal Hepatica for the Smile of Health."

The company, which for a few years in the early 1930s was part of a huge holding company called Drug Inc., returned to the pharmaceutical business in 1943 with the purchase of Cheplin Biological Laboratories. Cheplin had specialized in making a therapeutic preparation based on fermented cow's milk, but during World War II it ended up as part of the effort to mass produce penicillin. After the war Cheplin was renamed Bristol Laboratories and continued working with antibiotics.

This business got the company into legal trouble. In 1961 Bristol-Myers was one of three companies indicted for conspiring to fix the price of tetracycline (Squibb was one of the companies named as an unindicted coconspirator). A jury found the defendants guilty, but in 1970 a U.S. Appeals Court reversed the convictions and ordered a retrial, in which they were acquitted.

After World War II Bristol-Myers continued its aggressive advertising of such preparations as Vitalis hair tonic, Bufferin (the first buffered aspirin), and Ban roll-on deodorant. In 1959 the company expanded this line with the purchase of the Clairol hair-coloring business (with its famous advertising line "Does she . . . or doesn't she? Hair color so natural only her hairdresser knows for sure"). The company's current chief executive, Richard Gelb, is the son of the couple who founded Clairol.

Bristol-Myers continued its acquisitions in the 1960s and 1970s, purchasing such companies as Drackett (maker of Windex and Drano), Mead Johnson (infant formula), Zimmer (orthopedic and surgical products), Westwood (Keri skin-care products), and Unitek (dental equipment). The company suffered, however, from some new product failures.

It began to experience a resurgence in the late 1970s and used some of its new resources to expand its drug business. The company ended up becoming a leader in producing a new wave of anticancer medications, while also enjoying success with its cholesterol-lowering drug Questran and a tranquilizer called BuSpar. In 1987 it obtained an exclusive license to produce and test two new drugs for treating AIDS.

More frustrating was the company's attempt to hold on to its share of the over-the-counter analgesic market in face of the growing popularity of Johnson & Johnson's Tylenol. Bristol-Myers first responded by introducing a non-aspirin product called Datril. In 1984 it brought out Nuprin, a new, non-prescription form of Upjohn's ibuprofen pain reliever. The company's

Excedrin product suffered serious tampering incidents in 1982 and 1986. After the latter, which involved a nationwide recall, Bristol-Myers followed Johnson & Johnson—which had its own tampering problems with Tylenol—in ending the use of capsules for over-the-counter medications.

The company acquired two biotechnology firms, Genetic Systems and Oncogen, in 1986, but sold Genetic Systems to the French drug company Sanofi in 1990. To strengthen its position in coronary care, Bristol-Myers purchased SciMed Life Systems, a producer of balloon angioplasty catheters, in 1987.

Two years later Bristol-Myers decided to join forces with its old rival Squibb in a $12-billion friendly merger that created the world's second-largest drug company (after Merck). "The pharmaceutical industry is truly global," Richard Gelb told reporters. "To compete successfully you clearly have to have critical mass around the world." Squibb, which had been much more active abroad than Bristol-Myers, gave Gelb what he needed.

The combined company began taking an aggressive posture in the pharmaceutical field. For example, to pave the way for worldwide marketing of its Pravachol cholesterol-lowering drug, the company simultaneously prepared applications for twenty-one countries—all before the product was approved by U.S. regulators. Boldness can, however, get one into trouble. In 1991 the Food and Drug Administration (FDA) pressured Bristol-Myers Squibb to stop promoting several unapproved and unproven uses for its cancer medications. That same year, the FDA approved the company's application to market Videx (the commercial name for dideoxyinosine, or DDI), the first new treatment for AIDS since AZT was approved in 1986.

OPERATIONS

Pharmaceutical Products (53 percent of 1991 revenues). The largest parts of the company's prescription drug business derive from cardiovascular medications (especially Capoten) and antibiotics. Other products include the cholesterol-lowering agents Questran and Pravachol; chemotherapeutic agents, such as VePesid and Paraplatin; and the tranquilizer BuSpar.

Medical Devices (14 percent of revenues). This segment of the company's operations includes the Zimmer line of orthopedic implants, ostomy-care and wound-care products, surgical instruments, and other devices.

Nonprescription Health Products (17 percent of revenues). The largest part of this segment consists of infant formula products, such as Enfamil and Prosobee. The company is the second-largest producer in that market. Also included are Sustagen and other adult nutritional supplements; analgesics sold under the names Bufferin, Excedrin, Nuprin, and Tempra; Comtrex cold medications; Keri body lotion; and Theragran vitamins.

There was an uproar in 1989 over a decision by the company and Gerber Products Company, which together began marketing Gerber Infant Formula, to promote the product directly to parents, rather than the traditional practice of letting physicians provide the guidance on whether to use formula or breast-feed. This followed a related controversy concerning the promotion of infant formula in the third world. In early 1991 reports began to surface that the Federal Trade Commission was investigating Bristol-Myers Squibb and other infant formula producers for price-fixing in connection with sales to federal nutrition programs.

Toiletries, Beauty Aids, and Household Products (16 percent of revenues). Included here are Miss Clairol, Nice 'n Easy, and other hair-coloring preparations; Sea Breeze skin-care products; Ban antiperspirants; Windex glass cleaner; Drano drain openers; Renuzit air fresheners; Behold and Endust furniture polishes; and other products.

TOP EXECUTIVES

- Richard L. Gelb, chairman and chief executive
- Michael E. Autera, executive vice president
- Wayne A. Davidson, executive vice president
- Charles A. Heimbold, Jr., executive vice president

OUTSIDE DIRECTORS

- Robert E. Allen, chief executive of AT&T
- Richard M. Furlaud, retired president of Bristol-Meyers Squibb
- Ellen V. Futter, president of Barnard College
- Louis V. Gerstner, Jr., chief executive of RJR Nabisco
- Alexander Rich, professor of biophysics at MIT
- James D. Robinson III, chief executive of American Express
- Andrew C. Sigler, chief executive of Champion International

FINANCIAL DATA

In the following lists, the figures before 1989 are the sum of the separate results of Bristol-Myers and Squibb.

Revenues (in millions of dollars)

1991	11,159
1990	10,300
1989	9,189
1988	8,558
1987	7,558

Net Income (in millions of dollars)

1991	2,056
1990	1,748
1989	747
1988	1,254
1987	1,068

GEOGRAPHICAL BREAKDOWN

Revenues (in millions of dollars)

Year	United States		Foreign	
1991	7,686	(62%)	4,786	(38%)
1990	7,017	(61%)	4,421	(39%)
1989	6,478	(64%)	3,685	(36%)

Net Income (in millions of dollars)

Year	United States		Foreign	
1991	2,099	(69%)	929	(31%)
1990	1,747	(66%)	911	(34%)
1989	1,259	(76%)	387	(24%)

LABOR RELATIONS

A forerunner of the Oil, Chemical and Atomic Workers (OCAW) organized many of Squibb's employees during World War II. The major labor conflict at the company came in 1959, when two thousand Squibb employees (by then members of the OCAW) staged a six-week strike. The walkout was a success for the union in resisting a company attempt to have foremen do work that previously had been performed only by hourly workers in union jurisdiction.

Bristol-Myers was traditionally nonunion. Since the merger the company has been shutting down facilities and eliminating thousands of jobs, or else shifting them from unionized plants to nonunion ones.

ENVIRONMENTAL AND HEALTH RECORD

In 1977 the National Cancer Institute reported a link between an ingredient used in hair-coloring products like those sold by Bristol-Myers's Clairol subsidiary and cancer in laboratory rats. The company initially disputed these findings, but later its products were reformulated to eliminate the suspect substance. During the same period, the company took advantage of growing concern over the environmental effects of aerosol cans by heavily promoting its nonaerosol Ban roll-on deodorant.

As the parent company of Mead Johnson, Bristol-Myers has been one of the targets in an international campaign to restrict aggressive marketing of infant formula in the third world. Poor mothers in those countries often must mix the powder with unclean water and dilute the formula to the extent that it provides far less nutrition than breast milk. Along with other manufacturers, Bristol-Myers initially resisted strict curbs on marketing but later agreed to comply with a code issued by the World Health Organization.

Starting in the mid-1970s, Squibb was one of more than two dozen drug producers and distributors sued by large numbers of women who said they suffered from vaginal cancer and other ailments because their mothers had used the drug diethylstilbestrol, commonly known as DES. Despite evidence that it caused cancer in animals, for several decades the medication was widely prescribed for pregnant women to prevent miscarriages. Squibb lost a few big individual suits but successfully defended itself in several other cases, including one in which the California State Supreme Court found that the company's relatively small involvement in the DES market was not enough to make it liable. Many of the suits are still pending.

Squibb also has been named as a defendant in a suit brought by a group of people in Puerto Rico who say they suffered physical damages from toxic waste that Squibb and other companies dumped into a waterway.

In 1992 Bristol-Myers Squibb paid a fine of $3.5 million after pleading guilty to federal charges relating to violations of clean water and waste management regulations by the company at its manufacturing facility in Syracuse, New York.

Bristol-Myers Squibb paid $50,000 in 1991 to settle a complaint brought by a group of ten states charging that the company had misrepresented the environmental benefits of certain products, including hair sprays and household cleaners. That same year the company announced that it would shut down its Surgitek breast-implant business. This occurred during a period when the FDA indicated that it was considering taking action against producers of silicone breast implants because of questions about the safety of those products.

BIBLIOGRAPHY

Blochman, Lawrence G. *Doctor Squibb: The Life and Times of a Rugged Idealist.* New York: Simon & Schuster, 1958.

Braithwaite, John. *Corporate Crime in the Pharmaceutical Industry.* Boston: Routledge & Kegan Paul, 1984.

Chetley, Andrew. *A Healthy Business? World Health and the Pharmaceutical Industry.* London: Zed Books, 1990.

Mahoney, Tom. *The Merchants of Life: An Account of the American Pharmaceutical Industry.* New York: Harper & Brothers, 1959.

Mintz, Morton. *By Prescription Only.* Boston: Beacon Press, 1967.

BRITISH AIRWAYS PLC

Speedbird House
Heathrow Airport
Hounslow, Middlesex TW6 2JA
United Kingdom
(081) 759-5511

1991 revenues: $8.6 billion (year ending March 31)
1991 net income: $166.1 million
Publicly traded company
Employees: 54,427
Founded: 1924

OVERVIEW

Since the British government decided to privatize British Airways, the carrier has undergone a remarkable transformation. The joke used to be that BA actually stood for Bloody Awful; a glowing article in *Business Week* in 1989 suggests that Bloody Awesome would now be more appropriate. Under the leadership of John King (Lord King of Wartnaby) and Colin Marshall, the airline has indeed been remade into one of the world's most impressive carriers.

By some measures BA is the global leader in the industry, and it remains number one in the big transatlantic market. That latter position, however, has been threatened recently by changes among the U.S. carriers. BA's onetime powerful rivals, Pan American and TWA, which have been in decline for years, have been selling off many of their routes, including those to London, to stronger U.S. competitors, such as American Airlines and United Airlines.

BA, nonetheless, continues with its intention of being one of the mega-carriers that can survive the current turmoil of the industry. Not satisfied with its current route network of 153 destinations in 69 countries, BA sought (unsuccessfully) to buy a chunk of the Belgian carrier Sabena and has been

seeking a merger with KLM. BA has also formed a partnership with Aeroflot
to create a new Moscow-based carrier called Air Russia.

HISTORY

In the years after World War I the advocates of civil aviation were promoting
the idea of creating regular service between countries in the manner of shipping lines. The French government recognized the importance of airlines and
in 1933 helped combine the young, struggling carriers in the country into a
single operation named Air France.

In Britain there was more skepticism about the nonmilitary uses of flying.
Winston Churchill, for instance, who oversaw aviation as a government official
in the late 1910s, shared the view that there should be no subsidies for airlines.
Nonetheless, some British entrepreneurs were willing to take on the challenge.
In 1919 an operation called Aircraft Transport & Travel Ltd. began flying
between an airstrip at Hounslow outside London (later the site of Heathrow
Airport) and a field outside Paris. This is believed to have been the world's
first daily scheduled international airline service.

By the early 1920s the British state began to reassess its policy on civil
aviation, especially after a government-appointed commission strongly recommended the creation of a subsidized national airline. Thus in 1924 the
government created Imperial Airways out of several existing carriers, including the successor to Aircraft Transport & Travel. The operation was encouraged to have global ambitions, but it was not given a full-time chief. For more
than a dozen years the company was headed by Sir Eric Geddes, who was
kept busy by his other position as chairman of Dunlop Rubber. The company
also was hampered by the fact that it was required to fly only British-made
planes.

Imperial was appropriately named, since it focused its efforts on creating
air links between England and the various parts of the British Empire. The
first goal, to reach India, was accomplished in 1926, after refueling airports
were built in Cairo and Baghdad and an emergency facility was set up in the
desert between those two cities. The journey from London to India involved
flying via Paris to Basel, Switzerland, then taking a train to Genoa, Italy, and
then flying, in stages, east to Karachi, Pakistan. The trip took one week,
compared to the sailing time of three weeks. Service was soon extended to
Calcutta, Rangoon, and Singapore.

Service to Africa began in the early 1930s, and by 1933 the route was
extended to Cape Town—a ten-day journey. This international growth was
promoted by the British government in a way similar to that used in the
United States: subsidies in the form of airmail contracts.

Despite its steady growth, Imperial found itself criticized for ignoring the
European market and for Sir Eric's rigid management style. The government
thus decided to subsidize a new carrier, called British Airways, which was
founded in 1935 and was building a network across Europe. In the hope that
the two carriers would work better together, the British government in the

late 1930s nationalized and merged Imperial and British Airways into British Overseas Airways Corporation (BOAC).

During World War II BOAC was widely employed for military purposes, and after the war it had to confront the fact that the international airline business had become dominated by the United States through its "chosen instrument," Pan American Airways. In 1946 BOAC's European routes were split off and made part of a new government-owned company called British European Airways (BEA), which was allowed to purchase the most-advanced commercial planes of the day, especially Lockheed Constellations. BOAC's South American routes were assigned to a new state-owned carrier for several years before being reabsorbed by BOAC in 1949.

During the 1950s BOAC tried to bring together Qantas and the other airlines created in Commonwealth countries in a united operation, but the rivalries and differences were too strong. Also during this period BOAC had difficulties with its British-built de Havilland Comets, which were unable to withstand high altitudes. The company gradually began adopting American-made aircraft, acquiring its first Boeing jets in 1960.

In 1962 BOAC and Air France agreed to finance the construction of a supersonic transport (SST), and that same year BOAC formed an alliance with the steamship company Cunard. The British government pressured the carrier to suspend some unprofitable services and restructure its debt. BEA, meanwhile, was doing well by offering vacation travel packages under the auspices of its BEA Airtours operation. In 1974 BOAC and BEA were merged to form British Airways.

Two years later the first British Airways Concorde SST made its maiden flight, but by this time the supersonic plane had been overshadowed by the jumbo jets developed by Boeing with the encouragement of Pan American. The Concordes went into service, cutting the length of transatlantic flights nearly in half, but they remained an uneconomical proposition, even at the inflated fares charged to the elite clientele.

BA faced another challenge by the name of Freddie Laker. A longtime airline entrepreneur who gained fame for helping in the Berlin airlift of 1948, Laker set out to make transatlantic travel available to the masses. He created the idea of a Skytrain, a no-frills service that did not require advance reservations. Laker ran into bureaucratic hurdles on both sides of the Atlantic as well as opposition from BA and from a rival upstart carrier, British Caledonian. In 1977, after six years of haggling, Laker finally received permission to fly. For several years he was celebrated as a folk hero and prospered from the down-scale trade across the ocean.

By the early 1980s, however, Laker was in a financial squeeze. He also was confronted with a decision by British Airways and the other members of the transatlantic big three (Pan Am and TWA) to seek permission to offer their own discount fares to compete directly with Skytrain. The noose steadily tightened around Laker's neck, and in 1982 he ceased operations. Laker later brought an antitrust suit against BA and other carriers, which was settled out of court for $48 million.

In the meantime, the new Tory government led by Margaret Thatcher was moving to end state control of BA. In 1980 Thatcher appointed Lord (John) King of Wartnaby as the new chairman of BA and charged him with preparing the company for privatization. Lord King set out to shake up the airline by cutting costs and eliminating what were seen as unnecessary personnel. His chief executive, Colin Marshall, replaced many of BA's senior managers with a team of younger executives, many of them from nonairline backgrounds. Service was upgraded, efforts were made to improve punctuality, and consultants were brought in to give the company a new image. He even revitalized the Concorde.

British Airways was given the status of a public limited company in 1985, but actual privatization was delayed because of the need to reduce its debt and because of concerns of what the move would mean to British Caledonian. At first the government arranged for the two carriers to swap some routes, but when British Caledonian began to weaken, BA moved to take over its smaller rival for $458 million. This greatly expanded BA's route network and gave it a commanding position at both Heathrow and Gatwick, two of the busiest airports in the world.

When the sale of BA to the public finally occurred in February 1987, the Thatcher government focused its efforts on selling shares to institutional investors rather than to the general citizenry, since BA was considered a more risky proposition than previous privatizations, such as that of British Gas.

Once free of government control, BA chief executive Marshall became a leading advocate of international deregulation as he strengthened BA's position as a megacarrier able to survive the expected shakeout in the industry. He formed a marketing partnership with United Airlines in the United States and joined in a consortium called Galileo to develop a European computerized reservations system. In 1989 the company participated with management and worker groups in an attempt to buy United Airlines, but the deal collapsed.

By the late 1980s BA was being hailed by many industry observers as the leading airline in the world. This was not only because the company assumed the top spot in 1986 in terms of passengers carried and passenger miles flown, but because it was shaping itself into what one analyst called "the model global airline of the future."

In the last few years BA has continued to pursue its ambitious goals, but it is no longer so easy to achieve sterling results. BA tried to buy a stake in Sabena and turn Brussels' Zaventem Airport into a European hub. The plan ran into opposition in the European Commission, and then Sabena lost interest. Later the deal was revived but in the end it was Air France that ended up acquiring a piece of Sabena.

At the same time, BA began to confront new competition on its home turf as American Airlines and United began to purchase routes between U.S. cities and London from the ailing Pan Am and TWA. BA was stunned in 1991 when British and American authorities worked out a deal that gave American Airlines and United access to Heathrow Airport while allowing BA's plucky rival Virgin Atlantic greater access to the U.S. market. Yet the

United States also granted British carriers, including BA, the right to pick up passengers in the United States and carry them to destinations in Asia, Australia, Mexico, and South America.

BA also suffered on account of the crisis in the Middle East in 1990 and early 1991, which pushed the company's European operations into the red. To try to regain lost business, in March 1991 BA announced a bold promotional campaign in which all of the carrier's seats on international flights to and from Britain on April 23 would be free, the winners chosen by lottery. With some five million people from around the world applying for the free tickets, the plan was a marketing coup.

BA continues to plan for the long term. In July 1991 it signed an agreement with the Soviet carrier Aeroflot to create a new airline (31-percent owned by BA) called Air Russia to fly between Moscow and cities in Europe, North America, and the Far East. BA also owns 49 percent of Deutsche BA, a German company that in 1992 acquired a German regional carrier called Delta Air.

OPERATIONS

Airline Operations (98 percent of 1991 revenues). British Airways has one of the world's most-extensive route networks, serving 153 destinations in 69 countries on 6 continents. In fiscal year 1991 BA carried more than 24 million passengers a total of 64.7 million kilometers. BA also carried 506,000 tons of cargo. The company has a fleet of 230 aircraft, the largest number of which are Boeing 747s and 737s. BA's charter business is carried out mostly by its subsidiary Caledonian Airways.

Package Holidays and Other Services (2 percent of revenues). This small segment consists of several companies that provide surface arrangements in the United Kingdom for inbound and outbound package vacations. Also included here is BA's participation in the Galileo computerized reservations system in Europe and the Apollo system in the United States.

TOP EXECUTIVES

- Lord (John) King of Wartnaby, chairman
- Colin Marshall, deputy chairman and chief executive
- Michael Angus, deputy chairman
- Derek Stevens, chief financial officer

OUTSIDE DIRECTORS

- Michael Davies, chairman of Calor Group PLC
- Charles H. Price II, former U.S. ambassador to the United Kingdom
- Lord White of Hull, chairman of Hanson Industries

FINANCIAL DATA

Revenues (in millions of pounds) (years ending March 31)

1991	4,937
1990	4,838
1989	4,257
1988	3,756
1987	3,263

Net Income (in millions of pounds) (years ending March 31)

1991	95
1990	245
1989	175
1988	151
1987	152

GEOGRAPHICAL BREAKDOWN

Revenues (in millions of pounds)

Year*	Europe		The Americas		Elsewhere	
1991	1,919	(39%)	1,653	(33%)	1,365	(28%)
1990	1,825	(38%)	1,619	(33%)	1,394	(29%)
1989	1,622	(38%)	1,374	(32%)	1,261	(30%)
1988	1,609	(43%)	1,175	(31%)	972	(26%)

*Fiscal year ends March 31.

Operating Surplus (in millions of pounds)

Year*	Europe		The Americas		Elsewhere	
1991	−34	(0%)	158	(79%)	43	(21%)
1990	3	(1%)	249	(65%)	132	(34%)
1989	16	(5%)	181	(54%)	139	(41%)
1988	36	(15%)	131	(56%)	69	(29%)

*Fiscal year ends March 31.

LABOR RELATIONS

Nearly all of BA's workers in Britain are organized, with about half a dozen unions represented. The largest is the Transport and General Workers Union, which has about twenty-eight thousand members among both cabin crews and ground personnel.

After Lord King took over BA in 1980 he set out to weaken the power of the unions at the carrier. Encouraged by the Thatcher government, he eliminated twenty thousand jobs. The new BA management then sought to replace traditional labor relations with a more entrepreneurial approach. This included encouraging employee stock ownership and creating a profit-sharing plan.

In the United States, fourteen hundred BA workers are represented by the International Association of Machinists and Aerospace Workers. In 1990 the company signed a four-year contract with the union that guaranteed job security for the life of the pact while giving management greater freedom to use part-time workers.

ENVIRONMENTAL AND SAFETY RECORD

The maintenance practices of British Airways came under criticism in the wake of a 1985 incident in which an engine on one of its Boeing 737s exploded during takeoff. A piece of the engine punctured the fuel tank in the wing, causing a fire in which fifty-five persons were killed. The mechanics who serviced the plane had not been informed of a warning that had been issued by the engine's manufacturer, the Pratt & Whitney division of United Technologies, saying that cracks in the engine should not be welded without first subjecting the metal to a special treatment.

BA claims to be leading the airline industry in dealing with environmental issues. In 1991 the company completed a year-long "green" audit focusing on the atmospheric emissions of its aircraft, and it has begun seeking ways to reduce those emissions.

BIBLIOGRAPHY

Corke, Alison. *British Airways: The Path to Profitability*. New York: St. Martin's Press, 1986.

Penrose, Harald. *Wings Across the World: An Illustrated History of British Airways*. London: Cassell, 1980.

Sampson, Anthony. *Empires in the Sky: The Politics, Contests and Cartels of World Airlines*. New York: Random House, 1984.

BRITISH PETROLEUM COMPANY PLC

Britannic House
1 Finsbury Circus
London EC2M 7BA
United Kingdom
(071) 496-5027

1991 revenues: $61.0 billion
1991 net income: $716 million
Publicly traded company
Employees: 115,250
Founded: 1909

OVERVIEW

British Petroleum (BP), the largest company in Britain and the third-largest in Europe, grew out of moves by Western interests to capture control over the oil supply of Iran (then Persia) early in this century. BP, which for more than seventy years was in effect a subsidiary of the British government, developed into one of that elite group of oil companies known as the Seven Sisters.

After the company's Iranian assets were nationalized but then rescued by a CIA-led coup, BP began to expand its oil activities to other parts of the world and moved into new fields, such as chemicals and animal nutrition. Its petroleum business got major boosts in the late 1960s from big strikes in Alaska and the North Sea.

During the 1980s the once-sleepy company became a whirlwind, spending some $20 billion to gain control of Sohio in the United States and rival North Sea producer Britoil, while also buying back much of a huge stake taken in BP by Kuwait. In recent years BP has continued to buy and sell assets, has launched oil exploration efforts in new parts of the world, and has increased its profile in the United States.

HISTORY

In the early years of the twentieth century, as the automobile began to replace the horse, the United States was building a domestic oil industry. Yet Britain, the leading power of the day, was dependent on foreign producers. Various parties in Britain were looking to Persia for an oil supply that could be more directly controlled, although several early ventures, including one sponsored by news service founder Baron Julius de Reuter, had failed.

A more auspicious attempt was made by William Knox D'Arcy, an Englishman who had made a fortune from gold mining in Australia. With the assistance of Sir Henry Drummond Wolff, a former British official in Persia, and the encouragement of General Antoine Kitabgi, the director general of Persian customs, D'Arcy's representative managed to win a 480,000-square-mile concession in 1901.

D'Arcy quickly sent a team to begin drilling, but they had little luck. As the expenses mounted and funds dwindled, D'Arcy began a frantic search for additional capital. It was at the initiative of the Royal Navy, which was preparing for a switchover from coal to oil power in its ships, that Burmah Oil Company came to D'Arcy's rescue. Owned by Scottish interests, Burmah Oil provided the means for D'Arcy's people to go on drilling until they made a major strike—the first in the Middle East and one of the largest in the world—in 1908. The following year D'Arcy and Burmah Oil formed the Anglo-Persian Oil Company.

It took another two years to complete a pipeline from the remote location of the oil field to the port of Abadan on the Persian Gulf, where construction was begun on a refinery that would later become the biggest in the world. As World War I approached, the navy's concern for secure oil supplies prompted Winston Churchill, then first lord of the admiralty, to push through Parliament legislation calling for the government to purchase a majority interest in Anglo-Persian.

The company prospered during the early 1920s solely from the oil being produced in Persia. Yet when a major strike was made in neighboring Mesopotamia (Iraq) in 1927, Anglo-Persian benefited by virtue of the stake in the Turkish Petroleum Company (TPC) it had obtained in 1914. The United States, not wanting to be left out of the Middle East oil bonanza, began seeking a cut of TPC by promoting an open-door policy in Mesopotamia.

An agreement for U.S. participation in TPC, renamed Iraq Petroleum, was worked out in 1928. The American companies Standard Oil of New Jersey and Standard Oil Company of New York, along with Anglo-Persian, Royal Dutch/Shell, and the French state-owned Compagnie Française des Pétroles, agreed not to compete with one another for concessions in a huge area representing the old Ottoman Empire.

To supplement what came to be called the Red Line arrangement, the heads of Jersey Standard, Royal Dutch/Shell, and Anglo-Persian met secretly at Achnacarry, a hunting lodge in Scotland, in 1928. Forming what became known as the As-Is agreement, the oil giants pooled the world market (aside from the United States and the Soviet Union) and divided it up according to existing shares of the major producers. Any expansion of the business was supposed to preserve those relationships. This was the first international oil cartel.

Although the architects of As-Is continued to dominate the global oil market outside the United States, they were unable to prevent competitors from expanding. Standard Oil of California got a foothold in Bahrain, and Gulf Oil, in partnership with Anglo-Iranian (the new name taken by Anglo-Persian after the shah changed the name of his country to Iran in 1935), obtained a valuable concession in Kuwait.

After World War II many oil-producing countries, and especially Iran, began to demand greater control over their petroleum production. The National Front of Mohammed Mossadegh was not satisfied with the fifty-fifty arrangement established in countries like Venezuela, and Iranian nationalists demanded complete control over their country's oil industry. Thus in 1951, after Mossadegh became prime minister, Anglo-Iranian's assets were expropriated.

The company retaliated by seeing to it that Iran's oil output was effectively boycotted by the other large petroleum producers. The coup de grâce was provided by the Central Intelligence Agency, which in 1953 helped to overthrow the Mossadegh government and put the shah back in power. The United States enjoyed the fruits of its efforts when a consortium was formed to reestablish foreign control over Iranian oil. Anglo-Iranian—which changed its name to British Petroleum in 1954—ended up with 40 percent of the new entity, while 8 percent went to each of five U.S. companies: Standard Oil of New Jersey, Standard Oil of New York, Standard Oil of California, Gulf Oil, and Texas Company. Another 14 percent went to Royal Dutch/Shell and the remaining 6 percent to the Compagnie Française des Pétroles. In addition the Iranian government was to pay BP £25 million in compensation over ten years, and the other companies in the consortium agreed to pay BP £32 million and ten cents a barrel in recognition of Anglo-Iranian's investments over the preceding decades.

Although BP was back in operation in Iran, it expanded its exploration activities in many other parts of the world, including Nigeria, the territory of Papua, Trinidad, and Canada. Yet the biggest strikes came in Alaska and the North Sea. In 1965 BP discovered natural gas in the North Sea and five years later struck oil there. The company also made a major oil find in Alaska's Prudhoe Bay in 1969. BP found itself the owner of some of the largest petroleum reserves in the world.

The company took advantage of the situation to make its first foray into the American market. This was done by merging its Alaska assets with Standard Oil of Ohio (Sohio) in exchange for a 25-percent holding (later increased to 55 percent) in the company, which was the original base of the Rockefeller empire.

BP began to expand its chemical activities in the late 1960s following the purchase of the interest of Distillers Company in the joint venture the two firms had formed in Scotland in 1951. BP later bought the European chemical and plastics operations of the U.S. companies Union Carbide and Monsanto. During the 1970s BP also got into coal, purchasing properties in Australia, Canada, and South Africa. The company later diversified into animal feed as well, aided by a 1986 purchase of Purina Mills in the United States.

In the late 1980s BP also consolidated its oil holdings, first by ousting the top executives of Sohio and spending $8 billion to acquire the remaining shares of the company—a step that made BP the third-largest oil company in the world. The move came after a number of years of unfriendly relations between BP and the management of Sohio, which had experienced disappointing results from further oil exploration and from the acquisition of Kennecott Copper in 1981. BP expanded its presence in the North Sea in 1988 by acquiring Britoil for some $4 billion.

The ownership structure of BP itself changed in 1987, when the Thatcher government decided to sell off its shares. Those holdings had risen to 68 percent after the government bought the holdings of the failed Burmah Oil in 1975 and then declined to 32 percent after the government sold a $1-billion stake to the public in 1977. The Kuwait Investment Office was the largest purchaser in the 1987 sale, ending up with a 21.6-percent stake in the entire company. Under pressure from the British government, that holding was later reduced to a less-threatening 9.9 percent. BP brought that about by buying back the other shares with the $4.4 billion in proceeds from the sale of its minerals operation to RTZ.

The company continued to shuffle its assets. It sold minority interests in its North Sea and Alaskan operations and traded some of its service stations in the eastern and midwestern United States for similar facilities and a refinery on the West Coast. It also got rid of its London real estate.

Faced with declining output in its established fields, BP has been aggressively exploring for new sources of supply in many parts of the world, especially virgin territories. In 1991 the company also announced plans to resume exploration in Nigeria, where BP's holdings were nationalized in 1979 because of allegations that the company was indirectly shipping oil to South Africa. BP's Nigerian project, along with several other exploration efforts, was to be carried out through a joint venture with Statoil, the Norwegian government–owned company.

OPERATIONS

Exploration and Production (20 percent of 1991 revenues). BP's exploration activities are focused on Alaska and the United Kingdom portion of the North Sea. The company has reduced the number of exploration projects in recent years and is now focusing on efforts in China, Russia, Vietnam, and West Africa. In 1991 the company produced more than 400 million barrels of crude oil, condensate, and natural gas liquids. At the end of that year BP had proven reserves of some 4.6 billion barrels of oil and 11 trillion cubic feet of natural gas.

Refining and Marketing (64 percent of revenues). BP operates five refineries in the United States, five in Europe, two in Australia, and one in Singapore. These facilities processed 1.8 million barrels of crude oil per day during 1991. BP sells refined oil products throughout the world. Most of its gasoline output was sold through BP service stations, which number more than seventy-four hundred in the United States and seventy-seven hundred in Europe.

Chemicals (8 percent of revenues). BP is a major producer of chemicals in the United States, Europe, and elsewhere. Its products include petro-chemicals and polymers, especially ethylene and derivatives, used in packaging, housewares, construction materials, and cables; acetyls, used in paints, textiles, solvents, and drugs; nitriles, used in synthetic rubber and plastic; and specialty products for such industries as aerospace, automotive, electronics, and plastics.

Nutrition (8 percent of revenues). BP is one of the world's largest producers of animal feed for the livestock industry. It also makes products for fish farming and poultry breeding and has a limited involvement in food for humans.

Other Operations (0.4 percent of revenues). These include BP's solar energy business, its few remaining coal and other mineral assets, and its finance activities.

TOP EXECUTIVES

- John Baring, chairman
- David Simon, chief executive
- Hugh Norton, managing director
- John Browne, managing director
- Russell Seal, managing director

OUTSIDE DIRECTORS

- James Glover, chairman of IT Security International
- Carl H. Hahn, chairman of the Volkswagen board of management
- Charles F. Knight, chairman of Emerson Electric
- Robin Nicholson, executive director of Pilkingtons
- Patrick Sheehy, chairman of B.A.T. Industries
- Peter Sutherland, chairman of Allied Irish Banks
- Patrick Wright, former permanent undersecretary of state at the Foreign and Commonwealth Office and head of the Diplomatic Service

FINANCIAL DATA

Revenues (in millions of pounds)

1991	32,613
1990	33,039
1989	29,641
1988	25,922
1987	28,328

Net Income (in millions of pounds)

1991	383
1990	1,726
1989	1,789
1988	1,254
1987	1,602

GEOGRAPHICAL BREAKDOWN

Revenues (in millions of pounds)

Year	United Kingdom		United States		Elsewhere	
1991	12,997	(35%)	9,164	(24%)	15,487	(41%)
1990	12,209	(34%)	10,402	(29%)	13,757	(38%)

Replacement Cost Operating Profit (in millions of pounds)

Year	United Kingdom		United States		Elsewhere	
1991	502	(20%)	1,043	(41%)	1,010	(40%)
1990	406	(14%)	1,470	(50%)	1,086	(37%)

LABOR RELATIONS

Standard Oil of Ohio was swept up in the oil industry union organizing of the 1940s, though the company was one of the more difficult employers that the Oil Workers International Union (the precursor to the Oil, Chemical and Atomic Workers) had to deal with. In recent years the company has tended to follow industry patterns in labor policy.

BP's North Sea operations were hit with a wave of wildcat strikes by construction workers in 1989. The workers, who technically were employed by contractors, used sit-ins on oil platforms to press for improved safety conditions and union recognition.

ENVIRONMENTAL RECORD

BP is unpopular with environmentalists because of its role, as majority owner of the Alaska pipeline, in resisting government regulation of oil activities in that state and in seeking permission to extend drilling activities to the Arctic National Wildlife Refuge. BP also is responsible for a large volume of toxic releases. According to EPA data, the company's American operation was the fourth biggest emitter of toxics into the air, water, and land in 1989, with total releases of more than 123 million pounds.

The company caused a stir in Britain in 1990 when it launched an ad campaign that promoted a new brand of unleaded gasoline with the claim that it caused "no pollution." BP later apologized for the statement.

In 1990 BP agreed to pay a $2.3-million fine as part of a settlement of an $11-million suit brought against the company in 1986 by the EPA in connection with illegal discharges from BP's Marcus Hook refinery into the Delaware River. Several months later the company was sued by the state of California because of a four hundred thousand–gallon spill of crude oil that occurred in February 1990 near Huntington Beach. In January 1991 an explosion at a BP refinery in Washington State killed one worker and injured six. BP was penalized $135,000 by the Washington Department of Labor in connection with the incident.

In July 1991 BP was one of ten major oil companies cited by the EPA for discharging contaminated fluids from service stations into or directly above underground sources of drinking water. BP agreed to pay a fine of $74,000 and to clean up the contaminated water sources by the end of 1993. The company was also among a large group of coal producers fined by the U.S. Department of Labor for tampering with dust samples submitted to the federal agency in charge of monitoring mine health conditions.

On the positive side, BP has continued to develop its solar energy business, has replaced steel gasoline storage tanks at many of its service stations with noncorroding fiberglass ones, and has developed new techniques to treat hazardous oil wastes at refineries.

BIBLIOGRAPHY

Ferrier, R. W. *The History of the British Petroleum Company: The Developing Years, 1901–1932*. Cambridge: Cambridge University Press, 1982.

Longhurst, Henry. *Adventure in Oil: The Story of British Petroleum*. London: Sidgwick and Jackson, 1959.

Sampson, Anthony. *The Seven Sisters: The Great Oil Companies and the World They Made*. New York: Viking Press, 1975.

BROKEN HILL PROPRIETARY COMPANY LTD.

BHP House
140 William Street
Melbourne, Victoria 3000
Australia
(03) 609-3333

1991 revenues: $11.9 billion (year ending May 31)
1991 net income: $1.1 billion
Publicly traded company
Employees: 51,000
Founded: 1885

OVERVIEW

Broken Hill Proprietary (BHP), for decades the largest company in Australia, grew out of a big mineral discovery in the outback in the late nineteenth century. BHP shifted into the steel business in 1915 and did little else to distinguish itself until the 1960s. It was then that the company ended up in the oil and gas business via a joint venture with what is now Exxon.

Yet it was not until the 1980s that BHP started to become an important player in the global arena. It returned to the mining business in a big way by purchasing most of the operations of Utah International from General Electric. The company also spent heavily on independent oil and gas companies in the United States, in part to take on debt meant to discourage a long-playing takeover attempt by Australian financier Robert Holmes à Court.

Today BHP, with operations in more than two dozen countries, is a major international mining company and a petroleum explorer and producer of growing importance.

HISTORY

Amid the mining boom of southeastern Australia in the late nineteenth century, a ranch hand named Charles Rasp working near the western border of New South Wales found some intriguing rocks. Tests of the specimens showed them to contain silver and lead. He brought in about a dozen coworkers and acquaintances to form a mining operation, which they named Broken Hill Proprietary, after a nearby town.

Before long, they were all rich. BHP hit on one of the greatest deposits of silver ever discovered, and within a few years of its founding in 1885, the company was employing hundreds of workers to extract and process the ore, which also included scores of other minerals. By the beginning of the new century BHP was also mining iron ore in South Australia, and in 1915 the company began using that ore to make steel at a facility at Newcastle in New South Wales. This pushed the company into coal mining to provide coking coal for the mill.

The steel business took off with the demand created by World War I. After the acquisition of Australian Iron and Steel in 1935, BHP gained near monopoly control over steel production in the country. In 1939 BHP finally abandoned its exhausted mines in Broken Hill. In the early 1940s the company got involved in shipbuilding, and during World War II it produced munitions and participated in a consortium that made aircraft.

The management of BHP decided in the 1960s to expand its mining activities beyond that required to supply its steel operations. This strategy was pursued first through a joint venture with the Australian subsidiary of Standard Oil of New Jersey (now Exxon). The partners struck natural gas and then oil in the Bass Strait between the mainland and the island of Tasmania. BHP then began mining iron ore, manganese, and later coal for export.

By the 1980s BHP was working hard to turn itself into a global natural resources company. The biggest step in this direction was the 1984 acquisition of most of Utah International, the big mining operation that the U.S. company General Electric had bought in 1976 for what was then the astounding sum of $2.2 billion. The purchase gave BHP a major presence in North America and South America, including coal mines in the United States, a copper mine in Canada, and a 49-percent interest in an iron ore project in Brazil. BHP went on to acquire a series of U.S. petroleum companies, including Energy Reserves Group, Monsanto Oil, and Pacific Resources.

These purchases were not merely part of a diversification strategy. They also served to thwart a long-running takeover effort by Australian raider Robert Holmes à Court by swelling the company's debt. Yet Holmes à Court was not deterred, and by 1986 he had built up his holding in BHP to 28 percent. His takeover did not succeed, though he did win a place on the company's board of directors.

Since then the company has continued its far-flung mining and other natural resources activities. In 1987 BHP moved further into the U.S. petroleum business by purchasing a minority interest in Hamilton Oil; four years later it bought the rest of the company. The company also expanded at home, purchasing the Mount Goldworthy iron ore project in Western Australia in 1990.

OPERATIONS

Steel Production (43 percent of 1991 revenues). BHP is Australia's sole integrated producer of basic iron, raw steel, and related steel products; it supplies some 80 percent of the company's needs in this area. BHP also makes sheet steel, wire products, and refractory products. Some 36 percent of BHP's steel output is exported to countries in Asia, North America, Europe, and the Middle East. Since 1982 the company's steel operations have been restructured and output substantially reduced in accordance with a plan promulgated by the Australian government.

Mineral Exploration and Production (25 percent of revenues). BHP mines minerals including iron ore, coal (both coking and energy), manganese ore, copper concentrate, gold, and, to a lesser extent, ferro alloys, zircon, lead, zinc, and nickel. Mining operations are located in Australia, Papua New Guinea, Indonesia, Mali, Brazil, Chile, Canada, and the United States. The Chilean operation involves a joint venture with RTZ Corporation and other companies to mine Escondida, one of the largest-known copper ore bodies in the world.

Oil and Gas Exploration, Production, and Refining (32 percent of revenues). BHP has petroleum exploration interests in such countries as Papua New Guinea, Indonesia, China, Myanmar, Madagascar, India, Oman, Tunisia, Algeria, Egypt, Congo, Denmark, and Canada. The company is a participant in the North West Shelf Project in Western Australia, and it has five exploration permits in the Timor Sea off the coast of Australia's Northern Territory. BHP has proven reserves of seven hundred million barrels of oil and more than five trillion cubic feet of natural gas. The company also has a refinery in Hawaii, acquired through the purchase of Pacific Resources, with a capacity of ninety-five thousand barrels a day.

TOP EXECUTIVES

- Arvi Parbo, chairman
- Brian T. Loton, deputy chairman
- John B. Prescott, managing director and chief executive
- G. E. Heeley, executive general manager, finance
- Ron McNeilly, executive general manager, BHP Steel
- Peter J. Willcox, executive general manager, BHP Petroleum
- Jerry Ellis, executive general manager, BHP Minerals

OUTSIDE DIRECTORS

- D. J. Asimus, director of Australian Eagle Insurance
- J.B. Gough, chairman of Pacific Dunlop Ltd.
- J. A. L. Hooke, chairman of Tubemakers of Australia Ltd.
- W. D. McPherson, director of Tubemakers of Australia Ltd.
- Eric Neal, chairman of Westpac Banking Corporation
- A. W. Ogilvy, chairman of PWB Anchor Ltd.
- J. B. Reid, chairman of James Hardie Industries Ltd.
- D. W. Rogers, chairman of Woodside Petroleum Ltd.

FINANCIAL DATA

Revenues (in millions of Australian dollars) (years ending May 31)

1991	15,608
1990	13,421
1989	10,485
1988	9,820
1987	8,762

Net Income (in millions of Australian dollars) (years ending May 31)

1991	1,465
1990	1,145
1989	1,008
1988	909
1987	725

GEOGRAPHICAL BREAKDOWN

Operating Revenues (in millions of Australian dollars)

Year*	Australia		North America		Elsewhere	
1991	11,621	(69%)	3,666	(22%)	1,650	(10%)
1990	9,600	(68%)	3,143	(22%)	1,315	(9%)

*Fiscal year ends May 31.

LABOR RELATIONS

From the very beginning BHP had a union presence. The Amalgamated Miner's Association (AMA) of Australasia began organizing at the company in 1886, but it took some time to sign up a majority of the company's employees. By 1889 the union was powerful enough to win a strike called in support of the demand for a closed shop. The following year the directors of BHP briefly shut down the mines in support of the management drive to crush a longshoremen's strike. This in turn prompted a three-week strike at BHP that ended with an agreement between the two sides to settle disputes through arbitration.

Two years later relations between labor and management at BHP and other mines in the area deteriorated after the employers decided to institute a piecework-type system in place of the exclusive employment of unionized hourly wage workers. The AMA took the miners out on strike, while the employers brought in outside police to protect their property and the strike-breakers, also recruited from outside. After four months the impoverished workers ended their walkout, and the AMA lost its recognition from the employers.

Labor did not stay beaten for long. The AMA and other unions rebuilt their power, and in 1909 a clash over wage cuts led to a management lockout and the arrest of union leaders. An arbitrator ruled in favor of the workers, which helped persuade the management of BHP to cut back the company's operations in Broken Hill. Labor militancy in the town continued during the following years—including a year-long walkout in 1919–20—inspired in part by the local activities of the Industrial Workers of the World.

After BHP became primarily a steel company, it found itself in a long-running contest with a group of militant unions in that industry. BHP originally created a U.S.-style company union and used a blacklist to avoid hiring union activists. During the labor shortages of World War II BHP could not be so selective in its hiring, and soon it was forced to recognize independent unions. The tension in relations with those unions has abated since 1982, when the Australian government instituted a restructuring plan for the steel industry that included measures to limit strikes. The plan also reduced employment in the company's steel operations by 40 percent.

ENVIRONMENTAL AND HEALTH RECORD

The lead BHP started mining in Broken Hill in the late 1880s was dangerous to the health of both the miners and nearby residents. The workers came in direct contact with ore dust, while townspeople were exposed through the emissions of the smelter furnaces. Accidents, often fatal, were a fact of life for the miners and their families.

Today the company says that its activities are in compliance with environmental regulations in the countries of operation. There have, however, been oil spill problems at a government-owned oil storage facility operated by BHP in American Samoa. In addition, a BHP subsidiary in Washington State has been named a responsible party in connection with groundwater contamination near some petroleum storage tanks. BHP's steel operations in Australia have received numerous summonses for excessive emissions.

BIBLIOGRAPHY

Blainey, Geoffrey. *The Rush That Never Ended: A History of Australian Mining.* 3d ed. Melbourne, Australia: Melbourne University Press, 1978.

Kennedy, Brian. *Silver, Sin, and Sixpenny Ale: A Social History of Broken Hill, 1883–1921.* Melbourne, Australia: Melbourne University Press, 1978.

CABLE & WIRELESS PLC

New Mercury House
26 Red Lion Square
London WC1R 4UQ
United Kingdom
(071) 315-4000

1991 revenues: $4.5 billion (year ending March 31)
1991 net income: $862 million
Publicly traded company
Employees: 39,426
Founded: 1872

OVERVIEW

Cable & Wireless (C&W), which bills itself as "the world telephone company," started out as a telegraph system linking Britain with its far-flung empire in the second half of the nineteenth century. The company reluctantly accepted the advent of wireless communications and merged with the Marconi interests in 1929.

C&W was taken over by the British government after World War II but was privatized again by the Thatcher government in the early 1980s. Since that time C&W has been an aggressive player in the world telecom business. At home it took over Mercury Communications, which was challenging the monopoly of British Telecommunications, and abroad it acquired the phone company of Hong Kong and expanded its hold on the telephone systems of the eastern Caribbean.

In recent years the company has touted what it calls its "global digital highway," a network of high-quality fiber-optic lines connecting the business capitals of North America, Europe, and Asia. It remains to be seen how well C&W can compete outside the former colonies of its home country.

HISTORY

The "cable" part of Cable & Wireless dates back to the early days of telegraphy. In the 1850s and 1860s a variety of companies in Britain were seeking to expand the telegraph, then a new-fangled invention, from a strictly land-locked mode of communication to one that could cross the seas. Laying cable on the ocean floor was a tricky process, and many ventures ended in failure.

A man named John Pender tried to rationalize this treacherous business. Having made a fortune speculating in the cotton market, Pender got involved in a series of telegraph companies. In 1872 he merged four of them to create the Eastern Telegraph Company, which by 1880 operated, along with several allied companies, more than thirty thousand miles of submarine cable with which they sent and received messages throughout most of the British Empire.

A few weeks before Pender died in 1896, a crucial event took place regarding what would be the "wireless" aspect of C&W. It was then that an Italian inventor named Guglielmo Marconi applied in Britain for the world's first patent for wireless telegraphy. The following year Marconi formed the Wireless Telegraph and Signal Company. There was considerable resistance to the new technology at first, both because of doubts about its efficiency and because of resistance to a system that would compete with the existing wire telegraph network.

Marconi overcame some of the technical problems and succeeded in sending the first wireless message across the Atlantic in 1901. But the telegraph interests, led by Eastern Telegraph, did everything possible to deter the competing mode of communication. The rivalry continued for two more decades. Telegraphy received a boost from the expansion of wire traffic during World War I—even though British and German forces took steps, whenever possible, to sabotage each other's communications facilities.

The Marconi company, meanwhile, kept pressing the British government to subsidize the creation of a network of wireless stations that would span the British Empire. By the mid-1920s the government was coming to appreciate the virtues of wireless communication, and even Eastern Telegraph began to hedge its bets by moving slowly into the wireless arena. When wireless systems connecting Britain with Australia and the Caribbean were developed by Marconi for the government, Eastern realized that it could no longer resist the inevitable. In 1928 the heads of Eastern and the Marconi company began to meet, and they decided that a "fusion" of the two firms was the best course of action. In 1929 all British-owned private and government cable and wireless operations were consolidated under the auspices of Imperial and International Communications Ltd.—the operating arm of a holding company named Cables and Wireless Ltd.

The new enterprise was created just in time to experience a sharp falling off of business as a result of the economic crisis spreading throughout the world. Imperial also had to contend with increasing competition from scores of wireless telegraphy services that were being set up in many different countries; even the spread of airmail service was siphoning off some business. At the same time, many countries in the British Empire—recently declared autonomous by the Balfour Declaration—wanted more control over their communications systems.

Imperial, which changed its name to Cable (without the "s") and Wireless in 1934, pressed the government to create a system that would ensure the company greater stability. This was finally done in 1938 with the passage of the Imperial Telegraphs Act, which set a flat rate for plain-language telegrams between all points in what had been the British Empire. It also provided C&W additional financial guarantees from the government, which was given the right to appoint a director to the company's board. C&W, by now operating in 146 locations around the globe, considered this plan a new charter.

As World War II began, C&W facilities became frequent targets for the German Luftwaffe; the company's London headquarters also were bombed during the blitz. Stations in such places as Athens, Hong Kong, and Singapore were taken over by Axis forces, but the rest of the system stayed in operation throughout the war.

After the surrender of the Germans and the Japanese, C&W faced a new challenge. Many of the Commonwealth countries were demanding a restructuring of the telecommunications system based on government ownership in each country. In Britain the new Labour government embraced the idea and moved to transfer C&W to state ownership, making it an arm of the post office.

C&W continued to operate its international network—in Britain, in the Crown Colonies, and in a number of other countries, such as Indonesia and the Philippines, in which it had concessions. It also operated five inland telephone systems and provided broadcasting services in Nairobi and Hong Kong.

The future of both cable and wireless international telegraphy was put into question by the development of submarine telephone cables. In 1956 the first transatlantic phone cable, TAT-1, was laid by the British Post Office, AT&T, and the Canadian Overseas Telecommunications Corporation. C&W was asked to help develop a lightweight coaxial cable and then became involved in a massive project called the Commonwealth Round-the-World Telephone System to link all of the Commonwealth nations.

The demand for submarine telephone cables gave new life to C&W, which had always performed better with cable as opposed to wireless communications. Yet technology continued to advance, and soon the focus was on a new form of wireless transmission: satellites. AT&T put the first communications satellite, Telstar, into orbit in 1962. This form of communication grew rapidly, aided by the 1964 formation of the International Telecommunications Satellite Consortium (INTELSAT), which launched "birds" for use by many countries. C&W joined the move into satellites, beginning with the construction of an earth station on Ascension Island to provide support communications for the U.S. Apollo space program.

C&W used yet another technology, called tropospheric scatter radio transmission, to provide expanded telephone, telegraph, and telex services in the Caribbean. The system was later supplemented by microwave links. This helped to solidify C&W's hold on the telecommunications business in the eastern Caribbean.

During the 1970s C&W expanded its satellite facilities and undertook such projects as the laying of a three-hundred–channel telephone cable from Hong Kong to Canton. The company also branched out into continental Europe to provide a variety of telecommunications services and equipment. C&W also moved into the United States, beginning with an investment in a telephone management company called TDX. In 1977 TDX was taken over by C&W and became a subsidiary with the name Cable & Wireless Communications Inc. A controlling interest also was acquired in Carterfone Communications, the company that had successfully challenged AT&T's equipment monopoly. (The holding was sold in 1987.)

After Margaret Thatcher took office in 1979, the privatization of C&W was a key goal of the Tory government. To oversee the return to private ownership, which took place in 1981, the government chose Eric Sharp. He sold off some operations but also acquired 79 percent (later reduced to 59 percent) of Hong Kong Telecommunications and all of an upstart company, Mercury Communications, that was challenging the monopoly of British Telecommunications over domestic telephone service.

Mercury began an ambitious program of building a fiber-optics network to serve corporate customers. Once privatized, British Telecom turned out to be a more formidable competitor, but Mercury displaced its rival from such deals as the 1991 alliance it entered with AT&T, Deutsche Bundespost Telekom, France Telecom, and the Netherlands' TTT to install two new transatlantic submarine cables.

That same year, Lord Young of Graffham, the former Conservative trade and industry minister who took over as chairman of C&W in 1990, announced that Mercury would not take on British Telecom in the U.K. residential telephone market. Instead the company would focus on corporate customers and niche monopoly situations abroad.

In August 1991 Lord Young forced out his managing director, Gordon Owen, in a dispute over this strategy. Owen was a strong proponent of C&W's so-called global digital highway: a system of fiber-optic lines providing multinational companies with high-quality voice, data, and video links. Lord Young, wary of competing with the likes of AT&T, put emphasis on local opportunities. Whichever of the two strategies C&W ends up pursuing, it will remain a major player in global telecommunications.

OPERATIONS

International Telephone Services (46 percent of 1991 revenues). C&W provides telecommunications services in fifty countries. In eighteen countries, mainly in the Caribbean, it owns the local phone company; it also owns 59 percent of Hong Kong Telecommunications Ltd. In more than thirty countries it is the provider of overseas communications services. C&W has constructed a network of broad-band fiber-optic lines linking the major business centers of Europe, North America, and the Pacific Rim. In the United States C&W acquired TRT/FTC in 1990, making it the fourth-largest long-distance carrier in the country. In 1991 the company launched its first local service in a European Community country by offering a specialized fax service in Italy. The company also formed a joint venture with Toyo Information Systems as part of a plan to become a significant player in the Japanese telecommunications market. C&W was part of another joint venture that was chosen by the Australian government in 1991 to provide telephone services in competition with the country's state-owned telecommunications company. In 1992 C&W entered yet another joint venture, to provide long-distance and international communications networks for Russia's main business centers.

Domestic Telephone Services (22 percent of revenues). The company's Mercury Communications Ltd. is British Telecom's main competitor for domestic service in the United Kingdom. Until 1991, when the British government decided to expand competition, Mercury was part of a duopoly arrangement with British Telecom. C&W has decided not to compete with British Telecom in the residential market, but it has been aggressive in building a fiber-optics network to attract corporate customers. Mercury also is planning to emphasize wireless personal communications.

Other Telecommunications Services (15 percent of revenues). Included here are leased circuits, telex services, and maritime telecommunications services.

Other Operations (16 percent of revenues). This segment includes the sale and rental of telecommunications equipment manufactured by others, the operations of C&W's ships for laying and maintaining undersea cables, and telecommunications consulting.

TOP EXECUTIVES

- Lord Young of Graffham, executive chairman
- James Ross, chief executive
- Rodney J. Olsen, director, finance
- Jonathan H. M. Solomon, director, corporate business development
- Tom Chellew, director, Caribbean and the Middle East
- Michael G. Gale, director, Asia-Pacific

OUTSIDE DIRECTORS

- Winfried F. W. Bischoff, chairman of J. Henry Schroder Wagg & Company
- Peter Carey, senior adviser to Morgan Grenfell
- Janet P. Morgan, former special adviser to the director general of the British Broadcasting Corporation (BBC)
- N. Brian Smith, former chairman of Metal Box PLC

Also on the board is Gordon Brunton, former chairman of Mercury.

FINANCIAL DATA

Revenues (in millions of pounds) (years ending March 31)

1991	2,593
1990	2,316
1989	1,534
1988	1,244
1987	1,201

Net Income (in millions of pounds) (years ending March 31)

1991	493
1990	433
1989	346
1988	293
1987	267

GEOGRAPHICAL BREAKDOWN

Revenues (in millions of pounds)

Year*	United Kingdom and Europe		Asia and Pacific		Elsewhere	
1991	843	(32%)	1,176	(45%)	603	(23%)
1990	586	(25%)	1,154	(49%)	604	(26%)
1989	291	(19%)	894	(58%)	367	(24%)

*Fiscal year ends March 31

Trading Profit (in millions of pounds)

Year*	United Kingdom and Europe		Asia and Pacific		Elsewhere	
1991	128	(21%)	371	(61%)	113	(18%)
1990	84	(14%)	378	(64%)	130	(22%)
1989	35	(9%)	283	(72%)	75	(19%)

*Fiscal year ends March 31

LABOR RELATIONS

The people who worked for C&W and its predecessors enjoyed a certain esprit de corps, especially those posted to foreign stations. The staff association they formed was far from antagonistic toward the company, and when the depression hit they supported management's moves to cut expenses by reducing the size of the work force (which initially were done through voluntary retirements). There was some dissent when the company asked for pay cuts and longer working hours from those who remained, but management cut off any rebellion by dissolving the staff association.

An attempt was made in 1942 to revive the organization, but it was blocked by C&W chairman Edward Wilshaw. Since then several unions have come to represent the company's employees. Unionized workers at Hong Kong Telecommunications have held demonstrations and short strikes to protest layoffs announced after C&W took over the company.

BIBLIOGRAPHY

Baglehole, K. C. *A Century of Service: A Brief History of Cable and Wireless Ltd*. London: Cable and Wireless, 1969.

Barty-King, Hugh. *Girdle Round the Earth: The Story of Cable and Wireless and Its Predecessors to Mark the Group's Jubilee, 1929–1979*. London: Heinemann, 1979.

CHEVRON CORPORATION

225 Bush Street
San Francisco, California 94104
(415) 894-7700

1991 revenues: $37.3 billion
1991 net income: $1.3 billion
Publicly traded company
Employees: 55,123
Founded: 1879

OVERVIEW

Known until 1984 as Standard Oil of California, Chevron Corporation has been one of the more conservative of the oil majors but periodically has made dramatic moves. The first of these came in the 1930s, when the company began exploration in Saudi Arabia—which had been shunned by some of the larger oil players—and ended up discovering the biggest petroleum reserve in the world.

In 1984 Chevron was brought in as a white knight to purchase Gulf Oil, which was being threatened with a hostile takeover by raider T. Boone Pickens, Jr. The $13.2-billion deal stands as the second-largest merger in corporate history. Most recently the company has fought the bureaucracy in the former Soviet Union republic of Kazakhstan to move ahead with a plan—the largest Western project in the country—to explore for oil near the Caspian Sea.

HISTORY

During the 1860s there were numerous attempts in California to repeat Edwin Drake's 1859 discovery of oil in Pennsylvania, which gave rise to the U.S. petroleum industry. Although widespread drilling failed to yield dramatic results, a hardy band of entrepreneurs kept the faith while fighting among one another over leases and deeds. Among them was San Francisco businessman Charles N. Felton, who in 1879 formed the Pacific Coast Oil Company (PCO) and soon brought in other oil players, such as Frederick B. Taylor and Demetrius G. Scofield.

PCO's drilling began to achieve some success, and within a few years it had built pipelines from producing areas, such as Moody Gulch in Santa Clara County, to a refinery it constructed in Alameda, across the bay from San Francisco. The refinery was the largest facility of its kind west of Cleveland. PCO also built the first steel tanker, used to carry crude from the town of Ventura, near the Pico Canyon fields north of Los Angeles, to the Alameda refinery.

During the 1880s PCO faced increased competition, most notably from the Standard Oil empire, which was shipping oil from the east via ships traveling around Cape Horn. Using its Iowa subsidiary, Standard moved to capture much of the market for kerosene, gasoline, naphtha, and other products. Then in the 1890s, as oil was discovered underneath Los Angeles, Standard entered the production end of the business in the West, both by buying existing operations and by creating new ones. In 1900 PCO decided to give up the battle and sell out to Standard. Six years later the Rockefeller empire consolidated its West Coast holdings as Standard Oil Company (California).

California Standard got itself into a long-running battle with the federal government over its right to drill on federal land—a dispute that ended in compromise. A more profound legal confrontation for the company and the rest of the Standard empire came in 1906, when the federal government brought an antitrust suit against the group. After five years of legal proceedings the Supreme Court ordered the breakup of the Rockefeller trust into thirty separate companies, including Standard Oil (California).

Once independent, California Standard stepped up its exploration activities, sending drilling parties to such countries as Argentina, Colombia, Ecuador, Mexico, and the Philippines. In 1926 the company merged with Pacific Oil Company, a subsidiary of the Southern Pacific Railway, and through the resulting reorganization took the parentheses out of its name and began calling itself Standard Oil of California, or Socal for short. The following year it supplied the fuel used by Charles Lindbergh in his historic transatlantic flight.

During the 1930s Socal focused its exploration efforts on the Middle East, first by obtaining a concession in Bahrain. The effort paid off, but the company already had its eye on a much larger territory: the nearby kingdom of Saudi Arabia. Socal's more powerful competitors, Standard Oil of New Jersey and Royal Dutch/Shell, had shown little interest in the Saudi territory, which was part of the region covered by the 1928 Red Line Agreement. That pact committed the leading producers to cooperate with one another on any projects within the confines of the old Ottoman Empire.

Socal was not part of the Red Line arrangement, so it was free to explore in Saudi Arabia on its own. In 1933 it was granted a concession by King Ibn Saud that turned out to contain the largest oil reserves in the world. The oil was so plentiful that Socal brought in Texaco to form a joint marketing company they dubbed Caltex. Even that was not sufficient, so in 1944 the two companies formed the Arabian American Oil Company, or Armaco, which soon took on Jersey Standard and Socony as partners.

After World War II the company grew along with the development of the West Coast, but it also expanded its refining and marketing operations to the Eastern Seaboard. In 1961 Socal merged with Standard Oil Company (Kentucky), the leading marketer in five southern states. The company continued its foreign exploration and production in such places as Indochina, Libya, Nigeria, and the North Sea, but it remained highly dependent on the output from Saudi Arabia. Control of the Saudi operations was taken over by the government of that country in 1980.

The California company was slow in joining the diversification trend among the oil majors. It finally made its move in 1979 with a takeover bid for the mining giant AMAX. When the board of AMAX rebuffed Socal, it backed off. The same thing happened two years later, when Socal came courting again with a higher bid.

Socal next assumed the industry spotlight in 1984, amid the challenges being posed by maverick oilman T. Boone Pickens, Jr., to the petroleum giants. When Pickens turned his sights on Gulf Oil, the Pittsburgh company turn to Socal as a white knight. Socal, which changed its name to Chevron during this period, ended up acquiring Gulf for $13.2 billion.

Gulf had its beginnings in the discovery of oil in Texas in the first years of the century. The Mellon family of Pittsburgh helped finance the pioneering J. M. Guffey Petroleum Company and built a refining operation at Port Arthur on the Gulf of Mexico. In 1907 the two operations were combined as Gulf Oil, which became a formidable competitor to the Standard Oil trust. Gulf later was among the U.S. companies to participate in the Iraq Petroleum Company and was a party to the Red Line Agreement. It won a concession in Kuwait in partnership with Anglo-Iranian. In the 1970s Gulf was rocked by revelations that it had made large amounts of illegal campaign contributions in the United States and payoffs to government officials abroad. The scandal resulted in the resignations of several top executives.

Chevron's purchase of Gulf was hailed for greatly expanding the company's production capacity and its marketing network, but it also created a huge debt load. To help relieve the burden, Chevron sold just under half of Gulf's Canadian operations to the Reichmann family of Toronto for $2.5 billion.

Chevron came under fire by the Right in the late 1980s for maintaining its investment in Angola (which it inherited from Gulf) and from the Left for its operations in South Africa. In 1988 Chevron purchased Tenneco's oil and gas reserves in the Gulf of Mexico. The following year Chevron found itself the subject of a possible takeover after Pennzoil used much of the $3 billion it won in its legal battle with Texaco to buy a block of Chevron stock. The California company rebuffed Pennzoil by getting a large portion of its stock into friendly hands via an employee stock-ownership plan.

OPERATIONS

Petroleum Products (91 percent of 1991 revenues). Chevron is an integrated petroleum company. It carries out exploration and production activities primarily in the United States, Canada, Angola, Australia, Indonesia, the United Kingdom portion of the North Sea, and the South China Sea. The company also has negotiated exploration rights in Kazakhstan. Its reserves at the end of 1991 were 2.7 billion barrels of crude oil, condensate, and natural gas liquids and 9.4 trillion cubic feet of natural gas. Production in 1991 totaled 958,000 barrels of crude oil and natural gas liquids per day.

The company is a partner with Texaco in the Caltex Group of companies, which explores for and produces oil in Indonesia and refines and markets in Asia, Africa, Australia, and New Zealand.

Chevron operates eleven refineries in the United States, one in Canada, and one in the United Kingdom. Its affiliates, including Caltex, operate an additional fourteen foreign facilities. The company supplies 2,600 service stations in the United States, 240 in Canada (British Columbia), 420 in the United Kingdom, and 190 in Central America.

Chemicals (8 percent of revenues). Chevron manufactures a wide range of petrochemicals, fertilizers, and other agricultural chemicals, including consumer products sold under the Ortho label. It operates thirty chemical manufacturing facilities in sixteen states and owns a majority interest in plants in Brazil, France, and Japan.

Minerals (1 percent of revenues). The company's Pittsburg & Midway Coal Mining Company produces mainly steam coal at mines in New Mexico, Alabama, Wyoming, Kentucky, and Colorado. Other active mineral properties include a 50-percent–owned platinum and palladium mine in Montana, a copper and silver deposit in Chile, and a zinc and lead discovery in Ireland. In 1990 Chevron decided to sell its geothermal energy, uranium, gilsonite, and gold assets.

TOP EXECUTIVES

- Kenneth T. Derr, chairman and chief executive
- J. Dennis Bonney, vice chairman
- James N. Sullivan, vice chairman
- William E. Crain, vice president, exploration and production
- Ray E. Galvin, vice president

OUTSIDE DIRECTORS

- Samuel H. Armacost, partner in the investment firm Weiss, Peck & Greer; former chief executive of BankAmerica Corporation
- Sam L. Ginn, chief executive of Pacific Telesis

- Charles M. Pigott, chief executive of PACCAR Inc.
- Condoleezza Rice, professor of political science at Stanford University
- George P. Shultz, former secretary of state; professor of International Economics at the Stanford Graduate School of Business
- S. Bruce Smart, Jr., former chief executive of the Continental Group
- George H. Weyerhaeuser, chief executive of Weyerhaeuser Company
- John A. Young, chief executive of Hewlett-Packard

FINANCIAL DATA

Revenues (in millions of dollars)

1991	37,286
1990	39,633
1989	30,312
1988	26,331
1987	27,029

Net Income (in millions of dollars)

1991	1,293
1990	2,157
1989	251
1988	1,768
1987	1,250

GEOGRAPHICAL BREAKDOWN

Revenues (in millions of dollars)

Year	United States		Canada		Elsewhere	
1991	31,249	(75%)	1,227	(3%)	9,121	(22%)
1990	33,299	(77%)	1,486	(3%)	8,336	(19%)
1989	26,224	(79%)	1,184	(4%)	5,743	(17%)

Operating Income (in millions of dollars)

Year	United States		Canada		Elsewhere	
1991	465	(17%)	155	(64%)	2,071	(77%)
1990	1,896	(41%)	289	(6%)	2,462	(53%)
1989	-20	(0%)	240	(13%)	1,583	(88%)

LABOR RELATIONS

Like its brethren in the Standard Oil empire, the California company shifted from ruthless labor policies early in the century to a policy of paternalism after World War I. It offered wages, benefits, and working conditions that were generally superior to those of other companies in the industry. In the late 1910s the Oil Field, Gas Well and Refinery Workers Union was formed, motivated largely by the need to improve conditions at other petroleum companies. Nonetheless, in 1919 the union began a drive to organize California Standard's workers—with limited success.

It was not until the 1930s that significant organizing activity resumed in the oil industry. The union, which in 1937 changed its name to the Oil Workers International Union (OWIU), made some gains, but not at the Standard Oil companies, where there was a stubborn attempt to maintain company unions instead of independent collective-bargaining organizations. Although explicit company unions were barred by the Wagner Act, such organization continued to represent workers at Socal, even after a wave of strikes in the 1940s. It was not until the late 1950s that the Oil, Chemical and Atomic Workers (the successor to the OWIU) was able to organize most of the company. After that, Socal generally followed industry patterns in dealing with the union.

ENVIRONMENTAL RECORD

Despite a company program devoted to the reduction of toxics, Chevron facilities in California have a poor record of compliance with environmental regulations. The company also has been charged with selling pesticides banned in the West in third world markets. It also has been involved in oil spills in California, Delaware, and, through its Caltex participation, the Philippines.

Some of Chevron's worst problems have been in Richmond, California, where it has a refinery, a pesticide plant, and other facilities. In 1989 a local group called Citizens for a Better Environment published a report acknowledging that Chevron had reduced waste-water discharges at the facility but said that toxic air emissions were still at unacceptably high levels. In 1988 the company paid $550,000 to settle a state lawsuit brought in connection with toxic emissions at the plant.

That same year, the company paid a record fine of $1.5 million to the EPA for waste-water discharges at its El Segundo refinery near Los Angeles. The federal agency said that there had been some 880 violations of pollution laws at the facility since 1981. The federal government also has brought suits against the company in connection with benzene emissions at its Philadelphia refinery and effluent discharges at an offshore oil production platform in southern California.

An explosion and fire in 1989 at the Richmond refinery severely burned three workers. An Occupational Safety and Health Administration (OSHA) inspection following the accident found that workers who were responsible for assisting firefighters had not been provided with even basic safety equipment. OSHA later fined the company $877,000 for more than one hundred willful and serious violations.

In 1992 Chevron agreed to pay $8 million in fines after pleading guilty to violations of federal clean-water laws. The violations took place at a company oil-drilling platform in the Santa Barbara Channel off the coast of California.

According to a study of EPA data by the Citizens Fund, Chevron was responsible for the forty-fourth-largest volume (8.5 million pounds) of toxic releases into the air among the country's manufacturing companies in 1989 (the latest figures available).

On the positive side, the company has helped protect a butterfly on the endangered species list that is found around its El Segundo refinery. Chevron's refinery in Pascagoula, Mississippi, won an award from the Izaak Walton League of America for its advanced alert system for effluent problems and for the preservation of a wetlands area. The company also has been developing "naturally occurring or organic" pesticides and fertilizers.

BIBLIOGRAPHY

Davidson, Ray. *Challenging the Giants: A History of the Oil, Chemical and Atomic Workers International Union.* Denver: OCAW, 1988.

Haynes, H. J. *Standard Oil Company of California: 100 Years Helping to Create the Future.* New York: Newcomen Society, 1980.

O'Connor, Harvey. *History of Oil Workers Intl. Union (CIO).* Denver: Oil Workers Intl. Union, 1950.

Sampson, Anthony. *The Seven Sisters: The Great Oil Companies and the World They Made.* New York: Viking Press, 1975.

Tarbell, Ida M. *The History of the Standard Oil Co.* 1904. Reprint. New York: Macmillan, 1925.

White, Gerald T. *Formative Years in the Far West: A History of Standard Oil Company of California and Predecessors Through 1919.* New York: Appleton-Century-Crofts, 1962.

CIBA-GEIGY LTD.

Klybeckstrasse 141
CH-4002 Basel
Switzerland
(041) 696 11 11

1991 revenues: $15.5 billion
1991 net income: $943.6 million
Publicly held company
Employees: 91,665
Founded: 1970 (Ciba was founded in 1859, Geigy in 1758)

OVERVIEW

Ciba-Geigy is the result of the 1970 marriage of two of Switzerland's leading chemical and pharmaceutical firms. With operations in more than fifty countries, the combined company is a major player in both of those fields throughout the world. The company is especially known for its synthetic hormones, its insecticides (it was a Geigy scientist who invented DDT), and its dyes.

It also is known, however, for its less-than-diligent concern for health and environmental considerations. In several instances the company has been involved in the testing of toxic substances on human subjects, and it has been slow to remove certain products from the market after it was determined that they were harmful to human health.

HISTORY

The Geigy part of the company dates back to 1758, when a young man named Johann Rudolf Geigy became a dealer in drugs, dyes, and spices. He later joined with an apothecary named Nicolaus Bernoulli to sell such products as quinine bark, opium, gum arabic, and dyewoods. After Johann Geigy's death the business was split up, but in 1840 the sons of the partners, Carl Geigy and Leonhard Bernoulli, reunited it.

Under the name of J. R. Geigy, the firm focused its efforts on dyes, and starting in 1859 it was one of the first producers of synthetic dyes. The company went on to become a leader in that field, managing (like Ciba) to avoid being crushed by the powerful German dye companies by specializing in expensive specialty dyes rather than the commodity products the Germans concentrated on. In some cases there was outright cooperation between the Swiss and German companies.

World War I upset this comfortable arrangement, but the Swiss recovered by selling to the British. After the war the Swiss companies declined to join the German IG Farben cartel, forming their own cartel, Basle IG, instead. Ciba, Geigy, and Sandoz used the arrangement to pool their expertise and their profits. Of the three, Geigy, still dependent on vegetable dyes, was in the weakest position. Sandoz, which grumbled about subsidizing Geigy, formed a joint venture with the company that led to the creation of the Cincinnati Chemicals Works, which served as a foothold for Basle IG in the United States.

In 1929 the participants in Basle IG finally decided to join with IG Farben. This enlarged cartel, which later took in the French dye makers and the British Imperial Chemical Industries, existed until the onset of World War II.

Geigy also became involved in textile finishes, mothproofing agents, and insecticides, including the creation in 1940 of the chemical compound dichloro-diphenyl-trichloroethane, which went on to fame (and later disgrace) as DDT. Dr. Paul Müller, a Geigy chemist, received the 1948 Nobel Prize in medicine for DDT, which by then was in wide use to control the spread of insect-borne diseases like typhus and malaria.

Geigy's pharmaceutical operations, established in 1938, developed such products as an ointment to fight scabies, a medication for Parkinson's disease, an antituberculosis drug, anticoagulants, and sedatives. Butazolidin, synthesized in 1946, became widely used for gout and rheumatory arthritis.

Ciba is actually an acronym for part of the German name (Gesellschaft für Chemische Industrie im Basle) of a dye works that French silk weaver Alexander Clavel established in Basel in 1859. Ciba became well known for the production of fuchsin, a reddish purple dye, and martius yellow.

Soon after the turn of the century Ciba moved into pharmaceuticals with the introduction of an antiseptic called Vioform. It later diversified into a wide range of chemicals and built or acquired facilities around the world. Ciba entered the U.S. market in 1921 with the purchase of Aniline Dyes & Chemicals and set up an American drug subsidiary, Ciba Pharmaceutical Products, in 1937.

Ciba biochemists did some of the early research on sex hormones; in 1934 one team succeeded in isolating progesterone in pure crystalline form. The company went on to become a leader in the production of synthetic hormones.

Experiments with the root of the rauwolfia shrub yielded a sedative called Serpasil.

In the late 1960s executives of Ciba and Geigy, facing intensified international competition, began to explore the possibility of combining their textile and pharmaceutical research. This led to the decision to merge the two companies entirely—what the firms dubbed "the Basel marriage."

The biggest obstacles to the deal were antitrust regulations in the United States. To satisfy those rules and overcome opposition to the merger, Ciba sold its U.S. dye works and Geigy divested its American drug operations.

The general sentiment is that the merger has worked, with the two companies complementing each other's strengths and weaknesses. The combined operation has grown substantially, both through expansion of existing businesses and through acquisitions. The latter has included U.S. purchases, such as the pigments business of Hercules, Airwick air fresheners, Funk Seeds, and the laser company Spectra-Physics (sold in 1990). Ciba-Geigy also formed a joint venture with Corning Glass to operate a medical diagnostics business.

OPERATIONS

Pharmaceuticals (34 percent of 1991 revenues). Among the mainstays of this segment are Estraderm, a synthetic hormone; Anafranil, an antidepressant; Voltaren, an anti-inflammatory; Nitroderm TTS, for the treatment of angina; Tegretol, an anticonvulsant; and Actigall, a gallstone medication. Medications recently introduced include Nicotinell TTS, which reduces the urge to smoke; Foradil, an antiasthmatic; Cibacen, which lowers blood pressure; and Trileptal, an antiepileptic. Ciba-Geigy also is engaged in joint research on AIDS with the U.S. company Tanox Biosystems.

Dyestuffs and Chemicals (13 percent of revenues). This segment includes a variety of textile dyes, textile chemicals, detergents, and thermal papers. A new $70-million U.S. dye facility in St. Gabriel, Louisiana, came on line in early 1992. The company also has a joint venture with Du Pont to develop fluorochemical products with such applications as children's clothing and the waterpoofing of tents.

Agricultural (23 percent of revenues). Ciba-Geigy is a major producer of pesticides, herbicides, fungicides, and seeds. Its agricultural segment also includes animal health products, such as Interceptor, a heartworm and hookworm medication for dogs.

Additives (9 percent of revenues). Included here are additives for plastics, synthetic fibers, coatings, photography, and other applications.

Plastics (9 percent of revenues). Among the main products here are printed circuit boards, sealants used in automobile production, and lightweight parts for aircraft interiors.

Pigments (4 percent of revenues). Ciba-Geigy is a leader in the production of high-performance pigments for applications including auto body finishings, plastics, ceramics, and glass. The company has introduced a line of lead-free enamel colors for use in decorating drinking glasses and glass food containers.

Mettler-Toledo (5 percent of revenues). This operation produces a variety of instruments for scientific and industrial purposes.

Ciba Vision (4 percent of revenues). This segment includes traditional and disposable contact lenses and cleaning solutions. In 1990 the company introduced a new line, Focus lenses, which can be worn for a period of one to three months.

TOP EXECUTIVES

- Alex Krauer, chairman and managing director
- Albert Bodmer, deputy chairman
- Heini Lippuner, chairman of the executive committee
- Jacques Pierre Barman, member of the executive committee
- François L'Eplattenier, member of the executive committee

OUTSIDE DIRECTORS

- Max M. Burger
- Kaspar V. Cassani, member of the advisory council of IBM
- Franz Galliker, chairman of Swiss Bank Corporation
- Rainer E. Gut, chairman of CS Holding
- Hans Bernard Herzog
- Jean-Marie Lehn, professor of chemistry at the College of France–Paris
- Fritz Leutwiler, former cochairman of ABB ASEA Brown Boveri
- Helmut Sihler, chief executive of Henkel KGaA
- Robert Staubli, former president of Swissair
- Hugo E. R. Uyterhoeven, professor at Harvard Business School
- Frank Vischer, professor of law at the University of Basel

The company does not disclose the affiliations of its outside directors. Those given above were obtained from other sources.

FINANCIAL DATA

Revenues (in millions of Swiss francs)

1991	21,077
1990	19,703
1989	20,608
1988	17,647
1987	15,764

Net income (in millions of Swiss francs)

1991	1,280
1990	1,033
1989	1,557
1988	1,325
1987	1,100

GEOGRAPHICAL BREAKDOWN

Revenues (in millions of Swiss francs)

Year	Europe		North America		Elsewhere	
1991	9,274	(44%)	6,745	(32%)	5,058	(24%)
1990	8,866	(45%)	6,108	(31%)	4,729	(24%)

LABOR RELATIONS

Ciba-Geigy, like the other major Swiss chemical companies, has sought to keep the loyalty of its employees through paternalistic practices. As a result its employees were slow to heed the calls of the labor movement. Around 1917, however, a significant number of chemical workers in Basel began to join the Swiss Confederation of Trade Unions. Although the unions staged a general strike in the industry in 1919, the unrest did not lead to union recognition.

During the early 1940s union sentiments were rekindled, led by the left-wing textile workers' union, the Schweizerische Textil- und Fabrikarbeiter-Verband (STFV). In 1943 Ciba-Geigy and the other leading chemical companies in Basel recognized the STFV, and two years later the first collective-bargaining agreement in the industry was signed. Relations have generally been harmonious since then.

Ciba-Geigy's U.S. subsidiaries have generally friendly relationships with the two unions—the Oil, Chemical and Atomic Workers and the International Chemical Workers—that represent their employees.

ENVIRONMENTAL RECORD

After several decades of being lauded for its role in pest control, Geigy's DDT began to be seen as a threat to humans because the toxic substance became lodged in the food chain. This was only one of the instances in which Ciba, Geigy, and the combined company have been at the center of public controversies.

One of the most notorious cases occurred in Egypt, where it was revealed that in 1976, six boys were paid to stand in a cotton field while it was sprayed with a Ciba-Geigy insecticide called Galecron. The point of the experiment was to see how much of the chemical would be absorbed into the boys' bodies. The highly toxic Galecron, a suspected carcinogen, was later blamed for health problems of cotton workers around the world, but the company waited for a long time before taking the insecticide off the market.

In 1978 a Japanese court concluded that clioquinol, a Ciba-Geigy drug used to treat diarrhea, was responsible for a degenerative neurological disease that had killed or injured thousands of persons. The company, which was criticized for excessive marketing of the medication, ended up paying out several hundred million dollars in compensation.

During the early 1980s Ciba-Geigy learned that its antiarthritic drugs Butazolidin and Tanderil had been responsible for several thousand deaths and serious injuries in different parts of the world. After an internal document with that information was leaked to the press in 1983, the company advised health officials of the problem and suggested that the drugs be used only for acute conditions.

In 1985 Ciba-Geigy's U.S. subsidiary was fined a record $1.4 million by the state of New Jersey for illegally dumping hazardous wastes at three landfills near its Toms River dye works. The company also agreed to pay $2.6 million to remove thousands of drums of toxic wastes. Ciba-Geigy ended up in protracted litigation with the state of New Jersey over the issue of financial responsibility for the clean-up of underground reservoirs that had been contaminated by the pollution. Finally, in 1992, the company agreed to pay at least $50 million for groundwater purification.

In 1986 an accident at a Ciba-Geigy facility in Basel led to the release of a large quantity of the herbicide atrazine into the Rhine River. The incident occurred only several days after a fire at a Sandoz plant resulted in the release of highly toxic mercury compounds into the same waterway. In 1991 Ciba-Geigy was fighting a proposal to ban atrazine throughout Europe.

Ciba-Geigy ran afoul of the U.S. FDA in 1988 when it launched a publicity blitz for its new arthritis medication, Voltaren. The FDA claimed that the company was in effect marketing a prescription drug directly to consumers.

The EPA fined Ciba-Geigy's U.S. subsidiary $245,000 in 1991 for failing to meet federal standards relating to the sludge that was being generated by the company's waste-water treatment system.

BIBLIOGRAPHY

Braithwaite, John. *Corporate Crime in the Pharmaceutical Industry.* Boston: Routledge & Kegan Paul, 1984.

Chetley, Andrew. *A Healthy Business? World Health and the Pharmaceutical Industry.* London: Zed Books, 1990.

Erni, Paul. *The Basel Marriage: History of the Ciba-Geigy Merger.* Zurich: Neue Zurcher Zeitung, 1979.

Hansson, Olle. *Inside Ciba-Geigy.* Penang, Malaysia: International Organization of Consumers Unions, 1989.

Mahoney, Tom. *The Merchants of Life: An Account of the American Pharmaceutical Industry.* New York: Harper & Brothers, 1959.

CITICORP

399 Park Avenue
New York, New York 10043
(212) 559-1000

1991 revenues: $14.8 billion
1991 net income: −$457 million (loss)
1991 assets: $217 billion
Publicly traded company
Employees: 86,000
Founded: 1812

OVERVIEW

Citicorp is the troubled giant of the U.S. financial services industry. The descendant of one of the oldest banks in the country, it emerged in the twentieth century as the leading money-center commercial bank and for decades has led the crusade to liberalize government regulation of banking activities. The desire to become a global financial services company has been a central theme in the company's history.

Citicorp took major steps toward that goal starting in the 1960s. It expanded aggressively throughout the world, pushed for the right to enter new lines of business at home, plunged into the credit card business, and took advantage of the savings and loan crisis to win the right to acquire branches across state lines.

By the beginning of the 1990s reality was catching up with Citicorp. Its relatively thin capital base no longer sufficed in a period when nonperforming loans in the third world and domestic real estate were weakening the entire banking system. By 1991 Citicorp had to turn to a Saudi prince and a group of institutional investors for infusions of capital, and the company was compelled to slow down its quest to be the world's banker.

HISTORY

Citicorp's roots go back to the early nineteenth century, amid the financial reorganization that took place after the demise of the First Bank of the United States in 1811. Various competing petitions—in part reflecting divisions within the Democratic-Republican party—had been filed with the New York State legislature for permission to establish replacements for the New York City branch of the national bank. Samuel Osgood, a senior statesman of the party who had served as the country's first postmaster general, united the warring factions behind a petition brought by a group of merchants. The plan worked, and City Bank received its charter in 1812.

As Harold van B. Cleveland and Thomas F. Huertas wrote in their history of the financial institution, "like nearly all banks of the day, [City Bank] was intended to be a kind of credit union for its merchant-owners." But soon after it was founded the United States went to war against Britain, and City Bank began doing considerable business with the federal government.

After the war the weakness of the economy and the undisciplined borrowing practices of the bank's directors depressed the company's stock price and allowed a merchant named Charles Lawton to gain control. City Bank then developed along with the growth of New York City as a commercial center.

The demise of the Second Bank of the United States and the advent of the era of "free banking" created new opportunities for City Bank and other state-chartered financial institutions. Yet, this boon was cut short by the financial panic of 1837. City Bank, which was particularly hard hit, was saved from failure only by the support of John Jacob Astor, the wealthiest man in the country, whose representative, Moses Taylor, became a director of the bank.

Taylor, who later became president of City Bank and acquired a controlling interest, turned the bank into a vehicle for promoting his varied commercial activities, especially by serving as a ready source of liquidity. The bank, which switched to a national charter after the end of the Civil War, continued to grow, but it was far from the largest bank in New York.

Now known as the National City Bank of New York, the bank entered a new stage of its history with the selection of James Stillman as president in 1891. Stillman developed a close relationship with the Rockefellers and their Standard Oil empire, and National City Bank became Standard Oil's main bank. Stillman also moved into investment banking, and he made a breakthrough in that crowded and very competitive field when he arranged for National City Bank to join forces with Kuhn, Loeb to reorganize the Union Pacific Railroad.

By the early years of the twentieth century National City Bank was very much a financial institution for big business. It had set up a foreign-exchange department and had built a network of correspondent banks overseas to help in providing foreign trade financing for its customers. By 1912 National City maintained accounts with 132 banks in all corners of the world. It also served as the leading depository of federal government funds. In fact, National City had become the largest bank in the United States. The bank's relatively high reserves made it a source of stability during the banking panic of 1907.

Under the leadership of Frank Vanderlip, who took over as president in 1909, National City got around federal laws restricting the activities of banks by forming an affiliate called National City Company in 1911. The company started buying up shares in other banks around the country and quickly became the largest bank holding company in the nation. This brought about an uproar over the creation of a "money trust," prompting Vanderlip to sell off the company's domestic bank holdings, but it retained its foreign bank interests. Vanderlip was also one of the leading proponents of a central bank and helped to shape the Federal Reserve Act that Congress passed in 1913.

The creation of the Federal Reserve System reduced the dominance of National City over the country's banking system, but it freed the bank to enter new lines of business. Vanderlip solicited corporate customers from around the country, moved further into investment banking, and began to build an international branch network, aided by the acquisition of a majority interest in the International Banking Corporation in 1915.

Around this time, Vanderlip began to be concerned for his own future, fearing that Stillman's son (also named James), who was rising in the bank, could displace him. Vanderlip thus set out to acquire a majority holding in the bank, which he proposed to do with the help of the elder Stillman, who lived in Paris and managed his affairs at a distance. Stillman turned him down, but Vanderlip proceeded with a plan to create, on his own, a company called American International Corporation to invest in local enterprises in foreign countries where National City was setting up branches.

This caused tension between Vanderlip and the elder Stillman, and in 1918, in the wake of the seizure of the bank's Petrograd branch by the Bolsheviks, Vanderlip came close to being ousted; the only thing that saved his position was that Stillman fell ill and died. In 1919 Vanderlip decided to resign, and James A. Stillman was elected president. Yet the younger Stillman did not remain in that position for long. Heavy losses caused by the collapse of the Cuban sugar market prompted him to resign in 1921.

Stillman's successor, Charles Mitchell, advanced the goal of making National City an all-purpose financial intermediary by moving into retail banking. This was made possible by a series of changes in federal law, culminating in the McFadden Act of 1927, which allowed national banks to open new branches in their hometown. National City moved quickly to take advantage of the new rules, and by the end of 1929 it had thirty-seven branches in New York City. The bank's position in the trust business was strengthened by its 1929 merger with Farmers' Loan and Trust Company.

The stock market collapse and the ensuing depression halted the expansion of National City's financial supermarket. The bank had to write off tens of millions of dollars in loans, and its securities business all but evaporated. National City was weak, but other banks were weaker. One of these was the Bank of America, which had been acquired in 1928 by A. P. Giannini's Transamerica Corporation. In 1931 National City purchased Bank of America's thirty-two branches in New York, ending up with the largest retail network in the city.

Mitchell won praise for the Bank of America takeover, but he was soon at the receiving end of a great deal of criticism over National City's banking practices. Congressional hearings were held, during which Mitchell was grilled by senators who sought to paint National City's wheeling and dealing in the 1920s as a primary cause of the crash. Mitchell vigorously defended his actions, but the political pressure was too great; in 1933 he resigned from the bank.

Bank reforms passed during the Roosevelt administration forced National City to liquidate its securities operation (National City Company), but federal deposit insurance and other protective measures restored public confidence in the whole banking system. Mitchell's successor, James Perkins, used the new period of stability to build the bank's international network.

Yet the major expansion of the foreign as well as domestic operations of the bank did not come until after the end of World War II. National City took full advantage of the new position of the United States as the preeminent capitalist power in the world and the dollar as the dominant currency. During the 1950s it participated in the credit boom and built up its asset base by merging (in 1955) with a smaller New York rival called First National Bank. The combined institution took the name First National City Bank (FNCB).

When a shortage of deposits emerged in the late 1950s, FNCB moved into the growing Eurodollar market and introduced such innovative financial instruments as the negotiable certificate of deposit. It also greatly expanded what was already the largest foreign branch system of any U.S. bank. The Overseas Division was at the time led by Walter Wriston, who would later rise to the top of the bank's executive hierarchy. Between 1960 and 1967 the bank opened eighty-five new foreign branches, located everywhere from Paraguay to Singapore. Wriston was determined to make the bank indispensable to U.S. companies that were themselves branching out across the globe.

FNCB was just as active developing domestic business. It expanded its New York City branch network, led the commercial banks into the residential mortgage business, and cautiously moved into the new field of credit cards. Wriston, who rose to the presidency in 1967, took advantage of a loophole in federal law to create a one-bank holding company that could enter new businesses and not be subject to the same body of regulations as a bank.

Once a number of other banks began to take this step as well, Congress moved to restrict the loophole, but in the meantime, Wriston managed to enter such fields as equipment leasing, data-processing services, mortgage banking, travel services, and financial counseling. This was part of his grand plan to transform FNCB into a global financial services company. Wriston emerged as a leading advocate of greater freedom for banks.

During the 1970s he was also a proponent of another controversial cause. In the wake of the sharp rises in oil prices, banks like FNCB found themselves awash with deposits from oil-producing countries. Wriston led the way in recycling these petrodollars by aggressively lending to third world countries.

Between the end of 1970 and the end of 1974, private bank lending to those countries quintupled, going from about $6 billion to $29 billion. When concerns began to be raised about the ability of these nations to repay their debts, Wriston argued that there was nothing to worry about, since countries, unlike corporations and individuals, could not go bankrupt. Maybe so, but Wriston's bank later felt the consequences of the spread of problem loans in the third world.

At home Citicorp—the new name adopted by FNCB's holding company in 1974—weathered the financial instability brought on by failures of such companies as Penn Central and Franklin National Bank. Citibank was doing so well compared with the rest of the industry that, according to *Fortune,* some officials at the Federal Reserve referred to the bank as "Fat City."

During the early 1980s Citicorp was able to pursue its expansionary goals when regulators began to permit out-of-state commercial banks to take over ailing savings and loan associations. In 1982 Citicorp, the first bank to exploit this new policy, entered the lucrative California market by taking over Fidelity Savings of San Francisco.

Wriston's position as the leading crusader for financial deregulation was assumed—though with a somewhat more subdued manner—by John Reed, who took over Citicorp upon Wriston's retirement in 1984. The Federal Reserve rebuffed Citicorp's attempt to enter the insurance business, but Reed pushed the legal limits on commercial bank involvement in investment banking, and he got into the financial information business by taking over Quotron Systems. Citicorp, which purchased Diners Club and Carte Blanche and was one of the most aggressive issuers of Visa and MasterCard credit cards, became the leader of the "plastic" industry.

The consumer thrust was not limited to the United States. In the quest to become the world's first global consumer bank, Citicorp bought banks in such countries as Spain and France. The results were mixed, but by the end of the 1980s the company had amassed eight million customers in forty countries. "We want to be like Benetton—location indifferent," a Citicorp executive once told a reporter.

At the beginning of the 1990s one thing that Citicorp could not be indifferent to was the deterioration of the bank's financial condition. Although Reed had bitten the bullet on the third world debt problem in 1987 by adding $3 billion to the bank's loan-loss reserves, by 1990 Citicorp was facing a rising level of nonperforming assets both at home and abroad. The debt-laden empires of high-profile customers like Rupert Murdoch and Donald Trump were beginning to teeter. Citicorp earnings shriveled. The money market, worried about the bank's stability, forced Citicorp to pay high interest rates on its short-term borrowing. Reed responded to the pressure by cutting the company's dividend, eliminating thousands of jobs, and slashing expenses.

Reed also began scouring the world for several billion dollars in capital. He found one taker in Saudi prince Al-Waleed bin Talal, who invested $590 million in Citicorp in 1991 through the purchase of special convertible preferred stock. The deal potentially gave the prince a 9.9-percent interest in the company, but he did not join the board of directors. A few weeks later Citicorp sold another $600 million in preferred stock to a group of several dozen institutional investors.

These infusions of capital provided some measure of stability, but Citicorp's once-lofty position at the top of the U.S. banking industry continued to weaken. In 1991 mergers between New York's Chemical Bank and Manufacturers Hanover Trust and between Bank of America and Security Pacific in California were creating more formidable rivals. On the international stage Japanese and European banks continued to zoom past Citicorp in size; by 1990 it was no longer among the world's top-twenty bank holding companies. A further embarrassment came in August 1991, when a leading member of Congress described Citicorp as "technically insolvent." Two months later, while reporting more heavy losses, Citicorp suspended the dividend on its common stock. John Reed continues to look toward the future, but for now that future looks dangerously uncertain.

OPERATIONS

Global Consumer Business (61 percent of 1991 revenues). Citicorp provides retail banking and other financial services to individuals in some forty countries. The company sold its Italian retail banking operation in 1991. In the United States, where twenty-four million of the company's thirty-five million customer-households are located, Citicorp has more than five hundred bank branches in eight states and the District of Columbia. Many of these are at former thrift institutions Citicorp was allowed to take over and, since 1990, has been permitted to unite under the Citibank name.

Citicorp is also the leading issuer of credit cards in the United States, serving some eighteen million households with thirty-one million Visa, MasterCard, Choice, and Diners Club cards. The company has an additional 3.4 million credit card accounts in eighteen foreign countries. Since the beginning of 1990 the credit card business has become increasingly competitive. In addition to its traditional rivals—other banks and American Express—Citicorp has to contend with challenges from nonfinancial companies like AT&T and Sears, Roebuck.

Also included in this segment is the Citibank Private Banking operation, which Citicorp calls the largest non-Swiss private bank in the world. With offices in seventy-two cities in thirty-two countries, it had $70 billion in assets under management at the end of 1991.

Global Finance Business (37 percent of revenues). This segment consists of Citicorp's financial services to corporations and public sector entities. The company divides these activities into two sectors. JENA (Japan, Europe, North America, and Australasia) covers operations in what Citicorp calls the capital market economies. Among the services provided are traditional lending, asset-based lending, foreign exchange, underwriting, venture capital, and investment advice. The other sector, called International Banking and Finance, focuses on the third world. Citicorp does business in sixty-two third world countries. Citicorp also has a special unit called World Corporation Group, which provides international services to more than two hundred multinational corporations, including Sony, Siemens, and Fiat.

Information Business (2 percent of revenues). Citicorp has long been a proponent of the idea that information is at the heart of financial activities. Walter Wriston liked to say that "information about money has become as important as money itself." In line with this, Citicorp purchased Quotron Systems, a financial data service best known for providing stock price quotes, in 1986. Quotron is engaged in a heated competitive battle with Reuters, the Telerate subsidiary of Dow Jones, and Automatic Data Processing, Inc. Both Quotron and Telerate have been attempting to chip away at Reuters' strong lead in the market for systems that both provide foreign-exchange data and execute trades. To bolster its position Quotron announced in mid-1991 that it was working with a dozen big banks to develop a new currency-trading system.

TOP EXECUTIVES

- John S. Reed, chairman
- Richard S. Braddock, president
- Paul J. Collins, vice chairman
- H. Onno Ruding, vice chairman
- Pei-yuan Chia, senior executive vice president

OUTSIDE DIRECTORS

- D. Wayne Calloway, chairman and chief executive of PepsiCo
- Colby H. Chandler, former chief executive of Eastman Kodak
- Kenneth T. Derr, chief executive of Chevron
- John M. Deutch, professor at MIT
- Lawrence E. Fouraker, former dean of Harvard Business School
- H. J. Haynes, senior counselor to Bechtel Group
- C. Peter McColough, former chief executive of Xerox
- Rozanne L. Ridgway, president of the Atlantic Council of the United States
- Donald V. Seibert, former chief executive of J.C. Penney
- Frank A. Shrontz, chief executive of Boeing
- Mario H. Simonsen, vice chairman of the Brazil Institute of Economics
- Roger B. Smith, former chief executive of General Motors
- Franklin A. Thomas, president of the Ford Foundation
- Edgar S. Woolard, Jr., chief executive of Du Pont

FINANCIAL DATA

Revenues (in millions of dollars)

1991	14,750
1990	14,587
1989	13,752
1988	13,018
1987	12,353
1986	10,290

Net Income (in millions of dollars)

1991	−457 (loss)
1990	458
1989	498
1988	1,858
1987	−1,182 (loss)
1986	1,028

Assets (in millions of dollars)

1991	216,922
1990	216,986
1989	230,643
1988	211,657
1987	207,749
1986	200,099

GEOGRAPHICAL BREAKDOWN

Revenues (in millions of dollars)

Year	North America		Europe, Middle East, and Africa		Elsewhere	
1991	8,736	(59%)	2,993	(20%)	3,021	(20%)
1990	9,055	(62%)	3,137	(22%)	2,395	(16%)
1989	8,747	(64%)	2,495	(18%)	2,510	(18%)
1988	7,946	(61%)	2,409	(19%)	2,663	(20%)

Net Income (in millions of dollars)

Year	North America		Europe, Middle East, and Africa		Elsewhere	
1991	−885	(0%)	132	(31%)	296*	(69%)
1990	230	(50%)	212	(46%)	16†	(3%)
1989	965	(100%)	−117	(0%)	−350‡	(0%)
1988	933	(50%)	101	(5%)	824	(44%)

*In 1991 Citicorp had a net loss of $21 million in the Asia-Pacific region and a net profit of $317 million in the region encompassing the Caribbean, Central America, and South America.

†In 1990 Citicorp had a net profit of $125 million in the Asia-Pacific region and a net loss of $109 million in the region encompassing the Caribbean, Central America, and South America.

‡In 1989 Citicorp had a net profit of $362 million in the Asia-Pacific region and a net loss of $712 million in the region encompassing the Caribbean, Central America, and South America.

LABOR RELATIONS

In 1969 the *Wall Street Journal* wrote that in the U.S. banking industry, "unions have been as welcome as Bonnie and Clyde." The situation has not changed, especially at Citicorp. In 1981, when Ralph Nader formed Citiwatch to monitor the bank's activities, one of the areas emphasized was employee rights. The United Food and Commercial Workers International Union, which represents employees at a handful of financial institutions, briefly showed some interest in organizing at Citicorp, but the effort did not get off the ground.

BIBLIOGRAPHY

Citibank, Nader and the Facts. New York: First National City Bank, 1974.

Cleveland, Harold van B., and Thomas F. Huertas. *Citibank, 1812–1970*. Cambridge, Mass.: Harvard University Press, 1985.

Davis, Steven I. *Excellence in Banking: A Profile of Superior Management Based on Insight Into Citibank, Deutsche Bank, Morgan & 13 Other Selected Banks*. New York: St. Martin's Press, 1986.

Hutchison, Robert A. *Off the Books: Citibank and the World's Biggest Money Game*. New York: William Morrow, 1986.

Multinational Banks and Their Social and Labour Practices. Geneva: International Labour Office, 1991.

Leinsdorf, David, and Donald Etra. *Citibank: Ralph Nader's Study Group Report on First National City Bank*. New York: Grossman Publishers, 1973.

Miller, Richard B. *The Late Great Citicorp*. New York: McGraw-Hill, 1992.

COCA-COLA COMPANY

One Coca-Cola Plaza NW
Atlanta, Georgia 30313
(404) 676-2121

1991 revenues: $11.6 billion
1991 net income: $1.6 billion
Publicly traded company
Employees: 28,900
Founded: 1892

OVERVIEW

Coca-Cola is the best-known product name in the world, and the Coca-Cola Company is the undisputed leader of the international soft drink industry. The company gets more than three-quarters of its operating income from outside the United States, by cultivating markets large and small. A pioneer in national advertising, the company spends vast sums to etch its flowing-script logo onto the consciousness of people around the globe.

For the past two decades Coca-Cola has faced intensified competition from its perennial rival, PepsiCo. Despite the ill-fated introduction of a new Coke in 1985, the company has remained solidly on top. Less successful has been Coca-Cola's attempt at diversification. Forays into wines and movies were both abandoned.

HISTORY

The origins of the U.S. soft drink business can be found in the tonics and elixirs that drug stores used to prepare for customers as a cure for a variety of ailments. In the 1880s John Styth Pemberton, an Atlanta druggist, invented one of the more popular solutions by mixing together coca leaves and the kola nut. Asa Griggs Candler bought the right to market Pemberton's invention in syrup form and sold it to soda fountains around the country and abroad.

Not particularly interested in direct sales to customers, Candler sold that right to a group of Tennessee businessmen in 1899 for only a dollar. Candler turned out to be more excited about politics than commerce, and in 1919 ownership of the Coca-Cola Company was acquired by Ernest Woodruff, a Georgia financier. Four years later Woodruff's son Robert took over the company. He remained chief executive until 1955. Even after his retirement he continued to exert his influence over the company until his death in 1985.

Coca-Cola was one of the earliest companies to grasp the importance of image advertising. The company went to great lengths to project its product, overseas as well as at home, as a leading symbol of American life. Not surprisingly, the company rejected the nickname "Coke" for many years because of the association with cocaine. In fact, there had been a trace of the drug in the original Coca-Cola formula, but this was eliminated in 1903.

After the bombing of Pearl Harbor in 1941, Woodruff announced his intention to make Coca-Cola available to everyone in the military. General Eisenhower, who was keen on Coca-Cola himself, made it possible for the company to open dozens of bottling plants around the world, often right behind the frontline troops.

The refreshing beverage in the small green bottle dominated the soft drink market through the 1940s. Yet its determined competitor, Pepsi-Cola, was slowly gaining ground. Started by North Carolina pharmacist Cabel Bradham in the 1890s, the Pepsi-Cola Company took off around the turn of the century but later ran into serious financial difficulties. It was forced to declare bankruptcy and was sold to new owners on several occasions. Then, during the depression, the company rebounded by selling Pepsi in twelve-ounce bottles for the same nickle price as Coke's six-ounce serving.

Nonetheless, Pepsi remained an also-ran in the soft drink market until the 1950s, when it got a boost from a new advertising campaign that presented it as the preferred drink of the young "sociables." The company got a major lucky break in 1959, when Khrushchev was photographed drinking Pepsi at an exposition of American products in Moscow. Pepsi was now a true contender on a global scale. Indeed, the company was so impressed with the significance of the Khrushchev photo that it promoted Donald Kendall, the executive who arranged to have Khrushchev drink the product, to the position of chief executive of the company.

A decade later Kendall's friendship with Richard Nixon helped Pepsi become the first soft drink company to enter the Soviet market. Today the company supplies Pepsi in exchange for the right to sell Stolichnaya vodka in the United States. For its part, Coca-Cola demonstrated its ability to draw support from the White House in the late 1970s, when it used its contacts with Jimmy Carter (through Atlanta lawyer Charles Kirbo) to get the first shot at the Chinese market.

Coke and Pepsi escalated their rivalry in the 1960s with a series of advertising campaigns that attempted to tap into the changes in the American psyche. In the place of traditional slogans, such as Coke's "The pause that refreshes" and "Pepsi-Cola hits the spot," the companies spent millions of dollars promoting such notions as "You've got a lot to live, and Pepsi's got a lot to give" and "Coke is the real thing."

More advertising and more products greatly expanded the competition. Up until that time, Coke and Pepsi had only one soft drink brand apiece. A much smaller competitor, Royal Crown, then paved the way to a giant new market by bringing out the first major sugar-free soft drink. In 1963 Coca-Cola brought out Tab. Pepsi-Cola soon followed with its own low-calorie brands. The two also launched assaults on the market of the much-smaller Seven-Up Company by pushing their own lemon-lime drinks: Coke's Sprite and Pepsi's Mountain Dew.

Efforts to market additional products really took off in the early 1980s. At that time Seven-Up presented a significant challenge to its competitors by linking its product to the issue of caffeine. Coca-Cola and Pepsi took little notice of the caffeine controversy when it started. However, Pepsi soon got scared and decided to introduce its own Pepsi Free. Concerned about losing ground to its major competitor, the Coca-Cola Company, which had just introduced the sugar-free Diet Coke, decided to bring out caffeine-free versions of Tab, Coke, and Diet Coke. These six cola varieties were joined by Cherry Coke in 1985.

Addressing the caffeine challenge did not give Coke much relief. Around this time, Pepsi launched the most serious challenge ever in the intense competition for supermarket shelf space. Much of this battle centered around the issue of taste rather than on the traditional price basis, with Pepsi introducing a series of taste-test ads that proved successful. By the 1980s this "Pepsi Challenge" was paying off—Coke's market share slipped. The corporate share for the Coca-Cola Company was bolstered by the tremendous success of Diet Coke, but when regular Coke's share plunged several percentage points from 1983 to 1984, the company began to run scared.

In response to all of this, Coca-Cola management took the most radical step in the history of the company. In April 1985 chief executive Roberto Goizueta announced that Coca-Cola was in the process of making the first major change in Coke's formula in the ninety-nine-year life of the product. The new product was to have a smoother, sweeter taste; some people claimed that the taste of the new Coke was similar to that of Pepsi.

The company worked hard in an attempt to make the new Coke a success. Though it spent nearly four years evaluating the change in its formula, soon after the new Coke was introduced it became clear that consumer loyalty to the old taste was much stronger than the company had realized. The majority of consumers not only expressed their dislike of the new Coke, they began organizing to get the company to return to the traditional taste. Organizations like Old Coke Drinkers of America were formed and began talking of filing lawsuits against the switch.

It took very little time—only three months, to be exact—for Goizueta to admit defeat. He announced that alongside the new Coke, the company would return to selling the old Coke, which would be called Coca-Cola Classic. The company now had eight permutations of its syrup—a marketing nightmare. The new Coke was to remain the company's flagship brand, yet results began to come in showing that the Classic version was selling better in many parts of the country. As McDonald's and other leading restaurant chains abandoned the new Coke, the company struggled to keep the brand alive.

If Coca-Cola and Pepsi had been allowed to move ahead with acquisitions announced in 1986, their market strength would have grown tremendously. PepsiCo was planning to purchase Seven-Up for $380 million and Coca-Cola was ready to pay $470 million for Dr Pepper. However, the federal government stopped these mergers for antitrust reasons. Instead the domestic business of Seven-Up was purchased in a leveraged buyout by Hicks & Haas of Dallas, which had already purchased Dr Pepper in the same manner.

Coca-Cola succeeded in closing the deal in which it acquired two of its largest independent bottlers for a combined price of more than $2 billion. In addition it turned around and sold 51 percent of the bottling operation to the public through a stock offering. PepsiCo made a similar move, spending $1.7 billion to acquire the bottling business of General Cinema in 1989.

Competition in the cola sector reached new levels of intensity in the 1980s. Coca-Cola and PepsiCo engaged in frequent price-cutting and ran hard-hitting ad campaigns in the quest for market share. The results were mixed: Coca-Cola's share of the overall soft drink market expanded, yet PepsiCo's share of retail store sales continued to climb. In 1990 PepsiCo suffered a blow when Burger King announced that it was switching to Coke products in its fast-food restaurants. At the same time, Coca-Cola was seeking to salvage the new Coke it introduced in 1985 by relaunching it as Coke II.

Coca-Cola also has sought to strengthen its competitive position by diversifying. This strategy began in 1960 with the purchase of Minute Maid, the pioneer in the frozen orange juice field. The company bought Taylor Wines in 1977 and developed a sizable presence in the wine business, but the operation did not meet the company's profitability standards and was sold to Seagram in 1983.

In 1982 the company went Hollywood by purchasing Columbia Pictures for $750 million. Goizueta believed that Coca-Cola's marketing skills would apply to films, and he followed the Columbia purchase by entering into a joint venture to form Tri-Star Pictures, the first new major studio in decades. Yet the vagaries of the movie business did not suit the cola makers of Atlanta, so in 1989 Coca-Cola sold Columbia and Tri-Star (which had merged) to Sony Corporation for $3.4 billion.

In a departure from its usual solo efforts abroad, Coca-Cola in 1991 formed a joint venture with Nestlé to market ready-to-drink coffee, tea, and chocolate beverages on a worldwide basis (except for Japan). That year the company also took the unusual step of hiring Creative Artists Agency, the powerful

Hollywood talent agency led by Michael Ovitz, to help develop a global marketing and media strategy.

OPERATIONS

Soft Drinks (86 percent of 1991 revenues). The company's primary business consists of manufacturing soft drink concentrates and syrups that are sold to bottling and canning operations and to soda fountain wholesalers and retailers. Syrups are composed of flavoring concentrate (the company's secret formula), water, and sweetener, usually high-fructose corn syrup in the United States and sucrose abroad. In diet products aspartame (made by the NutraSweet subsidiary of Monsanto) is used instead.

Some 68 percent of syrup and concentrate sales are made to bottlers, and the rest are made to fountain retailers and wholesalers. About 38 percent of U.S. syrup and concentrate sales are to Coca-Cola Enterprises, the company's 49-percent-owned bottling subsidiary. In 1991 the company announced plans to acquire another major bottler, Johnston Coca-Cola Bottling Group, for about $450 million in stock. Coca-Cola also owns major equity interests in leading bottlers in Canada, Britain (a joint venture with Cadbury Schweppes), France, Australia, Taiwan, the Philippines, Holland, and other countries.

Coca-Cola has moved fast to take advantage of changes in Eastern Europe. Almost immediately after the Berlin Wall went down, the first cases of Coke were heading into eastern Germany. The company later announced plans for investing an astounding $450 million over two years for a bottling operation and marketing to capture the soft drink business in the former German Democratic Republic. In 1991 the company also announced that it would open a regional office in Kiev. Coca-Cola sees opportunities in Western Europe as well, and efforts are being made to increase soft drink consumption in countries like France.

In 1991 the company began negotiations to reintroduce its soft drinks in India. Coca-Cola had abandoned that country in 1977 following a government edict that foreign companies reduce their equity holdings in subsidiaries to 40 percent. The company also moved to challenge PepsiCo in the Middle East after the Arab League lifted its boycott of Coke products in 1991.

Foods (14 percent of revenues). After having abandoned a number of other businesses, the company's only significant non–soft drink operation consists of juices and a few other beverages. Coca-Cola Foods is the largest marketer of packaged citrus products, mainly through the sale of Minute Maid ready-to-serve and frozen concentrate juices. Other products include Five Alive beverages, Bright and Early breakfast drinks, Bacardi tropical fruit mixers (produced under license from Bacardi & Company), and the Hi-C line of fruit drinks. In 1992 Coca-Cola introduced Powerade, a product meant to challenge the dominant position of Gatorade (owned by Quaker Oats) in the sports drink market.

TOP EXECUTIVES

- Roberto C. Goizueta, chairman and chief executive officer
- Donald R. Keough, president and chief operating officer
- Jack L. Stahl, chief financial officer

OUTSIDE DIRECTORS

- Herbert A. Allen, chief executive of the Allen & Company investment banking firm
- Ronald W. Allen, chief executive of Delta Air Lines
- Warren E. Buffett, chief executive of Berkshire Hathaway
- Charles W. Duncan, Jr., private investor
- Susan B. King, senior vice president for public affairs at Corning, Inc.
- James T. Laney, president of Emory University
- Donald F. McHenry, professor of diplomacy at Georgetown University
- Paul F. Oreffice, chairman of Dow Chemical Company
- James D. Robinson III, chief executive of American Express
- William B. Turner, chairman of the executive committee of W. C. Bradley Company
- Peter V. Ueberroth, managing director of the Contrarian Group
- James B. Williams, chief executive of SunTrust Banks

FINANCIAL DATA

Revenues (in millions of dollars)

1991	11,572
1990	10,236
1989	8,622
1988	8,065
1987	7,658
1986	6,977

Net Income (in millions of dollars)

1991	1,618
1990	1,382
1989	1,724
1988	1,045
1987	916
1986	934

GEOGRAPHICAL BREAKDOWN

Revenues (in millions of dollars)

Year	United States		European Community		Elsewhere	
1991	4,125	(36%)	3,338	(29%)	4,063	(35%)
1990	3,931	(38%)	2,805	(27%)	3,501	(34%)
1989	3,679	(43%)	1,855	(22%)	3,089	(36%)

Operating Income (in millions of dollars)

Year	United States		European Community		Elsewhere	
1991	560	(21%)	767	(28%)	1,386	(51%)
1990	440	(23%)	667	(34%)	845	(43%)
1989	468	(27%)	541	(31%)	717	(42%)

LABOR RELATIONS

As an aggressive multinational Coca-Cola must contend with labor disputes in many countries. The most turbulent incident in the company's history took place in Central America in the 1970s, when workers at the Coca-Cola bottling operation in Guatemala organized a union. This fledgling organization experienced attacks, resulting in the deaths of more than a dozen people, from right-wing death squads. The International Union of Food and Allied Workers Associations mobilized an international campaign that prompted the Coca-Cola Company to put pressure on its Guatemala franchisee to see to it that the union's rights were recognized. Despite signs of improvement, the company decided to close the plant in early 1984. After the destitute workers occupied the facility for more than a year, however, Coca-Cola arranged to keep the operation going under the control of a new set of investors.

Coca-Cola also has had continuing problems concerning the wages and conditions for migrant workers employed at its Minute Maid subsidiary. Although a contract was signed with the United Farm Workers in 1972, Minute Maid and its parent company have frequently been charged with being insensitive to the miserable working conditions of these workers.

After announcing in 1986 that it was leaving South Africa, the company moved to sell its bottling plant to black entrepreneurs and move its syrup plant to neighboring Swaziland. But the move angered the divestment movement, which felt that the company would continue to profit from sales of its beverages in the apartheid society. There was unrest among Coca-Cola's South African workers, too, and they went on strike in 1988—while the change of ownership was still in progress—to protest the subcontracting of union work.

Most of the unionized employees of Coca-Cola and its bottlers in the United States are represented by the Teamsters.

ENVIRONMENTAL RECORD

Coca-Cola has come under attack by environmentalists for several reasons. The company's Minute Maid subsidiary was part of a consortium that purchased 685,000 acres of tropical forest in Belize in 1986 for use as an orange grove. After numerous protests about the destruction of this rain forest, the company agreed to preserve most of its share of the land in its pristine state. But there have been subsequent reports of the company buying rain forest land in Brazil. There also has been controversy in Brazil over plans for building a Coke bottling plant in an area that had been designated an environmental sanctuary.

Coca-Cola also has been criticized for its lobbying against bottle bills in state legislatures in the United States. And there has been controversy over the company's testing of what it claims to be a recyclable plastic can, which environmentalists say would be expensive to recycle. The company is faulted for using multilayered material (which is difficult to recycle) for Minute Maid products sold in aseptic packaging.

BIBLIOGRAPHY

Clairmonte, Frederick, and John Cavanagh. *Merchants of Drink: Transnational Control of World Beverages*. Penang, Malaysia: Third World Network, 1988.

Dietz, Lawrence. *Soda Pop: The History, Advertising, Art and Memorabilia of Soft Drinks in America*. New York: Simon & Schuster, 1973.

Enrico, Roger, and Jesse Kornbluth. *The Other Guy Blinked: How Pepsi Won the Cola Wars*. New York: Bantam Books, 1986.

Frundt, Henry J. *Refreshing Pauses: Coca-Cola and Human Rights in Guatemala*. New York: Praeger, 1987.

Kahn, E. J., Jr. *The Big Drink: The Story of Coca-Cola*. New York: Random House, 1960.

Louis, J. C., and Harvey Z. Yazijian. *The Cola Wars*. New York: Everest House, 1980.

Oliver, Thomas. *The Real Coke, the Real Story*. New York: Random House, 1986.

Reyes, Miguel A. *Soft Drink, Hard Labor: Coca-Cola Workers in Guatemala*. New York: Monthly Review Press, 1987.

Watters, Pat. *Coca-Cola: An Illustrated History*. Garden City, N.Y.: Doubleday, 1978.

COLGATE-PALMOLIVE COMPANY

300 Park Avenue
New York, New York 10022
(212) 310-2000

1991 revenues: $6.1 billion
1991 net income: $124.9 million
Publicly traded company
Employees: 24,900
Founded: 1806

OVERVIEW

Colgate-Palmolive has long operated in the shadow of its much larger competitors—Procter & Gamble and Unilever—in the mundane business of soap, toothpaste, and other personal and household products. Yet Colgate remains an important player because of its aggressive global reach. It operates in more than 160 countries and is not afraid to venture into risky areas. A plant in Saudi Arabia was opened in 1990—in the midst of the Persian Gulf crisis. Two-thirds of the company's revenues and operating profit come from outside the United States.

For a long time the company had a reputation for stodginess, but it worked up enough adrenaline to discourage a takeover attempt by Sir James Goldsmith. Colgate also has recovered from an ill-fated diversification strategy by selling off many of its acquisitions and reviving its core products.

HISTORY

In 1795 Robert Colgate arrived in America to take title to a farm, but when the title turned out to be defective he went into partnership with Ralph Mather in the manufacture of candles and soap. The venture was short-lived, yet in

1802 Colgate's son William went into the same line of work, first in Baltimore and then in New York.

Beginning with its founding in 1806, William Colgate & Company set as its goal convincing housewives that its manufactured soaps were superior to the homemade variety that was most widely used at the time. The enterprise grew steadily over the following decades and introduced other products, most notably Colgate toothpaste (originally sold in jars) in 1877.

Meanwhile, the B. J. Johnson Soap Company was making soap, candles, and cheese in Milwaukee, Wisconsin. Founder Caleb Johnson conceived the idea of making a soap from vegetable oils—palm and olive, to be exact. After obtaining French machinery for making hard-milled soap, the company introduced Palmolive soap, which by the early years of the twentieth century was becoming a leader in its field. The produce was so successful, thanks to aggressive promotional campaigns, that the Johnson firm changed its name to the Palmolive Company in 1917.

A decade later Palmolive merged with the Peet Brothers Company, a soap maker based in Kansas City, and in 1928 it joined forces with the Colgate firm. Planned mergers with Kraft-Phenix cheese and Hershey chocolate were derailed by the stock market crash.

Colgate-Palmolive-Peet defied the economic crisis and continued expanding, especially abroad. Soap manufacturers in Britain, France, and Germany were acquired, and subsidiaries were set up in Sweden, Italy, Poland, and Switzerland.

Even more aggressive foreign expansion occurred after World War II. Major plants in Manchester, Hamburg, Compiègne (outside Paris), and Anzio (south of Rome)—along with smaller plants in seven other countries—supplied all of Europe with Colgate toothpaste and Palmolive soap as well as powdered detergents, liquid cleaners, and shaving cream. Factories were later constructed in Malaysia and Thailand for the Asian market. Today the company operates 232 facilities (of which 88 are owned) in more than 40 countries.

In the 1970s, facing slower growth in its prime markets, the company began making major acquisitions in order to diversify. In 1972 the purchase was the Kendall Company of Boston, a producer of hospital products, bandages, sporting goods, and tape coatings for oil and gas pipelines. The following year the company bought Helena Rubinstein, one of the leading cosmetics houses. This was followed by a series of smaller sporting goods manufacturers and some food operations.

The diversification strategy was not a success, and the man who promoted it, chief executive David Foster, was ousted. The company entered the 1980s somewhat adrift and susceptible to a takeover. Colgate-Palmolive remained independent (even after Sir James Goldsmith bought 4 percent of its shares), but the company sold off a number of its acquisitions. Among these were the Bike Athletic and Etonic athletic shoe businesses; Riviana Foods, the maker of Carolina Rice; Hebrew National hot dogs; and the Kendall Company.

Under the leadership of Reuben Mark the company also has given facelifts to its core products, but it still finds it hard to keep up with the competition, especially when it comes to introducing new products. In 1992 Colgate-Palmolive returned to the acquisitions approach by spending $670 million in stock and cash to purchase Mennen Company, maker of Speed Stick deodorant, Skin Bracer aftershave, and Baby Magic lotion.

OPERATIONS

Oral Care (22 percent of 1991 sales). Colgate-Palmolive is the world leader in toothpaste, thanks in part to its success in getting gel toothpaste and pump dispensers to market before Procter & Gamble, but it trails in the United States. Its flagship brand, Colgate, is marketed in more than 160 countries. The company also has been pushing into the former Soviet Union and Eastern Europe, and in 1990 Colgate was the first toothpaste to receive the seal of approval from the Soviet Ministry of Health.

One product in this segment has been the subject of controversy. In 1985 Colgate acquired 50 percent of a Hong Kong company that marketed a toothpaste in Asia sold under the name Darkie and distributed in a package with a picture of Al Jolson in blackface and top hat. In the mid-1980s several religious organizations in the United States charged that the package promoted an offensive racial stereotype and asked Colgate-Palmolive to do something about it. The company resisted, but after three years of pressure it agreed to change the name to Darlie and to change the logo to a portrait of a man of undefined race.

Other products in this segment include oral rinse, toothbrushes, dental floss, and more sophisticated items, such as the Periogard Periodontal Tissue Monitor, used for professional diagnosis of gum disease. To strengthen its presence in the professional field, the company acquired the OraPharm Company of Australia and the dental therapeutics business of Scherer Laboratories in the United States in 1990.

Body Care (18 percent of sales). The company has been enjoying good growth in this segment of its operations, which is led by its Palmolive family of products (soap, shampoo, liquid bath foam, shower gel, and so on). The Palmolive line was relaunched beginning in 1989, with product improvements and new packaging aimed at projecting the image of gentle, natural care. Yet in the U.S. shampoo market, for instance, Colgate has been trounced by Procter & Gamble, which in 1985 introduced the innovative Pert Plus, a combination shampoo and conditioner.

Other products include the antibacterial soap Protex, the Care line of baby skin-care products, and the upscale Cleopatra lines of soaps and lotions. The company has been targeting growth for this sector in such countries as India, Pakistan, and the former Soviet Union.

Household Surface Care (20 percent of sales). The company has good positions in household cleaners, dishwashing products, and bleach. The Ajax brand, a world leader in cleaning products, is sold in more than one hundred countries. The company has introduced a no-rinse formula for Ajax all-purpose cleaner in Europe and will extend the rollout to other parts of the world.

Dishwashing liquids are sold under the Palmolive name and other brands, such as Axion. Bleach, which is used mainly as a fabric cleaner in the United States, is employed as a household cleaner in many other countries. The company has a joint venture with Clorox to market bleach in Asian and Pacific markets. In 1990 Colgate-Palmolive acquired Javex, the leading Canadian bleach company, and Unisol, a bleach and household-cleaning company in Portugal.

Fabric Care (23 percent of sales). Sold under such names as Fab, Axion, Cold Power, and Dynamo, the products of this segment are powdered detergents, liquid detergents, and fabric softeners. In this segment the company has had an especially hard time catching up to Procter & Gamble and Unilever. Fab One-Shot, a premeasured packet of detergent and softener introduced with great fanfare by the company in 1987, was a flop.

The company has been a major proponent of superconcentrates, extremely dense powdered detergents that require smaller quantities per load and are sold in smaller containers, supposedly making them more desirable in environmental terms. The superconcentrates, which have sold well for nearly a decade in Europe and Japan, were put on the market in the United States at the start of the 1990s.

Pet Dietary Care (11 percent of sales). This highly profitable segment consists of Hill's Prescription Diet products, which are dispensed exclusively through veterinarians for ailing cats and dogs, and Science Diet products, formulated for healthy animals. Both are sold in several dozen countries. Colgate acquired this business through the 1976 purchase of Riviana Foods—the rest of which was sold off later.

TOP EXECUTIVES

- Reuben Mark, chairman and chief executive officer
- William S. Shanahan, chief operating officer
- Roderick L. Turner, senior executive vice president
- Robert M. Agate, chief financial officer
- William G. Cooling, chief of operations
- Lois D. Juliper, chief technological officer
- Silas M. Ford, executive vice president

OUTSIDE DIRECTORS

- Vernon R. Alden, former chairman of the Boston Company
- Jill K. Conway, visiting scholar at MIT
- Ronald E. Ferguson, chief executive of General Re Corporation
- Ellen M. Hancock, vice president of IBM
- David W. Johnson, chief executive of Campbell Soup
- John P. Kendall, officer of Faneuil Hall Associates, a private investment company
- Delano E. Lewis, chief executive of Chesapeake & Potomac Telephone Company
- Howard B. Wentz, chairman of ESSTAR Inc.

FINANCIAL DATA

Revenues (in millions of dollars)

1991	6,060
1990	5,691
1989	5,039
1988	4,734
1987	4,366

Net Income (in millions of dollars)

1991	125*
1990	321
1989	280
1988	153
1987	1†

*Includes a net provision for restructured operations of $243 million.
†Includes a net provision for restructured operations of $144.8 million.

GEOGRAPHICAL BREAKDOWN

Revenues (in millions of dollars)

Year	United States and Canada		Europe		Elsewhere	
1991	2,196	(36%)	1,969	(32%)	1,896	(31%)
1990	2,059	(36%)	1,923	(34%)	1,710	(30%)
1989	1,937	(38%)	1,557	(31%)	1,545	(31%)

Operating profit (in millions of dollars)

Year	United States and Canada		Europe		Elsewhere	
1991	99	(33%)	26	(9%)	179	(59%)
1990	217	(39%)	153	(28%)	184	(33%)
1989	187	(39%)	119	(25%)	172	(36%)

LABOR RELATIONS

Colgate has reasonably good relations with the two major unions—the Oil, Chemical and Atomic Workers and the International Chemical Workers Union—representing the one-third of the company's U.S. employees who are organized, even though the restructuring of the 1980s brought about the loss of thousands of jobs. During the restructuring the company negotiated plant-closing provisions with the unions and provided outplacement counseling and job retraining. Plans for the elimination of two thousand more jobs were announced in September 1991.

ENVIRONMENTAL RECORD

Like many other large companies, in recent years Colgate has gotten religion about the environment. The company now publicizes its efforts to reduce the amount of packaging for its products and to use recycled paperboard for boxes. Also, the switch to superconcentrated detergents, which provide more washing capacity per volume of powder, is promoted as an environment-friendly initiative.

BIBLIOGRAPHY

Foster, David R. *The Story of Colgate-Palmolive: 169 Years of Progress.* New York: Newcomen Society in North America, 1975.

CS HOLDING

Talacker 42
CH-8021 Zurich
Switzerland
(01) 212 16 16

1991 revenues: $407.5 million (year ending March 31)
1991 net income: $198 million
Publicly traded company
Employees: 44,153
Founded: 1989 (Credit Suisse was founded in 1856)

OVERVIEW

CS Holding is an umbrella organization for Credit Suisse, one of Switzerland's largest commercial banks, and CS First Boston, one of the world's leading investment banks. The group also includes Electrowatt Ltd., a utility holding company, and Fides Holding, which engages in money management and management consulting.

Credit Suisse has been striving to become a major global financial services company, and despite some difficulties in its American investment banking operations, the Swiss company has made significant progress in that direction. Credit Suisse has a large network of international offices engaged in both commercial and investment banking. CS First Boston, the group's problem child, is nonetheless the world's most global investment bank, with powerful affiliates in New York, London, Tokyo, and other financial centers and a top position in Euromarket financing.

The group's aspirations were plainly expressed by chairman Rainer Gut to a reporter in 1991: "We should have the capability to manage and conceive any financial deal anywhere in the world."

HISTORY

Credit Suisse was founded in Zurich in 1856 by Alfred Escher, a politician from an eminent Swiss family. The bank, whose shares were sold to the public, was soon playing an important role in financing new industrial enterprises, railroads, and insurance companies. Among the institutions it helped establish was Basler Bankverein, forerunner of Swiss Bank Corporation, now the country's second-largest commercial bank.

In 1867 Credit Suisse suffered the only loss in its history, in connection with the financing of cotton imports from the United States. During the 1890s the bank, by then the largest in Switzerland, was instrumental in the development of hydroelectric power in that country, including the founding of Electrowatt Ltd.'s predecessor.

In the beginning of the twentieth century Credit Suisse moved from venture capital investing to greater emphasis on deposit and credit operations, foreign exchange, underwriting, and stock brokerage. Its clients in this period included Nestlé, Fischer Iron and Steel, and the forerunner of Alusuisse—all of which are represented on the bank's board of directors today. After five decades of conducting all of its business from Zurich, Credit Suisse opened a branch in Basel in 1905 and later expanded to Geneva, Lucerne, Lugano, and other cities.

World War I virtually brought the bank's foreign operations to a halt, but Swiss neutrality allowed domestic business to continue without serious interruption. After the armistice Credit Suisse put greater emphasis on cultivating foreign customers, especially German companies. The bank was active in bond issues used to finance reconstruction in countries like France.

Credit Suisse managed to keep afloat during the depression of the 1930s, despite a sharp rise in default rates among lenders and a sharp decline in deposits. This was done by selling off assets and by dipping into undisclosed reserves that had been accumulated. With the onset of war at the end of that decade, the bank looked to the United States for business. In 1939 a U.S.-oriented investment fund (Intercontinental Trust) was established, and the Swiss American Corporation was formed to facilitate this securities business. The bank opened its first foreign branch in New York City in 1940.

During World War II Credit Suisse again benefited from Switzerland's neutral status, and the bank entered the postwar period financially sound. It once again became heavily involved in financing hydroelectric power and providing reconstruction loans to countries that had been devastated by the war. Credit Suisse put more emphasis on its retail banking operations by promoting savings accounts and, later, credit cards among the population. At the same time, the bank expanded its export financing business along with leasing and factoring.

During the 1960s Credit Suisse became one of the leading players in the Euromarket by forming an alliance with the U.S. investment bank White Weld. It also moved heavily into precious metal trading, especially after the gold market was liberalized, and became a manufacturer of ingots and coins through the purchase of the metal refiner Valcambi. The bank created an extensive international network of offices, in both the developed and the third world.

In the late 1970s Credit Suisse faced a scandal when managers of its branch in Chiasso, Switzerland, were found to have diverted more than $1 billion of the bank's money into off-the-books investments for their personal benefit. The bank recovered the assets and prosecuted the managers. During this period the bank acquired Crédit Foncier Suisse and Alliance Credit Corporation, leaders, respectively, in the mortgage and consumer credit fields.

After White Weld merged with Merrill Lynch in 1978, Credit Suisse found a new Euromarket partner in another U.S. investment bank, First Boston. Created in the 1930s out of the investment banking subsidiaries of the First National Bank of Boston and the Chase National Bank (which had to be spun off to comply with the Glass-Steagall Act), the firm built a strong position in utility and railroad underwriting. It also prospered from the acquisition of Mellon Securities in 1946.

The firm then entered a period of tribulation. It was a defendant in the antitrust suit brought by the Truman administration against seventeen investment banks. Although the case was ultimately dismissed, it kept First Boston and the other firms in a legal morass for six years. In the mid-1950s the firm arranged financing for the construction of an oil refinery in Puerto Rico. The project turned out to be a disaster, and a First Boston executive had to step in to restructure the operation.

During the 1960s First Boston's position slipped as it maintained a conservative posture in a go-go environment. In the early 1970s, however, the company embarked on a new effort in the international arena. It challenged Salomon Brothers in the bond underwriting business, winning important issues from the World Bank and the Japanese Development Bank.

After Financière Credit Suisse–First Boston was formed in 1978 (40-percent owned by First Boston, which in turn was 40-percent owned by CSFB), the joint venture gained a dominant position in the Eurobond market and moved aggressively into new financial instruments, such as mortgage-backed securities and municipal bond index futures. The company also used its success in Eurobonds to expand into international equity underwriting.

Before long, CSFB was facing increasing competition from the likes of Goldman Sachs, Salomon Brothers, and even its own parent companies—with whom relations were strained. Yet in 1986 the parents and the child worked together on a $4-billion bond floated by General Motors Acceptance Corporation. First Boston was the lead manager, Credit Suisse provided a letter of credit, and CSFB placed the bonds in Europe.

Back home, First Boston embraced the takeover mania that started in the late 1970s, and its merger specialists, Bruce Wasserstein and Joseph Perella, became the hottest practitioners in the field. This led to fat profits in the mid-1980s, but the firm was seriously weakened by the aftereffects of the 1987 stock market crash. Another blow came early the following year, when Wasserstein and Perella, in disagreement with the strategy of top management, left to form their own mergers and acquisitions boutique.

First Boston sought to gain greater stability in 1988 by merging with its European affiliate, creating a new, privately held company called CS First Boston (44.5-percent controlled by CS Holding). In 1989 Metropolitan Life Insurance purchased a 10-percent stake in that new company. John Hennessy, who took over as chief executive of CS First Boston in 1989, had to contend with the collapse of the junk bond market and the financial collapse of one of First Boston's biggest clients, Canadian retail magnate Robert Campeau—which left the firm holding the bag on more than $1 billion in bridge loans. Hennessy streamlined operations and shuffled management but remained committed to expanding the firm's global reach.

Credit Suisse chairman Rainer Gut also holds fast to the goal of creating a worldwide financial services company. In 1990 he built up the commercial banking leg of that structure by acquiring Bank Leu, Switzerland's fifth-largest bank, in the first hostile takeover in that country's banking industry. The aim is to make Bank Leu the core of a private banking business for wealthy clients. It will join existing CS Holding private-banking entities, such as Clariden Bank, which is strong in North America and South America, and Bank Hofmann, which has many clients in northern Europe. Gut also has moved into a new area of financial services by creating an insurance company from scratch. At the same time, Credit Suisse, along with its competitors, has been forced by the Swiss government to abandon long-standing fee-fixing practices.

In late 1990 CS Holding stepped in to deal with the problems at CS First Boston by injecting $300 million of new capital and increasing its stake to 60 percent. The move allayed many of the fears about First Boston's problem loans and allowed the firm to make its way back to the top tier of the securities business. One of its first deals under the new ownership structure was to bring out a $40-million stock issue by Samsung, the first international equity offering by a South Korean company.

OPERATIONS

Credit Suisse (84 percent of group income in 1991). Credit Suisse is a full-service bank with 390 offices over 5 continents. It provides commercial, private, and investment banking services to a wide range of clients. Its subsidiaries primarily engaged in commercial banking are located in Switzerland, Germany, France, Italy, Luxembourg, and Canada. Investment banking subsidiaries are located in Switzerland, Germany, England, Japan, and the United States. Credit Suisse also has a group of specialized financial companies in such areas as leasing and real estate.

CS First Boston (0 percent of group income—had a loss in 1991). CS First Boston is 64-percent owned by CS Holding and is in turn a holding company for three investment banks: First Boston Corporation, based in the United

States; Financière Credit Suisse–First Boston, which has subsidiaries in twelve countries; and CS First Boston Pacific, with subsidiaries in five countries. These firms provide financial advisory services in areas like mergers and acquisitions and engage in capital-raising activities. CS First Boston employs its own capital resources to trade and underwrite securities and to engage in merchant banking.

Fides Holding (1 percent of group income). Fides Holding, which does money management and management consulting, has twenty-one branches in Switzerland and two foreign subsidiaries. The operation also includes Switzerland's largest independent software producer, which works mainly with banks, insurance companies, and hospitals.

Electrowatt Ltd. (11 percent of group income). Electrowatt Ltd., which is 42-percent owned by CS Holding, is the holding company for a group of Swiss and foreign companies engaged in energy, manufacturing, and engineering services. Its energy division consists of electric utilities heavily involved in hydroelectric power. The industry division produces electronics components, while the engineering services division provides construction services in Europe and North America.

CS Life. An insurance operation that was incorporated in 1989, CS Life is still in an early stage of development.

TOP EXECUTIVES

- Rainer E. Gut, chairman and president
- Hugo von der Crone, vice chairman
- Robert A. Jeker, president of Credit Suisse
- John M. Hennessy, president of CS First Boston
- Adolf Gugler, president of Electrowatt
- Peter Küpfer, member of the executive board
- Ruedi Stalder, member of the executive board
- Max C. Roesle, senior executive
- Peter W. Bachmann, senior executive

OUTSIDE DIRECTORS

- Albert Bodmer, vice chairman of Ciba-Geigy
- Henry C. M. Bodmer, chairman of Abegg Holding Company
- Ulrich Bremi, managing director of Bauer Holding
- Kaspar V. Cassani, member of the advisory council of IBM
- Walter Diehl, chairman of Swiss Reinsurance Company
- Artur Frauenfelder, executive vice president of Sulzer Brothers Ltd.
- Robert L. Genillard, vice chairman of Thyssen-Bornemisza Group
- Fritz Gerber, chief executive of Roche Holding

- Jean-Claude Gisling, managing director of Publicitas Holding
- Hermann J. M. Haerri, deputy chairman of the executive committee of Alusuisse-Lonza Holding
- Ernest Matthey, member of the board of André & Cie
- Helmut O. Maucher, chief executive of Nestlé
- Marc Moret, chief executive of Sandoz
- H. Berthold Saemann, member of the board of George Fischer Ltd.
- Thomas Schmidheiny, chairman of Holderbank Financière Glaris Ltd.

FINANCIAL DATA

Since CS Holding has existed in its current form only since 1989, the following figures refer to Credit Suisse alone.

Assets (in millions of Swiss francs) (years ending March 31)

1991	128,822
1990	125,767
1989	117,667
1988	113,383
1987	107,240

Income (in millions of Swiss francs) (years ending March 31)

1991	4,068
1990	3,217
1989	3,492
1988	3,039
1987	2,905

Net profit (in millions of Swiss francs) (years ending March 31)

1991	650
1990	471
1989	716
1988	592
1987	550

GEOGRAPHICAL BREAKDOWN

The following table shows Credit Suisse Group's assets.

Assets (in millions of Swiss francs)

Year*	Switzerland		Other Industrial Countries		Elsewhere	
1991	72,284	(46%)	74,396	(48%)	8,929	(6%)
1990	70,904	(47%)	69,152	(46%)	9,620	(6%)

*Fiscal year ends March 31

LABOR RELATIONS

Credit Suisse has long prided itself on taking good care of its employees. The bank set up a sports center for its workers in 1925 and there were no layoffs during the depression, although wages were cut during that difficult period. In 1975 the bank established an employee stock-purchase plan and set up a mechanism for allowing workers a greater say in decisions regarding working conditions.

BIBLIOGRAPHY

125th Anniversary of Credit Suisse: An Historical Survey. Zurich: Credit Suisse, 1981.
Multinational Banks and Their Social and Labour Practices. Geneva: International Labour Office, 1991.

DAEWOO GROUP

Major affiliate:

Daewoo Corporation
541, 5-GA Namdaemunno
Chung-Gu, Seoul 100-414
South Korea
(2) 759-2114

1991 revenues: Daewoo Group, $21.1 billion; Daewoo
    Corporation, $8.4 billion
1991 net income: Daewoo Group, $121.8 million; Daewoo
    Corporation, $39.6 million
Publicly traded company
Employees: Daewoo Group, 92,000; Daewoo Corporation, 9,000
Founded: 1967

OVERVIEW

Daewoo is one of the most diversified and ubiquitous of the *chaebol* conglomerates that dominate the South Korean economy. As a 1991 article in the *Financial Times* put it: "Visitors to Seoul can drive from the airport in a car made by Daewoo Motors, on a road built by Daewoo Corporation to a hotel owned by Daewoo Group. In their hotel room, furnished with fabric from Daewoo Corp., they will probably use a telephone made by Daewoo Telecom and watch a Daewoo Electronics television."

Daewoo has been dominated for twenty-five years by founder Woo-Choong Kim, who is said to work hundred-hour weeks year-round to be sure the company is operating at peak efficiency. Kim developed a reputation for turning around struggling companies while pursuing an international strategy of expanding through partnerships with Western companies.

A combination of worker militancy and poor competitive position in many of its operations served to throw the conglomerate into a slump in the late 1980s. In an attempt to regain the breathtaking growth that once characterized the country's economy, Daewoo, like the other *chaebol*, is now being pressured by the South Korean government to focus its operations on a handful of businesses.

HISTORY

The Daewoo Group emerged out of the drive by the South Korean government in the 1960s to turn the country into a leading exporter by encouraging the growth of giant manufacturing and trading conglomerates. It was in this context that thirty-year-old Woo-Choong Kim, a graduate of the elite Yonsei University, joined with Dae-Do To in 1967 to form a small company called Daewoo, a combination of their given names that also meant "great universe."

Kim, who soon bought out his partner, concentrated initially on clothing and textile production, selling to the likes of Sears, Roebuck and J.C. Penney in the United States. As third world competitors like Malaysia and the Philippines began moving into these labor-intensive fields, Daewoo, at the urging of the government, got involved in such businesses as electronics, shipbuilding, petrochemicals, and construction. Kim developed a structure in which Daewoo Corporation served as the main trading and construction entity while also acting as the parent for a variety of industrial and service companies. These firms are linked to Daewoo Corporation through a complicated system of cross-holdings.

Daewoo's tentacles spread throughout the Korean economy, and before long it seemed to have a hand in making just about everything. One of the most highly visible operations, especially in international terms, was automobiles. In 1979 the company was asked by the government to take over an ailing automaker that was half owned by General Motors (GM). This resulted in the formation of Daewoo Motor Company, which as a joint venture with GM began producing the Pontiac LeMans—initially for the U.S. market, where it was well received, and then for the Taiwanese and Canadian markets.

The arrangement with GM was only one of numerous joint ventures that Daewoo has formed with U.S. and European companies. Such an arrangement with the Sikorsky Aerospace division of United Technologies resulted in the first helicopters being produced in Korea. In 1987 Daewoo formed a partnership with another division of United Technologies, Carrier Corporation, to make air-conditioning equipment. (In 1991 Carrier increased its stake in the venture to 75 percent.)

Daewoo also has joint ventures with Caterpillar to make forklifts; with General Dynamics to make parts for the F-16 fighter plane; with Boeing to produce components for the 737, the 747, and 767 jet airliners; and with Northern Telecom to make telecommunications equipment. Daewoo's Model D personal computer, distributed by Leading Edge in the United States, was one of the first major challengers to IBM in the PC market, but the distributor later went bankrupt.

Daewoo has ventured out on its own, too. As part of an effort to develop advanced semiconductor technology, the company bought a controlling interest in U.S. chipmaker ZyMOS in 1986. Foreign manufacturing has been another element of Daewoo's strategy. A microwave oven assembly operation was established in France and VCR production was begun in Northern Ireland.

Daewoo has been especially active opening new markets. It was doing some $200 million a year in trade with Czechoslovakia, for instance, well before the political transformation of Eastern Europe. The company often exchanged its goods for credit for Libyan oil, which it then processed at its refinery in Belgium.

During this time, the company's shipbuilding operation, which makes some of the largest container vessels in the world (when there are customers), suffered along with the rest of the industry. Then, in the late 1980s, it had to cope with increasing militancy among its work force. The government provided some financial relief but forced Daewoo to inject more money into the operation by selling off other assets.

The problems in shipbuilding, along with the general rise in labor costs, have helped to dampen the once-rapid growth of the Daewoo Group. Also, the company's failure to achieve a dominant position in any of its many businesses has contributed to the weakness. Daewoo's top executives—led by Kim and Young-Suk Yoon, who was shocked at the state of the company after he returned from two years in the United States to take over the presidency of Daewoo Corporation in 1989—have responded to the stagnation by eliminating hundreds of middle managers and withdrawing from unprofitable businesses.

These problems have not deterred Daewoo, which moved ahead with such projects as the development of an auto parts manufacturing operation in the United States and a plan to produce a small passenger car called the Tico under license from Japan's Suzuki Corporation.

Yet in 1991 the company's expansionary ways came up against a government policy of forcing the *chaebol* to focus their operations on a smaller number of businesses. Daewoo proposed to specialize in shipbuilding, electronics, textiles, and construction. This left out Daewoo Motor Company, which soon appeared to be on the verge of dissolution anyway. However, the shipbuilding area actually included various other manufacturing operations, including the minicar project. In 1991 there were reports that General Motors was considering withdrawing from its joint venture with Daewoo.

OPERATIONS

Construction. This is one of the two main activities of Daewoo Corporation. The company acts as a general contractor for projects around the world. Among those completed in 1990 were highways in Botswana and the Ivory Coast, a railroad bed in Iran, and a candy factory in the Sudan. New contracts received during the year included a sports complex in Japan, a refinery in Iran, and roads in Nigeria, Botswana, and Cameroon. The company received domestic contracts for an airport, a thermal power plant, a municipal waste-disposal plant, and other projects.

Trading. Daewoo Corporation is also the trading arm of the Daewoo Group. In that capacity it exported some $6.1-billion worth of goods in 1991, the largest categories of which were electrical and electronic goods, ships, and steel and metal.

Other companies within the Daewoo Group include Daewoo Automotive Components, Daewoo Electronics (home appliances and audio and video equipment), Daewoo Heavy Industries (diesel engines, construction equipment, industrial vehicles), Daewoo Securities, Daewoo Shipbuilding & Heavy Machinery, and Daewoo Telecom (telephone equipment, semiconductors, personal computers).

TOP EXECUTIVES

Daewoo Corporation
- Woo-Choong Kim, cochairman
- Joon-Sung Kim, cochairman
- Woo-Bock Lee, vice chairman
- Suk-Heun Yun, vice chairman
- Young-Suk Yoon, president, general trading division
- Soung-Bu Hong, president, development division
- Young-Soo Chang, president, construction division

FINANCIAL DATA

Daewoo Corporation

Revenues (in millions of Korean won)

1991	6,380,667
1990	5,245,800
1989	4,789,627

Net Income (in millions of Korean won)

1991	30,067
1990	53,084
1989	215,106

LABOR RELATIONS

Daewoo, which for years took advantage of government policies that suppressed unionization, was one of the earliest targets of the new labor movement that emerged in South Korea in the 1980s. Workers at Daewoo Motor walked off the job in 1985, well before the wave of worker unrest that rocked the country in 1987. Their goal was both to get substantial wage increases and to shake up their union, which was part of the government-dominated Federation of Korean Trade Unions. A group of several hundred workers occupied the Pupyong plant until Daewoo chairman Woo-Choong Kim himself came to negotiate a settlement. The workers won a 10-percent wage increase, but later many of the militants were harassed by police and some were imprisoned.

In 1987, amid a national strike wave, Daewoo Motor was again shut down. Militant workers seized company offices adjacent to the plant and ransacked them. They then clashed with the riot police sent in to retake the facility. Similar confrontations took place in 1988 and 1989, resulting in substantial wage increases.

Daewoo Shipbuilding, too, has been a center of worker unrest. In addition to strikes during the wave of militancy in the late 1980s, the operation experienced a twelve-day walkout in 1991, when the general labor climate was calmer. That dispute ended with a settlement that gave workers annual bonuses equal to six months of pay, an increase in family allowances, and a greater role in setting company labor policy.

ENVIRONMENTAL RECORD

Although neither environmental consciousness nor reporting on environmental issues is as yet very advanced in South Korea, Daewoo announced in 1986 that it was introducing a dioxin-free version of the germicide hexachlorophene (HCP) developed by one of its subsidiaries.

BIBLIOGRAPHY

Amsden, Alice H. *Asia's Next Giant: South Korea & Late Industrialization.* Oxford: Oxford University Press, 1989.

Kearney, Robert P. *The Warrior Worker: The Challenge of the Korean Way of Working.* New York: Henry Holt, 1991.

Min-Ju No-Jo: South Korea's New Trade Unions. Hong Kong: Asia Monitor Resource Center, 1988.

Steers, Richard M., Yoo Keun Shin, and Gerardo R. Ungson. *The Chaebol: Korea's New Industrial Might.* Cambridge, Mass.: Ballinger, 1989.

DAI-ICHI KANGYO BANK, LTD.

1-5, Uchisaiwaicho 1-chome
Chiyoda-ku, Tokyo 100
Japan
(03) 3596-1111

1991 revenues: $35 billion (year ending March 31)
1991 assets: $459 billion
1991 net income: $651.6 million
Publicly traded company
Employees: 18,640
Founded: 1971 (Dai-Ichi Kokuritsu Ginko was founded in 1873,
     Nippon Kangyo Bank in 1897)

OVERVIEW

Dai-Ichi Kangyo (DKB) is the oldest and largest bank in Japan and since 1986 has been the biggest private-sector bank in the world. Having a customer base of some twenty million in a nation of savers has made DKB a financial powerhouse.

Although its business is still concentrated in Japan, in recent years DKB has been following its competitors abroad, in particular by making several large investments in the United States. It now has branches and agencies in twelve countries and representative offices in about twenty others.

Like the other big Japanese banks—which now dominate the list of the world's top banks—DKB has learned that size is not everything. It has been concentrating on ways to improve its less-than-dazzling profitability while continuing to take advantage of its position at the top of the banking industry in a country that has become the planet's most important source of capital.

HISTORY

DKB is the product of the 1971 merger of two prominent Japanese banks established in the late nineteenth century. Dai-Ichi Kokuritsu Ginko, or First National Bank, was formed in 1873 by industrialist Eiichi Shibusawa, a key figure in the development of modern Japanese business. As the first bank organized under the National Bank Act of 1872, Dai-Ichi was allowed to issue currency until the Bank of Japan took over that function.

Shibusawa introduced joint-stock companies to Japan to check the power of the family-based *zaibatsu* conglomerates that controlled so much of the economy. He put Dai-Ichi up against the giant *zaibatsu* banks that had a lock on much of industry by virtue of close relationships with their sister companies in the Mitsui, Mitsubishi, Sumitomo, and other conglomerates.

Dai-Ichi nevertheless managed to develop an impressive roster of customers, both from some of the smaller conglomerates (including Kawasaki and Furukawa) and from independent firms outside the industrial groups, such as Hitachi.

The Nippon Kangyo Bank was formed in 1897 to make long-term loans to farmers and companies with funds raised by issuing bonds. Sponsored by the Japanese government, Nippon Kangyo remained closely tied to agriculture and rural industries. In the early twentieth century it went through a series of consolidations, culminating in a 1943 merger with Mitsui Bank that created what was called Teikoku Bank.

After World War II Nippon Kangyo was severed from Teikoku and initially was given the role of helping to administer the national lottery. In 1950 it became a general deposit bank, and two years later it abandoned its bond-issuing activity.

Both Nippon Kangyo and Dai-Ichi grew steadily in the 1950s and 1960s, but they and other financial institutions faced a growing threat from the U.S. banks that were entering the Japanese market. To respond to this challenge the Ministry of Finance encouraged consolidation to create stronger Japanese competitors. In line with this policy, Dai-Ichi was supposed to merge with the larger Mitsubishi Bank in 1969, but the deal was abandoned after some of Dai-Ichi's clients expressed concern that they would become dominated by their competitors in the Mitsubishi group.

As an alternative, Dai-Ichi, then the sixth-biggest bank in the country, turned to Nippon Kangyo, the eighth largest. Dai-Ichi's strong position in Tokyo complemented Nippon Kangyo's nationwide branch network. The merger succeeded, and in 1971 the combined operation, Dai-Ichi Kangyo, emerged as Japan's largest bank.

To win over the public the new bank launched a large-scale promotional effort, and DKB's new heart logo soon became a familiar symbol to Japanese banking customers. It also introduced a number of new financial products—

including fifty-year home mortgages paid off by parents and children—peddled by bicycle-riding door-to-door salesmen.

Behind this new heartfelt concern for customers there were growing tensions within DKB, largely as a result of clashes between the Dai-Ichi and the Nippon Kangyo cultures. Nonetheless, DKB has managed to go on growing and has become a new *keiretsu* (the contemporary version of the *zaibatsu*) through holdings in a wide range of industrial companies. DKB organized the Sankin-kai, a group of executives from nearly fifty major firms—including Hitachi, Isuzu, and Kawasaki—that meets monthly to discuss matters of mutual concern.

Like many of its competitors, DKB began to expand overseas, though it preferred to create new operations rather than buying existing banks. One exception to that policy was the 1980 purchase of the Japan-California Bank in the United States.

DKB has been a strong opponent of Japanese laws prohibiting commercial banks from engaging fully in the securities business. Unable to get the law changed, DKB followed other Japanese banks in doing so abroad. DKB also has strengthened its position at home as a dealer in government bonds.

During the second half of the 1980s DKB prospered, thanks to low-interest rates and its expanding foreign operations. Actual growth and relative currency values (the appreciation of the yen) allowed DKB to zoom past the U.S. leader, Citicorp, in 1986 to become the largest bank in the world, measured by assets; Citicorp remained the most profitable.

That year, DKB and its Japanese brethren moved ahead of the U.S. banks as the world's largest group of international lenders, in part by their ability to underprice the American institutions. By the end of the 1980s DKB and other Japanese banks were becoming important players even in the U.S. leveraged buyout field. They also captured 25 percent of the banking market in California.

DKB expanded its presence in the United States in 1989 by purchasing a controlling interest in CIT Financial, an asset-based lending operation, from the big New York bank Manufacturers Hanover Trust. At the same time, DKB took a 4.9-percent stake in Manny Hanny itself. The $1.4-billion deal was the largest U.S. investment to date by a Japanese bank.

As the 1990s began, DKB and the other Japanese banks no longer seemed to be sitting on top of the world. Climbing interest rates at home, a decline in the value of the yen, and the end of the bull market in the Tokyo Stock Exchange combined to weaken the position of the Japanese financial giants. DKB and the others began to rethink the "big is beautiful" philosophy they had been following and began looking for ways to improve their mediocre profitability. They are finding the answer, in part, in their retail business, given the increasing interest of the Japanese population in consumer borrowing and credit cards.

OPERATIONS

Retail Banking. DKB is the only bank with branches in every one of Japan's forty-seven prefectures. With a total of some 400 branches, the bank receives an average of 760,000 customer visits every business day. In recent years the bank has introduced new products, such as Heart Super Loans (large loans that have no restriction on their use) and Heart Super MMCs (small-denomination money market certificates). In 1990 the bank began issuing DKB-MasterCard travelers checks. DKB also issues credit cards in cooperation with MasterCard and Visa. In 1991 DKB formed an alliance with Tokyo-based Jonan Shinkin Bank, the largest of Japan's community banks, to provide a variety of services.

Corporate Banking. DKB serves a wide range of large and small companies. In the case of large companies, DKB offers what it calls relationship management, which includes serving subsidiaries and affiliates at home and abroad. At the end of its 1991 fiscal year DKB had outstanding loans of ¥ 14.7 trillion (76 percent of the total) to companies with capitalization of less than ¥ 1 billion.

Securities Business. In addition to managing a portfolio of domestic and foreign stocks and bonds, DKB is involved in underwriting and trading Japanese government bonds and serves as a representative commissioned company for domestic and foreign companies issuing bonds in the Tokyo capital market. In countries like Germany, Switzerland, and Holland DKB subsidiaries engage in a wider range of securities activities, including equity underwriting. In the United States DKB has a subsidiary, formed in 1989, to deal in government securities. In late 1989 DKB formed an alliance with the British firm Hill Samuel to provide investment advisory services.

International Finance. DKB is actively involved in loan syndications, often working with insurance companies and other Japanese institutional investors to create yen-based finance packages. The bank also engages in project financing and structured financing, such as debt-to-equity conversions, in third world countries.

TOP EXECUTIVES

- Ichiro Nakamura, chairman
- Kuniji Miyazaki, president
- Hiroshi Arai, deputy president
- Yutaka Hayashi, deputy president

FINANCIAL DATA

Revenues (in millions of yen) (years ending March 31)

1991	4,920,387
1990	4,236,234
1989	3,043,706
1988	2,549,532
1987	2,092,383

Assets (in millions of yen) (years ending March 31)

1991	64,530,318
1990	68,765,075
1989	54,778,094
1988	47,073,956
1987	42,330,501

Net income (in millions of yen) (years ending March 31)

1991	91,613
1990	144,966
1989	199,004
1988	151,569
1987	101,538

GEOGRAPHICAL BREAKDOWN

Revenues (in millions of yen)

Year*	Japan		Europe		Elsewhere	
1991	3,149,048	(64%)	688,854	(14%)	1,082,485	(22%)
1990	2,668,827	(63%)	677,797	(16%)	889,609	(21%)
1989	2,039,283	(67%)	426,119	(14%)	578,304	(19%)

*Fiscal year ends March 31.

LABOR RELATIONS

Employees of DKB, like those of all major Japanese banks, are represented by labor unions. Labor relations are generally harmonious, but a 1992 report by the Tokyo Prefectural Labor Standards Office found that DKB was among those banks that were not observing the law requiring that employees receive overtime pay for all extra hours worked. One of DKB's foreign branches, which are not all unionized, ran into legal trouble with an American employee. The former manager of the bank's branch in San Diego, California, filed suit in late 1990 charging that he had been underpaid and forced out of his job because he was white. The suit also claimed that the manager, Karl Biniarz, had been told by Japanese executives not to hire blacks or women as commercial loan officers. The bank denied the charges.

BIBLIOGRAPHY

Multinational Banks and Their Social and Labour Practices. Geneva: International Labour Office, 1991.

DAIMLER-BENZ AG

Mercedesstrasse 136
D-7000 Stuttgart 80
Germany
(0711) 17-0

1991 revenues: $62.7 billion
1991 net income: $1.3 billion
Publicly traded company
Employees: 379,252
Founded: 1882

OVERVIEW

Daimler-Benz, which dates back to the operations set up by the two German engineers widely credited with having invented the automobile, is one of the leading industrial powerhouses of Europe. Since the mid-1980s Daimler-Benz, known for decades as the parent company of Mercedes-Benz, has made a series of acquisitions that have propelled it to the top of the aerospace industry outside the United States.

To solidify that uneasy position, Daimler-Benz—which is controlled by Deutsche Bank, with a big stake owned by Kuwait—has formed a series of international alliances with such competitors as the Pratt & Whitney division of United Technologies. The company also has struggled to cope with the less exciting result of its shopping spree: the money-losing electrical and electronic giant AEG. In addition to managing these difficult new businesses, the company has had to deal with increasing competition in its primary business, luxury automobiles, from the likes of Toyota and Nissan.

HISTORY

Daimler-Benz got its start and its name from two German engineers, Gottlieb Daimler and Carl Benz, each of whom set up a company in the 1880s to build engines. Both men had worked for firms that made locomotives and both had become fascinated with the possibilities of the internal combustion engine—the concept of which had been around for decades but had remained impractical. Both Daimler and Benz believed that such an engine, fueled by *benzin* (gasoline)—at that time considered a waste product in the refining of kerosene—could be the basis for a self-propelled vehicle.

In 1881 Daimler had been forced to resign as technical director of the Gasmotoren-Fabrik Deutz, a producer of stationary industrial engines fueled by gas, because of tensions between him and Nicholas Otto, inventor of the company's engine. The following year Daimler joined with his protégé Wilhelm Maybach to form a new business to produce a lightweight portable engine. After Otto's patent for a four-stroke engine was declared invalid, Daimler and Maybach moved ahead with their work, producing what was in effect the world's first motorcycle in 1885. The following year Daimler put an engine on a carriage he commissioned and turned it into a horseless carriage.

In 1883 Benz established a firm called Benz & Cie., Rheinische Gasmotorenfabrik, ostensibly to produce stationary gas engines. In actuality he used the opportunity to continue his experiments with the portable internal combustion devices that he had started four years earlier. By 1885 he, too, was testing a horseless carriage.

The world took little notice in 1886 of the arrival of an invention that eventually would transform everyday life. Customers did not flock to the Daimler and Benz companies, yet those entrepreneurs maintained their faith in automobiles. Over the next few years Daimler and his partner Maybach put their engines on streetcars and boats. They also sold the French rights to the device to a company that made the technology available to the industrial giant Peugeot, allowing that company to enter the automobile business. Yet Daimler was still facing resistance from his financial backers, who wanted him to concentrate on the established and reliable business of making stationary gas engines. Benz also faced obstacles, but by the early 1890s his cars were selling briskly in France, which embraced the automobile much more readily than did Germany.

It was in the final years of the nineteenth century that the automobile age truly began, and Benz was the largest producer of horseless carriages in the world. Both Benz and Daimler also created trucks, buses, and other motorized vehicles.

The next stage of automobile development was brought about at the instigation of Emil Jellinek, a German entrepreneur living in the French resort city of Nice. Jellinek commissioned Daimler to produce four cars if they could reach a speed of twenty-five miles per hour, ten more than the existing limit. Later he put in another order for six vehicles, with the stipulation that the cars have four- rather than two-cylinder engines and that they be located in the front.

Finally, in 1900—just after Daimler's death—Jellinek persuaded the company to build an entirely new car that was lighter, lower, wider, and longer, with a thirty-five-horsepower engine. Jellinek offered to purchase thirty-six of the cars—which he wanted to name Mercedes after his daughter—in exchange for the exclusive sales franchise for Austro-Hungary, France, Belgium, and the United States. The Mercedes made its first splash in 1901 at the week of road races held each spring in Nice. It dramatically outperformed all of the other vehicles and was tirelessly promoted by Jellinek. The car became the driving machine of choice for aristocrats and the wealthy, who at this time were just about the only people able to afford automobiles.

Initially Benz was left in the dust by the success of the Mercedes, but by the late 1900s the company followed the path of Daimler in setting up foreign sales operations. It also produced a racing car called the Blitzen, which, with a top speed of more than 130 miles per hour, was the fastest automobile in the world.

During World War I Daimler and Benz turned to military production, with Daimler making airplane engines and trucks while Benz made tanks. After the war both companies suffered from the shortage of raw materials and the slump in the car market brought on by the general instability of the German economy. Merger talks between the two companies, which had begun tentatively in 1919, became more serious. In 1924 Daimler and Benz combined their sales and promotion departments and coordinated their product lines; two years later the companies merged completely to form Daimler-Benz AG.

During the 1930s Daimler-Benz enjoyed the support of the Hitler government, which regarded the success of the Mercedes in auto racing as a boost to the country's prestige. Hitler himself liked to appear in parades and other public events in his Mercedes convertible. In 1933 the company began receiving a government subsidy for its racing activities, although an equal amount was given to Auto Union (the result of the 1928 merger of Audi and DKW), whose racing department was being built by former Mercedes designer Ferdinand Porsche. Daimler-Benz also benefited from Hitler's elimination of the tax on auto sales and his *autobahn* highway construction program.

Yet Hitler, inspired by Henry Ford, also was determined to see the development of a low-cost automobile for the masses. Daimler-Benz was privately opposed to the plan, which was being promoted by Porsche as well, but the company carried out its instructions to produce prototypes for the small car. This vehicle, the *Volkswagen* (people's car), was not produced in significant numbers until after World War II.

During the war Daimler-Benz was an important component of the German military effort, producing aircraft engines as well as trucks, tanks, and other martial products. In 1944 the company's factories were heavily bombed by Allied planes. After the defeat of Germany, Mercedes had the stigma of having been Hitler's personal car, but the company set out to rebuild itself. By 1950 Daimler-Benz was producing nearly thirty-four thousand cars a year, a record for the firm. A new series of Mercedes, the 300 line, was well received and went on to become the favorite luxury car for many of the world's most famous persons.

By the mid-1950s Daimler-Benz came to be controlled by industrialist Friedrich Flick, who had bought up shares at depressed prices soon after the war. The other major investors were the Quandt brothers (who controlled BMW) and Deutsche Bank, which had long held roughly one-quarter of the company. Together these three investors controlled some 80 percent of Daimler-Benz shares.

The company had made great strides since the war and was reviving its reputation through participation in high-profile auto races. At the urging of Flick, it also bought 80 percent of its rival, Auto Union (later sold to Volkswagen). Yet Daimler-Benz was still light-years behind the mighty U.S. automakers. The company realized that the American market was key to its growth. Initially sales were limited to New York and Los Angeles, where dealer Max Hoffman set up showrooms. Later in the decade the company arranged for Studebaker-Packard to distribute the Mercedes, but that company (whose days were numbered) was not adept at selling luxury cars. In the mid-1960s Daimler-Benz set up its own sales company, Mercedes-Benz of North America.

Daimler-Benz was not hard hit by the oil crisis of the early 1970s because Mercedes customers, the world's elite, were undeterred by higher gasoline prices. Its trucks were also enjoying strong demand, though that ended by the early 1980s, just about the time that Daimler-Benz acquired the U.S. heavy-truck maker, Freightliner. In 1982 the company bowed to the new interest in smaller cars and introduced a compact Mercedes, known as the Baby Benz. It initially became quite popular, attracting many customers who had never before dared to buy a Mercedes, yet its foreign sales later fell victim to the strong deutsche mark.

The ownership of Daimler-Benz changed during the mid-1970s—the Quandt family sold its shares to Kuwait and Flick sold most of his to Deutsche Bank. In the mid-1980s the company sought to shield itself against the vagaries of the auto business by diversifying. Within the space of only a year it purchased Motoren- und Turbinen-Union (MTU), a producer of aircraft engines and diesel motors for ships and tanks; 66 percent of Dornier, a manufacturer of space systems, commuter planes, and medical equipment; and 80 percent of AEG, a leading appliance and electronics company.

Competition in the luxury car field began to heat up in the early 1980s, with BMW, Audi, Jaguar, Volvo, and Saab all trying to take market share away from the leading company, Mercedes. Daimler-Benz, which avoided frequent model changes, responded by bringing out a new line of midsize cars. There turned out to be technical problems with those cars, however, the responsibility for which was an issue in a squabble among the company's top executives. The discord was most pronounced between chairman Werner Breitschwerdt and finance chief Edzard Reuter, who narrowly lost a board election for the top spot in 1983. The confrontation, which also involved a dispute over the wisdom of the company's diversification moves (which Reuter designed), reached a head in 1987. Breitschwerdt resigned under pressure (mainly from Deutsche Bank) and was succeeded by Reuter.

Once in power, Reuter set out to pull the company together and prepare it for European integration in 1992. He created a new subsidiary, Deutsche Aerospace, based on MTU, Dornier, and AEG assets as well as the 1989 acquisition of a majority interest in Messerschmitt-Bölkow-Blohm (MBB), the aerospace company that was Germany's representative in the Airbus Industrie consortium. This positioned Daimler-Benz to become Europe's leading aerospace and military supplier. Reuter's high-tech preoccupation extended to all of the company's products; even AEG's washing machines were to adopt microelectronics and sophisticated new materials.

While this transformation was taking place, Daimler-Benz began to face greater competition in its primary business. The Japanese automakers were moving upscale, challenging the European leadership of the luxury car market with striking new vehicles, such as the Lexus from Toyota and the Infiniti from Nissan. Ford purchased Britain's Jaguar and sought to inject new life into that high-end rival of Mercedes. At the beginning of the 1990s Daimler-Benz decided to focus on that high end with the introduction of a new line of S-class Mercedes, which in the United States sold for up to $100,000.

In 1990 the auto, aerospace, and electronics industries were jolted by the news that Daimler-Benz and the huge Japanese conglomerate Mitsubishi were negotiating a plan for "intensive cooperation" between their operations in those fields. Reuter was motivated by the desire to get access to Mitsubishi's electronics technology, while the Japanese group wanted access to Daimler's aerospace operations, especially MBB.

Shortly after that bombshell was dropped, Daimler-Benz announced another strategic alliance, this one with the U.S. aerospace company United Technologies. The plan here was to link United Technologies' Pratt & Whitney engine subsidiary to MBB through cross-investments.

The state of Daimler-Benz took a turn for the worse in 1991. The alliance with Mitsubishi had not yet brought any significant benefits, both AEG and Deutsche Aerospace were struggling, and the parent company found itself involved in an investigation of illegal sales of truck parts to Iraq. Questioning whether the company's diversification strategy made sense any longer, the London *Economist* headlined an article on the company THE FLAWED VISION OF EDZARD REUTER.

OPERATIONS

Passenger Cars (40 percent of 1991 revenues). The company's wholly owned Mercedes-Benz subsidiary is the producer of one of the world's leading luxury passenger cars. In 1991 the company sold some 577,000 automobiles, half of which went abroad (the largest number going to the United States). The company, which in 1991 introduced the new S-class, has eleven manufacturing plants in Germany and nineteen abroad.

Commercial Vehicles (28 percent of revenues). Mercedes is the world's leading producer of heavy trucks and a major manufacturer of vans and buses. In 1991 it sold a total of 295,000 commercial vehicles. In 1990 the company took over a heavy-truck production plant near Berlin in eastern Germany, and two years later it entered into a joint venture with two truck makers in Czechoslovokia.

AEG (14 percent of revenues). This 80-percent-owned subsidiary makes a wide range of electrical and electronic products. Its main businesses include factory automation, rail systems, office equipment, mobile communications equipment, power transmission and distribution equipment, household appliances, lighting devices, and the Telefunken electronics operation. This ailing company had a loss of about $400 million in 1991. That year AEG sold its cable business to Alcatel Alsthom and continued efforts to sell its most unprofitable operation, the Olympia office equipment business.

Deutsche Aerospace (13 percent of revenues). Deutsche Aerospace, or DASA, combines the operations of Dornier (airplanes, space systems, and medical equipment), Messerschmitt-Bölkow-Blohm (the German partner in the Airbus consortium), Motoren- und Turbinen-Union (aircraft engines), and the former aerospace operations of AEG (Telefunken radar, radio, and other products). Since early 1990 DASA has formed alliances with the Pratt & Whitney engine division of United Technologies, France's Aérospatiale, and Alenia of Italy.

Daimler-Benz InterServices (4 percent of revenues). This operation, known as Debis, began operations in 1990. The aim is to provide customers with access to Daimler-Benz's expertise in software, financial services, and marketing. In 1991 Daimler-Benz acquired a 34-percent interest in France's Cap Gemini Sogeti, the largest computer services company in Europe.

TOP EXECUTIVES

- Edzard Reuter, chairman of the board of management
- Werner Niefer, deputy chairman of the board of management
- Manfred Gentz, member of the board of management
- Gerhard Liener, member of the board of management
- Jürgen E. Schrempp, member of the board of management
- Helmut Werner, member of the board of the management

OUTSIDE DIRECTORS

- Gerd Binnig, head of the IBM Physics Group
- Horst J. Burgard, member of the board of management of Deutsche Bank
- Martin Kohlhaussen, Speaker of the Commerzbank management board

- Hilmar Kopper, speaker of the board of management of Deutsche Bank
- Rudolf Kuda, member of the board of management of the union IG Metall
- Hans-Georg Pohl, chairman of the board of management of Deutsche Shell
- Wolfgang Röller, speaker of the board of management of Dresdner Bank
- Roland Schelling, attorney at law in Stuttgart
- Frank Steinkühler, first chairman of the union IG Metall
- Hermann Josef Strenger, chairman of the board of management of Bayer AG
- Bernhard Wurl, member of the board of management of the union IG Metall

The supervisory board also includes seven worker representatives and Werner Breitschwerdt, former chairman of the board of management.

FINANCIAL DATA

Revenues (in millions of deutsche marks)

1991	95,010
1990	85,500
1989	76,392
1988	73,495
1987	67,475

Net Income (in millions of deutsche marks)

1991	1,942
1990	1,795
1989	6,809*
1988	1,702
1987	1,782

*Includes extraordinary income items that make it noncomparable with other years.

GEOGRAPHICAL BREAKDOWN

Revenues (in millions of deutsche marks)

Year	Germany		Rest of Europe		Elsewhere	
1991	44,443	(47%)	23,083	(25%)	26,764	(28%)
1990	36,674	(43%)	24,164	(28%)	24,662	(29%)
1989	29,562	(39%)	21,427	(28%)	25,403	(33%)

LABOR RELATIONS

In its home country Daimler-Benz traditionally has had a cooperative relationship with unions. In 1984 the company was caught up in a national strike carried out by the union IG Metall that succeeded in reducing the standard workweek in the auto industry from forty to thirty-eight and one-half hours with no reduction in pay.

Labor relations have been less harmonious in other parts of the world. At a 1988 meeting of rank-and-file workers from half a dozen countries there were reports of serious tensions between Daimler-Benz management and unions in various locations, especially in Brazil and South Africa. In the latter country there have been numerous strikes over such issues as the firing of shop stewards. In 1990 two thousand workers occupied the Mercedes plant in South Africa for several weeks, an action that was in part triggered by a dispute between rank-and-file workers and the National Union of Metalworkers. Many of the workers were opposed to the union's policy of national wage negotiations, because they felt that Mercedes could afford bigger raises than other producers.

ENVIRONMENTAL RECORD

In recent years Daimler-Benz has joined the trend of being more sensitive to the environmental impact of its operations. The new line of S-class Mercedes luxury cars introduced in 1991 practically eliminated the use of ozone-destroying CFCs, and the company is involved in developing electric vehicles as well as other alternatives to gasoline and diesel engines. In 1991 it bought a 10-percent stake in Metallgesellschaft, a German company active in recycling. That same year, however, Daimler-Benz angered environmentalists with its plan to build a large vehicle test track across moorland in Lower Saxony.

BIBLIOGRAPHY

Bellon, Bernard P. *Mercedes in Peace and War.* New York: Columbia University Press, 1990.

IMF Guide to World Aerospace Companies and Unions. Geneva: International Metalworkers' Federation, 1987.

Kimes, Beverly Rae. *The Star and the Laurel: The Centennial History of Daimler, Mercedes and Benz.* Montvale, N.J.: Mercedes-Benz of North America, 1986.

Maxcy, George. *The Multinational Automobile Industry.* New York: St. Martin's Press, 1981.

Sobel, Robert. *Car Wars.* New York: E. P. Dutton, 1984.

DEUTSCHE BANK AG

Taunusanlage 12
D-6000 Frankfurt am Main 1
Germany
(69) 71500

1991 revenues: $28.3 billion
1991 net income: $930.6 million
1991 assets: $296.4 billion
Publicly traded company
Employees: 71,400
Founded: 1870

OVERVIEW

Deutsche Bank, born at the time of German unification, is prospering 120 years later from the *re*unification of the country. By far the country's largest financial institution, it has moved aggressively into what was East Germany, in many cases taking over the same bank buildings it owned before the expropriations following World War II. Its might is enhanced by its ownership of substantial shares of many of Germany's largest companies, which has given Deutsche Bank executives seats on the supervisory boards of more than one hundred firms. At Deutsche Bank those executives serve on a relatively egalitarian management board that includes a *sprecher* (spokesman) rather than a chief executive or chairman.

Deutsche Bank's aspirations go far beyond Germany. It has been building itself into one of the world's premier financial services companies, in part by purchasing a major investment bank in Britain and commercial banks in such countries as Italy and Spain. Deutsche Bank, which is also a major player in the Euromarket, is among the institutions that will benefit most from both the collapse of communism in Eastern Europe and the economic unification of Europe.

HISTORY

Deutsche Bank was founded in Berlin in 1870 with the aim of conducting "banking business of every kind but above all to promote and facilitate trade relations between Germany, the other European countries and overseas markets." Following this principle and taking advantage of the opportunities created by the unification of Germany, Deutsche Bank opened branches in Bremen and Hamburg, the country's major seaports, and in 1873 set up an office in London.

The bank's foreign emphasis helped it survive the financial crisis of the mid-1870s and enabled it to acquire a number of other, weaker financial institutions. Deutsche Bank was soon one of the leading banks in Germany.

Deutsche Bank went on to finance major projects, both in Germany and throughout the world. These included many in the emerging electric power industry, for which Deutsche Bank helped finance generating plants, municipal lighting systems, and electric railways. In the transportation area, Deutsche Bank also was involved in financing the Northern Pacific Railroad in the United States and the Anatolian and Baghdad railways in the Ottoman Empire, not to mention the expansion of the German rail system.

In the early twentieth century Deutsche Bank continued to acquire other financial institutions and was involved in the creation of the Banca Commerciale Italiana. The bank also expanded its branch system and otherwise developed the retail side of its business.

Germany's defeat in World War I and Allied demands for reparations put the country's banking system in a precarious position. It also forced Deutsche Bank to turn from its international focus to a domestic orientation. To cope with the financial instability Deutsche Bank merged with its main rival, Disconto-Gesellschaft, in 1929.

The combined operation, now far and away the leading bank in Germany, was able to weather the depression, while ensuring its political survival by providing financial support to the Nazis. During World War II Deutsche Bank continued this policy of compliance by accepting the increasingly worthless financial instruments issued by the government.

After the war Allied authorities determined that Deutsche Bank had actively supported the Nazi regime, had maintained close ties to Nazi officials, such as SS chief Heinrich Himmler, and had been involved in appropriating assets of financial institutions in countries overrun by the Nazis. The occupying forces ended up dividing the bank first into ten and then three regional institutions, one each for the north, central, and southern regions of West Germany. In 1957 the operations were reunited and allowed to function, with headquarters in Frankfurt, under the Deutsche Bank name once again.

The bank set out to build both its retail business (in part by creating the Eurocheck system) and its international operations, which had been dismantled after the war. Foreign offices were opened first in South America and then in such cities as Tokyo, Istanbul, Cairo, Beirut, and Teheran. Deutsche Bank also entered the international bond business. Its 1958 offering for Anglo American Corporation of South Africa was the first deutsche mark–denominated foreign bond issue in forty-four years. The bank went on to become one of the leading participants in the Eurobond market.

In 1968 Deutsche Bank joined with Britain's Midland Bank, Belgium's Société Générale de Banque, and Holland's Amsterdam-Rotterdam Bank to form the U.S.-based European-American Bank & Trust Company in New York, which in 1974 took over the failed Franklin National Bank. In 1972 the same group established the European Asian Bank.

During this time, Deutsche Bank expanded its investments in a wide range of German companies, and the bank soon held seats on the supervisory boards of more than one hundred firms, among them the biggest names in German industry. Deutsche Bank was under some pressure to reduce its holdings, but that sentiment was put aside after the run-up in oil prices during the early 1970s, since German authorities were concerned about German companies being too vulnerable to takeovers from abroad. In 1975 the bank spent more than $1 billion to acquire Friedrich Flick's 29-percent holding in Daimler-Benz to keep it out of the hands of the Shah of Iran. The shares later were converted into a holding company that sold the stock to the public.

Deutsche Bank used the 1980s to widen its international network, in both commercial and investment banking. The first U.S. branch was opened in New York in 1979, and the bank began trading securities in that city as well as in London and Tokyo. In 1984 Deutsche Bank purchased a 4.9-percent interest in the British securities firm Morgan Grenfell, and in 1986 it spent $603 million to purchase Banca d'America e d'Italia from the ailing Bank of America. In 1989 the bank created an insurance subsidiary that was seen as a challenge to Germany's Allianz, Europe's leading insurer. Deutsche Bank made itself a leader in the European mergers and acquisitions field in 1989 by purchasing the remainder of Morgan Grenfell for $1.5 billion.

By the late 1980s Deutsche Bank was actively pursuing the goal of becoming a global investment bank and a Europe-wide universal bank, offering corporate and consumer services as well as mutual funds and asset management. To do so, the bank, led by Alfred Herrhausen as a sole *sprecher* (rather than the usual cospokesmen arrangement), was trying to change its traditionally conservative corporate culture into something more aggressive. (Herrhausen's tenure was cut short when he was killed in a terrorist attack in 1989.)

The bank demonstrated its new assertiveness in 1990, when it wasted no time taking advantage of the collapse of communism in East Germany, forming a joint venture with the Deutsche Kreditbank (which four decades earlier had expropriated many Deutsche Bank operations). Along with its rival Dresdner Bank, Deutsche Bank left U.S. banks in the dust in the rush east.

The importance of Deutsche Bank was made apparent on July 1, 1990, when thousands of former East Germans mobbed its branch in East Berlin to convert their savings into West German currency. Since then Deutsche Bank has opened more than 290 branches in the former German Democratic Republic, many of them in buildings it owned before 1945. The bank has also made inroads in other parts of Eastern Europe, opening offices in Budapest, Prague, and Warsaw.

OPERATIONS

Corporate Banking. With more than 230,000 corporate customers worldwide, Deutsche Bank provides traditional credit services as well as management consulting, leasing, and pension services. In addition to its German operations, Deutsche Bank owns Banca d'America e d'Italia in Italy, Banco Comercial Transatlántico in Spain, Banco de Montevideo in Uruguay, H. Albert de Bary & Company in Holland, and Deutsche Bank subsidiaries in France, Belgium, Luxembourg, Austria, Canada, Singapore, and Australia.

Consumer Banking. Deutsche Bank has been building its retail banking business by leading the way in the introduction of automatic teller machines in Germany. Also included in this segment is the life insurance operation set up in 1989.

Securities. Deutsche Bank manages the equivalent of mutual funds and fixed-income funds for both individuals and institutional investors. The bank also has been active in the German Futures and Options Exchange since it was launched in January 1990.

Underwriting. In 1990 Deutsche Bank acted as lead manager in seventy-four domestic offerings of additional equity and nine initial public offerings. On the international level the company participated in thirty-eight foreign share placements and maintained its leading position in the Eurobond market, serving as lead manager for such borrowers as Unilever and the World Bank.

Deutsche Bank's investment banking activities also include ownership of the British firm Morgan Grenfell, the Canadian company McLean McCarthy, the Australian firm Bain & Company (50-percent owned), and other operations in Germany, the United States, Britain, Switzerland, Portugal, and Luxembourg.

Structured Financing. The bank participates in syndicated credit facilities, such as the $1.2-billion multiple facility agreement arranged for Thyssen AG in 1990. Deutsche Bank also remains an important supplier of project finance for such ventures as the Brenner Tunnel and the Mobilfunk mobile communications system. It is active in international leasing through subsidiaries in Germany, Italy, Spain, Indonesia, and the United States. Other activities include interest-rate swaps, foreign-exchange trading, money market operations, and precious metals trading.

TOP EXECUTIVES

- Hilmar Kopper, *sprecher* (spokesman) of the board of managing directors
- F. Wilhelm Christians, chairman of the supervisory board
- Georg Krupp, managing director, retail banking
- Carl L. von Boehm-Bezing, managing director, private banking
- Herbert Zapp, managing director, corporate banking

OUTSIDE DIRECTORS

- Marcus Bierich, chairman of the board of management of Robert Bosch GmbH
- Hellmut Kruse, member of the supervisory board of Beiersdorf AG
- Heribald Närger, chairman of the supervisory board of Siemens
- Michael Otto, chairman of the board of management of Otto-Versand GmbH & Company

The supervisory board, which represents shareholders and labor, also includes ten representatives elected by the employees of the company.

FINANCIAL DATA

Assets (in millions of deutsche marks)

1991	449,079
1990	400,160
1989	343,984
1988	305,295
1987	268,341
1986	257,223

Net Income (in millions of deutsche marks)

1991	1,410
1990	1,067
1989	1,340
1988	1,203
1987	670
1986	1,068

LABOR RELATIONS

Deutsche Bank employees are highly unionized—mainly through the main German bank union, Gewerkschaft Handel, Banken und Versicherungen—and, as required by law, there are union representatives on the bank's supervisory board. The bank's 1990 annual report says: "We would like to thank all employee representatives for the good and reliable cooperation." That cooperation broke down in early 1992, when Deutsche Bank was among those German financial institutions targeted by bank workers for token strikes meant to dramatize the demand for higher wages.

BIBLIOGRAPHY

Davis, Steven I. *Excellence in Banking: A Profile of Superior Management Based on Insight Into Citibank, Deutsche Bank, Morgan & 13 Other Selected Banks.* New York: St. Martin's Press, 1986.
Seidenzahl, Fritz. *100 Jahre Deutsche Bank*. Frankfurt am Main: Deutsche Bank, 1970.

DOW CHEMICAL COMPANY

2030 Dow Center
Midland, Michigan 48674
(517) 636-1000

1991 revenues: $18.8 billion
1991 net income: $935 million
Publicly traded company
Employees: 62,200
Founded: 1897

OVERVIEW

Dow, the sixth-largest chemical company in the world and the second largest in the United States, manufactures more than 2,000 products at 181 locations in 32 countries. Most of the products are for industrial use in making drugs, paper, automobiles, housewares, electronics, aircraft, and other chemicals. Dow also sells directly to the consumer with such products as Saran Wrap plastic film, Ziploc plastic bags, and Fantastik cleaner.

For much of the past twenty years the company has been attempting to remove the stigma of having produced napalm during the Vietnam War. In recent years its image problems have been compounded by its involvement with dioxin and Agent Orange.

To help overcome these blemishes, Dow spent tens of millions of dollars during the 1980s on an ad campaign showing college graduates going to work for the company on socially responsible projects—accompanied by the slogan "Dow lets you do great things."

HISTORY

In the mid-1880s Herbert Henry Dow was an industrious engineering graduate with a dream. While studying at Cleveland's Case School of Applied Science (now Case Western Reserve), Dow had discovered that the brine brought to the surface during oil and gas drilling contained a great deal of lithium and bromine. He had then devised a new method of extracting the bromine, which was used in the production of patent medicines and the developing of film. Dow was convinced that he had the makings of a successful business.

After managing to find a few backers to put up his initial capital, Dow set up a modest one-man operation to extract the bromine from a saltwater well in Canton, Ohio. While struggling with this miniplant he refined his ideas and worked out a system for accomplishing the extraction via electrical currents. Dow abandoned the Canton operation and, after getting new seed money, headed for the town of Midland, Michigan—about 125 miles north of Detroit—where Dow had found natural brine deposits that were particularly rich in bromine and easier to pump. Then a logging town past its prime, Midland would turn out to be one of the key sites in the emergence of the American chemical industry.

Dow, an inveterate tinkerer, was the subject of some amusement among the locals as he set up his contraption in a barn. He also had difficulty raising adequate capital, and relations with his main investor were rocky—so much so that he eventually lost control of Midland Chemical.

Undaunted, Dow raised money to start another enterprise to extract chlorine from saltwater. After operating briefly in Ohio, he moved the business to Midland, where he set up right next to his former company and made a deal to use their waste brine for his process. At the time, the market for chlorine bleaching powder, used in textile and paper production, was, like that of most chemicals, controlled by European interests—in this case the British combine United Alkali.

In 1897 Dow engineered a merger of his new firm with Midland Chemical, forming a new company to be known as Dow Chemical. The firm was much better capitalized than Dow's previous ventures, and after some initial technical problems it began to prosper in the bleach business. It also sold a full line of bromides for pharmaceutical houses and photographic supply companies.

Dow was confident enough to begin selling abroad, challenging the dominance of the big British and German producers. The German bromide cartel issued threats to drive Dow out of business by flooding the U.S. market with cheap product, but Dow was not intimidated. In fact, he responded by expanding his exports to Germany and underselling the cartel. The Germans tried to pressure Dow into a settlement that would divide up the world market on terms favorable to them. Dow refused, but as a result of the stalemate the Germans withdrew from the American market and Dow gradually ended its shipments to Germany.

Dow then embarked on an expansion of its product line. Among the new items were lime sulfur and lead arsenate sprays, iron chloride for engraving, zinc chloride for use as a soldering flux, and carbon tetrachloride, which functioned as a household cleanser and fire extinguisher. Dow also moved from simple extraction of bromine and chlorine from brine to a more sophisticated process that produced additional useful chemicals.

The onset of World War I and the blockade of German goods put Dow

Chemical in a critical position for the American economy. Dow recognized that there would soon be a serious shortage of the dyes used by the textile industry, so he brought in a chemist from the University of Michigan to develop a process for making the first domestically produced synthetic indigo. Once the United States entered the war, Dow was called on to produce huge quantities of mustard gas, monochlorbenzol and phenol for explosives, acetic anhydride for coating airplane wings, and a variety of other substances.

Dow pioneered the production of the lightweight metal magnesium, which it promoted as a material in automobiles after the war. The company also persuaded Detroit to use Dow's ethylene dibromide as an additive for gasoline to prevent engine knocking.

Dow Chemical's growth continued after Herbert Dow's death in 1930. He was succeeded by his son Willard. A plant was set up in North Carolina to extract bromine from seawater (Dow was falsely rumored to be trying to extract gold as well). The magnesium business was slowly growing (after peace was made with German competitor IG Farben), and the company was developing many new products from its research. Dow also began working in the new field of plastics. By 1939 Dow was the fifth-largest chemical company in the United States.

With the start of World War II Dow was called on to expand its output of magnesium and other strategic substances. In the midst of this buildup, the company was hit with a federal indictment charging that Willard Dow and treasurer Earl Bennett had conspired with a subsidiary of the Aluminum Company of America to monopolize the magnesium market. Despite the company's efforts to get the case dropped in the interests of wartime mobilization, Dow and the other defendants had to plead no contest to settle the case. The federal government brought more players into the magnesium business—which had become essential to aircraft production—by forcing Dow to share its technology.

After the war Dow began to expand its output and took steps in two new directions. First, it entered the consumer market by selling sheets of thin flexible plastic for use in the kitchen. Saran Wrap soon became a standard item in millions of households. Second, the company moved into foreign production after being approached by Japan's Asahi Chemical Company with an offer to form a joint venture to make plastics. This was followed in the 1950s by similar partnerships in England, India, Australia, Brazil, and other countries, while Dow subsidiaries were set up in such nations as Italy, France, Holland, and Argentina.

Among the most successful of the company's new products was Styrofoam, which proved useful in everything from flotation devices to insulation for television signal towers. Dow Corning, a joint venture with Corning Glass Works that was formed during the war to make silicone sealants for the ignition systems of airplanes, turned out hundreds of new silicone products for industrial and consumer markets. In the late 1950s the company also entered the synthetic fiber business.

By the early 1960s Dow was the world's largest producer of chlorine and caustic soda and was at or near the top in vinyl chloride, propylene, hydrochloric acid, magnesium, plastics, and other products. Yet in the latter part of the decade the company was best known as the producer of napalm, a jellylike inflammable substance widely used by U.S. troops during the Vietnam War. The antiwar movement branded Dow a war criminal for producing a substance that often ended up being used against civilians. Boycotts of Dow products were launched, and the company's campus recruiters were targets of angry protests.

As much as the company tried to promote its other activities, such as a measles vaccine it had developed, for a whole generation of Americans, Dow Chemical was inextricably linked to napalm. By the 1980s the memory of napalm was beginning to fade, but it was replaced by controversy over the company's involvement in the production of the defoliant Agent Orange, which also was used during the Vietnam War. In addition, the company built the Rocky Flats nuclear weapons plant in Colorado for the Department of Energy and managed it from 1952 to 1975.

Dow was relatively unscathed by the oil price hikes of the 1970s because it had its own petroleum feedstocks. More significant was the decline in price and demand for basic chemicals, for the company remained heavily dependent on commodity products like chlorine and ethylene. In 1985 Dow wrote off some $600 million in unneeded plants and other assets.

To add a bit of predictability the company has moved into specialty chemicals, such as superstrong ceramics and plastics, and into nonchemical markets. In 1981 Dow purchased the pharmaceutical house Merrell Drug, and four years later it acquired the Texize operations (spot removers, detergents, cleansers, and so on) of Morton Thiokol. In 1989 a joint venture was formed with Eli Lilly & Company to produce agricultural chemicals; called DowElanco, it is now one of the largest companies in the field. That same year, Merrell Dow was merged with Marion Laboratories to create a subsidiary with its own publicly traded stock.

OPERATIONS

Chemicals and Performance Products (24 percent of 1991 sales). This segment consists of a wide range of products primarily used as raw materials in the manufacture of chemicals, pulp and paper, pharmaceuticals, and personal-care products. Among the chemical and metal products are chlorinated solvents (used in dry cleaning, electronics, and paints), chlorine (used in bleaching paper), ethylenamines (among other things, used as an antiknock gasoline additive), magnesium, calcium chloride, propylene and ethylene glycols, vinyl chloride, caustic soda, and propylene oxide. Dow's performance products include latex coatings and binders (especially for paper and carpets), ion exchange resins (used for water purification, sugar processing, and drugs), superabsorbents, and membranes.

The raw material for many of the products are obtained from salt deposits the company owns in Louisiana, Michigan, Texas, Ontario, Alberta, and Germany; natural brine deposits in Michigan; and limestone deposits in Texas.

This segment has already begun to feel a drop in demand for chlorine as a result of environmental concerns in the pulp and paper industry and various efforts—including federal Clean Air Act regulations—to reduce the use of chlorinated solvents.

Plastic Products (36 percent of sales). Dow is one of the world leaders in plastics for markets including packaging, automobiles, electronics, construction, appliances, housewares, furniture, flooring, recreation, and health care. Dow's plastics include polystyrene resins, polyethylenes, and adhesive polymers. Also included in this segment are Styrofoam-brand plastics, packaging foams, and adhesive and plastic films.

Consumer Specialties (29 percent of sales). This segment of Dow's operations is actually composed of three businesses: agricultural products (including herbicides, insecticides, and fumigants), pharmaceuticals, and consumer products. The pharmaceuticals operation, Marion Merrell Dow Inc., includes prescription products, such as Cardizem (a cardiovascular medication), Seldane (an antihistamine), Carafate (an antiulcer drug), and Nicorette (a smoking-cessation aid). Over-the-counter products include Cepacol oral hygiene aids, the antacid Gaviscon, and Os-Cal calcium supplements.

Consumer products include Saran Wrap and Handi-Wrap plastic films, Ziploc plastic bags, Spray 'n Wash laundry stain remover, Fantastik and Dow household cleaners, and Perma Soft and Style hair-care products.

Hydrocarbons and Energy (10 percent of sales). Dow calls itself the world leader in the production of olefins, styrene, and aromatics. This segment also is involved in coal gasification and cogeneration of power used in other Dow operations. Destec Energy, the Dow subsidiary involved in cogeneration, became a publicly traded company in 1991 with an initial public offering of 28 percent of its shares.

TOP EXECUTIVES

- Paul F. Oreffice, chairman
- Frank P. Popoff, president and chief executive
- Enrique C. Falla, chief financial officer
- Andrew Butler, senior vice president

OUTSIDE DIRECTORS

- Willie D. Davis, chief executive of All Pro Broadcasting, Los Angeles
- Harold T. Shapiro, president of Princeton University
- Paul G. Stern, chief executive of Northern Telecom
   Also on the board are Dow family members Michael L. Dow and Herbert H. Dow.

FINANCIAL DATA

Revenues (in millions of dollars)

1991	18,807
1990	19,773
1989	17,600
1988	16,682
1987	13,377

Net Income (in millions of dollars)

1991	935
1990	1,378
1989	2,486
1988	2,398
1987	1,240

GEOGRAPHICAL BREAKDOWN

Revenues (in millions of dollars)

Year	United States		Europe		Elsewhere	
1991	9,079	(48%)	5,881	(31%)	3,847	(20%)
1990	9,494	(48%)	6,278	(32%)	4,001	(20%)
1989	8,084	(46%)	5,523	(31%)	3,993	(23%)

Operating Income (in millions of dollars)

Year	United States		Europe		Elsewhere	
1991	1,136	(68%)	372	(22%)	173	(10%)
1990	1,622	(58%)	692	(25%)	504	(18%)
1989	1,876	(47%)	1,160	(29%)	974	(24%)

LABOR RELATIONS

Dow had a tradition of paternalism—a profit-sharing plan was established as early as 1900—but Midland factory workers were organized by District 50 of the United Mine Workers. The first strike occurred in 1948, when the union was seeking bigger postwar raises than the company could abide. The walkout lasted four weeks, ending with a compromise.

District 50 later became part of the United Steelworkers of America, and the employees at Dow's Midland operations, by far the largest organized group in the company, became members of Local 12075 of the USWA. In 1974, amid fat times for the company, Dow withstood a 121-day strike in Midland by using employees outside union jurisdiction to maintain operations. Earlier, during the 1960s, Dow had broken several locals of the International Chemical Workers Union. Today about 15 percent of the company's U.S. employees are represented by unions. The company says in its 10-K filing that it "generally has a good relationship with these unions."

ENVIRONMENTAL AND HEALTH RECORD

Although terms like "environment" and "pollution" were not used at the time, Dow Chemical had problems with noxious emissions from its operations in Midland almost from the very beginning.

Only much later did the issue move from one of the annoyance of local residents at offensive odors to charges of serious health hazards. For as long as possible the company sought to keep these hazards quiet. Dow fought the attempts of the EPA to collect data on air pollution in Midland.

When Dr. D. Jack Kilian, medical director at Dow's huge facility in Freeport, Texas, began reporting evidence of genetic damage in workers exposed to benzene and epichlorohydrin, the company did not want the employees to be notified of the danger. A 1981 study by the Council on Economic Priorities found that Dow had one of the worst records in occupational health among the leading chemical companies.

During the 1980s Dow led the campaign to reverse a ban on the production of an herbicide called 2,4,5-T that was an ingredient in the defoliant Agent Orange used by U.S. troops during the Vietnam War. Remaining stocks of the defoliant, which had been produced by Dow since 1948, continued to be used after the war to spray rice fields and range lands in the United States. The manufacture of 2,4,5-T created dioxin, one of the most toxic substances known. Dioxin had been detected in waterways near Dow's Michigan plants.

The company also found itself the target of thousands of lawsuits filed by Vietnam veterans charging that the dioxin in Agent Orange had caused liver damage, nervous disorders, birth defects, and other health problems. Dow executives insisted that there was no evidence that dioxin caused anything worse than skin rashes. Yet, after the Agent Orange lawsuits were consolidated, documents were disclosed showing that Dow was aware as early as 1965 that dioxin was exceptionally toxic. The case was settled out of court with the creation of a $180-million fund.

Dow also has been at the center of controversies regarding the pesticide DBCP, the crop fumigant EDB, methylene chloride, and other danger substances. Federal researchers have found an unusually high incidence of brain cancer among Dow workers in Texas.

The company's Merrell Dow Pharmaceuticals subsidiary has been the target of several hundred lawsuits charging that its Bendectin morning sickness drug caused birth defects. Many of the suits were consolidated in a class action case that Dow won in 1985, but the company discontinued the drug. In October 1991 a state court jury in Texas awarded nearly $34 million in damages in an individual case brought by a couple whose daughter had been born with birth defects they said were linked to the drug.

The Dow Corning joint venture has found itself at the center of a controversy about the safety of silicone breast implants. The gel from the implants, which are used both for breast enlargement and for breast reconstruction after a mastectomy, sometimes migrates into the body and is believed to cause immune-system disorders.

Internal company documents made public in 1992 suggested that Dow Corning was lax in conducting safety studies and in notifying physicians of potential problems. In the wake of these revelations there was a shake-up in the top management of Dow Corning. At the same time, the Food and Drug Administration was grappling with the question of whether to make a moratorium on the use of the implants a permanent restriction. In the meantime, Dow Corning decided to abandon the silicone gel implant business.

Dow's 1990 annual report boasts of having fully eliminated ozone layer–depleting halogenated CFCs from its polystyrene and polyethylene foam products as well as from about 75 percent of its Styrofoam insulation. The company also has contributed money to efforts aimed at preserving wetlands and promoting recycling. In 1991 Dow created an outside board of advisers to help the company improve its environmental practices.

A compilation of EPA data by the Citizens Fund found that Dow ranked twenty-eighth among U.S. manufacturing companies in terms of total releases of toxic chemicals in 1989 (the latest figures available). It ranked seventh in terms of releases of known or suspected carcinogens.

BIBLIOGRAPHY

Nader, Ralph, and William Taylor. *The Big Boys: Styles of Corporate Power.* New York: Pantheon, 1986.

Sorey, Gordon K. *The Foreign Policy of a Multinational Enterprise: An Analysis of the Policy Interactions of Dow Chemical & the U.S.* Salem, N.H.: Ayer, 1980.

Whitehead, Don. *The Dow Story: The History of the Dow Chemical Company.* New York: McGraw-Hill, 1968.

DOW JONES AND COMPANY

200 Liberty Street
New York, New York 10281
(212) 416-2000

1991 revenues: $1.7 billion
1991 net income: $72.2 million
Publicly traded company
Employees: 9,459
Founded: 1882

OVERVIEW

Dow Jones, a major provider of business information, is best known as publisher of the *Wall Street Journal*, which circulates throughout the United States and has separate editions in Europe and Asia. The company is also the leading supplier of on-line business data in the United States. Other activities include publishing the financial weekly *Barron's*, twenty-three daily newspapers in the United States, and business magazines in Asia. Dow Jones also has investments in media and telecommunications companies in North America, Europe, Asia, and South America.

Dow Jones has a long tradition of being run by business journalists who have risen through the ranks; ownership of the company's stock is dominated by the descendants of the man who bought the company from its founders and began building it into an information powerhouse. While still a major force in its field, recently Dow Jones has been suffering a slump in both the print and electronic parts of its operations.

HISTORY

Business reporting was still in a primitive state when Charles H. Dow and Edward D. Jones formed a stock market news service in New York City in

1882. Dow and Charles M. Bergstresser, who soon joined the firm as a partner, gathered the information while Jones did the editing of the handwritten bulletins that were provided to subscribers during the day. Later the bulletins were combined as the *Customers Afternoon Letter*, which in 1889 was transformed into the *Wall Street Journal*.

In 1887 the firm commissioned Clarence W. Barron to report from Boston. Barron turned out to be more than a correspondent. By the first years of the new century the clever financier had bought out the original partners and embarked on a plan of building the *Journal*'s circulation. He later founded a weekly investment paper, which he named after himself, and expanded a primitive news ticker that Dow Jones had established in 1897. Descendants of Barron still control the voting stock of the company.

When Barron died in the late 1920s the *Journal* was a growing publication, but it still focused on the New York City financial scene. Barron's successor, Kenneth Hogate, made the wise move of expanding, rather than cutting back on, coverage during the depression. He also hired a series of energetic editors. Chief among them was Bernard "Barney" Kilgore, who encouraged in-depth reporting and developed many of the page-one features that remain in use today.

Thanks to the efforts of Kilgore, who ascended to the presidency of Dow Jones, circulation of the *Journal* rose steadily, reaching one million by Kilgore's retirement in 1966. During the 1960s Dow Jones also began diversifying, while remaining careful not to stray too far from its core business of information. In 1962 the company created the *National Observer*, a weekly general-interest newspaper. The paper, which never managed to build a solid circulation or advertising base, was finally shut down in 1977. More successful were the information service AP–Dow Jones Economic Report, a joint venture started in 1960, and the purchase of the Ottaway Newspapers chain in 1970.

A bit farther afield was the book-publishing venture that Dow Jones formed with textbook house Richard D. Irwin in 1965. Although the two companies produced a successful series of business and financial titles, books never seemed to fit in with the overall Dow Jones strategy. Irwin was acquired by Dow Jones in 1975, then the combined Dow Jones-Irwin was sold in 1988 to Times Mirror—a newspaper company that was more committed to the book business.

The reputation of the *Journal* was tarnished in 1984, when it was revealed that R. Foster Winans, one of the writers of its popular "Heard on the Street" stock gossip column, had given market-sensitive information to several brokers before it was published. In an attempt to salvage its reputation, the *Journal* conducted an extensive investigation into the matter and published a series of stories that went into lurid detail about Winans's personal life.

At the end of 1990 Warren Phillips, who pushed the company into the information services area and grappled with the slump that began in the late 1980s, relinquished the chief executive's post to Peter Kann, who had been serving as president of the company and publisher of the *Journal*. Phillips also retired from the chairman's post in 1991.

In 1991 the company was defeated by General Electric in a contest to take over the Financial News Network, a cable television service that GE dismantled to reduce the competition faced by its CNBC channel.

OPERATIONS

Business Publications (43 percent of 1991 revenues). The company's flagship operation is the *Wall Street Journal*, the leading U.S. business newspaper and the daily with the largest circulation. The *Journal* is edited in New York City, published in four regional editions, and printed at eighteen plants across the country. Its daily circulation is about 1.8 million.

The *Asian Wall Street Journal*, established in 1976, is edited and printed in Hong Kong and transmitted by satellite to additional printing plants in Singapore and Japan. Material from this daily is used to produce the *Asian Wall Street Journal Weekly*, which is published in New York City for North American readers with a special interest in Asia.

The *Wall Street Journal/Europe*, founded in 1983, is edited in Brussels and printed in the Netherlands, Switzerland, and England. Its circulation is fifty-two thousand.

The *Wall Street Journal* has far and away the leading position among business newspapers in the United States. At times the paper—which has grown from one to three daily sections—has been in the enviable position of having to turn down ads because of space limitations. However, in the wake of the 1987 stock market plunge, the *Journal* began to experience a decline in circulation and ad revenues—a slide that accelerated as the recession began in 1990. At the end of that year the cover price was raised 50 percent, to seventy-five cents, to try to recoup some of the lost revenue.

While the *Journal* may not be able to restore its breakneck growth rates, it remains a very lucrative and near-monopoly business. The only direct competition comes from the relatively tiny circulation of *Investor's Daily* and the *Financial Times* of London. Less-direct competition comes from *USA Today* and the national edition of the *New York Times*. In other parts of the world, particularly Europe, the *Journal* is in the underdog position, trying to catch up to the *Financial Times*.

Barron's National Business and Financial Weekly, edited in New York City, has a circulation of about 240,000. Its readers are mainly individual investors attracted by the exhaustive financial data and irreverent writing, such as Alan Abelson's "Up and Down Wall Street" front-page column.

Other business publications include the *Far Eastern Economic Review*, a leading Asian business and political publication based in Hong Kong; *Asia Technology*, launched in 1989; and *American Demographics*, a monthly devoted to trends in consumer markets.

Dow Jones has formed a joint venture with Germany's von Holtzbrinck publishing group (publisher of the business daily *Handelsblatt*) to develop

English-language publishing in Europe. The two companies are also equity partners in a number of other European enterprises, including French business publisher Groupe Expansion, S.A., and its Eurexpansion holding company, which manages a network of business publications in Belgium, Czechoslovakia, France, Germany, Hungary, Ireland, Italy, Luxembourg, Poland, Portugal, Spain, Sweden, and Switzerland.

Among the company's other investments are a majority interest in *AmericaEconomia*, a business magazine in South America, and minority interests in Thailand's Nation Publishing Group and in Mediatex Communications, publisher of the *Texas Monthly*.

Information Services (44 percent of revenues). In this segment, which accounts for a majority of the company's operating income, the best-known product is the Dow Jones News Service, commonly called "the broadtape." This is the service that brings breaking news—via some 131,000 teleprinters and video displays—into the offices of stock brokerages, institutional investors, and other close followers of financial markets. It is the news medium of record during the business day.

Another set of leading products in this segment are supplied by Telerate Inc., which was established in 1969. Dow Jones began distributing Telerate's services overseas in 1977, bought a 32-percent stake in the company in 1985, and later increased its holdings to 67 percent. Telerate became a wholly owned subsidiary of Dow Jones in early 1990 after a nasty brawl over an unsolicited bid by Dow Jones to purchase the remaining 33 percent. Telerate provides investors and traders with price quotations, transaction services, analytic software, and other information on a wide range of markets. With offices in more than sixty countries, Telerate provides services that are received at some eighty-nine thousand terminals worldwide.

Telerate is stronger in the United States (especially with data on the government securities market) than it is abroad, where it is attempting to break the grip held by Reuters in such areas as foreign-exchange transaction services. The problem with Telerate is that its main customers—brokerage houses and banks—have been cutting back. This has sharply reduced Telerate's growth and by extension has been a drag on Dow Jones as a whole. The company's balance sheet, once virtually free of debt, is now highly leveraged as a result of the $1.6-billion Telerate acquisition.

The slowdown came just as Telerate was coping with the heavy start-up costs of its Trading Service, the product intended to challenge Reuters (as well as Citicorp's Quotron) in the foreign-exchange area. Telerate has been slow in developing new software to enable users to analyze data.

In 1992, Dow Jones announced plans to test two innovative information services with regional phone companies: a project with BellSouth to deliver news via cellular telephones and a plan with NYNEX to transmit video news programs over phone lines.

Other information services of Dow Jones:

- AP–Dow Jones Economic Report brings news and data on financial markets to subscribers in fifty-six countries.
- Professional Investor Report, begun in 1988, provides specialized information for traders, arbitrageurs, and other equity market professionals.
- Capital Markets Report covers fixed-income and financial-futures markets worldwide.
- Dow Jones News/Retrieval provides current and archival text and data on a wide range of business subjects; it is the only on-line source for the text of articles from back issues of the *Wall Street Journal*. In addition to data bases that require users to master a set of special commands, News/Retrieval also includes a text-retrieval service, called DowQuest (introduced in 1989), that responds to plain-English queries. Another data base available through the News/Retrieval is DataTimes, which provides full-text access to back issues of more than fifty national and regional newspapers and other publications. Dow Jones owns 15 percent of Oklahoma Publishing Company, parent of DataTimes.
- DowPhone is a telephone information service that provides real-time stock quotes, breaking news reports, and investment advice.
- DowVision, launched in 1990, provides delivery of a stream of data from various Dow Jones information systems to corporate subscribers; the information is customized to meet the particular needs of each subscriber.
- Federal Filings, Inc., provides rapid on-line reports about filings with the Securities and Exchange Commission (SEC).

Community Newspapers (13 percent of revenues). The lowest-profile segment of the company consists of twenty-three general-interest dailies published by Ottaway Newspapers, which is wholly owned by Dow Jones. Average daily circulation of these dailies is about 566,000, which puts Dow Jones (the *Wall Street Journal* excluded) at about number twenty-three among the newspaper chains.

TOP EXECUTIVES

- Peter R. Kann, chairman, chief executive, and publisher of the *Wall Street Journal*
- Kenneth L. Burenga, president and chief operating officer
- James H. Ottaway, Jr., senior vice president; president of Magazine Group and International Group
- Peter G. Skinner, senior vice president and general counsel
- Carl M. Valenti, senior vice president; publisher and president of Information Services Group

OUTSIDE DIRECTORS

- William M. Agee, chief executive of Morrison Knudsen Corporation
- Rand Araskog, chief executive of ITT Corporation

- Irvine O. Hockaday, Jr., chief executive of Hallmark Cards
- Vernon E. Jordan, senior partner in the law firm of Akin, Gump, Hauer & Feld
- Rene C. McPherson, former dean of Stanford Business School
- Donald E. Petersen, former chief executive of Ford Motor Company
- James Q. Riordan, president of Bekaert Corporation
- Richard D. Wood, chairman of Eli Lilly & Company

The board also includes William C. Cox, Jr., Bettina Bancroft Klink, and Martha S. Robes, all members of the family that controls the stock of Dow Jones, as well as former chief executive Warren H. Phillips.

FINANCIAL DATA

Revenues *(in millions of dollars)*

1991	1,725
1990	1,720
1989	1,688
1988	1,603
1987	1,314

Net Income *(in millions of dollars)*

1991	72
1990	107
1989	317
1988	228
1987	203

GEOGRAPHICAL BREAKDOWN

Revenues (in millions of dollars)

Year	United States		Foreign	
1991	1,275	(74%)	450	(26%)
1990	1,302	(76%)	417	(24%)
1989	1,337	(79%)	350	(21%)
1988	1,295	(81%)	308	(19%)
1987	1,200	(91%)	114	(9%)

Operating Income (in millions of dollars)

Year	United States		Foreign	
1991	166	(65%)	90	(35%)
1990	180	(74%)	64	(26%)
1989	263	(74%)	91	(26%)
1988	282	(77%)	86	(23%)
1987	298	(95%)	16	(5%)

LABOR RELATIONS

Dow Jones, which now has ninety-five hundred employees, has traditionally used a combination of paternalism and pressure to get the best performance from its work force, especially the reporters at the *Journal*.

One employee's reaction to this mixed policy is vividly expressed in a 1972 article in the now-defunct journalism review [*More*]. A. Kent MacDougall, who had just resigned from the paper, recounts how he announced his departure by sending out a memo on the paper's internal wire: "AFTER 10 YEARS AND 3 MONTHS OF DJ PEONAGE, I WILL BE FREE AT LAST, FREE AT LAST, GREAT GAWD ALMIGHTY, FREE AT LAST." And yet his resentment was tempered by a genuine affection for the *Journal*.

As for formal labor relations, the editorial employees of the *Journal* and *Barron's* have been represented since the 1930s by an unaffiliated union called the Independent Association of Publishers' Employees (IAPE). Long regarded as essentially a company union (it has never gone on strike), the IAPE came to life in the 1980s when some more-aggressive leaders sought to affiliate with a larger labor organization. The majority of the membership felt differently, and two affiliation attempts—one with the Graphic Communications International Union in 1987 and another with the Communications Workers of America in 1990—were defeated.

ENVIRONMENTAL RECORD

The company's impact on the environment comes from its use of newsprint. Dow Jones is a limited partner in two ventures that supply about 40 percent of its newsprint needs. The remainder of the 200,000 metric tons consumed in 1991 came from more than a dozen other suppliers.

A 1990 survey by the House Committee on Ways and Means listed the *Wall Street Journal* as the worst of the "Dirty Dozen"—a group of major papers that used less than 10-percent recycled material. The company has since announced plans to raise that proportion to 30 percent.

BIBLIOGRAPHY

Kerby, William F. *A Proud Profession: Memoirs of a Wall Street Journal Reporter.* Homewood, Ill.: Dow Jones–Irwin, 1981.

Rosenberg, Jerry M. *Inside the Wall Street Journal: The History and Power of Dow Jones and America's Most Influential Newspaper.* New York: Macmillan, 1982.

Scharff, Edward E. *Worldly Power: The Making of the Wall Street Journal.* New York: Beaufort Books, 1985.

Wendt, Lloyd. *The Wall Street Journal: The Story of Dow Jones and the Nation's Business Newspaper.* Skokie, Ill.: Rand McNally, 1982.

Winans, R. Foster. *Trading Secrets: An Insider's Account of the Scandal at the Wall Street Journal.* New York: St. Martin's Press, 1986.

E. I. DU PONT
DE NEMOURS AND COMPANY

1007 Market Street
Wilmington, Delaware 19898
(302) 774-1000

1991 revenues: $38 billion
1991 net income: $1.4 billion
Publicly traded company
Employees: 133,000
Founded: 1802

OVERVIEW

Du Pont, the leading chemical company in the United States, is one of the country's oldest and most powerful industrial empires. Since its early days as a gunpowder producer, the company has played an influential role in American life, at times seeming to have the top elected officials of the land at its beck and call. For decades the du Pont family was a virtual aristocracy, and although no longer closely involved in the company's affairs, the family remains wealthy and powerful, at least in the state of Delaware, which is essentially a du Pont fiefdom. One branch of the family alone is estimated by *Forbes* to be worth nearly $9 billion.

Once disdained as a war profiteer and "merchant of death," the company has for the past half century cultivated a more benign image through the introduction of nylon, cellophane, and other aspects of "better living through chemistry," as the Du Pont slogan put it.

The company, though one of the nation's ten biggest industrial firms, no longer has the kind of clout it possessed when it controlled General Motors and many other large corporations. In fact, since 1981 the Seagram Company, which ended up with more than 20 percent of Du Pont's stock as a result of a complicated takeover battle, has come to have the greatest influence on the Wilmington company.

Du Pont spent the 1980s trying to recover from a slump in its large synthetic fibers business, but it has not had an easy time moving into new fields like pharmaceuticals, imaging systems, and electronics. The company also has had to contend with a host of pressures stemming from its role as the single largest industrial polluter in the United States.

HISTORY

In 1802 thirty-one-year-old young Éleuthère Irénée du Pont de Nemours set up a mill along Brandywine Creek near Wilmington, Delaware, to produce gunpowder. Du Pont had emigrated from France two years earlier with his wife, his father, and his brother to escape the turmoil of the post–revolutionary period. In France he had been apprenticed to the famed chemist Antoine Lavoisier and in particular had developed skill in making black powder, on which basis he decided that he could produce better powder than that being supplied by U.S. mills.

The first powder carrying the Du Pont name was shipped in 1804; the first foreign sale, to the government of Spain, was made the following year. Business was helped by the connections of du Pont's father, Pierre Samuel, an economist and entrepreneur who counted among his acquaintances Thomas Jefferson. That contact resulted in government contracts, and Du Pont powder was used by the navy in its assault on the pirates of Tripoli.

The company went on selling black powder exclusively for the next three decades, surviving frequent accidents, such as the 1818 disaster that killed forty workers and nearby residents. In 1832 the product line was expanded to include refined saltpeter, pyroligneous acid, and creosote. As the country grew, Du Pont prospered, its products being used both for peaceful purposes (blowing out tree stumps to clear land) and for bellicose ones. It seemed that there was always a war or conflict in which men needed gunpowder to blow one another up.

An improved type of blasting powder (based on sodium nitrate rather than potassium nitrate) was introduced in 1857 by Lammot du Pont, grandson of the founder. Two years later the company made its first move out of the Wilmington area by purchasing the Wapwallopen powder mills near Wilkes-Barre, Pennsylvania. In 1880 the company opened a plant near Gibbstown, New Jersey, to make a more powerful explosive—dynamite, which Du Pont had initially resisted but then realized could be as profitable as black powder.

Du Pont thrived during the Civil War by selling powder to the Union Army, but after the war the company found itself in a crisis as the government dumped surplus powder on the market, driving prices down to as little as five cents a pound (compared to the wartime high of thirty-three and a half cents). Another problem was that a company called California Powder Works, which had been formed by miners to produce low-cost blasting powder, was underselling the established mills by using low-paid Chinese workers and taking advantage of the fact that it could get saltpeter (a key ingredient) from its source in India more cheaply than the Eastern firms.

Du Pont, then run by the founder's son Henry, solved the problem by bringing his competitors together to form the Powder Trust—officially known as the Gunpowder Trade Association—which set prices and made rules limiting competition. The trust overwhelmed the rest of the industry; even California Powder succumbed, selling a large share of itself to Du Pont. By 1889 the trust controlled 95 percent of powder production in the United States, enabling Du Pont, in particular, to make a fat profit off the Spanish-American War.

In the late 1890s the trust faced a challenge from the European powder cartel, which decided to enter the U.S. market for the first time. Appalled at this competition, Du Pont sent a delegation to Europe to work out a pact. The result was an agreement in which the Powder Trust in effect paid the cartel to keep out of the American market.

The company, which changed from a family partnership to a corporation in 1899, was purchased and reorganized in 1902 by three great-grandsons of the founder: T. Coleman du Pont, Alfred I. du Pont, and Pierre S. du Pont. The three used a variety of methods, both legal and questionable, to create a virtual monopoly in the powder market; they also grabbed a market share of more than 50 percent for other explosives.

As part of this process they branched out into new fields and created a complex organizational structure that is considered the beginning of the modern American corporation. That structure, which for the first time gave managers clear areas of responsibility, was applied to General Motors, which Du Pont gained control of in the later 1910s (and maintained until the mid-1960s).

Du Pont came to assume such a commanding position in the explosives market that the federal government began antitrust proceedings against the company in 1907. Five years later Du Pont and the Gunpowder Trade Association were deemed an illegal monopoly. As a result the company was compelled to sell off some of its holdings, which were turned into two new companies, Atlas Powder and Hercules Powder. (Some time later, in 1942, Du Pont, Atlas, Hercules, and several other companies pleaded no contest to criminal antitrust violations.) Yet Du Pont was allowed to maintain a complete monopoly in the sale of smokeless powder. There was internal turmoil in the company as well. Following intense disagreements about corporate strategy among the three du Ponts, Coleman and Pierre effectively stripped Alfred of his power.

After prospering during World War I—Du Pont produced 40 percent of all explosives shot from Allied cannons—the company resumed its expansion and diversification. Du Pont went on such a spending spree in the 1920s and 1930s that it virtually turned into a holding company. Among these purchases were major stakes in National Ammonia, United States Rubber, Remington Arms, and U.S. Steel (which ended up being sold after the Federal Trade Commission began an investigation). Du Pont also formed cartels and joint ventures throughout Europe, South America, and other parts of the world.

The most important new line of products was fibers. In 1920 Du Pont purchased rights from the French company Comptoir de Textiles Artificiels to a new, cellulose-based fiber that served as a cheap substitute for silk. The product, introduced by the Delaware company under the name "rayon," brought about a revolution in clothing. Inexpensive but smart-looking apparel became available to a large segment of the population. Du Pont also caused a sensation with another product derived from a Comptoir patent: cellophane, which was introduced in 1924. When Du Pont chemists managed to create a moisture-proof version, the product was widely adopted for packaging food, cigarettes, and an endless number of other items. In the search for cheaper labor and a compliant government, Du Pont located much of its textile production in the South, thereby becoming one of the first "runaway" employers.

During the 1920s the company also began production of synthetic ammonia, photographic film, industrial alcohol, and tetraethyl lead (the antiknock additive for gasoline). Freon fluorocarbon refrigerant was introduced through a joint venture with General Motors in 1931. That same year, Du Pont brought out neoprene, the first successful general-purpose synthetic rubber. The 1930s also saw the introduction of Lucite, a clear, hard plastic resin, and Teflon, a slippery resin that was later used for nonstick cookware.

Yet the biggest splash came with the discovery of nylon, the first truly synthetic textile fiber. Back in 1931 Du Pont scientist Wallace H. Carothers presented the first paper on nylon to the American Chemical Society, and after years of frustrating research he perfected the technique for making artificial silk. Production was located at a plant in Seaford, Delaware, which became known as the Nylon Capital of the World. In 1940 Du Pont introduced nylon stockings and sold sixty-four million pairs that first year. Nylon also came to be used for brushes, shower curtains, strings for musical instruments, tires, and many other products.

According to author Gerard Colby, the du Ponts, as major backers of the right-wing Liberty League, were involved in a short-lived plot to overthrow the U.S. government during the 1930s because of the policies of the Roosevelt administration. (The du Ponts later made their peace with Roosevelt, as symbolized by the 1937 marriage of the president's son to Ethel du Pont, granddaughter of Eugene du Pont, who ran the company in the late nineteenth century.) The company also was slow in ending its ties to Nazi Germany and Japan.

By the time the United States entered World War II, however, the company was brimming with patriotism. In addition to selling its usual products to the military, the company was chosen in 1942 to oversee the development of the atomic bomb. Du Pont built facilities for the bomb's production, lent many of its scientists to the effort, and in effect managed the Manhattan Project. After the war the company was called on to manage the Savannah River nuclear weapons plant in South Carolina, which it did until 1989.

After World War II Du Pont expanded its investment in the South and used its political muscle to help ensure that that region remained largely antiunion and probusiness. Among the new products being made were Orlon, an acrylic fiber; Dacron, a polyester fiber; and Mylar, a polyester film.

On the national level, the company and the du Pont family faced an antitrust suit brought by the Justice Department in 1949. The government charged that General Motors was simply too large an economic force to be controlled by one family or financial group. Du Pont used an elaborate public relations campaign to present an innocent image of itself and also managed to win over the judge in a juryless trial.

In 1955, less than a year after the favorable verdict, Du Pont took the brazen step of announcing that it would increase its holdings in GM by $75 million. This time the Delaware dynasty had gone too far. Even within the business community there was dismay over the move, and in 1957 the Supreme Court overturned the judge's ruling and declared that Du Pont's control of GM was indeed in violation of the antitrust law. Four years later the high court ordered Du Pont to sell its holdings in GM over the course of ten years. Because of the effect that such a sale would have on the stock market, even spread out over a decade, the company decided to distribute its sixty-three million GM shares to Du Pont stockholders. The process was completed in 1965.

Although Du Pont had enjoyed cooperative arrangements with foreign companies for many years, it was not until the late 1950s that it began to establish a direct presence abroad. An international department was set up in 1958, and soon the company had plants in such countries as Ireland, Belgium, the Netherlands, Mexico, Brazil, and Argentina.

The Vietnam War brought another period of prosperity for Du Pont, and the company introduced such new products as the fibers Lycra, Nomex, Tyvek, Qiana, and Kevlar (later to become famous for its use in bulletproof vests). It also entered the precision instrument field and began to get involved in pharmaceuticals. Yet by the late 1960s, conditions began to deteriorate. The company faced overcapacity and increased competition, both domestic and foreign, in its fibers business. Corfam, a synthetic leather the company had spent $60 million to develop, was a flop. There was unrest among the poor black population of Wilmington. A group of researchers working with Ralph Nader published an unflattering book on the company's stranglehold over the state of Delaware. And Du Pont was coming under public criticism for its production of ozone-destroying fluorocarbons.

Such an array of problems prompted the Du Pont board to take the remarkable step of elevating Irving Shapiro to the chairmanship of the company. Not only was Shapiro not a relative, but he was a lawyer, a Jew (the du Ponts had a history of anti-Semitism), and a Democrat. What he did offer was a knack for solving problems and for advancing the interests of the company in Washington. During the 1970s he led the company's challenge to various environmental regulations and ended up as the major spokesman for business during the Carter administration, a period when corporate interests became exceedingly bold in advancing their agendas in Washington.

Soon after Shapiro's retirement in 1981, his successor, Edward Jefferson, took the company in a new direction by joining in what would become an epic battle for Continental Oil Company, known as Conoco. That company, founded as Continental Oil and Transportation Company in Utah in 1875, was later absorbed into Standard Oil and regained its independence after the Rockefeller trust was broken up in 1913. Conoco acquired Consolidation Coal in 1966 and during the 1970s began oil and gas production in the North Sea.

The takeover saga began when the Canadian company Dome Petroleum bid for 20 percent of Conoco's shares in an effort to get at its Canadian oil reserves. All of Conoco was put in play as Seagram made an unwanted offer for an even larger portion of the company. The management of Conoco turned to Du Pont, a company with which it already had a joint exploration agreement, and asked it to serve as a white knight. The bidding war that ensued involved Mobil as well. After the dust settled, Du Pont was the winner, with what was at the time an unprecedented offer of $7.2 billion. Du Pont, however, had to hand over more than 20 percent of its own shares to Seagram in order to obtain that company's holdings in Conoco. Since that time, Seagram and the Bronfman family, which now controls five of eighteen seats on Du Pont's board, have played a central role in the affairs of the Wilmington company.

During the 1980s Du Pont formed a large number of joint ventures, among them an arrangement with Japan's Idemitsu Petrochemical Company to produce butanediol, with Mitsubishi Gas Chemical to make pyromellitic dianhydride, with Philips to market optical discs (this partnership later dissolved), and with Imperial Chemical Industries to sell automotive products. The company also has built up a large health business through such moves as buying an interest in companies developing diagnostic tests for AIDS and signing marketing agreements with several large drug companies. A major move into the electronic-imaging business has yet to pay off. In 1987 the company abandoned its explosives operations in the United States and Canada.

Fibers were not forgotten during this period: Du Pont led a successful effort to transform polyester's frumpy image to that of a high-fashion material. The company used heavy advertising to expand the market for its Stainmaster carpet fibers (made from a mixture of nylon and Teflon). Lycra spandex, originally intended for use in girdles, became popular in biking shorts and other exercise wear while also being adopted by several top-name clothing designers.

In 1990 Du Pont put its $500-million pharmaceutical business into a joint venture with Merck. The combined operation is marketing Du Pont's Percodan painkiller, Coumadin heart medication, and two other drugs, along with three medications from Merck. Facing weakness in numerous areas, Du Pont announced in July 1991 that it would cut at least $1 billion in fixed costs, including several thousand jobs, by the end of 1992.

OPERATIONS

Chemicals (9 percent of 1991 revenues). This segment consists of a wide range of commodity and specialty products, including titanium dioxide, used in paints and coatings; Freon and other fluorochemicals; polymer intermediates; acid products; peroxygens and additive chemicals used in such industries as paper, petroleum, textiles, and mining.

Fibers (16 percent of revenues). Included here are a variety of specialty fibers used for clothing (Dacron, Lycra, and so on), protective apparel (Kevlar), carpeting (Stainmaster), and industrial applications like tire reinforcement, health care, and aerospace.

Polymers (14 percent of revenues). Du Pont produces a diversified assortment of engineering polymers (for appliances, machinery, and so on), elastomers (including synthetic rubber), fluoropolymers (used in Teflon cookware and industrial applications like wire and cable), ethylene polymers (packaging, adhesives, and so on), auto finishes, and related products, such as Lucite and Mylar.

Petroleum (41 percent of revenues). The Conoco subsidiary is a fully integrated international petroleum company. Its crude oil production is located in the United States, Canada, Europe, the Middle East, and the Asia-Pacific region. Conoco has proven reserves of more than one billion barrels of oil and nearly four trillion cubic feet of natural gas.

Coal (5 percent of revenues). Consolidation Coal's operations consist of mining steam coal that is sold mainly to electric utilities and metallurgical coal that is sold to steel producers. Coal production is located in ten states and in Canada, the largest portion coming from West Virginia. The company has proven and probable reserves of more than five billion tons. In 1991 Du Pont agreed to sell a 50-percent stake in Consolidation to the German company Rheinbraun AG for a price that analysts estimated at roughly $1 billion.

Diversified Businesses (15 percent of revenues). This segment consists of agricultural products (herbicides, fungicides, and insecticides); electronic components (subassemblies and printed circuit boards); imaging systems (photographic and printing materials and systems); medical products (diagnostic imaging, in vitro diagnostics, and pharmaceuticals); and Remington firearms.

TOP EXECUTIVES

- Edgar S. Woolard, Jr., chairman and chief executive
- John A. Krol, vice chairman
- Constantine S. Nicandros, vice chairman; chief executive of Conoco

OUTSIDE DIRECTORS

- Percy N. Barnevik, chief executive of ABB Asea Brown Boveri
- Andrew F. Brimmer, president of the economic consulting firm Brimmer & Company

- Charles R. Bronfman, cochairman of Seagram
- Edgar M. Bronfman, chief executive of Seagram
- Edgar Bronfman, Jr., president and chief operating officer of Seagram
- Louisa C. Duemling, director of the World Resources Institute
- Edward B. du Pont, chairman of Atlantic Aviation Corporation
- Charles M. Harper, chief executive of ConAgra
- Howard W. Johnson, president emeritus of MIT
- E. Leo Kolber, chairman of the Canadian holding company Claridge Inc.
- Dean R. McKay, member of the advisory board of IBM
- Margaret P. MacKimm, former senior vice president of Kraft General Foods
- John L. Weinberg, senior chairman of Goldman Sachs

The board also includes former chief executive Richard E. Heckert.

FINANCIAL DATA

Revenues (in millions of dollars)

1991	38,031
1990	39,589
1989	35,099
1988	31,957
1987	29,687

Net Income (in millions of dollars)

1991	1,403
1990	2,310
1989	2,480
1988	2,190
1987	1,786

GEOGRAPHICAL BREAKDOWN

Revenues (in millions of dollars)

Year	United States		Europe		Elsewhere	
1991	24,076	(57%)	13,419	(32%)	4,462	(11%)
1990	25,107	(58%)	13,424	(31%)	4,714	(11%)
1989	23,865	(62%)	10,610	(27%)	4,175	(11%)
1988	21,834	(62%)	9,648	(27%)	3,727	(11%)

After-Tax Operating Income (in millions of dollars)

Year	United States		Europe		Elsewhere	
1991	938	(49%)	961	(51%)	−50	(0%)
1990	1,442	(52%)	1,215	(43%)	138	(5%)
1989	1,985	(69%)	777	(27%)	119	(4%)
1988	1,607	(65%)	653	(27%)	194	(8%)

LABOR RELATIONS

Throughout its long history Du Pont has been driven by a strong antiunion animus. The company successfully warded off independent organizing among its employees through a combination of intimidation (extensive networks of spies were used in plants to identify and eliminate "malcontents") and paternalism (the company was a leader in the introduction of such fringe benefits as employer-paid pension plans). Yet according to author Gerard Colby, the company abruptly terminated famed sharpshooter Annie Oakley without a pension after she worked for more than thirty years testing and promoting the company's sporting gunpowder.

Union-organizing efforts—including some by the United Mine Workers' old District 50 in the late 1930s—were crushed mercilessly at Du Pont. Once the labor movement made collective bargaining inevitable, Du Pont responded by fostering the creation of company-dominated employee associations. While these evolved into organizations that were technically unions, they operated at an extremely low level of militancy. The 1973 Nader study of Du Pont (*The Company State*, by James Phelan and Robert Pozen) quoted an official of one of these unions as saying, "We're not company dominated. We're so weak the company doesn't have to dominate us." One major union, the International Chemical Workers, did manage to organize a few Du Pont facilities.

The company sought to keep these independent unions isolated from one another, even though they became joined in the Federation of Independent Unions–Du Pont Systems. When the local at a plant in Niagara Falls, New York, went on strike in 1970, no other locals staged any job actions in support—even though Du Pont brought in employees from other plants to serve as strikebreakers. The company encouraged promanagement employees to bring about a change in the leadership of the Niagara Falls local, and after six months the strike ended ignominiously with a sweetheart contract.

Some of the unions joined forces with Nader in the 1970s to challenge the company's pension policies and other practices. Many employees were sympathetic to the organizing efforts of the United Steelworkers during the 1970s. Yet Du Pont continued to do things its own way. When elections were held at fourteen plants in 1981, the United Steelworkers were defeated—due, in no small part, to the firing of activists and other unfair labor practices by

Du Pont. The company also has continued to take a tough line with the independent unions.

Du Pont has refused to negotiate with the unions on some legally mandatory subjects of bargaining and has strongly resisted any forms of coordination by the different locals. When the union at Old Hickory, Tennessee, in the early 1980s demanded data on wage rates at Du Pont's other textile plants, the company refused, even after the National Labor Relations Board (NLRB) ordered it to supply the information. And when the members of the Ampthill Rayon Workers union at the Spruance plant in Richmond, Virginia, voted in November 1985 to affiliate with the United Steelworkers, the company insisted on negotiating only with the independent union. Du Pont also resisted recognizing the International Brotherhood of Du Pont Workers, formed in 1981. It did, however, inherit some contracts with the Oil, Chemical and Atomic Workers after taking over Conoco.

In 1988 the company introduced an unusual incentive plan for all employees in its fibers business. The scheme, designed to raise productivity and foster a team environment, tied everyone's pay, from hourly workers to the group vice president, to the unit's profitability. The firm's unionized workers, for whom the plan was voluntary, had mixed feelings about it; nonunion workers had no choice but to participate. In late 1990 the plan was dropped amid frustration among employees at the loss of part of their raises because of industrywide conditions that were depressing profitability in the fibers business. A year later the company introduced a stock-option plan for most of its employees.

In 1991 the NLRB charged that the company was using workplace committees, which were supposed to discuss matters like safety, to bypass unions and unlawfully implement changes in working conditions.

ENVIRONMENTAL AND HEALTH RECORD

The business of Du Pont has been dangerous from the start. The black powder that the company produced during its early decades was extremely volatile, and fatal explosions were a frequent occurrence for its work force. So perilous was the powder that the company had difficulty getting ships and trains to transport it to customers. For a long time the most common means of conveyance was the mule train, although that became controversial after three Du Pont wagons loaded with 450 kegs of powder exploded in 1854 while traveling through the middle of Wilmington, Delaware, killing the drivers, the mules, and several bystanders while also digging a large crater in the street. Many towns consequently passed ordinances barring powder wagons from their thoroughfares.

Du Pont has continued to expose its employees to extremely dangerous working conditions and frequently has run afoul of occupational safety and health laws. In the 1920s there was a controversy over the deaths of eight Du Pont workers and the poisoning of several hundred others in connection with the production of tetraethyl lead for gasoline. Similar conditions arose at a plant of Standard Oil of New Jersey (now Exxon), which was producing gasoline with the tetraethyl lead in a joint venture, called Ethyl Gasoline Corporation, with General Motors, then controlled by Du Pont.

During the early 1970s, evidence began to emerge of high levels of bladder cancer among Du Pont production workers, especially at the Chambers Works in New Jersey. Since at least the 1930s there had been evidence linking beta-nephthylamine (BNA), a chemical used in dye bases, to cancer. Yet the company went on producing BNA at Chambers until 1955, and after it was dropped, Du Pont went on making benzidine, another carcinogen, for ten more years.

In 1987 a New Jersey Superior Court jury found that Du Pont officials and company doctors had deliberately concealed medical records that showed that six veteran maintenance workers had asbestos-related diseases linked to their jobs. Also in 1987, Du Pont subsidiary Consolidation Coal was cited by the Mine Safety and Health Administration for "reckless disregard" in failing to report worker injuries. Conoco paid $250,000 in 1988 to settle charges brought by the EPA for air pollution violations. In 1991 Consolidation was among a group of coal companies fined for falsifying air samples provided to federal inspectors testing for conditions that could cause black lung disease.

Du Pont was also at the center of a controversy regarding the practice of genetic screening. A series of articles in the *New York Times* in 1980 revealed that many major companies in the chemical and related industries had begun testing employees to determine which ones might have a genetic makeup that made them more susceptible to toxics and carcinogens they might be exposed to in the workplace. Among these, Du Pont was cited as the only firm that gave blood tests to black job applicants to determine which ones were carriers of the trait for sickle-cell anemia. Although Du Pont defended the practice, there were accusations later that the company had pressured the *Times* to demote the writer of the article, Richard Severo.

In the mid-1970s Du Pont was put on the defensive by growing evidence that Freon, used in aerosol cans and in refrigerants, was contributing to the destruction of the earth's ozone layer. The company found its own experts, who downplayed the danger of CFCs like Freon. At the same time, Du Pont officials warned that curtailing production could result in the loss of several hundred thousand jobs. It was not until the late 1980s, after more than a decade of resistance, that the company conceded that CFCs might be a problem. In 1988 Du Pont announced with great fanfare that it would phase out production of Freon and other CFCs, but environmental groups charged the company with moving too slowly and warned that some of the substitutes Du Pont was introducing for CFCs were also harmful to the ozone layer. A newspaper in Wilmington, Delaware, reported in 1991 that Du Pont had used human subjects during the 1960s in experiments on the use of Freon for dry-cleaning women's hair.

In 1989 evidence emerged that the Savannah River nuclear weapons plant, which Du Pont had built and operated for the federal government since 1951, had serious structural flaws and safety problems that the company had failed to report. Numerous accidents at the plant, which made plutonium and the tritium gas needed in nuclear warheads, were kept secret as well. The Department of Energy tried to exonerate the company by saying that the problems had been reported and that it was the government that had kept them secret. A number of former government officials, however, said they had never been informed. The facility was turned over to Westinghouse in 1989.

Most of Du Pont's facilities are responsible for substantial emissions of toxics into the land, water, and air. In 1991 the company was fined $1.9 milllion for dumping corrosive acids and toxic solvents at the Chambers Works. Analysis of EPA data by the Citizens Fund has found that Du Pont has the largest aggregate amount of toxic releases of any industrial company in the United States.

BIBLIOGRAPHY

Carr, William H. A. *The du Ponts of Delaware*. New York: Dodd, Mead, 1964.

Chandler, Alfred D., Jr., and Stephen Salsbury. *Pierre S. duPont and the Making of the Modern Corporation*. New York: Harper & Row, 1971.

Colby, Gerard. *Du Pont Dynasty*. Secaucus, N.J.: Lyle Stuart, 1984. (This is a revised and updated version of a book called *Du Pont: Behind the Nylon Curtain*, which the author published under the name Gerard Colby Zilg in 1974. Promotion of the book abruptly ended after du Pont family members complained to the publisher, Prentice-Hall.)

Du Pont: The Autobiography of an Enterprise. Wilmington, Del.: Du Pont, 1952.

Du Pont Fiddles While the World Burns: Industry Inaction on Ozone Depletion. Washington, D.C.: U.S. Public Interest Research Group, 1989.

Hold the Applause! A Case Study of Corporate Environmentalism as Practiced at Du Pont. Washington, D.C.: Friends of the Earth, 1991.

Mosley, Leonard. *Blood Relations: The Rise and Fall of the du Ponts of Delaware*. New York: Atheneum, 1980.

Phelan, James, and Robert Pozen. *The Company State: Ralph Nader's Study Group Report on Du Pont in Delaware*. New York: Grossman, 1973.

Taylor, Graham D., and Patricia E. Sudnik. *Du Pont and the International Chemical Industry*. Boston: G. K. Hall, 1984.

EASTMAN KODAK COMPANY

343 State Street
Rochester, New York 14650
(716) 724-4000

1991 revenues: $19.4 billion
1991 net income: $17 million
Publicly traded company
Employees: 133,200
Founded: 1880

OVERVIEW

Although numerous companies are chipping away at its status, Eastman Kodak remains the world leader in the big business of picture taking. For a century its yellow boxes of film have been a familiar sight to amateurs and professionals alike. (The company itself is often called Big Yellow.) In fact, it was company founder George Eastman who created widespread amateur photography with a succession of easy-to-use cameras and films. Devices like the Brownie and the Instamatic allowed the average person to record both significant events and moments of fun with a minimum of skill and bother.

Kodak also has had its share of failures, such as its late entry into the instant photography market and the resulting patent infringement suit brought by Polaroid, which cost Kodak more than $900 million. The company's disc camera was another disappointment, and various Japanese companies took the lead in the 35-mm camera market.

The top management of Kodak sought to cope with these challenges by buying into new businesses, forming joint ventures, and carrying out sweeping structural changes in the company, including the abandonment of its long tradition of lifetime job security. The $5-billion purchase of Sterling Drug in 1988 gave the company a bigger foothold in the health business but also imposed a heavy financial burden.

HISTORY

In the 1870s George Eastman, a young bookkeeper at the Rochester Savings Bank in upstate New York, developed an interest in photography. The mechanical reproduction of images was advancing steadily in the nineteenth century, but when Eastman adopted his new hobby, taking pictures was still a cumbersome process involving heavy equipment and a variety of chemicals.

Despite his amateur status, Eastman developed a method for coating photographic plates with emulsion, thereby replacing the messy wet plates with dry ones. To produce and distribute these dry plates he established a company in 1880.

Eastman's major contribution came in 1888, when he introduced a small-box camera that was so easy to use that it ended the monopoly of the professional photographer and put picture taking into the hands of the masses. The devices were sold under the brand Kodak (a name invented by Eastman) and marketed with the soon-to-be-famous line, "You press the button—we do the rest."

The Kodaks, as they came to be called, were a sensation. Soon the boxes and their carrying cases were standard equipment on outings and vacations and at family events. Having one's picture taken—which had previously been an uncomfortable experience involving the need to stay absolutely still for long stretches—was suddenly enjoyable.

The roll of film in the camera could be used for one hundred shots before the whole device had to be returned to Kodak for processing. Yet it was not long before the company introduced film cartridges that could be processed by the new photofinishing operations that were springing up.

Kodak's celluloid roll film was also instrumental in the development of the first practical motion picture camera—Thomas Edison's kinetograph. The corresponding viewing device, called the Kinetoscope, was first demonstrated in New York in 1894. Eastman also helped spread the use of X rays. Soon after Wilhelm Roentgen discovered the properties of the rays, Eastman developed photographic plates that could record X-ray images.

At the same time, the company—which in 1892 was renamed Eastman Kodak—was making photography increasingly simple and convenient. In 1900 an even smaller box camera was introduced. Priced at one dollar and named Brownie, the device was immensely popular, especially with youngsters. Color film began to appear just before World War I, and the first home movie cameras and projectors were introduced by Kodak in 1923. A color movie system came five years later.

During those early years Eastman Kodak grew rapidly, initially by extending the sale of its products to more corners of the globe. A London sales office was opened in the mid-1880s, and by the end of that decade there was a British subsidiary, which was soon manufacturing Kodak products as well as selling them in many countries outside the United States.

Kodak also expanded by taking over many of its smaller competitors. A 1921 court ruling forced Kodak to divest six of the companies it had acquired and to end the practice of requiring Kodak dealers to sell exclusively Kodak products at fixed prices. Later the company also ran into legal problems because of the dominance it and Technicolor Corporation enjoyed in the field of color cinematography.

Eastman Kodak inspired and benefited from the increasing importance of photography in the twentieth century. Spot news photos, aerial photography, advertising images, and the rise of illustrated magazines like *Life* all contributed to the company's growing prominence as the leader of the industry.

The company's amateur photography business was especially buoyant after World War II. Rising living standards and reduced working hours allowed people more leisure time, and their activities almost always included the taking of snapshots. Also, competition was limited. The German camera industry, which had begun to challenge Kodak in the early part of the century, was in disarray.

But this charmed existence for Eastman Kodak was not lasting. The company was again faced with antitrust problems. The charge was that the practice of including the cost of processing in the price of Kodachrome film restrained trade in the photo-finishing industry. As part of a 1955 consent decree, the company ended the practice and released the formulas necessary to process the film.

Competition also began to intensify in the late 1950s as Japanese companies began producing high-quality, low-priced 35-mm cameras. Kodak fought back with the Instamatic, a compact and extremely easy-to-use device that ushered in a new snapshot craze. Some seventy million of these "point and shoot" cameras, including a pocket version introduced in 1972, were sold during the 1960s and 1970s.

Emboldened by this success, in 1976 the company plunged into the instant photography market pioneered by Polaroid. Although Kodak said it had developed its own techniques, Polaroid sued, embroiling the two companies in an epic lawsuit. In 1985 a federal judge ruled that Kodak's instant film and cameras infringed on some of Polaroid's patents. The following year, after losing its appeal, Kodak was obliged to remove its product from the market and recall the sixteen million cameras in the hands of consumers. In 1991 the two companies finally settled the dispute, with Kodak agreeing to pay Polaroid a whopping $925 million in damages.

While the Polaroid suit was pending, Kodak also had some disappointment with a more original innovation: the Disc system it introduced in 1982. The tiny cameras, with discs rather than rolls of film inside, were supposed to join the list of historic Kodak products. Some twenty-five million were sold—far fewer than had been projected—and photo finishers resisted the new format.

Part of the problem was the rise of the new low-cost, highly automated 35-mm cameras promoted by the Japanese producers. Kodak, which had abandoned the 35-mm market amid the success of the Instamatic in the 1960s, moved back in, but it had a hard time catching up to the likes of Nikon and Minolta.

In the 1980s Kodak also confronted increasing competition in the film market, especially from Japan's Fuji Photo Film Company, which humiliated Kodak by winning the sponsorship of the 1984 Los Angeles Olympics. At the same time, growth in the amateur picture-taking market began to decline.

To regain the allegiance of serious photographers, Kodak introduced the high-speed Kodacolor Gold 1000 film and the fine-grain Ektar line. The company also began producing the controversial Fling and other disposable cameras.

Kodak made a major foray into the health-care field in 1988, when the company acted as a white knight for Sterling Drug, which was being pursued by the Swiss pharmaceutical house Hoffmann–La Roche. Kodak paid more than $5 billion for Sterling, best known as the U.S. producer of Bayer aspirin. Sterling acquired the business seven decades ago in an auction of the American interests of the German chemical company Bayer, which had been seized by the U.S. government during World War I. Sterling went on to develop a reputation for aggressive marketing and frequent run-ins with federal regulators.

In an attempt to navigate the perilous waters of the 1980s, Kodak embarked on an ambitious project of restructuring and diversification. Special emphasis was placed on electronics and biotechnology. In the former area the company made a $20-million investment in Sun Microsystems and used that firm's well-regarded workstations in an electronic-publishing system Kodak put on the market. Companies making floppy disks and digital image-processing equipment were acquired, and three joint ventures in biotechnology were established.

Most recently Kodak has sought to protect its film and photo-finishing businesses from the threat posed by the all-electronic cameras introduced by various Japanese companies. The solution is a system that uses traditional photographic film and allows consumers to convert their pictures into electronic images that would be stored on compact discs. With the use of the appropriate equipment the images could be displayed on a television screen or computer display.

OPERATIONS

Imaging (36 percent of 1991 revenues). Kodak's best-known products are used for capturing, recording, and displaying photographic images. These products—most of which are made in and around Rochester—include cameras, projectors, other audiovisual equipment, films, processing services, photographic papers, batteries, and chemicals. Other manufacturing facilities are located in Australia, Brazil, Canada, France, Mexico, and the United Kingdom.

For more than a decade Kodak has had to contend with a rising challenge to its film business from Japan's Fuji. After a long time on the defensive, Big Yellow turned the tables by making a major offensive in Fuji's home market, where it has long been as dominant as Kodak has been in the United States. Yet Kodak has been unable to win more than 10 percent of the Japanese market for color film. In addition, Fuji has been steadily increasing its market share in Europe, where it is taking on both Kodak and the lower-profile Agfa-Gevaert of Germany. Kodak, in turn, has been taking great pains to woo back professional photographers in the United States who defected to Fuji.

Kodak is leading the way in combining film and electronic imaging with its new Photo CD system, which digitizes photographs to extremely high resolution and allows the image to be analyzed, displayed, stored, and transmitted in much more sophisticated ways. The system is expected to be available to consumers in 1992. Kodak announced plans in 1991 to purchase the Image Bank, a leading agency for stock photographs.

Information (20 percent of revenues). The roots of this segment of Kodak's operations, which consists of businesses that serve the imaging and information needs of business, industry, and government, go back to the early decades of this century. Microfilming began with the 1928 founding of the Recordak Corporation. Kodak entered the photocopier business in 1952, but its Verifax device employed technology that lost out to competing methods. Yet starting in 1975 the company introduced a line of high-powered copiers with the name Ektaprint. In 1981 Kodak acquired Atex Inc., a leading supplier of text-editing systems for publishers. The purchase of Verbatim Corporation in 1985 instantly made Kodak one of the leading producers of floppy disks; nonetheless, that business was sold in 1990.

Today's products include graphic arts film, microfilm, high-end copiers, printers, and other business equipment. The main production facilities are in Rochester, New York, and in Windsor, Colorado, as well as in Germany, Mexico, and the United Kingdom.

Among the new products are the company's first fully digital copier, the Ektaplus 7016 multifunction printer (which works with both IBM-compatible and Macintosh machines), and the Diconix ink-jet color printer. Kodak has also introduced the widely accepted PhotoYCC software standard for translating color into electronic form. The company's Atex products, however, are steadily being overtaken by systems using desktop publishing software.

In addition, the Photo CD technology is being marketed to business users, with applications in such fields as desktop publishing, graphics design, architecture, and interior design.

Chemicals (18 percent of revenues). The main products of this segment, which dates back to the creation of the Tennessee Eastman Company in 1920 to manufacture wood alcohol, are olefin, acetyl, polyester, and specialty and fine chemicals. Olefin consists of ethylene and propylene, which are used as intermediates in the manufacturing of alcohols, solvents, and plasticizers sold to makers of paint, chemical, and plastics. Acetyl products are used in a variety of processes that result in acetate yarn, photographic film base, cellulosic plastics, and other substances.

Polyester products—which began with the establishment of the Carolina Eastman Company in 1968—are used for beverage bottles, threads, and some film base. The specialty products include photographic chemicals, health and nutrition products, and high-technology organic chemicals. Chemical facilities are located in New York (Rochester), Tennessee, Texas, South Carolina, Arkansas, and in Canada and the United Kingdom.

Health (25 percent of revenues). This segment includes X-ray film and supplies as well as blood analyzers, pharmaceuticals, over-the-counter drugs, and household, personal-care, and do-it-yourself products. These products are manufactured in numerous states and in Canada, France, Germany, Puerto Rico, and the United Kingdom.

The best-known consumer brands in the health segment, which consists largely of Sterling's operations, include Bayer aspirin, Midol pain relievers, Phillips' Milk of Magnesia, and Lysol disinfectants.

Sterling has turned out to be something of an albatross for Kodak. Its drug development process ran into obstacles, and its leading products faced intensified competition. To bolster the struggling company, in 1991 Kodak combined Sterling's operations with those of the French company Sanofi S.A., a majority of which is owned by Société Nationale Elf Aquitaine, the state-controlled oil and chemical group. Kodak subsequently renamed its subsidiary Sterling Winthrop Inc.

TOP EXECUTIVES

- Kay R. Whitmore, chairman, president, and chief executive
- Paul L. Smith, senior vice president
- Leo J. Thomas, president of the imaging division
- Wilbur J. Prezzano, president of the health division
- Earnest W. Deavenport, Jr., president of the chemical division

OUTSIDE DIRECTORS

- Richard S. Braddock, president of Citicorp
- John F. Burlingame, vice chairman emeritus of General Electric
- Colby H. Chandler, former chairman of Eastman Kodak
- Martha Layne Collins, president of St. Catharine College
- Charles T. Duncan, senior counsel to the law firm Reid & Priest
- Alice F. Emerson, former president of Wheaton College
- Roberto C. Goizueta, chairman and chief executive of Coca-Cola

- Paul E. Gray, chairman of the Corporation of the Massachusetts Institute of Technology
- John J. Phelan, Jr., former chairman of New York Stock Exchange
- Richard A. Zimmerman, chairman and chief executive of Hershey Foods

FINANCIAL DATA

Revenues (in millions of dollars)

1991	19,419
1990	18,908
1989	18,398
1988	17,034
1987	13,305

Net Income (in millions of dollars)

1991	17*
1990	703†
1989	529‡
1988	1,397
1987	1,178

*After deducting $1.6 billion in restructuring costs.
†After deducting $888 million related to a litigation judgment (and postjudgment interest), which reduced net earnings by $564 million.
‡After deducting restructuring costs of $875 million, which reduced net earnings by $549 million.

GEOGRAPHICAL BREAKDOWN

Revenues (in millions of dollars)

Year	United States		Europe		Elsewhere	
1991	10,882	(56%)	5,053	(26%)	3,484	(18%)
1990	10,663	(56%)	5,165	(27%)	3,080	(16%)
1989	10,869	(59%)	4,556	(25%)	2,973	(16%)

Earnings from Operations (in millions of dollars)

Year	United States		Europe		Elsewhere	
1991	108	(14%)	222	(29%)	448	(58%)
1990	1,698	(60%)	675	(24%)	474	(17%)
1989	785	(49%)	470	(30%)	337	(21%)

LABOR RELATIONS

Eastman Kodak has long prided itself as a good employer. George Eastman was a pioneer in the practice of profit sharing and that of soliciting ideas from workers for the improvement of the production process. Such paternalism by the "Great Yellow Father" has allowed the company to remain union-free (though it inherited several contracts after taking over Sterling Drug).

In the wake of the thousands of layoffs in the mid-1980s, however, the International Union of Electronic Workers (IUE) initiated efforts to organize workers at Kodak. But that campaign has yet to result in any union contracts.

In 1990 Kodak instituted a so-called tin parachute plan, which guaranteed all employees severance pay, health insurance, and other benefits if they were to lose their jobs as a result of a change in ownership of the company. The primary purpose of the plan was to deter potential raiders by sharply escalating the cost of a takeover.

ENVIRONMENTAL RECORD

The company's relatively clean image was sullied in 1987, when tests at Kodak's main facilities in Rochester revealed that toxic chemicals were migrating into the groundwater of nearby residential neighborhoods, where some households were reporting chemical smells in their basements. Corporate and local officials downplayed the risks, but Kodak responded vigorously. The company announced a $100-million program to upgrade chemical storage tanks, set up a program to stabilize property values in the affected area, and promised to pay for all environmental testing.

This was a reasonable corporate response to an environmental problem, but Kodak found itself under increased pressure in 1988, when thirty thousand gallons of liquid methylene chloride spilled near a school. Tests conducted in 1989 showed that this substance—regarded as a probable carcinogen by the EPA—and eleven other dangerous chemicals were present in local groundwater in amounts exceeding state guidelines.

In 1990, after a state grand jury investigation, Kodak pleaded guilty to two misdemeanor violations of New York State environmental law and paid $2 million in criminal and civil fines. It also agreed to reduce its methylene chloride releases and to allow an independent review of its environmental record. The case stemmed from both spillage of methylene chloride and a 1986 incident in which Kodak contracted with an unauthorized company to dispose of some fifty thousand pounds of contaminated soil.

Kodak has responded to criticism of its solid-waste impact—especially that of its disposable cameras—by instituting a program for collecting and recycling metal film cartridges and the plastic containers they are distributed in.

Rochester is not the only Kodak location with environmental problems. According to 1989 EPA data tabulated by the Citizens Fund, Kodak was responsible for the ninth-largest volume (some seventy-nine million pounds) of toxic releases among all industrial companies in the United States. When the analysis is limited solely to releases of known or suspected carcinogenic substances, Kodak had the third-highest volume of releases.

BIBLIOGRAPHY

Collins, Douglas. *The Story of Kodak*. New York: Harry N. Abrams, 1990.
Mann, Charles C., and Mark L. Plummer. *The Aspirin Wars: Money, Medicine, and 100 Years of Rampant Competition*. New York: Alfred A. Knopf, 1991.

ELECTROLUX AB

Lilla Essingen
S-105 45 Stockholm
Sweden
(8) 738 60 00

1991 revenues: $14.3 billion
1991 net income: $68.1 million
Publicly traded company
Employees: 134,229
Founded: 1901

OVERVIEW

As a result of three decades of aggressive buying, Electrolux has transformed itself into one of the world's leading producers of white goods (that is, appliances like refrigerators, ranges, and washing machines). Demolishing the idea that cultural differences prevented appliance makers from selling abroad, Electrolux made itself the first truly global producer in the industry. It owns more than six hundred operating companies in forty countries.

The hundreds of firms collected by Electrolux—which itself is nearly 50-percent owned by the Swedish company ASEA AB—represent many businesses beyond Electrolux's traditional focus on vacuum cleaners and refrigerators. It is, for example, the world's largest producer of chain saws and a leading manufacturer of automobile safety belts.

Electrolux leads the appliance market in Europe but faces tough competition both from a joint venture of Bosch and Siemens and from the U.S. company Whirlpool, which in 1989 formed a joint venture with Philips and two years later bought out the Dutch company's share. In the United States, where Electrolux lags behind General Electric and Whirlpool, it is not able to market products under its own name, the rights to which were sold off long ago.

HISTORY

Electrolux has its origins in two companies founded early in the century. AB Lux, created in 1901, launched the Lux lamp, a kerosene-powered device for outdoor lighting in harsh conditions. The product was well received and ended up being widely used in lighthouses as well. In 1910 another electrical products firm, Elektromekaniska AB, was established. Soon both companies were producing copies of a new-fangled device from America: the vacuum cleaner.

The man responsible for uniting these two companies and putting them on the path to success was a salesman and promoter by the name of Axel Wenner-Gren. In 1910, while working for a predecessor of the Swedish company Alfa-Laval, he was inspired by an American-made vacuum cleaner he saw in Vienna. Convinced that there was a huge potential market for lightweight cleaners, he eventually returned to Sweden and managed to engineer a joint venture between Lux and Elektromekaniska to exploit that market.

The Lux I, introduced in 1913, was well received, but Wenner-Gren was not satisfied. He pushed for a lighter and less-expensive product, which is what he got with the Lux II, which came out a year later. Further improvements followed regularly, but what made Elektrolux—the company formed by the 1919 merger of the joint-venture partners—was not technology but salesmanship. Wenner-Gren, by this time president of the company, sent salesmen out to ring doorbells all over Sweden. They demonstrated the product and clinched their hard sell by arranging for the customer to pay in installments.

Under the slogan "Every home an Elektrolux home," Wenner-Gren began expanding abroad, beginning with Denmark and, during the 1920s, extending throughout Europe. In his most famous feat of marketing prowess, Wenner-Gren himself persuaded Pope Pius XI to allow Elektrolux vacuums to be used in the Vatican by agreeing to take care of the cleaning for a year, free of charge.

There was some concern about the rapid growth of the company when Elektrolux went public in 1930. Yet the firm managed to go on expanding, aided by the company's 1925 purchase of Arctic AB, a Swedish company that pioneered the development of the refrigerator. The international presence of Elektrolux also was enhanced by the establishment of manufacturing operations abroad, starting with Germany in 1926. U.S. vacuum cleaner production began in Connecticut in 1931.

Operations were inhibited by World War II, but Elektrolux did manage to continue its diversification by purchasing companies that produced laundry equipment for apartment houses and outboard motors. After the war Elektrolux introduced a washing machine for households, along with freezers, dishwashers, a new generation of refrigerators, and other appliances. In 1957 the spelling of the company's name was changed to Electrolux. The large electrical firm ASEA, controlled by leading Swedish industrialist Marcus Wallenberg and now part of ABB ASEA Brown Boveri, bought a major stake in the company in the mid-1960s.

Wallenberg pushed the rather stodgy company to think big. Yet these new global ambitions came up against the fact that the white goods business was dominated by a handful of much larger corporations, such as Siemens, Philips, and Zanussi. Hans Werthén, who took over as president in 1967 at Wallenberg's behest, embraced a strategy of making it to the major league through acquisition. The process began with the purchase of Elektra, the Norwegian range manufacturer owned by ASEA. This was soon followed by Atlas, a Danish maker of refrigerators.

The buying spree was interrupted by a divestiture—the sale of 39 percent of American Electrolux to Consolidated Foods (now Sara Lee Corporation). Several years later Consolidated made a bid for all of Electrolux, but the Swedish minister of finance quashed the deal.

The company proceeded to acquire numerous small and medium-sized appliance companies as well as firms in other industries. The most significant example of the latter was the ailing Swedish office equipment manufacturer Facit, which Electrolux held on to for ten difficult years. After unloading Facit in 1974 the company returned to the United States, purchasing rival vacuum cleaner manufacturer Eureka and the Tappan line of appliances.

It was in the 1980s, once the company began to imagine it could be the world's leading white goods maker, that Electrolux undertook its most ambitious acquisitions. A bid for the German firm AEG was unsuccessful, but the well-regarded Italian appliance giant Zanussi was scooped up for $150 million in 1984. The next major target was White Consolidated Industries, a U.S. company that, like Electrolux, had made a specialty of taking over troubled manufacturing operations. It had amassed such well-known appliance brands as Frigidaire, Kelvinator, White-Westinghouse, and Gibson. By paying $740 million for it in 1986, Electrolux gave itself a major presence in the United States and propelled itself into the number-one position in the world appliance industry. It subsequently slipped behind Whirlpool.

That did not end the urge to merge. The appliance and food-service equipment lines of Britain's Thorn EMI were bought in 1987. The following year Electrolux extended its presence to the American backyard with the purchase of the outdoor power equipment business of Roper Corporation. The company began a move into Eastern Europe by acquiring Lehel, the leading Hungarian appliance maker, in 1991.

OPERATIONS

Household Appliances (58 percent of 1991 revenues). Nearly three-quarters of this segment consists of major appliances—refrigerators, washing machines, ranges, and dishwashers—and smaller kitchen devices. In the United States its major appliances are marketed under such brand names as White-Westinghouse, Kelvinator, Gibson, and Tappan. In Scandinavia and the rest of Europe the main brands are Electrolux and Zanussi.

The second-largest portion of this segment consists of floor-care products, including vacuum cleaners, floor polishers, and carpet-shampooing equipment. Electrolux is the world leader in this industry, with a global market share of about 20 percent.

Other products in this segment are room air conditioners (mainly in the United States), sewing machines, and kitchen and bathroom cabinets.

Commercial Appliances (11 percent of revenues). Electrolux is the European leader in the production of food-service appliances for restaurants and institutions. The company has aggressively built its position in this industry through acquisitions, including operations obtained from Thorn EMI in Britain and Buderus in Germany. It also makes a leading line of institutional refrigeration and freezing equipment.

Electrolux is the world leader in heavy-duty washing equipment for apartment houses, launderettes, and industrial laundries. It also makes machinery for dyeing and processing textiles. The company is one of the largest producers of industrial vacuum cleaners and other institutional cleaning systems.

Outdoor Products (11 percent of revenues). Electrolux is the world's largest manufacturer of chain saws, with a global market share of about 30 percent. This product line also includes equipment for clearing forests as well as protective clothing and tools for forestry work.

The company also leads in the production of portable garden equipment, such as grass trimmers and blowers, lawn mowers, and garden tractors. This segment also includes a rather unsuccessful operation that makes agricultural equipment, such as plows, sowing machines, and fertilizer spreaders.

Industrial Products (18 percent of revenues). The Gränges subsidiary, obtained via a 1980 acquisition, consists of several lines of business. The first is an aluminum-producing operation in Sweden, which has an annual capacity of one hundred thousand tons. Extruded aluminum products are fabricated in Sweden, Denmark, Britain, Holland, and Germany. A subsidiary is the leading Swedish company in the business of recycling metals. Gränges also has an automotive division that makes bumpers, hubcaps, and other parts. Other industrial products include materials handling equipment, automobile safety belts, and valves.

Commercial Services (2 percent of revenues). Most of the operations in this segment, which consists of cleaning services, were sold in 1990 and 1991. What remains are primarily cleaning companies operating in Brazil, the Middle East, and the Far East.

TOP EXECUTIVES

- Anders Scharp, chairman and chief executive
- Peter Wallenberg, deputy chairman
- Gösta Bystedt, deputy chairman
- Leif Johansson, president

- Lennart Ribohn, senior executive vice president
- Per-Olof Aronson, executive vice president
- Gunnar Bark, executive vice president
- Hans G. Bäckman, executive vice president

OUTSIDE DIRECTORS

- Claes Dahlbäck, president of the Wallenberg family investment firm AB Investor
- Carl Løwenhielm, member of the group executive committee of Scandinaviska Enskilda Banken
- Sven Olving, professor at the Chalmers Institute of Technology
- Bertil Danielsson, president of the Fourth National Pension Insurance Fund

As required by Swedish law, the board also includes three employee representatives and their deputies.

FINANCIAL DATA

Revenues (in millions of Swedish kronor)

1991	79,027
1990	82,434
1989	84,919
1988	73,960
1987	67,430
1986	53,090

Net Income (in millions of Swedish kronor)*

1991	377
1990	741
1989	2,579
1988	2,371

*Comparable figures are not available for 1986 and 1987 because of changes in accounting procedures.

GEOGRAPHICAL BREAKDOWN

Revenues (in millions of Swedish kronor)

Year	Europe and Scandinavia		North America		Elsewhere	
1991	51,125	(65%)	21,523	(27%)	6,379	(8%)
1990	53,965	(65%)	22,533	(27%)	5,936	(7%)
1989	52,571	(62%)	25,874	(31%)	6,474	(7%)

LABOR RELATIONS

Although in its home country Electrolux has reasonably good relations with trade unions—several officials of which serve on the company's board—the appliance conglomerate has taken a different labor stance overseas.

The company's foreign antilabor posture has been seen most clearly in Mexico and the United States. In 1988 three hundred workers at the Eureka plant in Juarez, Mexico, went on strike to demand union recognition. Management remained adamantly opposed and the strike was finally called off. Those workers who tried to return to their jobs were not taken back.

Electrolux has alienated U.S. labor groups by hiring antiunion consultants to fight against organizing drives like that initiated by the United Steelworkers in Springfield, Tennessee. The union lost the election but succeeded in raising a stink in Sweden about the U.S. subsidiary's practices. The parent company was compelled to send a top-level investigating team to Tennessee. As a result, when the next U.S. organizing drive occurred, this time by the United Paperworkers International Union, the company took a less hostile position and the union won the representation election.

At a gathering in 1989 unions from Sweden, the United States, and other countries agreed to form an Electrolux Unions World Council to coordinate activities.

ENVIRONMENTAL RECORD

In 1990 Electrolux made the switch from chlorofluorocarbons (CFCs)—coolants that contribute to the erosion of the ozone layer and thus increase the risk of skin cancer—to less-harmful hydrofluorocarbons.

BIBLIOGRAPHY

Electrolux and the Global Strategy Game. Geneva: International Metalworkers Federation, 1989.

SOCIÉTÉ NATIONALE ELF
AQUITAINE

Tour Elf
Cedex 45
92078 Paris-La Défense 6
France
(1) 47 44 45 46

1991 revenues: $38.7 billion
1991 net income: $1.9 billion
Publicly traded company
Employees: 86,900
Founded: 1941

OVERVIEW

Elf Aquitaine is the most aggressive of the international petroleum companies outside the clique known as the Seven Sisters. It is engaged in exploration activities around the world. So tireless is the company's pursuit of new sources of supply that it has even put trucks with seismic equipment in the middle of Paris to hunt for reserves under such landmarks as the Arc de Triomphe. Oil wells have not sprouted in the City of Light, but Elf has arranged to start drilling in Kazakhstan and Russia.

Aside from oil and gas, Elf is heavily involved in chemicals, pharmaceuticals (through its subsidiary Sanofi), and perfumes (it makes expensive fragrances like Van Cleef & Arpels).

As part of the French privatization program pursued since 1986, the government's holding in Elf has been reduced from two-thirds to about 55 percent. The company is bracing for increased competition in France, where it dominates the domestic oil business, as a result of European integration in 1992. To prepare for this, Elf has aggressively acquired properties elsewhere in Europe and the United States.

HISTORY

During the 1930s, when most of the petroleum industry was focused on countries like Venezuela and Saudi Arabia, a group of French officials decided to use a modest amount of public funds to finance some exploration efforts in France. The fruits of these endeavors were limited: one small oil field at Gabian in the Hérault, which soon dried up, and a natural gas deposit at Saint-Marcet in the Haute-Garonne.

Yet they formed the basis of the state-owned petroleum industry in France, which formally came into existence in 1939 with the creation of the Régie Autonome des Pétroles (RAP). During 1941, while the northern part of the country was being occupied by the Germans and the southern part was run by the collaborationist Pétain regime, a new semipublic body (majority owned by the state but with numerous private shareholders) called Société Nationale des Pétroles d'Aquitaine (SNPA) was formed to continue the exploration effort. After France was liberated, General de Gaulle set up another organization, Bureau de Recherches de Pétrole (BRP), to oversee oil activity.

In 1949 that activity started to become more meaningful; SNPA found a small deposit of oil at Lacq, in the southwest corner of the country, just north of the Pyrenees. Two years later drillers discovered a much bigger quantity of natural gas farther below the ground. Because the gas had an exceptionally high hydrogen sulfide and carbon dioxide content—a corrosive and toxic mixture—it took another five years before the first deliveries of gas to customers could take place. Lacq became the center of the natural gas industry in France, and the techniques used there to separate the gas have been adopted around the world.

During the 1950s the French oil effort turned to the country's colonies. In 1956 a subsidiary of RAP, working with Royal Dutch/Shell, struck oil in the Sahara. That same year, another Algerian discovery, involving a huge gas field, was made by a BRP subsidiary operating in a joint venture with the Compagnie Française des Pétroles (which was set up by the French government in the 1920s to hold France's interest in the Iraq Petroleum Company). Strikes also were made during this period in Gabon on the west coast of Africa.

Now that it had adequate sources of supply, the French petroleum companies decided to join forces to refine the oil and market it. Thus was formed the Union Générale des Pétroles in 1960. Over the next several years the group constructed three refineries in France and one in Germany. As of 1966, BRP and RAP were joined in a single state-owned body called the Enterprise de Recherches et d'Activités Pétrolières (ERAP), which was placed under the direction of Pierre Guillaumat, a key figure in France's postwar energy policy. Because BRP had been the majority shareholder in SNPA, that latter company became ERAP's main subsidiary.

With great fanfare ERAP introduced its retail brand name, Elf, in 1967. The Elf trademark, the blue-and-red cross-section of a drill bit, has been a familiar site at French gas stations ever since. In 1970 ERAP gained control of Antar, which greatly increased its refining capacity and marketing network.

In the meantime, ERAP's explorers were hard at work all around the world. These efforts became all the more important in 1971, when the Algerian government, frustrated at financial problems with the French companies, decided to nationalize the country's oil holdings. It was not until discoveries were made in the North Sea several years later that ERAP regained the lost production volume.

Following the oil crisis of the early 1970s, ERAP closed down several refineries because of the decline in demand for oil for uses other than transportation. The company also responded by diversifying into pharmaceuticals and cosmetics. This was done by acquiring two drug companies—Labaz and Robillart—and taking a minority position in the cosmetics firm Yves Rocher. To manage these operations ERAP formed a holding company called Sanofi.

In 1976 the assets and personnel of ERAP and SNPA were combined to form the Société Nationale Elf Aquitaine, two-thirds of which was owned by the government through ERAP and the remainder of which was held by some 150,000 private investors.

Under the leadership of Albin Chalandon, who took over after the retirement of Guillaumat in 1977, Elf focused on two major initiatives: expanding its presence in the United States and enlarging its chemical business.

The French government quashed Chalandon's 1980 plan to try to take over the American energy company Kerr-McGee, but the following year he was given a free hand to negotiate a $3-billion purchase of the minerals company Texasgulf. The acquisition gave Elf vast reserves of phosphate; and Texasgulf's extensive sulfur production, when combined with Elf's activity in that business at Lacq, made the French company the world's leading producer of the mineral. Elf's takeover was supported by the government-owned Canada Development Corporation, which had owned 37 percent of Texasgulf and which ended up with Texasgulf's Canadian assets as part of the deal.

Elf's predecessor companies for years had limited involvement with chemicals through the production of ethylene, benzene, and other intermediate chemicals. These operations were combined in 1970 with those of Total Chimie to form a joint venture called Ato Chimie. In 1980 Elf and Total Chimie took over some operations of Rhône-Poulenc and formed another venture named Chloé Chimie ("chloé" being a combination of the words *chlorine* and *ethylene*). As a result of a restructuring of the French chemical industry in the early 1980s, Elf ended up the sole owner of Ato and Chloé and also took over the chlorine and fluorine operations of Produits Chimiques Ugine Kuhlmann. All of these activities were brought together in 1983 as a new company called Atochem, a wholly owned subsidiary of Elf.

Elf's next major foray in the United States came in 1989, when it spent $1 billion to purchase Pennwalt Corporation, a big chemical producer. To satisfy objections from the U.S. Federal Trade Commission, Elf agreed to sell off plants producing polyvinylidene fluoride and vinylidene fluoride.

The Pennwalt acquisition, along with an unsuccessful bid for British oil and gas producer Tricentrol, was in line with the company's strategy of reducing dependence on the French domestic market and becoming a global player in petroleum, chemicals, pharmaceuticals, and related products.

In 1990 Elf bought a 25-percent stake in the Spanish oil refiner Compañía Española de Petróleos (CEPSA). The following year Elf gained control over CEPSA's smaller rival, Ertoil, and then sold it to CEPSA in a deal that increased Elf's holdings in that company to 35 percent. At the same time, Elf's Sanofi subsidiary formed three joint ventures with Sterling Drug (owned by Eastman Kodak) to sell both prescription and over-the-counter drugs around the world. Elf also expanded its exploration activities by forming a joint venture with the British company Enterprise Oil to acquire the North Sea assets of Occidental Petroleum. As part of the $1.3-billion purchase, Elf agreed to reduce its holdings in Enterprise Oil from 25 to 10 percent.

OPERATIONS

Petroleum Exploration and Production (19 percent of 1991 revenues). Currently Elf is engaged in oil and gas exploration in twenty-five countries and held exploration interests in six others. These activities are concentrated in France, the North Sea, West African countries that border the Gulf of Guinea (such as Gabon), the Middle East, the Far East, and the Gulf of Mexico. In 1990 the company signed an agreement to begin exploration in the Soviet Union. Elf's proven reserves of crude oil amount to more than two billion barrels and those of natural gas six trillion cubic feet. The company's principal production areas are located in the North Sea, the Gulf of Guinea region, and France.

Refining, Marketing, and Trading (49 percent of revenues). Elf's involvement in refining, marketing, and other downstream activities is concentrated in France, but it has expanded in such countries as Spain (through its holdings in CEPSA) and Britain (where in 1990 it purchased 230 service stations and other assets from a subsidiary of Amoco). Elf owns and operates three refineries in France, holds a majority stake in one in the United Kingdom, and has minority interests in nine others, six of which are in western Africa. Elf's marketing efforts are concentrated in France and other parts of Europe.

Chemicals (24 percent of revenues). Through its 99-percent ownership of Atochem, Elf is a major producer of basic chemicals in France and other parts of Europe and makes specialty chemicals in those areas and in the United States (through Pennwalt Corporation). By means of its American subsidiary Texasgulf, Elf is a leading producer of minerals and derivative chemicals in the United States.

Human Health Care, Bioactivities, and Perfumes (9 percent of revenues). Elf owns 61 percent of Sanofi (the second-largest human health care company in France), which was formed by Elf in 1973 and now trades on the Paris Bourse. Sanofi's pharmaceutical business, which contributed 54 percent of 1991 revenues in this segment, consists primarily of products for treating cardiovascular disorders and central nervous system diseases. Its leading product in this area in Ticlid, an antithrombotic.

The bioactivities area (37 percent of Sanofi's revenues) includes gelatines, flavors, fragrances, food additives, and animal health and nutrition products. The perfumes business (9 percent of revenues) includes Sanofi's production of such well-known brands as Van Cleef & Arpels, Oscar de la Renta, and Perry Ellis. Sanofi also holds minority interests in Parfums Nina Ricci and Yves Rocher SA.

TOP EXECUTIVES

- Loïk Le Floch-Prigent, chairman and chief executive
- Frederic Isoard, executive vice president, hydrocarbons division
- Jean-François Dehecq, executive vice president, human health care, and chief executive of Sanofi
- Raphaël Hadas-Lebel, senior vice president and corporate secretary
- Philippe Hustache, senior vice president and chief financial officer
- Jacques Puechal, executive vice president, chemicals division
- Bernard de Combret, executive vice president
- François de Wissocq, senior vice president

OUTSIDE DIRECTORS

- Pierre Boisson, president of Enterprise de Recherches et d'Activités Pétrolières
- Raymond H. Lévy, former chairman of Renault
- Jacques Mayoux, honorary president of Société Générale
- Jean Meo, president of the French Petroleum Institute
- Patrick Ponsolle, chief executive of Compagnie de Suez
- Betrand Schwartz, member of Le Conseil Economique et Social
- René Thomas, chief executive of Banque Nationale de Paris
- Alain de Wulf, vice chairman of Cie. Financière de Paribas

The board of directors also includes (in addition to Boisson) two French government representatives and, as required by law, six employee representatives. Gilbert Rutman, former vice chairman of Elf, is also a member.

FINANCIAL DATA

Revenues (in millions of French francs)

1991	200,674
1990	175,479
1989	149,802
1988	126,097
1987	127,353

Net Income (in millions of French francs)

1991	9,796
1990	10,625
1989	7,218
1988	7,205
1987	4,149

GEOGRAPHICAL BREAKDOWN

Revenues (in millions of French francs)

Year	France		Rest of Europe		Elsewhere	
1991	136,109	(60%)	55,094	(24%)	37,245	(16%)
1990	123,604	(61%)	40,399	(20%)	39,869	(20%)
1989	107,479	(61%)	31,155	(18%)	36,907	(21%)

Operating income (in millions of French francs)

Year	France		Rest of Europe		Elsewhere	
1991	8,386	(45%)	5,141	(27%)	5,208	(28%)
1990	7,370	(36%)	4,829	(24%)	8,232	(40%)
1989	8,313	(65%)	3,544	(28%)	955	(7%)

LABOR RELATIONS

The Confédération Générale du Travail and the other four principal French labor unions are represented at Elf's facilities in France. As required by French law, management holds annual meetings with a delegation of union representatives, and employees are directly represented on the company's board of directors. There have been no significant strikes or work stoppages in recent years.

ENVIRONMENTAL RECORD

Elf's Atochem subsidiary joined forces with the U.S. company Allied-Signal in 1988 to develop substitutes for CFCs.

In 1990 several million gallons of crude oil belonging to an Elf subsidiary spilled into the Gulf of Mexico as a result of an explosion aboard a Norwegian supertanker. Although Elf was not legally responsible for the spill, the company spent about $8 million to help in the cleanup.

According to an analysis of data from the U.S. EPA, Elf's American subsidiaries were responsible for the twelfth-largest volume (seventy-three million pounds) of toxic releases among all U.S manufacturing companies in 1989 (the latest figures available).

EXXON CORPORATION

225 East John W. Carpenter Freeway
Irving, Texas 75062
(214) 444-1000

1991 revenues: $104.3 billion
1991 net income: $5.6 billion
Publicly traded company
Employees: 101,000
Founded: 1863

OVERVIEW

Exxon, which emerged out of John D. Rockefeller's Standard Oil trust, is one of the behemoths of the oil industry and one of the largest companies in the world. With operations in eighty countries and 78 percent of its revenues coming from outside the United States, Exxon is only nominally an American corporation.

Despite its size, the company has experienced some major stumbles. Efforts to diversify into such areas as office machinery and electrical equipment were conspicuous failures. In recent years the company has been in the public eye mainly because of the giant oil spill by one of its tankers off the coast of Alaska in 1989.

Still, Exxon, which underwent an extensive restructuring and cost-cutting regime during the 1980s, is considered a formidable competitor in the oil business, and it continues to vie with Royal Dutch/Shell for leadership of that industry.

HISTORY

Edwin Drake's discovery of oil in Pennsylvania at the end of the 1850s led to the birth of the U.S. petroleum industry. Within a short time kerosene produced from oil replaced the coal-derived variety as the major source of artificial light. But the new commodity was not available on a regular basis. Financed by a large number of undercapitalized entrepreneurs, the commodity's price was continually changing, as was its supply.

Such conditions made the business ripe for consolidation, and the man who stepped in to capture this opportunity was the young entrepreneur John D. Rockefeller. Along with two partners, he set up a kerosene-refining business in Cleveland in 1863. He soon bought out the co-owners and embarked on a single-minded drive to take over as much of the business as he could—that is, the refining and transportation aspects of the industry, since Rockefeller decided that the exploration end was too risky.

Rockefeller's company went public in 1870 under the name of Standard Oil Company. For the rest of the century Standard employed every device, legal and not so legal, to dominate the industry. It grew large enough to dictate terms to the railroads and thus enjoyed freight charges substantially lower than those paid by its dwindling rivals. Rockefeller allowed competitors to operate in limited areas, but if they grew too large, Standard waged unbridled price wars to keep them in place or take them over.

To get around an Ohio law limiting a corporation's ownership of shares of companies in other states, Rockefeller created an arrangement that became known as the Standard Oil trust, in which Standard's subsidiaries were nominally independent but were controlled by a centralized board of trustees. In 1892 the Ohio Supreme Court struck down the plan, so the holding company for the trust was converted to Standard Oil (New Jersey). That state was chosen because it had adopted more liberal rules regarding out-of-state ownership.

The first challenge to Standard's domination came with the development of the Baku fields in Russia by the Nobel brothers of Sweden. Working with the Rothschilds of France, the Nobels provided Europe with an alternative source of supply. Then the industry in the United States was transformed with the discovery of oil in Texas. Beginning with the 1901 gusher at the Spindletop oil field, near Beaumont, the Texas wells began producing at levels far in excess of those in Pennsylvania. The dominance of the Southwest was clinched when additional finds were made in Oklahoma and Louisiana.

Just as Standard's predominance began to erode a bit, public opposition to the trust reached its height, helped by muckraking books such as Ida Tarbell's unflattering history of Standard. The Roosevelt administration brought antitrust charges against the Rockefeller empire, and in 1909 a federal court ruled that the Standard Oil trust was illegal under the Sherman Act. The case went all the way to the Supreme Court, which in 1911 upheld the ruling and ordered the dissolution of Standard into more than thirty independent companies.

The largest of the spin-offs was Standard Oil of New Jersey, often called Jersey Standard. Although the Standard Oil trust was no more, the New Jersey company came to assume a powerful position in the world oil industry. This took some adjustment, for, as Anthony Sampson points out in *The Seven*

Sisters, at the time of the breakup, Jersey Standard had little oil of its own and served more as a bank and trading company.

Under the authoritarian leadership of Walter Teagle, the company dealt with this problem first by quietly purchasing a 50-percent interest in a Texas company called Humble Oil (which later would be fully integrated and form the basis of the company's U.S. operations) and then by amassing properties in Venezuela and the Caribbean. The company also made the more ambitious move of challenging the British domination of petroleum supplies in much of the rest of the world. Jersey Standard (along with Standard of New York, or Socony) used U.S.-government pressure to become a partner in the Western-run Turkish Petroleum Company, which was developing oil supplies in a vast area of the old Ottoman Empire. In 1928 Teagle met secretly with his counterparts at Royal Dutch/Shell and Anglo-Persian (now British Petroleum) at Achnacarry, a hunting lodge in Scotland. The three companies carved up much of the world market and in effect created the first international oil cartel.

This arrangement remained in effect for decades, but at home Teagle found himself in hot water in 1941 for having maintained a noncompetition deal with Germany's IG Farben chemical combine since the 1920s. As part of that deal, Jersey Standard had handed over crucial patents, such as that for tetraethyl lead gasoline additive, after Hitler came to power. The American company also had agreed to hold back on research into synthetic rubber. To settle the affair, Jersey Standard signed a consent decree that provided for royalty-free licensing of the patents.

While it was busy dividing up the world with Royal Dutch/Shell, Jersey Standard passed up an opportunity to participate in what turned out to be an oil jackpot: Saudi Arabia. That boon went instead to one of the lesser of the Seven Sisters—Standard Oil of California, or Socal. The Saudi reserves discovered in the 1930s were so great that Socal needed help in developing them. It turned first to Texaco, and then the two firms formed a consortium called Arabian American Oil Company, or Aramco, which Jersey Standard finally joined in 1945.

In the mid-1950s Jersey Standard was among the U.S. companies that got shares of Iranian production after a CIA-led coup overthrew a nationalist leader who had expropriated the holdings of Anglo-Persian. Toward the end of that decade the company made a major discovery of oil in Libya, and in 1960 it found large supplies of natural gas in the Netherlands. Strikes were made later in Alaska, the North Sea, Alabama, and Florida. The company also moved into uranium, copper, and other minerals.

During the 1960s and 1970s Jersey Standard was at the forefront of efforts by the Seven Sisters to respond to the challenge of the oil-producing countries, which in 1960 formed the Organization of Petroleum Exporting Countries (OPEC) cartel. The company, which changed its name to Exxon in 1972, was one of the prime targets of the criticism directed against the ways in which the oil industry exploited the price increases of the 1970s. The company later paid a fine of more than $2 billion for overcharging its customers. At the same time, the company found its holdings in Saudi Arabia, Libya, Iraq, and Venezuela nationalized.

Exxon's hopes of using diversification as a new engine of growth did not succeed. Its $500-million foray into the office equipment business was poorly planned and was abandoned in the mid-1980s. Another failure was the company's $1.2-billion purchase of Reliance Electric in 1979; the promise of a device that could greatly raise the efficiency of electric motors turned out to be a pipedream. And a multi-billion-dollar shale oil project was abandoned in 1982.

Yet all of these expensive dead ends did not put much of a dent in the huge company, which in the mid-1980s was sitting on some $11 billion in cash. Much of this was used to buy back stock, but Exxon refused to get involved in the oil merger mania of the decade. The slump in oil prices did, however, make itself felt, and the company responded by slashing expenses and eliminating jobs—more than forty thousand of them. Even the company's Manhattan headquarters building was sold off (to Japanese investors), and the head office was moved to a suburb of Dallas. These measures did not please the company's employees, but investors enjoyed a buoyant stock price and high earnings per share.

Some of that contentment disappeared in 1989 after the *Exxon Valdez* tanker struck a reef off the coast of Alaska and spilled eleven million gallons of crude oil into Prince William Sound. An attempt to settle government charges brought against Exxon for some $1 billion collapsed in 1991, and the case was sent back to court. Later that year, however, another settlement was reached. This pact called for Exxon to pay an additional $25 million in criminal fines. According to one analysis, the company actually would come out $5 million ahead in the new plan, since it was structured to allow more of the payments to be tax deductible.

OPERATIONS

Petroleum (91 percent of 1991 revenues). Exxon is an integrated oil producer. It is involved in exploration and production in the United States (especially Alaska), Canada (through Imperial Oil Ltd., 69.6-percent owned by Exxon), the United Kingdom portion of the North Sea, Norway, France, Holland, Germany, Egypt, Yemen Arab Republic, Niger, Australia, Malaysia, Indonesia, Thailand, and Colombia. At the end of 1991 the company had net proven developed and undeveloped crude oil and natural gas liquid reserves of 6.2 billion barrels. Natural gas reserves were nearly twenty-five trillion cubic feet.

The company operates refineries in the United States, Canada, Latin America, Europe, Africa, and the Far East. In the United States refined products are marketed along the Atlantic seaboard from Maine to Florida, in the Lower Mississippi Valley, the Midwest, the Southwest, the West Coast, and Rocky Mountain areas. Distribution facilities include a vast network of bulk plants, retail outlets and service stations, and a system of owned or affiliated pipelines.

Natural gas is sold to gas pipeline companies. In 1989 the Imperial Oil subsidiary acquired Texaco's Canadian operations for $4.1 billion.

Chemicals (9 percent of revenues). This segment consists of three major areas: basic petrochemicals, including olefins and aromatics; additives for fuels and lubricants; and specialty rubbers, a market in which Exxon is the world leader. Chemical plants are located in the United States, Canada, Britain, Scotland, France, and other countries.

Other operations include coal mines in the United States, Colombia, and Australia; a copper mine in Chile; and a zinc mine in Australia. Exxon also has an interest in an electric power generation operation in Hong Kong.

TOP EXECUTIVES

- Lawrence G. Rawl, chairman and chief executive
- Lee R. Raymond, president
- Jack G. Clarke, senior vice president
- Donald K. McIvor, senior vice president
- Charles R. Sitter, senior vice president

OUTSIDE DIRECTORS

- Randolph W. Bromery, professor emeritus of geophysics at the University of Massachusetts at Amherst
- D. Wayne Calloway, chief executive of PepsiCo
- Jess Hay, chief executive of Lomas Financial Corporation
- William R. Howell, chief executive of J.C. Penney
- Lord (Hector) Laing, life president of United Biscuits (Holdings) PLC
- Philip E. Lippincott, chief executive of Scott Paper
- Marilyn Carlson Nelson, vice chairman of Carlson Holdings
- John H. Steele, president emeritus of Woods Hole Oceanographic Institution
- Joseph D. Williams, retired chief executive of Warner-Lambert

FINANCIAL DATA

Revenues (in millions of dollars)

1991	104,271
1990	106,665
1989	87,768
1988	80,868
1987	77,668
1986	71,456

Net Income (in millions of dollars)

1991	5,600
1990	5,010
1989	3,510
1988	5,260
1987	4,840
1986	5,360

GEOGRAPHICAL BREAKDOWN

Revenues (in millions of dollars)

Year	United States		Other Western Hemisphere		Eastern Hemisphere	
1991	25,919	(22%)	18,422	(16%)	72,377	(62%)
1990	27,396	(23%)	20,195	(17%)	70,348	(60%)
1989	24,044	(25%)	16,612	(17%)	55,539	(58%)

Net Income (in millions of dollars)

Year	United States		Other Western Hemisphere		Eastern Hemisphere	
1991	1,478	(24%)	150	(2%)	4,567	(74%)
1990	1,691	(29%)	344	(6%)	3,840	(65%)
1989	505	(14%)	366	(10%)	2,687	(76%)

LABOR RELATIONS

The Standard Oil trust tends to be depicted as a villain in labor histories because of the infamous Ludlow Massacre of 1914. The dispute began in 1913, when some nine thousand miners employed by the Rockefeller-controlled Colorado Fuel and Iron Company and other companies went on strike to demand union recognition as well as better working and living conditions. Several months into the walkout the state militia was sent in to attack the strikers' tent village. During a battle with the workers, the militiamen poured oil on the tents and set them afire. Two women and eleven children were killed in the blaze.

By the 1920s Jersey Standard was projecting a very different image for itself. It led the way in using paternalistic policies as a way of discouraging unionization. When labor organizations became more active in the 1930s, Jersey Standard, like many other companies, created company unions to "represent" its workers. Those unions ostensibly became independent after company-dominated unions were outlawed. Yet, while such independents at other oil companies eventually gave way to representation by the Oil, Chemical and Atomic Workers, Jersey Standard's unions remained isolated, weak, and largely under the domination of management.

Morale among both unionized and nonunion workers at the company plummeted during the 1980s as Exxon eliminated tens of thousands of jobs and put the squeeze on those who remained. These policies may have had consequences outside the company. A front-page article in the *Wall Street Journal* (March 16, 1990) suggests that accidents like that in New Jersey, where hundreds of thousands of gallons of oil leaked into New York Harbor, were the result of the company's restructuring moves. One analyst is quoted as saying that Exxon's operations were "overworked and undermanned."

Exxon also has been no great friend to labor abroad. In 1990, for example, the company's International Colombia Resources subsidiary pressured the government of Colombia to crack down on a group of coal miners who had walked off the job at one of its facilities. Worker demands included improved housing and a shorter workweek. Colombian authorities declared the strike an economic detriment to the country and ordered the miners back to work. The miners' union then reached a settlement with the company that included some of what they were seeking.

ENVIRONMENTAL RECORD

Exxon was never a particularly green company, but an event on March 24, 1989, gave it a prominent place in the environmental rogues gallery. On that day its supertanker *Valdez* struck Bligh Reef and spilled eleven million gallons of crude oil into the Prince William Sound, polluting more than seven hundred miles of Alaskan shoreline. Although much of the guilt was laid to the captain of the vessel, who was intoxicated and away from his post at the time of the accident, Exxon was blamed, too. Among the charges were that the company did not act quickly enough in dealing with the spill and that it did not adequately cooperate with state and federal officials.

A coalition of environmental groups launched a boycott of Exxon and urged customers to return their credit cards to the company. They also called on the oil giant to roll back recent gasoline price increases, to pay for the cleanup, and to establish a $1-billion trust fund for protecting endangered areas of Alaska. When institutional investors pressured the company to appoint an environmentalist to its board of directors, Exxon named John H. Steele of the Woods Hole Oceanographic Institution—a choice that was not entirely satisfactory to many environmental groups. Exxon also vowed to spend $1.3 billion on the cleanup.

In February 1990 the company was indicted by a federal grand jury on criminal felony and misdemeanor charges. The indictment was based on pollution and marine safety statutes. The company also was hit with civil charges. In March 1991 Exxon agreed to settle the criminal charges by pleading guilty to one charge and paying a fine of $100 million; at the same time, the civil charges were to be settled with the company agreeing to pay $900 million in damages over ten years.

Many environmentalists and some members of Congress criticized the terms of the settlement, saying that Exxon was being let off too lightly. In fact, shortly after the deal was reached, federal environmental officials announced that research was indicating that the damage to wildlife and the ecology of Prince William Sound was turning out to be greater than had been expected.

In April 1991 federal judge H. Russel Holland rejected the settlement of the criminal charges, saying that the $100-million fine was too low. When the Alaska legislature rejected the deal on the civil charges, that part of the settlement collapsed as well. Another settlement announced in September 1991, which increased the criminal penalty by $25 million, was accepted by Judge Holland.

The Alaska spill was not the only recent accident involving Exxon. In December 1989 an explosion at its Baton Rouge, Louisiana, refinery was so powerful that debris was spread for miles; two men were killed in the incident. On January 1, 1990, a cracked underwater pipeline at the company's Bayway Refinery in New Jersey leaked six hundred thousand gallons of heating oil into part of New York Harbor. That leak continued for six hours as operators doubted the validity of an alarm that had sounded. The company settled criminal and civil charges brought in connection with the leak by agreeing to fund $15 million in environmental initiatives.

In 1990 the Occupational Safety and Health Law Center released a report stating that Exxon had the worst corporate mine safety record among the nation's twenty-largest underground coal producers. At the company's two large coal mines in Illinois, operated by its subsidiary Monterey Coal Company, serious or fatal accidents had befallen 7.8 out of every 100 full-time miners.

Exxon was one of ten major oil companies cited by the EPA in 1991 for discharging contaminated fluids from service stations into or directly above underground sources for drinking water. Exxon agreed to pay a fine of $125,000 and to clean up the conditions by the end of 1993.

A study of EPA data by the Citizens Fund found that Exxon was responsible for the twenty-eighth-largest volume (thirteen million pounds) of toxic chemicals released into the air among all of the nation's manufacturing companies in 1989 (the latest figures available).

BIBLIOGRAPHY

Davidson, Art. *In the Wake of the Exxon Valdez: The Story of America's Most Devastating Oil Spill.* San Francisco: Sierra Club Books, 1990.

Davidson, Ray. *Challenging the Giants: A History of the Oil, Chemical and Atomic Workers International Union.* Denver: OCAW, 1988.

Gibb, George S., and Evelyn H. Knowlton. *The Resurgent Years: History of Standard Oil Co. (New Jersey), 1911–1927.* New York: Harper & Brothers, 1956.

Hidy, Ralph W., and Muriel E. Hidy. *Pioneering in Big Business: History of Standard Oil Co. (New Jersey), 1882–1911.* New York: Harper & Brothers, 1955.

Josephson, Matthew. *The Robber Barons: The Great American Capitalists, 1861–1901.* New York: Harcourt, Brace, 1934.

Keeble, John. *Out of the Channel: The Exxon Valdez Oil Spill in Prince William Sound.* New York: HarperCollins, 1991.

Larson, Henrietta, Evelyn H. Knowlton, and Charles S. Popple. *New Horizons: History of Standard Oil Co. (New Jersey), 1927–1950.* New York: Harper & Row, 1971.

O'Connor, Harvey. *History of Oil Workers Intl. Union (CIO).* Denver: Oil Workers International Union, 1950.

Sampson, Anthony. *The Seven Sisters: The Great Oil Companies and the World They Made.* New York: Viking Press, 1975.

Tarbell, Ida M. *The History of the Standard Oil Co.* 1904. Reprint. New York: Macmillan, 1925.

FANUC LTD.

Oshino-mura, Minami-Tsurugun
Yamanashi Prefecture 401-05
Japan
(0555) 84-5555

1991 revenues: $1.3 billion (year ending March 31)
1991 net income: $267.9 million
Publicly traded company
Employees: 2,041
Founded: 1955

OVERVIEW

Fanuc, an acronym for Fuji Automatic Numerical Control, started out as a subsidiary of Fujitsu and made its way to the top of the factory automation business. The company is a leader both in numerical control devices (the systems that turn lathes and other machine tools into precision instruments) and in robotics.

The company is run by Seiuemon Inaba, an authoritarian manager obsessed with improving his products. He has adopted the German engineering slogan *"weniger teile"* ("fewer parts") as his own. Fanuc's main operations, located near the base of Mt. Fuji, include a showcase factory that probably has gone farther than any other facility in using robots to make other robots. As a result, Fanuc employs few production workers; most of the company's small labor force is engaged in research and development or sales and administration.

Inaba is one of the most ardent apostles of automation, even though the spread of robotics has substantially slowed down (outside of Japan). A succession of major American companies have left the robotics business, and the leading U.S. machine-tool firm in the field, Cincinnati Milacron, sold its robotics operation to ABB ASEA Brown Boveri in 1990. Ironically, it has been Fanuc that has kept the computerized numerical control and robotics industries alive in the United States through its joint ventures with General Electric and General Motors. Automation is the stuff of the future, and Fanuc will be an important part of it.

HISTORY

Fanuc was established in 1955 as a subsidiary of Fujitsu. Initially the operation, headed by a young engineer named Seiuemon Inaba, focused on research and development. This was necessary because at the time, Japan produced no numerical control equipment; the field was dominated by U.S. companies.

Within a decade the operation, known as Fujitsu Fanuc, had caught up with Western technology. By the late 1960s it was selling numerical control devices in Japan and soon gained a domestic market share of 80 percent. In 1972 the operation was spun off into an independent company, although Fujitsu retained a sizable minority interest (39 percent today).

Once independent, Fujitsu Fanuc, as the company continued to call itself until 1982, set its sights beyond Japan. In 1975 it entered the United States by licensing the Pratt & Whitney division of United Technologies to market its drilling machines. It reached a similar agreement with Siemens covering the distribution of Fanuc products throughout Europe, although that deal later ran afoul of European Community antitrust rules. Fanuc got into the South Korean market more directly, by setting up a manufacturing operation in that country in 1978. Working with the United Nations, the company also helped to create numerical control capacity in countries like Bulgaria.

By the early 1980s Fanuc had risen to the top of the numerical control industry, with some 50 percent of the world market. Inaba then moved into the robotics field, challenging the leading position of Kawasaki Heavy Industries and Hitachi. In 1981 the company demonstrated its prowess by establishing a showcase factory in which robots and numerical control machines were used to manufacture robot components. The following year Fanuc formed a joint venture with General Motors to produce and market robots in the United States. GM was a desirable partner, since it was also the largest customer for the robots. Before long the operation, called GMFanuc Robotics, was the largest supplier of robots in the world. (It should be noted, however, that 90 percent of its sales were to GM.)

Although the automation business (outside Japan) went into a slump in the mid-1980s, Fanuc persevered and solidified its position in 1987 by forming a joint venture with General Electric to make computerized numerical control equipment. The arrangement represented a setback for GE, which only a couple of years earlier had made a much-ballyhooed entry into the industrial automation market. After losing $200 million in the effort, GE decided to turn to tiny Fanuc for help. GE's involvement with Fanuc increased after Siemens dropped out of its joint venture with the Japanese company in 1990.

Then Fanuc expanded its alliance with GM to include the marketing of robots in Europe, and it joined with Mitsui and a Soviet machine-tool service operation called Stanko to form a company to repair robots in the Soviet Union. Fanuc also set up joint ventures in Indonesia, China, and India.

In 1990 Fanuc sought to buy a 40-percent share in Moore Special Tool Company, a U.S. machine-tool manufacturer whose products include devices used in the production of nuclear weapons. For this reason the proposed purchase ran into problems with the national security–minded federal government. Fanuc was able, however, to proceed with a plan to work with Moore on a new product. The plan was for Fanuc to develop a computerized numerical controller and software for a new plunge-type, electrodischarge machine that uses a laserlike electric charge to cut intricate metal parts.

Fanuc was among the companies that in 1991 expressed interest in participating in a Japanese research project to develop extremely tiny devices. The New Energy and Industrial Technology Development Organization, the sponsor of the micromachine project, planned to choose the participants in 1992. That same year General Motors sold its 50-percent interest in GM Fanuc to Fanuc.

OPERATIONS

Computerized Numerical Control Equipment and Electrodischargers (83 percent of 1991 revenues). Fanuc is the world's largest producer of numerical control equipment for machine tools. It produces both the basic controllers—the electronic brains—of sophisticated machine tools and other components, such as motors and drills. The company's joint venture with General Electric makes programmable logic controllers.

Industrial Robots (14 percent of revenues). Fanuc is also one of the leading manufacturers of industrial robots for applications such as laser cutting, laser welding, spot welding, stud welding, and handling of materials. Until 1992 much of the company's robotics work was done through the GMFanuc Robotics Corporation, a joint venture with General Motors that operated in both the United States and Europe.

Other Products (3 percent of revenues). Fanuc's other significant business involves the production of plastic injection molding machines.

TOP EXECUTIVES

- Seiuemon Inaba, president and chief executive
- Shigeaki Oyama, senior executive vice president
- Kohei Ito, executive vice president
- Ryoichiro Nozawa, executive vice president
- Yoshihiro Hashimoto, executive vice president

FINANCIAL DATA (NOT CONSOLIDATED)

Revenues (in millions of yen) (years ending March 31)

1991	184,576
1990	178,119
1989	149,086
1988	116,742
1987	118,571

Net Income (in millions of yen) (years ending March 31)

1991	37,669
1990	34,772
1989	21,986
1988	16,654
1987	19,035

LABOR RELATIONS

Given its extensive use of automation, Fanuc employs an extremely small group of production workers. Most of its nonadministrative employees are in research and development. The company has a policy of paying higher-than-average wages, but it demands extremely long hours of work. Many employees spend weekday nights in facilities at the company and go home only on weekends.

BIBLIOGRAPHY

Lynn, Leonard. "Japanese Robotics: Challenge and—Limited—Exemplar." *Annals of the American Academy of Political and Social Science* 470 (November 1983): 16–27.

Noble, David F. *Forces of Production: A Social History of Industrial Automation.* New York: Alfred A. Knopf, 1984.

FIAT SpA

Corso Marconi 10
10125 Turin
Italy
(011) 65651

1991 revenues: $50.6 billion
1991 net income: $971 million
Publicly traded company
Employees: 287,957
Founded: 1899

OVERVIEW

Fiat is the largest private company in Italy, controlling, through a vast network of subsidiaries, a wide swath of that country's economy. The company, dominated by the flamboyant Agnelli family, is best known as a producer of automobiles, the firm's original product when it was established at the end of the nineteenth century. Its small, relatively inexpensive cars came to dominate the Italian market, thanks to government support (especially during the Mussolini regime) in the form of high tariffs on imports.

Fiat grew rapidly after World War II and became one of the world's leading automakers, yet the company failed to gain a foothold in North America and eventually abandoned that market. In addition to its own production, the company helped establish auto production facilities in places like the former Soviet Union.

In recent years Fiat has responded to rising competitive challenges by forming a series of alliances with such companies as Ford Motor and Alcatel Alsthom. There have been frequent reports that the company was negotiating a merger with one of its foreign rivals.

HISTORY

The founder of the Fiat empire was a former cavalry officer named Giovanni Agnelli, who just before the turn of the century decided to enter the new business of producing horseless carriages. In 1899 he joined with a group of aristocrats in Turin to form the Fabbrica Italiana di Automobili Torino.

The company, which became known by its initials FIAT (and took Fiat as its official name in 1906), got off to a good start in the car business and soon branched out to trucks, buses, and marine engines. But Agnelli, the managing director, engaged in some suspicious practices, and in 1908 criminal charges were brought against him and the rest of the board—all of whom resigned. The prosecutors failed to prove their case, however, so Agnelli was acquitted and returned to his post.

Agnelli developed close ties with Italian politicians, which helped Fiat gain orders from the government for military vehicles and equipment. By the mid-1910s the roster of such politicians included Benito Mussolini, who received Fiat financial support for the founding of his propaganda newspaper *Il Popolo d'Italia*. The advent of World War I was a boon for Fiat, which became one of the leading suppliers of vehicles, munitions, and other military items to the government. It also began to make airplanes. Protected by high tariffs, the company controlled virtually the entire Italian auto market, with the exception of luxury cars like Lancias and Alfa Romeos.

In the wake of the Bolshevik revolution, Fiat was a prime target of worker unrest and in 1920 experienced factory occupations at its plants in Turin, by then the Italian counterpart of Detroit. Agnelli was not deterred by the militancy; in fact, he began a process of buying up other industrial companies as well as the leading Turin newspaper, *La Stampa*. With the help of Vittorio Valletta, a professor of banking hired in 1921, Agnelli turned Fiat into a vertically integrated enterprise, producing its own steel, paint, and other materials for its cars. Other activities included the production of railway cars and tractors and a construction operation called Impresit. In 1927 the various Agnelli holdings were put under the umbrella of a holding company called Istituto Finanziario Industriale.

The influence of Agnelli, who became known as *Il Senatore* after Mussolini made him a senator for life in 1923, widened as the Fascists rose to power. This is not to say that he was an ardent believer in *Il Duce*, but simply that he knew how to take advantage of the situation. As Alan Friedman writes in his provocative book on the Agnellis, "[*Il Senatore*] never liked Mussolini very much, but nor had he allowed principles to stand in the way of his profits. His emphatic policy, from the early days of the 1900s until 1945, was not Fascist or anti-Fascist, it was opportunism and collaboration with anyone, regardless of their political beliefs, on behalf of his beloved Fiat."

Indeed, when Mussolini's power began to wane in about 1943, Agnelli started making contacts with the Allies. Agnelli died in 1945, shortly after the end of World War II. His gestures may have played a role in the decision of the United States not only to allow Agnelli's protégé Vittorio Valletta to remain in charge of the company but also to grant Fiat Marshall Plan funds to rebuild.

Valletta made full use of those resources to expand and modernize Fiat's operations in automaking as well as steel, heavy equipment, marine engines, aircraft, and other industrial products. The company also began to expand its manufacturing operations abroad and licensed its automobile technology to the Spanish government–owned automaker SEAT. During the 1950s Fiat continued to benefit from trade policies that blocked foreign companies from gaining much of a position in the Italian car market.

Those practices finally were challenged in 1961, when the European Economic Community pressured Italy to lower its tariffs and drop its import quotas. Fiat, never enamored of competition, kicked up a fuss, using *La Stampa* to campaign against imports. Fiat held onto its dominant position in the domestic market and continued to widen its influence abroad. An important step in the latter process was the mid-1960s agreement with the Soviet Union to construct an entirely new auto-producing complex on the Volga River. The facility, with a capacity of six hundred thousand cars a year, was located in a town renamed Togliattigrad, in honor of Palmiro Togliatti, one of the founders of the Italian Communist party. Fiat also expanded in the third world, building plants in such countries as India, Egypt, Morocco, and Argentina.

After running Fiat for more than two decades, Vittorio Valletta retired in 1966 at the age of eighty-two. He was succeeded as chairman by Giovanni Agnelli II, grandson of the founder. Known as Gianni or *L'Avvocato* (he received a degree in law but never practiced), Agnelli had grown up in luxurious surroundings and had been groomed, especially after the death of his father when he was fourteen, as the heir to the Fiat empire. But by the time he had reached adulthood, he had no interest in such a responsibility, and he had gladly let Valletta control the company after the end of the war while he spent the next two decades leading the life of a playboy and bon vivant. Enjoying a personal income of about $1 million a year, he traveled in high society and spent much of his time yachting along the French Riviera.

Agnelli took over the company at a time when the world auto industry was becoming more competitive. To deal with the challenges, Agnelli brought his younger brother Umberto, who had been running the company's French operations, to headquarters as a co–managing director. In an attempt to overtake Volkswagen as the world's number-three automaker (behind General Motors and Ford), Agnelli sought to acquire the ailing French company Citroën, but he managed to gain only a minority position. (The alliance ended in 1973.) Fiat did, however, take over Italian luxury producer Lancia and 50 percent of sports-car maker Ferrari in 1969 (a stake that increased to 90 percent in 1988). The company's earthmoving equipment business was merged with that of Allis-Chalmers in 1973, but the alliance was terminated several years later, with the U.S. company charging that Fiat had tried to dominate the relationship.

The oil crisis of the early 1970s and the resulting slump in the auto business took a heavy toll on Fiat. In an effort to turn the company around, the Agnellis brought in a well-respected young businessman named Carlo De Benedetti (who later would gain fame as the head of Olivetti) to take over the nonautomotive aspects of the company. At the same time, Umberto Agnelli was chosen as a senator and devoted his time to politics. Both of these changes did not work out. Umberto did not receive the kind of respect he had hoped for as a politician, while De Benedetti's bold proposals clashed with the entrenched corporate bureaucracy at Fiat. He left the company within a matter of months, and Umberto returned. Shortly thereafter, Fiat announced that it had sold nearly 10 percent of itself to the government of Libya for some $415 million.

The late 1970s were a difficult period for the company. Worker militancy escalated once again, and terrorist groups like the Red Brigades targeted Fiat executives, more than two dozen of whom were wounded in ambushes. In 1979 Carlo Ghiglieno, a high-level executive in Fiat's auto operation, was shot and killed on a Turin street. The following year the Agnellis withdrew from day-to-day involvement in Fiat and managerial control of the company was handed over to Cesare Romiti, a no-nonsense executive who had come to Fiat in 1974. Romiti, who came to be known as *Il Duro* (The Tough One), successfully took on the company's militant unions, expanded the use of robots in auto production, and embarked on a restructuring of Fiat's operations. Unprofitable activities, both at home and abroad, were abandoned, including the ill-fated sales operation in North America. At the same time, Fiat introduced a new model called the Uno, a small car that was well received in Europe, and expanded its military-contracting operations. After Libya sold its stake (which had risen to 15 percent) in the company back to the Agnellis, Fiat was permitted to become a contractor for the Reagan administration's Strategic Defense Initiative (Star Wars).

All of this contributed to an impressive revival by the company. Productivity soared, profits rose, and Fiat was once again the darling of the international investment community. The Agnellis were not very disappointed when merger talks with Ford Motor collapsed, but Fiat did combine its truck operations with those of Ford in Europe. In 1986 Fiat acquired Alfa Romeo after using all of its political muscle to defeat a proposed sale of the loss-ridden, state-owned company to Ford. As a result Fiat ended up with some 60 percent of the domestic market, and by the late 1980s it had the highest market share in Europe.

In 1990 Fiat agreed to purchase a 6-percent stake in Compagnie Générale d'Électricité and formed a strategic alliance with the French company, which subsequently renamed itself Alcatel Alsthom. The agreement involved coordination of manufacturing operations through a series of mergers and other cooperative endeavors. Those mergers were to be in such fields as auto parts, railroad equipment, and telecommunications systems. For example, Fiat took over Alcatel's auto battery business, while Alcatel gained control of Fiat's Telettra subsidiary. The overall Alcatel-Fiat deal caused some concern in the

European Commission, which used its recently adopted powers to review cross-border business alliances to set certain conditions on the transactions between the two companies. Merger talks with U.S. car maker Chrysler were terminated shortly after the Alcatel alliance was announced.

In 1991 Fiat formed another alliance with Ford, when the two companies merged their farm and construction equipment operations into a venture called N.H. Geotech N.V. Fiat also expanded its involvement in what used to be known as the Soviet bloc. The company licensed a design for a new minicar to the Polish state-owned automaker Fabryka Samochodow Malolitrazowych (FSM). The Polish company, along with another state-owned firm called Fabryka Samochodow Osobowych (FSO), had already been licensing other Fiat designs. In September 1991 the Polish government began the process of privatizing FSM, and Fiat agreed to purchase a 51-percent stake (later increased to 90 percent) in the company. During the same period, Fiat was negotiating with the Russian government to purchase a 30-percent stake in VAZ (the Russian initials for Volga Auto Works), producer of the Lada sedan. Another possible project, involving construction by Fiat of a new auto complex in the former Soviet Union, was put on hold.

The company entered into another foreign alliance in October 1991, when it joined with the U.S. company Raytheon to pursue opportunities in such fields as petrochemicals, waste management, and dismantling of chemical weapons. Meanwhile, at home Fiat continued to experience an erosion of its position in what used to be a virtually captive market. The company's market share in early 1991 fell below 50 percent as imports from Ford and Renault poured into the country. That raised a disturbing specter for the company of what would happen if Japanese producers were allowed to sell their wares in Italy in significant numbers. This threat is part of the reason why there continue to be rumors of a merger between Fiat and one of its foreign competitors.

OPERATIONS

Automobiles (43 percent of 1990 revenues). Fiat is by far the largest auto producer in Italy (with a market share of 53 percent in 1990) and the second largest in Europe. The company makes a full range of cars, from subcompacts to full-sized luxury models, under the names Fiat, Lancia-Autobianchi, Alfa Romeo, Innocenti, and Ferrari. Those products are sold primarily in Italy and other countries of Europe, though the company also ranks fourth in the Brazilian market. It has thirty-three auto-manufacturing facilities in Italy and one each in Brazil, Portugal, and Venezuela.

Commercial Vehicles (12 percent of revenues). The company makes a wide range of trucks and related vehicles, quarry and construction vehicles, buses, fire engines, diesel engines, and forklifts. This segment operates under the auspices of its Iveco N.V. subsidiary, which is based in the Netherlands.

Manufacturing facilities for commercial vehicles are located in Italy, Germany, France, the United Kingdom, and Venezuela. In 1990 Iveco ranked second in the European truck market, behind Mercedes-Benz. That year Iveco agreed to purchase 60 percent of Enasa, Spain's largest producer of commercial vehicles.

Farm and Construction Equipment (4 percent of revenues). This segment includes the production of tractors, combine harvesters, hay- and forage-harvesting equipment, grape harvesters, lawn mowers, bulldozers, backloaders, excavators, and other heavy equipment. In 1990 the company had a market share of 33 percent in Italy and 10 percent in the rest of Europe. It operated eight manufacturing facilities for agricultural equipment (in Italy, the United States, France, and Spain) and four for construction equipment (Italy and Brazil). In 1991 Fiat merged these operations with Ford Motor's New Holland subsidiary to create a venture called N.H. Geotech N.V. That same year Fiat joined with Deere & Company and Hitachi in a venture to produce construction equipment in Europe.

Automotive-related Sectors (13 percent of revenues). Included in this segment are automotive components produced under the auspices of the subsidiary Magneti Marelli. Manufacturing facilities are located in Italy, France, Spain, the United Kingdom, Portugal, Brazil, and Mexico. This segment also includes metallurgical products (iron and aluminum casting, and steel components), various other industrial components, and production systems (including the robotic devices made by its Comau subsidiary).

Other Industrial Sectors (16 percent of revenues). This segment covers a variety of activities, including large-scale engineering projects, production of rolling stock and railway systems, military and commercial aircraft engines, fibers, chemicals, biotechnology, newspaper publishing, and telecommunications. In 1991 Fiat transferred its controlling interest in its Telettra telecommunications subsidiary to Alcatel Alsthom as part of its alliance with the French company.

Service Sectors (12 percent of revenues). Included here are credit, leasing, and other financial services; casualty and life insurance; and department stores and other retailing operations.

TOP EXECUTIVES

- Giovanni Agnelli, chairman
- Umberto Agnelli, vice chairman
- Cesare Romiti, managing director
- Giorgio Garuzzo, group chief operating officer
- Paolo Cantarella, president and chief executive of Fiat Auto

OUTSIDE DIRECTORS

- Henry Carl Martin Bodmer, chief executive of Abegg Holding Company
- Michel David-Weill, chairman of Lazard Frères
- Étienne Davignon, director of Société Générale de Belgique
- Wisse Dekker, chairman of the supervisory board of Philips Electronics
- Gianluigi Gabetti, chief executive of the Agnelli family holding company IFI
- Mario Monti, dean of Bocconi University
- Giampiero Pesenti, general director of ITALCEMENTI SpA
- Franzo Grande Stevens, legal adviser to the Agnelli family
- Pierre Suard, chairman and chief executive of Alcatel Alsthom
- Richard A. Voell, president of Rockefeller Center
- Ulrich Weiss, member of the board of management of Deutsche Bank

FINANCIAL DATA

Revenues (in billions of Italian lire)

1991	58,029
1990	57,209
1989	52,019
1988	45,512
1987	39,644
1986	29,873

Net Income (in billions of Italian lire)

1991	1,114
1990	1,613
1989	3,306
1988	3,026
1987	2,373
1986	2,162

GEOGRAPHICAL BREAKDOWN

Revenues (in billions of Italian lire)

Year	Italy		Rest of Europe		Elsewhere	
1990	39,483	(69%)	15,315	(27%)	2,411	(4%)
1989	34,854	(67%)	14,598	(28%)	2,567	(5%)
1988	30,425	(67%)	12,594	(28%)	2,493	(5%)

Operating profit (in billions of Italian lire)

Year	Italy		Rest of Europe		Elsewhere	
1990	1,725	(80%)	442	(20%)	− 38	(0%)
1989	3,518	(75%)	775	(17%)	377	(8%)
1988	2,871	(75%)	694	(18%)	258	(7%)

LABOR RELATIONS

Fiat has always been the main arena of the often-contentious labor relations of Italy. The company has employed a mixture of paternalism and repression in its attempts to control the work force. Founder Giovanni Agnelli created an extensive social welfare system for the tens of thousand of workers who were lured to Turin to work in the company's huge factories. Yet in 1920, when workers were inspired by the Bolshevik revolution to occupy those factories, Agnelli quickly asked the prime minister to send in the army. It was one of the few Agnelli requests to be turned down by the government, but the general strike failed nonetheless, paving the way for the rise of fascism.

The labor movement, which had been suppressed during the Mussolini era, was revived soon after World War II with the creation of the Confederazione Generale Italiana del Lavoro (CGIL) union alliance. Although CGIL was supposed to be nonpartisan, the largest group within it was the Communist party. Amid an atmosphere of anticommunism, several political parties soon broke away from CGIL and formed two rival union federations, the Confederazione Italiana Sindacati Lavoratori (CISL) and the Unione Italiana del Lavoro (UIL).

During the 1950s the labor movement remained weak. At Fiat the three federations were represented, but union membership declined and management felt free to fire militants or send them to remote parts of the company. The tide began to turn in 1962, when a routine walkout over a contract turned into an uprising against the right-wing UIL federation, which had negotiated a sweetheart settlement with the company. But the real explosion came in 1969, when Fiat's production workers were at the forefront of a wave of worker unrest that came to be known as the Hot Autumn.

Emerging out of rank-and-file frustrations over working conditions, the struggle at Fiat began in July 1969, when thousands of workers clashed with police at the massive Mirafiori plant in Turin. Wildcat walkouts continued over the next few weeks, prompting Agnelli to suspend the entire work force at the factory. The unions, which had lost control of the situation, finally pulled themselves together and signed an agreement with Fiat and other large employers that increased wages in an egalitarian way, shortened the work-week, improved conditions on the job, and gave more protection to union activity.

The unions at Fiat (and elsewhere in Italian industry) continued to make gains throughout the 1970s, though with less upheaval. The government pressured the company to pay substantial pay increases to help workers cope with the rise in oil prices and general inflation of the period. Yet both the unions and the rank and file also had to contend with the emergence of a terrorist campaign by groups like the Red Brigades against Fiat management. The unions, including the Communist party–dominated CGIL, condemned the terrorists and urged workers to align themselves with the government. Yet many workers, even if they did not condone the violence, could not bring themselves to support a state dominated by antilabor politicians.

Fiat had no ambivalence about the situation. The company began to take action against those workers it considered terrorist sympathizers. In October 1979 sixty-one workers were terminated for what management called lack of "diligence, propriety and good faith on the job." The firings became a test of strength between management and labor, and the unions backed down. The unions did, however, put up a fight a year later when Cesare Romiti, who had just been put in charge of the company, announced plans to eliminate more than fourteen thousand jobs—a move that was unheard of in Italy. This prompted a strike that was militant at first but quickly lost momentum when white-collar workers organized a back-to-work movement. After a demonstration to demand an end to the strike drew some forty thousand people, the unions quickly sued for peace.

The settlement of the five-week strike included a provision for rotating layoffs among twenty-three thousand workers rather than the company's original job-elimination proposal. An unspecified number of positions were to be abolished at a later date. The accord represented a turning point in labor relations at Fiat and in Italy as a whole. It marked the end of a period of rising labor power and the beginning of one in which management at Fiat and other companies have had a much freer hand in the pursuit of profit. Between 1980 and 1985 the company reduced employment in its overall operations by some one hundred thousand jobs.

Having been tamed, the unions formalized their cooperative relationship with Fiat in 1989 with an agreement that established a system of ongoing consultation between labor and management. The following year the company reached an agreement with the unions on a joint program to promote worker safety.

ENVIRONMENTAL RECORD

Fiat is one of a number of automakers that have been experimenting with electric vehicles. It began producing such a model, called the Panda, in small numbers in 1990. The company announced in 1991 that beginning in 1992 it would equip its entire passenger car line with exhaust emission controls designed to satisfy European Community standards scheduled to take effect in 1993.

BIBLIOGRAPHY

Barkan, Joanne. *Visions of Emancipation: The Italian Workers' Movement Since 1945.* New York: Praeger, 1984.

Friedman, Alan. *Agnelli: Fiat and the Network of Italian Power.* New York: NAL Books, 1989.

Maxcy, George. *The Multinational Automobile Industry.* New York: St. Martin's Press, 1981.

Sobel, Robert. *Car Wars.* New York: E. P. Dutton, 1984.

FORD MOTOR COMPANY

The American Road
Dearborn, Michigan 48121
(313) 322-3000

1991 revenues: $88.3 billion
1991 net income: − $2.3 billion (loss)
Publicly traded company
Employees: 332,700
Founded: 1903

OVERVIEW

Ford, one of the great names of the automobile industry, is a company that has played a major role in shaping both the horizons of everyday life and the conditions of toil on the job.

Founder Henry Ford transformed automobiles from an amusement for the wealthy to a conveyance for the common person. His Model T was for many the stepping stone to modern life, a means of escape from an isolated rural existence. The impact of Ford—who exhibited eccentric views ranging from pacifism to anti-Semitism—was felt by those who built his cars as well as by those who drove them. He introduced mass production on an unprecedented scale and sought to shape his employees into ideal workers, which meant both maximum effort on the job and clean living off the job. The latter was enforced through an elaborate system of surveillance organized by the company's so-called Sociological Department.

Ford stuck to his no-nonsense approach to automaking even when more elaborate car styles started to emerge. The result was that the company lost its lead and went into a period of instability that lasted for decades. The difficulties were exacerbated by Ford family problems that intruded on the company even after it went public in 1956, since the family continued to hold a controlling interest.

The 1980s saw an impressive rebound by the company, which for the first time was free of family managerial control. Yet by the beginning of the 1990s that magic was wearing off as Ford suffered along with the rest of the industry. For all its ups and downs, Ford remains a reasonably strong competitor both in the United States and in Europe. It may not regain the glory it had early in this century, but it will survive the challenge from Japan and remain one of the world's leading automakers.

HISTORY

The story of Ford Motor begins, of course, with the life of Henry Ford. Born in 1863 on a farm in rural Michigan, he had an aptitude for things mechanical. While working as an engineer for the Edison Illuminating Company in Detroit in the 1890s he tinkered first with a small internal combustion engine and then with a vehicle propelled by such a device. In 1896 he completed his first version of a horseless carriage—an invention that was then only a decade old.

The crude product, which Ford called a Quadricycle, was a stepping stone to a more refined vehicle completed in 1898. The following year he left his job at Edison and formed the Detroit Automobile Company, the city's first car maker. The venture survived only about a year, however, being forced to dissolve when Ford's backers declined to invest any more in the money-losing operation.

Ford rebounded by setting out to build cars on his own, and the effort gained credibility when Ford drove one of his creations in a car race in Grosse Point in 1901 and won an upset victory. The achievement encouraged his backers to set up Ford in a new company. Yet after Ford showed himself to be more interested in a new racing car he was designing than in the vehicle the company was planning to sell, the investors gave him the boot. After Ford's departure they adopted the name Cadillac Automobile Company, which would later become the luxury car division of General Motors.

For a while Ford continued to pursue his racing car ambitions, but in 1902 he and a new partner, Alex Malcolmson, joined the hundreds of entrepreneurs seeking their fortunes in the production of passenger cars. The following year the venture, now known as Ford Motor Company, began producing (with the help of various subcontractors) an automobile designated the Model A.

The car was well received, and the company soon reached an output of twenty-five vehicles a day. In 1904 three new products—the Model B, the Model C, and the Model F—were announced. With a price range of $800 to $2,000, they appealed to customers with varying means. Malcolmson believed that making more expensive cars would be more profitable, so he pushed Ford to go further upscale with the Model K, a luxurious touring car with a six-cylinder engine.

Ford, however, was beginning to develop the strategy that would make him famous. He pushed the idea of making an inexpensive car that would be affordable to a much wider portion of the population. Introduced in 1908, the Model T was not only relatively inexpensive ($825); its appeal was also based on its innovative transmission, its novel ignition system (which did away with the need for dry-storage batteries), and its use of components made of lightweight but sturdy vanadium.

The Model T revolutionized daily life, first in the United States and then in many other parts of the world. Automobiles were transformed from a novelty for the rich to the basis for mass mobility. The change was most dramatic in rural areas, where the car—which was especially well suited to bumpy country roads—made farm life much less isolated. By the end of World War I nearly half of all the cars in the world were "Tin Lizzies," as the Model T came to be called. Eventually more than fifteen million of them would be sold.

The triumph of the Model T was nearly snatched away from Ford by a patent dispute. An inventor named George Selden had filed back in 1879 for a patent based on a particular kind of gasoline engine he had seen at the Philadelphia Centennial Exposition in 1876. Selden engaged in legal maneuvers that resulted in the issuance of the patent being delayed until 1895—that is, until an industry that could exploit the technology had developed. In 1899 the Electric Vehicle Company bought the rights to the Selden patent and began challenging the right of auto producers to produce gasoline-powered cars without paying a license fee.

Many automakers gave in to the pressure and banded together in the Association of Licensed Automobile Manufacturers to restrict entry into the market. The association sought to undermine independents by publishing ads that warned potential customers, "Don't buy a lawsuit with your car." Henry Ford refused to recognize the claims of the association, which brought suit against the creator of the Model T in 1909. Ford lost the initial case but was vindicated at the appellate level in 1911. Ford was free to go on producing cars without paying tribute to the association, which was forced to disband.

The Model T also was significant because of the way it was made. Ford applied the time and motion techniques of Frederick Taylor to his factories, and in 1913 he introduced the first moving assembly line. Ford also shook up the industry by raising the wages of his workers, a step that was taken to reduce labor turnover. In addition, Ford kept lowering the price of the Model T, and he even gave rebates to customers when sales rose above a certain level.

During World War I Henry Ford spent a large amount of money subsidizing an independent peace initiative, but he also won a contract from the U.S. Navy to produce Eagle boats, which were designed to fight German submarines. After the war Ford, who bought out his fellow shareholders in 1919, stepped up production of tractors, and in the mid-1920s he started producing airplanes. Yet he resisted updating the Model T, which had come to look drab and old-fashioned next to the flashier cars being produced by General Motors (GM) and other companies. After much anguish—including pressure from his son Edsel, who had been given the title of president in 1918—Ford relented, and in May 1927 the Model T production line was shut down.

That same year the company introduced, with great fanfare, a new Model

A, which incorporated many of the advances in automobiles that had emerged since the birth of the Model T two decades earlier. Yet the retooling required for the new car was far behind schedule, so that production fell well below demand. Other companies filled the void, and Ford Motor lost its first-place position in the industry to GM. The company faced further travails during the depression but used price cuts to raise demand for its products. By this time Ford was also producing in Canada, Britain, Germany, and a dozen other countries; there was even a licensing arrangement with the Soviet Union.

Although Henry Ford was soft on naziism—he accepted an award from the German government in 1938—he was quick to offer the services of Ford Motor when the U.S. government began its military mobilization two years later. He built a huge plant called Willow Run to produce B-24 Liberator bombers. The facility, initially hyped as a veritable Eighth Wonder of the World, turned instead into a national embarrassment because of production problems. Edsel Ford, then trying to exercise real control in the company as his aging father grew increasingly out of touch with reality, had personal problems as well. His health steadily deteriorated, and he died of cancer in 1943.

Henry Ford wanted to name his crony Harry Bennett as Edsel's successor as president, but the family would not hear of it. To resolve the immediate problem, Henry Ford himself took over the position, but that was obviously not a permanent solution. Then the founder's grandson, Henry Ford II, was released from the navy and brought back to Detroit. The young Ford had to deal with hostility from Bennett and sometimes even from his own grandfather, but finally in 1945 he was given the presidency of the company. Henry Ford I died two years later.

The automaker that Henry Ford II took over was a troubled company. The introduction of upscale Lincoln cars and the middle-range Mercury models had not prevented Ford from falling farther behind both the Chevrolet division of GM and Chrysler. Ford was no genius, but he realized that he needed help. Only a few weeks after he took over the presidency, an offer of such assistance came from an unusual source—a group of ten young men who had gained recognition during the war for their skills in the Office of Statistical Control, which played an invaluable role in planning large-scale movements of supplies. As the war ended, the group, headed by Charles "Tex" Thornton—at thirty-two a colonel in the army air force—decided to stay together and hire themselves out to a corporation. After learning about the situation in Dearborn, they decided that Ford was that corporation.

As it turned out, Henry Ford II agreed, and the group, which also included Robert McNamara and Arjay Miller, began work at the company in early 1946. Before long they were known collectively as the "Whiz Kids." The group adopted a take-charge attitude, but Ford brought in Ernest Breech, a financial expert who had worked for GM, to oversee their work. It was Breech who pushed the company to develop an entirely new car—the 1949 Ford—which had a sleek, aerodynamic design and was the first passenger car to have an overdrive option. The success of the new car caused Breech's stock to soar and thus prompted the ambitious Tex Thornton to depart for Hughes Aircraft. He later founded the conglomerate Litton Industries.

Between the efforts of Breech and those of the remaining Whiz Kids, Ford enjoyed a dramatic comeback in the early 1950s. Yet the bulk of the company's sales remained less-expensive cars, which threw off a lot less profit than the pricier models. So the decision was made to develop a new, medium-priced car. Actually, the design was not entirely new, but Ford's public relations people cooked up the image of something that had been a decade in the making. Although thousands of names had been considered, the final choice was Edsel.

The ill-fated Edsel arrived in September 1957, in the middle of a recession and amid a turn in the market toward less-expensive cars. The much-ballyhooed product was a flop. The only consolation for the company was that a significant number of people who passed up the Edsel purchased Ford's new Fairlane, a less-expensive car introduced during the same period. A few years later Ford, like GM, reluctantly responded to the rising demand for compact cars with the introduction of the Falcon. And when GM scored with its upscale small car, the Monza, Ford responded in 1964 with the Mustang.

The man who took much of the credit for the great success of the sporty Mustang was Lee Iacocca, an aggressive salesman who had been promoted to the head of the Ford Division in 1960. Iacocca, who intended to rise much further in the company, was incensed when a high-ranking GM defector, Semon Knudsen, was hired as president by Henry Ford in 1968. Knudsen lasted only a year amid the ruthless corporate politics of the company. Fifteen months later Iacocca was a large step closer to this ultimate ambition—being the ruler of the Ford empire—when he was named president of the company. Yet Iacocca was not to have his final triumph. Henry Ford grew to dislike the man, and in 1978 he forced him out. A year later Ford, tired of fighting off shareholder lawsuits charging financial improprieties, stepped down and handed over the reins to Philip Caldwell.

Caldwell certainly had his hands full. As a result of the highly publicized problems of the Pinto (described later in this chapter), the quality of the company's cars had come into question. Ford, like the other two big car companies, had been caught off guard by the soaring demand for small, fuel-efficient cars brought on by the oil crisis. But GM had moved quickly to bring out its compact X-cars, while Ford struggled to find a replacement for the Pinto.

For some time the true dimensions of the company's problems in the United States were concealed by profits from abroad. It was during the 1970s, in fact, that Ford made great strides toward internationalizing its operations. The first step was to standardize designs internationally so that what was essentially the same car could be marketed around the world. The leading example of this was Ford's Fiesta, introduced in 1976.

The next stage involved producing what came to be called the global car. Plants in various countries were used to produce components that were brought together in several centralized assembly facilities. Ford began assembling its Escort in three countries with components manufactured by Ford factories in nine nations. This technique of "global sourcing" allowed Ford to take advantage of maximum economies of scale in the component plants and also made it less vulnerable to strikes or other disruptions in any one country. In 1979 the company also took a 25-percent stake in Japanese automaker Toyo Kogyo (now known as Mazda), which began producing components and later engineered whole cars for Ford.

By the early 1980s Ford's declining position in Europe meant that the company's foreign exploits were no longer making up for its domestic travails. Ford experienced three years of heavy losses. Yet those abysmal conditions did not last for long. A turnaround began in 1983 (helped in part by union concessions), and by the middle of the decade Ford was rapidly gaining market share, thanks to the popularity of its European-looking new Taurus and Mercury Sable models. In 1986 Ford, then run by Caldwell's successor, Donald Petersen, had a larger net income than GM for the first time since 1924. The company felt confident enough to pay a hefty $2.5 billion to acquire Britain's luxury car maker, Jaguar, in 1989.

The good times were not permanent. When Harold "Red" Poling took over as chairman in 1990, the company's money-making machine was sputtering. The Japanese onslaught was continuing, and Ford was slow in updating its product line. The losses started piling up in late 1990 and continued into the new year.

The plunge was especially dramatic in Ford's European operations. After gaining the top spot in Europe for the first time in 1984, Ford began slipping behind Volkswagen, Fiat, and even Peugeot. Part of the problem was that Ford was strongest in the sluggish British market, while the real growth was to be found in places like Germany, where the rival GM dominated. By 1990 GM enjoyed profits of nearly $2 billion in Europe; Ford's earnings there plunged to $145 million.

Also compounding Ford's problems was the poor state of one of its financial subsidiaries. In 1985 Ford had purchased First Nationwide Financial Corporation, then the country's ninth-largest savings and loan association. Three years later First Nationwide took over a group of insolvent thrifts in Colorado, Illinois, and Ohio. Problem loans mounted up at First Nationwide to the point that federal regulators ordered the company to tighten up its credit controls.

Like many other large companies, Ford has responded to its troubles in part by forming alliances with its competitors. In addition to its long-standing relationship with Mazda, the company announced in 1991 that it would produce a minivan in cooperation with Nissan and that it had asked another Japanese company, Yamaha, to design and develop a small engine to be used in Ford's European cars in the mid-1990s. That same year, Ford formed a joint venture with Volkswagen to establish a factory in Portugal to make multipurpose family vehicles for the European market. Ford already had such a cooperative relationship with Volkswagen in Brazil, where the two companies operated jointly through a company called Autolatina. Ford's farm equipment operations, which included the New Holland division of Sperry

Corporation it acquired in 1985, were put into a joint venture 80-percent owned by Italy's Fiat.

OPERATIONS

Automotive (82 percent of 1991 revenues). Ford produces a full line of passenger cars and a variety of trucks in the United States and other countries. In 1991 the company had a domestic market share of 20.1 percent for automobiles and 28.9 percent for trucks; in both cases it trailed GM by at least four percentage points. Outside the United States, Ford's most-extensive operations are in Britain, Germany, Canada, and Spain. The company also has strong positions in Australia and Taiwan.

Financial Services (18 percent of revenues). Ford has five major financial subsidiaries. Ford Motor Credit Company provides wholesale financing and capital loans to franchised Ford dealers. First Nationwide Financial Corporation is a savings and loan holding company that has run into financial difficulties and has been forced by federal regulators to initiate stricter management controls. Associates First Capital Corporation, American Road Insurance, and U.S. Leasing engage in consumer finance, commercial finance, insurance underwriting, and leasing.

TOP EXECUTIVES

- Harold A. Poling, chairman and chief executive
- Philip E. Benton, Jr., president and chief operating officer
- Allan D. Gilmour, executive vice president and president of the Ford Automotive Group
- Stanley A. Seneker, executive vice president and chief financial officer
- William C. Ford, chairman of the executive committee

OUTSIDE DIRECTORS

- Colby H. Chandler, retired chief executive of Eastman Kodak
- Michael D. Dingman, chairman of the Henley Group
- Roberto C. Goizeuta, chief executive of Coca-Cola
- Irving O. Hockaday, Jr., chief executive of Hallmark Cards
- Drew Lewis, chief executive of Union Pacific Corporation
- Ellen R. Marram, senior vice president of Nabisco Brands, a subsidiary of RJR Nabisco
- Kenneth H. Olsen, chief executive of Digital Equipment Corporation
- Carl E. Reichardt, chief executive of Wells Fargo & Company
- Clifton R. Wharton, Jr., chief executive of the Teachers Insurance and Annuity Association–College Retirement Equities Fund

FINANCIAL DATA

Revenues (in millions of dollars)

1991	88,286
1990	97,650
1989	96,146
1988	92,446
1987	79,893

Net Income (in millions of dollars)

1991	−2,258 (loss)
1990	860
1989	3,835
1988	5,300
1987	4,625

GEOGRAPHICAL BREAKDOWN

Revenues (in millions of dollars)

Year	United States		Europe		Elsewhere	
1991	53,809	(61%)	24,075	(27%)	10,402	(12%)
1990	61,771	(63%)	25,398	(26%)	10,481	(11%)
1989	64,182	(67%)	20,971	(22%)	10,993	(11%)

Operating Income (in millions of dollars)

Year	United States		Europe		Elsewhere	
1991	−1,447	(0%)	−961	(0%)	150	(100%)
1990	628	(70%)	263	(30%)	−31	(0%)
1989	1,627	(42%)	1,289	(34%)	919	(24%)

LABOR RELATIONS

Henry Ford gained fame as the man who instituted the five-dollar day for his workers in the 1910s. The facts were somewhat more complicated; not all workers qualified for that amount, which in any event was not the base pay. A large part of the five dollars consisted of a so-called profit-sharing bonus that had to be earned—by working at a high level of intensity on the job and by living in a style that Ford considered appropriate off the job.

To enforce the life-style regulations, Ford created a Sociological Department, which had inspectors who visited the homes of workers and interviewed family members and neighbors. The company wanted to be sure that workers were not spending their share of Ford profits in a frivolous or irresponsible manner.

Ford also became famous for the diversity of the workers he hired. Critics have pointed out that the varied nationalities and languages made union organizing more difficult, yet at the same time, Ford pioneered the hiring of ex-convicts, the disabled, and blacks in industrial jobs.

The benign image of Ford Motor began to dissolve during the depression. In 1932 a protest march to the company's Rouge plant in Dearborn was met with tear gas and machine-gun fire, which killed four persons. Dearborn police officers were supplemented by members of the Service Department, Ford's own security force. Headed by Henry Ford's right-hand man, Harry Bennett, the Service Department became notorious for its surveillance of workers, both on and off the job.

Over the next few years, labor relations in the automobile industry were transformed. A wave of job actions in the industry paved the way for the creation of the United Automobile Workers of America (UAW) in 1935 as an affiliate of the American Federation of Labor (AFL). The commitment of the UAW's activists to industrial unionism clashed with the craft orientation and general conservatism of the AFL. In 1936 the UAW joined the newly established Committee for Industrial Organization (CIO) and set out to organize the big automakers.

GM was the first target. Short strikes at various sites around the country were followed by a nationwide action against the company in January 1937. The UAW successfully employed the tactic of sit-down strikes and plant occupations, most notably at the Fisher Body plant in Flint, Michigan. GM capitulated in February 1937 and Chrysler followed suit later in the year.

Things were more difficult at Ford. The organizing effort was curtailed after the infamous "Battle of the Overpass," in which UAW organizers were attacked by Bennett's security force and free-lance thugs when they attempted to distribute leaflets outside the Rouge plant in May 1937. Although the company clearly had violated the National Labor Relations Act, Bennett bought time by co-opting some UAW leaders and exploiting divisions within the union (which included the creation of a new UAW allied with the AFL). Shortly after the charges against Ford were finally upheld by the Supreme Court in 1941, a wildcat strike spread through the company's plants. Henry Ford, reportedly under pressure from his son Edsel, finally relented and agreed to a representation election. The CIO-affiliated union won the vote overwhelmingly.

Once the presence of the union was an established fact, Bennett took an entirely different approach toward the UAW. Apparently seeking to co-opt the union, he negotiated an extremely generous contract, agreeing to a closed shop, dues checkoff, and a provision that Ford would match the highest wage rate paid by anyone in the industry.

Labor unrest escalated again after World War II. Yet while GM suffered a 113-day strike over wage increases, Ford settled with the UAW without any interruption of work. In the following years the UAW won steady improvements for its members, including such pioneering provisions as supplementary unemployment benefits and company-paid pensions. The union's cooperative relationship with management averted strikes, but it heightened tension between rank-and-file workers and the UAW leadership. The result was periodic insurgencies on the shop floor, especially when a new generation of workers entered the factories in the late 1960s.

The ability of the UAW to win steady contract improvements came to an end with the auto industry crisis of the late 1970s. In 1979 the union agreed to $243 million in concessions to ailing Chrysler, and the federal government insisted on another $200 million as one of the terms for the government bailout of the company. By the early 1980s, with several hundred thousand autoworkers out of work indefinitely, the UAW felt it had to give in to concessions sought by Ford and GM as well. In some cases Ford was ruthless in its demands for givebacks. At a plant in Sheffield, Alabama, for instance, the company told workers in 1981 that it would close the plant unless they took a 50-percent cut in pay and benefits or else bought the money-losing operation.

Some of this lost ground was regained when the industry rebounded in 1983, yet there remained a tug-of-war between company claims that the labor-cost differential with Japan had to be narrowed and worker resistance to an erosion in living standards. The leadership of the UAW, taken over by Owen Bieber in 1983, dealt with the problem by promoting a more cooperative relationship with management while seeking to expand job security and worker participation. The union also agreed to take part of a wage increase in the form of bonuses tied to the company's profit level.

The UAW has continued to cooperate with Ford management in easing work rules and raising productivity in exchange for modest improvements in job security. The union's strategy of using "jointness" as a way of trying to save jobs has also been applied at the joint manufacturing operations set up by Japanese companies and the big three in the United States, including the Ford-Mazda plant in Michigan. The contract at that facility went particularly far in allowing flexibility, giving management the right to make broad use of temporary workers.

Ford has had a mixed labor relations record abroad as well. One major hot spot has been Britain, the site of major walkouts in 1978 and 1988. In the latter case more than thirty thousand British Ford workers went on strike to resist company demands for additional workplace reorganization (beyond what the unions had consented to in 1985), which Ford claimed was necessary to compete with the Japanese car makers then entering the British market.

Another site of contention has been the plant in Mexico City, where the company laid off all of the workers in 1987 and then reopened with a smaller work force that was compelled to toil at lower wages and with new equipment that greatly increased the speed of the assembly line. Many of the rehired rank-and-file workers supported a group of those who remained jobless in their protests against the company, including a thirty-five-day hunger strike in 1989. Workers also clashed with the government-controlled union, which failed to oppose the company's actions.

In 1985 the first worldwide conference of rank-and-file Ford workers took place in Liverpool, England. Representatives came not only from plants in Europe—which had held such meetings previously—but also from Brazil, Malaysia, South Africa, Australia, New Zealand, Japan, and North America. Subsequent gatherings of Ford workers from different parts of the world have been held under the auspices of the International Metalworkers Federation and the Transnational Information Exchange.

ENVIRONMENTAL AND SAFETY RECORD

Ford's reputation as an automaker was seriously blemished in the 1970s, when its new compact, the Pinto, turned out to have a fatal flaw: its fuel tank was unshielded and was located near the back bumper in the fragile car, meaning that rear-end collisions frequently resulted in horrible explosions. There was later evidence that Ford was aware of the vulnerability of the gas tank but went ahead with production of the car. In one civil case a jury awarded $125 million in damages (reduced by the judge to $3.5 million), but the company executives were found innocent of murder charges in another Pinto case.

Ford also was embarrassed by reports that many of its cars with automatic transmissions produced during the 1970s had a tendency to slip from park into reverse. In 1981 federal regulators forced the company to send warning notices to purchasers of some twenty-three million vehicles about the problem. Ford might not have been happy about this, but it was a lot less onerous than the massive recall of the cars that had been urged by public interest groups.

The company has had difficulty meeting federal standards for auto emissions and fuel efficiency. In 1973 the company was fined $7 million for falsifying tests results submitted to the federal government on emissions testing. In 1991 more than sixty thousand Ford pickup trucks and vans were recalled for emissions that exceeded federal standards. Also, Ford was the last of the big three automakers to introduce air bags.

In 1991 Ford warned consumers of a potential transmission defect on several pickup, minivan, and utility vehicle models produced at the company's plant in Louisville, Kentucky. Ford said it would soon announce a recall to deal with the defect, which could allow the vehicles to roll even when the transmission is in the park position.

In 1992, Ford introduced two new models that were billed as the cleanest-running mass-production cars ever developed. The updated version of the Ford Escort and the Mercury Tracer were engineered to meet strict emission controls scheduled to go into effect in California in 1997.

BIBLIOGRAPHY

Collier, Peter, and David Horowitz. *The Fords: An American Epic.* New York: Summit Books, 1987.

Doody, Alan F., and Ron Bingaman. *Reinventing the Wheels: Ford's Spectacular Comeback.* New York: Harper Business, 1988.

Ford and Its Workers. Geneva: International Metalworkers Federation, 1980.

Ford Motor Co. Anti-Report. London: Counter Information Services, n.d.

The Ford Report: A Public Inquiry into the Ford Motor Company. London: Greater London Council Industry and Employment Branch, 1986.

Katz, Harry C. *Shifting Gears: Changing Labor Relations in the U.S. Automobile Industry.* Cambridge, Mass.: MIT Press, 1985.

Lacey, Robert. *Ford: The Men & the Machine.* Boston: Little, Brown, 1986.

Maxcy, George. *The Multinational Automobile Industry.* New York: St. Martin's Press, 1981.

May, George S., ed. *The Automobile Industry, 1885–1920.* Encyclopedia of American Business History and Biography series. New York: Facts on File, 1990.

———. *The Automobile Industry, 1920–1980.* Encyclopedia of American Business History and Biography series. New York: Facts on File, 1989.

Meyer, Stephen, III. *The Five Dollar Day: Labor Management and Social Control in the Ford Motor Company, 1908–1921.* Albany: State University of New York Press, 1981.

Nevins, Allan. *Ford.* 3 vols. New York: Charles Scribner's Sons, 1954–63.

Petersen, Donald E., and John Hillkirk. *A Better Idea: Redefining the Way Americans Work.* Boston: Houghton Mifflin, 1991.

Rae, John. *The American Automobile: A Brief History.* Chicago: University of Chicago Press, 1965.

———. *The American Automobile Industry.* Boston: Twayne, 1984.

Shook, Robert L. *Turnaround: The New Ford Motor Co.* New York: Prentice-Hall, 1990.

Sinclair, Upton. *The Flivver King: A Story of Ford-America* (1937). Chicago: Charles H. Kerr, 1987. (A novel based on the Ford story.)

Sobel, Robert. *Car Wars.* New York: E. P. Dutton, 1984.

Taub, Eric. *Taurus: The Making of the Car that Saved Ford.* New York: E. P. Dutton, 1991.

White. Lawrence J. *The Automobile Industry Since 1945.* Cambridge, Mass.: Harvard University Press, 1971.

FUJITSU LTD.

6-1, Marunouchi 1-chome
Chiyoda-ku, Tokyo 100
Japan
(03) 3216-3211

1991 revenues: $21.1 billion (year ending March 31)
1991 net income: $588 million
Publicly traded company
Employees: 145,872
Founded: 1935

OVERVIEW

Fujitsu began as a producer of telephone equipment, and although it remains in that field, the company's preoccupation has been to challenge IBM's dominance of the global computer market. Fujitsu has not even come close in that effort in most of the world, but it did manage to surpass Big Blue in Japan. It paid a price (specifically, $800 million) for its imitation of IBM's operating systems, but if it results in a bigger share of the mainframe market, it will have been money well spent.

While trying harder as number two in the computer industry (a position it gained with the 1990 purchase of most of the British company International Computers Ltd., or ICL), Fujitsu has become a more important force in other fields as well. It is one of the top Japanese—which these days means top world—producers of memory chips and in 1991 introduced the smallest cellular telephone and the lightest laptop computer.

HISTORY

Fujitsu started out in life as the telephone equipment subsidiary of Fuji Electric, itself a joint venture of Furukawa Electric of Japan and Germany's Siemens. In 1935 Fujitsu was spun off as an independent company, and although it went on supplying that equipment, it also was pulled by the government into military production. The company made military communications gear, and during World War II it produced antiaircraft weapons.

After the war Fujitsu returned to the production of civilian telecommunications gear, serving as one of the main suppliers to the newly created utility company Nippon Telegraph and Telephone. At the urging of the Ministry of International Trade and Industry (MITI), Fujitsu diversified into the then-young field of automatic data processing. In 1954 it introduced the FACOM 100, Japan's first commercial computer. The business developed slowly, however, until the Japanese government adopted a policy that restricted imports while it was negotiating a deal with industry leader IBM that would give that company the right to set up a Japanese manufacturing subsidiary in exchange for licensing crucial patents to Fujitsu and other companies.

Fujitsu, which, unlike its competitors, declined to form research alliances with IBM, was pushed by MITI to focus on integrated circuits as well as mainframes. The Japanese producers were set back by IBM's introduction of the revolutionary 360 Series in 1964, yet they benefited from low-interest loans from the government-created Japanese Electronic Computer Company. Fujitsu brought out its next-generation machine, the FACOM 230, in 1965.

Although the company was advancing in telecommunications equipment and factory automation (the latter business was spun off in 1972 and became known as Fanuc), its computer operation remained in the shadow of IBM. MITI, growing increasingly anxious about the survival of the Japanese computer industry, pressured the top companies to form alliances; Fujitsu ended up with its rival Hitachi.

But it was another alliance that allowed Fujitsu to move ahead. In 1972 the company decided to back a former IBM engineer named Gene Amdahl who set up a company to make what became known as plug-compatible computers—machines that were more efficient and less expensive than those of Big Blue but could run on the same software. For about a decade Amdahl (and other companies that rushed into the field) put IBM on the defensive, and Fujitsu benefited from Gene Amdahl's knowledge of IBM operating systems. The Japanese company brought out its first plug-compatible machine in 1974 and was soon supplying Amdahl with mainframe subassemblies. By the end of the decade Fujitsu surpassed IBM Japan as the largest computer maker in its home country.

Fujitsu increased its market penetration overseas through additional alliances with Western companies, including its onetime parent Siemens and ICL in Britain. It also joined with the U.S. company TRW in 1980 to make cash register terminals and bought out its partner three years later. Yet Fujitsu also faced legal troubles abroad. IBM accused Fujitsu of stealing proprietary software for use in its IBM-compatible systems. The case went to arbitration, with the result that Fujitsu was required to pay IBM $833 million but was allowed to go on selling its plug-compatible systems. The Japanese company also won limited access to new IBM operating systems. By 1990 Fujitsu was able to steal the spotlight from IBM by announcing a new generation of mainframes just before Big Blue was scheduled to do the same.

During the 1980s Fujitsu (along with Hitachi and NEC) entered the supercomputer market, challenging the dominance of the U.S. company Cray Research, though it found it difficult to attract customers outside Japan. Its position in telecommunications has been stronger. Still aided by its close ties to Nippon Telegraph and Telephone, Fujitsu has become a leader in the development of Integrated Services Digital Networks, the sophisticated systems designed to carry audio, video, data, and text.

Fujitsu is also one of the world's largest producers of semiconductors. It was one of five companies chosen by MITI in the 1970s to focus on chips at a time when new methods of production were making possible much denser integrated circuits. Fujitsu and its Japanese counterparts overwhelmed the U.S. producers of memory chips to such an extent that even the free trade–oriented Reagan administration felt compelled to impose dumping penalties against the Japanese firms. U.S. government opposition also forced Fujitsu in 1987 to drop a plan to purchase 80 percent of Fairchild Semiconductor.

Fujitsu had more success in Europe, where in 1990 it paid $1.3 billion for an 80-percent stake in ICL, Britain's only producer of mainframes. The deal allowed Fujitsu to jump ahead of the U.S. company Digital Equipment into the number-two spot among the world's computer makers. That position was further enhanced in 1991, when Fujitsu, through ICL, acquired the computer division of the Finnish company Nokia Group. ICL also agreed that year to purchase a 50-percent interest in the European computer-maintenance operations of the U.S. telephone company Bell Atlantic.

Although it has continued to challenge IBM directly in the mainframe market, Fujitsu has hedged its bets by producing computers using the rival UNIX operating system developed by AT&T. In 1990, moreover, Fujitsu, NEC, and Toshiba each purchased small stakes in the Ma Bell operation.

Fujitsu also has been making a name for itself as an innovator in areas other than mainframes. In 1991 it introduced the world's smallest portable cellular telephone (it weighs 10.2 ounces and can fit inside a shirt pocket) and the lightest laptop computer, a two-pound notebook-style model that uses memory cards instead of disks. Fujitsu announced in 1991 that it was investing $40 million in a new U.S. company called Hal Computer, which planned to introduce an assortment of products ranging from workstations to superminicomputers. At about the same time, Fujitsu joined a consortium of five Japanese companies to promote CD-ROM electronic publishing.

OPERATIONS

Computers and Information-Processing Systems (69 percent of 1991 revenues). Fujitsu continues to lead the mainframe computer market in Japan with its M Series machines; they are used in such high-profile applications as the Tokyo Stock Exchange and Japan Railways. In 1990 the company delivered its first VP2000 Series supercomputer, with which Fujitsu is among those

Japanese firms challenging industry leader Cray Research. Fujitsu is also a major supplier of large-scale storage systems; in 1990 it began marketing a disk system with a capacity of 30 gigabytes. Foreign sales of mainframes are done primarily through Amdahl Corporation (44-percent owned) in the United States and ICL (80-percent owned) in Europe.

Fujitsu has followed the trend away from mainframes in many applications by developing a series of powerful minicomputers and PCs. The company is also on the multimedia bandwagon (the ability to process data, sound, and images), having introduced its FM TOWNS 32-bit hypermedia PC in 1989. With the settlement of the dispute with IBM, Fujitsu has been freer to promote systems software. The company also is active in developing artificial intelligence systems. Although Fujitsu spun off much of its Fanuc factory automation subsidiary (it retained 39 percent), in 1991 the company announced an alliance in that field with McDonnell Douglas.

Communications Systems (15 percent of revenues). Fujitsu provides a wide range of telecommunications equipment, including transmission systems, large-scale switching systems and PBXs, cellular phones, private communication networks, and ISDN systems. In 1991 the company purchased a 75-percent stake in Fulcrum Communications, an equipment division of British Telecom.

Semiconductors and Electronics Components (12 percent of revenues). Fujitsu is one of the leading producers of state-of-the-art memory chips, the 1-megabit versions of which are in wide use today. In 1990 the company announced the first 4-megabit chip for processing three-dimensional images. In mid-1991 Fujitsu went to court in Japan to challenge the patent that U.S. chip maker Texas Instruments had been granted in the country in 1989 on basic semiconductor technology. Fujitsu also produces semicustom chips, microprocessors, and amplifiers used in satellite broadcast receivers. In 1991 Fujitsu ranked sixth in the world semiconductor business, with a market share of 4.8 percent.

Other Operations (4 percent of revenues). Included in this segment are automobile audio equipment and security devices.

TOP EXECUTIVES

- Takuma Yamamoto, chairman
- Matami Yasufuku, vice chairman
- Tadashi Sekizawa, president
- Kazuo Watanabe, executive vice president
- Mikio Ohtsuki, executive vice president

FINANCIAL DATA

Revenues (in millions of yen) (years ending March 31)

1991	2,971,462
1990	2,549,773
1989	2,387,442
1988	2,046,802
1987	1,789,417

Net Income (in millions of yen) (years ending March 31)

1991	82,673
1990	86,758
1989	69,948
1988	42,115
1987	21,609

GEOGRAPHICAL BREAKDOWN

Revenues (in millions of yen)

Year*	Domestic		Foreign	
1991	2,233,493	(75%)	737,969	(25%)
1990	1,941,075	(76%)	608,698	(24%)
1989	1,859,129	(78%)	528,313	(22%)
1988	1,594,193	(78%)	452,609	(22%)

*Fiscal year ends March 31.

LABOR RELATIONS

Relations between unions and management at Fujitsu's domestic plants are generally harmonious, but the company has clashed with unions in Britain. After it took over ICL in 1990, the unions representing workers at that company charged that Fujitsu was not observing a ten-year-old agreement that required management to consult with the union on alternatives to job eliminations.

ENVIRONMENTAL RECORD

Fujitsu is among the companies that have taken steps to eliminate the use of ozone-destroying CFCs from electronics production. In 1989 Fujitsu said it would cease its use of CFCs by 1995.

BIBLIOGRAPHY

Anchordoguy, Marie. *Computers, Inc.: Japan's Challenge to IBM*. Cambridge, Mass.: Harvard University Press, 1989.

Campbell-Kelly, Martin. *ICL: A Business and Technical History*. Oxford: Clarendon Press, 1989.

Sobel, Robert. *IBM vs. Japan: The Struggle for the Future*. Briarcliff Manor, N.Y.: Stein & Day, 1985.

GENERAL ELECTRIC COMPANY

3135 Easton Turnpike
Fairfield, Connecticut 06431
(203) 373-2211

1991 revenues: $60.2 billion
1991 net income: $2.6 billion
Publicly traded company
Employees: 284,000
Founded: 1878

OVERVIEW

The company does not like the term, but General Electric (GE) is a classic conglomerate. Its original businesses—electrical equipment, light bulbs, and appliances—are now small parts of an industrial and financial empire that includes a television network, an investment bank, and the production of medical equipment, plastics, and nuclear weapons.

GE is not a major brand name abroad, but it is a powerhouse of an exporter (more than $7 billion in 1991), especially in big industrial items like jet engines and locomotives. The company has gone through a wrenching reorganization since the early 1980s—so much so that the company began to refer to itself almost exclusively by its initials rather than to utter the word *electric*, which increasingly does not describe what it does. Traditionally GE has been thought of as a paradigm of modern management methods, though by the late 1980s there was a growing view that it had become an unwieldy collection of disparate businesses.

Chief executive Jack Welch nonetheless continues his constant reshuffling of GE's assets. At the same time, he pushes the concept of GE as a "boundaryless company," that is, one in which internal divisions blur, suppliers and customers are partners, and there is no separation between domestic and foreign operations.

HISTORY

The story of General Electric begins with Thomas Edison. In 1879 Edison and his assistant, Francis Jehl, created the first long-lasting incandescent light bulb. The announcement of the device, which consisted of a carbon filament in a vacuum globe, made the stock market go wild. The shares of gas companies, which had dominated the energy business, plunged as investors flocked to the Edison Electric Light Company, a start-up firm financed by J. P. Morgan and Western Union president Hamilton Twombly.

Edison's vision of electricity transforming commerce and everyday life captured the imagination of the country. And Edison was determined to capture the market, both for light bulbs and for the energy needed to illuminate them. The wizard of Menlo Park set up the Edison Electric Illuminating Company to build the first central-station generating plant. He shrewdly chose as his initial service area a section of downtown Manhattan that included the financial district.

After the Pearl Street station successfully started operation in 1882, competitors rushed into the new business, both to generate electricity and to make light bulbs. Edison's poorly written patent application for the bulb had been rejected, and so the legal monopoly went to a rival. The rights to a refined version of that bulb were scooped up by an aggressive young inventor and entrepreneur named George Westinghouse, who also began producing generating equipment.

Despite this setback, Edison's company made money by expanding its service and licensing its equipment designs to others. Yet Edison the mechanical genius was less than brilliant as a manager. He missed a number of important opportunities and insisted on using direct current (DC) rather than alternating current (AC). The latter, adopted by Westinghouse and other companies, allowed higher-voltage power to be transmitted over much longer distances. Edison held to the belief that AC was too dangerous, and as a way of highlighting the point he urged New York State to use a Westinghouse AC generator in building the first electric chair.

The battle between DC and AC was only one of the many differences in standards among the various purveyors of electricity in any given city. The desire to resolve this problem and the quest for economies of scale prompted numerous generating companies to merge with one another. J. P. Morgan, the apostle of corporate consolidation, wanted to extend this to the manufacturing of electrical equipment. He gained control over Edison General Electric (formed in 1889 to consolidate the Edison holdings) and in 1892 combined it with another firm, Massachusetts-based Thomson-Houston, to form General Electric. Edison had no place in either the name of the new firm or its management. He went back to his laboratory, and GE, under the leadership of Charles A. Coffin, went on to become an industrial giant.

One of GE's major businesses was electric railways. Thomson-Houston had brought two such operations into the combined company, and the Edison side had included the Sprague Electric Railway and Motor Company, a pioneer in electric streetcar systems. GE gained a great deal of publicity by providing an elevated electric train line at the Chicago World's Fair in 1893.

Before long GE was dominating virtually all aspects of electrification in the United States, from generating and transmitting power to making the trolleys, motors (including large ones for industry), elevators, fans, and bulbs that used it. Around the turn of the century the company developed high-speed steam turbines, and in 1903 it acquired the Stanley Electric Manufacturing Company, whose founder, William Stanley, had invented the transformer.

In 1900 GE established the country's first corporate research facility, which, among other things, improved on Edison's light bulb and devised the tungsten filament still in use today. In 1913 the lab developed the first X-ray tube, thus forming the basis of GE's medical equipment business. Later, as a result of its research on insulation for electric wiring, the research lab began doing early work on plastics.

Yet the company realized that electricity would have to be employed much more widely if its power generation and equipment operations were to continue growing. Thus GE began to introduce new electric appliances, beginning with the toaster and the iron in 1905. The following year a rather awkward electric range was brought out. During the 1910s GE came out with a waffle iron and an experimental household refrigerator. In 1918 the company merged with its two major competitors—Pacific Electric Heating Company, maker of the popular Hotpoint iron, and Hughes Electric Heating Company, which made an electric range. By the 1920s GE was selling an affordable household refrigerator and soon introduced vacuum cleaners, washing machines, and other electric devices for the home.

While GE's appliance business was blossoming, government concern about the company's market dominance was growing. In 1924 GE and Westinghouse were forced out of the power generating business, and a later antitrust action forced GE to make its light bulb patent available to competitors.

But at the same time, GE was boldly entering new lines of business, most notably the young field of broadcasting. Following the achievement of the first wireless voice transmission in 1906, the radio business was being developed by the Marconi Wireless Company of America; GE was working on the technology as well. In 1919 the federal government was alarmed at the attempt of American Marconi, as the subsidiary of a foreign firm (British Marconi), to purchase certain essential patents owned by GE. As an alternative the Wilson administration worked with GE to create a new company called Radio Corporation of America (RCA), which absorbed the assets of American Marconi.

RCA, essentially a subsidiary of GE with a large minority interest owned by AT&T, was the vehicle by which a small group of companies attempted to dominate the new industry through the pooling of patents—so much so that soon after Westinghouse Electric entered the arena, it was invited to join the combine, as was United Fruit, which made use of radio to communicate with its banana boats going to and from Central America.

Westinghouse went on to create the first commercial broadcasting station in 1920; soon radio stations were popping up everywhere and people were clamoring for listening devices. Tensions among the partners in RCA over who could do what led to a 1922 agreement that gave the phone company the exclusive right to produce and sell radio transmission equipment, while receiving apparatuses were to be manufactured by GE and Westinghouse and marketed by RCA. In 1926 AT&T decided to quit broadcasting in exchange for a monopoly on wire connections between stations.

That same year, a new entity called National Broadcasting Company (NBC) was formed to operate AT&T's former stations and RCA's outlets. It was agreed that NBC—50 percent owned by RCA, 30 percent by GE, and 20 percent by Westinghouse—would pay AT&T generous rates for guaranteed access to land-line connections.

NBC began its network broadcasting with a November 1926 gala production originating at the old Waldorf-Astoria Hotel in New York City and at other sites. By early 1927 NBC had two radio networks, NBC-Red and NBC-Blue. Even though a competing operation called the Columbia Broadcasting System (CBS) was formed in 1927, the federal government felt that NBC was too dominant in the industry. In 1930 the Justice Department brought antitrust charges against RCA, GE, and Westinghouse.

The industry was stunned but worked out a consent decree they could live with. The final deal was for GE and Westinghouse to give up their ownership interests in RCA. The latter was allowed to keep its radio-manufacturing facilities and GE and Westinghouse would be allowed to compete in that business after a thirty-month interval.

GE kept up its stream of new products—including electric dishwashers and fluorescent lighting—during the depression, but with the onset of World War II the company shifted its focus to military needs. GE produced radar systems and power plants for ships while also building some of the first jet engines for airplanes.

After the war GE resumed production of its consumer goods, but it also branched into new areas. Among these were silicone-based sealants and lubricants and, on a much bigger scale, nuclear power. GE produced the first nuclear reactors for submarines and, after the federal government opened up atomic energy to civilian purposes, nuclear reactors for power plants.

During the 1950s the company was a fount of innovations—among them, turbine engines for jet aircraft, gas turbines for electric power generation, synthetic diamonds, and self-cleaning ovens. GE promoted its products with the slogan "Progress is our most important product" and sent then-actor Ronald Reagan around the country as a goodwill ambassador.

Yet the old bugaboo of the company—antitrust—returned to torment it. In 1961 the Justice Department indicted several dozen companies, GE among them, for criminal price-fixing in the electrical equipment business. (A couple of years before the indictments Senator Estes Kefauver had conducted an investigation that found that GE and its "competitors" were submitting identical bids to major customers like the Tennessee Valley Authority.) All of the defendants decided to plead guilty to the charges. GE was fined $437,000 and ended up paying tens of millions of dollars in damages in civil suits brought by customers. Several company executives paid personal fines and received short jail sentences.

In the following years the company went through a massive reorganization, reducing the number of its operating units from some two hundred to several dozen. GE also reassessed its position in the computer industry. The company had started making mainframes in 1956 and ended up as one of what were called the seven dwarfs trying to compete with industry giant IBM. In 1970 GE got tired of its losses in the business and sold out to Honeywell. GE later decided that it needed a foothold in electronics and purchased semiconductor maker Intersil (though it was sold in 1988).

As some of GE's core businesses—especially nuclear reactors—went into a slump in the 1970s, the company made a bold diversification move. It spent more than $2 billion in 1976 to acquire Utah International, a natural resources company involved in oil, uranium, copper, coal, and other minerals.

Utah added substantially to GE's earnings, but the larger company was still in something of a rut when Jack Welch took over as chief executive in 1981. The go-getter Welch set out to do something about that, vowing to retain only those businesses in which GE was number one or two. Over the next decade he sold and bought scores of operations. In the course of this shake-up Welch eliminated some one hundred thousand jobs, earning him the nickname Neutron Jack. Among those businesses divested was Utah International, which (except for its Ladd Petroleum unit in the United States) was sold in 1984 to Australia's Broken Hill Proprietary. The housewares division (toasters, irons, and other small appliances) went to Black & Decker.

On the acquisition side, Welch made several dramatic moves. In 1985, amid a merger wave in the media, he agreed to spend $6.3 billion to purchase RCA and its subsidiary NBC, one of the three major television networks.

After GE had given up its interest in RCA in the 1930s, RCA, under the leadership of "General" David Sarnoff, played an important role in the development of television technology and became a leading military and civilian electronics producer, though, like GE, it abandoned the computer business. In the period before the GE buyout it was suffering from instability in its top ranks. Its NBC subsidiary, which in the 1940s was pressured by the federal government to sell one of its two radio networks (giving rise to the third network, ABC), moved aggressively into television in the 1950s, though it was later overshadowed in that medium by CBS. It was not until the 1980s, when the legendary programmer Grant Tinker took over, that the network was able to rise toward the top in the ratings war.

In addition to taking on RCA, GE got more heavily involved in financial services. The General Electric Credit Corporation, founded decades earlier in order to help consumers finance the purchase of GE refrigerators, had come into its own in the 1980s by plunging into areas like leasing. To this GE first added Employers Reinsurance Corporation, bought from Texaco for more than $1 billion in 1984. Two years later GE went Wall Street by purchasing 80 percent of the investment banking firm Kidder, Peabody & Company for

$600 million. During the early 1980s Kidder, founded in the mid-nineteenth century, was propelled to the top ranks of the mergers and acquisitions game by hotshot Martin Siegel, yet in the overall securities business it ranked only number fifteen.

Welch also resumed some of his housecleaning, extending the process to the assets of RCA. In 1987 he sold the combined GE-RCA business in consumer electronics (televisions, VCRs, and so on) to the French firm Thomson SA for cash (somewhere between $500 million and $1 billion) plus that company's medical diagnostic operations, adding to GE's existing strong position in that business. Thomson arranged to go on using the GE brand name.

Since 1986 GE has had to contend with a boycott of its products launched by the organization INFACT to protest the company's involvement in nuclear weapons production. INFACT later extended its boycott to GE's medical products and succeeded in getting several major institutions to cancel orders for expensive diagnostic equipment.

In 1989 GE added a new dimension to one of its oldest businesses by agreeing to purchase 50 percent (later increased to 75 percent) of the Hungarian lighting company Tungsram for $150 million. Two years later GE took another step in Europe by acquiring the light bulb business of Thorn EMI for $360 million.

OPERATIONS

Aerospace (8 percent of 1991 revenues). This segment includes GE's military and NASA contracts involving electronics, avionic systems, missile system components, spacecraft, communications systems, radar, and sonar. In fiscal year 1991 GE was the third-largest Pentagon contractor, with prime contract awards totaling $4.9 billion.

GE has been involved in major military projects ranging from the B-1 bomber to the MX missile, the Trident submarine, the Stealth bomber, and Star Wars. GE built and operated the Pinellas plant near St. Petersburg, Florida, for the federal government. It was at this plant that GE produced all of the country's neutron generators, which are known as the "trigger" for nuclear bombs. (In 1990 GE notified the federal government that it wanted to end its involvement at Pinellas.) From 1946 to 1964 GE operated the federal government's Hanford Nuclear Reservation in Washington State, and since 1946 the company has run the federally owned Knolls Atomic Power Laboratory.

GE has managed to go on doing a substantial amount of work for the Pentagon, despite having been involved in a number of contracting scandals. In 1985 GE was temporarily suspended as a military supplier after being indicted on charges of falsifying claims regarding work on Minuteman missiles. After admitting its guilt, the company refunded $800,000 to the government and paid a penalty of just over $1 million. In 1988 the company was indicted by a federal grand jury for trying to defraud the Defense Department of $22 million in connection with a battlefield computer system. GE was later convicted in that case and paid a penalty of more than $18 million.

Aircraft Engines (13 percent of revenues). GE was encouraged by the federal government to become involved in the development of jet engines during World War II, when the established engine makers, such as Pratt & Whitney, were busy meeting the military's insatiable demand for piston engines. The first U.S.-built jet plane, with an engine built by GE, made its trial flight in 1942. After the war GE continued in the jet market and by the 1960s was established as one of the three main engine producers, along with Pratt & Whitney and Britain's Rolls Royce. In 1974 it formed a joint venture with the French company Société Nationale d'Étude et Construction de Moteurs d'Aviation (SNECMA).

When a competing consortium—International Aero Engines, formed in 1983 by Pratt & Whitney, Rolls Royce, and companies from Japan, Italy, and West Germany—stumbled in its development of engines for the Airbus A340, GE-SNECMA (now known as CMF International) moved in to fill the void. GE also shot ahead of Pratt & Whitney in the two companies' individual efforts, although one of GE's projects, an unducted fan engine that was developed at great cost in cooperation with Boeing as an energy-saving technology, was abandoned when oil prices moderated.

GE also took advantage of Pratt & Whitney's problems in the military arena. During the early 1980s Pratt & Whitney had serious difficulties with the F100 it was developing for a joint air force–navy program. The Pentagon did its best to help its favorite engine maker but finally decided to give money to GE to develop an alternative product. This encouraged GE to be more aggressive in both its military and its civilian engine operations. In 1990 GE announced its GE90, which at eighty thousand pounds of thrust was even more powerful than Pratt & Whitney's top-of-the-line PW4000. By this time, though, Pratt & Whitney was beginning to rebound. In 1991 Pratt & Whitney was chosen by the U.S. Air Force to power the Advanced Tactical Fighter— a contract that over time could be worth $12 billion.

Despite the continuing rivalry between the two companies, there are areas of cooperation between GE and Pratt & Whitney. In 1990 the two companies announced that they would work together on a new commercial supersonic engine, and the following year they were among a group of companies chosen by the Japanese government to work on an engine that could enable a plane to fly five times the speed of sound.

In 1991 GE signed a cooperation agreement with the Czechoslovakian engine company Motorlet. That same year, the Justice Department accused GE of conspiring with an Israeli military officer to defraud the Pentagon of more than $30 million on the sale of jet engines and support services to the Israeli Air Force.

Appliances (9 percent of revenues). This segment, which has suffered from the weak housing market in the United States in recent years, includes kitchen and laundry equipment, such as refrigerators, ranges, microwave ovens, dishwashers, clothes washers and dryers, and room air conditioners. Products are sold under the GE, Hotpoint, RCA, and Monogram brands or under the private brand names of retailers. GE may be facing legal problems in this segment. In 1991 the Federal Trade Commission confirmed news reports that the agency was investigating whether GE and other producers of major kitchen appliances had engaged in price-fixing.

In 1989 GE agreed to pay $575 million for 50 percent of the European appliance business of Britain's General Electric Company (no relation). The move helped GEC (with whom GE is often confused outside the United States) fight off a takeover effort by Plessey Company. In 1991 Toshiba agreed to help GE sell refrigerators in Japan as a way of helping to relieve trade tensions between the two countries.

Broadcasting (5 percent of revenues). It was only a few months after GE announced its intention in December 1985 to purchase RCA that the NBC subsidiary of that company for the first time came out on top in the prime-time ratings contest, thanks to programs like "The Cosby Show." GE shook up NBC by naming someone with no television experience—Robert Wright, head of GE's financial operations—to head the network. In addition to cutting costs, Wright spent money to acquire additional TV stations and moved the network into cable by creating a news-and-information channel called CNBC. At the same time, he sold off NBC's radio networks to a company called Westwood One.

In 1990 NBC joined with Rupert Murdoch's News Corporation, Cablevision Systems, and the Hughes Communications subsidiary of General Motors in a $1-billion joint venture called Sky Cable to deliver up to 108 channels of programming to subscribers, who would use small receiving dishes costing about $300 each. In 1991 GE bought CNBC's rival, Financial News Network, and then shut it down. These initiatives did not make up for the fact that by 1991, NBC had lost its lead in network ratings and its profits were sinking. In mid-1991 reports began to appear to the effect that GE was trying to sell the network; about the same time, the Sky Cable project was abandoned.

Industrial (11 percent of revenues). This segment encompasses lighting products, electrical distribution and control equipment for industrial and commercial construction, motors, transportation systems, and industrial automation products.

A rare innovation in the light bulb business came in the late 1980s, when GE introduced a much smaller bulb for use as headlights in automobiles, which would allow car designers to improve aerodynamics and create sleeker styling. GE, the world's second-largest lighting producer (behind Philips), sought to improve its mediocre position in Europe by purchasing half (later 75 percent) of the Hungarian company Tungsram in 1989. GE further expanded its European business in 1991 through the purchase of the light bulb operations of Thorn EMI.

In the industrial automation area, GE made a major commitment in the 1980s in order to unseat the Japanese company Fanuc as the industry leader (though the two companies now have a joint venture operating in the United States, Europe, and Japan). Pushing the slogan "Automate, emigrate or evaporate," GE spent $300 million on a model renovation of the company's locomotive plant in Erie, Pennsylania. But it turned out to be more difficult than expected to put all of the pieces together, and the demand for automation systems (not to mention locomotives) turned out to be erratic.

Materials (8 percent of revenues). Included in this segment are high-performance engineered plastics, silicones, superabrasives (such as synthetic diamonds), and laminates. In 1988 GE bolstered its plastics business through the acquisition of Borg-Warner's chemical operations for $2.3 billion. Borg-Warner was the leader in the production of acrylonitrile-butadiene-styrene (ABS) resins, widely used in plastics for computers, appliances, and car interiors. Also in this segment, until it was sold in late 1990, was Ladd Petroleum Corporation, the remaining portion of Utah International that GE had held on to.

Power Systems (10 percent of revenues). GE is the leader in most products used in the generation, transmission, and distribution of electricity. Yet the company has suffered from the decline of nuclear power in the United States, where there has not been an order for a new reactor in nearly twenty years. Still, GE continues to develop technology in this area, both to service existing nuclear plants and to be ready if atomic energy makes a comeback.

At the same time, GE has been plagued with problems stemming from old nuclear business. In 1987 the company was embarrassed when there was an accidental release of secret documents from the 1970s in which GE engineers discussed flaws in the reactors they were producing. Those problems had never been disclosed to customers. This occurred as a result of one of a series of lawsuits brought by utilities against GE because of design flaws in reactors.

Nonetheless, GE was chosen for a $1-billion contract to build the world's first advanced nuclear power facility. In 1991 GE was approved for the project by the Japanese government. Joining GE in constructing the reactor for Tokyo Electric Power will be Hitachi and Toshiba.

Technical Products and Services (8 percent of revenues). This segment consists mainly of medical equipment and communications and information services. In the medical area, GE is a major producer of magnetic resonance scanners and computed tomography scanners as well as X-ray, ultrasound, nuclear-imaging, and other diagnostic equipment. GE's medical equipment executives were embarrassed in 1991 when five employees of their Japanese joint venture with Yokogawa Electric Works were arrested on charges of bribing officials at university medical centers in that country to get them to purchase GE diagnostic equipment.

The other products include data network services, electronic messaging, application software packaging, and maintenance and leasing for computers. In 1989 GE's mobile communications business was put in a joint venture with the Swedish company Ericsson.

GE Financial Services (26 percent of revenues). This segment, known by the initials GEFS, consists of a variety of financing activities (commercial and industrial loans, revolving credit and inventory financing for retailers, and so on), property and casualty reinsurance, and (through Kidder, Peabody) investment banking and securities services. GEFS has been a rapidly growing part of General Electric over the past decade and is now its single largest source of revenues; it also contributes nearly a fifth of the entire company's profits. Yet GEFS has been rocked by defaults on a number of loans made in leveraged buyouts of companies (including some Kidder, Peabody clients) that ended up being unable to service their debt.

GE was so eager to get into the securities business that it paid a very generous price for Kidder, Peabody. The company came to regret that eagerness, for in 1987 Kidder was pulled into the insider trading scandal when Martin Siegel admitted that he had passed confidential information to crooked arbitrageur Ivan Boesky in exchange for suitcases filled with cash. Siegel, who had left the firm in early 1986, also told authorities that he had helped Kidder trade on inside information on its own account. This led to Richard Wigton, the head of Kidder's arbitrage department, being arrested and led away in handcuffs (though the charges were later dropped). The firm later paid $25 million to settle federal charges relating to insider trading. The stock market plunge in 1987 was another blow to the GE subsidiary. Low morale at the firm caused a series of resignations by top executives in the late 1980s, and in 1990 GE had to inject $550 million of additional capital into the firm.

TOP EXECUTIVES

- John F. Welch, Jr., chairman and chief executive
- Edward E. Hood, Jr., vice chairman
- John D. Rittenhouse, senior vice president, technology programs
- Eugene F. Murphy, senior vice president, aerospace
- Brian H. Rowe, senior vice president, aircraft engines
- J. Richard Stonesifer, senior vice president, appliances
- Gary C. Wendt, president of GE Financial Services
- David C. Genever-Watling, senior vice president, industrial and power systems
- John D. Opie, senior vice president, lighting
- John M. Trani, senior vice president, medical systems
- Robert C. Wright, president of NBC
- Gary L. Rogers, senior vice president, plastics
- Paolo Fresco, senior vice president, international

OUTSIDE DIRECTORS

- H. Brewster Atwater, Jr., chief executive of General Mills
- D. Wayne Calloway, chief executive of PepsiCo
- Silas S. Cathcart, retired chairman of Illinois Tool Works
- Lawrence E. Fouraker, former dean of the Harvard Business School
- Henry H. Henley, Jr., retired chief executive of Cluett, Peabody
- Henry L. Hillman, chairman of the Hillman Company investment firm
- David C. Jones, former chairman of the Joint Chiefs of Staff
- Robert E. Mercer, retired chairman of Goodyear Tire & Rubber Company
- Gertrude G. Michelson, senior vice president of R. H. Macy & Company
- Barbara Scott Preiskel, former senior vice president of the Motion Picture Associations of America
- Lewis T. Preston, retired chairman of J. P. Morgan & Company
- Frank H. T. Rhodes, president of Cornell University
- Andrew C. Sigler, chief executive of Champion International
- Walter B. Wriston, former chairman of Citicorp

FINANCIAL DATA

Revenues (in millions of dollars)

1991	60,236
1990	58,414
1989	54,574
1988	50,089
1987	48,158
1986	42,013

Net Income (in millions of dollars)

1991	2,636
1990	4,303
1989	3,939
1988	3,386
1987	2,915
1986	2,492

GEOGRAPHICAL BREAKDOWN

Revenues (in millions of dollars)

Year	United States		Foreign	
1991	52,812	(85%)	9,736	(16%)
1990	51,270	(85%)	9,165	(15%)
1989	48,912	(87%)	7,458	(13%)

Operating Profit (in millions of dollars)

Year	United States		Foreign	
1991	7,062	(89%)	903	(11%)
1990	6,862	(89%)	883	(11%)
1989	6,070	(86%)	974	(14%)

LABOR RELATIONS

Radical groups like the Industrial Workers of the World won converts at General Electric during World War I and staged a major strike at the company in 1918. This upsurge of militancy was short-lived, however. During the 1920s GE, like many other companies at the time, indirectly discouraged independent unionization (there was a company union) by engaging in a form of welfare capitalism. At the same time, GE president Gerard Swope met secretly with the head of the American Federation of Labor and said that the company would accept being organized as long as it was on an industry rather than a craft basis. The craft-oriented AFL was not ready for such an idea.

When the depression hit, GE instituted work-sharing plans and made loans to its employees. Yet this was not enough. The 1930s saw the rise of widespread industrial unionism in the electrical equipment business, especially after the creation of the United Electrical and Radio Workers Union (UE) in 1936. That same year, GE consented to a request from UE for a representation election at some of the company's main facilities. UE won the vote and before long had much of the company organized.

After the war UE pushed for substantial wage improvements, but in the new cold war climate it found itself under attack because of the Communist party influence in the union. UE was raided by other unions, and after ceasing to pay dues to the CIO, UE was expelled from that organization. In place of UE the CIO chartered a new union called the International Union of Electrical, Radio, and Machine Workers (IUE). UE lost members to the IUE and was a target of McCarthyism in the 1950s.

Eventually UE and the IUE realized that they needed to cooperate to be able to confront companies like GE effectively. This was especially important because in the 1950s the company adopted a labor relations policy known as Boulwarism. This approach, named after labor relations director Lemuel R. Boulware, involved making a supposedly reasonable proposal and adamantly sticking to it rather than engaging in back-and-forth negotiations. In other words, the company's initial offer was its final offer.

UE and the IUE began to cooperate in the 1960s, and after a series of strikes in the latter part of that decade they managed to get the company to soften its hard line in labor relations. (A National Labor Relations Board ruling that Boulwarism was an unfair labor practice also helped.) Whatever progress was made was largely lost in the 1980s as chief executive Jack Welch ruthlessly set out to eliminate jobs as part of his restructuring of the company. Numerous unionized plants were shut down, with the work transferred to nonunion facilities in the South or low-wage havens like Mexico. Although GE was far from unprofitable, the company began to demand wage and benefit concessions or work-rule changes from those unionized workers who were not terminated. GE workers began to make up some lost ground in national contracts negotiated in mid-1991. The wage increases were modest, but workers got major improvements in medical benefits.

Welch applied his same labor-squeeze policy at NBC after GE purchased the network in 1985. Management demanded major concessions from the National Association of Broadcast Employees and Technicians (NABET) in the 1987 contract talks, prompting a walkout by twenty-eight hundred members of the union. After seventeen weeks NABET, whose striking members had been quickly replaced by NBC, called off the strike without winning a single major concession from the company. NBC, on the other hand, won the right to hire temps to fill jobs previously done by regular staff members. The network went on to eliminate hundreds of jobs and to introduce the use of robot cameras for some of its programs.

GE also has a less-than-sterling labor record abroad. In 1988 the International Metalworkers Federation held a convention of delegates from GE factories in twenty-three countries. Reports delivered at the gathering showed that the company had been depressing wages and weakening unions just about everywhere. Some of the strongest antiunion postures had been taken by GE in Brazil and Colombia.

ENVIRONMENTAL RECORD

GE has been embroiled since the early 1980s in a controversy over the estimated half a million pounds of toxic polychlorinated biphenyls (PCBs) dumped by two of its plants into New York's Hudson River (a source of drinking water) for several decades. For several years GE resisted calls to end the dumping, but it finally agreed to cease the practice in 1977. Although GE used political pressures to get itself absolved of responsibility at the state level, the company was ordered by the EPA to remove the PCBs from the riverbanks. The company has been experimenting with bioremediation (that is, the use of anaerobic bacteria) to break down the PCBs into less-toxic substances.

According to evidence collected by INFACT, GE was responsible for substantial emissions of airborne radioactive waste from the smokestacks at the Hanford Nuclear Reservation in Washington State during the two decades it was run by GE. There is also evidence that the facility contaminated the Columbia River and groundwater beneath Hanford with radioactive substances. There has been an abnormally high incidence of cancer among families living near the facility. INFACT also has documented radioactive hazards, including lethal exposures to workers, at the Knolls Atomic Power Lab.

Other environmental matters include a 1990 action brought against the company by the state of Ohio alleging violations of air pollution regulations at its Circleville facility, and 1991 charges by New York State that GE's power equipment plant in Schenectady violated water pollution regulations.

According to a study of EPA data by the Citizens Fund, GE was responsible for the second-largest volume (nearly thirteen million pounds) of releases of known or suspected carcinogens of any U.S. industrial company in 1989 (the latest figures available). GE ranked twenty-second in terms of overall toxic releases.

BIBLIOGRAPHY

Barnouw, Erik. *A History of Broadcasting in the United States.* 3 vols. New York: Oxford University Press, 1966, 1968, 1970.

Fuller, John. *The Gentlemen Conspirators.* New York: Grove Press, 1962.

General Electric: A Profile for Metalworkers. Geneva: International Metalworkers Federation, 1988.

Hertsgaard, Mark. *Nuclear Inc.: The Men & Money Behind Nuclear Energy.* New York: Pantheon Books, 1983.

INFACT. *Bringing GE to Light: How General Electric Shapes Nuclear Weapons Policies for Profits.* Philadelphia: New Society, 1988.

Loth, David. *Swope of G.E.: The Story of Gerard Swope and General Electric in American Business.* New York: Simon & Schuster, 1958.

Schatz, Ronald W. *The Electrical Workers: A History of Labor at General Electric and Westinghouse, 1923–60.* Urbana and Chicago: University of Illinois Press, 1983.

Sobel, Robert. *RCA.* New York: Stein & Day, 1986.

GENERAL MOTORS CORPORATION

3044 West Grand Boulevard
Detroit, Michigan 48202
(313) 556-5000

1991 revenues: $123.1 billion
1991 net income: −$4.4 billion (loss)
Publicly traded company
Employees: 756,300
Founded: 1908

OVERVIEW

For decades General Motors (GM) held a commanding position in the international motor vehicle industry. After emerging from the consolidation of a string of car makers, parts producers, and other operations early in this century, GM went on to become the major influence on the way people got from point A to point B. For many, it also became the cornerstone of the U.S. economy. It was widely believed, in the words of GM president Charles "Engine Charlie" Wilson's famous remark to Congress, that "what was good for our country was good for General Motors—and vice versa."

Founder Billy Durant realized from the beginning that to a great extent, the industry was selling an image. He laid the groundwork for what would become a basic part of the GM philosophy: attract customers by frequent changes in the superficial aspects of automobiles. Thus was the world blessed with tail fins and acres of chrome. This is not to say that GM ignored what went under the hood. The company relentlessly pushed the idea that bigger and more powerful was better. This notion became so rooted in the thinking of the U.S. auto industry that GM and its domestic rivals had a hard time responding to the shift in preference to smaller cars that began in the late 1950s and escalated dramatically with the oil crisis of the 1970s.

For the past two decades GM also has had to confront the most serious challenges to its dominance. Japanese car makers came from out of nowhere to win the loyalty of a substantial portion of drivers in the United States and many other countries. In effect GM acknowledged that it had something to learn from the Japanese when it formed a joint venture with Toyota to make cars using Toyota's manufacturing techniques.

GM's market share dropped precipitously during the 1980s, but the company has employed a variety of means to bounce back. It has slashed costs and jobs, persuaded the United Auto Workers to embrace the team concept, redesigned its cars to make them look more like the popular imports, and spent more than $7 billion to get into computer services and military electronics. Yet its reputation sank so low that a 1989 film—Michael Moore's *Roger & Me*—ridiculing the company was a smash hit.

Reports of GM's death may be exaggerated, but the company once called the Chrome Colossus continues to ail. Particularly in its home market, the 1990s for GM will be a time of retrenchment and desperate attempts to find a strategy for survival.

HISTORY

In the early years of the twentieth century the U.S. auto business consisted of countless small producers struggling to survive in an industry that was anything but orderly. The man who set out to rationalize things was William Crapo Durant, an indefatigable entrepreneur who, among many other things, had taken over a small cart company and by 1904 turned it into the country's largest manufacturer of carriages.

That year Durant decided to take the plunge into the motor car business, which he had been observing with great interest. His first step was reorganizing the Buick Motor Car Company, a struggling producer founded by inventor David Buick in 1901 and later taken over by James H. Whiting, a wagon maker in Flint, Michigan.

Once he had assumed the position of general manager at Buick, Durant began planning the promotion of the Model-C car the company was about to introduce. He quickly built up a network of dealers and attracted a large volume of orders—more, in fact, than the company's capacity to produce. Durant, however, was not interested in the production side of things. He kept selling, and by 1908 Buick was the nation's leading car maker.

In 1908 Durant was approached by Benjamin Briscoe, owner of the country's leading auto parts producer, who had once controlled Buick and was now backing John Maxwell. Briscoe proposed a plan to get J. P. Morgan to finance a consolidation of several leading automakers. Since this was in line with Durant's long-standing goal for the industry, he responded favorably to the initiative. After some discussions, a proposal was drawn up to combine Buick, Ford Motor, Maxwell-Briscoe, and Olds. Olds, founded by Ransom E. Olds, was one of the earliest entrants in the car business. Henry Ford's company was just beginning its climb to fame as the producer of the Model T.

The negotiations did not go smoothly; Ford, for instance, decided that he wanted to remain independent. The result was that in 1908 Durant formed a holding company called General Motors that first took control of Buick and then Olds. Then Durant went on one of the most remarkable buying sprees in U.S. business history. Racing around the country, Durant snapped up car makers and parts producers. Among the former were Cadillac and Oakland (later renamed Pontiac); among those that got away were Goodyear Tire & Rubber and, again, Ford Motor.

By 1910 Durant's ambitions had moved too far ahead of the reality of General Motors. The company was running out of cash and Durant was scrambling to get new bank loans. After a number of rejections, GM finally did receive an infusion from a group of banks, but the terms were severe. The banks in effect took charge of the company by setting up a five-member management committee that they controlled. Durant was a member of that group, but his desire for bold expansion was overruled by the fiscal conservatives who dominated the committee. He gradually withdrew from his GM activities.

The prudent policies continued after Charles Nash took over as president of GM in 1912, but the company did make innovations, such as the "self-starter" (to replace the often-perilous cranks) and the eight-cylinder (V-8) engine. Durant, in the meantime, was building a new empire of his own. He gained control of the company founded by auto designer Louis Chevrolet and in 1915 introduced an inexpensive car, the Model 490, meant to compete directly with Ford's Model T.

At the same time, Durant began accumulating shares of GM stock, siphoning off profits from Chevrolet to assist in the effort. Then he gained even more of GM by announcing that he would exchange five shares of Chevrolet stock for one share of GM. Now firmly in control of GM once again, Durant embarked on an expensive expansion. He acquired a car maker called Sheridan, 60 percent of Fisher Body Corporation, and the Canadian factories of McLaughlin Motor (later to become GM of Canada). He also diversified into farm equipment and refrigerators (through the purchase of Frigidaire).

During World War I the company converted to military production—trucks, ambulances, airplane motors, and so forth—but quickly resumed civilian operations after the armistice. Postwar sales were boosted by the creation of General Motors Acceptance Corporation, which financed purchases of the company's products.

However, a weakened stock market put Durant, who was extremely over-extended in his purchases of GM shares, in an impossible position. As GM's stock price sank, Durant desperately sought to meet margin calls from his brokers. Finally, in 1920, he could hold out no longer. He agreed to a bailout that once again stripped him of control, which was now in the hands of the du Pont family and J. P. Morgan & Company.

Pierre S. du Pont, who took over as president of GM, embarked on a reorganization of the company along the lines of a plan devised by Alfred P.

Sloan, Jr., a GM executive who had joined the company after it acquired the Hyatt ball-bearing operation from the Sloan family. Sloan, who rose to the presidency in 1923, rationalized the company's varied and sometimes overlapping product line and set out to retake some of the ground gained by Ford's wildly popular Model T.

He accomplished that task with the introduction of the 1925 Chevrolet, which generated far more excitement than did Ford's seventeen-year-old entry. He arranged GM's other offerings to appeal to a wide range of income groups, or as Sloan put it, "a car for every purse and purpose." He also began to modernize car design, abandoning the box-on-wheels look that had dominated the industry. Henry Ford finally saw the writing on the wall. In 1927, as Ford announced that production of the Model T would end, Chevrolet rose to the top spot in U.S. car sales. While Ford was reluctantly changing, Sloan was developing a strategy based on the introduction of a new model each year.

Sloan also expanded the company by acquiring a majority stake in Yellow Cab Manufacturing and interests in several aviation companies. GM set up assembly operations in Europe, New Zealand, and South Africa, and purchased Vauxhall Motors in Britain and 80 percent of Adam Opel, Germany's largest automaker.

GM was set back by the depression, though it remained the leader in what little automobile business there was to be had. It was also during this period that GM emerged as the largest industrial corporation in the United States. When the mobilization for World War II began, GM plunged into military production, converting its factories to make such things as airplanes, machine guns, artillery shells, gyroscopes, and antiaircraft guns.

Even before the war was over, GM executives were planning for the anticipated explosion of demand that would follow the cessation of hostilities. There was some talk of a small car (along the lines of Germany's *Volkswagen*), but the preference for bigger (and more profitable) models won out. The postwar cars were larger and more powerful than ever.

So was General Motors. As Ford struggled with its management crisis, GM solidified its dominance in the auto market and assumed a major position in other fields, becoming, for example, the country's largest military contractor. Not coincidentally, when Dwight Eisenhower was elected president in 1952 he asked GM president Charlie Wilson to be his secretary of defense. In what would be the decade of the automobile, GM was one of the most important institutions in American life. It was an especially imposing figure in the business world. In 1955 GM became the first company in the world to attain an annual profit of $1 billion.

Not all was well with the company, however. Its vast size had made it a target of critics of economic concentration. The Justice Department was pursuing an attempt to get Du Pont to divest itself of its 23-percent holding in GM, which dated back to the du Pont family's bailing out of William Durant in 1920. (The case was brought in 1949, but not until the mid-1960s would

Du Pont finally cease to be the controlling shareholder in GM.) During the late 1950s, after the Justice Department sued GM for monopolizing the bus business, there was even talk that the company should be broken up, in the manner of the Standard Oil trust back in 1911.

GM's "big is beautiful" philosophy in car design was coming into question, too. The recession of 1957–58 prompted a surge in demand for smaller, more economical cars—a fact that Ford learned the hard way in its Edsel disaster. The mood was changed enough that even another automaker—American Motors president George Romney, who was promoting his company's previously obscure small car, the Rambler—lashed out at the "dinosaurs" being produced by his larger counterparts.

GM responded by developing a compact called the Corvair. The poorly designed car became an albatross for the company. When consumer advocate Ralph Nader publicized the Corvair's problems, GM responded by spying on Nader in an attempt to come up with dirt to discredit him. In the end, however, it was GM and the Corvair that were discredited.

The demand for small cars continued to rise, and increasingly it was the foreign producers, including the recently arrived Japanese, who were filling that demand. The trend took a dramatic leap forward in the mid-1970s in the wake of the oil embargo. The resulting gasoline shortages turned panicked U.S. drivers away from the gas-guzzling offerings from Detroit.

To its credit, GM was quick to respond to the new mood. The company's engineers plunged into a down-sizing effort that resulted in a shrunken Cadillac as well as a U.S. version of the German-designed Chevette, which was no great success. GM also spent more than $2 billion to develop a line of other front-wheel-drive compacts known as X-cars. Although GM started to experience red ink, the company's market share shot ahead, as did its reputation. By 1981 *Fortune* wrote that "the complacent giant that used to dominate its industry by sheer size is now an aggressive, inventive product leader."

It was that year that GM brought out its J-car, a subcompact specifically meant to take on the Japanese imports that were flooding the U.S. market. In addition to fighting the Japanese, GM decided to join them. In 1983 the company stunned the industry by forming a joint venture with Toyota—the New United Motor Manufacturing Inc.—to produce a subcompact in California using the Japanese company's manufacturing techniques. Two years later GM announced that it would create a new subsidiary, Saturn Corporation, to produce small cars at a Japanese-style factory in Tennessee.

The company, then run by Roger Smith, also made some bold moves outside its core business. In 1984 it agreed to pay $2.5 billion to acquire Electronic Data Systems (EDS), the computer services firm built by H. Ross Perot, and in 1985 it made a winning $4.7-billion offer for Hughes Aircraft. In addition, GM engaged in a series of smaller investments and joint ventures in fields ranging from robotics to artificial intelligence. The intention, Smith said, was to find "the key to the twenty-first century."

In the short term, however, these investments provided a number of headaches. Ross Perot, who became a GM director and the company's largest shareholder as a result of the EDS deal, embarked on a highly visible campaign to make GM competitive again—a process he likened to "teaching an elephant to tap dance." At the same time, the integration of EDS into GM proved to be no easy task. In fact, Roger Smith apparently lost hope in the possibility, for in 1986 he made an unsuccessful attempt to sell the operation to AT&T. Finally GM got rid of Perot rather than EDS. The company spent more than $700 million to buy out him and his soapbox.

Although Perot went away, the problems he had pointed to remained. GM continued to lose ground in the U.S. auto market, not only to the Japanese but also to a newly resurgent Ford, which in 1986 even managed to make more money than its much larger rival. GM responded by slashing capacity, eliminating tens of thousands of production jobs, and axing large numbers of salaried staff. At the same time, it put more emphasis on its so-called captive imports—cars made for GM by companies in other countries for sale in the U.S. market. A new line called Geo was created to market cars made by Japan's Suzuki and Isuzu (in which GM had purchased a 34-percent interest in 1970). The company also was pushing the Pontiac LeMans, made by a joint venture with Daewoo in South Korea.

Although the cost cutting resulted in some improvements in profitability, the overall decline continued. By 1990 the situation had deteriorated to the point that some of the company's large institutional shareholders were taking a more active interest in GM's operations. A plan to boost the pensions of Smith and his heir apparent, Robert Stempel, came under attack. As the first Saturn cars were finally about to go on sale in late 1990, production problems limited the number available to dealers, and five months after the launch, the company had to recall almost a third of the cars for repairs. GM took a huge, $2.1-billion write-off to cover the cost of plant closings, which put the company's net income far into the red for 1990. In late 1991 the company gave a clearer and startling indication of how extensive that retrenchment would be. Stempel announced that over several years GM would shut down more than twenty plants in the United States and Canada, resulting in the elimination of more than seventy thousand jobs.

Stempel's leadership—further darkened by the $4 billion loss the company posted for 1991—began to unravel. In April 1992 the outside directors of GM issued a sharp rebuke to Stempel by removing his heir apparent, Lloyd Reuss, as president and installing one of their number, John Smale, as chair of the executive committee.

While cutting back at home, GM has continued to expand abroad. In 1989 it purchased a 50-percent stake in Swedish automaker Saab for $500 million. The following year GM signed a $1-billion agreement to sell auto parts to the Soviet Union. The company's European operations, which began to show new vigor, moved eastward by taking over an assembly plant in Hungary and investing in Poland. In 1992 GM formed a joint venture with a Chinese company called Gold Cup to assemble pickup trucks for sale in China.

OPERATIONS

Automotive Products (79 percent of 1991 revenues). General Motors is the largest motor vehicle producer in the world. In 1991 some 17 percent of the forty-three million vehicles sold on the planet were made by GM; 35 percent of new vehicles in the United States were GMs. The company sells cars in six lines: Chevrolet, Buick, Pontiac, Oldsmobile, Cadillac, and Saturn, which began sales in 1990. Vehicles are distributed through more than ten thousand dealers in the United States and five thousand in other countries. GM has thirty automotive assembly operations in the United States and twenty-nine distribution and warehousing facilities. Major foreign manufacturing operations are located in Canada, the United Kingdom, Germany, Spain, Belgium, Austria, Australia, Brazil, and Mexico.

Financing and Insurance Operations (9 percent of revenues). The major portion of this segment is General Motors Acceptance Corporation, which finances the purchase of GM products. The company also provides insurance services to dealers and customers and engages in mortgage banking, marine financing, and investment services.

Other Products (12 percent of revenues). Two main operations are included in this segment. The first is Electronic Data Systems Corporation, which is a leader in data-processing and telecommunications services. A major user of mainframe computers, EDS joined with Hitachi in 1989 to buy a controlling interest in the National Advanced Systems computer business of National Semiconductor Corporation. In 1991 EDS took over the British computer service company SD-Scicon.

The other operation is GM Hughes Electronics Corporation, the result of the merging of Hughes Aircraft and Delco Electronics. Hughes, acquired by GM in 1985, is a leading military electronics producer. Its business with the Defense Department, especially in missile systems, helped make GM the country's fourth-largest military contractor in fiscal year 1991. In 1990 Hughes pleaded guilty to unlawfully obtaining secret Pentagon budget documents. Hughes was indicted by a federal grand jury in 1991 on charges that the company falsified test results on electronic circuits for a wide range of high-tech weapons. Hughes is also the leading supplier of commercial satellites. The main auto innovation Hughes has provided GM is a "heads-up" display system that allows a driver to view dashboard data through projections onto the windshield rather than having to look down. Delco has been a captive supplier of car radios and automotive electronic components for GM since 1936. It also has done work for the Pentagon.

TOP EXECUTIVES

- Robert C. Stempel, chairman and chief executive
- John F. Smith, Jr., president

- Robert J. Schultz, vice chairman
- William E. Hoglund, executive vice president
- Robert T. O'Connell, executive vice president
- F. Alan Smith, executive vice president

OUTSIDE DIRECTORS

- Anne L. Armstrong, chairman of the board of the Center for Strategic and International Studies
- Thomas E. Everhart, president of the California Institute of Technology
- Charles T. Fisher III, chairman of NBD Bancorp Inc.
- Marvin L. Goldberger, professor of physics at the University of California at Los Angeles
- Ann D. McLaughlin, former U.S. secretary of labor
- J. Willard Marriott, Jr., chief executive of Marriott Corporation
- Edmund T. Pratt, Jr., chairman of Pfizer, Inc.
- John G. Smale, retired chief executive of Proctor & Gamble
- Leon H. Sullivan, pastor emeritus of the Zion Baptist Church of Philadelphia
- Dennis Weatherstone, chairman of J. P. Morgan & Company
- Thomas H. Wyman, former chief executive of CBS, Inc.

The board also includes former chief executive Roger B. Smith.

FINANCIAL DATA

Revenues (in millions of dollars)

1991	123,056
1990	124,705
1989	126,932
1988	123,642
1987	114,870
1986	115,610

Net Income (in millions of dollars)

1991	−4,453 (loss)
1990	−1,986 (loss)
1989	4,224
1988	4,856
1987	3,551
1986	2,945

GEOGRAPHICAL BREAKDOWN

Revenues (in millions of dollars)

Year	United States and Canada		Europe		Elsewhere	
1991	113,544	(77%)	25,365	(17%)	8,337	(6%)
1990	114,273	(78%)	24,443	(17%)	8,445	(6%)
1989	120,995	(81%)	19,740	(13%)	8,024	(5%)

LABOR RELATIONS

Autoworkers at General Motors and the other large car companies remained largely unorganized until the 1930s. After collective bargaining was sanctioned by the federal government, organizing efforts began to emerge, and in 1935 the American Federation of Labor gave a charter to the United Automobile Workers of America. UAW activists were interested in building an industrial union, which ran contrary to the AFL's craft orientation, so the union ended up allying itself with the recently formed Committee for Industrial Organization.

When the UAW set out to organize the industry, GM was made the primary target. The company, petrified at the thought of having to deal with a union, made extensive use of detective agencies to keep track of the UAW's activities. Nonetheless, workers began to pressure the company by engaging in short sit-down strikes, usually to protest the speeding up of the assembly line. The UAW made a special target of the Fisher body plant in Flint, which was one of only two sites where the company had dies for its new models. In late December 1936 the workers at the Fisher plant staged a sit-down strike that was to last six weeks. The dispute was settled when GM agreed to recognize the UAW.

During the 1940s GM and the UAW developed a cooperative working relationship; in fact, company president Charlie Wilson and Walter Reuther, head of the union's GM department, became quite chummy. The harmony was shattered in 1945 when the UAW responded to the lifting of the wartime wage freeze by demanding a 30-percent wage increase (about thirty-four cents an hour) from the industry. The union also asked that the companies open their books so that the UAW could show that such a raise would be possible without boosting prices for cars. The union accepted eighteen-and-a-half cent increases from Ford and Chrysler but went on strike against GM to get more. The walkout lasted 113 days, but in the end the union had to settle for the same raises won at the other two major automakers without a strike.

In the 1948 bargaining, GM and the UAW created a system whereby wage increases were made automatic, tied to the cost of living and annual improvement factors. Two years later the union won health insurance and a pension plan, thus opening up collective bargaining to the area of employee benefits.

For the next twenty years the UAW went easy on General Motors, targeting instead the weaker Ford Motor and Chrysler for setting industry contract terms. Then in 1970 the union decided once again to "take on the big guy," as a UAW official put it. When the company failed to give in to the union's demands, which included full pensions after thirty years of service, regardless of one's age, the UAW struck. The walkout, which was peaceful (some said ritualistic), ended after fifty-nine days with a compromise on the issues.

Far less placid was the situation that soon emerged at the plant in Lordstown, Ohio, where the company was assembling its ballyhooed new subcompact, the Chevrolet Vega. The young work force assembled at the factory rebelled against the inhuman pace of the line, and their strike became the leading symbol of what came to be known as the "blue collar blues."

By the early 1980s the crisis in the industry brought on by the rising tide of imports put an end to the UAW's ability to win steady contract improvements. When Chrysler used contract concessions from the UAW as part of its survival strategy, GM and Ford were inspired to make such requests from the union as well.

Faced with the loss of hundreds of thousands of its members' jobs, the UAW was in no position to resist. The union also began to move away from its adversarial tradition and adopt a stance more like that of Japanese unions. When GM and Toyota formed their New United Motor Manufacturing Inc. (NUMMI) joint venture in California, the union signed a contract that gave the operation an extraordinary degree of flexibility in managing the labor process.

The UAW again embraced what became known as "jointness" when GM decided to open a Japanese-style factory on its own in Tennessee. The union ceded so much in its contract at the Saturn plant that one of the union's founders, Victor Reuther, charged it with betraying the principles of the labor movement.

GM and the UAW nonetheless attempted to introduce jointness at other plants. The 1987 contract agreement committed the union to such a path, in exchange for greater guarantees on job security. Yet the hoped-for shop revolution did not proceed very smoothly. Productivity gains were slow in coming, and the move widened a split in the union between advocates of the team concept and those who still thought that the union was supposed to maintain an arm's-length relationship with management. The production system at the NUMMI plant in California and at Saturn, which involved a more intense pace of work, came under attack by some critics for being "management by stress." In a 1989 election at GM's Van Nuys, California, plant, workers ousted UAW officials who supported jointness. Two years later the UAW negotiated a new agreement with Saturn that moved closer to a traditional auto industry contract.

The UAW continued to allow greater managerial flexibility in the 1990 national contract talks, despite evidence that the company's job security promises were not doing much good and despite increasing rank-and-file unrest over working conditions. In 1991 thirty-two hundred UAW members at a GM plant in Baltimore walked off the job, complaining that reductions in staff and a speedup of production had made it impossible for them to perform their work safely.

ENVIRONMENTAL AND SAFETY RECORD

Although the entire automobile industry is partly responsible for the decline of public transportation in the United States, GM has played a more direct role. In 1936 GM joined with Firestone Tire and Standard Oil of California to create National City Lines, which purchased municipal streetcar systems, converted them to bus lines and then sold out, with the stipulation that the new owners use only gasoline-powered vehicles. Between 1936 and 1949 National City Lines was involved in the dismantling of rail systems in forty-five cities.

In the mid-1960s General Motors became a symbol of industry insensitivity to safety concerns as a result of the controversy over the Corvair compact introduced by GM in 1960 to respond to the growing demand for smaller cars. The Corvair had some serious design problems, making it rather unstable and dangerous to drive. Substantial information on the problems was amassed by a young lawyer named Ralph Nader, who ended up as a consultant to Senator Abraham Ribicoff of Connecticut. Ribicoff held hearings in 1965 in which GM president James Roche and GM chairman Frederic Donner were grilled about the company's meager commitment to improving auto safety.

That same year, Nader published a book called *Unsafe at Any Speed*, which focused on the defects of the Corvair. The book galvanized public opinion on the issue and unnerved GM to such an extent that the company hired private detectives to dig up dirt on Nader. Instead the surveillance plan backfired, and Roche was compelled to apologize for the spying before Congress. The controversy helped bring about the passage of the National Traffic and Motor Safety Act of 1966.

GM was also at the forefront of the industry's resistance to pollution control. The company was aware that even a simple inexpensive device—a positive crankcase ventilation (PCV) valve—could substantially cut down on emissions, yet it declined to use it. When the federal government finally established the first modest emissions standards in the mid-1960s, GM and the other big auto companies successfully pleaded for delays in enforcement. After the Clean Air Act of 1970 established more-stringent regulations, the big three again got delays, even though a number of foreign car makers were able to meet the standards.

GM also dragged its feet when presented with reports that poorly sealed panels on some of its cars could cause dangerous levels of carbon monoxide to leak into the passenger compartment. After some deaths were attributed to the problem in the late 1960s, the company recalled two and a half million cars to repair the defect.

Over the past two decades the company has been criticized frequently by environmentalists and consumer advocates for its efforts to weaken federal rules on emissions and for its resistance to the establishment of regulations that would require passive restraints, such as airbags, in all automobiles. In 1990 the Public Interest Research Group published a report stating that GM spent $2 million over the previous decade in lobbying against clean-air and fuel-efficiency regulations. In August 1990 GM finally agreed to put air bags in all of its U.S. cars starting in 1995.

GM also has had problems with health and safety conditions on the job. In 1987 the company was fined $500,000 by the Occupational Safety and Health Administration for violations of record-keeping requirements at four plants. A study of conditions at the Lordstown plant in Ohio found that workers there were experiencing an abnormally high level of cancer. In September 1991 OSHA proposed fining the company $2.8 million for fifty-seven willful safety violations at an Oklahoma City plant that the agency said contributed to a fatal accident at the factory.

Toxic releases have been another blemish on GM's environmental record. In 1991 the EPA proposed fines of more than $14 million on the company's foundry in upstate New York, which the agency said had improperly disposed of PCBs in a landfill. That same year, GM's Hughes Aircraft subsidiary agreed to pay $85 million to settle a suit brought by residents in Tucson, Arizona, who said their drinking water had been contaminated with trichloroethylene from a government-owned missile site operated by Hughes. Hughes was one of a group of companies and public entities identified by the EPA as potentially responsible parties in connection with the site.

A 1991 study of EPA data by the Citizens Fund found that GM had the eighth-largest volume (eighty-six million pounds) of toxic releases among all U.S. industrial companies in 1989 (the most recent data available).

GM's main positive accomplishment in the environmental area has been its work on electric vehicles. In 1990 it displayed a prototype of an electric car that the company said could be on the market by the middle of the decade. The following year it chose a site in Lansing, Michigan, to produce the car, which was named Impact, and set a team of engineers to work on finding ways to extend its range to at least one hundred miles per charge.

BIBLIOGRAPHY

Cray, Ed. *Chrome Colossus: General Motors and Its Times*. New York: McGraw-Hill, 1980.

Katz, Harry C. *Shifting Gears: Changing Labor Relations in the U.S. Automobile Industry*. Cambridge, Mass.: MIT Press, 1985.

Keller, Maryann. *Rude Awakening: The Rise, Fall, and Struggle for Recovery of General Motors*. New York: William Morrow, 1989.

Lee, Albert. *Call Me Roger: The Story of How Roger Smith, Chairman of General Motors, Transformed the Industry Leader into a Fallen Giant*. Chicago: Contemporary Books, 1988.

Levin, Doron P. *Irreconcilable Differences: Ross Perot Versus General Motors*. Boston: Little, Brown, 1989.

Mann, Eric. *Taking on General Motors: A Case Study of the Campaign to Keep GM Van Nuys Open*. Los Angeles: Center for Labor Research and Education/ UCLA, 1987.

Maxcy, George. *The Multinational Automobile Industry*. New York: St. Martin's Press, 1981.

May, George S., ed. *The Automobile Industry, 1885–1920*. Encyclopedia of American Business History and Biography series. New York: Facts on File, 1990.

———. *The Automobile Industry, 1920–1980*. Encyclopedia of American Business History and Biography series. New York: Facts on File, 1989.

Nader, Ralph, and William Taylor. *The Big Boys: Power and Position in American Business*. New York: Pantheon Books, 1986.

Rae, John. *The American Automobile: A Brief History*. Chicago: University of Chicago Press, 1965.

———. *The American Automobile Industry*. Boston: Twayne, 1984.

Serrin, William. *The Company and the Union: The "Civilized Relationship" of the General Motors Corporation and the United Automobile Workers*. New York: Alfred A. Knopf, 1973.

Sloan, Alfred P., Jr. *My Years With General Motors*. Garden City, N.Y.: Doubleday, 1963.

Smith, Roger B. *Building on 75 Years of Excellence: The General Motors Story*. New York: Newcomen Society, 1984.

Sobel, Robert. *Car Wars*. New York: E. P. Dutton, 1984.

Weisberger, Bernard A. *The Dream Maker: William C. Durant, Founder of General Motors*. Boston: Little, Brown, 1979.

White, Lawrence J. *The Automobile Industry Since 1945*. Cambridge, Mass.: Harvard University Press, 1971.

Wright, J. Patrick. *On a Clear Day You Can See General Motors: John Z. DeLorean's Look Inside the Automotive Giant*. Grosse Pointe, Mich.: Wright Enterprises, 1979.

GLAXO HOLDINGS PLC

Lansdowne House
Berkeley Square
London W1X 6BP
United Kingdom
(071) 493-4060

1991 revenues: $5.5 billion (year ending June 30)
1991 net income: $1.5 billion
Publicly traded company
Employees: 43,384
Founded: 1873

OVERVIEW

Glaxo, which had its origins in the powdered milk business, jumped to the top ranks of the international pharmaceutical industry during the 1980s on the basis of one product, the extraordinarily popular ulcer drug Zantac. The company, which now manufactures in 30 countries and sells in 150, cannot rest on its laurels much longer, however. Just as Zantac overcame the previous leader, SmithKline's Tagamet, generic imitators and other competitors are looking to dethrone Zantac.

Glaxo is preparing for its post-Zantac future by developing new drugs that eliminate migraine headaches and that control the side effects of chemotherapy. The latter may be effective in treating anxiety and schizophrenia as well. And Glaxo's ambitions do not stop there. The company has said that it aspires to find a cure for cancer.

HISTORY

Glaxo began its existence in the 1870s with the trading activities of English entrepreneur Joseph Nathan in New Zealand. Nathan was importing and exporting goods ranging from whalebone to patent medicines when one of his sons, on a business trip to London, learned of a new process to produce powdered milk. The Nathans were taken with the idea and purchased the rights to it. Production of powdered milk soon began in New Zealand and later was expanded to Britain.

The powdered milk venture was not, in general, a great hit, but the Nathans did find a receptive market for the baby food version of the product, which was sold under the brand name Glaxo. Sales rose steadily after the company published a child-care book called the *Glaxo Baby Book,* which promoted the soon-to-be-famous slogan that Glaxo products "build bonnie babies." After World War I the company, led by Louis Nathan after his father's death, expanded its distribution to India and South America.

A turning point in the company's history occurred in 1923, when Harry Jephcott, who had been hired to head a research operation, attended a dairy convention in Washington, D.C., and learned of research on identifying and isolating vitamin D. Jephcott persuaded the company to license the technology and to begin fortifying its products with the vitamin. Glaxo also introduced a liquid vitamin D concentrate called Ostelin and a vitamin-fortified dairy product called Ostermilk. Foreign sales continued to expand as markets like Greece and China were penetrated.

During World War II Glaxo began producing penicillin and anesthetics along with vitamin supplements. After the war the company, now led by Jephcott, moved more heavily into penicillin production and sold off various unrelated operations. The parent company, Joseph Nathan & Company, was dissolved, and Glaxo went public.

The company's biggest advance in this period was its isolation of Vitamin B_{12}. This discovery, which took place almost simultaneously across the Atlantic at Merck, was a major advance in the treatment of pernicious anemia. Glaxo also succeeded in synthesizing the hormone needed for the treatment of hypothyroidism.

During the 1950s Glaxo grew through a series of acquisitions, including chemical and medical supply operations. Most important for the future of the company was the purchase of Allen & Hanburys, a pharmaceutical house founded in 1715. Glaxo also developed a line of anti-inflammatory cortisone products.

Glaxo fought off a takeover bid by Beecham, another leading British drug house, in the 1970s by arranging a friendly merger with the Boots Company, a pharmaceutical company and retailer. Government antitrust authorities prohibited both deals, so Glaxo remained independent. It did not thrive in this state, however, because of serious marketing problems, not the least of which was the company's absence from the world's largest drug market, the United States.

These problems came to an end in the early 1980s, when the company introduced its new antiulcer medication, Zantac. Arranging to use the sales force of the Swiss company Hoffmann–La Roche (which was underemployed because of the declining sales of that firm's Librium and Valium tranquilizers),

Glaxo challenged SmithKline's ulcer drug, Tagamet, which had become the most widely prescribed medication on earth.

Thanks to aggressive marketing, Zantac was very well received, especially in the United States, where Glaxo finally had formed a subsidiary. The product benefited from the fact that it was taken only twice a day (half the frequency of Tagamet) and that it seemed to be free of the side effects that afflicted some Tagamet users. The ulcer drug soon overtook the SmithKline product for the number-one spot, and by virtue of this success Glaxo became one of the largest pharmaceutical companies in the world.

Ernest Mario, an American who took over as chief executive in 1989, continued to seek new markets for Zantac, in part to make up for a roadblock that appeared in Japan, where an ulcer drug developed by Yamanouchi turned out to be a formidable competitor. Another of Glaxo's new products, the injectable antibiotic ceftazidime (which is sold under various brand names), was nonetheless a success in that country. The company also proposed a nonprescription version of Zantac in the United States.

Deciding to focus all of its energies on prescription drugs, Glaxo sold off its food business, its animal health line, and other operations. At the same time, Glaxo spent $350 million to establish a U.S. research and development facility in North Carolina. The company has been using its worldwide $700-million annual research budget to develop products that will compensate for the expiration of Zantac's patent. Glaxo also has formed marketing alliances with Gilead Sciences, a small biotechnology firm in California, and with Japan's Sankyo. In 1991 Glaxo announced that it was beginning human trials for a new AIDS drug.

OPERATIONS

Having sold off its nondrug businesses, Glaxo operates in a single industry segment. With that segment, its products are divided into five major therapeutic areas:

Antiulcerants (47 percent of 1991 sales from continuing operations). This area consists of the company's leading product, Zantac (the brand name for ranitidine), a histamine H_2 blocker used in the treatment of peptic ulcers and related diseases of the alimentary tract.

Zantac, the world's best-selling prescription medicine, has taken a comfortable lead over SmithKline's Tagamet, the previous leader of the industry, but it has been facing growing competition from Losec (Prilosec in the United States), made by Astra AB of Sweden.

Glaxo also has had to contend with questions regarding the expiration of Zantac's patent. In 1991 a small Canadian company called Genpharm filed an application with the U.S. Food and Drug Administration to develop a generic version of Zantac, in anticipation of the expiration of the first patent on the drug in 1995. Yet Glaxo insists that the initial patent was for a form of Zantac that never was marketed. The relevant patent for the lucrative product, the company maintains, is one that does not expire until the year 2002. Observers say Glaxo has reason to be nervous, since Genpharm is owned by the Tabatznik family, which has a string of generic drug firms in Britain, Australia, and New Zealand, and has already won numerous patent fights with big pharmaceutical companies.

Respiratory Medicines (23 percent of sales). The principal product in this area is Ventolin, the world's leading asthma medication, which was introduced in 1969. Glaxo also sells the same medication in controlled-release tablets under the name Volmax as well as another asthma medicine, an inhaled steroid preparation called Becotide, which is also sold as an intranasal hay fever medication under the name Beconase.

Systemic Antibiotics (18 percent of sales). Included here are injectable antibiotics, such as ceftazidime, and oral ones, such as Ceporex. Ceftazidime, introduced in 1983, is sold in more than forty countries.

Dermatologicals (4 percent of sales). This area includes such products as Betnovate and Dermovate (Temovate in the United States), used for steroid-responsive skin conditions, such as psoriasis and eczema.

Cardiovascular Medicines (1 percent of sales). The principal drug in this area is Trandate, which is used to control hypertension.

Other Products (7 percent of revenues). The company's remaining revenues come from the sale of bulk pharmaceuticals and Zofran, a drug that controls vomiting associated with chemotherapy, launched in 1990. Zofran is also under study as a treatment for anxiety and schizophrenia. Glaxo is seeking approval for the sale of a medication called sumatriptan for severe migraine headaches. Some analysts believe that sumatriptan, which Glaxo wants to sell under the name Imitrex in the United States, could become a billion-dollar product by the mid-1990s.

TOP EXECUTIVES

- Paul Girolami, chairman
- Ernest Mario, chief executive
- Mario Fertonani, managing director, Europe, Middle East, northern and eastern Africa
- John M. Hignett, managing director, finance
- Franz B. Humer, managing director, product development
- Hiroshi Konishi, managing director, Japan
- Arthur M. Pappas, managing director, Latin America, southern Asia, Far East (except Japan), Australasia
- Charles A. Sanders, managing director, United States and Canada
- Richard B. Sykes, managing director, research and development

OUTSIDE DIRECTORS

- Ronald Arculus, former British ambassador to Italy
- Anne L. Armstrong, former U.S. ambassador to Britain
- John Cuckney, chairman of 3i PLC and Royal Insurance Holdings
- Ralf Dahrendorf, warden of St. Antony's College, Oxford University
- James L. Ferguson, former chief executive of General Foods
- Geoffrey Howe, former chancellor of the exchequer

FINANCIAL DATA

Revenues (in millions of pounds) (years ending June 30)

1991	3,397
1990	3,179
1989	2,570
1988	2,059
1987	1,741

Net Income (in millions of pounds) (years ending June 30)

1991	912
1990	807
1989	688
1988	571
1987	496

GEOGRAPHICAL BREAKDOWN

Revenues (in millions of pounds)

Year*	Europe		North America		Elsewhere	
1991	1,481	(44%)	1,359	(40%)	557	(16%)
1990	1,338	(42%)	1,316	(41%)	525	(17%)
1989	1,081	(42%)	1,163	(45%)	326	(13%)

*Fiscal year ends June 30.

LABOR RELATIONS

The company reports that a majority of its employees are represented by labor unions and describes relations with those unions as "good." In 1988 Glaxo announced that it was withdrawing recognition from one union, an affiliate of the Electrical, Electronic, Telecommunications and Plumbing Union (EETPU) that represented professional employees at a research center, because membership had dropped to an insignificant level.

ENVIRONMENTAL AND HEALTH RECORD

Before Glaxo's infant formula business was sold off in the late 1980s, that operation was the subject of controversy. Like many other formula producers, Glaxo had been accused of violating World Health Organization (WHO) standards for the marketing of formula in poor countries. Religious and public health advocates had pressured the WHO to adopt guidelines to discourage aggressive marketing of the formula in situations where mothers were often compelled to mix the powder with impure water or dilute the formula to the extent that it became much less nutritional than breast milk.

BIBLIOGRAPHY

Chetley, Andrew. *A Healthy Business? World Health and the Pharmaceutical Industry*. London: Zed Books, 1990.

Jephcott, Harry. *The First Fifty Years: The Early Life of Joseph Edward Nathan and His Merchandise Business That Became the Modern Glaxo Group*. London: Glaxo Group, 1969.

Lynn, Matthew. *Merck v Glaxo: The Billion Dollar Battle*. London: Heinemann, 1991.

Tweedale, Geoffrey. *At the Sign of the Plough: 275 Years of Allen & Hanburys and the British Pharmaceutical Industry, 1715–1990*. London: John Murray, 1990.

GOODYEAR TIRE & RUBBER COMPANY

1144 East Market Street
Akron, Ohio 44316
(216) 796-2121

1991 revenues: $10.9 billion
1991 net income: $96.6 million
Publicly traded company
Employees: 99,952
Founded: 1898

OVERVIEW

For decades Goodyear was the world's leading tire maker. Its winged-foot logo was a familiar sight on automobiles and on the fleet of blimps it operated. It did the most to make Akron, Ohio, the global center of the rubber industry.

For the past quarter century the company has faced intensified competition from foreign producers. By the 1980s those competitors were taking over virtually all of Goodyear's domestic rivals, and today the company is the last major tire maker based in the United States.

Along with the competition, there have been problems stemming from the steps the company took in 1986 to avoid a takeover by Sir James Goldsmith. Loaded with debt, Goodyear has had to sell off many of its nontire operations and has shut down numerous factories and eliminated large numbers of jobs in its core business.

Amid all of this, its French rival, Michelin, has taken over the top spot, and Japan's Bridgestone is challenging Goodyear for second place. In 1991 Goodyear's chief executive resigned under pressure from the board of directors. Although it has fallen on hard times, Goodyear, with operations in twenty-six countries, remains a leading player in the world tire industry.

HISTORY

When Frank A. Sieberling founded Goodyear in 1898 he was a wheeler-dealer who knew little about the rubber and tire business. His father had started a varied and generally successful group of ventures, including a rubber company, in Akron, Ohio, but most of the family fortune was wiped out during the economic crisis of the 1890s. Looking to the tire business as a new way to make money, Sieberling bought a factory in Akron and named his new company in honor of Charles Goodyear, an inventor whose 1839 discovery of the vulcanization process made him the founder of the tire industry.

The company initially focused on bicycle tires (mostly pneumatic) and carriage tires (mostly solid), but it also made horseshoe pads, rubber bands, poker chips, and other miscellaneous items. The first automobile tire was sold in 1901.

In those early years Goodyear had to contend with messy patent litigation, but the company emerged from its legal problems and rose through the ranks of the industry thanks to technical innovations. The most important of these were a change in the flange (which held the tire to the rim) that allowed the tire to be removed much more easily, and a rivet fabric that reduced tread separation and distributed road shock more evenly. This straight-sided Quick Detachable tire with a Universal Rim was introduced with great fanfare in 1905. Full-page advertisements were placed in the leading magazines of the day, and Goodyear arranged for race car drivers to use the new product. The company also won over a number of automakers, and the Quick Detachable became original equipment on many models.

Several years later the company improved the traction of its tires by developing a diamond-shaped tread with four-way edges. Known as the All-Weather Tread, this design came to be widely identified with Goodyear for many years to come. Another advance was the introduction of a tougher tire cord, inserted with multiple plies placed at right angles to one another. These tires, called No Rim-Cuts to emphasize the protection at the base, brought another boost to the company's sales.

By the beginning of World War I Goodyear was the dominant tire producer in the United States, and Akron, also the home of such producers as Goodrich and Firestone, was becoming the rubber capital of the world. Goodyear also began expanding geographically, purchasing a manufacturing plant in Ontario, obtaining a two thousand–acre rubber plantation in Indonesia, and opening a branch office in London. In 1916 Goodyear became the world leader in tire sales. That year the company also got involved in cotton growing in Arizona.

Along with automobiles, Goodyear helped to build the market for trucks. To demonstrate the durability of its cord pneumatic truck tires, in 1917 the company sent a five-ton Packard truck on what was then an unprecedented journey from Akron to Boston. The following year Goodyear further publicized the possibilities of long-distance hauling by sending two trucks from

Boston across the country to San Francisco, down the coast to Los Angeles, and back to Akron. The convoy traveled some seventy-seven hundred miles— more than 70 percent of which was on unpaved roads.

Goodyear experienced a slump in the early 1920s that was so severe that the company came close to bankruptcy. Wall Street financiers, previously shunned by Goodyear, were brought in to arrange a recapitalization of the firm and a reorganization that involved the resignation of the company's directors, including founder Frank Sieberling. Goodyear rebounded and went on to expand production overseas (in Brazil, Argentina, Sweden, and Indonesia) and move into new products, including footwear, packaging and cushioning material, and a paint base and waterproofing compound called Pliolite.

The company also expanded its involvement in the production of dirigibles, those huge airships filled with lighter-than-air gases like hydrogen and helium. In the mid-1920s, at the urging of the U.S. Navy, Goodyear formed a joint venture with the German producer Zeppelin to gain access to that company's unique methods. The venture soon produced what would become the famous airships *Akron* and *Macon*.

Although the dirigible era declined with the spectacular explosion of the *Hindenburg* in 1937, Goodyear continued to make the smaller airships, blimps, which lacked the rigid internal framework of dirigibles. Besides being used by the military for various missions, they were (and have continued to be) a promotional tool for Goodyear.

The company, then run by Paul Litchfield, participated in the industrial mobilization initiated by the federal government with the advent of World War II. Along with tires, blimps, and its other usual products, Goodyear produced Corsair fighter planes and components for other aircraft, gas masks, rubber boats, rafts, and life jackets. Another unusual effort involved making inflatable decoys of planes, artillery, and other equipment, which were used to confuse the Nazis as to Allied military plans in the period leading up to the invasion of Normandy. The company also participated in the program to begin large-scale production of synthetic rubber when natural rubber supplies from the Far East were cut off.

After the war the company prospered from the postwar growth in consumer spending and also regained its facilities in Indonesia, which had been seized by the Japanese during the war. Goodyear continued its aircraft production and began moving into the rocket and missile field. Concern about shortages in rubber supplies during the Korean War led the federal government to ask for expanded output of synthetic rubber at government-owned plants operated by Goodyear. The company itself developed an improved synthetic rubber called Natsyn in 1955. During that same period, Goodyear was contracted by the Atomic Energy Commission to operate a uranium enrichment plant. Starting in the 1950s the company accelerated its overseas expansion by setting up factories in such countries as Germany, Italy, Luxembourg, Turkey, Singapore, and Zaire.

Goodyear also struggled to keep up with changes in tire technology. In 1946 the radial tire was introduced by France's Michelin, and over the following decade that new design was widely adopted in Europe. Goodyear responded by setting out to devise a new substance for tire cord to replace rayon and nylon. Finally, in 1962, the company introduced polyester cord tires. Because there was a growing demand for high-performance tires yet continued resistance to radials—or so the domestic producers said—in the United States, Goodyear developed a transitional product called the bias-belted tire, which it introduced in 1967. This tire was well received and helped pave the way to the acceptance of radials in the 1970s.

Yet, by that decade Michelin had entered the U.S. market and was making inroads with Detroit's automakers. The French company enhanced its competitive position in North America by opening plants in Canada and the United States. The Japanese company Bridgestone also was developing an American presence. Goodyear met the competition by introducing a gas-saving all-weather tire called Tiempo in the late 1970s and an improved version called Arriva in 1980. That year it also brought out the Eagle tire, designed for speed and performance rather than long life.

Goodyear moved into the oil and gas business in the early 1980s through the purchase of Celeron Corporation for $825 million in stock, and within a few years the company was building a $900-million pipeline to transport crude oil from California to refineries on the Gulf Coast. The pipeline ran into problems because of concerns over its effect on water supplies in Texas, but the company faced a much bigger challenge in 1986, when Anglo-French financier Sir James Goldsmith made an unsolicited $4.7-billion offer to buy the company.

Goodyear's management got rid of Goldsmith—who strongly opposed the company's diversification moves—by buying his holdings at a hefty premium. The company also made a tender offer for other shares, resulting in a total stock buyback of $2.6 billion. To help pay for the purchases, Goodyear sold off Celeron, its cotton-growing business, and its aerospace operations. The latter included the blimp production business, though the company went on operating its fleet of airships. The All American Pipeline system could not be unloaded.

The debt-laden company was thus left with its tire business (very little of which remained in Akron) in a period when sales of that product were slowing down because of the greater durability of radials. Competition in the United States also intensified as foreign rivals acquired domestic competitors: Bridgestone bought Firestone, Germany's Continental bought General Tire, Italy's Pirelli bought Armstrong, and Michelin bought Uniroyal-Goodrich. The Michelin purchase allowed it to topple Goodyear as the world's number-one tire maker.

An attempt by Goodyear in 1989 to raise prices backfired when its competitors failed to follow suit. Amid an all-out battle for market share, the once untouchable leader found itself not only surpassed by Michelin but also tailgated by Bridgestone, a company it had helped rebuild after World War II. Goodyear's oil pipeline was also running at well below capacity. In 1990 the company suffered its first net loss in half a century.

One casualty of this dismal situation was chief executive Tom Barrett, who resigned under pressure in 1991. He was replaced with Stanley Gault, the recently retired chairman of Rubbermaid who was serving on Goodyear's board of directors. The unusual appointment of an outsider to head the tire maker was an apparent signal from the board that tough measures were required to rescue the company. Soon it was announced that one of those measures would be to sell off its remaining nontire operations. Tire assets were not immune either; one tire plant in Alabama was sold to the Dutch company Azko.

At the same time, Gault moved to win market share in its core business by announcing a new tire that was designed to reduce fuel consumption and related exhaust emissions. Goodyear also formed a technology-sharing arrangement with South Korea's Hyundai Petrochemical.

OPERATIONS

Tires and Related Products (82 percent of 1991 revenues). Goodyear produces a wide range of rubber tires and tubes for automobiles, trucks, buses, tractors, earth-moving equipment, airplanes, industrial equipment, and other vehicles, both for sale to original equipment manufacturers and in the replacement market. Passenger tires are sold mainly under the names Tiempo, Eagle, Invicta, and Corsa. Tires also are sold by the subsidiaries Kelly-Springfield, Lee Tire & Rubber, and Brad Ragan.

Tires and related products are manufactured at facilities in about a dozen states as well as in Argentina, Brazil, Canada, Chile, Colombia, France, Germany, Greece, Guatemala, India, Indonesia, Italy, Jamaica, Luxembourg, Malaysia, Mexico, Morocco, Peru, the Philippines, Taiwan, Thailand, Turkey, the United Kingdom, and Venezuela.

General Products (18 percent of revenues). This segment of Goodyear's operations includes vehicle components (belts, hoses, springs, and so on), industrial rubber products, synthetic rubber, polyester products, packaging products, footwear products, and roofing products. The company's All American Pipeline operation accounted for less than 1 percent of 1991 revenues. In 1992 Goodyear sold its polyester business to Shell Oil.

TOP EXECUTIVES

- Stanley C. Gault, chief executive
- Hoyt M. Wells, president
- Oren G. Shaffer, executive vice president

OUTSIDE DIRECTORS

- John G. Breen, chief executive of Sherwin Williams Company
- Thomas H. Cruikshank, chief executive of Halliburton Company

- Gertrude G. Michelson, senior vice president of R. H. Macy & Company
- Steven A. Minter, president of the Cleveland Foundation
- Russell E. Palmer, chief executive of the Palmer Group
- Charles W. Parry, retired chairman of ALCOA
- Agnar Pytte, president of Case Western Reserve University
- George H. Schofield, chief executive of Zurn Industries
- William C. Turner, chief executive of the counsulting firm Argyle Atlantic Corporation

FINANCIAL DATA

Revenues (in millions of dollars)

1991	10,907
1990	11,273
1989	10,869
1988	10,810
1987	9,905

Net Income (in millions of dollars)

1991	97
1990	−38 (loss)
1989	207
1988	350
1987	771

GEOGRAPHICAL BREAKDOWN

Revenues (in millions of dollars)

Year	United States		Europe		Elsewhere	
1991	6,231	(57%)	2,282	(21%)	2,394	(22%)
1990	6,460	(57%)	2,301	(20%)	2,512	(22%)
1989	6,421	(59%)	2,039	(19%)	2,409	(22%)

Operating income (in millions of dollars)

Year	United States		Europe		Elsewhere	
1991	423	(54%)	124	(16%)	237	(30%)
1990	237	(53%)	36	(6%)	249	(41%)
1989	491	(53%)	132	(14%)	303	(33%)

LABOR RELATIONS

Goodyear founder Frank Sieberling was a paternalistic employer who in 1912 launched a model residential community for his workers near the plant in Akron. Sieberling enabled employees to buy low-cost homes in the community without having to make a down payment. The company also established Goodyear Hall, a large, elaborate facility devoted to employee education and recreation.

In the factory the company devised a plan that involved the training of fifty workers in all aspects of the manufacturing process. Members of this "Flying Squadron," who were given special, superseniority rights, were sent into lagging departments to speed up output, or to overburdened areas during periods of high-volume production. Later they were called on to intimidate union supporters.

Despite these policies, Goodyear workers did join a strike that was promoted in 1913 by the Industrial Workers of the World at the major tire companies. The walkout was abandoned after forty-eight days, but the following year the company did shorten the workday and institute a vacation policy.

In 1919 the company created the Goodyear Industrial Assembly, a legislative body modeled on the U.S. Congress, in which employee representatives set policy on wages, benefits, safety procedures, and other aspects of working conditions. The assembly, which remained in effect until 1937, was a remarkable experiment in industrial democracy—but one that was not emulated by other corporations.

Goodyear workers were among the targets of an organizing drive instituted by the American Federation of Labor in the early 1930s, amid the depression and the enactment of New Deal reforms in employment policy. Several thousand Goodyear workers signed union cards, but in a vote conducted by the Industrial Assembly, an overwhelming majority of employees opposed the call for a strike to pressure the tire companies to recognize the union.

Yet in 1935, after several years of limiting the day to six hours to spread the work in a time of high unemployment, the Industrial Assembly voted to rescind a decision by the company to return to the eight-hour day. Management vetoed the assembly's action, but then the company was overruled by the U.S. Department of Labor.

The confrontation worked to the benefit of the newly formed United Rubber Workers (URW), which called a strike at Goodyear in 1936. The result was a huge walkout in which some ten thousand demonstrators overwhelmed local authorities who tried to enforce an injunction against mass picketing. The URW ended the strike after thirty-four days when it won reforms in working conditions, but in the following months there were frequent work stoppages and sit-down actions.

In 1937 Goodyear workers voted under National Labor Relations Board supervision to make the URW, by then affiliated with the Congress of Industrial Organizations, their collective-bargaining representative. This meant the demise of the Industrial Assembly. Although Goodyear was then compelled to bargain with the union, it stretched out the negotiations as long as possible. It was not until 1941 that the company and the union entered into their first formal contract.

Disputes over wage guidelines and other practices during World War II led to two strikes. A fifty-one-day nationwide walkout of Goodyear workers took place in 1954. The longest work stoppage in company history—130 days— occurred in 1976, when the URW sought to close down all of the major producers. In an attempt to erode the power of the URW, Goodyear announced in 1977 that the company would build its first nonunion plant, in Oklahoma.

During the 1980s the hard times facing the company and the rest of the U.S. tire industry made Goodyear workers willing to accept contract concessions. The contract talks of 1988, which came while the company was still recovering from the takeover attempt by Sir James Goldsmith, resulted in a contract that improved pension benefits but included no general wage increase. A contract settlement reached in 1991 raised wages and benefits about 18 percent over its three-year term.

At the end of 1990 some 46 percent of the company's domestic employees were represented by unions, mostly the URW.

ENVIRONMENTAL RECORD

In 1988 the company reached a settlement with the EPA on the cleanup of the Superfund toxic-waste site at the Phoenix-Goodyear Airport in Arizona. The company agreed to extract and treat groundwater contaminated with industrial solvents such as trichloroethylene. The Defense Department, for which Goodyear's aerospace division had been working at the site, agreed to help pay for the estimated $30-million cleanup cost.

Goodyear was among the responsible parties cited in connection with toxic-waste dumping at the Forest Glen Superfund site near Niagara Falls, New York. In 1989 the EPA ordered Goodyear and the other parties to purchase the homes of and relocate fifty families living in mobile homes atop the contaminated site.

In 1990 Goodyear was one of nine major companies that reached an agreement with the EPA on cutting emissions of carcinogens by the beginning of 1993.

A study by the National Institute for Occupational Safety and Health, released in 1991, concludes that workers exposed to orth-toluidine and aniline, chemicals used in making rubber and other products, faced a highly elevated risk of developing bladder cancer. The study focuses on workers at Goodyear's plant in Niagara Falls, New York.

BIBLIOGRAPHY

Allen, Hugh. *The House of Goodyear: A Story of Rubber and of Modern Business*. 1943. Reprint. Salem, N.H.: Ayer, 1976.

French, Michael J. *The U.S. Tire Industry: A History*. Boston: Twayne, 1991.

O'Reilly, Maurice. *The Goodyear Story*. Elmsford, N.Y.: Benjamin Company, 1983.

Roberts, Harold S. *The Rubber Workers: Labor Organization and Collective Bargaining in the Rubber Industry*. New York: Harper & Brothers, 1944.

GRAND METROPOLITAN PLC

20 St. James's Square
London SW1Y 4RR
United Kingdom
(071) 321 6000

1991 revenues: $15.3 billion (year ending September 30)
1991 net income: $756.4 million
Publicly traded company
Employees: 122,178
Founded: 1934

OVERVIEW

Grand Metropolitan has evolved from the owner of a group of seedy hotels
to a world leader in the food, beverage, and restaurant industries. Frustrated
by antitrust problems in Britain, the company went on a buying spree in the
United States in the 1980s, ending up with some of the country's most famous
brand names.

Grand Met made itself into a global leader in the wine and spirits business,
but the company had to sell off its brewing operations to meet U.K. government requirements for holding on to its huge network of pubs. While Grand
Met has tried to build an identity for itself in food, drink, and retailing, the
company is best known as a shrewd buyer and seller of properties of all kinds.

HISTORY

Grand Met was created single-handedly by Maxwell Joseph, who left school
in 1926 at the age of sixteen to work in real estate in North London. Joseph
was a precocious entrepreneur, and he was soon buying and selling properties
on his own. In 1934 he established a firm called MRMA Ltd. to acquire the
leasehold interest in premises known as Mount Royal Marble Arch.

The depression made it easy for Joseph to purchase properties cheaply but at the same time made them much more difficult to resell. It was not until after World War II that his growing portfolio began to have some real value. He then began a hotel-buying spree, beginning with blitz-damaged and run-down establishments and later moving on to more prestigious ones. The first of the latter was London's Mount Royal Hotel, purchased for $2.8 million in 1957. This was followed by the Lotti in Paris, the Carlton in Cannes, and the Hotel d'Angleterre in Copenhagen. Joseph changed the name of the company to Mount Royal Ltd. in 1959 and Grand Metropolitan Hotels in 1962.

In the late 1960s Joseph began to diversify, focusing on companies that provided some of the things served in hotels. In short order he acquired Express Dairies, Berni Inns, Truman Hanburg brewers, and the Watney-Mann brewery (which had put in an unsuccessful counterbid for Truman Hanburg). The controversial 1972 Watney-Mann purchase—the largest up to that time in British business—brought with it International Distillers and Vintners, producer of such famous liquor brands as J&B Scotch, Bombay gin, and Bailey's Irish Cream.

Having run up more than £500 million in debt through these acquisitions, Grand Metropolitan (the shortened name was adopted in 1973) took some time to consolidate. The company's next major move came in 1980, when it made an unsolicited bid for the Liggett Group, the U.S. cigarette company that was of interest mainly because it owned the American distributor for Grand Met's leading liquor brand, J&B. Liggett's management fought fiercely against the takeover, but in the end it succumbed to Grand Met's sweetened offer of $600 million.

In his last major deal before his death in 1982, Joseph paid $500 million to cash-starved Pan American World Airways for its chain of Inter-Continental Hotels. This gave Grand Met such toney establishments as the Mark Hopkins in San Francisco.

Joseph's successor, Stanley Grinstead, unloaded Liggett's tobacco business and then jumped on the health-care bandwagon. Grand Met bought Quality Care Inc., a producer of medical equipment, and Pearle Health Services, owner of a large chain of eye-care stores in the United States.

Allen Sheppard, who took over as chief executive in 1986, put the acquisition focus back on food and drink, especially in the United States. The first of a series of major deals was the 1987 purchase of Heublein Inc., marketer of dozens of major brands of wines and spirits, for $1.2 billion. This made Grand Met the world leader in alcoholic beverages, though Seagram remained larger in hard liquor alone.

Heublein has its origins in a family restaurant in Hartford, Connecticut, whose owners devised the first bottled cocktails in the late nineteenth century. The company, which survived Prohibition by pushing A-1 steak sauce, bought the rights to Smirnoff vodka in 1939 at a time when the drink was largely unknown in the United States. Heublein skillfully created a market for the stuff after the war with a promotion of new mixed drinks containing vodka, including an ad campaign stating that vodka left the drinker "breathless."

The company got into the wine business with the purchase of United Vintners in 1969 and then took a plunge in fast food with the acquisition of Kentucky Fried Chicken in 1971. In 1982 Heublein was acquired by cigarette maker R. J. Reynolds, which divested a number of its operations before selling the company to Grand Met five years later.

The Heublein acquisition was dwarfed by Grand Met's purchase of Pillsbury Company, one of a series of megamergers that rocked the U.S. food industry in 1988. The $5.8-billion deal, which went through after Pillsbury's poison-pill defense was struck down in court, gave Grand Met one of the most famous names in U.S. food processing.

Pillsbury was founded in 1869 by Charles Pillsbury, who went on to become one of the pillars of the Minneapolis milling business. Known mainly as a producer of flour and other baked goods (its Doughboy is one of the most widely recognized advertising characters), the company got into the restaurant business in the 1960s with the purchase of Burger King. William Spoor, who ran Pillsbury from 1973 to 1985, arranged the acquisition of Green Giant (the largest packer of peas and corn), Häagen-Dazs ice cream, and Van de Kamp's (a specialty food producer).

After the company faltered under the leadership of Spoor's successor, John Stafford, Spoor was temporarily brought out of retirement to resume his old job. After taking over the weakened company, Grand Met sold off Van de Kamp's and the Bumble Bee tuna business and converted Burger King and Häagen-Dazs from Pillsbury units into free-standing operations.

During the late 1980s Grand Met also sold off the Inter-Continental Hotel chain (for four times what it had paid Pan Am) to Japan's Seibu/Saison Group, bought restaurant chains in Germany and Switzerland, increased its ownership of legal betting shops in Britain, acquired the Christian Brothers winery in California, and sold off a Pepsi bottling operation.

OPERATIONS

Food (40 percent of 1991 revenues from continuing businesses). This segment has five divisions. The first is Pillsbury Brands, which operates mainly in the United States and consists of three major businesses. Its baked-goods operation produces refrigerated ready-to-bake dough products (a market in which it ranks first), pancake mix, dessert mix, frozen pizza, and other foods. Its vegetable business is based primarily on Green Giant, the market leader in various kinds of frozen and canned vegetables. The third of the Pillsbury businesses consists of flour milling and the production of processed feed ingredients for the poultry, hog, beef, and dairy industries.

The second division in this segment is Grand Metropolitan Foods Europe, which includes the Express dairy foods operation in the United Kingdom and Ireland and Pillsbury Foods Europe. The third division is Häagen-Dazs, the largest manufacturer and distributor of superpremium ice-cream products (that is, those with high butterfat content). Grand Met has been expanding the ice-cream business in Canada, Japan, and Europe. The fourth division is

Alpo, maker of premium canned and dry foods for dogs and cats. The final division is GrandMet Foodservice USA, which provides bakery mixes, canned vegetables, dehydrated potatoes, and other food products for institutional food operations.

Drinks (32 percent of revenues). This segment includes IDV, the world leader in wines and spirits, and, until recently, GrandMet Brewing. Because of pressures from the U.K. Monopolies and Merger Commission, Grand Met has reached an agreement to sell its brewing and beer distribution operations to Courage, the U.K. subsidiary of Foster's Brewing Group, the Australian company formerly known as Elders IXL. The two companies also planned to form a joint venture called Inntrapreneur to manage all of the tenanted pubs of Courage and some of Grand Met's.

The wine and spirits operation includes such well-known liquor brands as Smirnoff, the world's most popular vodka; J&B Scotch, the number-two whiskey; Popov, the number-two vodka; and Bailey's Irish Cream, the second-ranking liqueur. In total the company has eleven of the top one hundred brands in the world. IDV also has the U.S. distribution rights for such brands as Absolut, José Cuervo, Wild Turkey, Cinzano, Grand Marnier, and Amaretto di Saronno.

Grant Met's wine operation—which includes Almaden, Inglenook, and Lancers—has its largest operation in the United States, where it enjoys more than 10 percent of the market for nonfortified wines. The company also sells an herbal fruit drink called Aqua Libra. In 1991 Grand Met and Allied-Lyons each acquired a 25-percent share in New Zealand Wine & Spirits, a producing and distributing subsidiary of brewer Lion Nathan.

Retailing (27 percent of revenues). The largest portion of this segment is the Burger King chain of fast-food restaurants. Burger King, which became a subsidiary of Pillsbury in 1967, has engaged in a perennial battle with industry leader McDonald's. The company suffered frequent management changes in the late 1970s and early 1980s but emerged as an aggressive challenger to McDonald's, especially in the advertising arena. By the latter part of the 1980s Burger King was suffering from a string of unsuccessful ad campaigns and began falling further behind McDonald's. Grand Met has sought to revitalize the chain, in part by removing it from Pillsbury's control. The chain's new chief executive, Barry Gibbons, also accelerated a plan to build new outlets in unconventional locations, such as in hospitals and prisons. Burger King has jumped on the health bandwagon. In 1991 it agreed to begin posting nutrition information at its restaurants in New York City, and at about the same time, it began an experiment in which food provided by Weight Watchers International was added to the menu at one outlet.

At the end of fiscal 1991 Burger King had approximately fifty-five hundred restaurants in the United States and eight hundred abroad. Some 83 percent were franchises and the rest were owned by the company.

This segment also includes sixteen hundred pubs in the United Kingdom operating under the Chef & Brewer and Clifton Inns names. In 1991 Grand Met sold its Pizzaland and Pastificio restaurant chains in the United Kingdom, and it announced plans to put up for sale its Wienerwald restaurants in Germany and its Spaghetti Factory eating establishments in Switzerland.

Other retail operations include the Pearle chain of eye-care stores in North America, Europe, and the Far East.

TOP EXECUTIVES

- Allen Sheppard, chairman and group chief executive
- George J. Bull, chief executive, drinks sector
- Ian A. Martin, chief executive, food sector
- David P. Nash, group finance director
- David E. Tagg, chief executive, retailing and property sector

OUTSIDE DIRECTORS

- Richard V. Giordano, deputy chairman of the BOC Group
- John Harvey-Jones, former chairman of Imperial Chemical
- Colin Marshall, chief executive of British Airways
- David A. G. Simon, deputy chairman of British Petroleum

FINANCIAL DATA

Revenues (in millions of pounds) (years ending September 30)

1991	8,748
1990	9,394
1989	9,298
1988	6,029
1987	5,706

Net Profit (in millions of pounds) (years ending September 30)

1991	432
1990	1,069
1989	1,068
1988	702
1987	461

GEOGRAPHICAL BREAKDOWN

Sales from continuing businesses (in millions of pounds)

Year*	United Kingdom and Ireland		United States		Elsewhere	
1991	1,731	(23%)	4,433	(59%)	1,238	(17%)
1990	1,698	(23%)	4,537	(62%)	1,101	(15%)
1989	1,586	(27%)	3,467	(59%)	820	(14%)

*Fiscal year ends September 30.

Operating Income From Continuing Businesses (in millions of pounds)

Year*	United Kingdom and Ireland		United States		Elsewhere	
1991	304	(31%)	517	(52%)	169	(17%)
1990	273	(31%)	472	(53%)	141	(16%)
1989	214	(30%)	358	(51%)	131	(19%)

*Fiscal year ends September 30.

LABOR RELATIONS

Grand Met has been a villain for U.S. unions since late 1989, when the company's Green Giant subsidiary announced that it planned to shut down a frozen food–processing plant in Watsonville, California, and move the work to Mexico. Workers at the facility in Watsonville—a town that in 1986 and 1987 was the site of a successful struggle of food packers against another company—were mainly Hispanic and were members of the Teamsters. They were being paid up to eight dollars an hour; the workers at Green Giant's Mexican operation earned four dollars a day. A union-organizing drive at the Mexican plant in 1984 was quashed by management.

In response to Green Giant's plans, the Watsonville workers launched a product boycott and a corporate campaign against Grand Met. During October 1990 there was a coordinated series of protests against Grand Met operations in the United States, Britain, Japan, and Mexico. The workers also have charged the company with irresponsible environmental practices at its Mexican plant.

Burger King, like other fast-food chains, has strongly resisted unionization of its employees, who are often teenagers. In 1990 the Department of Labor filed suit against Burger King for violation of child labor laws at many of the company-owned outlets in the United States. The complaint charged that Burger King assigned more hours to workers under the age of sixteen than

was permitted by law, and that those young workers were performing prohibited duties, such as cooking and baking.

ENVIRONMENTAL RECORD

In the late 1980s Grand Met's Burger King subsidiary was the target of a
boycott led by the Rainforest Action Network, which criticized the company
for using beef from Central America. The ranchers who produce that beef
are responsible for the conversion of large quantities of rain forest to pasture
for cattle. Environmentalists argue that the preservation of rain forests is
essential to maintaining the ecological balance of the planet.

Burger King promised in 1987 to suspend its use of Central American beef
but resisted a proposed system of verification. But by 1989 the Rainforest
Action Network was persuaded that the company had indeed complied, so
the boycott was called off.

In 1991 Burger King began phasing out coated-paper sandwich boxes and
bleached-paper bags in favor of packaging that is easier to recycle.

In 1990 Pillsbury was ordered by the EPA to pay a fine of $100,000 and to
reimburse the city of Joplin, Missouri, $75,000 in costs relating to the com-
pany's illegal discharge of pollutants into the Silver River.

BIBLIOGRAPHY

Cavanagh, John, and Frederick Clairmonte. *Alcoholic Beverages: Dimensions of
Corporate Power*. New York: St. Martin's Press, 1985.

Clairmonte, Frederick, and John Cavanagh. *Merchants of Drink: Transnational
Control of World Beverages*. Penang, Malaysia: Third World Network, 1988.

Jacobson, Michael, Robert Atkins, and George Hacker. *The Booze Merchants*.
Washington, D.C.: Center for Science in the Public Interest, 1983.

Pillsbury, Philip W. *The Pioneering Pillsburys*. New York: Newcomen Society,
1950.

HEWLETT-PACKARD COMPANY

3000 Hanover Street
Palo Alto, California 94304
(415) 857-1501

1991 revenues: $14.5 billion (year ending October 31)
1991 net income: $755 million
Publicly traded company
Employees: 89,000
Founded: 1939

OVERVIEW

Hewlett-Packard (H-P), the preeminent instruments company, is most famous for developing the hand-held scientific calculator that made the slide rule obsolete. The highly regarded firm also pioneered a management strategy based on breaking down the rigid chain of command.

H-P, the first Silicon Valley start-up, also has wanted to become a major presence in the computer industry. The company has faced many obstacles in this quest, but by the early 1990s it was far ahead in the laser printer market and was gaining ground with a new series of powerful workstations and an innovative hand-held computer. Though H-P has never quite made it to the top of the computer business, its twelve thousand products and aggressive research and development make it one of the world's most important companies in the electronics industry.

HISTORY

Back in the 1930s, when the area now called Silicon Valley consisted mainly of orchards, a Stanford University engineering professor named Frederick Terman had a mission. He encouraged his students to remain in the area after graduation and start new ventures rather than going to work for large corporations in the East. Two students who took this appeal to heart were William Hewlett and David Packard.

In 1938, with an initial investment of $538, they began tinkering in a garage in Palo Alto. At the beginning of 1939 they established a formal partnership and were already selling their first product based on work Hewlett had done for his master's thesis—a resistance-capacity audio oscillator used to test sound equipment. Walt Disney Studios ordered eight of them for the production of the movie *Fantasia*. The following year, with a product line of eight instruments, Hewlett and Packard took the big step of moving into a building in the commercial district of town.

The modest operation blossomed as a result of government orders during World War II, including a contract from Terman, who was doing antiradar research for the military. This work put H-P in a position to benefit from the electronics boom after the war. With Hewlett focusing on technology and Packard on management, the company expanded steadily, reaching $2 million in sales with 146 employees in 1950. The following year the company introduced a high-speed frequency counter that reduced measurement time from ten minutes to one or two seconds. The device was of special use to radio stations in determining that they were broadcasting on the correct frequency.

In 1957 the growing company made its first public stock offering, and the following year it carried out its first acquisition, buying F. L. Moseley Company, a producer of graphic recorders. This was soon followed by the purchase of a medical instruments manufacturer by the name of Sanborn Company.

H-P, now bringing in more than $100 million a year in sales, gained a great deal of publicity in the mid-1960s as the producer of a cesium-beam instrument that measured time to within one-millionth of a second. The device, dubbed the "flying clock," was sent on a thirty-five-day round-the-world tour to coordinate the national time standards of various countries.

During this time H-P was expanding its international presence. In 1959 a marketing organization was established in Geneva and a manufacturing facility in Böblingen, West Germany. Four years later a joint venture was formed with the Japanese company Yokogawa Electric Works.

H-P produced its first computer, which served as a controller for some of the company's test and measurement instruments, in 1966. Two years later it introduced the first desktop scientific calculator. That was well received, but H-P made a much bigger splash with the first hand-held scientific calculator, the HP-35, in 1972. It, more than any other product, was responsible for ending the age of the slide rule.

Its success with the HP-35 encouraged H-P to think it could score in the emerging market for small computers. H-P had some success with the minicomputers it introduced in the 1970s, but when the company brought out its first personal computer, the HP-85, in 1980, the reaction was less than overwhelming. With John Young now serving as chief executive, H-P centralized its computer research and development and soon launched a new line called Spectrum. As part of that switch, H-P invested more than $250 million developing its Precision Architecture system, which was based on a concept called reduced instruction set computing, or RISC, which greatly enhanced computing speed by eliminating many routine instructions.

H-P became even better known during the 1980s as a producer of printers. It pioneered ink-jet technology and then made laser printing available to a much wider range of computer users through its LaserJet series. The LaserJet turned out to be the best-selling product in H-P's history.

H-P increased its standing in the processor part of the business through an acquisition—the 1989 purchase of Apollo Computer, a leader in the work-station market, for $500 million. Through the deal, H-P's share of the market initially jumped ahead of leader Sun Microsystems. But later it slipped behind Sun because of delays in receiving new microprocessors from Motorola and inadequate software. H-P also was falling behind in laptops and other PCs. Better progress was being made in the minicomputer field, where H-P began to gain market share from IBM and Digital Equipment in the late 1980s after spending $400 million to redesign its machines.

H-P sought to remedy some of its deficiencies via joint ventures. Such arrangements were set up, for example, with Hitachi (both for developing RISC chips and for developing artificial intelligence software) and Samsung (for workstation development). In 1991 H-P even began an effort with its workstation rival Sun to develop an advanced software that would allow machines from the two companies to share information within networks.

Despite this cooperation with Sun on software, H-P launched an uncharacteristically aggressive promotional campaign for its new workstations, explicitly highlighting the advantages of its machines over Sun's products. Also in 1991 the company challenged the Japanese dominance in the "palmtop" market by introducing its own hand-held PC. Many analysts called this device, formally called the HP 95LX but nicknamed "Jaguar," the product that would cause the tiny machines to be regarded as serious business tools.

OPERATIONS

Measurement, Design, Information, and Manufacturing Equipment and Systems (36 percent of 1991 revenues). This product grouping includes both hardware and software involved in general-purpose instruments and computers (especially workstations and minicomputers), hand-held calculators, and equipment for design, manufacturing, and other information processing. This includes a software package called New Wave, which ended up making H-P (along with Microsoft) a defendant in an unsuccessful copyright suit brought by Apple Computer. That company claimed that the H-P product and Microsoft's Windows infringed on its copyrights relating to the Macintosh.

Peripherals and Network Products (31 percent of revenues). This grouping includes printers, plotters, magnetic disc and tape drives, terminals, and network products. The most successful product is the LaserJet series, which gives H-P a commanding lead (some 60 percent in the United States) in the market for laser printers. In 1991 H-P announced a new, low-cost ink-jet printer capable of printing in color on plain paper.

Service for Equipment, Systems, and Peripherals (20 percent of revenues). This segment includes support and maintenance services relating to most of the products in the previous two groupings.

Medical Electronic Equipment and Service (6 percent of revenues). H-P is a leading manufacturer of products that perform patient monitoring, diagnostic, therapeutic, and data-management functions. This grouping also includes applications software, support, and maintenance for these products.

Analytical Instrumentation and Service (5 percent of revenues). Included here are gas and liquid chromatographs, mass spectrometers, and spectrophotometers used to analyze chemical compounds.

Electronic Components (2 percent of revenues). This segment consists of microwave semiconductor and optoelectronic devices that are sold primarily to manufacturers for incorporation into electronic products.

TOP EXECUTIVES

- David Packard, chairman of the board
- John A. Young, president and chief executive
- Dean O. Morton, executive vice president and chief operating officer
- Richard A. Hackborn, executive vice president, computer products
- Lewis E. Platt, executive vice president, computer systems
- William E. Terry, executive vice president, measurement systems

OUTSIDE DIRECTORS

- Thomas E. Everhart, president of the California Institute of Technology
- John B. Fery, chief executive of Boise Cascade
- Harold J. Haynes, retired chief executive of Chevron
- Walter B. Hewlett, independent software developer (and son of cofounder William Hewlett)
- Shirley M. Hufstedler, partner in the law firm Hufstedler Kaus & Ettinger
- George A. Keyworth II, director of research at the Hudson Institute
- Paul F. Miller, Jr., senior partner in the investment firm Miller Anderson & Sherrerd
- David Woodley Packard, president of Ibycus Corporation (and son of chairman David Packard)
- Donald E. Petersen, retired chief executive of Ford Motor Company
- Condoleezza Rice, associate professor of political science at Stanford University

- Hicks B. Waldron, retired chief executive of Avon Products
- T. A. Wilson, chairman emeritus of Boeing

FINANCIAL DATA

Revenues (in millions of dollars) (years ending October 31)

1991	14,494
1990	13,233
1989	11,899
1988	9,831
1987	8,090

Net Income (in millions of dollars) (years ending October 31)

1991	755
1990	739
1989	829
1988	816
1987	644

GEOGRAPHICAL BREAKDOWN

Revenues (in millions of dollars)

Year*	United States		Europe		Elsewhere	
1991	9,613	(51%)	5,789	(31%)	3,457	(18%)
1990	8,841	(52%)	5,050	(30%)	3,079	(18%)
1989	8,195	(53%)	4,402	(29%)	2,808	(18%)
1988	6,827	(54%)	3,554	(28%)	2,221	(17%)

*Fiscal year ends October 31.

Operating Income (in millions of dollars)

Year*	United States		Europe		Elsewhere	
1991	1,191	(70%)	292	(17%)	224	(13%)
1990	1,069	(62%)	363	(21%)	281	(16%)
1989	881	(54%)	359	(22%)	379	(23%)
1988	858	(61%)	235	(17%)	325	(23%)

*Fiscal year ends October 31.

LABOR RELATIONS

Hewlett-Packard has long adopted a position of paternalism in its dealings with employees. The company adopted policies of avoiding layoffs, allowing people to work flexible hours, and sending gifts when a staff member got married or had a baby. Practices like these have engendered a strong sense of loyalty among the employees and lessened the appeal of unions.

Yet the company has come under some criticism for its policy of using large numbers of temporary workers (who enjoy no benefits or job security) to work on short-term projects and to fill in for permanent employees on vacation or leave.

ENVIRONMENTAL RECORD

Although H-P prides itself on good corporate citizenship, the company has been ranked the dirtiest of a "dirty dozen" of polluting electronics companies by the Silicon Valley Toxics Coalition. The company has been named a potentially responsible party at two Superfund cleanup sites in Colorado.

H-P has been a heavy user of ozone-destroying CFCs, but in 1990 the company said it would phase out its use of CFC solvents.

HITACHI, LTD.

6, Kanda-Surugadai 4-chome
Chiyoda-ku, Tokyo 101
Japan
(03) 3258-1111

1991 revenues: $55 billion (year ending March 31)
1991 net income: $1.6 billion
Publicly traded company
Employees: 309,757
Founded: 1910

OVERVIEW

Hitachi is the largest electrical and electronics producer in Japan and the second-largest industrial firm in the country (after Toyota). With manufacturing operations in sixteen countries, it competes in world markets with both high-tech items like advanced semiconductors and more mundane items like electric fans. At home the company also sells a huge number of products, ranging from nuclear power plants to refrigeration equipment.

Although Hitachi is, along with NEC and Toshiba, one of the world's biggest chip makers, it is not as well known around the globe as some other Japanese electronics companies. In part this is because for years many of its products were sold abroad under other names (for instance, VCRs marketed by RCA). Another problem has been that Hitachi stumbled in some high-visibility areas. It built, for example, one of the first personal computers but never made it anywhere near the top of that intensely competitive field.

Hitachi is still trying to get rid of the stigma of having been caught trying to buy IBM trade secrets in 1982. To improve its image the company set up the Hitachi Foundation in the United States, with former government official Elliot Richardson as its head. Yet some of Hitachi's public relations efforts

were undermined in 1991 when the company was caught up in another industrial espionage scandal at home.

HISTORY

The Hitachi story began with the frustration of an engineering graduate over
the fact that Japan was importing so much of its technology from Europe and
the United States. In 1910 Namihei Odaira, while working in the repair shop
at Kuhara Mining, began putting together his own small electric motors. The
devices were used in the copper mine, but Odaira did not immediately attract
other customers. It was not until the outbreak of World War I, when Japanese
power companies found it difficult to get generators from Europe, that Odaira
was able to build his business.

In 1920 he formally established an independent company, naming it after
the town of Hitachi (which means "rising sun") in which he worked. Over
the next decade Odaira expanded his operations and acquired a series of other
companies, turning Hitachi into the country's leading producer of pumps and
other mechanical equipment. In 1924 the company built Japan's first electric
locomotive, and later it moved into vacuum tubes and light bulbs.

With the advent of militarism in the 1930s, Hitachi was pressured to work
for the armed forces. Odaira agreed to produce radar and sonar equipment
but managed to avoid making weapons. During the war many of the company's
factories were destroyed in bombing raids.

Following the defeat of Japan, the Allied occupation forces removed Odaira
from the leadership of the company and stripped Hitachi of many of its plants.
It was only during the Korean War, when the U.S. military purchased materiel
from Hitachi and other Japanese firms, that the company was able to regain
its footing. During the 1950s, under the leadership of Chikara Kurata, Hitachi
grew along with the recovery of the Japanese economy and the development
of the electronics industry. The company established technology-sharing pacts
with American firms like General Electric and RCA and was chosen as a
supplier by government-owned Nippon Telegraph and Telephone.

Hitachi soon moved into household appliances and consumer electronics.
It also entered information processing, and with assistance from the Ministry
of International Trade and Industry it began to develop mainframe computers
that could compete with those of industry leader IBM. In the 1970s, following
the lead of the U.S. company Amdahl (which got financing from Fujitsu),
Hitachi began producing so-called plug-compatible mainframes—computers
that were superior to but compatible with those made by IBM. Hitachi's
machines were distributed first by the U.S. company Itel and then by the
National Advanced Systems (NAS) division of the National Semiconductor
Corporation.

Hitachi was not satisfied cloning IBM's technology; it wanted Big Blue's
secrets. In 1982, after being caught in a sting operation by the FBI, the
company and eleven of its employees were indicted on charges of commercial
bribery and theft of confidential software design material from IBM. On the

criminal charges the company was fined only $24,000 and two employees were given jail sentences. But as a result of a civil suit brought by IBM, Hitachi ended up paying about $40 million a year in royalties to Big Blue. IBM also was given the right for five years to inspect new Hitachi software products before they were released. The scandal cost the Japanese company a great deal of business as well.

Hitachi, nonetheless, kept on making computers for sale in the United States by NAS, including machines to compete with the new Sierra generation of mainframes introduced by IBM in 1985. Hitachi's products are sold in Europe by Olivetti and other companies. In 1989 the Japanese company bought 80 percent of NAS, with the remainder sold to the Electronic Data Systems division of General Motors. Renamed Hitachi Data Systems, the operation took direct aim at IBM and Amdahl, Big Blue's largest competitor in the compatible mainframe market.

In 1990 Hitachi announced its new mainframe even before IBM and Amdahl launched their own new machines. Hitachi, which had about 7 percent of the IBM-compatible mainframe market in 1989, was expected to nearly double that within several years. At the same time, Hitachi has been one of the main Japanese companies seeking to challenge the U.S. company Cray Research in the production of supercomputers.

An even better record has been achieved by Hitachi in semiconductors. In the 1970s it was one of five participants in a research and development effort called the Very Large Scale Integration (VLSI) Project, which was encouraged by the Japanese government. Consequently, Hitachi and NEC led the way in the late 1970s as the Japanese electronics industry swept ahead of the American producers in the production of 16-kilobit memory chips. The Japanese surge continued during the development of the 64K chip—so much so that most of the U.S. producers dropped out of the market. The Japanese approach to capturing market share was expressed most clearly in a 1985 Hitachi memo that became public. The document instructed distributors to go on cutting prices in 10-percent increments to undercut U.S. suppliers—and "don't quit until you win." Hitachi was one of six Japanese companies accused of dumping (the selling of goods abroad at below the home market price) when the Reagan administration felt compelled to take some action to stem the Japanese tide.

In more recent years Hitachi has adopted a new posture in the United States—that of a joint venture partner. The company formed a chip development partnership with Texas Instruments in 1988, began work on an artificial intelligence software product with Hewlett-Packard in 1991, and, that same year, agreed to work with TRW on developing space technologies.

Hitachi also has been at the center of efforts to create increasingly dense memory chips, now measured in megabits rather than kilobits. While most companies were getting ready to produce 4-megabit chips and were starting work on 16-megabit ones, Hitachi jumped a generation ahead. In 1990 it announced the first prototype for a 64-megabit memory chip, which is expected to be on the market in the mid-1990s. The company expects the device to be the basis of most electronic products at the end of the decade.

While Hitachi was enjoying this status as a technological leader, it got pulled into more scandals in 1991. Amid revelations that Nomura Securities had paid large sums to major corporate clients to reimburse them for stock market losses, it came out that Hitachi had received $23 million of that money. Two weeks later it was reported that Hitachi was among several companies that had paid an industrial spy who was arrested while breaking into the offices of construction equipment producer Komatsu Ltd.

OPERATIONS

Information Systems and Electronics (34 percent of 1991 revenues). Hitachi produces computers, terminals, peripheral devices, workstations, magnetic disks, semiconductors, integrated circuits, and Japanese word processors. Other products in this segment include broadcasting equipment, telephone equipment, facsimile machines, test and measurement equipment, and medical electronics equipment.

Power and Industrial Systems (28 percent of revenues). Included in this segment are nuclear, hydroelectric, and thermal power plants; automobile components; chemical plants; construction machinery; elevators and escalators; refrigeration and air-conditioning equipment; electric locomotives; industrial robots; environmental control equipment; and other products.

Consumer Products (13 percent of revenues). This segment consists of a wide range of consumer electronic devices (televisions, VCRs, video cameras, audio equipment, and so on); major appliances (such as washing machines and refrigerators); and smaller household devices (microwave ovens, vacuum cleaners, space heaters, and others).

Materials and Other Products (25 percent of revenues). Hitachi produces electric wire and cable, rolled copper products, optical fiber cable, forged and cast steel products, pipe fittings, electric insulating materials, carbon and graphite products, printed circuit boards, and ceramic materials.

TOP EXECUTIVES

- Katsushige Mita, chairman
- Tsutomu Kanai, president
- Yutaka Sonoyama, executive vice president
- Sutezo Hata, executive vice president
- Takeo Miura, executive vice president
- Toshi Kitamura, executive vice president
- Tadashi Okita, executive vice president
- Iwao Matsuoka, executive vice president

FINANCIAL DATA

Revenues (in millions of yen) (years ending March 31)

1991	7,736,961
1990	7,077,855
1989	6,401,417
1988	5,716,962
1987	5,543,247

Net Income (in millions of yen) (years ending March 31)

1991	230,185
1990	210,963
1989	185,587
1988	136,806
1987	98,676

GEOGRAPHICAL BREAKDOWN

Revenues (in millions of yen)

Year*	Japan		Elsewhere	
1991	7,175,268	(85%)	1,286,537	(15%)
1990	6,632,684	(86%)	1,080,099	(14%)
1989	6,042,155	(87%)	916,518	(13%)

*Fiscal year ends March 31.

LABOR RELATIONS

Hitachi has never been a great fan of labor unions. During a major strike in 1950 the company dismissed several thousand workers. Formal relations have been more harmonious since then, but there have been reports of discontent at the rank-and-file level.

One of the major points of contention has been the company's insistence that its employees make superhuman efforts at work. Hitachi is notorious in labor circles for keeping people on the job for extremely long hours. An employee named Hidyuki Tanaka, who was dismissed for refusing to work overtime in 1967, has been carrying on a crusade for reinstatement ever since. A labor union report published in 1989 states that the rate of suicide among Hitachi workers has been abnormally high. In a few instances, according to the report, the wives of workers who committed suicide then killed themselves in protest against the inhuman overwork of their husbands.

Hitachi has been one of a group of Japanese companies that have managed to establish single-union, no-strike relationships with unions in Britain. In

1984 it converted a television factory in Wales, which it had been operating in a joint venture with Britain's General Electric Company, into a single-union plant. That union was the Electrical, Electronic, Telecommunications, and Plumbing Union, which has been one of the unions most willing to abandon traditional adversarial practices.

In 1990 one thousand employees at a Hitachi plant in Malaysia went on strike in support of a group of coworkers dismissed for trying to form a union. The company fired all of the strikers, who were given their jobs back only after signing a letter of apology to the company.

ENVIRONMENTAL RECORD

Hitachi is among the electronics companies that have plans to phase out the use of solvents containing ozone-destroying CFCs. In 1989 Hitachi said that it would end its CFC use by 1996.

The company is also among the electrical firms working to produce longer-lasting batteries for electric vehicles. In 1991 the Japanese government announced plans for installing, on an experimental basis, a device that can remove nitrous oxide (a major form of automobile pollution) from the air. The device, made by Hitachi, was to be placed near the ventilation system of a highway tunnel.

BIBLIOGRAPHY

Anchordoguy, Marie. *Computers, Inc.: Japan's Challenge to IBM*. Cambridge, Mass.: Harvard University Press, 1989.

Sobel, Robert. *IBM vs. Japan: The Struggle for the Future*. Briarcliff Manor, N.Y.: Stein & Day, 1985.

HOECHST AG

Brüningstrasse 50
D-6230 Frankfurt am Main 80
Germany
(69) 305 0

1991 revenues: $31.1 billion
1991 net income: $895.7 million
Publicly traded company
Employees: 179,332
Founded: 1863

OVERVIEW

Hoechst is one of the big three German chemical companies that formed the giant IG Farben combine in the 1920s and were split up again after World War II. Like BASF and Bayer, Hoechst enjoyed a dramatic resurgence during the 1950s and rose to the top tier of the industry.

Like Bayer, Hoechst is heavily involved in drugs. It owns a majority interest in the French company Roussel-Uclaf, which is best known as the producer of the abortion pill RU 486. Hoechst, which is 20-percent owned by the government of Kuwait, also has made major investments in the United States, including the $2.9-billion purchase of Celanese Corporation in 1987.

HISTORY

Hoechst was founded in a village of that name in 1863 by a chemist named Eugene Lucius. The aim of the firm—originally called Meister, Lucius & Company—was to join in the new business of synthetic dyes. The company rigged up a small engine and a boiler to mix anilin oil and arsenic acid, and soon it was producing fuchsia dye—only the first in what would be a huge portfolio of coloring agents created by the rapidly growing company.

In 1883 the company made its first move beyond dyes when one of its chemists discovered antipyrine, one of the early analgesics. This led to work on the anesthetic novocaine and salvarsan, the first effective medication for syphilis. The company went on to achieve the first synthesis of adrenaline in 1906 and the isolation of insulin in 1923, by which time the firm had been renamed Hoechst.

The dye industry in Germany (as well as in other countries) had a strong propensity for anticompetitive practices. Hoechst went along with this by joining the Dreiverband cartel (BASF and Bayer were part of the Dreibund cartel). The cartels carved up the market among themselves and undermined the growth of the dye industry in countries like the United States. During World War I the German dye companies altered their formulas to produce mustard gas and explosives.

In 1916 the two dye cartels joined forces to create the Interessengemeinschaft der deutschen Teerfarbenfabriken (Community of Interests of the German Tar Dye Factories). Known later as the Little IG, this combine had complete control over the dye industry and soon acquired extensive coal mining operations to carry out a plan initiated by BASF to create liquid fuel through the hydrogenation of coal.

By the 1920s dye industry leaders, led by Carl Duisberg of Bayer and Carl Bosch of BASF, were pushing for a complete consolidation of the industry— that is, the merger of the dye makers into a single company. This is what happened in 1925 with the creation of the Interessengemeinschaft Farbenindustrie AG (Community of Interests of the Dye Industry, Inc.), or IG Farben.

This huge corporation, which soon included related industries, such as explosives and fibers, was the biggest enterprise in all of Europe and the fourth-largest in the world, behind General Motors, United States Steel, and Standard Oil of New Jersey. With Standard Oil IG Farben entered into a noncompetition arrangement for oil and chemicals while agreeing to cooperate on the development of synthetic rubber (though Jersey Standard later came under fire because of evidence that the German company was impeding its progress in this crucial area).

Although Carl Bosch, the head of IG Farben's managing board, opposed the anti-Semitism of the Nazis, the company gave financial support to Hitler and (without Bosch, who resigned in 1935) became indispensable to the German military effort during World War II. The company made use of slave labor, locating one of its synthetic rubber facilities in Auschwitz in order to be near the captive labor supply of the infamous concentration camp. Lethal gas made by IG Farben was used in the death camps. For such practices a group of IG Farben executives were convicted of war crimes at the Nuremberg trials. Several years later, in 1952, the company was redivided into several independent firms, including BASF, Bayer, and Hoechst.

Hoechst rebounded rapidly from the war, since its manufacturing facilities had escaped heavy damage. The company emphasized synthetic fibers like polyester along with polyethylene and petrochemicals. By the 1960s the company, once again a leader in the chemical industry, was making investments in countries like Holland, Austria, Spain, and France. Also, a major investment in a pharmaceutical company was made in France.

That company was Roussel-Uclaf, founded in 1920 by Dr. Gaston Roussel and built over the following decades by Roussel and his son Jean-Claude into one of Europe's leading producers of drugs, chemicals, and related products. In 1968 the younger Roussel met a Hoechst director and was inspired to pursue a policy of "Europeanizing" his family's firm. Although the French government was uneasy about the deal, Roussel sold a 43-percent interest in the company to Hoechst.

The two firms proceeded to share many of their marketing and research operations and jointly launched new products, such as the broad-spectrum antibiotic Claforan. After Roussel was killed in a helicopter crash in 1972, Hoechst ended up taking a majority stake in the company, with the French government holding most of the rest. Hoechst itself also has experienced foreign ownership: in 1982 the government-owned Kuwait Petroleum took a 24-percent interest in the company and gained a representative on Hoechst's supervisory board.

Meanwhile, Hoechst continued its international expansion, acquiring British paint maker Berger, Jenson & Nicholson (later sold) and Hystron Fibers in the United States. The company also has opened new foreign markets for its drugs, becoming a world leader in diuretics, oral insulin, steroids, and hookworm medication. During the 1980s Hoechst plunged into biotechnology through a large investment in a genetic laboratory at Massachusetts General Hospital in Boston. (Research in this area in Germany has been stalled because of environmental protests.)

A much bigger American initiative was taken by Hoechst in 1987 when it acquired Celanese Corporation, the eighth-largest chemical producer in the United States, for $2.9 billion. This put Hoechst at the head of the invasion of the U.S. market by the leading European chemical companies.

In the early 1990s Hoechst found itself involved in two controversies regarding pharmaceuticals. Groups on both sides of the abortion issue have criticized the company's Roussel-Uclaf subsidiary (now 35-percent owned by Rhône-Poulenc) in connection with RU 486, a pill that terminates pregnancies. The antiabortion forces do not like the fact that the company makes the product, while prochoice groups are unhappy that the product has not been introduced in the United States. The decision to limit the sale of RU 486, which also appears to be an effective medication for breast cancer and other diseases, was reportedly made by Hoechst, which does not want to become embroiled in the abortion controversy.

The other issue that stirred up debate is a commercial one. In the late 1980s the U.S. biotechnology firm Genentech (now 60-percent owned by Roche) introduced a blood-dissolving drug called TPA to compete with products like Hoechst's streptokinase. Genentech promoted the drug heavily, but in 1990 a study was released showing that TPA was no more effective than streptokinase, which costs only about one-tenth as much.

OPERATIONS

Chemicals and Color (24 percent of 1991 revenues). Hoechst produces a wide range of chemical products for the plastics, paint, paper, ink, building materials, automotive, and electrical industries. The company also makes pigments and dyes for plastics, textiles, and other products. This segment also includes the company's artificial sweetener Sunett as well as surfactants used in detergent production and superabsorbers used in disposable diapers.

Fibers (15 percent of revenues). A large part of this segment consists of synthetic fibers, such as Trevira, used in clothing and other fibers and in such industrial applications as tarpaulins, belting, tire cord, and roofing materials.

Polymers (18 percent of revenues). Hoechst is the world leader in high-density polyethylene, with plants in Europe, the United States, and Australia. A joint venture with Lucky-Goldstar in South Korea includes building a plant with a capacity of 120,000 tons that is expected to begin operations in 1992. Hoechst is also a major producer of polypropylene and polyvinyl chloride. Amid the overcapacity and intense price competition in the polyvinyl chloride (PVC) market, the company sold its PVC film operations in 1989. In partnership with Japan's Mitsubishi, Hoechst still makes polyester film used in audiotape and videotape. This segment also includes synthetic resins and paints used in automotive and other industries.

Health (22 percent of revenues). Among the best-selling drugs made by Hoechst are Claforan (an antibiotic), Trental (for circulatory disorders), Daonil (for diabetes), and Lasix (a diuretic). In 1991 the U.S. FDA approved the company's ACE inhibitor Altace, used to control high blood pressure. This segment also includes the operations of Schwarzkopf (77-percent owned by Hoechst), a leading German maker of hair- and personal-care products.

Engineering and Technology (15 percent of revenues). Included in this segment are printing plates, optical storage disks, industrial gases, welding equipment, engineering ceramics, and carbon products.

Agriculture (6 percent of revenues). The largest part of this segment consists of crop-protection products, such as herbicides and insecticides. The company also makes parasite-control products for animals, feed additives, and seeds. The company's Biotech Australia affiliate is working on vaccines for the control of ectoparasites, such as cattle ticks.

TOP EXECUTIVES

- Wolfgang Hilger, chairman of the board of management
- Günter Metz, deputy chairman of the board of management

- Rolf Sammet, chairman of the supervisory board
- Jürgen Dormann, member of the board of management
- Martin Frühauf, member of the board of management
- Heinz Harnisch, member of the board of management
- Karl Holoubek, member of the board of management
- Hans Georg Janson, member of the board of management
- Justus Mische, member of the board of management
- Ernst Schadow, member of the board of management
- Karl-Gerhard Seifert, member of the board of management
- Uwe Jens Thomsen, member of the board of management

OUTSIDE DIRECTORS

- Werner H. Dieter, chairman of the board of management of Mannesmann AG
- Dietrich-Kurt Frowein, member of the board of management of Commerzbank
- Kurt Furgler, former president of the Swiss Confederation
- Robertus Hazelhoff, deputy chairman of the board of management of ABN Amro Holding NV
- Horst K. Jannott, chairman of the board of management of Münchener Rückversicherungs-Gesellschaft
- Hubert Markl, president of the German Society for the Advancement of Scientific Research
- Abdul Baqi Al-Nouri, Petrochemical Industries Company of Kuwait
- Peter-Michael Preusker, head of the economics section of the central committee of the union IG Chemie
- Wolfgang Röller, spokesman of the board of management of Dresdner Bank
- Egon Schäfer, deputy chairman of IG Chemie

The supervisory board also includes eight employee representatives and Erhard Bouillon, a former member of the board of management.

FINANCIAL DATA

Revenues (in millions of deutsche marks)

1991	47,186
1990	44,862
1989	45,898
1988	40,964
1987	36,956

Net Income (in millions of deutsche marks)

1991	1,357
1990	1,696
1989	2,130
1988	2,015
1987	1,528

GEOGRAPHICAL BREAKDOWN

Revenues (in millions of deutsche marks)

Year	Europe		North America		Elsewhere	
1991	27,134	(58%)	9,143	(19%)	10,909	(23%)
1990	27,756	(62%)	8,551	(19%)	8,555	(19%)
1989	26,497	(58%)	10,265	(22%)	9,136	(20%)

LABOR RELATIONS

Forty-one percent of Hoechst's workers in Germany are members of labor unions, mainly IG Chemie. Relations are quite harmonious and there has not been a strike since the 1920s. In the United States fewer than one-quarter of Hoechst Celanese's employees are represented by unions.

ENVIRONMENTAL AND HEALTH RECORD

Hoechst has not had quite as much environmental and health trouble as the other two big German chemical companies, BASF and Bayer, but its record is not spotless.

Hoechst has been a target of environmentalists because of its production of CFCs. After years of pressure, Hoechst, like other manufacturers, such as Du Pont, has agreed to phase out the use of CFCs and has developed alternative products, hydrofluorocarbons, that are less harmful to the ozone layer.

In 1991 the company was fined $202,000 by the U.S. FDA for failing to inform the agency that its antidepressant drug nomifensine had caused several deaths in Europe. In 1984 the FDA had approved the drug for sale in the United States under the name Merital.

A group of residents of Pampa, Texas, brought a lawsuit against the company's Hoechst Celanese subsidiary in 1990, charging that toxic emissions from its chemical plant had caused near-epidemic levels of leukemia and Down's syndrome in the area. The company denied that the plant was responsible for the health problems and said it would fight the suit.

Hoechst Celanese was among twenty-three companies that agreed in 1990 to pay a total of $3 million for the clean-up of a Superfund site near Louisville,

Kentucky. Hoechst Celanese has been named as a potentially responsible party in connection with a total of eighty-five Superfund sites.

A study of EPA data by the Citizens Fund found that Hoechst Celanese was responsible for the seventeenth-largest volume (forty-eight million pounds) of toxic releases among all American manufacturing companies in 1989 (the most recent figures available).

On the positive side, the company has taken steps to reduce waste water and solid waste in its plastics production and has begun recycling projects for those products. One such project is a joint venture with the auto company Opel to produce auto parts from recycled polypropylene bumpers and other car components.

BIBLIOGRAPHY

Borkin, Joseph. *The Crime and Punishment of I.G. Farben*. New York: Free Press, 1978.

Grant, Wyn, William Paterson, and Colin Whitston. *Government and the Chemical Industry: A Comparative Study of Britain and West Germany*. Oxford: Oxford University Press, 1989.

Hayes, Peter. *Industry and Ideology: IG Farben in the Nazi Era*. Cambridge: Cambridge University Press, 1987.

HONDA MOTOR COMPANY, LTD.

1-1, Minami-Aoyama 2-chome
Minato-ku, Tokyo 107
Japan
(03) 3423-1111

1991 revenues: $30.6 billion (year ending March 31)
1991 net income: $542.5 million
Publicly traded company
Employees: 85,500
Founded: 1946

OVERVIEW

Established soon after the end of World War II, Honda was one of
the great entrepreneurial success stories of modern Japan. Founders
Soichiro Honda, a flamboyant mechanic, and the more businesslike Takeo
Fujisawa built the company from a modest operation that made engines to
motorize bicycles into the world's leading producer of motorcycles and then
one of the most aggressive of automakers.

But Honda depended on backing from Mitsubishi Bank, the company
did not get pulled into any of the large Japanese conglomerates that dominate
much of that country's economy. Honda also showed a great deal of independence in moving into the auto business against the wishes of government
economic planners, who thought the field was crowded enough already.

But Honda was not simply another car maker. The company made major
innovations in engine design—including ones that drastically cut polluting
emissions—and played a leading role in opening the huge North American
market to Japanese producers. Although Honda remained far behind Toyota
and Nissan in domestic auto sales, it ended up shooting ahead of its rivals in
the United States, where the company also created a sensation by opening

the first Japanese auto assembly operation. Later Honda led the way in the Japanese automakers' move into the U.S. luxury car market.

Honda, in fact, became so firmly entrenched in the United States that its American operations became regarded by many as a U.S. company, especially after Honda made the bold move of beginning to manufacture engines in that country rather than importing them from Japan. Although the company, like the rest of the industry, was thrown for a loop by the recession of the early 1990s, it is likely to remain near the top of the industry in the all-important U.S. auto market.

HISTORY

Soichiro Honda, the son of a blacksmith, finished eight years of schooling and then went to Tokyo in 1922 to serve as an apprentice in an auto repair shop. After awhile Honda, with the encouragement of his racing enthusiast boss, began spending his free time building racing cars and soon was entering his creations in competitions. In one of those races, the All-Japan Speed Rally of 1936, Honda was seriously injured in a crash.

In 1937 Honda started a business to produce piston rings, but his lack of familiarity with casting created serious obstacles for the enterprise. Honda solved the problem by enrolling part time in a technical school, and by 1941 the company was supplying piston rings to Toyota Motor, which purchased a 40-percent share of the company. During World War II Honda also made parts for ships and airplanes.

After the war Honda sold the rest of the company to Toyota and used the proceeds to spend a year at leisure and then to start a new business. Operating under the grandiose name Honda Technical Research Institute, the company used recycled military engines to make motorized bicycles, a vehicle that was especially popular with the black marketeers at the time, given the shortage of automobiles.

After getting financial backing from Takeo Fujisawa, Honda renamed the firm Honda Motor Company in 1948 and began designing a motorcycle. With Fujisawa running the business side and Honda the technical end of things, the company finished the prototype of what became known as the Dream Type D in 1949 and began production the following year. The Type D was not a great success, so Honda set himself to work on a new motorcycle with a more powerful, 5.5-horsepower engine. Designated the Type E, the new product was an instant hit. Demand was so strong that the company expanded its work force at breakneck speed, hiring virtually everyone who responded to Honda Motor's constant help-wanted advertising.

The company was also buoyed by the popularity of the compact engine, the Cub Type F, that it created for giving motorized bicycles more oomph. Taking advantage of the cash flow generated by the advance payments made for many of its products, Honda Motor embarked on a bold expansion drive that included the construction of two large factories and the purchase of the most modern machine tools from the United States.

After overcoming some technical problems with his engines in the mid-1950s, Honda embarked on the development of a new motorbike that he thought would be the product to create a mass market for two-wheelers. The result was the 4.5-horsepower Super Cub, which many consider Honda's masterpiece. The bike had a light design that made it attractive to those who were not motorcycle enthusiasts. It had a polyester resin body and an electric ignition and it was cheap to maintain.

The company, by now the leading Japanese motorcycle producer, once again went out on a limb to expand its capacity. In fact, it built the largest motorcycle factory in the world. Honda Motor also began to enter foreign markets, focusing at first on Southeast Asia and then, after getting financial help from the Japanese government, the United States. American Honda Motor Company was established in 1959. One of the major goals of the U.S. operation was to change the image of motorcycles, which typically were associated with delinquents and other antisocial types. Using an ad campaign that focused on the message "You meet the nicest people on a Honda," the company built up a large volume of business.

Honda Motor also entered the European market, establishing a moped factory in Belgium—the first overseas Japanese manufacturing facility to be set up in a developed country. It was during this period that Honda and Fujisawa decided to add cars and light trucks to their product line. Returning to the activity of his youth, Honda moved toward the auto business by starting to design racing cars. Then he insisted that the company develop an air-cooled engine, despite the belief of most of his engineers that abandoning the customary water-cooling technology would make it difficult to control engine temperature and emissions.

Honda had his way, however, and in 1967 the company introduced its first mass-produced automobile to the domestic market. The air-cooled N-360 minicar, the first Japanese car to employ front-wheel drive, was an immediate success. The company brought out another car, the 1300, with a more powerful air-cooled engine two years later, but it was so expensive to produce that money was lost on each one sold. Honda pushed the company to concentrate on developing an even higher-performance air-cooled engine, but Fujisawa and the company's engineers, concerned that such a system would be unable to meet newly enacted emission controls in the United States, finally got Honda to relent.

The company faced a crisis in 1970 when the newly formed Japan Automobile Users' Union demanded heavy damages from Honda for the family of a man who had died in a crash while driving an N-360. This helped create a public controversy in Japan about auto defects in the products of all of the car makers. Although the head of the union was later convicted of trying to extort large payments from the auto companies, the negative publicity surrounding the affair caused Honda's sales to plummet.

Honda quickly bounced back with the introduction of the Civic and its innovative Compound Vortex Controlled Combustion (CVCC) engine, which greatly reduced auto emissions. It also had the advantage of being able to use leaded or unleaded fuel (unlike cars with catalytic converters) at a time when the availability of unleaded gasoline was still limited. The enthusiastic welcome received by the Civic in the United States is considered a milestone in the shift to small cars and the realization that the Japanese producers could have a major impact on the American auto market. At this high point of the company's fortunes, Honda and Fujisawa retired and Kiyoshi Kawashima took over as president. In 1976 the company went upscale from the Civic and brought out the Accord, followed by the sporty Prelude.

In 1978 Honda began producing motorcycles in Marysville, Ohio, and four years later the company became the first Japanese company to assemble automobiles in the United States. The heavily robotized plant quickly reached its capacity of 150,000 Accords and then doubled that capacity while beginning production of the Civic as well. Later Honda began producing automobile engines in Ohio, once again leading the way in the extension of Japanese manufacturing in the United States. In 1985 output of Honda's Ohio operations surpassed American Motors, in effect making the Japanese company the fourth-largest U.S. automaker. Taking into account both its Ohio output and its imports, Honda also shot ahead of Toyota and Nissan to gain the highest U.S. market share of any foreign-based car maker. In 1989 the Honda Accord became the best-selling car in the United States—the first time a foreign car had ever attained that position.

During this period, Honda indirectly entered the European market by licensing Britain's Rover Group to use Honda designs to produce and market cars in Europe. The two companies later formed a further alliance to co-produce a larger car intended to be sold as the Honda Legend and as the Rover Sterling.

In order to market a line of luxury cars in North America, Honda created a new division, Acura, in the mid-1980s. The Legend was put under its auspices, along with the Integra. The Legend, introduced in 1986, was the leading wedge in the assault by Japanese car makers on the high end of the market. However, the Legend was soon overshadowed by Toyota's Lexus and Nissan's Infiniti entries. Honda then went after another segment of the auto market, announcing in late 1990 that it would produce a station wagon version of the Accord in the United States.

Amid the recession of the early 1990s, Honda's U.S. production began to slump, and the company came nowhere near to reaching its ambitious goals for exporting its U.S.-made cars back to Japan. Faced with problems both at home and in its largest export market, in 1991 the company underwent a management reorganization that gave top officers more direct control over auto operations.

OPERATIONS

Automobiles (81 percent of 1991 revenues). Honda, the third-largest automaker in Japan, sold more than 1.9 million passenger cars in its 1991 fiscal year, half of them in North America. Its main models are the subcompact Civic, the compact Accord, the midsize Legend, the subcompact, sporty Prelude, and the subcompact Integra. Models sold only in Japan include the City subcompact, the Beat minivehicle, and the Acty minitrucks and minivans. Honda's cars are produced at three factories in Japan, two in the United States, and one each in Canada and New Zealand. Honda also has a licensing and subcontracting relationship with the Rover Group in Britain, in which Honda took a 20-percent interest in 1990.

Motorcycles (12 percent of revenues). Honda has been the world's largest producer of motorcycles since 1960. In fiscal 1991 it sold some 3.4 million two-wheeled vehicles, most of them in third world countries. The company's product line ranges from 50-cc to 1,500-cc engines, including machines designed both for everyday use and for racing. Honda's motorcycles are produced at three sites in Japan and by subsidiaries in the United States, Mexico, Belgium, Italy, Spain, Thailand, and Brazil.

Power Products (7 percent of revenues). The company's smallest segment consists of power tillers, portable generators, general-purpose engines, lawn mowers, outboard engines, snowblowers, lawn tractors, and all-terrain vehicles. These products are manufactured in Japan, the United States, France, and Thailand.

TOP EXECUTIVES

- Koichiro Yoshizawa, chairman
- Nobuhiko Kawamoto, president
- Yoshihide Munekuni, executive vice president
- Nobuyuki Otsuka, senior managing director
- Hiroyuki Yoshino, senior managing director
- Masaru Miyata, senior managing director
- Koichi Amemiya, senior managing director

FINANCIAL DATA

Revenues (in millions of yen) (years ending March 31)

1991	4,301,518
1990	3,852,905
1989	3,489,258
1988	3,498,531*
1987	2,960,985

*This figure represents the thirteen months ending March 31, 1988, because of the company's change of its fiscal-year end.

Net Income (in millions of yen) (years ending March 31)

1991	76,273
1990	81,684
1989	97,299
1988	107,510*
1987	83,689

*This figure represents the thirteen months ending March 31, 1988, because of the company's change of its fiscal-year end.

GEOGRAPHICAL BREAKDOWN

Net Sales (in millions of yen)

Year*	Japan		North America		Elsewhere	
1991	1,392,962	(32%)	2,017,987	(47%)	890,569	(21%)
1990	1,320,483	(34%)	1,855,479	(48%)	676,944	(18%)

*Fiscal year ends March 31.

LABOR RELATIONS

In the early years of the company, when workers were virtually being pulled in off the street to increase production, Soichiro Honda ran the factory with an iron fist. He is even reputed to have "motivated" slow learners by assaulting them with a wrench.

It is thus not surprising that in 1953 Honda's workers decided to form a union. The company accepted the advent of collective bargaining, which paid off a couple of years later, when Honda was facing severe financial difficulties. The union called on its members to give up their days off and work long hours to help the company over the hurdle.

The honeymoon was not permanent, however. In 1957 a dispute over wages led to a strike and later a lockout, which some workers resisted by occupying the roof of the company's headquarters. Honda responded by firing several union leaders, but later this action was overturned in court. Since then the company has enjoyed relatively harmonious relations with the All Honda Workers Union, which is affiliated with the Japan Council of the International Metalworkers Federation.

Honda imported this style of labor relations to the United States in 1979 when it began producing motorcycles, and later automobiles, in Marysville, Ohio. The company deliberately chose a rural area where it could attract employees who had not previously worked in auto plants. This made it easier to engender the esprit de corps and cooperative environment—one in which everyone was called an associate—thought to be necessary for efficient operation.

The United Auto Workers targeted the Marysville facility for organizing, and the union won a battle over the right of UAW supporters to wear union hats and buttons along with their Honda uniforms. The company claimed to be neutral about unionization, but the UAW charged that management had sponsored an antiunion group and otherwise attempted to discourage support for the UAW. An election scheduled for 1985 was postponed because of these charges, which were made to the National Labor Relations Board. After the board dismissed the charges, the UAW decided to withdraw its call for an election. Honda's U.S. operations have remained nonunion ever since.

Yet this does not mean that there were no personnel problems at the U.S. operation. Honda found itself charged with discriminating against women and blacks in its hiring practices. In 1988 the company agreed to pay $6 million to settle a discrimination suit brought by a group of 370 persons who said they had been turned down for jobs because of race and/or sex.

ENVIRONMENTAL AND SAFETY RECORD

As far back as the 1960s, Honda engineers were preoccupied with the issue of automobile emissions. When the Clean Air Act of 1970 in the United States made emission control an imperative, Honda approached the problem in a different way than other automakers. Instead of relying on catalytic converters to treat the hydrocarbons and carbon monoxide created by the running of the car, Honda sought a way to reduce the pollutants at the source. This was accomplished through the creation of an auxiliary combustion chamber in which the ratio of air to fuel was low while the ratio was raised much higher than normal in the main chamber. The system, known as Compound Vortex Controlled Combustion, or CVCC, was introduced in the early 1970s and was the first to meet the standards of the Clean Air Act.

Honda has continued to increase the efficiency of its engines, and in 1991 the company announced that its 1992 Civic VX would receive a fuel-efficiency rating of an astounding fifty-five miles per gallon for highway driving and forty-eight miles per gallon in city driving. The company also displayed a prototype of a two-seat passenger car that could get one hundred miles per gallon.

Honda also has responded, albeit less promptly, to safety issues. In 1990 the company announced that starting in 1993, all Hondas sold in the United States would be equipped with air bags on both the driver's and front passenger's sides.

According to a study of U.S. EPA data by the Citizens Fund, in 1989 Honda's Ohio plant released four million pounds of toxic chemicals either known to cause or suspected of causing birth defects. The plant ranked twentieth among all manufacturing facilities in the United States in terms of such releases.

BIBLIOGRAPHY

Gelsanliter, David. *Jump Start: Japan Comes to the Heartland*. New York: Farrar, Straus & Giroux, 1990.

Sakiya, Tetsuo. *Honda Motor: The Men, the Management, the Machines*. Tokyo and New York: Kodansha International, 1987.

Sanders, Sol. *Honda: The Man and His Machines*. Boston: Little, Brown, 1975.

Shook, Robert L. *Honda: An American Success Story*. New York: Prentice-Hall, 1988.

Sobel, Robert. *Car Wars*. New York: E. P. Dutton, 1984.

HYUNDAI GROUP

Major affiliate:

Hyundai Motor Company
14-2 Ke-Dong, Jongro-Ku
Seoul
South Korea
(02) 746-1114

1991 revenues: $7.4 billion
1991 net income: $70.9 million
Publicly traded company
Employees: 41,700
Founded: Hyundai Group was founded in 1947, Hyundai Motor in
    1967

OVERVIEW

Hyundai Motor is the best-known branch of the Hyundai Group, one of the
giant *chaebol* conglomerates that dominate the economy of South Korea.
Closely controlled by founder Ju-Yung Chung and his family, the group's
twenty-seven affiliates are involved in everything from semiconductors to furniture.

   Unlike rival Daewoo, which expanded through partnerships with Western
companies, Hyundai plowed ahead on its own, relying on the willingness of
its employees to work long hours at maximum intensity. Hyundai, which
started out as a construction company and went on to do massive engineering
projects in places like Saudi Arabia, gained a reputation for getting jobs done
quickly and cheaply by bringing in an army of single-minded workers.

   In the late 1980s, however, that devotion to work and to the company began
to falter. Hyundai's operations—especially the massive shipyard in Ulsan—
became a focus of militant strikes and other job actions by a revitalized labor

movement. The industrial disputes were especially frustrating for Hyundai, since they came just as the group was enjoying the enthusiastic reception its inexpensive automobiles were receiving in the United States.

Like the other *chaebol*, Hyundai has had to contend with rising public disillusionment with its activities. Yet Chung clearly believes that Korea will become more prominent on the world stage thanks in no small part to the activities of Hyundai. To help make that happen, Chung, who had just lost a battle with the government over tax evasion charges, formed a new political party that won 17 percent of the vote in national elections held in March 1992.

HISTORY

The Hyundai empire was built by Ju-Yung Chung, who was born to a poor farm family and had little formal schooling. During the 1940s he started an auto repair shop, and soon after World War II he raised his sights by establishing Hyundai Engineering and Construction Company.

By making good contacts with U.S. military officials in Korea and pushing himself and his employees to the limit, Chung won progressively larger contracts for projects that eventually included dams, roads, harbors, and large housing complexes. In 1958 he founded Keumkang Cement to produce building materials. Hyundai soon moved abroad, developing an international reputation for completing large jobs on time and within budget.

In the mid-1960s Chung was ready to take on new challenges. He formed Hyundai Motor Company, initially to assemble Ford models for local sale, but then the company designed and began producing (with technical help from Mitsubishi, which owns 15 percent of the company) Korea's first homegrown passenger car, the Pony.

A few years later, in 1973, Chung decided to plunge into shipbuilding, despite the fact that large-scale naval construction did not exist in the country. He sent dozens of employees to study naval architecture in Britain and then proceeded to construct the largest shipbuilding complex in the world in Ulsan. Under the name Hyundai Shipbuilding and Heavy Industries, the operation soon began to outbid established producers in Japan and Europe. The growth of the operation was stunted by the crisis in the international shipbuilding business brought on by the escalation of oil prices, but Hyundai survived by making marine engines and smaller vessels.

At the same time, Hyundai's engineering operation became one of the leading contractors in the Middle East. The contract to build the Jubail Industrial Harbor Complex in Saudi Arabia by itself was worth nearly $1 billion. The company's position in the region was in question for a while after an employee was convicted of bribing a government official in Saudi Arabia.

Chung formed Hyundai Corporation in 1976 as the general trading company for what was now one of South Korea's largest *chaebol*. He then embarked on further diversification by splitting off various parts of the shipbuilding and heavy industry company into separate firms. New lines of business included locomotive parts, furniture, and metals. The latter was accomplished through the takeover of Inchon Iron & Steel and Aluminum of Korea. Hyundai also entered the electronics field. It established a semiconductor plant in California in 1984, only to close it two years later when business slumped, but it stayed in the chip business at home. Hyundai also moved into the personal computer field, introducing a machine called Blue Chip that in the U.S. market was priced below the Leading Edge Model D, made by Daewoo.

Hyundai Motor raised its international profile in the mid-1980s when it began exporting its low-priced Excel to the United States. With the Japanese producers moving upscale, Hyundai was able to capture a large share of the market for inexpensive cars. In its first year selling in the U.S. market, the company, promoting its product as "cars that make sense," moved more than 160,000 units—the most successful launch ever achieved by an import. The company also initiated North American production with the opening of an auto plant near Montreal; however, sales began to decline over the next few years. To compensate for the sagging business in the United States, Hyundai Motor began a drive to expand exports to such countries as Germany, Poland, Yugoslavia, Malaysia, and Vietnam.

Hyundai and the other *chaebol* came under increasing criticism in the late 1980s as many Koreans began to doubt that the big conglomerates were still the key to economic progress. The government of President Roh Tae Woo responded to the public mood by taking steps to control the spread of the *chaebol*. In 1991 the conglomerates were asked to focus their activities on several key businesses. Hyundai chose to concentrate on automobiles, shipbuilding, and petrochemicals.

While Hyundai has gone along with the government's industrial policy, Chung, now the honorary chairman of the group, has been busy developing commercial ties between his company and both the former Soviet Union and China. One result of these efforts was a $30-million timber joint venture project in eastern Siberia. Part of Chung's motivation was to create relationships that might raise the chances of Korean reunification.

OPERATIONS

Hyundai Group's operations consist of the following four main affiliates.

Hyundai Motor Company. Hyundai Motor makes passenger cars, trucks, buses, and specialized vehicles for sale in eighty countries. In addition to its subcompact Excel, which made a splash in the United States when it was introduced in 1986, the company exports the midsized Sonata (introduced in 1989), the Scoupe (1990), and the Elantra sedan (1991).

Hyundai Corporation. This is the trading and marketing arm of the group. Its 1990 sales of $8.9 billion were broken down as follows: 32 percent in electronics and electrical equipment, 22 percent in ships and plants, 30 percent in machinery, 8 percent in steel and metal, 5 percent in general merchandise, and 4 percent in resources and energy.

Hyundai Electronics Industries Company. Hyundai Electronics makes semi-conductors, personal computers, telecommunications equipment, automotive electronic components, and industrial electronic systems. In the memory chip field it is racing to be one of the first producers to introduce a 16-megabit chip.

Hyundai Heavy Industries, Ltd. This company builds a wide range of tankers, container ships, and other vessels, marine engines and components, steam-generating plants, and industrial plants.

TOP EXECUTIVES

Hyundai Motor
- Se-Yung Chung, chairman
- Sung-Won Chon, president

LABOR RELATIONS

Like the other South Korean *chaebol*, the Hyundai Group was built on cheap and obedient labor. Founder Ju-Yung Chung demanded almost fanatical devotion from his employees, and by many accounts, he got it.

The era of unquestioning loyalty came to an abrupt end in 1987, when Hyundai was one of the main targets in a dramatic surge of worker unrest. In July of that year more than twenty thousand workers walked off their jobs at the giant shipyard in Ulsan to press their demands for higher wages and the right to form an independent union. They later occupied the facility as well. After several days of protests and clashes between workers and police, Chung reluctantly agreed to recognize the union.

Yet the dispute did not end there. Workers at the shipyard and many other Hyundai operations stayed on strike to push for wage increases as high as 25 percent. Faced with heavy police repression, the workers returned to their jobs, but they staged several brief walkouts and occupations to protest the arrests of numerous activists after special police investigations.

Hyundai Motor experienced further upheaval in 1988 as twenty thousand workers went on strike to demand sizable wage increases from a company that was enjoying great success in its U.S. sales. At the same time, strikers at Hyundai Precision Industry held eight company officials hostage, including one of Chung's sons. Employee anger was intensified by revelations that Hyundai executives had hired gangsters to kidnap a union leader.

In 1989 the Ulsan shipyard was the scene of a 109-day wildcat sit-down strike that ended only when the facility was retaken by a force of some ten thousand riot police. Although the formal walkout was crushed, there were reports that those back on the job were doing little work. There was a repetition of these events in 1990, when thousands of riot police again stormed the giant shipyard—this time using helicopters, boats, and bulldozers—to put down a strike and occupation called to protest the refusal of the government to release several jailed leaders of the 1989 job actions.

Hyundai Motor employees challenged management again in early 1992. As a protest against overtime and the failure of the company to pay a year-end bonus, the workers occupied the auto plant in Ulsan for several days.

ENVIRONMENTAL RECORD

Since the environmental impact of industry is not yet a major issue in South Korea, the main environmental incident Hyundai has had to confront occurred abroad, though, oddly enough, the foreign country was the former Soviet Union. The company's joint venture with Russian authorities to develop timberland in eastern Siberia has run up against strong opposition from the indigenous Udege people, who are supported by environmental groups. The Udege, who in 1991 threatened armed resistance if the project went ahead, insisted that the cutting of trees in the targeted area would undermine their way of life, while environmentalists pointed to the ecological damage caused by previous timber projects.

BIBLIOGRAPHY

Amsden, Alice H. *Asia's Next Giant: South Korea & Late Industrialization*. Oxford: Oxford University Press, 1989.

Kearney, Robert P. *The Warrior Worker: The Challenge of the Korean Way of Working*. New York: Henry Holt, 1991.

Min-Ju No-Jo: South Korea's New Trade Unions. Hong Kong: Asia Monitor Resource Center, 1988.

Steers, Richard M., Yoo Keun Shin, and Gerardo R. Ungson. *The Chaebol: Korea's New Industrial Might*. Cambridge, Mass.: Ballinger, 1989.

IMPERIAL CHEMICAL INDUSTRIES PLC

Imperial Chemical House
Millbank
London SW1P 3JF
United Kingdom
(071) 834-4444

1991 revenues: $23.3 billion
1991 net income: $1 billion
Publicly traded company
Employees: 128,600
Founded: 1926

OVERVIEW

Widely known as ICI, Imperial Chemical Industries is the fourth-largest chemical producer in the world (after the German big three)—or fifth, if Du Pont's nonchemical revenues are counted. ICI was Britain's version of the cartelization process that swept through much of the world's dye, explosive, and chemical industries early in this century.

ICI, however, never had quite the dynamism of the German IG Farben or Du Pont, and the lumbering giant struggled for decades to hold its own. It was only in the early 1980s that it began to experience a revitalization. The flamboyant chairman at the time, John Harvey-Jones, became something of a folk hero for engineering the turnaround—though not to the thousands of workers who lost their jobs as a result of his efforts. The makeover also included some ambitious acquisitions, which made ICI the world leader in the paint business and an important player in drugs and seeds.

In 1991 ICI, the second-largest industrial company in Britain (third if you count the binational Royal Dutch/Shell) was thrown into a panic when Hanson

Industries, a conglomerate with a record as a raider, purchased a stake in the company. ICI's management rallied widespread opposition to a Hanson bid while taking further steps to restructure the company.

HISTORY

Imperial Chemical was created amid the merger wave of the dye and chemical industries in the period after World War I. In 1926, at about the same time that the IG Farben combine was being formed in Germany and Du Pont was taking over many of its competitors in the United States, four British producers were joined to make ICI: Nobel Industries Ltd., United Alkali Company Ltd., British Dyestuffs Corporation Ltd., and Brunner, Mond & Company Ltd.

The oldest of these was Nobel Industries, whose direct ancestor, the British Dynamite Company, was founded in 1871. The company has its origins, of course, in the invention of dynamite by Alfred Nobel, who patented the explosive in Britain in 1867. Four years later British Dynamite (half owned by Nobel) was established, with headquarters in Scotland to avoid the strict regulations on dynamite that had been adopted in Britain. When production began, shipments often had to be smuggled to customers. Yet the company grew rapidly, and by World War I its successor, Nobel Industries, was a major supplier of munitions.

Brunner, Mond & Company was established by Ludwig Mond, a German Jew with university training in the sciences who emigrated to England in 1862, and by John Brunner, the son of a schoolteacher. In 1873 the two men formed a partnership to produce soda (sodium carbonate) using a new system developed by the firm of Solvay & Cie. in Belgium to replace the standard Leblanc process. Brunner, Mond went on to divide up the world soda market with Solvay.

United Alkali started out as a cartel of Lancashire producers of bleaching powder. The companies, which used the Leblanc process, merged in 1891 to form United Alkali but still had trouble competing with Brunner, Mond and the other users of the Solvay method.

The fourth component of ICI, British Dyestuffs, was established in 1919 as a holding company for British Dyes Ltd.—formed in 1915 at the encouragement of the government to cope with the consequences of the embargo of German dyes during World War I—and competitor Levinstein Ltd.

After its creation ICI produced various chemicals, but it put special emphasis on fertilizers. To protect this market it made an agreement with IG Farben to split up the market for nitrogen, the main component of fertilizer. Nonetheless, ICI's business in this field faltered, as did its foray into synthetic fuel. The company made various cooperative arrangements with Du Pont (which the two companies were forced to abolish after World War II).

In the 1930s ICI belatedly expanded its product line after two of its scientists devised the first method for making polyethylene, which would become a widely used plastic. During World War II the company made weapons, ammunition, and other military products in plants constructed by the government.

After the war, in the 1950s, ICI did not enjoy the kind of rapid growth seen by the German chemical companies, because many of its production facilities were becoming obsolete. One exception to this was the large chemical complex opened in the town of Wilton in 1952. As befit the word *imperial* in its name, ICI focused much of its business in Britain and its former colonies.

It was not until the 1960s that ICI, having fought off bankruptcy, took further steps to modernize its plants. An ethylene cracker was built in Britain, fiber operations were begun in Germany, and a polyvinyl chloride facility was constructed in the United States. Like its German competitors, ICI continued to put emphasis on American investments. Atlas Chemical was purchased in 1971 (although antitrust problems forced ICI to sell off the company's explosives business) and a paraquat plant in Texas was acquired in 1977.

Although cheap natural gas from the North Sea allowed ICI to reduce the cost of making its fertilizers, the company continued to be inefficient relative to many of its foreign competitors. The company posted its first loss in 1980 and lowered its dividend.

The first signs of improvement were seen after John Harvey-Jones took over leadership of the company in 1982. He cut costs ruthlessly, closing dozens of plants and laying off workers by the thousands. He reduced ICI's dependence on bulk chemicals and focused on specialty products and pharmaceuticals. He also dumped polyethylene and bulk production of polyester fibers.

Harvey-Jones, known for his shaggy hair and flamboyant manner, also embarked on an acquisitions drive that included the chemical division of the U.C. food company Beatrice in 1985 and Glidden Paint a year later. That latter deal, which cost ICI $580 million, propelled the company to the top of the world paint industry. In 1988, after Harvey-Jones retired and was replaced by Denys Henderson, the company spent $1.7 billion to acquire U.S.-based Stauffer Chemical from Unilever. ICI later sold off all but Stauffer's agrochemicals business.

Ironically, the company that sold Glidden to ICI, Hanson Industries, was later perceived as a menace to the chemical giant. In mid-1991 Hanson purchased a stake of nearly 3 percent in the company, and although the conglomerate—which has a history as a corporate raider—said it did not intend to carry out a hostile takeover, ICI felt very threatened indeed. The management of the chemical giant rallied widespread opposition to Hanson and embarked on further restructuring. The company sold off its British and Kenyan soda ash operations and began seeking a partner or buyer for its thriving pharmaceutical business. The takeover threat evaporated in 1992 when Hanson sold its holdings, but ICI's top managers continued to take steps to make their stewardship look more impressive.

OPERATIONS

Bioscience (22 percent of 1991 revenues). This segment comprises two main business areas. The more lucrative of these (contributing half of the entire company's operating income) is pharmaceuticals, an area that has grown steadily in recent years thanks to the cardiovascular drugs Tenormin, Inderal, and Zestril. To these ICI has added the well-received Zoladex (a hormonal treatment for prostate and breast cancer). ICI is also one of the world's largest producers of agrochemicals, including herbicides, pesticides, and fungicides. The company is a leading supplier of seeds, which are sold in some fifty countries.

Specialty Chemicals and Materials (41 percent of revenues). A major part of this segment is the paint business, which is not very profitable despite the fact that ICI is the world's leading supplier of surface coatings. The company has joint ventures in this area with Swire Pacific in Hong Kong and Nippon Oils & Fats in Malaysia.

The other portions of this segment are colors and fine chemicals (including products for the textile, leather, and paper industries); polyurethanes (used in products ranging from shoes to automobiles); specialty chemicals (inks, coatings, adhesives, lubricants, and so forth); advanced materials (high-performance substances for aircraft, spacecraft, and the automotive and electronics industries); biological products (biodegradable plastics, genetic fingerprinting, and so on); industrial explosives; and fibers (nylon fibers for apparel, carpets, tires, and conveyor belts).

Industrial Chemicals (27 percent of revenues). This segment includes general chemicals (chlorine, caustic soda, and chlorine derivatives, such as polyvinyl chloride) and petrochemicals and plastics (olefins, aromatics, polypropylene, polyethylene terephthalate resins and acrylics, and so on). ICI is a partner with the Italian company EniChem in the joint venture European Vinyls Corporation.

The final portion of this segment is the fertilizer business. A move by the company to sell its wholesale fertilizer operations in the United Kingdom to the Finnish company Kemira Oy was blocked by the British government in 1990. Instead ICI is moving to shut down some of its fertilizer business and restructure the rest.

Regional Businesses (9 percent of revenues). In 1991 ICI created this new segment, which brings together localized businesses, including plastics in Australia, soda ash in Pakistan, and nitrogen products in Canada.

TOP EXECUTIVES

- Denys Henderson, chairman and chief executive
- R. C. Hampel, chief operating officer

- F. Whitely, deputy chairman
- J. D. F. Barnes, executive director
- P. Doyle, executive director
- C. Hampson, executive director
- A. T. G. Rodgers, executive director
- C. M. Short, executive director

OUTSIDE DIRECTORS

- Lord Chilver, chairman of English China Clays PLC
- Patrick Meaney, chairman of the Rank Organisation
- Jeremy Morse, chairman of Lloyds Bank
- Antony Pilkington, chairman of Pilkington PLC
- Ellen R. Schneider-Lenné, member of the board of managing directors of Deutsche Bank
- Paul A. Volcker, chairman of James D. Wolfensohn Inc. and former chairman of the U.S. Federal Reserve
- Thomas H. Wyman, former chairman of CBS

FINANCIAL DATA

Revenues (in millions of pounds)

1991	12,488
1990	12,906
1989	13,171
1988	11,699
1987	11,123
1986	10,136

Net Income (in millions of pounds)

1991	542
1990	670
1989	1,057
1988	837
1987	760
1986	557

GEOGRAPHICAL BREAKDOWN

Revenues (in millions of pounds)

Year	United Kingdom		Rest of Europe		Elsewhere	
1991	5,650	(37%)	3,194	(21%)	6,249	(41%)
1990	6,126	(40%)	3,152	(20%)	6,101	(40%)
1989	6,231	(40%)	2,928	(19%)	6,427	(41%)

Profit (in millions of pounds)

Year	United Kingdom		Rest of Europe		Elsewhere	
1991	300	(29%)	191	(18%)	555	(53%)
1990	295	(30%)	157	(16%)	547	(55%)
1989	612	(41%)	225	(15%)	663	(44%)

LABOR RELATIONS

ICI continued the paternalistic labor policies of its predecessor company, Brunner, Mond. In an attempt to make workers identify with the company, ICI adopted the practice of exempting production workers with five years of experience from layoffs and paying them a weekly salary rather than an hourly wage. Extensive employee benefits also were provided. These policies did not prevent unionization of the work force—as they were intended, at least in part—but they did keep ICI relatively free of industrial disputes.

In the late 1960s the company expanded the practice of paying production workers a weekly salary and gave them increased responsibility in overseeing the production process. The result was a substantial increase in productivity. There was less harmony in the 1980s, when the new chairman, John Harvey-Jones, eliminated more than thirty thousand jobs without consulting the unions.

When the company was threatened with a possible takeover by Hanson Industries in 1991, the unions rallied in support of ICI management. Shortly before Hanson appeared on the scene, ICI had reached agreement with the unions on a 14-percent pay increase and a reduction in the workweek in exchange for a relaxation of work rules by the unions.

ENVIRONMENTAL RECORD

ICI has come under fire from environmentalists for its role as one of the world's largest producers of ozone-destroying CFCs. For years ICI and other producers (like Du Pont) resisted calls for cutting back production of CFCs—until the late 1980s, when an international agreement called the Montreal

Protocol set a timetable for phasing them out. Like Du Pont, ICI has developed alternative substances, hydrochlorofluorocarbons, but there has been evidence that these HCFCs may be toxic.

In Britain ICI has been fined numerous times in recent years for spills of oil, phenol, and other substances from its Billingham facility into the river Tees. The company has subsequently installed a system at Billingham that treats sewage and industrial effluent through the use of naturally occurring bacteria that inhabit the roots of marsh reeds.

Greenpeace has reported that an Italian subsidiary of ICI was involved in the dumping of four thousand tons of toxic waste in the Nigerian town of Koko. The waste was said to have caused widespread illness among area residents and among the Nigerian workers hired to clean up the dump site.

In the early 1980s an ICI subsidiary in Malaysia fired seven union officials for complaining to the government of that country about health hazards faced by employees of the company. In 1986 a worker at the company's fertilizer plant died after being overcome by chlorine fumes.

BIBLIOGRAPHY

Grant, Wyn, William Paterson, and Colin Whitston. *Government and the Chemical Industry: A Comparative Study of Britain and West Germany*. Oxford: Oxford University Press, 1989.

Pettigrew, Andrew M. *The Awakening Giant: Continuity and Change in Imperial Chemical Industries*. Oxford: Basil Blackwell, 1985.

Reader, W. J. *Imperial Chemical Industries: A History*. 2 vols. Oxford: Oxford University Press, 1970, 1975.

INTERNATIONAL BUSINESS MACHINES CORPORATION

Old Orchard Road
Armonk, New York 10504
(914) 765-1900

1991 revenues: $64.8 billion
1991 net income: −$2.8 billion (loss)
Publicly traded company
Employees: 344,396
Founded: 1910

OVERVIEW

IBM—for years those three letters were virtually synonymous with computers. Starting out as a producer of punch-card tabulators and other low-tech office machines, IBM seized the leadership of the data-processing industry that emerged in the 1950s. It used aggressive sales tactics and carefully planned technological advances to win intense devotion from customers while keeping the rest of the industry guessing.

IBM was so successful in making its systems the industry standard that many rivals decided that the only way to compete was to build machines that were compatible with, but more efficient or less expensive than, those of Big Blue. IBM's dominance also made it the subject of numerous antitrust suits, brought both by competitors and by the federal government. One of these suits lasted fourteen years before being dropped by the Reagan administration.

In the early 1980s IBM, which traditionally had focused on selling or leasing large-scale systems to major corporate or government customers, stunned the computer industry by plunging into the young field of personal computers. Shrewdly using Charlie Chaplin in its advertising to make the new machines seem less forbidding, IBM created a new standard in the field, though many of the PCs employing that standard came to be made not by IBM but by so-called clone producers.

Big Blue's position in all of its major businesses had been significantly eroded by the end of the 1980s, and a malaise seemed to set in. Chairman John Akers tried to shake up what he saw as a complacent work force with unusually blunt words. He also embarked on a series of alliances with other companies in the early 1990s, most notably a tie-up with Apple Computer that seemed to assure that together the two former rivals would dominate the PC market for many years to come. Akers also sought to inject new life into Big Blue by giving the major divisions of the company much greater autonomy. IBM's reputation has lost some of its luster, but the company remains a powerful presence in a world that increasingly depends on electronic devices for work, education, and play.

HISTORY

IBM began rather modestly as a result of the 1910 merger of three companies: International Time Recording Company, a leading producer of time clocks; Computing Scale Company of America, a lackluster manufacturer of scales and slicing machines; and Tabulating Machine Company, the pioneer in the field of punch cards. The first two were creations of entrepreneur Charles R. Flint, while Tabulating Machine was founded by inventor Herman Hollerith, who had built calculating machines for the Census Bureau but was not much of a businessman. He apparently hooked up with Flint because of financial problems.

The marriage of the three companies was given the clumsy name Computing-Tabulating-Recording Company, or CTR. In 1914 Flint hired a marketing wizard named Thomas Watson to serve as general manager of the firm. Watson had recently been fired, as many others had, by John Patterson, the autocratic head of National Cash Register (NCR).

Being dismissed by the temperamental Patterson was no stigma, but Watson had just been convicted (along with Patterson) of criminal antitrust violations in connection with a scheme that used a dummy company set up with NCR funds to drive competitors out of the business. While the verdict was being appealed, Dayton, Ohio—NCR's headquarters city—was hit with a disastrous flood. Patterson immediately devoted all of the company's resources to helping flood victims. Patterson was hailed as a national hero, so that when the appeals court ordered a new trial on a technicality, the Justice Department decided to drop the case. By this time Watson, who had been hired on the assumption that his legal problems would somehow evaporate, was already hard at work at CTR, and when the legal cloud was lifted, he was promoted to the presidency.

Watson demonstrated his usual zeal at CTR, applying many of the motivational and marketing methods he had learned at NCR. He fired up his sales force (with such devices as THINK signs) and brought about a steady expansion in the revenues of the company, especially in its tabulating-machine line. In

1924 Watson pursuaded CTR's board to change the company's name to the more grandiose sounding International Business Machines.

IBM was not alone in the business equipment field. Competitors included NCR, of course, as well as Burroughs Adding Machine and two new creations, Remington Rand and Underwood Elliott Fisher. Yet IBM avoided highly competitive products like typewriters, cash registers, and simple adding machines, concentrating instead on the larger tabulating systems for major corporations and government agencies. The company also put more emphasis on leasing rather than selling the equipment, and it prospered by insisting that customers use its punch cards.

This strong market position allowed IBM to weather the depression, and in the late 1930s the company even managed to enjoy fairly rapid growth, especially in the rental part of the business. The New Deal proliferation of federal government agencies was an important source of new business. Watson also brought IBM into an emerging market by purchasing Electromatic Typewriter, one of the few companies seeking to lure people away from manual typewriters. This period also saw the first antitrust action against IBM. As a result of the case, which went all the way to the Supreme Court, IBM could no longer require its customers to purchase its punch cards. However, given that there were no significant competitors in the field, the 1936 decision had little practical effect.

Another development of the 1930s was the creation of links between IBM and the acadmic world. A Columbia University psychology professor received support from the company for work on a machine to score standardized tests automatically. Astronomers at the same university were adapting IBM equipment to perform complex mathematical calculations. The company also ended up funding the efforts of a Harvard graduate student named Howard Aiken, who wanted to develop a more sophisticated kind of calculator, one that would perform according to preprogrammed instructions. The result was the Automatic Sequence Controlled Calculator (later known as the Mark I), one of the precursors of the computer. When the device finally was unveiled in May 1944, Aiken barely mentioned the support of IBM, angering Watson and probably contributing to his resistance to electronic-computing machines.

While Watson stuck to his punch cards, there were other advances in automatic computing. J. Presper Eckert and John Mauchly of the University of Pennsylvania constructed a huge contraption based on electronic vacuum tubes. They introduced the machine, dubbed Electronic Numerical Integrator and Calculator, or ENIAC, on February 14, 1946—which many consider the birth date of the computer age. Eckert and Mauchly went on to develop more computing devices under the name UNIVAC, and in 1950 their operation was purchased by Remington Rand. The company, which merged with Sperry Corporation in 1955 to form Sperry Rand, took the lead in the young computer industry.

Thomas Watson, Jr., who became president of IBM in 1952, did not share his father's skepticism about electronic computers. He gave the go-ahead for the development of a device for scientific applications that became known as the Defense Calculator, or 701. That product was adapted for commercial use as the 702 and subsequent models in the 700 series. Although the 702 was technically inferior to the UNIVAC, IBM's formidable salesmanship made it a great success. By 1956, only three years after the introduction of the 701, IBM had taken over virtually the entire market. As other players—such as RCA, NCR, and General Electric—were entering the field, Watson junior spent heavily on research and development. Yet the company, enjoying its wide lead in the industry, took its time in making the transition from vacuum tubes to transistors.

The results of IBM's efforts were revealed in April 1964, when the company announced—amid fanfare that included simultaneous press conferences in sixty-two U.S. cities and fourteen foreign ones—its System 360. The product of a $5-billion investment, the 360 was an entirely new generation of computers, meant to address any data-processing need. It was also a huge success, despite some significant delays in actually getting the machines to customers.

By this time the company's position was so dominant that analysts began describing the industry as "IBM and the Seven Dwarfs," the latter referring to the struggling competition: Sperry, Control Data Corporation, Honeywell, RCA, NCR, General Electric, and Burroughs. IBM's leadership extended outside the United States as well. The company, which had first moved overseas after World War I, by the mid-1960s was the market leader in every country where there was a computer market, with the exception of Britain and Japan. In Japan it ran neck and neck with Nippon Electric, and in Britain the government brought the leading domestic producers together to form International Computers Ltd., which gave IBM a run for its money. All of the company's foreign operations were conducted under the auspices of the IBM World Trade Corporation, run by the younger Watson son, Dick.

Back at home, IBM's hard-sell approach, which often included promises of new, improved products that were far from completed, were becoming intolerable to the company's competitors, who were losing business from customers waiting to see the next offering from what became known as Big Blue. William Norris, founder and chief executive of Control Data Corporation (CDC), began complaining to the Justice Department, and when he got no satisfaction he filed an antitrust suit against IBM in 1968. The suit accused IBM of promoting "paper machines and phantom computers." It turned out that the Justice Department had been pursuing its own investigation of IBM, and a month after the CDC action, the federal suit was filed.

While the Justice Department suit dragged on for more than a decade (and finally was dropped by the Reagan administration in 1982), IBM settled with Norris in 1973 by agreeing to sell its Service Bureau subsidiary to CDC at its asset value and to pay out some $101 million to CDC over seven years. (The Service Bureau had been created in 1956 as an independent operation as part of a consent decree signed by IBM to settle federal antitrust charges relating to the tabulating business.) The CDC settlement also included a provision for destroying the computerized index compiled by Control Data for the seventy-five thousand pages of internal IBM documents it had gotten during the discovery phase of the case. The Justice Department had coveted that index to assist its case.

Other competitors found new ways to challenge IBM in the marketplace. One group discovered that it was profitable to purchase IBM 360 computers and then lease them to others at lower rates than IBM was charging for rentals. Another batch of companies began producing peripheral equipment, such as disk drives and printers, that could work with IBM mainframes (that is, were "plug compatible," in industry jargon) and were cheaper and/or more efficient than the peripherals sold by IBM itself. Yet other companies, led by Digital Equipment Corporation, began selling what became known as minicomputers—smaller, more flexible systems that sold for a fraction of the cost of the typical mainframe.

IBM tried to outmaneuver these rivals in the market through such steps as the introduction in 1970 of the 370 Series, which was priced to the disadvantage of the leasing companies and included design changes that forced the plug-compatible companies to modify their products. But most of the confrontation ended up taking place in court. The company found itself embroiled in a seemingly endless series of antitrust suits brought by the leasing companies and the plug-compatible producers. The wave of litigation, which *Fortune* once described as "IBM's travails in Lilliput," generally turned out in Big Blue's favor.

While disposing of these challenges, IBM was facing a new assault in its primary business—mainframes. The threat did not come from the Seven Dwarfs, who, after RCA and General Electric dropped out of the field, were renamed the BUNCH (an acronym for Burroughs, the UNIVAC division of Sperry, NCR, Control Data, and Honeywell). It arose, instead, from an engineer named Gene Amdahl, who had worked for IBM on the 360 and now intended to produce mainframes that were more efficient than IBM's but were compatible with them.

Amdahl got backing from Japan's Fujitsu, German computer maker Nixdorf, and U.S. venture capitalists. Amdahl's first machine, the 470 V/6, was introduced in 1975. When it became clear that major users would accept the product, a number of other small companies rushed into the IBM-compatible mainframe business. Before long these upstarts were chipping away at IBM's market share.

That was one thing Big Blue could not tolerate. In 1979 IBM turned the industry upside down by introducing a new generation of medium-scale mainframes that were priced substantially below existing levels. Customers responded to this 4300 line with far more enthusiasm than IBM had anticipated. The company was overwhelmed with orders for the new machines—some forty-two thousand of them within the first three weeks of the announcement. Deliveries had to be stretched out over four years.

This was too much of a good thing. Customers frustrated with the long waiting periods turned to the competition, while users of the large-scale machines held back on purchases in anticipation of price cuts comparable to those offered on the 4300 systems. The result for IBM was a severe financial squeeze.

IBM recovered from the confusion and achieved its goal of regaining some of the market share lost in the 1970s. It also moved to gain access to the most advanced semiconductor technology by taking a stake in Intel. Positive results were more difficult to come by in the field of telecommunications, which IBM had entered in 1975 by forming the Satellite Business Systems (SBS) joint venture with Aetna Life & Casualty and the Communications Satellite Corporation. SBS, which was not a great success, was handed over to MCI when IBM purchased an interest in the long-distance carrier in 1985. Big Blue also stumbled with telecommunications equipment producer Rolm, which was acquired in 1984 and sold to Siemens four years later.

The biggest splash made by IBM was in the newest segment of the information business—microcomputers. Big Blue had watched in the late 1970s as small companies like Apple Computer built a substantial market for devices that took computing power out of the big, climate-controlled mainframe facilities and put it in the hands of individuals. By 1980 IBM's planners had decided to violate the traditional orientation of the company and enter this new business.

The result was the IBM PC, which was introduced in August 1981 and took the world by storm. Unlike the System 360, the PC was not a leap forward in technology. Its components were standard ones provided by outside vendors. Yet it had the IBM name, and the fact that its operating system was an open one meant that independent software companies could write programs for it.

IBM managed to seize a large share of the personal computer market in short order, aided by the fact that its PC came on the scene at a time when Apple was having trouble with its new machines. By October 1983 *Business Week* was able to declare: "The battle for market supremacy is suddenly all over, and IBM is the winner." IBM was especially successful, given its strong ties to corporate customers, in making its product the one that large companies turned to as they joined the desktop revolution.

Yet, as had happened with mainframes, IBM's success prompted a group of companies to enter the field with machines that were compatible with Big Blue's operating system but were cheaper or more efficient. Start-up companies like Compaq, which was formed in 1983 by venture capitalist Ben Rosen and former Texas Instruments engineer Rod Canion, seized a significant portion of the market by selling what became known as IBM clones.

Compaq, in particular, became a technology leader, introducing the first PC with the advanced Intel 80386 microprocessor. The advent of these 32-bit devices paved the way for powerful desktop machines that could replace mainframes and minicomputers for many applications. Compaq also pioneered the portable PC market (although its initial, twenty-eight-pound entry would have been more accurately described as "luggable")—a field in which IBM struck out with its ill-fated PCjr. By 1986 the clone makers were selling more PCs than IBM was, and Big Blue's entry in the booming laptop market went nowhere.

In 1987 IBM struck back with a new line of PCs called Personal System/2, which used the new OS/2 operating system developed by Microsoft and had a graphical interface resembling Apple's Macintosh. The new system employed a proprietary architecture called Micro Channel and other exclusive designs, the patents on which IBM vowed to defend vigorously. As it turned out, there was not a lot of business for the company's lawyers, because the OS/2 never caught on. Most of the major clone producers stuck with an architecture that was closer to the existing standard.

Meanwhile, in the mainframe market IBM continued to battle the plug-compatible makers while scrambling to respond to the movement away from big computers to powerful desktop machines. Big Blue introduced a new generation of high-end mainframes, the Sierra or 3090 Series, in 1985, but it was not enough of a leap forward to persuade large numbers of users to move up. IBM also had limited success in persuading customers who were switching to PCs and more powerful workstations that mainframes were still needed to coordinate the networking of the smaller machines.

All of these troubles added up to a slump for IBM at the end of the decade. In 1989 the company announced that it would eliminate ten thousand jobs and take a $2.3-billion charge against earnings for restructuring. Wall Street recognized the gravity of the company's problems, and IBM's stock price sagged.

Beginning in 1990 IBM sought to ease its troubles with an approach that was foreign to the company's traditions—it began cultivating new markets and forming alliances with other firms for product development. This included:

- joining with Siemens to work on a new generation of memory chips;
- introducing a new line of workstations that used AT&T's UNIX operating system and included easy-to-use software created by Apple Computer cofounder Steven Jobs's Next Inc.;
- forming a partnership with a small company called Metaphor Inc. to develop software that could run on different operating systems (IBM later purchased the company);
- selling and supporting the Netware operating system made by Novell Inc. with its local-area-network products;
- participating in a campaign of major computer companies in Japan to break NEC's hold on the PC market in that country;
- establishing a marketing alliance with Wang Laboratories in which IBM agreed to invest up to $100 million in the ailing company;
- entering into a joint development agreement with Thinking Machines Corporation to integrate that company's supercomputer technology with IBM's mainframe systems;
- and, most dramatically, allying itself in 1991 with rival Apple Computer by agreeing to codevelop a new operating system, whereby each company

would employ the system and modify its products to make them more compatible with the other's.

While the Apple alliance created the groundwork for future dominance of the PC market by the two companies—and put software leader Microsoft on the defensive—the immediate situation for IBM remained bleak. Market share continued to stagnate, profitability was still sliding, and the company's stock price remained depressed. IBM chairman John Akers was so exasperated by the situation that he read the riot act to his managers. Saying, according to a leaked memo, that IBM's work force was "too damn comfortable," he called for the dismissal of any employees who were not performing up to par. In another effort to revitalize the company, Akers announced an extensive decentralization move in late 1991. The plan, which also involved the elimination of about twenty thousand jobs, will in effect turn Big Blue into a group of relatively autonomous and presumably more dynamic Little Blues.

For all of its recent financial problems, IBM has remained a formidable force in the industry. It also has continued to break new ground in technology. In 1991 the company said it would introduce a hand-held PC that could communicate with larger computers via radio or cellular telephone. About the same time, company researchers announced that they had succeeded in manipulating single atoms and made a switch that depended on the motion of one of those atoms, raising the possibility of circuits at that submicroscopic level. One part of the company, at least, is looking beyond the current troubles to the distant future.

OPERATIONS

Processors (23 percent of 1991 revenues). IBM is far and away the world leader in the sale of large-scale general-purpose computers, known as mainframes. This business, in which IBM has a market share of about 60 percent, is estimated to account for about half of the company's gross profits. This segment also includes midrange hardware like the AS/400 minicomputer.

Personal Systems and Other Workstations (18 percent of revenues). IBM barged into the PC business in 1981 and for a while looked like it might have the entire market to itself. That did not happen, but IBM did take a strong lead. By the beginning of the 1990s the resurgence of Apple Computer and the clone makers had reduced IBM's market share to about 17 percent. The company's OS/2 operating system, introduced in 1987, did not become a new standard, and in 1991 IBM formed an alliance with Apple to develop a new operating system, one that would draw their products closer together. In 1992 IBM made its debut in the laptop computer market in the United States and entered the pen-based PC field.

Peripherals (16 percent of revenues). This segment includes a variety of printers, storage devices, and telecommunications equipment. IBM is especially dominant in high-end disk drives, where it controls 80 percent of the market.

Software (16 percent of revenues). Extracting information from large IBM systems used to require the services of a programmer, but as part of the Personal System/2 introduced in 1987 IBM brought out software called OfficeVision to simplify that task. The plunge into software for PCs and networks was taken a step further in 1991, when IBM and Apple formed an alliance that included joint work on developing a new operating system. That move was a direct challenge to software leader Microsoft and its Windows program, which has been hailed as the means for making IBM-compatible PCs as user-friendly as Macintoshes.

Support Services (11 percent of revenues). Maintenance is the largest category of the company's support services.

Federal Systems (3 percent of revenues). This segment consists of specialized information technology products and services provided to the Department of Defense, the National Aeronautics and Space Administration (NASA), and other federal agencies. The company also does work for foreign governments. In 1991 it won a $2.5-billion contract from Britain's Royal Navy to modify forty-four helicopters with electronic equipment designed for antisubmarine warfare. In fiscal 1991 IBM was the twenty-seventh-largest military contractor in the United States, with prime contract awards totaling $773 million.

Other Products (12 percent of revenues). The company identifies this segment as consisting of "customer solution services, financing revenue and supplies."

TOP EXECUTIVES

- John F. Akers, chairman
- Jack D. Kuehler, president
- Frank A. Metz, Jr., senior vice president, finance and planning
- John R. Opel, chairman of the executive committee

OUTSIDE DIRECTORS

- Stephen D. Bechtel, Jr., chairman emeritus of the Bechtel Group
- Harold Brown, chairman of the Foreign Policy Institute of the Johns Hopkins University and former U.S. secretary of defense
- James E. Burke, retired chairman of Johnson & Johnson
- Thomas F. Frist, Jr., chief executive of Hospital Corporation of America
- Fritz Gerber, chief executive of Roche Holding Ltd.
- Judith Richards Hope, senior partner in the law firm Paul Hastings Janofsky & Walker

- Nannerl O. Keohane, president of Wellesley College
- Richard W. Lyman, president emeritus of Stanford University
- J. Richard Munro, chairman of the executive committee of Time Warner
- Thomas S. Murphy, chairman of Capital Cities/ABC
- Helmut Sihler, chief executive of Henkel KGaA
- John B. Slaughter, president of Occidental College
- Edgar S. Woolard, Jr., chief executive of Du Pont

FINANCIAL DATA

Revenues (in millions of dollars)

1991	64,792
1990	69,018
1989	62,710
1988	59,681
1987	55,256
1986	52,160

Net Income (in millions of dollars)

1991	−2,827 (loss)*
1990	6,020
1989	3,758
1988	5,806
1987	5,258
1986	4,789

*Reflects a restructuring charge of $3.4 billion and a $2.3 billion charge to implement a new accounting standard for retiree benefits.

GEOGRAPHICAL BREAKDOWN

Revenues (in millions of dollars)

Year	United States		Europe, Middle East, Africa		Elsewhere	
1991	32,102	(41%)	26,974	(34%)	19,834	(25%)
1990	33,327	(42%)	28,210	(36%)	17,763	(22%)
1989	31,221	(43%)	24,271	(34%)	16,929	(23%)
1988	30,271	(44%)	22,555	(33%)	15,888	(23%)

Net Income (in millions of dollars)

Year	United States		Europe, Middle East, Africa		Elsewhere	
1991*	− 2,394	(0%)	1,264	(66%)	650	(34%)
1990	1,459	(24%)	2,977	(50%)	1,571	(26%)
1989	− 325	(0%)	2,676	(65%)	1,469	(35%)
1988	1,408	(26%)	2,349	(43%)	1,722	(31%)

*Before charge relating to change in accounting standard for retiree benefits.

LABOR RELATIONS

IBM is the classic example of a company that has used good pay and benefits and a general policy of paternalism to eliminate the incentive for its employees to unionize. For decades it also maintained a no-layoffs policy.

Feelings of loyalty to the company have not, however, been universal in its work force. In 1976 a group of employees formed an underground organization called IBM Workers United out of discontent with hazardous working conditions and overly strict personnel practices at a facility in upstate New York where circuit boards were made—a process that includes the use of toxic chemicals. The group began publishing a newsletter, which was distributed by supporters from outside the company. At about the same time, another group formed Black Workers Alliance of IBM Employees to fight against racism in the company.

For eight years IBM Workers United remained underground in the sense that its leaders kept their identities secret. Still, the organization was active in getting its message out. The leaders spoke regularly with the press, though they used pseudonyms and refused to be photographed. They also made contact with IBM workers in other countries, including the small numbers that were unionized in France, Sweden, Spain, Italy, Greece, and Japan. The first international meeting of IBM workers took place in Tokyo in 1984.

The following year the Communications Workers of America (CWA) announced plans for a large-scale organizing drive against IBM in cooperation with IBM Workers United, whose head, Lee Conrad, had by this time gone public. Formal organizing proceeded slowly, but IBM Workers United gained increased support in 1986 when the company began to take steps to reduce its payroll. The group argued that even though the company did not call them layoffs, pressuring people to take early retirement and other means of raising attrition amounted to the same thing. In 1987 the CWA helped organize an international gathering of unions from two dozen countries to discuss organizing Big Blue. A study prepared for that meeting (*The IBM File*) concludes that some ten thousand of the company's four hundred thousand employees worldwide were members of labor unions.

One organizing success came in South Korea, where, amid a general upsurge in labor militancy, workers used sit-ins and hunger strikes to pressure IBM's local subsidiary to recognize the newly formed IBM Korea Union in 1989.

ENVIRONMENTAL RECORD

Since the early 1980s there has been a heated controversy over the issue of whether the electromagnetic fields created by video display terminals are a health hazard. IBM has not publicly disagreed with the industry view that there is no definitive evidence that this is the case, despite numerous reports of clusters of problem pregnancies among women whose jobs involved working at terminals.

However, in 1989 IBM did announced that it was modifying some of its terminals to substantially lower the radiation they emitted. The company insisted that this did not imply that its previous monitors were dangerous; the new products, according to IBM, were simply a response to the demand for low-radiation monitors.

IBM has been cited as one of the largest users of ozone-destroying CFCs. The company pledged to eliminate CFCs by 1993 after being pressured by environmental groups.

The company also has had problems with toxic releases. In 1981 leaks from the IBM facility in Manassas, Virginia, contaminated groundwater in an area within a radius of more than a mile from the plant. The company spent more than $10 million in a clean-up effort. IBM also has been responsible for seepage of industrial solvents at such facilities as the one in San Jose, California.

According to a study of EPA data conducted by the Citizens Fund, IBM's Endicott, New York, facility was among the fifty manufacturing facilities with the highest volume of toxic releases into the air in 1988. Its releases that year totaled more than 4.4 million pounds. Those emissions were reduced by more than 80 percent in 1989 (the latest information available) thanks to changes in production procedures.

IBM was confident enough in its environmental prowess that in 1991 its British subsidiary announced that it would begin to offer environmental consulting services to other companies.

BIBLIOGRAPHY

Anchordoguy, Marie. *Computers, Inc.: Japan's Challenge to IBM*. Cambridge, Mass.: Harvard University Press, 1989.

Brock, Gerald. *The U.S. Computer Industry*. Cambridge, Mass.: Ballinger, 1975.

DeLamarter, Richard T. *Big Blue: IBM's Use and Abuse of Power*. New York: Dodd, Mead, 1986.

Engelbourg, Saul. *International Business Machines: A Business History*. New York: Arno, 1976.

Fisher, Franklin M. *IBM & the U.S. Data Processing Industry: An Economic History*. Westport, Conn.: Greenwood, 1983.

Fishman, Katharine. *The Computer Establishment*. New York: Harper & Row, 1981.

The IBM File. Geneva: International Metalworkers Federation, 1987.

McKenna, Regis. *Who's Afraid of Big Blue? How Companies Are Challenging IBM—and Winning*. Reading, Mass.: Addison-Wesley, 1988.

Mercer, David. *The Global IBM: Leadership in Multinational Management*. New York: Dodd, Mead, 1988.

Rodgers, William. *Think: A Biography of the Watsons and I.B.M.* Briarcliff Manor, N.Y.: Stein & Day, 1969.

Sobel, Robert. *IBM: Colossus in Transition*. New York: Times Books, 1981.

———. *IBM vs. Japan: The Struggle for the Future*. Briarcliff Manor, N.Y.: Stein & Day, 1985.

Watson, Thomas J., Jr., and Peter Petre. *Father, Son & Co.: My Life at IBM and Beyond*. New York: Bantam Books, 1990.

INTERNATIONAL PAPER
COMPANY

Two Manhattanville Road
Purchase, New York 10577
(914) 397-1500

1991 revenues: $12.7 billion
1991 net income: $184 million
Publicly traded company
Employees: 70,500
Founded: 1898

OVERVIEW

International Paper (IP), one of the world's leading forest products companies, makes a wide range of paper and packaging, including copier paper, stationery, coated paper for magazines, pulp lining for diapers, milk cartons, cardboard boxes, and paper bags.

IP started out as a producer of newsprint and later moved into paper bags and cartons, spending decades plodding along as a large but unexciting player in those fields. In the 1980s the company began to show more signs of life. It embarked on a multibillion-dollar acquisitions drive that brought it properties like Hammermill Paper, which put IP into the higher-quality end of the paper business.

Although IP lost its position at the top of the paper industry when Georgia-Pacific took over Great Northern Nekoosa in 1990, the company has made itself into an important international force by gobbling up a series of leading European producers of paper and photographic and printing supplies. Yet at home it still has to contend with a dismal record in its environmental and labor policies.

HISTORY

IP was formed in 1898 when a group of twenty pulp and paper mills in five northeastern states (Maine, New Hampshire, Vermont, Massachusetts, and New York) were consolidated. The main product of the company was newsprint. After World War I the government of Canada, the source of much of IP's pulp, decided to block such exports in order to encourage the manufacture of finished products in that country. IP thus formed the Canadian International Paper Company, which built a newsprint mill in Quebec and purchased the papermaking operations of the Canadian company Riordan.

During the 1920s IP built a hydroelectric power plant on the Hudson River in New York State and restructured its paper operations. Newsprint production was concentrated in Canada, while the U.S. mills were converted to make book and writing paper. The company also entered the kraft market (strong brown paper used for bags and heavy-duty wrapping) through the purchase of Bastrop Pulp & Paper, a mill in Louisiana. By the 1930s IP also was making kraft containerboard.

Soon after World War II IP, now controlled by the Hinman family, entered the milk carton business by acquiring Single Service Containers Inc. The company moved further into the packaging business in the 1950s with such purchases as carton maker Lord Baltimore Press.

It was in the 1960s that IP first began to expand outside North America. In 1960 it bought from W. R. Grace a half interest in a paper mill in Colombia that made paper from bagasse (crushed sugar cane) fibers, another bagasse mill and packaging operation in Puerto Rico, and a folding box company in Mexico. Two years later IP bought shares in Cartonajes International SA in Spain and a paper company called Silca in Italy.

Back in the United States IP began to diversify, with mixed results. Its purchase of the Davol hospital supply company in 1968 turned out well (though the business was sold in 1980), but a disposable diaper venture was a failure. The company also was embarrassed by its involvement in a series of price-fixing scandals involving paper labels, folding cartons, and corrugated containers. This came amid a period of management instability as the board of directors brought in several outside chief executives after the Hinman family's reign ended. One of these outsiders, J. Stanford Smith, conceived of IP as a "land resources management business," and toward this end, the company purchased General Crude Oil Company in 1975.

Smith's successor, the flamboyant (especially for stodgy IP) Edwin A. Gee, sold off the oil business four years later and used the $800 million in proceeds to acquire a forest products company called Bodcaw. He also sold the Canadian newsprint operation.

John Georges, who succeeded Gee in 1985 and who, like Gee, was a veteran of Du Pont, took advantage of an improving forest products market to modernize many of IP's facilities and to launch a major acquisitions drive. In 1986 he spent $1 billion to acquire Hammermill Paper, which had been under assault by raider Paul Bilzerian. Hammermill, a leading producer of writing and copier paper, gave IP a strong position in the high end of the market. Other purchases included Anitec Image Technology, the Kendall nonwoven fiber business from Colgate-Palmolive, and USG's Masonite operation, the leading producer of wood composite products. Georges put the company's land holdings into a partnership called IP Timberlands.

The buying spree continued into the new decade, despite a sharp downturn that afflicted IP and the rest of the pulp and paper industry. In 1991 the company purchased distributor Dillard Paper and the packaging equipment division of United Dominion Industries.

Since the late 1980s Georges also has raised IP's profile in Europe, with such acquisitions as Swedish chemical processor Bergvik Kemi, Ciba-Geigy's Ilford Group photographic paper business, French papermaker Aussedat Rey, German coated-paper producer Zanders Feinpapiere, and the British graphics equipment company Cookson Group.

OPERATIONS

Pulp and Paper (31 percent of 1991 revenues). IP is a leading producer of uncoated printing and writing papers. These include Springhill and Hammermill reprographic and printing papers; Strathmore, Beckett and Ward premium printing, writing, and art papers; Aussedat Rey (in France) reprographic and printing papers; and Zanders (in Germany) carbonless copy, writing, and specialty papers. IP also makes a variety of coated papers that are used in many major magazines, in brochures, and for other purposes. Also included here are pulp products used in disposable diapers and cigarette filters.

Paperboard and Packaging (26 percent of revenues). The company makes a wide range of industrial packaging products (linerboard, boxes, and specialty items, such as silicone-coated papers for medical purposes); packaging for consumer products, including milk and juice cartons; and kraft products used in industrial and consumer paper bags.

Distribution Businesses (20 percent of revenues). This segment consists of wholesalers that distribute paper and other office supplies, chemicals used by printers, industrial chemicals, and other products.

Specialty Products (15 percent of revenues). Included in this segment are Ilford photographic products (films, papers, processing chemicals, equipment), Anitec products for commercial printers, Masonite specialized wood composite products (such as garage door panels), nonwoven textiles, ingredients for inks and adhesives, and oil and gas exploration.

Wood Products and Timber (9 percent of revenues). This segment includes Masonite wall paneling and hardboard siding products, timber sales (through the company's majority ownership of the partnership IP Timberlands), and land development.

TOP EXECUTIVES

- John A. Georges, chairman and chief executive
- John T. Dillon, executive vice president, packaging
- Dana G. Mead, executive vice president, pulp and paper
- Robert C. Butler, senior vice president and chief financial officer

OUTSIDE DIRECTORS

- Willard C. Butcher, former chairman of Chase Manhattan
- Frederick B. Dent, chairman of Mayfair Mills
- William M. Ellinghaus, former president of AT&T
- Stanley C. Gault, chief executive of Goodyear Tire & Rubber
- Thomas C. Graham, chairman of Washington Steel Corporation
- Arthur G. Hansen, educational consultant
- William G. Kuhns, chairman of General Public Utilities
- Donald F. McHenry, professor of diplomacy at Georgetown University
- Jane C. Pfeiffer, management consultant
- Samuel R. Pierce, Jr., former secretary of housing and urban development
- Edmund T. Pratt, Jr., former chief executive of Pfizer
- Roger B. Smith, former chief executive of General Motors

FINANCIAL DATA

Revenues (in millions of dollars)

1991	12,703
1990	12,960
1989	11,378
1988	9,587
1987	7,800

Net Income (in millions of dollars)

1991	184
1990	569*
1989	864
1988	754
1987	407

*Includes a $212-million pretax business improvement charge.

GEOGRAPHICAL BREAKDOWN

Revenues (in millions of dollars)

Year	United States		Europe		Elsewhere	
1991	9,811	(76%)	2,833	(22%)	318	(2%)
1990	10,119	(77%)	2,730	(21%)	314	(2%)

Operating Profit (in millions of dollars)

Year	United States		Europe		Elsewhere	
1991	871	(84%)	143	(14%)	24	(2%)
1990	1,139	(85%)	177	(13%)	29	(2%)

LABOR RELATIONS

At the same time IP was established at the end of the nineteenth century, workers in the pulp and paper industry were beginning to form collective-bargaining organizations. The process was made more difficult by the tensions that existed between pulp and paper workers and, among the latter group, between the elite machine tenders and other members of the crews that ran the huge papermaking machines. In 1908 IP experienced its first strike, called in response to a reduction in wages mandated by management. The fledgling papermakers union was no match for the company, and the walkout ended in failure. IP then introduced an elaborate spy system and instituted a yellow-dog contract (a requirement that employees vow not to engage in union activity).

Two years later—after the paper and pulp workers had ended their rivalry and together formed the International Brotherhood of Pulp, Sulphite, and Paper Mill Workers—IP employees went on strike again. This time labor unity prevailed, and the workers won the twelve-week walkout.

In the following year workers at IP joined the union in great numbers, and in 1921 the union felt confident enough to ask for a 10-percent increase in pay from IP and other leading companies. The employers responded with a demand for a wage reduction, lengthening of the work day, and elimination of premium pay for overtime work. The workers thus voted to strike IP, but the company wasted no time bringing in strikebreakers and managed to maintain production, though at a substantially lower level. The strike dragged on for five years, until the decimated unions finally conceded defeat. They did not regain recognition from the company. It was only in the late 1930s that unions once again gained a foothold at IP, beginning with the Canadian operations. The union was then recognized at the kraft operations and finally at the book and bond paper mills.

The IP labor-management confrontation of the 1920s was re-created in the late 1980s. The dispute began in early 1987, when members of the United Paperworkers International Union (UPIU) at IP's mill in Mobile, Alabama, voted to reject management demands for contract concessions (including the elimination of premium pay for Sunday work) and were locked out of their jobs by the company. The Mobile workers then made a coordinated bargaining pact with their counterparts at three other IP mills—in Jay, Maine, Lock Haven, Pennsylvania, and De Pere, Wisconsin—where contracts were expiring and the rank and file had decided to strike rather than concede. Altogether some thirty-five hundred workers moved to re-create the old practice of pattern bargaining by declaring all for one and one for all.

As in 1921, IP did not hesitate to bring in replacement workers from around the country, many of them recruited by BE&K, an Alabama-based construction company that had diversified into strikebreaking. UPIU members at the four locations waged an aggressive battle against the company. In Maine, for example, the union pressured the state legislature to pass a bill outlawing the use of strikebreaking firms, but business-oriented Governor John McKernan, Jr., vetoed the measure. The Jay strikers were more successful in using local political power to pressure the company; they got the town to pass a set of local ordinances that put IP's environmental practices under close scrutiny.

The striking and locked-out locals also launched a broader campaign against the company, with the assistance of Ray Rogers's labor-consulting outfit, Corporate Campaign Inc. That campaign included sending strikers on caravans to garner support from around the country, including from IP locals that were not on strike. Substantial pressure was put on the company and its outside directors (especially Donald McHenry), but in the end it was not enough. IP held fast, and finally in October 1988 the UPIU abandoned the strike. IP, however, kept the replacement workers in Jay, Lock Haven, and De Pere on the job (the locked-out workers in Mobile were required by law to be rehired) and took back former strikers only as vacancies opened up.

ENVIRONMENTAL RECORD

IP is one of the biggest polluters in an industry infamous for its impact on the environment. Aside from water and air pollution, the company is a major contributor to the dioxin problem as a result of the chemicals used in the bleaching process to produce white papers.

These issues were highlighted in the course of the labor dispute in the late 1980s, described earlier. Unskilled strikebreakers hired by the company in Jay, Maine, were responsible for a series of accidents that nearly had fatal consequences for the town. The most serious of these occurred in February 1988, when several of the replacement workers accidentally broke the valve on a tank containing chlorine dioxide gas in pressurized liquid form. About 112,000 gallons of the liquid poured out and vaporized into a huge green cloud that floated out from the mill, forcing the evacuation of some three thousand people from homes, schools, and businesses. If the weather had been warmer and the winds weaker, it is thought that many could have died.

In response to incidents like these—and because of IP's long history of discharging large quantities of waste water into the Androscoggin River and creating toxic-laden sludge at the mill—town officials and residents of Jay (including strikers) moved to establish local ordinances to control IP's activities. The company challenged the rules in court, saying that the town had no right to regulate in areas covered by state and federal law.

The town's enactment of the rules, which was upheld by a U.S. appeals court in 1991, served to prompt state and federal regulators to get tougher with IP. In August 1988 the state attorney general filed suit against the company, saying that it had violated "virtually every environmental law" in its operations in Jay. The company later paid $885,000 to settle the charges.

At about the same time, IP paid $873,000 to settle charges brought by OSHA in connection with unsafe conditions at the Jay mill. IP also agreed to carry out a program to identify and correct health and safety hazards at all of the company's mills engaged in chlorine bleaching.

IP remains at the center of controversy over the creation of dioxins in the chlorine bleaching process. A 1989 EPA study of dioxin levels in fish near eighty-one paper mills found the highest concentration near an IP mill in Bastrop, Louisiana. Another study of the country's 104 bleaching mills found the worst dioxin problem at an IP facility in Georgetown, South Carolina. In December 1990 a group of people living near paper mills in Mississippi filed a $2-billion lawsuit against IP and Georgia-Pacific, charging the companies with endangering their health by dumping dioxins into three rivers in the state.

In 1991 the paperworkers' union formed an unprecedented alliance with the militant environmental group Greenpeace to campaign against IP's ecological sins. The UPIU and Greenpeace began staging joint actions to highlight the health problems for both workers and communities.

The EPA joined the chorus of critics of IP by charging the company with criminal violations of laws regarding the storage and disposal of hazardous wastes in Jay, and with knowingly making false statements to federal authorities about the presence of certain toxic substances at the mill. In July 1991 the company pleaded guilty to five felony charges and paid a fine of $2.2 million.

A study of EPA data by the Citizens Fund found that IP was responsible for the thirty-seventh-largest volume (twenty-three million pounds) of toxic releases among all U.S. manufacturing companies in 1989 (the latest figures available).

BIBLIOGRAPHY

Graham, Harry Edward. *The Paper Rebellion: Development and Upheaval in Pulp and Paper Unionism*. Iowa City: University of Iowa Press, 1970.
United Paperworkers International Union. *A Union Member's Guide to International Paper Company*. Nashville: United Paperworkers International Union, 1991.

JOHNSON & JOHNSON

One Johnson & Johnson Plaza
New Brunswick, New Jersey 08933
(908) 524-0400

1991 revenues: $12.4 billion
1991 net income: $1.5 billion
Publicly traded company
Employees: 82,700
Founded: 1887

OVERVIEW

By pioneering the production of antiseptic surgical dressings, Johnson &
Johnson (J&J) built itself into the most prominent manufacturer of hospital
supplies and first-aid material. Seventy years ago it revolutionized the treatment of minor injuries with the introduction of the Band-Aid—which, despite
the company's efforts to protect its trademark, is widely used as a generic
term for any adhesive bandage. J&J's name is also closely associated with
baby powder and other infant-care items, which often are used by adults as
well. These and the company's other health-care products—most sold with
the familiar red-cross symbol on the package—are widely used across the
globe. Now the largest diversified health-care company in the world, J&J has
some 166 operating units in 52 countries.

J&J also has sought to establish itself in the prescription drug business and
recently has been expanding its efforts in biotechnology. The company is also
heavily involved in reproductive health, with a range of products that both
prevent and promote ovulation. Retin-A, a medication originally designed to
treat acne, caused a sensation when tests suggested that it eliminates wrinkles.
The company's well-known painkiller Tylenol has overcome a series of highly
publicized tampering incidents and remains the leader in its field.

HISTORY

In 1861 sixteen-year-old Robert Wood Johnson left his home in Pennsylvania and headed for Poughkeepsie, New York, where he was taken on as an apprentice in his uncle's apothecary shop. Johnson developed an interest in the plaster preparations used to treat wounds, and in 1873 he formed a partnership in New York City with George Seabury to produce and distribute these and other medical products.

The relationship with Seabury was rocky, especially after Johnson brought his two younger brothers, James and Edward Mead, into the business. In 1886 the Johnsons struck out on their own and set up operations in New Brunswick, New Jersey. The focus of the company was the production of various plasters and other wound dressings treated to make them antiseptic. The latter quality, now taken for granted in medical products, was just becoming accepted in the late nineteenth century, as a result of Joseph Lister's pioneering work showing how germs caused disease.

In 1888 Johnson & Johnson, which was incorporated the year before, published what was to become a standard handbook on the antiseptic treatment of wounds. It also included a catalog of the young company's products. The wide dissemination of the volume rapidly built the firm's reputation. By the end of the century it was a leading supplier of medicinal plasters, antiseptic dressings, and absorbent cotton, all sold in packages with the red-cross symbol. The company was a pioneer in the development of antiseptic sutures for the sewing up of wounds.

J&J also dabbled in the tonics and digestive aids that were popular at the time. Mead Johnson became particularly interested in the area of infant digestion and ended up leaving to form his own firm, which grew into a leading supplier of infant formula.

Yet J&J's most widely recognized product turned out to be its baby powder, which was introduced after a physician wrote for advice on dealing with skin irritation being experienced by a patient using a J&J medicated plaster.

Robert Wood Johnson used every opportunity to promote his company's goods. Large quantities of medical supplies were donated to the military during the Spanish-American War and to rescue workers after the San Francisco earthquake. The company published the first comprehensive handbook on first aid and encouraged railroads to make first-aid kits standard equipment on trains and in stations.

In 1921 the company introduced another product that would become virtually synonymous with J&J—the Band-Aid. The adhesive bandage was invented by a J&J employee, Earle E. Dickson, to help his undextrous wife treat the frequent cuts she was inflicting on herself while slicing food. Dickson took the idea to his employer and eventually was rewarded with a vice presidency for giving the company what turned into its leading product.

Following an extensive foreign tour in 1923 by James Johnson (who took over the company after his brother's death in 1910), J&J began to expand overseas. In 1924 a manufacturing plant was opened in England, and during the 1930s subsidiaries were formed in South Africa, Mexico, Australia, Brazil, and Argentina.

The company's stature grew as a result of initiatives as far apart as a then-daring advertising campaign for its Modess sanitary napkins in the 1930s and its record-breaking production of medical supplies during World War II.

In the late 1950s the top management of J&J decided to expand the company's Band-Aid and baby powder image by taking a plunge into the prescription drug business. This was accomplished, first, by the 1959 purchase of McNeil Laboratories, a family-owned business that traced its origins to a drugstore opened in Philadelphia in 1879. McNeil specialized in sedatives and muscle-relaxing drugs and later introduced Tylenol. The Swiss drug house Cilag-Chemie and Janssen Pharmaceutica in Belgium were purchased as well.

J&J's carefully cultivated image was threatened in 1982, when someone began adding cyanide to capsules of Extra-Strength Tylenol on sale in Chicago. Seven people were killed, and suddenly Tylenol was associated with death. J&J quickly embarked on a public relations campaign that subsequently received high praise for its candor, its speed in removing the product from the market, and its success in restoring public confidence in Tylenol by reissuing the drug in tamper-resistant packages. J&J also took swift action when the contamination was repeated in New York State in 1986. This included discontinuing the sale of all of the company's over-the-counter medications in capsule form.

OPERATIONS

Consumer Products (37 percent of sales in 1991). This segment is led by Band-Aid adhesive bandages, various baby products, and Tylenol acetaminophen pain relievers. It also includes feminine hygiene products, antacids, sun-care products, toothbrushes, and children's cold and allergy medications.

J&J's hold on the baby market does not extend to disposable diapers, a market that it lost to Procter & Gamble and Kimberly-Clark in the United States. The company also has had problems in the feminine hygiene business. Its OB tampon, a popular item in Europe, did not catch on in the United States. In 1989 J&J abandoned a plan to purchase the tampon business of Playtex Inc.

The company is awaiting U.S. government approval to market sucralose, the first noncaloric sweetener derived from sugar. It is said to taste like sugar and can be used almost anywhere sugar is used, including in baked goods. J&J's McNeil Specialty Products subsidiary developed sucralose in partnership with Tate & Lyle PLC of the United Kingdom.

In 1989 J&J formed a joint venture with Merck & Company to develop nonprescription drugs. The venture has purchased a group of nonprescription products, including the antacid Mylanta, from the U.S. subsidiary of Imperial Chemical Industries.

Pharmaceutical Products (30 percent of sales). This segment consists of prescription drugs, including contraceptives, therapeutics, antifungal medications, and veterinary products. Prescription drugs include Haldol, an antipsychotic; Chemet, an oral medication for treating lead poisoning; the Ortho-Novum group of oral contraceptives; and Lutrepulse, a synthetic hormone that is pumped intravenously into women to induce ovulation. J&J is supporting research at the University of Virginia aimed at developing a contraceptive vaccine that would stimulate the immune system of women to produce antibodies that would prevent fertilization. Hismanal, an antihistamine that does not cause drowsiness, was developed at J&J's Janssen Pharmaceutica unit and is now sold in more than one hundred countries.

Retin-A, a dermatological cream for acne, became wildly popular in the late 1980s when tests suggested that the vitamin-A derivative could smooth wrinkled skin. Wall Street went wild for awhile, thinking that J&J had discovered a fountain of youth, although later studies of Retin-A's effectiveness on wrinkles were less encouraging and the FDA did not approve the drug's use for that purpose. The company came under fire for allegedly promoting Retin-A for this unapproved use. J&J also faced a lawsuit from the University of Pennsylvania, which said it was entitled to a share of profits from the medication because its inventor was on the faculty of the school. The company settled the suit in 1992 by agreeing to pay the university a royalty if Retin-A is approved as an anti-aging medication.

J&J also has moved into biotechnology. Its Ortho Biotech subsidiary pioneered the production of monoclonal antibodies for research purposes. The company's Orthoclone OKT-3, which reverses rejection of transplanted kidneys, was the first monoclonal antibody product approved by the FDA as a treatment in humans.

Procrit (marketed outside the United States as Eprex), a genetically engineered version of the human hormone erythropoietin (which stimulates red blood cell production), was approved by the FDA in 1990. Yet J&J faced delays in getting it on the market in the United States because of contract disputes with its partner, Amgen Inc. Also approved by the FDA in 1990 were Floxin, a broad-spectrum oral antibacterial, which J&J licensed from Daiichi Seiyaku Company of Japan; and Vascor, a drug for treating cardiovascular problems.

Professional Products (33 percent of sales). J&J's professional products include ligatures and sutures, surgical dressings, surgical instruments, surgical gowns and other accessories, diagnostic products, ophthalmic products (including contact lenses), dental products, and a variety of other items for physicians, dentists, nurses, therapists, hospitals, diagnostic laboratories, and clinics. These products are distributed through subsidiaries, including Codman & Shurtleff (surgical supplies), Critikon (intravenous devices), Ethicon (sutures, ligatures, and so on), and Iolab (ophthalmic products).

Ethicon's leadership in its field has been challenged by U.S. Surgical Corporation, which in 1990 moved into sutures seeking the same dominance it has in the other two major segments of the surgical supplies business: the staplers used to close incisions and endoscopic devices used to do gall bladder operations and other surgery through small holes in the abdomen.

J&J was embarrassed in 1991 when a special master for the federal district court in Minneapolis ordered the company to pay $116 million to Minnesota Mining and Manufacturing (3M) for willful violations of 3M's patents on fiberglass tape used for medical casts. The case began in 1985, when a disgruntled employee at 3M sent some samples of his company's new casting tape to several of the firm's rivals. The special master concluded that J&J had incorporated aspects of 3M's tape in its own product.

J&J has seventy-eight manufacturing facilities in the United States, thirty-one in the rest of the western hemisphere, forty-nine in Europe, and thirty-eight in Africa, Asia, and the Pacific. Among the most recently formed subsidiaries are ones in Hungary, Poland, and Yugoslavia. The company's products are sold throughout the world.

TOP EXECUTIVES

- Ralph S. Larsen, chairman and chief executive officer
- Robert E. Campbell, vice chairman
- Robert N. Wilson, vice chairman

OUTSIDE DIRECTORS

- James W. Black, M.D., professor of analytical pharmacology at the Rayne Institute of King's College School of Medicine, London
- Joan Ganz Cooney, chairman of the executive committee of the Children's Television Workshop
- Philip M. Hawley, chief executive of Carter Hawley Hale Stores
- Ann Dibble Jordan, former director of social services at the Chicago Lying-In Hospital
- Arnold G. Langbo, chief executive of Kellogg Company
- Robert Q. Marston, president emeritus and professor of medicine at the University of Florida at Gainesville
- John S. Mayo, president of Bell Laboratories
- Thomas S. Murphy, chairman of Capital Cities/ABC
- Paul J. Rizzo, dean of the business school at the University of North Carolina at Chapel Hill
- Maxine F. Singer, president of the Carnegie Institution of Washington
- Roger B. Smith, former chief executive of General Motors

FINANCIAL DATA

Revenues (in millions of dollars)

1991	12,447
1990	11,232
1989	9,757
1988	9,000
1987	8,012

Net Income (in millions of dollars)

1991	1,461
1990	1,143
1989	1,082
1988	974
1987	833

GEOGRAPHICAL BREAKDOWN

Revenues (in millions of dollars)

Year	United States		Europe		Elsewhere	
1991	6,248	(50%)	3,750	(30%)	2,449	(20%)
1990	5,427	(48%)	3,418	(30%)	2,387	(21%)
1989	4,881	(50%)	2,687	(27%)	2,189	(22%)

Operating Profit (in millions of dollars)

Year	United States		Europe		Elsewhere	
1991	1,022	(46%)	934	(42%)	261	(12%)
1990	904	(46%)	875	(45%)	170	(9%)
1989	699	(40%)	737	(42%)	322	(18%)

LABOR RELATIONS

From its earliest years J&J was a paternalistic employer, pioneering such employee benefits as pension plans and life insurance. The company's credo—a statement of principles taken very seriously at J&J—places responsibility to employees second to the commitment to customers but before the obligation to stockholders and the community.

Most of J&J's employees remain unorganized, although the Amalgamated Clothing and Textile Workers Union does represent workers at several Ethicon plants. That relationship has grown more strained as the company has shifted work away from the organized workplaces. One nonunion Ethicon facility in New Mexico was the focus of a book by sociologist Guillermo Grenier, who argued that the company's use of quality circles was an antiunion device.

ENVIRONMENTAL AND HEALTH RECORD

Like all companies in the drug business, J&J has had its share of problems with harmful side effects. One of the most serious of these cases involved the antiinflammatory drug Zomax, introduced by J&J's McNeil Pharmaceutical subsidiary in 1980. It was very well received by physicians, but patients began to experience severe allergic reactions known as anaphylaxis, which can lead to shock, seizures, or death. J&J removed the product from the market in 1983 but was hit with nearly six hundred lawsuits. In 1990 two former J&J researchers filed a racketeering suit against the company, claiming that they had lost their jobs because they had warned of the problem with the drug.

The company also has been the target of product liability suits relating to its contraceptive products. In 1985 a woman who alleged that use of a J&J contraceptive gel caused her daughter to be born with severe birth defects won a judgment of $5.1 million (later reduced to $4.7 million).

BIBLIOGRAPHY

Foster, Lawrence G. *A Company That Cares: One Hundred Year Illustrated History of Johnson & Johnson.* New Brunswick, N.J.: Johnson & Johnson, 1986.
Goldsmith, Barbara. *Johnson vs. Johnson.* New York: Alfred A. Knopf, 1987.
Grenier, Guillermo. *Inhuman Relations: Quality Circles and Anti-Unionism in American Industry.* Philadelphia: Temple University Press, 1988.

KYOCERA CORPORATION

5-22 Kitainoue-cho, Higashino
Yamashina-ku, Kyoto 607
Japan
(075) 592-3851

1991 revenues: $3.3 billion (year ending March 31)
1991 net income: $229.4 million
Publicly traded company
Employees: 14,031
Founded: 1959

OVERVIEW

Still relatively unknown outside of Japan, Kyocera Corporation is one of the most aggressive high-tech companies in that country. Founded by Kazuo Inamori, an unorthodox businessman who promotes a philosophy that *Fortune* once described as "a rich mixture of Zen Buddhism and Soviet-style exhortations to Stakhanovite performance," played a major role in introducing advanced ceramic materials for use in electronics and machine tools.

Kyocera has gained respect for technical innovations in its core business and has branched out into products ranging from ceramic sushi knives (which leave no metal odor) to prosthetic devices like artificial hips. Following a period in which it made laptop computers and VCRs for other companies, Kyocera now sells personal computers, laser printers, cameras, and other consumer and office products under its own name.

Despite the fact that it has manufacturing operations in seven countries stretching from Hong Kong to Brazil, the company is still relatively small compared to the giants of the electronics industry. Yet increasingly it is seen as a leading contender to become a global giant in the decades to come.

412

HISTORY

After completing a degree in applied chemistry at the un-elite Kagoshima University, Kazuo Inamori began work as a ceramics engineer for Shofu Industries. In 1959, at the age of twenty-seven, he obtained financial backing and struck out on his own, forming a company called Kyoto Ceramic to make electrical components.

Inamori drove himself and his employees to the limit, in part because the founder was obsessed with paying off the company's debt. Some progress, however, came by chance rather than from hard work. During the early years Inamori was trying to solve the problem of how to hold magnesium oxide powder together during firing in the production of insulators. After he tripped over a block of paraffin wax in the lab it occurred to him that wax could be mixed with the powder to make it easier to process.

An early breakthrough came in 1963, when the U.S. semiconductor company Texas Instruments gave Inamori a contract for making an insulating component. This led to orders from Fairchild Semiconductor and Sony. In the latter case, the company solved the problem of producing a small and delicate ceramic part by employing a technique like that used in making spaghetti.

The ambitions of the company were international from the start. In 1969 Inamori set up a U.S. subsidiary in California and two years later purchased a plant from Fairchild to produce ceramic components. At about the same time, the company formed a joint venture with the German company Feldmühle AG. In the following years the company created a subsidiary called Crescent Vert to make recrystallized jewels and acquired Cybernet, a Japanese producer of citizens band (CB) radios and audio equipment.

In 1982 the company and its subsidiaries were reorganized as Kyocera Corporation. The following year Kyocera bought the Japanese camera company Yashica, and in 1984 Inamori put together Dai-Ni Denden Kikau Company, a consortium of twenty-five companies, with the aim of competing with the government-owned Nippon Telegraph and Telephone in providing long-distance telephone and other telecommunications services. NTT, which previously had blocked Kyocera's attempt to challenge its monopoly in the sale of cordless telephones, was privatized in 1986.

Kyocera, which by the mid-1980s had captured 70 percent of the world market for integrated circuit ceramic packaging, has continued to expand aggressively in the United States, Europe, and other parts of the world. In 1985 it formed a joint venture with the Dutch company Philips to develop new media. Inamori's aggressive practices have sometimes gotten him into trouble. He has been criticized for paying insufficient attention to government export regulations and for marketing a bioceramic medical implant without official approval.

In 1989 the company acquired Elco Corporation, a U.S. producer of electronic connectors, and the following year it spent $560 million (in stock) to purchase AVX Corporation, a U.S.-based manufacturer of tantalum, glass, and ceramic multilayer capacitors with plants in ten countries. At the start of the 1990s Kyocera raised its profile by selling more products directly to consumers, including laser printers, the Refalo notebook-type personal computer, and (in Europe) the Multilight PC.

OPERATIONS

Electronic Components (34 percent of 1991 revenues). This segment, which now includes the operations of AVX and Elco, involves the production of chip capacitors, quartz oscillators, ceramic filters, resonators, piezoelectric buzzers, liquid crystal displays, thermal printheads, and other electronic parts.

Semiconductor Parts (23 percent of revenues). Included in this segment are multilayer chip packages, ceramic modules, motherboards, and various other semiconductor components.

Electronic Equipment (17 percent of revenues). Kyocera makes cellular telephones, cordless telephones, compact disc players, personal computers, laser printers, image scanners, and bar-code equipment. The company also makes a video-conferencing system compatible with Integrated Services Digital Network standards, which are increasingly being adopted in advanced telecommunications systems.

Optical Instruments (10 percent of revenues). The company makes single-lens reflex cameras (sold under the names Kyocera, Yashica, and Contax), lens-shutter cameras (Samurai), 8-mm video camcorders (Kyocera Finemovie), and 8-mm VCRs.

Consumer-related Products (8 percent of revenues). This diverse segment includes Crescent Vert jewelry, jeweled watches, dental and orthopedic implants, other dental and medical equipment, solar energy systems, kerosene water heaters, and ceramic knives and scissors.

Fine Ceramic Parts and Other Products (8 percent of revenues). Included in this segment are hybrid substrates, cathode holders, and other parts for machine tools, fiber optics, pumps, and other industries. The company also makes automotive components, such as ceramic rotors for turbochargers.

TOP EXECUTIVES

- Kazuo Inamori, chairman
- Kinju Anjo, vice chairman
- Kensuke Itoh, president
- Sadao Yamamoto, senior managing director
- Katsumi Nishimura, senior managing director
- Masao Kadota, senior managing director
- Shoichi Hamamoto, senior managing director
- Marshall D. Butler, chief executive of AVX Corporation

OUTSIDE DIRECTORS

- Stuart Lubitz, chairman of the law firm Spensley Horn Jubas & Lubitz

FINANCIAL DATA

Revenues (in millions of yen) (years ending March 31)

1991	461,233
1990	421,032
1989	391,099
1988	344,177
1987	309,595

Net Income (in millions of yen) (years ending March 31)

1991	32,250
1990	33,827
1989	33,293
1988	25,170
1987	17,905

GEOGRAPHICAL BREAKDOWN

Revenues (in millions of yen)

Year*	Japan		United States		Elsewhere	
1991	352,115	(60%)	119,952	(20%)	113,963	(19%)
1990	317,494	(61%)	111,772	(21%)	93,354	(18%)
1989	303,916	(64%)	104,327	(22%)	68,008	(14%)
1988	274,639	(65%)	91,584	(22%)	55,793	(13%)

*Fiscal year ends March 31.

Operating Profit (in millions of yen)

Year*	Japan		United States		Elsewhere	
1991	52,894	(91%)	1,794	(3%)	3,621	(6%)
1990	56,107	(79%)	6,225	(8%)	8,616	(12%)
1989	56,508	(78%)	8,947	(12%)	6,679	(9%)
1988	48,987	(81%)	6,628	(11%)	4,521	(8%)

*Fiscal year ends March 31.

LABOR RELATIONS

Kyocera founder Kazuo Inamori has always made great demands on his employees and has insisted on complete devotion. This apparently extends past death, given that Kyocera established a company cemetery. The work force is organized into "amoebas"—flexible, relatively autonomous teams.

Such policies were not looked kindly upon by the labor union at Cybernet, the CB radio maker acquired by Kyocera in 1979. An article in the U.S. business magazine *Forbes* in 1985 suggests that many of the public relations problems the company was having were due to leaks of embarrassing information by officials at that union.

ENVIRONMENTAL RECORD

Kyocera professes to be driven by "green" considerations in its design and production activities, and the company takes pride in its production of solar energy products. Its AVX subsidiary, however, was a defendant in federal and state actions brought against a group of companies in connection with PCB contamination in New Bedford, Massachusetts. In 1990 AVX reached an agreement with government authorities on a plan for the company to pay at least $66 million for clean-up operations at the Superfund site.

In 1992 Kyocera introduced a new laser printer that employed a permanent ceramic print engine and thus eliminated disposable cartridges.

BIBLIOGRAPHY

Halberstam, David. *The Next Century*. New York: William Morrow, 1991.

LEVI STRAUSS & COMPANY

1155 Battery Street
San Francisco, California 94111
(415) 544-6000

1991 revenues: $4.9 billion (year ending November 25)
1991 net income: $356.7 million
Privately held company
Employees: 32,100
Founded: 1853

OVERVIEW

Levi Strauss has been a major force in the transformation of the way the world dresses. Selling a product that was once mainly of appeal to manual laborers and cowboys, the company's blue jeans have become a key element in the move toward casual clothing that has swept many societies. Those durable trousers are also a leading symbol of U.S. culture, and as such, they have grown in popularity with the spreading appeal of things American.

Now the world's largest brand-name apparel manufacturer, with subsidiaries in twenty-three countries outside the United States, Levi Strauss has had to contend with declining blue jeans sales in its home country. Since going private in 1985 the company has met this challenge by ruthlessly cutting costs and introducing nondenim lines of casual clothing.

HISTORY

While still a teenager Levi Strauss sailed from Germany in 1847 to work for the dry goods business his older brothers had established in New York City. He was first put to work as an itinerant peddler, but in 1853 he moved to San Francisco to take advantage of the gold rush–induced boom—and to enjoy the greater tolerance of Jews that existed in that city.

Starting with a modest operation on the docks, Strauss built a successful firm, Levi Strauss & Company, that sold a wide range of clothing and dry goods. Among his customers were miners and laborers who demanded sturdy trousers, which Strauss fashioned out of tent canvas.

During this time, a tailor from the Baltic city of Riga, who was born Jacob Youphes but changed his last name to Davis when he came to America, was seeking to make his fortune. After failing at a number of ventures, he ended up tailoring in Reno, Nevada. In 1870 it occurred to him to use rivets to attach pockets to work pants more securely. The reinforced trousers caught on, but Davis did not have the money either to expand distribution or to patent the invention.

So in 1872 he sent a letter to the company that supplied his canvas, Levi Strauss & Company, proposing that the firm pay the $68 for the patent application in exchange for certain marketing rights. The dry goods company readily accepted the offer and soon set up a relationship with Davis in which it did all of the selling while he concentrated on production. Demand for the trousers, now made from denim (a corruption of *serge de Nîmes*—serge of Nîmes, France) colored with indigo dye, took off.

Control of the company, which enjoyed steady growth over the following decades, passed to the Stern family after the death of Levi Strauss in 1902. Strauss, who had never married, had long been pressured by his older sister Fanny to bequeath the business to his nephews—Fanny and her husband's children. Fanny's husband, David Stern, had been a partner in the company until his death in 1874.

After the earthquake of 1906 leveled the company's facilities, the Stern brothers rebuilt their offices as quickly as possible and also constructed a large factory, which was run by Jacob Davis's son Simon. While the younger Davis was something of a bon vivant, in 1912 he came up with the idea of a sturdy, one-piece garment for children, made, of course, from denim. Known as the Koverall, this product was the company's first to be distributed on a national basis.

The company's profitability began to erode around the time of World War I, and the Sterns seriously considered liquidating the operation. Yet Sigmund Stern's son-in-law Walter Haas accepted an offer to take over management of the firm and revive it. Haas brought in his brother-in-law Daniel Koshland to help in the task, which included coming to grips with the apparent fact that Simon Davis was not keeping close control on costs and that Davis's pet product, the Koverall, actually was losing money.

Haas and Koshland turned things around, and Davis resigned. The recovery, however, was interrupted by the depression, which the company survived by reducing costs through, among other things, putting its workers on short-time schedules. After World War II the company made the somewhat bold decision to expand into less-sturdy garments for casual wear.

Yet it was a movie star who was responsible for propelling the company into the business hall of fame. That actor was James Dean, whose Levi's became an essential part of his image as a youthful iconoclast, especially after his death in an auto accident in 1955. The antiestablishment mystique of blue jeans was reinforced by Marlon Brando's attire (which also included a leather jacket) in the film *The Wild Ones*.

The result was that Levi's were no longer identified primarily with cowboys and manual laborers, becoming a symbol of defiant youth instead. The company was encouraged to put more emphasis on its sportswear and in 1959 introduced the first preshrunk jeans. The cultural advantage continued during the following decade as blue jeans, especially the Levi's 501, became the uniform of the student movement and the counterculture.

Such developments encouraged Levi Strauss, now run by Walter Haas, Jr., to pay attention to foreign markets for the first time. In the early 1960s the company established a network of local distributors in Europe and purchased 75 percent of the dominant maker of blue jeans in Canada. Production was extended overseas as well.

Meanwhile, at home the company extended its product line with White Levi's, corduroy pants, and its first line of apparel for women. The company, which went public in 1971, also began licensing its name for such products as shoes and socks.

Then the company began devoting increasing portions of its resources to nonjean operations, both through acquisitions and start-ups. The motivation for the shift was clear—there were signs that the blue jeans market was maturing. But in many cases the new businesses were poorly chosen and ill fated. By the early 1980s the company was fleeing from the higher-priced, more fashionable markets it had entered and was putting emphasis once again on its traditional wares. This included substantial promotional efforts (especially in connection with the 1984 Olympics) and the formation of distribution links with Sears, Roebuck and J.C. Penney.

These efforts were made easier by the new popularity of jeans brought on by the clothes worn by John Travolta in the movie *Urban Cowboy*. But that was something of a flash in the pan. Blue jeans sales began to decline as clothing tastes of the young became more eclectic and a less egalitarian sense of style began to take hold in much of the population.

To try to recover some lost ground the company created a bunch of in-house entrepreneurs and asked them to come up with new product ideas. Then, in a step designed to remove the company from the short-term pressures of the stock market, a group of family members took the company private in a leveraged buyout in 1985. Being family-owned once again seems to suit Levi Strauss. During the late 1980s both sales and profits rose smartly, helped by a further streamlining of operations and by the success of a new line of casual clothes called Dockers.

With the Dockers line Levi Strauss also expanded the portion of its manufacturing that is done abroad. The company has been one of the most active exploiters of a U.S. customs provision called Tariff Item 807, which allows an American company to do some aspects of production overseas and then import the semifinished items back home and pay duties only on the value added abroad.

The company also is relying more on foreign sales, which have reached 39 percent of revenues. Taking advantage of the popularity of American culture in much of the world these days, Levi Strauss runs many of its ads abroad in English and uses symbols like James Dean. The company also takes advantage of the fact that in countries like France and Japan its blue jeans are considered more fashionable than they are at home. Most recently it has been looking to the jeans-starved population of Eastern Europe and the former Soviet Union as the next major growth area. In 1991 the first Rumanian shop to sell Levi's officially opened to large crowds. That same year the company invested $20 million in a jeans manufacturing and distribution business in Poland.

OPERATIONS

Men's Jeans (29 percent of 1991 sales). This segment, limited to domestic sales, represents the flagship operations of the company. It consists of the 501 family of jeans as well as the Red Tab and Silver Tab product lines. The closest competitor to Levi Strauss is VF Corporation, which makes Wrangler, Lee, and Rustler jeans.

Menswear (15 percent of sales). This segment consists of casual and dress slacks and branded knit and woven shirts. These sell under the names Dockers, Levi's for Men, Levi's Action, Levi's San Francisco, and Sutter Creek.

Womenswear (7 percent of sales). This segment consists of jeans and casual sportswear products sold under the 501, Dockers, Bend Over, and Levi's 900 Series names.

Britannia Sportswear (2 percent of sales). This operation, purchased in 1987, includes men's and women's jeans, tops, and casual sportswear sold under the Britannia, Brittgear, and Brittfitt labels.

Youthwear (7 percent of sales). This segment includes jeans and other casual products sold under the Dockers, Girls 900 Series, and Little Levi's names.

Levi Strauss International (39 percent of sales). This operation markets jeans and related apparel outside the United States. It is divided into divisions covering Canada, Latin America, Europe, and Asia and the Pacific. The company has affiliates in Australia, Belgium, Brazil, Canada, Denmark, Finland, France, Germany, Greece, Holland, Hong Kong, Italy, Japan, Malaysia, Mexico, New Zealand, Norway, the Philippines, Poland, Spain, Sweden, Switzerland, and the United Kingdom.

TOP EXECUTIVES

- Robert D. Haas, chairman and chief executive
- Peter E. Haas, Sr., chairman of the executive committee of the board of directors
- Thomas W. Tusher, president and chief operating officer

OUTSIDE DIRECTORS

- Tully M. Friedman, general partner in the private investment banking firm Hellman & Friedman
- James C. Gaither, partner in the law firm Cooley Godward Castro Huddleson & Tatum
- F. Warren Hellman, general partner in the private investment banking firm Hellman & Friedman
- John F. Kilmartin, principal of the retail-consulting firm Kilmartin Management
- James M. Koshland, partner in the law firm Ware & Freidenrich
- Patricia S. Pineda, general counsel of New United Motor Manufacturing, Inc.

Also on the board are Walter A. Haas, Jr., father of Robert D. Haas; and Rhoda H. Goldman, sister of Walter and Peter Haas; and Peter Haas, Jr.

FINANCIAL DATA

Sales (in millions of dollars) (years ending November 25)

1991	4,903
1990	4,247
1989	3,628
1988	3,117
1987	2,867

Net Income (in millions of dollars) (years ending November 25)

1991	357
1990	251
1989	272
1988	112
1987	135

GEOGRAPHICAL BREAKDOWN

Sales (in millions of dollars)

Year*	United States		Foreign	
1991	2,982	(61%)	1,894	(39%)
1990	2,561	(60%)	1,686	(40%)
1989	2,395	(66%)	1,233	(34%)

*Fiscal year ends in late November.

LABOR RELATIONS

When Levi Strauss and Jacob Davis first began selling riveted pants in the 1870s, the garments were made by seamstresses working in their homes on a piece-rate basis. But these domestic workers were unable to keep up with the growing demand for the product, so manufacturing was transferred to a workshop, where the piecework system continued to be used. Unlike many other California garment producers of the day, Levi Strauss avoided hiring Chinese workers.

Over the following decades the company adopted a policy of paternalism and was a strong opponent of unions. During the 1920s the Sterns were leaders of a business effort to drive unions out of San Francisco. During the wave of unionization in the 1930s, the company at first fought hard to remain an open shop. This position cost the company sales, since the building trades and other unions were urging workers to wear only union-made clothes. But in 1935, under the threat of a strike, management decided to recognize the United Garment Workers, which had authorization cards from a majority of the firm's production workers. The company did, however, draw the line at putting a union label on its products.

To encourage workers to identify with the company, Levi Strauss later introduced employee stock-option and profit-sharing plans. For this and other reasons, the company has experienced few strikes in its history and generally has good relations with its main union, the Amalgamated Clothing and Textile Workers.

Since the leveraged buyout, however, the company has closed dozens of plants and either automated or moved abroad many of the remaining jobs. In 1990, for example, the firm closed an eleven-hundred-worker plant in San Antonio, Texas, and moved the work to a lower-wage facility in the Caribbean. The workers, most of them Latina, formed a group called La Fuerza Unida, which launched a boycott of the company's products to protest the shutdown.

BIBLIOGRAPHY

Cray, Ed. *Levi's*. Boston: Houghton Mifflin, 1978.

LUCKY-GOLDSTAR GROUP

Major affiliate:

Goldstar Company, Ltd.
Lucky-Goldstar Twin Towers 20
Yoido-Dong, Youngdungpo-Gu
Seoul 150-721
South Korea
(02) 787-1114

1991 revenues: $4.9 billion
1991 net income: $24.8 million
Publicly traded company
Employees: 32,000
Founded: Lucky-Goldstar was founded in 1947, Goldstar Company
     in 1958

OVERVIEW

Goldstar is the electronics company—and the best-known portion abroad—of the Lucky-Goldstar conglomerate, one of the leading *chaebol* that dominate the South Korean economy. Lucky started out modestly enough, making face cream, but in the mid-1950s the Koo family–dominated group decided to follow the Japanese into the electronics export business.

Like Samsung, Goldstar started out supplying items like radios and televisions to U.S. retailers for sale under store brand names. But later the company began selling under its own name, and in recent years Goldstar has been attempting to move out of the low-end ghetto and into sophisticated markets like high-definition television and digital audio tape recorders. Goldstar's purchase of a 5-percent stake in Zenith in 1991 and the establishment of cooperative relations with the U.S. electronics company are part of this effort.

HISTORY

The Lucky-Goldstar Group began with the creation of the Lucky Chemical Company by In-Hwoi Koo in 1947. The firm began by making face creams and soon expanded to combs, toothbrushes, and other plastic items, including containers for the face cream. During the early 1950s it added toothpaste and laundry detergent.

From this modest base the company decided in the mid-1950s to emulate the Japanese and get into the business of producing and exporting electrical products. This was done through the formation of Goldstar Company Ltd. in 1958, which started out making fans. Within a year it became the first Korean company to manufacture radios (albeit unsophisticated ones), which were initially sold only in the domestic market. By the mid-1960s Goldstar, enjoying government loans and strict import controls, also was making the first refrigerators and television sets to be produced in the country. Washing machines and air conditioners soon followed. Once its products became more sophisticated, Goldstar started to export them, especially to countries like the United States, where they were supplied initially to retailers that sold them under their own brand names. By the late 1970s Goldstar, the most outward oriented of the Lucky-Goldstar companies, was exporting the equivalent of more than $100 million a year.

Lucky Chemical, meanwhile, formed a joint venture with Continental Carbon to make carbon black, used in producing rubber. It also built the first private oil refinery in Korea (in partnership with Caltex Petroleum). During the 1970s what became known as the Lucky-Goldstar Group created several dozen subsidiaries in a variety of fields, thus turning itself into a leading *chaebol*. Today the conglomerate includes, aside from Goldstar, more than three dozen companies involved in chemicals (Korea's largest company in the field), drugs, cosmetics, oil refining, oil exploration (in partnership with Chevron), petrochemicals, cables and wires, metals, insurance, construction, and other activities.

In recent years the group has grown, in part, by forming a series of joint ventures with the likes of AT&T (which helped Goldstar get into semiconductors), Dow Corning, Honeywell, Englehard, and Siemens. Following the lead of Japanese companies, Goldstar opened manufacturing facilities abroad, beginning with a television assembly plant in Huntsville, Alabama, that later expanded to microwave ovens. During the early 1980s it was the first Korean company to manufacture personal computers, compact disc players, and 8-mm camcorders. Yet Goldstar has not been an innovator in electronics. Its VCR, for example, came about through reverse engineering of Japanese models and some assistance from RCA. Goldstar had a long-standing relationship with Hitachi, but the Japanese company declined to share its VCR and camcorder technology.

Starting in the late 1980s, Lucky-Goldstar, like the other *chaebol*, came under increasing criticism for its dominant role in the Korean economy as well as for specific sins like driving up land prices. Emboldened by the end of authoritarian rule, workers organized themselves and succeeded in pushing up pay levels. This prompted Goldstar to shift some of its production to lower-wage bastions in Thailand and the Philippines. Lucky-Goldstar also brought in the U.S. consultant McKinsey & Company to develop a strategy that decentralized control and did not depend on being the lowest-cost producer. In 1991 the Korean government called on the *chaebol* to focus their activities, and Lucky-Goldstar responded by saying that it would specialize in electronics and petrochemicals.

Since 1988 the Goldstar part of the group has had to deal with a slump in its crucial exports to the United States. Its electronics business, which had been overtaken by that of rival Samsung, was suffering from rigid management and technical problems in its VCRs. By the early 1990s Goldstar was trying to revive itself by heavy promotion of its products, which have been upgraded with such enhancements as stereo sound for its color TVs.

In February 1991 the company bought a 5-percent share in Zenith Electronics, which had long promoted itself as the only remaining U.S.-owned producer of television sets. Also part of the deal were an agreement by Goldstar to promote Zenith's high-definition TV technology, especially in South Korea, and a licensing arrangement in which Goldstar would use Zenith technology for making flat picture tubes in its own TV sets. It later came out that the deal, the first major investment by a Korean company in a U.S. corporation, might involve more extensive joint development, manufacturing, and other activities.

OPERATIONS

Goldstar Company

Televisions (18 percent of 1990 revenues). Goldstar was the first Korean company to produce television sets and the first to export them. Its color TV plant in South Korea has a capacity of five million units a year. Additional manufacturing facilities are located in the United States, Germany, Mexico, and Malaysia. While export sales to the United States and Japan have declined, sales to the former Soviet Union and Eastern Europe have been on the rise.

Audio and Video Equipment (21 percent of revenues). The company makes radio-cassette players, CD players, stereo systems, VCRs, camcorders, and other audio and video devices. It has been moving into more sophisticated equipment, including digital audiotape recorders, CD-ROM players, digital pianos, and color video printers. In 1991 it signed a deal with the government of Libya to establish a VCR factory in that country.

Home Appliances (29 percent of revenues). Goldstar makes a variety of household appliances, including refrigerators, washing machines, microwave ovens, dishwashers, vacuum cleaners, air conditioners, fans, and heaters. The company is making some of these devices, especially washing machines and microwave ovens, more sophisticated through the addition of artificial intelligence features known as fuzzy logic.

Computer and Office Automation Equipment (12 percent of revenues). Starting with basic personal computers in the early 1980s, Goldstar now makes a variety of PCs, minicomputers, photocopiers, fax machines, cellular telephones, laser printers, and banking terminals. The company is seeking to move into advanced areas like color laser printers and computer-aided design.

Magnetic Recording Media (4 percent of revenues). Goldstar produces audiotapes, videotapes, computer disks, and magnetic cards. In 1990 its output included one hundred million videocassettes, one hundred million audiocassettes, and thirty million computer disks.

Components and Other Products (15 percent of revenues). The company produces a wide range of electrical and electronic components, including color picture tubes, cathode-ray tubes, magnetrons, compressors, and motors. The company also makes cameras (in a joint venture with Japan's Canon) and pumps.

TOP EXECUTIVES

Goldstar Company
- Hun-Jo Lee, president and chief executive
- Kwan-Hi Choe, executive vice president
- In-Ku Kang, executive vice president
- John Koo, executive vice president
- Yong-Ak Ro, executive vice president

FINANCIAL DATA

Goldstar Company

Revenues (in millions of Korean won)

1991	3,683,000
1990	2,978,602
1989	2,684,278

Net Income (in millions of Korean won)

1991	18,456
1990	33,653
1989	18,037

GEOGRAPHICAL BREAKDOWN

Net Sales (in millions of Korean won)

Year	Domestic		Overseas	
1990	1,505,394	(50%)	1,478,625	(50%)
1989	1,226,820	(47%)	1,378,168	(53%)
1988	1,031,613	(37%)	1,793,661	(63%)

LABOR RELATIONS

Lucky-Goldstar, like the other *chaebol*, was assisted in its growth by government policies that suppressed unionization of workers and encouraged low wages. That repressive system began to collapse with the strike wave that swept South Korea beginning in 1987. Lucky-Goldstar was not as hard hit as Hyundai was, for example, by the labor unrest. Yet in 1989 there were strikes at Goldstar's electronics operations, including some violent clashes between workers and police. The work stoppages that year cost the company some $600 million in lost production.

BIBLIOGRAPHY

Amsden, Alice H. *Asia's Next Giant: South Korea & Late Industrialization*. Oxford: Oxford University Press,1989.
Kearney, Robert P. *The Warrior Worker: The Challenge of the Korean Way of Working*. New York: Henry Holt, 1991.
Min-Ju No-Jo: South Korea's New Trade Unions. Hong Kong: Asia Monitor Resource Center, 1988.
Steers, Richard M., Yoo Keun Shin, and Gerardo R. Ungson. *The Chaebol: Korea's New Industrial Might*. Cambridge, Mass.: Ballinger, 1989.

MATSUSHITA ELECTRIC INDUSTRIAL COMPANY, LTD.

1006, Kadoma, Osaka
Japan
(06) 908-1121

1991 revenues: $46.9 billion (year ending March 31)
1991 net income: $1.8 billion
Publicly traded company
Employees: 210,848
Founded: 1918

OVERVIEW

Matsushita, one of the world's largest consumer electronics companies, followed its archrival Sony in moving from entertainment hardware to software by purchasing the U.S. company MCA, parent of Universal Pictures. Imitating, in fact, has always been Matsushita's strong suit. It has allowed more innovative companies like Sony to develop new products and then it has moved in to capture market share through lower prices.

The company was founded by self-made man Konosuke Matsushita, who supported Japan's militarists but after retiring devoted himself to promoting a homespun philosophy of Peace and Happiness through Prosperity. He died in 1989 at age ninety-four.

Matsushita has a huge list of products—from compact disc players to bicycles—sold all over the world, and it operates more than 350 manufacturing facilities throughout Japan, Southeast Asia, Europe, and North America. In recent years it has moved from the maturing consumer electronics arena to new businesses like industrial automation, semiconductors, and satellite equipment.

HISTORY

Matsushita Electric was the product of the ambitions of a man named Ko-nosuke Matsushita, who dropped out of school at the age of nine and began his business career. Working to help support his family—his farmer father had lost their savings speculating on commodity futures—Matsushita first took a job with a bicycle shop, and as a teenager he was hired by the Osaka Electric Company.

In 1918, at the age of twenty-three, he was ready to strike out on his own. With his wife and her brother, Matsushita formed a small company to produce electric adapter plugs. They slowly built the venture, and by the early 1920s they diversified into bicycle lights and electric heaters. To these Matsushita later added radios, batteries, electric motors, and light bulbs. The operation was incorporated as Matsushita Electric Industrial Company in 1935.

During the 1930s Matsushita was an ardent supporter of the militarist forces that came to dominate Japanese politics, and his company was rewarded with easy access to new foreign markets opened as a result of the country's expansionist policies. In turn, the company produced a variety of products for the military, including wooden planes and ships.

After the war the American occupation forces removed Matsushita from his position with the company as punishment for his support of the Japanese war effort. The company deteriorated in his absence, and thanks to pressure from his employees, the American authorities finally reinstated him in 1950.

The founder wasted no time reviving the company. He began producing television sets, washing machines, refrigerators, and vacuum cleaners, enjoying steady growth along with the recovery of the Japanese economy. A 1952 joint venture with the Dutch electronics company Philips gave Matsushita access to the latest technology. During this time, Matsushita purchased a 50-percent interest in the ailing Japan Victor Company, but JVC's management remained independent. Matsushita also pioneered the use of five-year business plans in Japan.

By the early 1960s Matsushita—which had added tape recorders and stereos to its product list—was the leading appliance maker in Japan. Its products, sold mostly under the National brand, were priced low in order to build customer loyalty. To keep those prices down, Matsushita was one of the first Japanese companies to cut production costs by setting up manufacturing operations in less-developed countries such as Taiwan.

On the sales end, the company also was beginning to establish a presence in the United States through a subsidiary formed in 1959. By the mid-1960s Matsushita's Panasonic and Technics brands were becoming well known to American consumers, even if the company itself remained obscure. In 1974 Matsushita acquired the television division of Motorola, thereby adding Quasar to its stable of brands—though Motorola's market share problems persisted. Matsushita also moved into air conditioners and microwave ovens.

During the early 1970s the company was developing a home video system for recording and playing television programs on cassettes. When Matsushita executive Akio Tanii, who headed the VCR effort (and now leads the company), saw JVC's version of the technology, he decided that it was better. Thus he persuaded his superiors to delay entering the market until JVC's Video Home System, or VHS, could be perfected. This meant allowing competitor Sony, which had a different system called Betamax, to bring out the first product.

The Betamax initially caused quite a stir, but it was overwhelmed when JVC and Matsushita entered the market, along with a slew of other manufacturers (including RCA, General Electric, Philips, and Toshiba) that were allowed to license the VHS system. In one of Sony's rare failures, Betamax lost out to VHS in the race to become the industry standard.

By the 1980s there were fewer opportunities for growth in consumer electronics, so Matsushita turned to such areas as semiconductors, factory automation, and business machines. At the same time, it continued to expand its core businesses abroad, setting up new production facilities in such countries as Spain, Germany, and China.

Yet the company's most dramatic move came in 1990, when it acquired the U.S. company MCA, parent of Universal Pictures. In making the $6-billion purchase, Matsushita followed a path blazed by archrival Sony, which the year before had paid more than $3 billion for another Hollywood studio, Columbia Pictures. Matsushita's deal was the largest American investment ever made by a Japanese company.

MCA, which started out as a small talent agency in 1924, was built by Lew Wasserman into one of the leading entertainment companies. It got into films in 1962 with its purchase of Decca Records, then owner of Universal Pictures. Universal, which had emerged in the 1920s as one of the second-tier major studios (it did production and distribution but owned no theaters), did not have many big stars under contract before 1940 and originally made its name by creating the horror genre with such films as *Frankenstein* and *Dracula*. After being taken over by MCA, Universal took the lead among film studios in television production, and by the mid-1970s it was making more than 25 percent of prime-time programs. In the 1980s Universal enjoyed a comeback in films with *E.T.* and several other hits. MCA, which had long been rumored to have organized-crime connections, had been looking for a merger partner for several years when Matsushita came along.

OPERATIONS

Matsushita did not begin consolidating MCA until after the end of its 1991 fiscal year.

Video Equipment (26 percent of 1991 revenues). Matsushita leads the world in the production of videocassette recorders and related equipment sold primarily under the Panasonic name. The company is a leading producer of conventional television sets (with screens as large as forty-three inches) and large-screen projection television systems. It also makes videodisc players and satellite broadcast receivers. In 1991 Matsushita decided to cooperate with Sony and Hitachi in the development of the next generation of VCRs.

Audio Equipment (9 percent of revenues). The company produces a wide range of radio receivers, stereo equipment, audiocassette recorders, radio-cassette combinations, compact disc players, digital audio tape recorders, car audio products, and electronic musical instruments. Matsushita gave its support in 1991 to a new system of digital compact cassettes developed by Philips.

Home Appliances (14 percent of revenues). This segment includes refrigerators, freezers, air conditioners, washing machines, dryers, vacuum cleaners, microwave and conventional ovens, food processors, and electric heaters. To increase demand in this area Matsushita has introduced such products as larger refrigerators, low-noise room air conditioners, fuzzy logic–controlled washing machines, and cordless steam irons. In 1991 the company opened a high-tech kitchen appliance showroom in Tokyo that allowed customers to use virtual-reality devices to experience what their dream kitchen would look and feel like.

Communications and Industrial Equipment (23 percent of revenues). In this fast-growing segment the company makes facsimile machines (for which Panasonic has about 18 percent of the market), word processors, personal computers, workstations, plain paper copiers, optical disc filing systems, PBX and cellular telephone equipment, industrial robots, vending machines, broadcasting equipment, and numerous other related products. In 1991 the company agreed to supply laptop computers to a joint venture involving AT&T and Marubeni Corporation, and it announced plans to produce PCs at a Texas factory in cooperation with Tandy Corporation.

Electronic Components (13 percent of revenues). Matsushita produces integrated circuits, charge-coupled devices, transistors, resistors, magnetic-recording heads, cathode-ray tubes, and other electronic items. In 1990 the company established its first semiconductor operation in the United States by purchasing a plant from National Semiconductor Corporation.

Batteries, Kitchen-related Products, and Other Products (15 percent of revenues). The company makes dry batteries, automobile batteries, solar batteries, gas hot water supply systems, and gas cooking appliances. Other products include bicycles, cameras, electric pencil sharpeners, and water purifiers.

With the acquistion of MCA the company added the following to its roster: film and television production and distribution operations; the Universal Studios theme parks in California and Florida; a strong book-publishing operation, including the highly successful G. P. Putnam imprint; and an $800-million record business (which may not include the legendary Motown label, whose owners announced plans in 1991 to terminate their relationship with MCA). Also, in 1991 Universal Pictures agreed to join with the French pay-TV service Canal Plus to coproduce films for worldwide distribution.

TOP EXECUTIVES

- Masaharu Matsushita, chairman
- Akio Tanii, president
- Hiroyuki Mizuno, executive vice president
- Tsuzo Morishita, executive vice president

OUTSIDE DIRECTORS

- Kyonosuke Ibe, adviser to the Sumitomo Bank, Ltd.
- Sohei Nakayama, special adviser to the Industrial Bank of Japan

FINANCIAL DATA

Revenues (in millions of yen) (years ending March 31)

1991	6,599,306
1990	6,002,786
1989	5,504,250
1988	5,067,188
1987	1,572,241*

*Figures for 1987 represent operations for only four months because of the switch from a fiscal year ending in November to one ending March 31.

Net Income (in millions of yen) (years ending March 31)

1991	258,914
1990	235,561
1989	213,462
1988	164,623
1987	49,423*

*Figures for 1987 represent operations for only four months because of the switch from a fiscal year ending in November to one ending March 31.

GEOGRAPHICAL BREAKDOWN

Revenues (in billions of yen)

Year*	Domestic		Foreign	
1991	3,632	(55%)	2,967	(45%)
1990	3,382	(56%)	2,621	(44%)
1989	3,207	(58%)	2,297	(42%)
1988	2,966	(59%)	2,101	(41%)

*Fiscal year ends March 31.

LABOR RELATIONS

Matsushita workers in Japan are widely represented by the Matsushita Electric Industrial Workers Union, an enterprise union that is affiliated with the All-Japan Electric Equipment Workers Union. The union, which has more than eighty thousand members, traditionally has pursued a cooperative relationship with management and was in fact key to the reinstatement of founder Konosuke Matsushita after his removal by Allied authorities following World War II.

The company's overseas operations have not been heavily unionized except in Britain, Indonesia, and Malaysia—the latter occurring in the late 1980s after the Malaysian government ended its policy of prohibiting unionization in the electronics industry. In the United States, the Teamsters and the International Brotherhood of Electrical Workers have organized employees at several Matsushita operations.

In 1991 a federal court in the United States found that Matsushita's Quasar subsidiary had discriminated against non-Japanese employees. The company, which was ordered to pay damages of $2.5 million, said it would appeal the ruling.

ENVIRONMENTAL RECORD

Matsushita is one of the numerous electronics companies that have announced plans to phase out the use of solvents made of ozone-destroying CFCs. The company has said that it will end its CFC use by 1995.

BIBLIOGRAPHY

Gould, Rowland. *The Matsushita Phenomenon*. Tokyo: Diamond Sha, 1970.
Workers, Unions and International Solidarity in Matsushita. Geneva: International Metalworkers Federation, 1988.
Yamashita, Toshihiko. *The Panasonic Way: From a Chief Executive's Desk*. Tokyo and New York: Kodansha International, 1987.

McDONALD'S CORPORATION

McDonald's Plaza
Oak Brook, Illinois 60521
(708) 575-3000

1991 revenues: $6.7 billion
1991 net income: $860 million
Publicly traded company
Employees: 168,000
Founded: 1955

OVERVIEW

McDonald's is the pioneer and behemoth of the fast-food industry. For the past three decades the company's restaurants have transformed eating habits in the United States and, increasingly, in many other parts of the world. Homemade food and local eateries have been overwhelmed by the standardized and predictable, yet highly popular, fare produced and served with assembly-line efficiency in some twelve thousand restaurants. During the 1980s more than five hundred new outlets a year were opened.

Two indicators of the company's status in sociological and business terms: the original outlet in the McDonald's chain, in Des Plaines, Illinois, has been turned into a museum; and the shares of McDonald's Corporation are now part of the elite group that make up the Dow Jones Industrial Average.

While McDonald's still remains the clear industry leader, in the late 1980s the magic started to disappear, at least in its home country. Sales in the United States began to stagnate, thanks to intensified competition and a decline in the American penchant for hamburgers. While the company has been forced to cut costs to deal with this problem, McDonald's continues to perform well abroad. It is now in more than fifty countries, and nearly 40 percent of systemwide sales come from outside the United States. One of the most successful restaurants is the seven-hundred-seat outlet in Moscow, which is widely regarded as a symbol of the Westernization of the Russian economy. A similar outpost was established in Beijing in 1992.

HISTORY

Ray Kroc, the man responsible for the McDonald's phenomenon, was a some-time piano player and paper cup salesman. He was fifty-two and a distributor of milkshake machines when he had a pivotal experience in 1954. It occurred while he was visiting a customer, the McDonald Brothers, who operated a roadside hamburger stand in San Bernardino, California.

Kroc was astounded to see the volume of business the McDonalds did in serving up burgers, french fries, and milkshakes with factorylike efficiency. While the brothers were content with their modest success, Kroc imagined a string of such establishments across the country. He signed a deal with the McDonalds, under which Kroc got the right to use their name and techniques in franchising the concept and the brothers would get a bit more than a quarter of the 1.9 percent of the franchisee's gross, to be collected by Kroc.

The McDonald's concept was an immediate success. The number of stores quickly went from dozens to hundreds, and the number of hamburgers sold—displayed on the golden arches sign—soared into the millions and later the billions. Kroc set down strict rules by which the stands had to be operated; in fact, he turned the management of a McDonald's into a kind of science, the principles of which were taught to aspiring store managers at an institution called Hamburger University.

The system devised by Kroc amounted to the industrialization of food service—the use of equipment and procedures that were so defined that an inexperienced teenager (the preferred employee) could be inserted into the system and function with no difficulty. The result was a perfectly tuned machine turning out food in a wholesome and unthreatening environment. Kroc summarized his approach as "Quality, Service, Cleanliness, and Value."

McDonald's success served as the catalyst for the emergence of a national fast-food industry. The diners and greasy spoons that had lined the country's roads were steadily replaced by the familiar outlets of a small number of major chains. The go-go atmosphere of fast food in the 1960s brought the business to the attention of large corporations. Pillsbury acquired Burger King in 1967, General Foods bought the Burger Chef chain in 1968, and Heublein purchased Kentucky Fried Chicken in 1971. Later PepsiCo acquired Pizza Hut and Taco Bell and Hershey Foods bought Friendly Ice Cream Corporation.

Growth continued in the 1970s, helped by demographic changes such as the migration of more women into the paid labor market and by economic changes like the sharp rise in the cost of food used to prepare meals at home. By spending large sums on marketing and advertising, the chains were able to turn fast-food "dining" into a socially acceptable way for a family to feed itself. Employing such devices as the Ronald McDonald character, Mc-Donald's in particular gained the loyalty of children, who became increasingly influential in determining where a family was going to eat out. In 1972 McDonald's reached $1 billion in total store sales and surpassed the U.S. Army as the nation's biggest dispenser of meals.

The dominance of McDonald's in the hamburger business began to be challenged in the 1970s. After initially holding back the necessary investment in Burger King, Pillsbury gave its subsidiary the money to compete more effectively with the industry leader. At the same time, an executive of Arthur Treacher's Fish & Chips decided to establish a chain that would serve higher-quality and more-substantial burgers than the ones sold by McDonald's. R. David Thomas named the firm after his daughter, and Wendy's eventually became one of the largest chains in the country.

The contest intensified in the 1980s. Burger King introduced successful nonhamburger menu items and in 1982 initiated the aggressive advertising campaign that came to be known as the Battle of the Burgers. Later Wendy's joined the fray with its now-famous "Where's the beef?" commercials, which exploited the fact that McDonald's had traditionally been stingy with the portion of meat in its hamburgers.

These assaults shook up McDonald's, but the industry leader continued to grow at a handsome rate, thanks in part to popular new offerings, such as the Egg McMuffin (which opened the breakfast market to the chains), Chicken McNuggets, and, later, the McD.L.T. The chain reached the milestone of ten thousand outlets in 1988.

At the same time McDonald's was gaining ground, Burger King was slipping in what the industry calls "share of stomach." A series of ill-fated ad campaigns and an inability to maintain consistently high standards among its outlets kept Burger King's average sales per store flat during the second half of the 1980s. Britain's Grand Metropolitan, which purchased Burger King's parent, Pillsbury, in 1988, installed a new management team and began a restructuring program, but the chain continued to suffer.

While McDonald's has done a good job at keeping ahead of the competition, all has not been well in the market they share. The burger business in particular no longer has a sizzling rate of growth, and increasing numbers of customers are getting tired of the same old fare. The growing concern about nutrition and the revival of sophisticated dining among yuppies and other groups have cast a fair amount of disrepute on fast food.

McDonald's has responded by upgrading its restaurants with a more sophisticated decor and ambience aimed at attracting diners interested in an evening out rather than just a quick bite. The dinner market also has been pursued through experiments with new menu items, such as pizza, spaghetti, spare ribs, grilled steak, and chicken fajitas. At the same time, McDonald's joined with its competitors in attracting business by discounting prices.

McDonald's has become increasingly dependent on foreign operations. Sales outside the United States rose from 19 percent of the total in 1980 to 35 percent a decade later. The first foreign restaurant was established in Canada in 1967. Today there are more outlets in Japan alone than there were in the entire system in the mid-1960s.

OPERATIONS

The company's business consists entirely of restaurants that prepare, package, and sell a limited menu of quickly prepared, moderately priced foods. The restaurants are operated either by the company (2,547 at the end of 1991), by a franchisee (8,735), or through a joint venture between the company and local businesspeople (1,136). The company has established uniform standards for quality of product, cleanliness and efficiency, and speed of service in all of these outlets.

McDonald's restaurants offer a substantially uniform menu consisting mainly of hamburgers (Big Mac, Quarter Pounder, McLean Deluxe), Filet-O-Fish and McChicken sandwiches, Chicken McNuggets, french fries, salads, milkshakes, and soft drinks. In the United States restaurants also serve a breakfast menu that includes Egg McMuffin, Sausage McMuffin with Egg, biscuits, muffins, and cereals.

The company has three domestic subsidiaries concerned with foreign operations—McDonald's Australian Property Corporation, McDonald's Deutschland, and McDonald's System of France—as well as foreign subsidiaries in Australia, Canada, England, France, Germany, and the Netherlands Antilles.

Among the fifty-nine countries in which there were McDonald's restaurants at the end of 1991, the largest numbers were in the United States (8,764), Japan (865), Canada (642), England (400), Germany (391), and Australia (304).

In 1991 the company announced that it was considering its first diversification—indoor playgrounds where parents would spent about five dollars to spend time cavorting with their children. A prototype of the venture, which was given the name Leaps & Bounds, was set up in suburban Chicago.

TOP EXECUTIVES

- Michael R. Quinlan, chairman and chief executive
- Fred L. Turner, senior chairman
- James R. Cantalupo, president and chief executive officer of McDonald's International
- Jack M. Greenberg, vice chairman
- Gerald Newman, senior executive vice president
- Edward H. Rensi, chief executive officer and president of McDonald's USA
- Paul D. Schrage, senior executive vice president

OUTSIDE DIRECTORS

- Gordon C. Gray, chairman of the Canadian real estate firm Royal Le Page Ltd.
- Donald G. Lubin, partner in the law firm Sonnenschein Nath & Rosenthal

- Andrew J. McKenna, chief executive of Schwarz Paper Company
- Terry Savage, financial analyst and syndicated newspaper columnist
- Ballard F. Smith, chief executive of Sun Mountain Broadcasting
- Roger W. Stone, chief executive of Stone Container
- Robert N. Thurston, retired executive vice president of Quaker Oats
- B. Blair Vedder, Jr., former chief operating officer of Needham Harper Steers
- David B. Wallerstein, business consultant

FINANCIAL DATA

Revenues (in millions of dollars)

1991	6,695
1990	6,640
1989	6,066
1988	5,521
1987	4,853

Systemwide Sales (in millions of dollars)

1991	19,928
1990	18,759
1989	17,333
1988	16,064
1987	14,330

Net Income (in millions of dollars)

1991	860
1990	802
1989	727
1988	646
1987	549

GEOGRAPHICAL BREAKDOWN

Revenues (in millions of dollars)

Year	United States		Europe		Elsewhere	
1991	3,710	(55%)	1,806	(27%)	1,179	(18%)
1990	3,871	(58%)	1,636	(25%)	1,133	(17%)
1989	3,887	(64%)	1,164	(19%)	1,104	(18%)

Operating Income (in millions of dollars)

Year	United States		Europe		Elsewhere	
1991	1,000	(60%)	361	(22%)	317	(19%)
1990	986	(62%)	325	(20%)	284	(18%)
1989	989	(69%)	192	(13%)	257	(18%)

LABOR RELATIONS

McDonald's, like the rest of the fast-food industry in the United States, has remained almost entirely nonunion. The company has gone to great lengths to maintain total control of its underpaid work force, using such techniques as rap sessions. These discussions serve both to allow workers to air their gripes and to allow supervisors to get a reading of the attitudes of the troops.

This nonunion philosophy has not gone unchallenged. When McDonald's sought to open its first stores in San Francisco in the early 1970s, the company was confronted by unions and local politicians who opposed city approval because of the company's labor policies. It took a long court battle before McDonald's prevailed. In the late 1970s the fast-food chains faced an intensive campaign in Detroit by an independent group called the Fastfood Workers Union.

Unions have been a bit more evident among McDonald's operations in other parts of the world. In Ireland, Sweden, and a few other countries unions have been successful in negotiating working conditions, but the company and its franchisees still seek to keep unions out wherever possible. This policy became a target of a militant labor campaign when the company opened its first outlet in Mexico in 1985. The restaurant workers' union laid siege to the facility and forced it to shut down until a successful representation election was held. Unions in Denmark launched a boycott of the company in 1988 after franchisees refused to sign a collective-bargaining contract. After about eight months the company relented and agreed to join the employers' group that negotiates with the Danish hotel and restaurant union.

Apart from resisting unions, McDonald's has long lobbied in the United States for a lower minimum wage for teenagers, who make up the large majority of the company's labor force. After years of debate, the "teenwage" concept finally was adopted by Congress when the minimum wage was revised in 1989. However, by the late 1980s, with demographic trends reducing the size of the teenage labor force, McDonald's and other chains began hiring older workers and the disabled. In 1990 a coalition of church, labor, and community groups in Philadelphia launched a boycott of McDonald's to protest the fact that workers in its inner-city outlets were being paid a dollar an hour less than those employed in suburban facilities.

ENVIRONMENTAL AND HEALTH RECORD

In the area of the environment, McDonald's has come under attack for the huge volume of waste generated by the food packaging used in its restaurants. In the late 1980s the Citizen's Clearinghouse for Hazardous Wastes and other groups launched a campaign to get the company to end its use of non-biodegradable, nonrecyclable polystyrene plastic foam containers. It was estimated that McDonald's used 1.6 billion cubic feet of the stuff each year. Citizen's Clearinghouse dubbed its effort the McToxics Campaign to highlight the little-publicized health effects of the foam particles that migrate from the containers into the food. Customers were urged to mail their used hamburger containers (known as clamshells because of their design) back to the company in protest.

Both McDonald's and the plastics industry reacted with alarm to the campaign, spending many millions of dollars to defend the clamshell. The company later agreed to work with the Environmental Defense Fund on developing ways to cut down trash by recycling packaging and testing reusable utensils and cups. This did not satisfy environmentalists, who were skeptical of the claims about the recycling of the foam containers, so the campaign continued. Then, in 1990, McDonald's announced that it would phase out its use of plastic foam in favor of paper packaging. The change applied to food containers only; Styrofoam coffee cups and plastic utensils would still be used.

The following year the company announced a more ambitious effort, in cooperation with the Environmental Defense Fund, to cut down its generation of solid waste. At the same time, the company opposed a proxy resolution put forth by a group of religious organizations to require observance of the Valdez Principles—a comprehensive commitment to reducing pollutants, conserving natural resources, reducing waste, and using energy more efficiently.

McDonald's also has been taken to task for the adverse effects of its products on the internal environment of its customers. The standard McDonald's menu contains items quite high in saturated fats and sodium. Even the highly touted McD.L.T. was found to have ten teaspoons of fat (even more than its regular hamburgers), and the company's traditional recipe for its highly praised french fries called for frying in beef fat.

Faced with pressure from nutrition groups, the company switched to vegetable oil for its french fries and introduced low-fat milkshakes and frozen yogurt desserts. In 1991 the company went a step further by introducing its McLean Deluxe hamburger, which used a process that substituted about half of the fat with water and a seaweed extract.

BIBLIOGRAPHY

Boas, Max, and Steve Chain. *Big Mac: The Unauthorized Story of McDonald's.* New York: Mentor Books, 1976.

Emerson, Robert L. *Fast Food: The Endless Shakeout*. New York: Lebhar-Friedman, 1979.

Kroc, Ray. *Grinding It Out*. Chicago: Contemporary Books, 1977. The autobiography of the founder of the McDonald's empire.

Love, John F. *McDonald's: Behind the Arches*. New York: Bantam Books, 1986.

Luxenberg, Stan. *Roadside Empires: How the Chains Franchised America*. New York: Viking, 1985.

Working for Big Mac. London: Transnational Information Centre, 1987.

McDONNELL DOUGLAS CORPORATION

P.O. Box 516
St. Louis, Missouri 63166
(314) 232-0232

1991 revenues: $18.4 billion
1991 net income: $423 million
Publicly traded company
Employees: 109,123
Founded: 1967 (McDonnell Aircraft was founded in 1939, Douglas
    Company in 1920)

OVERVIEW

McDonnell Douglas is the largest U.S. military contractor and the world's
leading manufacturer of combat aircraft, but its status as a major producer
of commercial aircraft has been slipping. For the past quarter century the
company has experienced both good times and bad for the two operations
(McDonnell in military, Douglas in civilian) that were wed in a 1967 merger.

Douglas was the original star in the commercial air transport business, but
it was later overtaken by Boeing and yet later by the European consortium
Airbus Industrie as well. Despite the fall to third place, the company still
enjoys the support of many of the world's airlines. On the military side, the
company has held on to the top spot among contractors and continues to
provide the F-15 and other fighters that are popular with the Pentagon and
various foreign governments. It was, however, stung by the abrupt cancellation
in 1991 of the A-12 attack plane it was building with General Dynamics.

By the early 1990s the condition of McDonnell Douglas was uncertain
enough that some observers were speculating about a possible bankruptcy.
That threat abated in late 1991 when the company announced that it planned
to sell a 40-percent stake in its jetliner business to Taiwan Aerospace Corporation for $2 billion, but the deal was strongly opposed by members of

Congress and the unions representing the company's workers. A substitute plan was devised that as of this writing is still being negotiated. If the Taiwanese rescue does not succeed, the most likely alternative is a Pentagon-arranged bailout of its leading supplier. One way or another McDonnell Douglas will remain a major force in the aerospace industry.

HISTORY

Donald Douglas became so fascinated with airplanes while a midshipman at the U.S. Naval Academy that he left Annapolis after his third year to study the brand-new subject of aeronautical engineering at the Massachusetts Institute of Technology. After graduating with MIT's first degree in the field Douglas worked briefly for a dirigible company and then was hired as chief aeronautical engineer by aviation pioneer Glenn L. Martin's company.

Douglas was not content to be someone else's employee. So, starting out in the back room of a Los Angeles barbershop, Douglas launched a business in 1920 with the support of wealthy aviation enthusiast David R. Davis. The firm built a biplane called the Cloudster, which crashed on a trial flight. Davis lost interest in the enterprise, but Douglas proceeded on his own.

Soon an opportunity arose to do business with the military. An acquaintance from MIT helped Douglas get a contract from the U.S. Navy to produce a plane capable of carrying a full-sized torpedo. The contract, and financial backing from a group of local businessmen led by Harry Chandler, publisher of the *Los Angeles Times*, also enabled Douglas to turn out a series of new planes for civilian customers.

One of those customers was the airline TWA, which sent out requests in 1932 to plane makers for a product that would compete with Boeing's 247. This new plane was to hold twelve passengers and fly at a cruising speed of 145 miles per hour. Douglas came up with a design that was more powerful than the 247 and had an intended cruising speed of 170 miles per hour, even faster than TWA's specifications. Douglas was chosen for the job, and he produced a prototype called the DC-1 (Douglas Commercial 1). Then, improving on the design and increasing the passenger capacity to fourteen, he created what would be one of the most important advances in the history of the industry—the DC-2.

The DC-2, and its twenty-one-passenger successor, the DC-3, took the aviation world by storm. Making use of new developments in engine technologies, the Douglas planes were enthusiastically received by the young airline industry, and soon DC-2s and DC-3s were carrying nearly all of the nation's civil air traffic. By the time the last DC-3 was delivered in 1945, more than ten thousand copies of the plane had been produced.

During this time, the Douglas Aircraft Company avoided being absorbed into a large holding company, as was happening to many of its competitors, including Boeing. In 1932 Douglas created a subsidiary that was 49-percent owned and run by the prominent aircraft designer Jack Northrop. Five years later Douglas took over the operation completely and Northrop went on to form his own company.

In the late 1930s Douglas increased his involvement in military aircraft, producing the B-18 bomber, which was based on the DC-3 design. The next plane in the Douglas series, the DC-4, began as a military aircraft designated the C-54 (a version of which was fitted for President Roosevelt—the first presidential plane).

During World War II Douglas built huge quantities of the C-47 (also based on the DC-3) for the military and began work on a new plane to compete with the innovative design of Lockheed's new Constellation. The eventual result was the DC-7, which was the first commercial transport to cross the United States nonstop against prevailing winds. The last of the great piston-engined transports, it also became a popular plane for many airlines in the United States and abroad.

During the 1950s the company prospered from the increased military spending prompted by the cold war. By the time the company's founder passed the mantle to his son Donald Douglas, Jr., in 1958 the situation was beginning to deteriorate. Boeing had successfully gambled on the jet plane, while Douglas had held back. When it became clear that jets were becoming the new standard, the Douglas company had to hastily develop its own model, the DC-8.

By the mid-1960s Douglas had a strong jet contender, the DC-9, to compete with Boeing's 727, but the costly development of the plane had eroded the company's financial position. The solution, according to the firm's Wall Street advisers, was a merger. So in 1967 Douglas Aircraft was wedded to the McDonnell Company of St. Louis. The Douglases ended up playing a limited role in the combined company, whose name, McDonnell Douglas, tellingly put the once-invincible Douglas name second.

The McDonnell firm had been founded just before World War II by James Smith McDonnell, an MIT graduate and pilot who had worked for the Glenn L. Martin Company. After serving as a subcontractor for Douglas on the C-47, McDonnell first gained recognition as the producer of the carrier-based Phantom jet in the early postwar period. The company went on to develop a series of fighters, including the F2H Banshee and the F3H Demon for the navy and the F-101 for the air force. (The planes' names reflected the fact that McDonnell, known as Mr. Mac, was fascinated with the paranormal.)

The second generation of Phantoms, designated the F-4, was introduced in 1958 and was adopted by the marines and the air force as well as the navy. It also was sold widely to foreign governments, helping to make it one of the best-known fighter planes in the world. In 1959 McDonnell was chosen as the prime contractor for Mercury, the first manned spacecraft in the West. The company went on to become a prime contractor for the Gemini spacecraft.

During the late 1960s the combined McDonnell Douglas company was challenged by the 747 jumbo jet that Boeing had developed at the urging of Pan American. Yet it turned out that there was a substantial demand for jets that were large, but not quite as jumbo as the 747. Both McDonnell Douglas and Lockheed fought hard for what was called the airbus market. McDonnell Douglas moved ahead of Lockheed with its DC-9, but then Boeing came on the scene with the wide-body 767 and the narrow-body 757—products that gave it a strong lead. The competition also was intensified through the entry of Airbus Industrie, a consortium of French, British, German, and Spanish aircraft companies. The travails of McDonnell Douglas were increased as the result of a series of accidents involving DC-10s.

McDonnell Douglas managed to recover from the DC-10 debacle and returned to the market, not by investing billions (like Boeing) in an entirely new product but rather by producing derivatives of the DC-9 and DC-10. Observers were originally skeptical about the willingness of airlines to buy what was essentially old technology, but models like the twin-engine MD-80 (based on the DC-9) proved to be successes. Lockheed, meanwhile, threw in the towel and left the commercial aircraft business.

By the mid-1980s the demand for new planes had improved considerably. The plunge of oil prices bolstered the airlines' earnings, enabling them to proceed with previously postponed expansion of their fleets. The rivalry among McDonnell Douglas, Boeing, and Airbus intensified as the three leaders of the industry fought for these orders. For customers eager to replace aging DC-10s with a longer-range wide-body, McDonnell Douglas spent heavily to develop the MD-11, which was to fit in between Boeing's 747 jumbo jet and its smaller 767. Yet Boeing responded by downsizing the 747 and stretching the 767.

Airbus, meanwhile, brought out a long-range A340 to compete directly with the MD-11. Able to price aggressively because of its government subsidies, Airbus began to take market share from McDonnell Douglas and was making Boeing uneasy. In 1988 Boeing solidified its position by introducing new versions of the 747 and the medium-range 737. Soon Boeing's main challenge was keeping up with demand. The order books of McDonnell Douglas were also fattened (to a lesser extent), and the value of its civilian backlog jumped ahead of military orders. Its profitability, however, remained poor.

While struggling with this intense competitive environment in the 1980s, McDonnell Douglas was having an easier time of it on the military side. The rapid escalation of Pentagon spending during the Reagan years was a boon for the company, despite the fact that McDonnell Douglas pleaded guilty in 1981 to federal charges of fraud and making false statements regarding foreign payoffs in the 1970s. McDonnell Douglas jumped to the top of the list of military contractors through hefty sales of its fighter planes, missiles, and (through the 1984 purchase of Hughes Helicopter) attack helicopters.

McDonnell Douglas entered the 1990s in a state of confusion. Demand for its commerical products, especially the MD-80/90 series, was strong, but the bottom line was weak and the morale of employees was low because of a series of unsettling reorganizations. Lots of money was still coming in from the Pentagon, but the company was falling behing in one of its key projects— the development of the C-17 transport for the air force.

Another blow came in early 1991, when the Defense Department decided to scrap the A-12 navy attack plane that McDonnell Douglas was building in cooperation with General Dynamics. The cancellation of the project, which was over budget and behind schedule, led to the elimination of thousands of jobs. McDonnell Douglas and General Dynamics responded by filing a $3-billion lawsuit against the Pentagon. The whole affair, combined with the other difficulties of McDonnell Douglas, cast a shadow over the company's future. The company attempted in 1991 to get back on its feet by arranging for a cash infusion of $2 billion from Taiwan Aerospace, a recently formed joint venture of the Taiwanese government and various private interests in that country. That plan was widely criticized in the United States, and by early 1992 the Taiwanese were having second thoughts as well. In May 1992 Taiwan Aerospace officials said they no longer wanted to invest in McDonnell Douglas. Instead, they would spend their $2 billion purchasing 20 of the company's new MD-12 jumbo jets, which would then be leased to airlines.

OPERATIONS

Combat Aircraft (32 percent of 1991 operating revenues). The company's current products in this segment are the F-15 Eagle, the F/A-18 Hornet, the AV-8B Harrier II, the T-45 Goshawk, and the AH-64 Apache attack helicopter. A program to develop and produce the A-12 navy attack plane was terminated in 1991.

The F-15 is a supersonic tactical fighter flown by Israel, Saudi Arabia, and Japan as well as by the U.S. Air Force (which alone has taken delivery of more than a thousand copies). The F/A-18 is a multimission strike fighter produced primarily for the navy and the marine corps, but it also is used by Canada, Australia, and Spain. In 1988 it was chosen by the government of Kuwait as its new fighter aircraft. Switzerland and South Korea also have begun procurement of the plane.

The AV-8B Harrier II is a vertical/short takeoff and landing attack aircraft that began to be deployed by the U.S. Marine Corps in 1984. The T-45 Goshawk is a single-engine trainer plane used by the U.S. Navy. The Apache helicopter is used by the U.S. Army, and the Pentagon also purchases copies to provide to foreign governments, such as Israel and Egypt.

Transport Aircraft (47 percent of operating revenues). The commercial segment of the company currently produces the MD-80 twin jet, the wide-body MD-11 trijet, and the new MD-90 twin jet (an advanced version of the MD-80 with engines that are more fuel efficient, are less noisy, and produce less in the way of emissions). As of the end of 1991 the company had a backlog of 235 firm orders and 335 options and reserves for the MD-80/90 as well as 138 firm orders and 160 options and reserves for the MD-11. In 1991 the company announced the formation of a joint venture with Shanghai Aviation Industrial Corporation to build planes in China.

Overall McDonnell Douglas has been receiving about 17 percent of worldwide commercial orders, trailing Boeing (53 percent) and Airbus (24 percent). This segment also includes development work on the C-17 transport for the U.S. Air Force.

Missiles, Space, and Electronic Systems (16 percent of operating revenues). McDonnell Douglas produces the Harpoon antiship missile for the U.S. Navy; the standoff land attack missile (SLAM), a derivative of the Harpoon, also for the navy; and long-distance Tomahawk sea-launched cruise missiles. In the space field the company produces the Delta launch vehicle for propelling civilian and military payloads into orbit and is involved with NASA's plans for a manned space station. McDonnell Douglas has been a major participant in work on the Strategic Defensive Initiative, or Star Wars, and has done research on the National Aero-Space Plane, a vehicle that would be able to take off from Earth and fly into orbit. This segment also includes civilian and military electronic systems for aviation and communication.

Financial Services and Other Products (5 percent of operating revenues). Included here are financing and leasing activities as well as software products for computer-aided design and computer-aided manufacturing. In 1991 the company formed an alliance with Fujitsu to develop and market factory automation equipment worldwide.

TOP EXECUTIVES

- John F. McDonnell, chairman and chief executive
- Gerald A. Johnston, president of McDonnell Douglas Corporation and of McDonnell Aircraft
- Robert H. Hood, Jr., president of Douglas Aircraft
- Kenneth A. Francis, president of McDonnell Douglas Space Systems
- E. Randolph Jayne II, president of McDonnell Douglas Missile Systems
- Edward C. Aldridge, Jr., president of McDonnell Douglas Electronic Systems Company

OUTSIDE DIRECTORS

- John H. Biggs, president of Teacher's Insurance and Annuity Association and College Retirement Equities Fund
- B. A. Bridgewater, Jr., chief executive of the Brown Group
- Willam E. Cornelius, chief executive of Union Electric
- William H. Danforth, chancellor of Washington University
- Kenneth M. Duberstein, chief executive of the Duberstein Group and former White House chief of staff
- Julian B. Goodman, retired chief executive of the National Broadcasting Company
- William S. Kanaga, retired chairman of Arthur Young & Company

- Roscoe Robinson, Jr., retired general in the U.S. Army
- George A. Schaefer, retired chief executive of Caterpillar Inc.

The board also includes chairman emeritus Sanford M. McDonnell and retired vice president James S. McDonnell, III.

FINANCIAL DATA

Revenues (in millions of dollars)

1991	18,448
1990	15,904
1989	14,233
1988	14,090
1987	12,710

Net Income (in millions of dollars)

1991	423
1990	306
1989	219
1988	350
1987	313

GEOGRAPHICAL BREAKDOWN

Revenues (in millions of dollars)

Year	United States		Europe		Elsewhere	
1991	12,284	(66%)	3,689	(20%)	2,475	(13%)
1990	12,463	(78%)	2,195	(14%)	1,246	(7%)
1989	11,457	(80%)	1,916	(13%)	860	(6%)

LABOR RELATIONS

Donald Douglas, like most of his fellow aircraft entrepreneurs, was unhappy about the passage of the National Labor Relations Act in 1935 and resisted the idea of his employees being represented by an independent union. He set up a company union instead, but amid the wave of labor militancy of 1937, his workers wanted more.

Inspired by the successful sit-down strike at the Flint, Michigan, plant of General Motors, Douglas workers at the firm's main plant in Santa Monica,

California, launched their own sit-down on February 23, 1937, to protest the firing of three union organizers and to demand wage increases, overtime pay, and recognition of the United Auto Workers. Douglas was unmoved. He accused the strikers of trespassing—a charge that was backed up by a grand jury indictment. Faced with an imminent assault by a heavily armed force of 350 police officers, the workers decided to leave the plant. Within several weeks, however, the workers chose the UAW as their collective-bargaining representative in an election supervised by the National Labor Relations Board.

The unrest continued at the company's Northrop division after Douglas bought out Jack Northrop's share in the operation. Another sit-down occurred at the Northrop plant in September 1937, which prompted Douglas to shut the facility down. When it was reopened a month later, it was staffed only by those workers who were willing to sign reemployment agreements in which they promised not to strike or occupy company property. Later those agreements were deemed illegal by the NLRB.

The company eventually learned to accept the presence of the UAW (and in some places the International Association of Machinists) as the bargaining representative for its production workers. That is not to say that the company was a pushover in negotiations. McDonnell Douglas, along with other companies in the industry, took a particularly hard line with the unions in the early 1980s. In 1983 the company insisted that the UAW accept the same contract concessions that had been forced on IAM members at Boeing. The workers refused and went on strike for sixteen weeks. But because the company remained intransigent, the workers ended up accepting virtually the same terms McDonnell Douglas had offered before the walkout, including lump-sum payments instead of increases in the base wage and the establishment of a two-tier pay system.

Chastened by that experience, the UAW did not hasten to call a strike when its contract expired in 1986. Instead, the UAW, along with the IAM, responded to new company demands for concessions by using an in-plant strategy. This involved asking workers to remain on the job without a contract and using various forms of shop floor action (punctilious observance of safety rules, for example) to pressure the company to reach a reasonable settlement. This tactic also had the advantages of allowing workers to go on getting paid during the struggle and of avoiding the risk that strikers face of being permanently replaced. The unions, nonetheless, ended up accepting a contract that was heavily weighted toward lump-sum payments.

As the company's worsening financial condition led to several drastic reorganizations and the layoffs of thousands of workers, labor-management relations continued to deteriorate. Despite this climate, the UAW managed to win a contract in 1991 that included modest increases in base pay but involved concessions on health benefits. Not satisfied with the pact, the union's rank and file twice voted to reject the terms and send their negotiators back to the table. A third, essentially identical, settlement was ratified in October 1991.

ENVIRONMENTAL RECORD

McDonnell Douglas was cited as a potentially responsible party by the EPA in connection with an area of toxic contamination around a missile plant in Tucson, Arizona. The company's share of the $17-million clean-up plan, which was approved by a federal court in 1991, was $500,000.

BIBLIOGRAPHY

Adams, Gordon. *The Iron Triangle: The Politics of Defense Contracting*. New York: Council on Economic Priorities, 1981.

Biddle, Wayne. *Barons of the Sky*. New York: Simon & Schuster, 1991.

Bluestone, Barry, Peter Jordan, and Mark Sullivan. *Aircraft Industry Dynamics: An Analysis of Competition, Capital and Labor*. Dover, Mass.: Auburn House, 1981.

Douglas, Donald W. *Wings for the World: The DC Family in Global Service*. New York: Newcomen Society, 1955.

Gansler, Jacques S. *The Defense Industry*. Cambridge, Mass.: MIT Press, 1980.

IMF Guide to World Aerospace Companies and Unions. Geneva: International Metalworkers Federation, 1987.

Newhouse, John. *The Sporty Game*. New York: Alfred A. Knopf, 1982.

Rae, John B. *Climb to Greatness: The American Aircraft Industry, 1920–1960*. Cambridge, Mass.: MIT Press, 1968.

Shaw, Linda, et al. *Stocking the Arsenal: A Guide to the Nation's Top Military Contractors*. Washington, D.C.: Investor Responsibility Research Center, 1985.

MERCK & COMPANY, INC.

P.O. Box 2000
Rahway, New Jersey 07065
(908) 594-4000

1991 revenues: $8.6 billion
1991 net income: $2.1 billion
Publicly traded company
Employees: 37,700
Founded: 1891

OVERVIEW

Merck is one of the most highly regarded companies in the international pharmaceutical industry. Its reputation rests above all on its research. The company, which spent nearly $1 billion on research and development in 1991, has some seventeen research centers with forty-five hundred employees in North America, Japan, and several European countries. Merck's manufacturing is also international, with forty-seven facilities in eighteen countries.

Merck has developed goodwill by such actions as offering to discount drugs purchased through the Medicaid system and giving away its medication to treat onchocerciasis, or "river blindness," which spreads through parasites endemic in tropical areas of the third world.

The company has steered clear of the merger mania that has afflicted much of the drug industry but has formed a series of strategic alliances with the likes of Du Pont and Johnson & Johnson.

HISTORY

Today's Merck is a descendant of an unbroken line of prominent drug producers dating back to 1668, when Friedrich Jacob Merck took over a pharmacy in the German town of Darmstadt. The early Mercks were men of learning and were in contact with the leading intellectuals of the day.

Heinrich Emmanuel Merck, born in 1794, was a protégé of Justus von Liebig, the father of organic chemistry. Putting Liebig's theories into practice, Merck started manufacturing morphine in 1827. The firm E. Merck went on to produce codeine, quinine, and other substances. By the middle of the century the company had an international reputation as a manufacturer of alkaloids.

In 1891 chemist Theodore Weicker, who had been sent to the United States to represent Merck's interests in the New World, and George Merck, the founder's grandson, who had been sent to learn from Weicker, set up a business to exploit the American market. By the turn of the century they were producing chloral hydrate, iodides, alkaloids, and other drug and chemical products. This was not a happy partnership, however, and in 1904 Weicker sold his share to George Merck (and went on to gain control of rival drug house E. R. Squibb). Merck prospered on his own, both from the production of pharmaceuticals and from publishing the *Merck Manual of Diagnosis and Therapy*, which would become one of the most widely used medical texts in the world.

During World War I Merck took the initiative of handing over to the Alien Property Custodian a block of stock representing the 80-percent interest in his firm owned by relatives in Germany. This enabled Merck to go on operating during the war. So diligent was he in meeting his adopted country's wartime needs that after the armistice the Alien Property Custodian sold the securities to investment bankers friendly to the company, thus ensuring that Merck would retain control.

The firm, which passed into the hands of the boss's son, George W. Merck, after his father's death in 1925, used Germany's defeat to move into foreign markets that had been abandoned by the German Merck. In 1932 the two firms signed an agreement for the exchange of technical information and for dividing up the world to avoid having two different Mercks competing in the same area. The arrangement lasted until 1945, when it was dissolved as part of a consent decree in an antitrust suit.

George W. Merck was a great proponent of research, and in 1933 he established the Merck Institute for Therapeutic Research. Yet it was another institution, Bell Laboratories, that brought Merck its next big product. In 1934 a researcher at Bell contacted the head of the Merck to report that he had isolated vitamin B_1 but needed help in synthesizing it. The Merck people lent a hand, and when the synthesis was perfected, Merck obtained a license to produce and sell B_1.

After this Merck made a big push in vitamins and figured out how to synthesize B_2, C, B_6, E, and others. Although the company set out to separate the health-promoting substances from natural sources, Merck scientists found that it was easier to make them from petroleum or coal-tar chemicals. In 1948 the company announced the discovery of a new vitamin, B_{12}, which was extremely effective in combating serious anemia.

Merck also became involved with antibiotics. In 1941 two researchers from Britain, concerned that the war in Europe would interfere with their work, brought a strain of penicillin to Merck for further development. Unfortunately, it turned out to be impractical to synthesize. In 1943, however, a researcher at Rutgers University working with funds from Merck discovered a new antibiotic he called streptomycin. Because of the importance of the drug, Merck declined an exclusive patent right, though the company did become its leading producer.

Later in the 1940s, Merck chemists played a key role in the synthesis of cortisone, which originally was planned as a treatment for arthritis but ended up being used for rheumatic fever, bronchial asthma, and a variety of other ailments. Merck later produced a more powerful version called hydrocortisone as well as other steroids.

Despite these advances, Merck, which went public in 1946, had difficulty in the postwar period. Competition, both domestic and from Europe and Japan, was intensifying, and new products kept pouring into the market. Merck was not well prepared to join the spreading practice of selling directly to doctors and dentists through a force of detail men. To shore up its position Merck merged with Sharp & Dohme, a century-old drug house, in 1953.

Merck maintained its reputation as a high-quality research operation, but the company's marketing of new products remained deficient. When Merck did try hard to promote one of its discoveries, the results could be disastrous. This was seen most clearly in the case of Indocin, which was introduced in 1965 to treat various arthritic disorders. Although the FDA approved the medication, it later came out that the company had not tested the drug adequately for efficacy and side effects.

It was not until John Horan took over as chief executive in 1976 that the company began to exploit its discoveries more deftly. Horan also devoted resources to improving existing products, such as its development of Enalapril, a high blood pressure inhibitor more potent than Squibb's Capoten. And he put more emphasis on licensing from foreign producers, including Astra of Sweden and Shionogi of Japan.

Merck was embarrassed by revelations in the mid-1970s that it was one of several hundred companies found to have made payoffs to obtain business abroad. In Merck's case, some $3.6 million had been disbursed in thirty-nine countries.

In 1983 Merck moved to expand its share of the Japanese market by purchasing a majority interest in Banyu Pharmaceutical of Tokyo, a company with which Merck had been in a joint venture since 1954. Yet this $313-million purchase, larger than any other acquisition by a foreign company in Japan, was not what the doctor ordered. Banyu turned out to be a managerial mess and the firm was the target of Japanese government efforts to restrain drug prices.

During the 1980s Merck also plunged into the emerging field of biotechnology, marketing the first genetically engineered human vaccine (for hepatitis B). The company's labs brought forth a wave of other new products, including

Mevacor, the first cholesterol-lowering drug, and Vasotec, another competitor to Squibb's Capoten. Merck's research effort—led until 1985 by P. Roy Vagelos, a biochemist who then took over as chief executive of the company—became the talk of the industry. Merck's technical prowess, along with its strong financial condition, allowed it to dislodge IBM from the position as America's "most admired" company in the 1987 edition of *Fortune* magazine's annual survey.

While many of its competitors got caught up with mergers in this period, Merck instead formed a series of joint ventures. They included an arrangement with Imperial Chemical Industries to comarket an antihypertension drug (called Prinivil by Merck, Zestril by ICI); a partnership with Johnson & Johnson to develop and market over-the-counter products; and the creation of a company with Du Pont to develop and market a variety of drugs. In 1991 the joint venture with Johnson & Johnson announced plans to purchase the German company Woelm Pharma, a subsidiary of Rhône-Poulenc Rorer that produces cold medications, laxatives, and vitamins.

In 1990 Merck announced that it was testing a new drug it had developed to fight the AIDS virus. The company has introduced a new prostate drug called Proscar, which analysts were predicting could be Merck's next blockbuster product.

OPERATIONS

Human and Animal Health Products (93 percent of 1991 revenues). Most of Merck's revenues come from prescription drugs, including antihypertensive and cardiovascular products (Vasotec, Mevacor, Prinivil, and so on); antibiotics (Primaxin, Mefoxin); antiulcerants (Pepcid, Prilosec); anti-inflammatory/analgesic products (Clinoril, Indocin); and vaccines/biologicals (M-M-R II for measles, mumps, and rubella and hepatitis B vaccines). The antihypertensives and cardiovasculars alone had sales of more than $3.8 billion in 1991. Its main over-the-counter products sold by its joint venture with Johnson & Johnson, is the antacid Mylanta.

Merck's animal products include antiparasites for livestock and dogs, coccidiostats for the treatment of poultry disease, and agricultural chemicals. The company says that its Ivomec antiparasitic is the largest-selling animal health product in the world.

Specialty Chemical Products (7 percent of revenues). This segment produces chemicals used in water treatment, paper manufacturing, oil drilling, food processing, skin and wound care, biodecontamination, and surface finishing.

TOP EXECUTIVES

- P. Roy Vagelos, chairman, president, and chief executive
- Robert L. Banse, senior vice president
- Jerry T. Jackson, senior vice president

- Richard J. Markham, senior vice president
- Edward M. Scolnick, senior vice president
- Francis H. Spiegel, Jr., senior vice president

OUTSIDE DIRECTORS

- H. Brewster Atwater, Jr., chief executive of General Mills
- William G. Bowen, president of the Andrew W. Mellon Foundation
- Carolyne K. Davis, health-care consultant with Ernst & Young
- Lloyd C. Elam, professor of psychiatry at Meharry Medical College
- Charles E. Exley, Jr., former chairman of NCR Corporation
- Ruben F. Mettler, former chairman of TRW
- Richard S. Ross, dean emeritus of the medical faculty of Johns Hopkins University School of Medicine
- Dennis Weatherstone, chairman of J. P. Morgan & Company

The board also includes John J. Horan, Merck's former chief executive, and Albert W. Merck, trustee of Merck family trusts.

FINANCIAL DATA

Revenues (in millions of dollars)

1991	8,603
1990	7,672
1989	6,551
1988	5,940
1987	5,061
1986	4,129

Net Income (in millions of dollars)

1991	2,122
1990	1,781
1989	1,495
1988	1,207
1987	906
1986	676

GEOGRAPHICAL BREAKDOWN

Customer Sales (in millions of dollars)

Year	United States		Other OECD		Elsewhere	
1991	4,616	(54%)	3,812	(44%)	174	(2%)
1990	4,039	(53%)	3,451	(45%)	181	(2%)
1989	3,487	(54%)	2,901	(45%)	162	(2%)
1988	2,996	(50%)	2,772	(47%)	171	(3%)

Income Before Taxes (in millions of dollars)

Year	United States		Other OECD		Elsewhere	
1991	2,252	(73%)	833	(27%)	−4	(0%)
1990	1,833	(68%)	823	(31%)	21	(1%)
1989	1,558	(69%)	722	(32%)	−13	(0%)
1988	1,090	(59%)	759	(41%)	−2	(0%)

LABOR RELATIONS

The major blemish on Merck's labor relations came in 1984, when the company locked out more than seven hundred workers at its Rahway, New Jersey, plant after contract talks broke down. The unions—including the Oil, Chemical and Atomic Workers, the International Chemical Workers, and the Amalgamated Clothing and Textile Workers—continued to resist management demands for contract concessions, which included a two-tier wage system, cuts in medical benefits, and changes in work rules that the unions said threatened job security.

A few weeks after the lockout some three thousand Merck workers around the country walked off the job in protest. The Oil, Chemical and Atomic Workers took the lead in launching a corporate campaign against Merck. This included taking out advertisements in newspapers, forming alliances with public interest groups to oppose Merck's high drug prices, and sending emissaries to gain support from unions representing Merck employees in Europe. The dispute was settled after three months when both sides agreed to a compromise package.

Since then labor relations have stabilized, and today about 21 percent of Merck's worldwide work force is covered by collective-bargaining agreements. In 1991 Merck joined a small group of companies that make stock options available to all employees, not just to top management.

ENVIRONMENTAL AND HEALTH RECORD

Starting in the mid-1970s, Merck was one of more than two dozen drug producers and distributors sued by large numbers of women who said they suffered from vaginal cancer and other ailments because their mothers had used the drug diethylstilbestrol (DES). Despite evidence that DES caused cancer in animals, for several decades the medication was widely prescribed for pregnant women to prevent miscarriages. The dispute, which now involves more than five hundred plaintiff groups, is still pending.

In 1990 the company reached an agreement with the New Jersey Department of Environmental Protection to settle charges the agency had brought against Merck for violating discharge limitations at its Rahway facility. The agreement called for the company to pay a fine of $575,000.

According to a Citizens Fund study of data from the EPA, Merck was responsible for the twentieth-largest volume (three million pounds) of releases of known or suspected carcinogens among all U.S. manufacturing companies in 1989 (the latest figures available).

BIBLIOGRAPHY

Braithwaite, John. *Corporate Crime in the Pharmaceutical Industry*. Boston: Routledge & Kegan Paul, 1984.

Chetley, Andrew. *A Healthy Business? World Health and the Pharmaceutical Industry*. London: Zed Books, 1990.

Lynn, Matthew. *Merck v. Glaxo: The Billion-Dollar Battle*. London: Heinemann, 1991.

Mahoney, Tom. *The Merchants of Life: An Account of the American Pharmaceutical Industry*. New York: Harper & Brothers, 1959.

Mintz, Morton, *By Prescription Only*. Boston: Beacon Press, 1967.

COMPAGNIE GÉNÉRALE des ÉTABLISSEMENTS MICHELIN

23, Place des Carmes-Dechaux
63040 Clermont-Ferrand
France
(73) 92-41-95

1991 revenues: $13.1 billion
1991 net income: −$195.6 million (loss)
Publicly traded company
Employees: 131,976
Founded: 1863

OVERVIEW

Michelin, which founded the modern tire industry in the 1890s, is now the largest producer in the business. The secretive company is organized as a partnership with outside shareholdings. Control remains firmly in the hands of family members through a special class of stock and through the presence of Michelins in two of the three top executive positions (called *gérants*, or managing partners) at the company.

Michelin has a long tradition of innovation. It developed the first radial tires, which were introduced right after World War II and eventually became the dominant design in the industry. Yet it was an acquisition—the 1989 purchase of the Uniroyal-Goodrich joint venture in the United States—that propelled the French company to the top spot.

Being biggest has not meant being the most profitable. Michelin, saddled with substantial debt from its aggressive international expansion, has been especially hard hit by the dismal conditions of the tire industry. The company entered the 1990s with a great deal of red ink and the need to eliminate thousands of jobs.

Aside from tires, Michelin is known for the travel and restaurant guides and maps it has produced since the beginning of the century. Especially in

France, the *Guide Michelin* is the source of the definitive rating systems for restaurants. Every chef in the country covets the top (three-star) rating for his or her establishment, since it is a guarantee of fame and a steady stream of customers.

HISTORY

The story of Michelin begins in the 1830s at a company founded by Edouard Daubrée and Aristide Barbier to manufacture farm implements. Daubrée's wife was the former Elizabeth Pugh Barker, niece of the famous Scottish chemist Charles Macintosh (inventor of the waterproofing method used on the first raincoats). As a girl in Scotland, Barker had played with rubber balls made by her uncle. When she had young children of her own, she asked Macintosh to send her some of the balls. They were so popular that Daubrée and Barbier began making them in their factory in Clermont-Ferrand in central France; eventually they started producing other rubber products as well.

In 1863 the partners decided to form a new company to formalize their involvement in the rubber business. Within a few years each of the men died, and the company remained adrift until 1886, when André Michelin, a grandson of Aristide Barbier, was invited to take control. Since André already had a successful iron business in Paris, he asked his brother Edouard, an artist who also was working in Paris, to go to Clermont-Ferrand and take charge of the firm, which was renamed Michelin & Cie.

Both Michelin brothers ended up involved in the business. They soon recognized the limitations of the standard tires of the day, which were permanently glued to a wooden rim. In 1891 Edouard invented a detachable pneumatic bicycle tire. After the product was used successfully in several high-profile races, it became a success. During the late 1890s the Michelins used the same design for a line of carriage tires and soon after that adapted it for the recent invention known as the horseless carriage. In these fields, too, the Michelin pneumatic tires soon became the new standard.

The spreading popularity of Michelin was aided by a unique logo adopted by the company. The roly-poly Michelin Tire Man, otherwise known as Mr. Bibendum, or simply "Bib," came from an idea Edouard had while viewing a display of tires that looked vaguely like the outline of a man. Shortly thereafter the Michelins commissioned an artist to draw a character made of tires. Inspired by a beer poster he had seen with the Latin phrase "Nunc est bibendum" (now is the time to drink), André suggested that the figure be shown standing at a banquet table and raising a champagne glass filled with road debris. The slogan with it read: "Nunc est bibendum—To your health—Michelin swallows obstacles!" Bib went on to become the company's mascot and one of the best-known advertising figures in the world.

In the early years of the twentieth century Michelin became one of the leading producers of tires. Manufacturing operations in France were supplemented with facilities in Italy and the United States. In 1905 the company introduced the Semelle (the Sole), a tire with a leather tread studded with steel rivets to give greater road grip. Michelin produced airplanes during World War I, and after the war, returning to its main business, it brought out the first tubeless tires and made changes in tire design that were the forerunner of modern treads. In 1937 Michelin pioneered the low-profile design that would become the industry standard. That same year, the company introduced the first steel-cord tires, designed for trucks.

Michelin continued its foreign expansion by building plants in England, Italy (its second in that country), Argentina, Spain, and Belgium; rubber plantations were established in Indochina. The U.S. factory, however, was shut down during the depression. In the same period, Michelin acquired control of Citroën when the automaker was unable to pay debts amounting to more than FF 700 million owed to the tire company. (Citroën would then be taken over by Peugeot in the 1970s).

During World War II many Michelin plants were in areas occupied by the Nazis, but the company did not collaborate. With the return of peace Michelin quickly revived its operations. Only a year after the end of the war, the company revolutionized the tire industry by introducing the first radial tire, which had been in development since 1930. Although the radial substantially improved tire wear and traction, the new product was slow in catching on, especially in the United States, where the big American tire makers, such as Goodyear and Firestone, downplayed the significance of Michelin's innovation.

François Michelin, the grandson of Edouard Michelin who took over management of the company in 1955, kept pushing the radial concept and extended it to tires for trucks and heavy equipment. He also continued the company's international expansion with the opening of factories in such countries as Germany, Algeria, and Nigeria. While radials became firmly entrenched in Europe, the breakthrough in the U.S. market did not come until the mid-1960s, when Ford Motor decided to put Michelin radials on some of its 1968 Lincoln Continentals as standard equipment. Then Sears, Roebuck began to sell radials in its auto centers.

As the tide began to turn, Goodyear came out with a bias-belted tire in 1967, which essentially bought the U.S. company time to catch up with Michelin's technology. During the 1970s radial fever reached the United States, brought about in part by Michelin's aggressive marketing drive and its decision to begin production of radials in South Carolina. By the end of the 1970s Michelin had four U.S. plants (two of which were making truck tires) and was steadily increasing its share of the American market.

During the 1980s Michelin entered the Asian market by setting up factories in South Korea and Thailand and later by acquiring a controlling interest in Japan's Okamoto Tire Company. In 1989 Michelin turned itself into the world's largest tire company by purchasing the Uniroyal-Goodrich Tire Company (a merger of two old-line producers) in the United States.

Uniroyal began life in 1892 as the United States Rubber Company, an amalgamation of nine of the leading producers of rubber footwear. The company, which came under the control of the du Pont family, later acquired some tire makers and began selling that product under the U.S. Royal name. In 1967 the company took the name Uniroyal. B.F. Goodrich was one of the earliest producers of automobile tires. The company created the modern golf ball and was a pioneer in the development of synthetic rubber. Goodrich was the first U.S. company to make radial tires, but it was always overshadowed by Goodyear. By the mid-1980s both Uniroyal and Goodrich had moved into other fields, especially chemicals, so they were eager to isolate their ailing tire operations by putting them in a joint venture, which remained troubled and then ended up in the hands of Michelin.

This American deal provided a boost to Michelin, which had borrowed heavily to finance expansion elsewhere in the world and had suffered heavy losses in the early 1980s. Yet all was not well with the company. The tire industry was now dominated by the big three—Michelin in Europe, Goodyear in the United States, and Bridgestone in Japan—but by the beginning of the 1990s, overcapacity and a soft auto market were taking their toll on all of the big tire makers. Goodyear reported a loss for 1990, and so did Michelin, although the latter's deficit was far greater—the equivalent of about $1 billion.

OPERATIONS

Tires and Wheels (98 percent of 1990 revenues). Michelin has almost entirely avoided the diversification that other tire makers embarked on in an attempt to achieve greater stability. Overwhelmingly focused on tires, the company has manufacturing operations and rubber plantations in a dozen countries in Europe, Africa, Asia, North America, and South America. It produces a wide range of tires for automobiles, trucks, heavy equipment, bicycles, and other vehicles.

General Rubber Goods, Maps, Guides, and Other Products (2 percent of revenues). The best-known product here is the *Guide Michelin*, the famous series of books that describe and rank restaurants and hotels.

TOP EXECUTIVES

- François Michelin, managing partner
- Edouard Michelin, managing partner
- René Zingraff, managing partner

OUTSIDE DIRECTORS

- Emmanuel Daubrée
- Gaston Defosse
- Michel Godret
- Annie Hauvette
- Grégoire Puiseux

The company does not disclose the affiliations of its outside directors.

FINANCIAL DATA

Revenues (in millions of French francs)

1991	67,649
1990	62,737
1989	55,256
1988	51,280
1987	46,936
1986	46,641

Net Income (in millions of French francs)

1991	−1,013 (loss)
1990	−5,273 (loss)
1989	2,653
1988	3,591
1987	2,647
1986	1,908

GEOGRAPHICAL BREAKDOWN

Revenues (in millions of French francs)

Year	France		Rest of Western Europe		Elsewhere	
1990	13,049	(21%)	26,287	(42%)	23,401	(37%)
1989	11,604	(21%)	25,970	(47%)	17,682	(32%)

LABOR RELATIONS

The Michelin brothers who built the company were ardent free marketeers, but they adopted a policy of paternalism toward their employees. The company town created in Clermont-Ferrand included subsidized housing, free medical care, and many other benefits for Michelin workers. Layoffs were unheard of—and for many years so were unions. The large French labor federations eventually gained a foothold in Clermont-Ferrand but remained rather weak.

Michelin carried its antiunion philosophy to its foreign facilities, often getting into bitter fights with the labor movement in those countries. During the early 1980s Canadian unions organized a boycott of the company because of its resistance to organizing drives at its plant in Nova Scotia. In Britain unions staged a militant strike that defeated Michelin's plan to institute continuous shifts, which would have forced workers to be on the job for three out of every four weekends. The company attempted to avoid such clashes in the United States by locating its factories in states like South Carolina and Alabama, where unions are weak.

At the Uniroyal-Goodrich operation, however, the company inherited a long-standing relationship with the United Rubber Workers (URW). Goodrich was one of the main organizing targets of the union after it was created in 1935. After Firestone agreed to recognize the union in 1937, Goodrich abandoned its company-dominated union, and the URW won a representation election at the firm. Goodrich initially took a hard line in negotiations, but a contract settlement was reached in 1938. U.S. Rubber, which accepted the advent of unionization without a fight, signed its first contract with the URW that same year.

In 1990 the International Federation of Chemical, Energy and General Workers announced plans for a worldwide campaign to organize the many Michelin workers who remain unrepresented by unions. The following year the company decisively broke with its no-layoffs tradition in France by announcing the elimination of forty-nine hundred jobs, or 13 percent of the domestic work force. There were indications that many thousands more would lose their jobs in the company's foreign factories.

Michelin has angered workers in the United States by announcing plans to shut down unionized Uniroyal-Goodrich plants and shifting production to the parent company's non-union facilities.

ENVIRONMENTAL AND HEALTH RECORD

Through the participation of its Uniroyal-Goodrich subsidiary in a joint venture with Texaco that makes synthetic rubber at a complex in Port Neches, Texas, Michelin has become embroiled in a health controversy in the United States. A group of workers at the plant have developed a form of cancer called non-Hodgkin's lymphoma that they charge is a result of exposure to such chemicals as butadiene on the job. This substance is also emitted in the air, creating a risk for nearby residents.

OSHA has long enforced a standard of exposure to butadiene but now believes that much stricter rules are required. Texaco and Uniroyal-Goodrich have taken steps to reduce butadiene emissions but insist that there is no definitive proof that the substance causes cancer.

BIBLIOGRAPHY

French, Michael J. *The U.S. Tire Industry: A History*. Boston: Twayne, 1991.
Report of the International Tyre Workers Conference: Turin, Italy, 24–26 March 1990. Amsterdam: Transnationals Information Exchange, 1990.
Roberts, Harold S. *The Rubber Workers: Labor Organization and Collective Bargaining in the Rubber Industry*. New York: Harper & Brothers, 1944.

MINNESOTA MINING AND MANUFACTURING COMPANY

3M Center
St. Paul, Minnesota 55144
(612) 733-1110

1991 revenues: $13.3 billion
1991 net income: $1.2 billion
Publicly traded company
Employees: 88,477
Founded: 1902

OVERVIEW

Minnesota Mining and Manufacturing Company, commonly known as 3M, has built a large industrial empire on a series of everyday products ranging from sandpaper to Scotch tape (which it invented) to Post-it adhesive note-pads (which it also created). Today the company boasts a product list of sixty thousand items, many of them unique.

Widely admired for its strong commitment to new product development, 3M's marketing efforts have been more uneven. It remains strong in areas like adhesives, abrasives, and coatings, but it lost the lead in the markets for such products as audiocassette tape, videotape, and floppy disks. With manufacturing facilities in forty-two countries and nearly half of its sales made outside the United States, 3M is one of the leading symbols of both low-tech and high-tech American innovation around the world.

HISTORY

Around the turn of the century the area of northern Minnesota near the shore of Lake Superior was experiencing a mining boom following the discovery of iron ore and the hope that gold and silver might be found as well. Yet it was a more mundane material that prompted the formation in 1902 of a company grandly named Minnesota Mining and Manufacturing. The five people, local professionals and businessmen, who incorporated the company were interested in mining corundum, a natural abrasive used for scouring, polishing, and sharpening metal, glass, and wood. The only commercially profitable mine for corundum in North America was located in northern Ontario.

Even before beginning mining operations, the company agreed to take over its competitor, Minnesota Abrasive, which also had set out to produce corundum but was faltering for lack of capital. Yet it was not long before 3M was struggling as well, since its expenses were mounting and mining had not yet begun. In 1905 the firm was saved by an infusion of capital from Edgar B. Ober and Lucius P. Ordway, two prominent Minnesota businessmen, who ended up with a controlling interest.

Ober and Ordway moved the company's operations from Two Harbors to Duluth and focused on the production of sandpaper. This was fortunate, given that they later learned that their mineral deposits contained not corundum but virtually worthless anorthosite. The company endured nearly a decade in which it was forced to sell a low-quality product and faced intense price competition from other producers.

It was not until 1914 that prospects for 3M began to look up. The company brought out an abrasive cloth called THREE-M-ITE that was well received by the growing automobile industry and became highly sought after as companies began mobilizing for war. The next breakthrough came in the early 1920s, when 3M was contacted by a printer named Francis G. Okie who had developed a waterproof sandpaper. The company bought the rights to the technology and introduced a product under the name WETORDRY that allowed dustless sanding; it too was embraced by automakers as well as by auto repainting shops.

In addition to increasing efficiency, the new product eliminated a great deal of the health hazard from sanding jobs. At this point 3M, whose new president, William L. McKnight, would lead the company for decades to come, was on its way to the top of the abrasives industry. Yet in order to gain a foothold in the European market, the company had to form a consortium (Durex Corporation) with eight of its competitors. In addition to aggressive salesmanship, 3M helped pave the way for its future success in 1930 by purchasing one of those competitors—Baeder-Adamson Company, the oldest sandpaper manufacturer in the United States.

The 3M name was further enhanced in the 1930s after it brought out the first effective masking tape, which, for reasons that are somewhat obscure, was given the brand name Scotch. Yet that brand was to become much more famous—and in fact it would become a generic term—for a cellophane tape that the company soon introduced. Americans embraced the transparent adhesive tape for a thousand and one purposes, from wrapping gifts to mending torn pages of books. Du Pont introduced its own version of cellophane around the same time, but it was used mainly for packaging.

During the 1930s and 1940s 3M brought out a line of colored asphalt roofing shingles, special adhesives for automobile production, and a variety of other adhesives, coatings, and sealants for industrial and consumer use. The company also helped modernize driving by creating Scotchlite reflective sheeting, which made possible road signs that were clearly visible at night. Using technologies developed in Germany, 3M introduced the first high-quality magnetic sound-recording tape shortly after World War II. The tape got a boost when Bing Crosby broke away from the tradition of live radio and began recording his popular show ahead of time.

Antitrust pressures from the federal government forced the dissolution of the Durex consortium in the early 1950s, but 3M took over that company's operations in Britain, France, and Brazil; some Durex assets in Canada and Germany were acquired as well.

While going international, 3M continued to spew out a stream of new products, and by the 1960s it had become a billion-dollar enterprise. Company-produced backdrops for the film *2001: A Space Odyssey* won an Academy Award. During the following decade, however, 3M suffered embarrassment from revelations of an illegal slush fund for political contributions and from a slowing down of sales. Japanese companies like TDK and Maxell took over the market for audiocassette tape, and 3M failed to take a strong position in computer products like floppy disks.

Taking over 3M amid these problems, Lewis Lehr restructured the company and encouraged additional innovation. The best-known result of the latter effort was the creation of Post-it adhesive notepads. The attempt to restore the rapid growth of the 1960s was taken up by Allen Jacobson when he assumed the chief executive's spot in 1986. He did this in part through a program called J−35 ("J" for Jacobson or his nickname Jake, and "35" for a desired 35-percent improvement in productivity). By the late 1980s 3M was cooking again, thanks in large part to a surge in exports and in overseas production.

Another boon for the company came in 1991, when a federal magistrate ordered Johnson & Johnson to pay the company more than $100 million in damages for willfully violating 3M patents on fiberglass tape used for medical casts.

OPERATIONS

Industrial and Consumer (38 percent of 1991 revenues). This segment serves customers in industries ranging from aerospace to textiles with such products as pressure-sensitive tapes, abrasives, specialty chemicals, adhesives, coatings, and sealants. The leading consumer products in this segment are the well-known Scotch-brand cellophane tapes, Post-it adhesive notepads, and Scotchgard fabric protector, as well as wood-refinishing products, packaging materials, and scouring pads and sponges.

Information, Imaging, and Electronic (34 percent of revenues). Included here are photographic films, lithographic plates, microfilm readers, floppy disks, videotape, document management systems, overhead projectors, X-ray film, electronic connectors, splicing material for copper wire, and fiber-optic cable, and many other products.

Life Sciences (28 percent of revenues). The company makes a wide range of products for medical, surgical, and dental markets, including wound closure and healing materials, heart-lung machines, orthopedic implants, surgical masks, intraocular lenses, and blood-gas monitors. Also included in this segment are closures for disposable diapers and reflective materials for traffic safety.

TOP EXECUTIVES

- Livio D. DeSimone, chairman and chief executive
- Harry A. Hammerly, executive vice president, international operations
- Lawrence E. Eaton, executive vice president, information, imaging, and electronic sector
- Ronald A. Mitsch, executive vice president, industrial and consumer sector
- Jerry E. Robertson, executive vice president, life sciences sector
- Giulio Agostini, senior vice president
- M. George Allen, senior vice president
- Charlton Dietz, senior vice president
- Christopher J. Wheeler, senior vice president

OUTSIDE DIRECTORS

- Edward A. Brennan, chief executive of Sears, Roebuck & Company
- George Fisher, chief executive of Motorola
- Allen E. Murray, chief executive of Mobil Corporation
- John G. Ordway, Jr., retired chairman of MacArthur Company
- Aulana L. Peters, partner in the law firm Gibson Dunn & Crutcher
- Rozanne L. Ridgway, president of the Atlantic Council of the United States
- F. Alan Smith, executive vice president of General Motors

Also on the board is Allen F. Jacobson, former chief executive of 3M.

FINANCIAL DATA

Revenues (in millions of dollars)

1991	13,340
1990	13,021
1989	11,990
1988	11,323
1987	10,004

Net Income (in millions of dollars)

1991	1,154
1990	1,308
1989	1,244
1988	1,154
1987	918

GEOGRAPHICAL BREAKDOWN

Revenues (in millions of dollars)

Year	United States		Europe		Elsewhere	
1991	6,875	(52%)	3,857	(29%)	2,608	(20%)
1990	6,802	(52%)	3,705	(28%)	2,514	(19%)
1989	6,601	(55%)	3,023	(25%)	2,366	(20%)
1988	6,275	(55%)	2,903	(26%)	2,145	(19%)

Operating Income (in millions of dollars)

Year	United States		Europe		Elsewhere	
1991	1,169	(60%)	409	(21%)	381	(19%)
1990	1,268	(58%)	463	(21%)	460	(21%)
1989	1,222	(57%)	452	(21%)	476	(23%)
1988	1,133	(56%)	477	(24%)	406	(20%)

LABOR RELATIONS

From its earliest years 3M cultivated good relations with its employees. When the company was still small, problems were resolved in group discussions. During the 1920s the company joined in the business trend of establishing profit-sharing plans for key employees. In 1937 the plan was revised to allow for participation by nearly all of the work force, but employees gradually grew disenchanted with the system and it was discontinued in 1952. The company introduced its own system of unemployment insurance in 1932, but it was soon superseded by government plans. Despite this paternalism, the company's main facilities were organized in the late 1940s by a predecessor of the Oil, Chemical and Atomic Workers.

The company found itself the target of a high-profile labor dispute in 1985 when it tried to shut down an audiotape and videotape manufacturing facility in Freehold, New Jersey. The OCAW local at the plant gained the support of rock star Bruce Springsteen (who had written songs about industrial decline in his native state of New Jersey) in its campaign to pressure 3M to keep the plant open. An advertisement headlined 3M: DON'T ABANDON OUR HOMETOWN! and signed by Springsteen and fellow singer Willie Nelson was published in major newspapers.

The OCAW also made contact with unions representing 3M workers in South Africa. In February 1986 three hundred black employees at 3M's plant near Johannesburg walked off the job in solidarity with the workers in New Jersey. The action also was meant to promote their own battle against layoffs and wage differentials between white and black workers. The campaign succeeded in keeping the plant open, but with a sharply reduced work force.

ENVIRONMENTAL RECORD

Thanks to its Pollution Prevention Pays program, launched in 1975 to encourage employees to find ways to reduce waste in the company's operations, 3M has enjoyed a favorable reputation among environmental groups. In 1990 the company began an effort to cut its toxic-air emissions at plants in the United States by 70 percent by 1993 and to reduce all toxic releases by 90 percent by the end of the century.

Nonetheless, 3M remains one of the largest industrial polluters, according to data from the EPA. In 1989 the company was responsible for emitting the sixth-largest volume (108 million pounds) among all U.S. manufacturing companies and the largest volume of substances known to cause or suspected of causing birth defects.

In 1989 Minnesota fined the company $1.5 million—the largest penalty ever levied by the state—for violations of emission limits from the incinerator at its Chemolite plant. The previous year 3M paid $158,000 to settle a lawsuit brought by environmental groups charging the company with violating federal water pollution regulations at the same facility.

The company has also been fined by the EPA for illegally importing hazardous chemicals and by the Nuclear Regulatory Commission for willfully violating federal rules governing distribution of a radioactive product—specifically, the company's static-eliminating air-ionizing guns, which were found to leak polonium 210.

3M's record in the area of occupational health also leaves something to be desired. According to an article by Jim Donahue in the May 1991 issue of

Multinational Monitor, 3M was cited by OSHA for workplace violations more than 150 times during the 1980s. In the early 1990s the National Institute for Occupational Safety and Health began investigating a high rate of heart and lung problems among workers at a 3M roofing products plant in Little Rock, Arkansas.

BIBLIOGRAPHY

Huck, Virginia. *Brand of the Tartan*: *The 3M Story*. New York: Appleton-Century-Crofts, 1955.

Our Story So Far: *Notes From the First 75 Years of 3M Company*. St. Paul, Minn.: 3M Company, 1977.

MITSUBISHI GROUP

Major affiliates:

Mitsubishi Corporation
6–3, Marunouchi 2-chome
Chiyoda-ku, Tokyo 100-86
Japan
(03) 3210-2121

1991 revenues: $140.3 billion (year ending March 31)
1991 net income: $464.4 million
Publicly traded company
Employees: 9,429
Founded: 1870

Mitsubishi Bank
7-1, Marunouchi 2-chome
Chiyoda-ku, Tokyo 100
Japan
(03) 3240-1111

1991 revenues: $30.9 billion (year ending March 31)
1991 net income: $725.5 million
1991 assets: $381.6 billion
Publicly traded company
Employees: 13,899
Founded: 1919

Mitsubishi Electric Corporation
Mitsubishi Denki Building
2-3, Marunouchi 2-chome

Chiyoda-ku, Tokyo 100
Japan
(03) 3218-2111

1991 revenues: $23.6 billion (year ending March 31)
1991 net income: $567.3 million
Publicly traded company
Employees: 97,002
Founded: 1921

Mitsubishi Heavy Industries
5-1, Marunouchi 2-chome
Chiyoda-ku, Tokyo 100
Japan
(03) 3212-3111

1991 revenues: $18.2 billion (year ending March 31)
1991 net income: $688.9 million
Publicly traded company
Employees: 44,272
Founded: 1884

Mitsubishi Motors Corporation
33-8, Shiba 5-chome
Minato-ku, Tokyo 108
Japan
(03) 3456-1111

1991 revenues: $19.9 billion (year ending March 31)
1991 net income: $183.9 million
Publicly traded company
Employees: 25,515
Founded: 1970

OVERVIEW

The Mitsubishi Group, one of Japan's leading *keiretsu* corporate families, consists of a massive trading company called Mitsubishi Corporation and scores of affiliates, among them leading manufacturers in all major industries. The most important of these are a core of about thirty large firms that are nominally independent but are tied to one another through cross-ownership, interlocking directorates, and regular meetings of their top managers to coordinate business strategies.

Mitsubishi Corporation is a *sogo shosha*, or general trading company, which means that it does not manufacture anything, but buys, sells, barters, and invests on a huge scale, racking up massive revenues but tiny profits. For many years it was the largest trading company in Japan, but it slipped to fifth place in 1986 because of the decline in oil prices and has remained there.

The group, which dates back to a shipping operation formed in the late nineteenth century, includes some of the largest Japanese players in such fields as aerospace, semiconductors, and banking. Mitsubishi Motors is a rising star in the international auto industry, and Mitsubishi Estate now owns 80 percent of one of the most famous pieces of real estate in the world—Rockefeller Center. The group's operations are so widespread that a 1990 *Business Week* article quotes a Japanese analyst as speaking of "the Mitsubishi-fication of the world."

HISTORY

Mitsubishi had its origins in the entrepreneurial efforts of Yataro Iwasaki, who started out as a manager in an Osaka trading house. In 1870 he acquired his own shipping company, originally called Tsukumo Shokai but renamed Mitsubishi Steamship four years later. The name Mitsubishi, which means "Three Diamonds," was derived from the symbols used on its ship flags.

Iwasaki developed close relations with the Japanese government by supplying ships for military actions and went on to create a virtual monopoly in the ocean transport business. Mitsubishi suddenly faced significant domestic competition in the early 1880s when the company's political allies fell out of power and the government encouraged the growth of a rival shipping operation, Kyodo Unyu (United Transport). Years of devastating price wars ended in 1887 with the merger of the shipping operations of the two firms into a new venture called Nippon Yusen Kaisha (Japan Shipping Company).

Mitsubishi, meanwhile, had expanded into coal production through the purchase of the Takashima Coal Mine and into shipbuilding by leasing the government-owned Nagasaki Shipyard. The family-run business, now known as Mitsubishi Company, also entered real estate, banking and other businesses, making it a true *zaibatsu* conglomerate.

By the 1920s the Mitsubishi octopus consisted of more than seventy enterprises, including ones involved in such heavy industries as chemicals, petroleum, electrical equipment, and engines. Drawn into the militarization process that overwhelmed Japan in the 1930s, the group's most famous contribution to the war effort was the Zero fighter plane. Mitsubishi companies also produced battleships, ammunition, and other military supplies.

After the war the Allied occupation authorities ordered the breakup of Mitsubishi and the other *zaibatsu*; more than seventy-five years of Iwasaki family control also came to an end. The separate companies struggled to survive the difficulties of the early postwar period on their own—and with different names, since the *zaibatsu* logos were banned.

Such restrictions were later eased by U.S. authorities as part of a decision to build up Japan as a bulwark against Communist expansion in Asia. By 1954 firms of Mitsubishi origin began restoring that name, and the group's central trading company was re-formed and moved quickly to create an international trading network. The trading company, which in 1971 was renamed Mitsubishi Corporation, followed the pattern of Japanese economic development by focusing on imports of raw materials and energy and exports of manufactured goods. Mitsubishi joined with Royal Dutch/Shell to develop a system of liquefying natural gas in order to exploit a large gas deposit discovered in Brunei.

Mitsubishi was thus reincarnated as one of the leading *keiretsu*, the postwar conglomerates that do not have quite the same degree of centralized control as the *zaibatsu* did but that constitute coherent groups nonetheless. Companies within the group fanned out into a wide range of businesses, among them synthetic fibers, aluminum, atomic power, and heavy equipment. In 1964 Mitsubishi Heavy Industries was reamalgamated, with operations in automobiles, nuclear reactors, and other fields as well as its original involvement in shipbuilding. Mitsubishi Bank emerged as one of the country's largest financial institutions.

Soon Mitsubishi seemed to be everywhere—from salt production in Baja California to the tourism industry in Kenya and forest products in Indonesia. Mitsubishi Electric began selling locomotives and satellite earth stations as well as smaller-ticket items like air conditioners, televisions, and, later, VCRs. During the 1980s it was one of the Japanese companies that took over the world market for memory chips. In 1983 Mitsubishi Electric pleaded no contest to charges that four of its employees had tried to steal trade secrets from IBM.

In 1970 the motor vehicle division of Mitsubishi Heavy Industries split off to form Mitsubishi Motors Corporation. The following year Chrysler bought 15 percent of the company and began selling its cars in the United States under the Chrysler Colt name. Mitsubishi later began selling its cars in the American market directly, although in 1985 the two companies joined forces again to create Diamond-Star Motors, which produces cars at a plant in Illinois. Chrysler increased its holdings in Mitsubishi to more than 20 percent but subsequently reduced them to about six percent. In late 1991 Mitsubishi Motors bought out Chrysler's share of the Diamond-Star operation.

Over the past decade the Mitsubishi Group has been an increasingly visible presence in world commerce. Mitsubishi Bank purchased the Bank of California in 1984, Mitsubishi Estate acquired a majority stake in Rockefeller Center in 1989, and a Mitsubishi consortium launched its own satellite that same year. Chemical company Mitsubishi Kasei purchased the Verbatim floppy disk business from Eastman Kodak and has moved into biotechnology. Mitsubishi Corporation acquired U.S. chemical company Aristech for $877 million and then sold pieces of it to other companies in its group. Mitsubishi Electric purchased the Apricot computer line in Britain. In 1990 the group formed a wide-ranging alliance with Germany's Daimler-Benz, but two years later, little had come of it.

Several parts of the Mitsubishi Group have had antitrust problems in recent years. In 1991 Mitsubishi Plastics Industries was accused, along with seven other companies, by Japan's Fair Trade Commission of fixing prices on food wrap. The following year Mitsubishi Electric paid $5 million in the United States to settle a suit brought by the states of Maryland and New York charging that the company had fixed prices on television sets.

OPERATIONS

Mitsubishi Corporation. The general trading arm of the group is Mitsubishi Corporation. Its main areas of activity are:

- Information systems and services and machinery (27 percent of 1991 trading transactions): consumer and medical electronics, semiconductor and computer systems, aerospace, telecommunications and multimedia systems and services, electrical equipment, automobiles, and various forms of industrial and agricultural machinery.
- Fuels (18 percent of trading transactions): petroleum, carbon materials, and related products.
- Metals (27 percent of trading transactions): raw materials for steel, steaming coal, steel products, nonferrous metal products, and nuclear fuel.
- Foods (12 percent of trading transactions): grains, sweeteners, oils, fats, meats, frozen foods, canned foods, dairy products, and other foods.
- Chemicals (8 percent of trading transactions): basic chemicals, plastics and high-performance chemicals, and fine and inorganic chemicals.
- Textiles and general merchandise (7 percent of trading transactions): fibers, pulp and paper, wood, construction materials, tires, cigarettes, and other products.

Mitsubishi Bank. Among the top ten commercial banks in the world, Mitsubishi Bank has 313 banking offices in Japan, mainly in Tokyo and Osaka. The bank provides a variety of financial services, including investment banking, securities brokerage, and project financing, in twenty-six countries. Some 75 percent of its international business is with non-Japanese clients. Its Bank of California subsidiary has offices in forty-two cities in California, Oregon, and Washington. The bank has a conservative approach to business and has avoided high-risk lending. This attribute caused the bank to be disparaged in the roaring 1980s but now is considered a virtue.

Mitsubishi Electric Corporation. The Mitsubishi Electric Corporation operates in four main areas:

- Information, telecommunications, and electronic systems and devices: a wide range of computers and peripherals, PBXs and other telephone equipment, fax machines, cellular phones, and integrated circuits. In 1991 the company agreed to develop high-performance gallium arsenide semiconductors in cooperation with AT&T.
- Heavy machinery: nuclear power equipment, electric locomotives, elevators and escalators, cooling systems, and other electrical equipment.

- Various kinds of industrial machinery and automation equipment.
- Consumer products: televisions, VCRs, audio equipment, and household appliances. The company makes the huge Diamond Vision display systems used in sports stadiums and has a leading position in the market for large-screen televisions.

Mitsubishi Heavy Industries. Mitsubishi Heavy Industries produces nuclear and fossil fuel power systems; cargo and passenger ships; machinery for industries like petroleum and paper; aircraft; cooling systems; and other machinery. In the aerospace area it produces components for such customers as Boeing, the Pratt & Whitney division of United Technologies, and the International Aero Engines consortium. Japan's largest military contractor, this company is also among a group of seven U.S., European, and Japanese companies working on a hypersonic jet engine that would cut air travel time between New York and Tokyo down to three hours. In 1991 the company was named as one of a group of firms that had employed an industrial spy who broke into the offices of Komatsu Ltd. to obtain information.

Mitsubishi Motors Corporation. Mitsubishi Motors Corporation is the sixth-largest automaker in Japan, with a product line that ranges from 660-cc minicars to heavy-duty trucks and large buses. Its leading models include the Galant, the Mirage, and the Eclipse. The Mirage is also sold by Chrysler in North America under the names Eagle Summit, Dodge Colt, and Plymouth Colt, while the Eclipse is made in the United States by Diamond-Star. Mitsubishi also has gone upscale, with luxury cars like the Diamante and Debonair. In 1990 it acquired 80 percent of Value Rent-A-Car in the United States but ended up in a messy legal dispute with the former owners of the company. In 1991 Mitsubishi became a partner in a three-way joint venture with the Dutch government and the Swedish car maker Volvo to operate Volvo's Dutch subsidiary.

TOP EXECUTIVES

Mitsubishi Corporation
- Yohei Mimura, chairman
- Minoru Makihara, president
- Takeshi Eguchi, executive vice president, new business
- Ichiji Kishimoto, executive vice president, Osaka Branch
- Shiro Shibuya, senior managing director, information systems
- Shinichiro Ohta, senior managing director, administration
- Akira Horie, senior managing director, Nagoya Branch
- Yoshiaki Shibata, senior managing director, machinery
- Nobuo Kobayashi, senior managing director, and chairman of Mitsubishi Euro-Africa and Mitsubishi Corporation (U.K.) Ltd.
- Enshiro Matsuyama, senior managing director, foods

FINANCIAL DATA

Mitsubishi Corporation

Revenues (in millions of yen) (years ending March 31)

1991	19,726,536
1990	18,522,931
1989	15,643,815
1988	13,364,883
1987	12,660,061

Net Income (in millions of yen) (years ending March 31)

1991	65,290
1990	60,356
1989	46,131
1988	31,167
1987	27,474

GEOGRAPHICAL BREAKDOWN

Mitsubishi Corporation

Revenues (in millions of yen)

Year*	Japan		Europe		Elsewhere	
1991	18,079,710	(71%)	3,037,340	(12%)	4,432,174	(17%)
1990	17,195,930	(73%)	2,926,067	(12%)	3,591,037	(15%)
1989	14,154,133	(70%)	3,043,760	(15%)	3,165,070	(16%)

*Fiscal year ends March 31.

Operating Profit (in millions of yen)

Year*	Japan		Europe		Elsewhere	
1991	101,270	(76%)	5,704	(4%)	26,187	(20%)
1990	100,806	(81%)	4,460	(4%)	18,713	(15%)
1989	70,415	(89%)	1,587	(2%)	6,914	(9%)

*Fiscal year ends March 31.

LABOR RELATIONS

While the Mitsubishi companies generally cooperate with unions in Japan, their policies in the United States have been more varied. In the Diamond-Star joint venture with Chrysler, Mitsubishi Motors accepted the presence of the United Auto Workers but managed to negotiate a contract that eased work rules and limited the number of job classifications to three—far fewer than in other unionized auto plants. In exchange for this management flexibility the workers were given much greater job security, including a ban on layoffs except when the long-term viability of the company is threatened.

By contrast, Mitsubishi Semiconductor America, a subsidiary of Mitsubishi Electric, strongly opposed an organizing drive among its employees in Durham, North Carolina, in 1987. The workers voted three to one against the International Brotherhood of Electrical Workers because, according to an IBEW official, "they had the hell scared out of them" by management.

ENVIRONMENTAL RECORD

The Mitsubishi Group has been the target of a consumer boycott by the Rainforest Action Network because of Mitsubishi Corporation's role in importing large quantities of lumber from tropical areas, thus contributing to the erosion of rain forests.

In 1990 Mitsubishi Motors had to recall ninety-two thousand cars and seventy-five thousand light trucks—many of them sold by Chrysler—in the United States because they were emitting excessive levels of carbon monoxide and hydrocarbons.

A nuclear reactor made by Mitsubishi Heavy Industries was involved in an accident at the Mihama nuclear power plant in Japan in 1991. The problem, which resulted in an automatic shutdown of the reactor, was traced to incorrect positioning of the antivibration bars, but it was not known whether the bars were installed improperly by Mitsubishi or whether they became loose during operation of the reactor.

On the positive side, Mitsubishi Corporation claims to recycle 70 percent of the paper used in its offices, and Mitsubishi Electric is the prime contractor for Earth Resources Satellite-1, scheduled for launching in 1992, and was selected as the integrator for the Advanced Earth Observing Satellite, which is supposed to go into orbit in 1995. These satellites, both projects of Japan's National Space Development Agency, will collect information on the ozone layer, global warming, and other environmental conditions.

BIBLIOGRAPHY

Bisson, Thomas Arthur. *Zaibatsu Dissolution in Japan*. 1954. Reprint. Westport, Conn.: Greenwood, 1976.
Kunio, Yoshihara. *Sogo Shosha: The Vanguard of the Japanese Economy*. Tokyo: Oxford University Press, 1982.

Mishima, Yasua. *Industrial Development and the Social Fabric*. Vol. 11, *Mitsubishi—Its Challenge and Strategy*. Greenwich, Conn.: JAI Press, 1990.

Wray, William D. *Mitsubishi and the N.Y.K., 1870–1914: Business Strategy in the Japanese Shipping Industry*. Cambridge, Mass.: Harvard University Press, 1984.

Yoshino, M. Y., and Thomas B. Lifson. *The Invisible Link: Japan's Sogo Shosha and the Organization of Trade*. Cambridge, Mass.: MIT Press, 1986.

Young, Alexander. *The Sogo Shosha: Japan's Multinational Trading Companies*. Boulder, Colo.: Westview, 1979.

MOBIL CORPORATION

3225 Gallows Road
Fairfax, Virginia 22037
(703) 846-3000

1991 Revenues: $56.9 billion
1991 net income: $1.9 billion
Publicly traded company
Employees: 67,500
Founded: 1866

OVERVIEW

Mobil Corporation, which, with British Petroleum, vies for third place among the world's oil companies, has emerged as the most ideologically combative of the group known as the Seven Sisters. The company, born out of the breakup of the Standard Oil trust in 1911, has been an outspoken defender of the oil industry and big business in general. Since the early 1970s this company has regularly bought space on the op-ed pages of newspapers around the country to trumpet its views.

Mobil, which traditionally was strongest in the lubricants business and took decades to build itself as a significant explorer for oil, failed at a diversification attempt launched in the 1970s. It is now almost entirely an oil and petrochemicals company, and like its brethren in the petroleum industry, it has spent the past decade shuffling its assets and streamlining its operations.

HISTORY

The origins of Mobil go back to only a few years after the U.S. petroleum industry was created by Edwin Drake's discovery of oil in Pennsylvania in 1859. In Rochester, New York, a carpenter and inventor named Matthew

Ewing devised a method of producing kerosene—then the dominant source of artificial light—by distilling crude oil in a vacuum. He claimed that this method would yield more kerosene from a barrel of oil than did other techniques.

Ewing persuaded a young entrepreneur named Hiram Bond Everest to invest in the project. It turned out that Ewing's method was not more efficient, but Everest noticed that it did create an oil residue that was odorless and unburned. He quickly recognized that the residue could serve as a lubricant for machinery and for leather that would be superior to the noxious and corrosive substances then being used for those purposes. In 1866 the two men formed Vacuum Oil to sell petroleum lubricants.

Yet the two partners did not see eye to eye on how to build the business. Everest wanted to concentrate on their Vacuum Harness Oil, while Ewing was still preoccupied with kerosene. When they could not resolve the dispute, Everest bought out Ewing's interest and aggressively built a market for his lubricants. He also introduced coach oil, axle grease, and additional lubricants for industrial purposes, among them a high-quality steam cylinder oil that accelerated the development of internal combustion gasoline engines and electric generators and motors.

In the 1870s Vacuum Oil came to the attention of the man who had given himself the task of consolidating (and later monopolizing) the young petroleum industry. That man was John D. Rockefeller, who started a kerosene-refining business in 1863 and in 1870 formed the Standard Oil Company. As part of his quest to dominate all aspects of the industry, Rockefeller purchased a controlling interest in Vacuum Oil in 1879.

To get around a law in Ohio (where the empire began) limiting a corporation's ownership of shares of companies in other states, Rockefeller created an arrangement that became known as the Standard Oil trust, in which Standard's subsidiaries were nominally independent but were controlled by a centralized board of trustees. The administrative arm of the trust was Standard Oil Company of New York, or Socony, which also dominated the refining and marketing of petroleum products in New York and New England.

Standard pushed Vacuum to expand abroad. By the late 1880s the company had branch offices or affiliates in Australia, Cuba, France, India, Italy, Japan, and other countries. Socony, too, was busy abroad, especially in selling kerosene to China. The company introduced millions of inexpensive kerosene lamps (given the name *mei foo*, from the Chinese symbols for Socony, meaning "beautiful confidence") to that country and then sent waves of clipper ships to satisfy the demand for the oil burned by those lamps.

By the early years of the twentieth century public opposition to the Standard Oil trust was growing, and the Roosevelt administration felt compelled to bring antitrust charges against the Rockefeller empire. In 1909 a federal court ruled that the trust was illegal under the Sherman Act. The case went all the way to the Supreme Court, which in 1911 upheld the ruling and ordered the dissolution of Standard into thirty-three independent companies, among them Socony and Vacuum.

Neither of the two companies was a fully integrated petroleum producer, so they had to scramble to gain access to crude oil supplies. In 1918 Socony purchased a 45-percent interest (later increased to 100 percent) in Magnolia Petroleum, one of the pioneers of the oil business in the Southwest. Eight years later Socony bought General Petroleum Corporation of California, and in 1930 it acquired White Eagle Oil & Refining. The company also became a partner in the Western-run Turkish Petroleum Company, which was developing oil supplies in a vast area of the old Ottoman Empire. Meanwhile, Vacuum built a refinery in New Jersey, and in 1929 it bought the Lubrite Refining Company. The following year it added Wadhams Oil Corporation and White Star Refining Company.

In 1931 the two offspring of the Standard Oil trust were reunited—with federal approval. The resulting company, Socony-Vacuum Corporation, had worldwide interests in refining, transportation, and marketing, along with popular brands like Flying Red Horse and Mobil. It became one of the Seven Sisters, the leading companies in the international oil business, but it was the smallest of the lot. In 1933 the company joined with another one-time sibling, Standard Oil of New Jersey, to create a joint venture—called Standard-Vacuum Oil Company, or Stanvac—for all of their operations in dozens of countries stretching from the east coast of Africa to New Zealand. (The arrangement was ended in 1962 in response to federal antitrust pressures.)

On its own Socony-Vacuum built new refineries in France and Italy, which it lost access to during World War II. After the war another refinery was built in Britain, and all of the European facilities began receiving more of their crude oil from Socony-Vacuum's production efforts, especially those in the Middle East. This was possible because in 1945 Socony-Vacuum joined the Aramco joint venture in Saudi Arabia, and in 1954 the company gained a share in Iranian production as part of a new consortium formed after a CIA-led coup overthrew the government that had expropriated the holdings of Anglo-Iranian Oil Company (later known as British Petroleum).

The company, which changed its name to Socony-Mobil in 1955, moved into petrochemicals in the 1960s. Then in 1966 it dropped the last reference to its Standard Oil origins by renaming itself Mobil Oil Corporation. Rawleigh Warner, who took over the company in 1969, moved to make Mobil a more aggressive player, a feat he accomplished in part by choosing as his president a lawyer-accountant named William Tavoulareas, the son of a Greek-Italian butcher from Brooklyn.

Mobil, which was highly dependent on its Mideast production, suffered through the periodic crises of that region—from the Suez dispute to the Six-Day War to the oil embargo of the early 1970s—but in the end the rise of petroleum prices helped to fill the company's coffers. In 1974 it used that wealth to acquire a majority interest (later increased to 100 percent) in Marcor, the parent company of retailer Montgomery Ward and the Container Corporation of America. Mobil Corporation was then established as a holding company. Additional investments were made in coal and uranium.

Oil exploration was not ignored during this period. The company made large finds in the Gulf of Mexico, on the Grand Banks off Newfoundland, in the North Sea, and elsewhere. In 1978 it began producing natural gas in Indonesia. Mobil also went exploring in the boardroom. It lost out to U.S. Steel in a 1982 contest for Marathon Oil but succeeded in purchasing Superior Oil for $5.7 billion in 1985.

Mobil was also in the public eye for the militant position it took on issues affecting business. Since the early 1970s the company has been a regular presence on the op-ed pages of major newspapers with its outspoken advertisements. One series of ads that ran in 1978 hailed the "capitalist revolution" and denounced government regulators as "the new reactionaries." Mobil also has sought to win friends in a less belligerent way—through large and conspicuous contributions to public television. One reason for the ideological crusade has been to counteract the bad publicity it received in scandals like the one stemming from the fact that the company supplied oil to the white supremacist regime in Rhodesia from 1966 to 1979—in violation of United Nations sanctions.

Under the leadership of street-smart Allen Murray, who took over in 1985, Mobil has shuffled billions of dollars worth of assets. The disappointing investments in Montgomery Ward and Container Corporation were sold off, while refineries were purchased in Louisiana and Australia. In 1990 the company's chemical division purchased Tucker Housewares, the second-largest producer of plastic products for the home.

OPERATIONS

Petroleum Exploration and Production (9 percent of 1991 revenues). Mobil is actively involved in drilling and production activities in the United States, Canada, Germany, Norway, the United Kingdom portion of the North Sea, the Netherlands, Nigeria, and Indonesia. It is seeking to develop oil supplies through exploration in such countries as Argentina, Australia, Peru, Turkey, Zambia, and Zimbabwe. Its net reserves of crude oil and natural gas liquids at the end of 1991 were 3.3 billion barrels; natural gas reserves were more than 18 trillion cubic feet.

Petroleum Refining and Marketing (84 percent of revenues). Mobil owns or has an operating interest in twenty-one refineries in twelve countries. Its worldwide refinery runs averaged 1.9 million gallons a day during 1991. The company's petroleum products—including automotive and aviation gasolines, industrial lubricants and greases, motor oils, and many others—are marketed in more than ninety countries around the world. Mobil has about nine thousand retail outlets in the United States, forty-five hundred in Europe, and smaller numbers in countries like Australia and Hong Kong.

Chemical and Other Products (6 percent of revenues). Mobil produces petrochemicals, plastics, and other chemical products at thirty-five plants in the United States and twelve abroad. Its best-known products in this area are Hefty trash bags and Baggies plastic food storage bags. The company also mines phosphates in the United States.

TOP EXECUTIVES

- Allen E. Murray, chairman, president, and chief executive
- Robert G. Weeks, senior vice president
- Paul J. Hoenmans, executive vice president of Mobil Oil
- Eugene A. Renna, executive vice president of Mobil Oil
- Lucio A. Noto, vice president and chief financial officer

OUTSIDE DIRECTORS

- Lewis M. Branscomb, director of science, technology, and public policy at the John F. Kennedy School of Government, Harvard University
- Donald V. Fites, chief executive of Caterpillar Inc.
- Allen F. Jacobson, former chief executive of 3M
- Samuel C. Johnson, chairman of S. C. Johnson & Sons
- Helene L. Kaplan, counsel to Skadden Arps Slate Meagher & Flom
- William J. Kennedy III, chairman of North Carolina Mutual Life Insurance Company
- J. Richard Munro, former co–chief executive of Time Warner Inc.
- Charles S. Sanford, Jr., chairman of Bankers Trust
- Robert G. Schwartz, chief executive of Metropolitan Life Insurance

FINANCIAL DATA

Revenues (in millions of dollars)

1991	56,910
1990	58,770
1989	50,976
1988	49,237
1987	46,927

Net Income (in millions of dollars)

1991	1,920
1990	1,929
1989	1,809
1988	2,087
1987	1,348

GEOGRAPHICAL BREAKDOWN

Revenues (in millions of dollars)

Year	United States		Canada		Elsewhere	
1991	20,006	(32%)	1,124	(2%)	41,542	(66%)
1990	21,198	(32%)	1,194	(2%)	43,155	(66%)
1989	19,191	(34%)	1,058	(2%)	36,544	(64%)

Net Income (in millions of dollars)

Year	United States		Canada		Elsewhere	
1991	334	(14%)	10	(.4%)	2,091	(86%)
1990	415	(16%)	113	(4%)	2,019	(79%)
1989	731	(32%)	95	(4%)	1,459	(64%)

LABOR RELATIONS

Like other companies born out of the breakup of the Standard Oil trust, Socony-Vacuum sought to use paternalism to discourage unionization. Like its brethren, it also used company unions to give the illusion of representation. Over time a number of these company unions gave way to real unions, such as the Oil, Chemical and Atomic Workers. Mobil generally follows industry patterns in bargaining.

After Mobil decided to sell its South African operations in 1989, the company found itself in a dispute with the Chemical Workers Industrial Union. The union, which represented most of Mobil's black workers in the country, protested the fact that the company had not consulted with it on the divestment. After a two-week strike the parties reached a settlement in which Mobil promised that the new owners would uphold union contracts and conditions of employment for at least one year. Mobil also agreed to give each worker one month's wages (about $690) as a form of severance pay.

ENVIRONMENTAL RECORD

In 1989 Mobil was sued by the city of Torrance, California, because of leaks of hydrofluoric acid and other health and safety problems at the company's refinery in that city. The suit, calling the facility a public nuisance, cited numerous instances of worker injury and death at the refinery as well as one case in which fumes from the plant had hospitalized eight students and two teachers at a nearby school. The city later filed criminal charges against the company and two of its managers in connection with a 1988 explosion at the refinery that killed one person and burned several others. In 1990 Mobil and the city reached a settlement of the public nuisance suit in which the company agreed to phase out or reformulate the use of hydrofluoric acid. Mobil also agreed to allow an independent consultant to monitor and control safety conditions at the refinery.

The state of Massachusetts in 1989 penalized Mobil for failing to report the discovery of a leaking gasoline tank at one of its service stations by requiring the company to take out newspaper advertisements urging other gasoline companies to comply with environmental laws and to upgrade their storage facilities.

Also in 1989, Mobil pleaded no contest to criminal charges in California relating to pipeline ruptures the year before that had spilled more than 130,000 gallons of crude oil, much of it into the Los Angeles River and the city's sewer system.

Mobil has come under attack for its attempt to portray its Hefty plastic trash bags as friendly to the environment. In 1990 half a dozen states filed lawsuits against the company charging it with deceptive advertising for calling the bags biodegradable. New York State Attorney General Robert Abrams called the company's claims for Hefty "green-collar fraud." Mobil settled the suits in 1991 by agreeing to end the claims about biodegradability and to pay each of the states $25,000.

On the positive side, the company has become involved in recycling by setting up a program with supermarkets to encourage customers to bring in used plastic grocery sacks, which are then recycled into Hefty bags. Mobil's chemical division has teamed up with Genpak Corporation to build a polystyrene recycling plant in Massachusetts and is a participant with other plastics companies in the National Polystyrene Recycling Company.

In 1990 Mobil finally began to take action to deal with an environmental hazard that has existed for decades. The problem was a veritable underground lake of petroleum resulting from years of storage-tank and pipeline leaks at the company's facility in the Greenpoint section of Brooklyn, New York. After years of resisting taking responsibility for the millions of gallons of oil, Mobil signed a consent order that required it to clean up the mess.

In recent years several former environmental managers at Mobil have brought suits against the company charging that they had been dismissed for refusing to conceal dangerous conditions at various facilities. In November 1990 one of those managers, Valcar Bowman, Jr., was awarded more than $1.3 million in damages by a federal jury in New Jersey.

In 1991 the EPA proposed a penalty of $575,000 against Mobil's facility in Paulsboro, New Jersey, for failure to report several accidental releases of hazardous substances. Mobil was also one of ten major oil companies cited by the EPA that year for discharging contaminated fluids from service stations into or directly above underground sources of drinking water. The company agreed to pay a fine of $125,000 and to clean up the problem by the end of 1993.

BIBLIOGRAPHY

Davidson, Ray. *Challenging the Giants*: *A History of the Oil, Chemical and Atomic Workers International Union*. Denver: OCAW, 1988.

Josephson, Matthew. *The Robber Barons*: *The Great American Capitalists, 1861–1901*. New York: Harcourt, Brace, 1934.

O'Connor, Harvey. *History of Oil Workers Intl. Union (CIO)*. Denver: Oil Workers International Union, 1950.

Sampson, Anthony. *The Seven Sisters: The Great Oil Companies and the World They Made*. New York: Viking, 1975.

Tarbell, Ida M. *The History of the Standard Oil Co*. 1904. Reprint. New York: Macmillan, 1925.

Warner, Rawleigh, Jr. *Mobil Oil*: *A View from the Second Century*. New York: Newcomen Society, 1966.

MOTOROLA, INC.

1303 East Algonquin Road
Schaumburg, Illinois 60196
(708) 576-5000

1991 revenues: $11.3 billion
1991 net income: $454 million
Publicly traded company
Employees: 102,000
Founded: 1928

OVERVIEW

Motorola is one of the most aggressive and generally successful U.S. companies seeking to resist the Japanese onslaught in high-tech areas like electronics and telecommunications. Motorola, which started out making car radios, has covered all the bases in the international competitiveness arena. At times it has been an outspoken opponent of unfair trade practices by the Japanese and has managed to pressure the U.S. government to penalize its foreign competitors for dumping.

Yet Motorola has been willing to compete in terms of efficiency. It is considered one of the most formidable U.S. manufacturing companies, thanks to its introduction of the most advanced industrial technology and its extraordinary efforts to improve quality control. Finally, Motorola has indulged in the "if you can't beat them, join them" approach by forming technology-sharing arrangements with the likes of Toshiba.

Motorola's main strength is in wireless communications; the company leads both the cellular telephone and paging businesses worldwide. It also has put forth an ambitious plan to ring the globe with satellites to provide cellular service virtually everywhere on earth.

Like other U.S companies, in the semiconductor field Motorola has been bloodied by the Japanese in the memory chip business but continues to be a dogged rival to Intel in the microprocessor field.

HISTORY

Paul Galvin returned home from serving in Europe during World War I with an entrepreneurial itch. Several ventures involving storage batteries failed, but then he found success making radios for use in an unusual place: automobiles. The Galvin Manufacturing Company, formed in 1928, came out two years later with the first commercially produced car radio. Galvin called his product Motorola, a combination of "motor" and "Victrola."

The Motorola radios, which at about $120 were priced at about half of what the custom-made units of the day cost, were heavily advertised and well received. The company went on to produce two-way radios for police cars and developed the portable two-way communications system that became known as the walkie-talkie. During World War II the company produced much of the communications equipment used by American troops.

After the war the company, which in 1947 changed its name to Motorola, bought Detrola, a competing car radio producer, and took over its role as a leading original equipment supplier to Ford Motor. During the same period, the company began making television sets that were priced well below the existing products and thus quickly gained a substantial market share.

The invention of the transistor at Bell Laboratories inspired Galvin's son Robert and Dan Noble, an engineer who played a key role at Motorola, to move into electronics. Paul Galvin was hesitant but ended up agreeing to the creation of an electronics operation. In the mid-1950s Noble developed germanium transistors, and the company ended up dominating the market for discrete (as opposed to integrated) devices. In the late 1950s Motorola became an important supplier to the U.S. space program.

During the 1960s the company flirted with further diversification and stumbled through several ill-conceived acquisitions. Robert Galvin, who took over the firm after his father's death in 1959, eventually decided to move out of consumer products and focus on high tech. In 1974 Motorola's Quasar television business was sold to Matsushita, and soon even the car radio operation was phased out.

In their place Motorola expanded its activity in electronics and sophisticated telecommunications. To help in the process it purchased technology firms like Codex, Universal Data Systems, and Four-Phase. Motorola became one of the leading U.S. producers of semiconductors, both memory chips and the more complicated business of making microprocessors, in competition with industry leader Intel. The grand plan seemed to be that Motorola would make components that would go into computers produced by Four-Phase, and that the computers would be linked to one another over long distances by Codex telecommunications equipment.

Motorola never achieved the grand synthesis, but it did make an important move into the field of cellular telephones, which began to develop during the

1970s. Despite some technical problems, the company became the leading U.S. producer of the mobile phones, but by the mid-1980s it was facing intense competition from Japanese producers. Motorola's position in the business was saved when the Department of Commerce brought dumping penalties against the Japanese firms.

Japanese competition has been an even more serious problem in the semiconductor business. With backing from their government, a group of Japanese companies charged into the memory chip business in the 1970s and by the early 1980s dominated the market. U.S. companies like Texas Instruments and Motorola were all but driven from the industry.

Motorola has survived in this field by forging alliances with some of its adversaries. In 1980 it formed a joint venture with Aizu-Toko to make integrated circuits in Japan, and later it bought out its partner. In 1986 the company entered into a technology-sharing relationship with Toshiba. The arrangement gave Motorola access to the Japanese company's expertise in manufacturing memory chips, while Toshiba was eager to learn Motorola's techniques for producing microprocessors—a field in which the Japanese remained behind. Motorola's 6800 family of microprocessors was widely adopted by Apple Computer and other producers of non-IBM-compatible systems.

The telecommunications equipment produced by Motorola is highly respected in Japan as well as elsewhere. In 1982 the company scored a major coup when Nippon Telegraph and Telephone, which has a long history of using its purchasing to assist in the development of Japanese communications and electronics companies, placed an order for Motorola pocket paging devices.

The company's reputation has been enhanced by its obsession with quality control. In the 1980s Motorola achieved a goal set by Galvin of reducing product defects by 90 percent. It also has reached high levels of efficiency through the construction of such facilities as a fully automated pager plant in Florida. Motorola was one of the first winners of the Commerce Department's Malcolm Baldrige National Quality Awards.

Motorola came up against Japanese protectionism again after it introduced the world's smallest portable telephone—the 12.3-ounce MicroTac—in 1989. The company was barred from selling the product in Tokyo or Nagoya, which together represented 60 percent of the Japanese market. With help from the U.S. government Motorola managed to remove some of the barriers.

Motorola is aggressively selling its cellular phones in other markets as well, including many third world countries that are jumping to cellular rather than bothering to expand and upgrade their inadequate wire-based networks. Enjoying its position as the worldwide leader in cellular phones, pagers, and two-way radios, Motorola made a bold announcement in 1990. The company unveiled plans for a $2-billion network of orbiting satellites that would provide cellular telephone service for remote areas of the world. Dubbed the Iridium project, the plan was designed as a major step toward global personal communications. Motorola later chose Lockheed to build the seventy-seven low-orbit satellites required for the system, but there are still questions about whether Motorola will be able to pull off the ambitious venture. It was made more complicated in 1991, when the International Maritime Satellite Consortium, or INMARSAT, announced a competing plan.

Despite the attention the company received for this project, Motorola entered the 1990s facing growing challenges in its key businesses. New competitors, such as a joint venture between General Electric and Sweden's L. M. Ericsson, moved into the lightweight cellular phone market and a recessionary climate slowed the growth of the business. Motorola responded by forming its own alliance with Northern Telecom, gaining a contract from the Chinese government for cellular equipment, and introducing an even smaller phone, the 7.7-ounce MicroTac Lite.

In the semiconductor arena Motorola was falling farther behind Intel in the microprocessor market, in part because its obsession with quality caused significant delays in new products. Nevertheless, the company persuaded Ford Motor to adopt Motorola chips for engine and transmission systems on its cars and trucks. Motorola got another boost when its microprocessors were chosen both for a new series of IBM laser printers and for a new generation of operating systems being developed jointly by IBM and Apple.

Motorola entered a new field in 1991 with the announcement that it would begin producing electronic ballasts for fluorescent lights. The company has also entered into a series of new joint ventures and other alliances, including a joint design program with Unisys for semiconductors and a cooperative marketing agreement with Northern Telecom covering cellular telephones. Motorola joined with Apple Computer in investing in a new company called General Magic, Inc. that is developing a portable device that combines features of personal computers and telephones. Another chip joint venture, with Philips, was announced in 1992.

OPERATIONS

Communications Products (31 percent of 1991 revenues). The first part of this segment consists of land mobile products, including two-way radio systems used by police and fire departments, taxicab operations, trucking companies, and other customers. The other part includes paging systems, a market in which Motorola is the world leader. The company was the first to introduce a pager designed to be worn on the wrist.

Semiconductor Products (31 percent of revenues). Motorola is the second largest U.S. supplier in the overall semiconductor market. It makes a wide variety of discrete components and integrated circuits, both memory chips and microprocessors. In the latter area it also trails behind industry leader Intel, but in 1991 it got a boost when its devices were chosen for a new generation of PC operating systems being developed jointly by IBM and Apple. In 1990 the company announced that it would produce its next generation of memory chips in Japan as part of its joint venture with Toshiba.

General Systems Products (24 percent of revenues). This segment includes cellular telephones—a business in which Motorola is the world leader—and cellular switching equipment. The company produces the smallest and lightest portable telephones on the market, and it supplies cellular infrastructure in joint ventures in such countries as Argentina, Hong Kong, Israel, Chile, and Mexico. Also included in this segment are several types of microcomputer components.

Information Systems Products (5 percent of revenues). Through its Codex Corporation and Universal Data Systems subsidiaries, the company produces high-speed leased-line and dial modems; data-voice, time division, and statistical multiplexers; network management and control systems; and other products for distributed data processing.

Government Electronic Products (6 percent of revenues). This segment consists of electronic systems and equipment supplied to the Department of Defense, NASA, and other U.S. government agencies. In fiscal year 1991 the company received prime contracts from the Pentagon worth $313 million, making it the country's fifty-seventh-largest military contractor. Motorola's military products include missile and aircraft instrumentation, surveillance radar systems, missile guidance systems, and tactical communications transceivers.

Other Products (3 percent of revenues). Included in this segment are automotive products, such as antilock braking system controls, gasoline and diesel engine controls, ignition modules, and vehicle navigation systems; industrial sensors; and software and hardware for hospital intensive care units.

TOP EXECUTIVES

- George Fisher, chairman and chief executive
- Gary L. Tooker, president and chief operating officer
- Christopher B. Galvin, senior executive vice president
- Robert W. Galvin, chairman of the executive committee
- John F. Mitchell, vice chairman of the board
- David K. Bartram, senior vice president

OUTSIDE DIRECTORS

- Erich Bloch, former director of the National Science Foundation
- David R. Clare, former president of Johnson & Johnson
- Wallace C. Doud, former vice president of IBM
- Anne P. Jones, partner in the law firm Sutherland Asbill & Brennan
- Thomas J. Murrin, dean of the School of Business and Administration at Duquesne University
- William G. Salatich, former vice chairman of Gillette Company

- Gardiner L. Tucker, former vice president of International Paper
- B. Kenneth West, chairman of Harris Bankcorp

The board also includes retired Motorola executives William J. Weisz, John T. Hickey, and Donald R. Jones.

FINANCIAL DATA

Revenues (in millions of dollars)

1991	11,341
1990	10,885
1989	9,620
1988	8,250
1987	6,727

Net Income (in millions of dollars)

1991	454
1990	499
1989	498
1988	445
1987	308

GEOGRAPHICAL BREAKDOWN

Revenues (in millions of dollars)

Year	United States		Foreign	
1991	8,802	(58%)	6,340	(42%)
1990	8,759	(60%)	5,896	(40%)
1989	8,123	(62%)	4,910	(38%)
1988	7,017	(64%)	3,968	(36%)

Operating Profit (in millions of dollars)

Year	United States		Foreign	
1991	452	(47%)	501	(53%)
1990	682	(69%)	308	(31%)
1989	623	(67%)	313	(33%)
1988	628	(73%)	228	(27%)

LABOR RELATIONS

Paul Galvin was a paternalistic employer who instituted a generous profit-sharing plan in the late 1940s. As a result of such policies the company has remained largely nonunion. There have, however, been organized employee protests against the company's strict drug-testing policy. In 1991 the National Labor Relations Board ordered Motorola to lift the restrictions it had placed on the protests.

Motorola workers in other countries have been even less complacent. In the late 1980s the company's operations in South Korea were caught up in the wave of worker militancy in that country. When a group of workers petitioned Motorola to recognize their union in 1987, the company, according to some reports, threatened to pack up and leave the country unless the workers gave up on the idea. In the following months there were clashes between prounion and antiunion Motorola workers and occupations of the company cafeteria and computer center by supporters of unionization.

Violence flared again in 1989, as union supporters claimed that the company had instigated attacks on them by a *kusadae* (save the company corps). The company denied the charge but agreed to give the union office space at its plant.

ENVIRONMENTAL RECORD

Motorola was one of several companies named by the EPA as potentially responsible parties in connection with a Superfund site in Scottsdale, Arizona. In 1991 the companies agreed to contribute $17 million toward the cost of cleaning up the site.

Motorola is among the electronics companies that have promised to phase out the use of ozone-destroying CFCs.

BIBLIOGRAPHY

Flamm, Kenneth. *Mismanaged Trade? Strategic Policy and the Semiconductor Industry*. Washington, D.C.: Brookings Institution, 1991.

Petrakis, Harry M. *The Founder's Touch: The Life of Paul Galvin of Motorola*. New York: McGraw-Hill, 1965.

Prestowitz, Clyde V., Jr. *Trading Places: How We Allowed Japan to Take the Lead*. New York: Basic Books, 1988.

NEC CORPORATION

7-1, Shiba 5-chome
Minato-ku, Tokyo 108–01
Japan
(03) 3454-1111

1991 revenues: $26.8 billion (year ending March 31)
1991 net income: $386.8 million
Publicly traded company
Employees: 117,994
Founded: 1898

OVERVIEW

Nippon Electric Company, founded at the end of the nineteenth century as
the Japanese subsidiary of Western Electric, has in recent years accomplished
the difficult feat of becoming a leading player in three of the most advanced
fields of modern industry: computers, telecommunications, and semiconductors. In doing so NEC boldly took on IBM, AT&T (its one-time parent), and
Texas Instruments.

The results of these specific challenges have been mixed. By the mid-1980s
NEC (the name was officially shortened in 1983) displaced Texas Instruments
as the leading semiconductor company in the world. It overtook IBM's Japanese subsidiary to become the second-largest computer maker in Japan (after
Fujitsu), although this was based on NEC's strength in the domestic PC market
rather than in the international mainframe business, in which NEC has been
stuck with a weak partner (Honeywell). In telecommunications NEC has a
strong position in large-scale switching equipment but is in the second tier of
PBX suppliers in the United States.

With eighteen overseas subsidiaries in eight countries and twenty-nine manufacturing operations in fifteen nations, NEC continues to preach the gospel

of C&C—the link between computers and communications—which in the coming years will be more of a reality rather than simply a catch phrase.

HISTORY

Nippon Electric Company was founded in 1898 as a partnership between Western Electric (the equipment subsidiary of AT&T) and a group of Japanese investors led by Kunihiko Iwadare. NEC, which went public the following year, initially functioned mainly as an importer of U.S.-made equipment.

Within a short period of time, however, Iwadare moved the company into manufacturing on its own, aided by sizable orders from the Japanese Ministry of Communications. In the following years the government increasingly looked to NEC to pioneer the development of new telecommunications technology in Japan.

When Western Electric wanted NEC to participate in a joint venture to produce electrical cables, NEC also brought in the cable-manufacturing division of Sumitomo, thereby initiating what would be a long-term relationship with that industrial group. In 1925 Western Electric's international operations were sold, under government pressure, to the upstart International Telephone & Telegraph, so NEC's American connection was transferred to ITT.

During the 1920s NEC branched out to broadcasting equipment, and by 1930 it installed its first transmitter at a radio station in Okayama. Over the following years the company was drawn into the process of militarization then overcoming Japan. NEC became heavily involved in microwave, radar, sonar, and other aspects of military communications, while ITT's holdings were transferred to Sumitomo, which took over the company completely during World War II and renamed it Sumitomo Communications. In the course of the war many of NEC's facilities were destroyed.

As part of the dissolution of the *zaibatsu* conglomerates after the war, Sumitomo Communications was split off and reassumed the name Nippon Electric. NEC's new managers received substantial help from the government in the form of public works projects, but they also redirected some of the company's military technology into civilian products, such as sonar devices for fishermen and radio receivers.

NEC reestablished its ties with ITT in 1950 and went on to prosper as one of the lead suppliers to the new Nippon Telegraph and Telephone. The company also moved into the production of television broadcasting equipment, computers, and consumer appliances. In the early 1960s NEC began opening sales offices in various foreign countries, including the United States in 1963.

Koji Kobayashi, who took over as president in 1964, restructured the company and instituted greater decentralization in management while pushing NEC into a wider range of electronics products, some of which were to be manufactured abroad. NEC formed an alliance with Honeywell in the computer field and was pushed, along with Hitachi and Fujitsu, by Nippon Telegraph and Telephone to bring computer and telecommunications equipment closer together.

NEC embraced the idea of that linkage, and by the late 1970s Kobayashi was promoting C&C (computers and communication) as the key to the future of NEC as well as of the entire broadly defined information industry. An important component of this evolution was semiconductor technology, so NEC became a leading player in the chip industry. It was one of the five companies chosen by the Japanese government to spearhead what turned out to be a successful move to dominate the international market for memory chips. NEC also purchased a U.S. chip company called Electronic Arrays.

In 1986 NEC produced one of the first prototypes of the 4-megabit memory chip, which will soon be the standard component in the electronics industry. By the mid-1980s NEC was the world's largest supplier of semiconductors. But when it moved from memory chips to microprocessors the leader in that latter field, Intel, accused NEC of illegally copying its microcode. In 1991 NEC reached an agreement with AT&T to share basic semiconductor technology.

NEC has had considerable success in the international market for telephone equipment. It has installed switching equipment in dozens of countries, though it has not managed to rise above fourth or fifth place in the highly competitive market for digital PBXs in the United States. In 1991 NEC again joined forces with AT&T, this time to submit a joint bid to Nippon Telegraph and Telephone for a contract to develop a digital mobile phone network.

In the computer field NEC began producing mainframes that were sold by Honeywell and used that company's software. Honeywell, however, turned out to be an ineffective competitor against IBM, and in 1986 its operations were turned into a joint venture with NEC and France's Groupe Bull. The following year, as Groupe Bull became the dominant party in the venture, the business was renamed Honeywell Bull. In 1991, however, NEC purchased a 4.7-percent stake in the ailing Bull.

NEC has had a greater impact in the personal computer field. It captured the lion's share of the PC market in Japan, and its IBM clones, after a slow start, were well received abroad. In the United States NEC was overshadowed by Toshiba in the laptop segment but held its own in desktop models. When the Reagan administration imposed a 100-percent tariff on the company's laptops, NEC transferred production to the United States. NEC was the first out with a notebook-style PC but was later overtaken by the likes of Compaq.

NEC has faced increased challenges on its home turf as well. In 1990 a U.S. company called AST Research began selling clones of NEC personal computers in Japan, and the following year IBM won support from a group of Japanese companies for an assault on NEC's control of the PC market.

At the other end of the spectrum, NEC is among a handful of Japanese companies that have entered the market for the largest and most powerful data-processing devices—supercomputers. Yet, like Hitachi and Fujitsu, it is having difficulty selling these expensive machines outside Japan.

OPERATIONS

Communications Systems and Equipment (28 percent of 1991 revenues). This segment covers, first of all, NEC's telephone equipment, including central office switching gear, transmission equipment, PBXs, teleconferencing systems, handsets, and fax machines. Also included are other telecommunications equipment for such technologies as fiber optics, microwaves, and satellites. Other products in this segment are broadcasting equipment, rocket guidance and control systems, and other aerospace and military equipment.

A subsidiary of NEC paid $34 million to the U.S. government in 1991 to settle charges that it and other companies had rigged bids on telecommunications contracts at U.S. military bases in Japan.

Computers and Industrial Electronic Systems (47 percent of revenues). NEC is the second-largest producer of computers in Japan. Its products range from laptop and desktop devices to minicomputers, mainframes, and supercomputers. In 1991 NEC introduced the first notebook-style PC that used a wireless system rather than a modem and phone lines to communicate with other computers. That same year, the company brought out the first notebook-type computers with screens capable of displaying color images comparable to those of a color television set.

NEC also makes peripheral devices and dedicated word processors. The industrial electronics part of this segment covers CAD/CAM, computer-aided engineering systems, and equipment for such fields as industrial automation, medical diagnostics, building control, postal automation, and fingerprint identification.

Electron Devices (18 percent of revenues). This segment covers semiconductors, including memory chips, microprocessors, and gate-arrays. NEC also makes transistors, electronic tuners, color display tubes, plasma display panels, capacitors, relays, keyboards, and other components. NEC, the world's leading noncaptive producer of chips, has a semiconductor technology–sharing agreement with AT&T.

Home Electronics (7 percent of revenues). Included in this segment are television sets, direct-broadcast satellite receivers, video projectors, videotex terminals, VCRs, compact disc players, videodisc players, kitchen appliances, air conditioners, and lighting products.

TOP EXECUTIVES

- Kenzo Nakamura, chairman
- Tadahiro Sekimoto, president
- Tomihiro Matsumura, senior executive vice president
- Yukio Mizuno, senior executive vice president
- Toshiro Kunihiro, senior executive vice president

FINANCIAL DATA

Revenues (in millions of yen) (years ending March 31)

1991	3,768,946
1990	3,504,308
1989	3,126,764
1988	2,755,217
1987	2,505,227

Net Income (in millions of yen) (years ending March 31)

1991	54,383
1990	85,219
1989	64,477
1988	25,363
1987	15,034

GEOGRAPHICAL BREAKDOWN

Sales (in millions of yen)

Year*	Domestic		Foreign	
1991	2,832,588	(77%)	866,210	(23%)
1990	2,552,059	(74%)	892,118	(26%)
1989	2,305,520	(75%)	777,280	(25%)
1988	1,969,207	(73%)	745,529	(27%)

*Fiscal year ends March 31.

LABOR RELATIONS

After the company was reorganized after World War II, the labor legislation sponsored by the Allied occupation authorities resulted in the formation of a powerful labor union. In 1946 NEC's workers staged a forty-five-day strike for higher wages. Three years later there was another major walkout, lasting 106 days, to protest the company's shutdown of several major plants. Labor relations since then have been generally harmonious.

ENVIRONMENTAL RECORD

NEC has launched a program to eliminate the use of ozone-depleting CFCs in all of its facilities worldwide by March 1995. The company's semiconductor operation ended its use of CFCs in 1991.

BIBLIOGRAPHY

Anchordoguy, Marie. *Computers, Inc.: Japan's Challenge to IBM*. Cambridge, Mass.: Harvard University Press, 1989.

Kobayashi, Koji. *The Rise of NEC: How the World's Great C&C Company Is Managed*. New York: Basil Blackwell, 1991.

———. *Computers and Communication: A Vision of C&C*. Cambridge, Mass.: MIT Press, 1985.

Sobel, Robert. *IBM vs. Japan: The Struggle for the Future*. Briarcliff Manor, N.Y.: Stein & Day, 1985.

NESTLÉ SA

Avenue Nestlé 55
CH–1800 Vevey
Switzerland
(21) 924 21 11

1991 revenues: $37.2 billion
1991 net income: $1.8 billion
Publicly traded company
Employees: 201,139
Founded: 1866

OVERVIEW

Nestlé, the world's number-one food producer, is one of the most multinational of companies. With more than four hundred manufacturing facilities in over sixty countries spread over six continents, the company seems determined to feed the entire human race.

Nestlé is best known for items like chocolate bars and instant coffee, but today it has an extensive product line that is adapted to local markets and cultures. For instance, to entice Japanese to switch from fish and rice breakfasts Nestlé developed cereals that had tastes like seaweed and papaya that are popular in that country. Many of the company's products are the result of a string of acquisitions over the past few decades, including (in recent years) the Carnation Company in the United States, Rowntree in Britain, and Buitoni in Italy.

Since the late 1970s Nestlé's name has been widely associated with a controversy over its marketing of infant formula in the third world. The company has adopted both hard and soft lines in response to the boycott of its products but has been unable to resolve the issue once and for all.

HISTORY

The multinational giant that is Nestlé grew out of the separate endeavors in Switzerland of a chemist and two American brothers in the 1860s. The chemist was Henri Nestlé, who in 1867 developed a form of sweetened cow's milk for infants who could not be breast-fed. Working in the town of Vevey, near Lausanne, Nestlé gained fame when his preparation saved the life of a baby who was dying of malnutrition because of an inability to digest his mother's milk. Soon his small operation, Farine Lactée Nestlé, was deluged with orders.

The American brothers were Charles and George Page. While serving as the U.S. consul in Zurich, Charles decided that Switzerland would be an ideal location for a factory to produce condensed milk, which had been invented a decade earlier by Gail Borden. In 1866 he and George acted on that idea by establishing an operation with the grandiose name Anglo-Swiss Condensed Milk Company. In truth there was no link with Britain; the brothers merely had anticipated—correctly, as it turned out—that the name would make it easier to sell to the English market.

The company prospered as condensed milk became a staple of European diets. In 1872 Anglo-Swiss opened a factory in Chippenham, England, and two years later purchased the London-based English Condensed Milk Company. Now the leading manufacturer of condensed milk in Europe, Anglo-Swiss broadened its product line to include cheese and infant formula.

Threatened by this challenge to its dominance, Nestlé, which had been purchased by a group of Swiss industrialists, retaliated by entering the condensed milk business. While battling one another, the two companies also expanded their operations abroad. Anglo-Swiss set up an American plant in upstate New York (later this was sold to Borden), while Nestlé bought a Norwegian condensed milk maker and opened facilities in the United States, Britain, Germany, and Spain. In the first years of the new century Nestlé also got into the chocolate business by investing in the Swiss General Chocolate Company, manufacturer of the Peter and Kohler brands—to which was soon added Nestlé brand milk chocolate.

In 1905 Nestlé and Anglo-Swiss decided to wed rather than go on fighting. The combined firm, called Nestlé & Anglo-Swiss Milk Company, enjoyed a strong position in the food industry. World War I disrupted operations, but the company used Swiss neutrality to expand outside of Europe, especially in Latin America. Nestlé had to slow down that expansion in the 1920s and reorganize its operations, but in 1928 the company did seize the opportunity to acquire Peter-Cailler-Chocolats Suisses (itself the product of a 1911 merger between Swiss General and Cailler, another chocolate maker).

Nestlé resumed its international expansion in spite of the depression, opening facilities in such countries as Argentina, Chile, Cuba, Mexico, Denmark, and Czechoslovakia. The company tried to counteract poor economic conditions by introducing new products, such as hot cocoa mix, the Nestlé Crunch candy bar, and a pioneering instant coffee called Nescafé.

Many of the company's operations and sources of raw materials were disrupted by World War II, but Nestlé sold large quantities of Nescafé, powdered milk, and chocolate bars to the U.S. military. Shortly after the end of the war Nestlé merged with Alimentana S.A., producer of Maggi dehydrated soup, bouillon, and seasonings.

Nestlé continued to expand, both by setting up operations in more countries of the world and by purchasing a variety of food companies. Among the latter were Crosse and Blackwell, a British maker of preserves and canned foods (in 1960); Locatelli, an Italian cheese producer (1961); Findus, a Scandinavian frozen foods company (1962); Libby, a U.S. fruit juice bottler (1970); Stouffer, a U.S. frozen foods producer that also had interests in hotels and restaurants (1973); and Beech-Nut, the U.S. baby food manufacturer (1979). Venturing entirely outside the food business, Nestlé bought a minority interest in the French cosmetics company L'Oréal. The company also introduced new products, such as Taster's Choice freeze-dried coffee.

In the 1980s Nestlé continued its buying spree, most notably with the $3-billion acquisition of the U.S. food company Carnation in 1985. Taking on Carnation, a pioneer in the production of evaporated milk and, later, nondairy creamers for coffee, also put Nestlé in the pet food business. Subsequent purchases included Hills Brothers Inc., the third-largest U.S. coffee company; Buitoni-Perugina, the Italian producer of pasta and candy; and Rowntree, the large British chocolatier. Beech-Nut was dumped in 1989 after several executives of the company were found guilty of intentionally selling adulterated apple juice. Nestlé scored with the Lean Cuisine line of low-calorie frozen dinners introduced by its Stouffer subsidiary.

In 1990 Nestlé formed an alliance with the Coca-Cola Company to market ready-to-drink coffees and teas under the Nescafé and Nestea brand names. That same year, Nestlé bought the Curtiss Brands chocolate division of RJR Nabisco, maker of Butterfinger and Baby Ruth candy bars. Nestlé also consolidated its $6 billion worth of U.S. operations into a single holding company. In 1991 Nestlé joined forces with the French food group BSN to take a majority position in Czechoslovakia's biggest food producer.

Nestlé plunged into a takeover battle for France's Source Perrier SA in 1992. The Swiss company made its offer (with the backing of Banque Indosuez) for the world's leading bottled water group after a bid had been made for Exor SA, which controls Source Perrier, by the Agnelli family of Italy. Within two months Nestlé defeated the Agnellis and won the right to acquire Perrier for about $2.8 billion.

OPERATIONS

Beverages (24 percent of 1991 revenues). The company's leading product in this sector is Nescafé instant coffee, which is a market leader in many parts of the world (though not in the United States). Other items include Nestea instant tea, Taster's Choice freeze-dried coffee, Hills Brothers roast and ground coffee, Quik hot cocoa mix, and Beringer wines.

Cereals, Milks, and Dietetics (20 percent of revenues). Nestlé is one of the leading producers of infant formula—a business that has made it a target of widespread protests (discussed later in this chapter). It also sells infant cereals and other baby food. Other products in this segment include sweetened condensed milk, evaporated milk, and coffee creamer. In order to improve its position in the dry cereal market in Europe, Nestlé formed an alliance, called Cereal Partners Worldwide, with the U.S. company General Mills.

Chocolate and Confectionery (16 percent of revenues). This segment includes one of the company's most famous products: the Nestlé Crunch candy bar. It also includes Perugina chocolates, KitKat bars (but not in the United States), and After Eight mints. The Baby Ruth and Butterfinger brands were acquired from RJR Nabisco in 1990.

Culinary Products (13 percent of revenues). This segment includes the Maggi line of dehydrated soups and seasonings as well as ready-to-microwave meals.

Frozen Foods and Ice Cream (10 percent of revenues). A major portion of this segment is the Stouffer line of frozen meals. Its Lean Cuisine brand had a commanding position in the market for low-calorie frozen dinners after it was introduced in the early 1980s but has since lost ground to less-expensive products. Also included are the Findus line of frozen foods and a new group of Buitoni products introduced in Europe.

Refrigerated Products (9 percent of revenues). This segment includes a variety of dairy products, such as yogurt, packaged fresh pasta and sauces, cold meat products, and refrigerated desserts.

Pet Foods (5 percent of revenues). Among the company's pet food brands are Friskies, Fancy Feast, and Mighty Dog.

Pharmaceutical and Other Products (4 percent of revenues). This segment consists mainly of products taken on through the purchase of Alcon Laboratories, a U.S. maker of ophthalmic products, in 1977. They include intraocular lenses, cleaning solution for contact lenses, and Betopic S, a medication for glaucoma.

TOP EXECUTIVES

- Helmut O. Maucher, chairman and chief executive
- José Daniel, general manager
- Reto F. Domeniconi, general manager
- Ramón Masip, general manager
- Camillo Pagano, general manager

OUTSIDE DIRECTORS

- Vincente Mortes Alfonso
- Carl L. Angst, director of Swiss Bank Corporation
- Bruno de Kalbermatten, chairman of Bobst SA
- Fritz Gerber, chief executive of Roche Holding
- Eric Giorgis
- Rainer E. Gut, chairman and president of CS Holding
- Pierre Lalive
- Fritz Leutwiler, former cochairman of ABB Asea Brown Boveri
- Jean-Pierre Meyers, director of L'Oréal
- Lucia Santa Cruz, director of Nestlé Chile
- Stephan Schmidheiny, chairman of various private holding companies
- Vreni Spoerry, vice chair of Schweizer Verband Volksdienst
- Robert Studer, president of Union Bank of Switzerland
- Paul A. Volcker, former chairman of the U.S. Federal Reserve

Nestlé does not disclose the affiliations of its outside directors. Those given above are the ones that could be obtained from other sources.

FINANCIAL DATA

Revenues (in millions of Swiss francs)

1991	50,486
1990	46,369
1989	48,036
1988	39,502
1987	34,183

Net Income (in millions of Swiss francs)

1991	2,470
1990	2,272
1989	2,412
1988	2,058
1987	1,879

GEOGRAPHICAL BREAKDOWN

Revenues (in millions of Swiss francs)

Year	Europe		North America		Elsewhere	
1991	24,350	(48%)	12,528	(25%)	13,608	(27%)
1990	22,567	(49%)	11,243	(24%)	12,559	(27%)

LABOR RELATIONS

Nestlé has good relations with unions at home, but its foreign labor record is mixed. The company is generally cooperative with unions in Europe, and it consults with the International Union of Food and Allied Workers Associations on European matters. Nestlé is much less friendly to unions in the third world and the United States.

One of the biggest confrontations in recent years came in the Philippines, where the company's manufacturing was shut down in 1986 in a dispute over wages. The company met a union demand to pay back holidays but refused to renegotiate the collective-bargaining agreement.

During the late 1970s Nestlé's U.S. subsidiary Libby, McNeil, Libby was one of the targets of a campaign by migrant farm workers in the Midwest. The workers, organized by the Farm Labor Organizing Committee (FLOC), were trying to win increased wages and improved working conditions from tomato growers operating under contract with companies like Libby and Campbell Soup.

After conducting a campaign that ended up focusing mainly on Campbell Soup, FLOC managed to pressure the big food companies to be signatories to a set of unusual three-way collective-bargaining agreements, thus putting significant pressure on the growers to treat the workers fairly.

Nestlé has contracts in the United States with several unions, including the Bakery, Confectionery and Tobacco Workers. Relations between that union and the company have been tense in recent years because of attempts by Nestlé, the union says, to use whipsawing to pressure workers in different locations to agree to contract concessions. The company was also the target of a boycott by U.S. construction unions to protest the fact that Nestlé was using nonunion labor to build a large ice-cream factory in California.

ENVIRONMENTAL AND HEALTH RECORD

During the mid-1970s Nestlé, then expanding steadily throughout the third world, was made the target of a campaign protesting the marketing of infant formula in poor countries. Activists from religious groups charged that the aggressive marketing of formula by companies like Nestlé was causing health problems, in that poor mothers often had to combine the powder with unclean water and frequently diluted the expensive formula to the extent that babies were remaining malnourished.

Nestlé initially responded to the boycott of its products by a counter-campaign, which included donating money to a research center that gave money to Herman Nickel, a writer for *Fortune* magazine, to produce a critical report on the boycott campaign. That report was never written, but Nickel published an article in *Fortune* that served the same purpose. The piece, entitled "The Corporation Haters," refers to the religious groups involved in the boycott as "Marxists marching under the banner of Christ." Nickel was later pushed off the *Fortune* staff, but he was rewarded by the Reagan administration by being named ambassador to South Africa.

Nestlé later changed its posture, agreeing to comply with a marketing code issued by the World Health Organization (WHO). As a result, the boycott was suspended in 1984. However, the protest campaign was resumed in 1988 because of evidence that Nestlé was violating the WHO code by continuing to distribute large quantities of free samples to hospitals in third world countries.

BIBLIOGRAPHY

The Global Chocolate Factory. Amsterdam: Transnational Information Exchange, n.d.

Social and Labour Practices of Multinational Enterprises in the Food and Drink Industry. Geneva: International Labour Office, 1989.

Wolflisberg, Hans J. *A Century of Global Operations*: *The Flavorful World of Nestlé*. New York: Newcomen Society, 1966.

NEWS CORPORATION LTD.

2 Holt Street
Sydney, New South Wales 2010
Australia
(02) 288-3000

1991 revenues: $8.4 billion (year ending June 30)
1991 net income: −$301.2 million (loss)
Publicly traded company
Employees: 38,400
Founded: 1923

OVERVIEW

News Corporation is the formal structure holding together the far-flung and eclectic media and entertainment empire assembled by Australian-born Rupert Murdoch. About 43-percent controlled by a Murdoch family company called Cruden Investments, News Corporation has holdings on four continents and in all of the major communications centers of the English-speaking world.

Murdoch's print properties run the gamut from the prestigious *Times* of London and the *Australian* to scandal-mongering tabloids like the *Sun* in Britain and the *New York Post*. He also has acquired a major Hollywood studio, a leading Anglo-American book publisher, and stakes in several publications in Eastern Europe. And he has been attempting to assemble a fourth television network in the United States. Other ventures include a direct-broadcast satellite operation in Europe and an electronic map–publishing business.

After a dazzling buying binge during the 1980s, News Corporation entered the 1990s loaded down with debt and suffering from sagging earnings. Murdoch had to sell a number of his assets and turn to his banks for a restructuring of his debt. He may be chastened, but Murdoch remains one of the prime movers of the international media business.

HISTORY

Rupert Murdoch in effect picked up where his father, Sir Keith Murdoch, left off. Murdoch père began in journalism in 1903 as a reporter for the *Melbourne Age*, gained some fame as a correspondent during World War I, was put in charge of the *Melbourne Herald*, and went on to take over some other Australian papers.

After toying with socialism while a student at Oxford and doing a stint as a copyeditor at London's *Daily Express*, the younger Murdoch returned to Australia in 1952 upon his father's death and at the age of twenty-three gained control of News Limited, Sir Keith's holding company. Murdoch proceeded to take over other newspaper properties and moved into magazines, radio, and television. He acquired the *Daily Mirror* in Sydney and launched the *Australian*, the country's first national daily.

Yet Australia was not big enough to satisfy Murdoch's ambitions. In 1969 he defeated Robert Maxwell in a battle for *News of the World*, Britain's largest-circulation Sunday paper. He went on to acquire the moribund *Daily Sun* and pumped up its circulation with blaring headlines and racy features that often were accompanied by photos of bare-breasted women.

Several years later he established a foothold in the New World by purchasing the *Express* and the *News* in San Antonio, Texas. He then took on the lowbrow supermarket tabloid *National Enquirer* by launching the *Star*. In 1976 Murdoch broadened his American interests by acquiring the *New York Post*, *New York* and *New West* magazines, and the *Village Voice*, a weekly paper in New York City.

After buying a Sydney television station and a 50-percent interest in the holding company for the Australian airline Ansett, Murdoch took the audacious step of taking over the *Times*, Britain's most prestigious daily.

Turning his sights back to the United States, Murdoch purchased the *Boston Herald-American* (renamed the *Boston Herald*) and the *Chicago Sun-Times*. To his newly acquired daily tabloids Murdoch brought the kind of sensationalized journalism, mixed with conservative politics, that had made him notorious abroad. A classic headline in the new *New York Post*: HEADLESS BODY FOUND IN TOPLESS BAR.

In the mid-1980s Murdoch both dabbled in hostile takeovers (he collected greenmail from Warner Communications in 1984) and accomplished a series of major U.S. purchases through News Corporation's News America subsidiary. In 1984 he acquired the Ziff-Davis Publishing Company's stable of twelve trade magazines for $350 million. The following year he became a broadcasting and film mogul by purchasing seven TV stations from Metromedia for $2 billion—a move that required him to become a U.S. citizen—and the Twentieth Century–Fox film company for $575 million.

Twentieth Century–Fox dates back to Fox Film Corporation, an independent producer that challenged the Edison monopoly early in the century. The studio, which merged with Twentieth Century Pictures in 1935, was ruled by Darryl Zanuck for more than a quarter of a century. For many years it churned out a succession of B movies (inexpensive formula films designed to fill out double bills). Fox had its ups and downs, barely avoiding bankruptcy on two occasions by producing what turned out to be blockbusters—*The Sound of Music* and *Star Wars*. After being purchased in the early 1980s by Denver oil tycoon Marvin Davis, the studio languished.

Murdoch ended up selling the *New York Post*, the *Chicago Sun-Times*, and the *Village Voice*, but he joined with France's Hachette to bring out a U.S. edition of the French fashion magazine *Elle* and a film magazine called *Premiere*. In 1988 he spent $3 billion to buy Triangle Publications, owner of *TV Guide*, *Seventeen*, and the *Daily Racing Form*.

Murdoch also was active outside the United States during this period, competing such deals as the acquisition of Hong Kong's *South China Morning Post* and the purchase of 20 percent of Pearson PLC, publisher of London's *Financial Times*.

He also spent more than $1 billion to take over Australia's largest newspaper group, the Herald and Weekly Times Ltd. Aside from consolidating Murdoch's control over the Australian newspaper business, this deal had important symbolic value—the company had once been run by his father, who was denied a significant equity interest in the firm. Since he was a young man Murdoch had felt that his father had been mistreated in the situation.

In 1987 Murdoch was again making a bold move in the United States. This time the arena was book publishing, and the target was the prestigious firm Harper & Row. Harper had its origins in the early nineteenth century, when James Harper and three of his brothers set up a printing company to service booksellers. The operation soon turned into a publishing house, and it grew so rapidly that by 1853 Harper & Brothers was the world's largest publisher, with authors like Herman Melville and Mark Twain. In the twentieth century the company, led by Cass Canfield, published popular writers like E. B. White and James Thurber.

The name Harper & Row was adopted in 1962 after a merger with textbook publisher Row, Peterson & Company. A few years later Canfield sought to protect the company against a takeover by selling a large block of stock to the Minneapolis Star & Tribune Company. Harper & Row purchased publishers Lippincott and Crowell in the late 1970s. When Harper itself was put into play in 1987, the winning bidder was News Corporation, which paid about $300 million.

Half ownership of Harper & Row was later transferred to British publisher William Collins, which was itself 42-percent owned by News Corporation and later came under the complete control of the Murdoch holding company. The combined company was renamed HarperCollins. In 1989 Harper purchased the Scott, Foresman textbook operation from Time Warner for $455 million.

The Murdoch media empire was extended to the heavens in the 1980s with the inauguration of a European satellite broadcasting service called Sky Television. Back on earth, Murdoch began to feel overextended as a result of the massive debt he had taken on to carry out his acquisitions. By the middle of

1990 News Corporation's debt was $8 billion and the company was having difficulty meeting its interest payments.

Murdoch began to speak uncharacteristically of growing from within rather than through acquisitions, and he moved to dispose of some assets to raise cash. In 1990 the Lippincott subsidiary of HarperCollins was sold for about $250 million, and the following year nine of Murdoch's U.S. magazines (including *Seventeen*, *New York*, and the *Daily Racing Form*) were handed over to Kohlberg, Kravis, Roberts & Company for $600 million.

OPERATIONS

Newspapers (28 percent of 1991 revenues). In the United States Murdoch retains two general-interest dailies—the *Boston Herald* and the *San Antonio Express-News*. In Britain News Corporation's newspaper role is far more prominent. It owns the country's two leading "quality" papers, the *Times* and the *Sunday Times*, as well as *Today*, the *Sun*, and the *News of the World*. The latter two are down-market but have the largest circulation of any newspapers in the English-speaking world.

In Australia and the Pacific Basin, News Corporation has extensive holdings, including more than one hundred newspapers in Australia alone. Among these are the national daily the *Australian*, the *Daily Telegraph Mirror* in Sydney, the *Herald-Sun* in Melbourne, and the *Courier-Mail* in Brisbane. News Corporation also owns 51 percent of the *South China Morning Post*, published in Hong Kong.

Magazines (12 percent of revenues). After the sale of the *Star* in 1990 for $400 million and the sale of nine publications to Kohlberg, Kravis, Roberts & Company in 1991, News America is left with two magazines: *TV Guide* and the fashion magazine *Mirabella*.

In Britain the company puts out the *Times Literary Supplement*, the *Times Educational Supplement*, the *Times Higher Education Supplement*, and *Sky Magazine* (published jointly with Hachette). In Australia the Murdoch organization publishes nine magazines, including three of the most popular ones in the country: *New Idea*, *TV Week*, and *Family Circle*. News Corporation has joined with the Burda media group in Germany to start a tabloid in Berlin called *Super*.

Filmed Entertainment (20 percent of revenues). The Twentieth Century–Fox operations acquired in 1985 are now known as Fox Film. The company, led until 1992 by TV and Hollywood veteran Barry Diller, is engaged in motion picture production, distribution, and exhibition. Among its recent successes have been *Home Alone*, *Die Hard* II, *The War of the Roses*, *The Abyss*, and *The Fabulous Baker Boys*. In 1991 the company released twenty movies and finished in fourth place with a market share of 11.6 percent. Fox also owns a 50-percent interest in CBS/Fox, which distributes home video-cassettes.

Fox Broadcasting produces and syndicates programming as part of an attempt to establish a fourth commercial television network in the United States. By mid-1991 Fox had 139 affiliates to which it was supplying about 20 hours of programming a week. The highly touted Joan Rivers late-night talk show was a flop, but Fox prime-time programs like "Married . . . With Children" gained a great deal of audience share beginning in the fall of 1988, when the big three networks were without new programs because of the Writers Guild strike. The budding network's biggest hit is the animated series "The Simpsons," whose starring character, Bart Simpson, has become a major icon of American popular culture. Fox's fledgling network consists mainly of lower-power UHF stations, but it reaches more than 90 percent of the country.

Television Broadcasting (12 percent of revenues). The Fox Television Stations company owns and operates broadcast stations in seven major U.S. cities: New York, Los Angeles, Chicago, Dallas, Houston, Salt Lake City, and Washington, D.C. These outlets, covering six of the top ten markets, allow the company to reach about 18 percent of U.S. homes with television.

In Europe News Corporation has transformed an operation originally called Sky Television, acquired in 1983, from a cable programming distributor to a direct-broadcast satellite service aimed mainly at households in Britain. The service was fairly successful in the mid-1980s, when it was still providing programming—mainly reruns of situation comedies and other English-language shows—to cable systems in thirteen countries. Yet it found the going tougher when customers had to purchase their own receiving equipment. The service was so desperate for advertisers that it was selling spots for ten pounds.

There was also the problem of competition, emanating from a rival called British Satellite Broadcasting (BSB). Losses from the business grew to hundreds of millions of dollars. In 1990 the company sought to solve the competition problem, at least, by merging with BSB, whose largest shareholder is Pearson. The new entity, called British Sky Broadcasting, or BSkyB, then began the formidable task of turning two money-losing operations into one profitable one.

News Corporation also pursued the satellite TV business in the United States by forming a joint venture called Sky Cable with NBC, Hughes Communications, and Cablevision Systems. That venture was abandoned in 1991.

Book Publishing (14 percent of revenues). HarperCollins, Inc. is the second-largest book publisher in the United States, with a major presence in general books, educational texts (through its subsidiary Scott, Foresman), and religious titles (through its Zondervan subsidiary, acquired in 1988). Since it has been under the complete control of News Corporation the company has taken a more ambitious approach to publishing, seeking to operate on a global basis.

HarperCollins also has begun to indulge in the blockbuster approach that characterizes much of modern publishing. In 1990 the house shocked the industry by purchasing the rights to three books by Jeffrey Archer for an amount reportedly in excess of $20 million. In 1992 Harper paid a similar amount for the next three novels by Barbara Taylor Bradford.

HarperCollins, Ltd., based in Glasgow and London, publishes general-interest, children's, reference, educational, and religious titles. In 1990 the company acquired British publisher Unwin Hyman Ltd. for approximately £16 million. In Australia HarperCollins books are published and distributed under the names Collins A&R, Golden Press, and HarperCollins Australia.

Other Operations (14 percent of revenues). News Corporation's other operations include commercial printing operations in Australia and the United Kingdom, a 50-percent interest in the holding company of Ansett Australia airlines, an aircraft-leasing joint venture, Etak electronic maps, and a three hundred thousand–acre sheep farm in Australia.

TOP EXECUTIVES

- K. Rupert Murdoch, managing director and chief executive
- Kenneth E. Cowley, executive director
- George Craig, chief executive of HarperCollins
- David F. DeVoe, chief financial officer
- Richard H. Searby, deputy chairman

OUTSIDE DIRECTORS

- Anna Murdoch, novelist and wife of Rupert Murdoch
- Stanley Shuman, executive vice president of the investment banking firm Allen & Company

FINANCIAL DATA

Revenues (in millions of Australian dollars) (years ending June 30)

1991	10,971
1990	8,763
1989	7,813
1988	5,976
1987	5,302

Net Income (in millions of Australian dollars) (years ending June 30)

1990	− 393 (loss)
1989	343
1988	1,164
1987	472
1986	826

GEOGRAPHICAL BREAKDOWN

Revenues (in millions of Australian dollars)

Year*	United States		United Kingdom		Australia and Pacific Basin	
1991	6,560	(60%)	2,249	(20%)	2,162	(20%)
1990	4,930	(56%)	1,739	(19%)	2,095	(24%)
1989	3,739	(48%)	1,692	(22%)	2,382	(30%)
1988	2,517	(42%)	1,678	(28%)	1,781	(30%)

*Fiscal year ends June 30.

Operating Income (in millions of Australian dollars)

Year*	United States		United Kingdom		Australia and Pacific Basin	
1991	1,028	(66%)	197	(13%)	332	(21%)
1990	799	(59%)	138	(10%)	426	(31%)
1989	585	(42%)	396	(29%)	414	(30%)
1988	352	(37%)	365	(38%)	233	(25%)

*Fiscal year ends June 30.

LABOR RELATIONS

Rupert Murdoch is notorious among newspaper-publishing unions for his actions in Britain, where he responded to a printers' strike in 1986 by moving production of his four papers to a heavily fortified and largely nonunion operation in the Wapping section of East London. The only unions tolerated at Wapping were the National Union of Journalists and the Electrical, Electronic, Telecommunications and Plumbing Union, the latter having signed a no-strike agreement.

Murdoch also outraged organized labor by contracting with TNT, a nonunion hauling company (and News Corporation's partner in the Australian airline Ansett), to distribute the papers. Murdoch's actions prompted militant mass picketing at Wapping, until the area was saturated with riot police and more than a thousand people were arrested.

Murdoch has not been quite so confrontational with newspaper unions in the United States. During a 1978 newspaper strike in New York he made a deal with the unions that allowed the *Post* to resume publication after fifty-six days, while the *Times* and *News* were out for eighty-eight days.

As for the company's book-publishing operations, in 1974 Harper & Row had an experience that was unusual in the publishing industry—its employees went out on strike. The unaffiliated Association of Harper & Row Employees, which represented editorial, clerical, and other workers, decided to take on the tradition of low pay that has long characterized the business.

In the early 1980s the workers at Harper & Row, by then represented by District 65 of the United Auto Workers, were again battling with management. This time the dispute centered on a move by the company to transform the employee pension fund into a stock-ownership plan. The switch allowed management to use a substantial amount of the assets of the terminated pension plan to repurchase stock that had been sold to the Minneapolis Star & Tribune Company—an action that the union charged was an improper attempt to keep the existing management entrenched.

After Murdoch took over the company, labor relations became less confrontational. In 1989 District 65 and Harper signed a new five-year contract following amicable negotiations.

BIBLIOGRAPHY

Block, Alex B. *Outfoxed: Marvin Davis, Barry Diller, Rupert Murdoch & the Inside Story of America's Fourth Television Network.* New York: St. Martin's Press, 1990.

Exman, Eugene. *The House of Harper: 150 Years of Publishing.* Boston: Houghton Mifflin, 1958.

Kiernan, Thomas. *Citizen Murdoch.* New York: Dodd, Mead, 1986.

Leapman, Michael. *Arrogant Aussie: The Rupert Murdoch Story.* Secaucus, N. J.: Lyle Stuart, 1985.

Regan, Simon. *Rupert Murdoch: A Business Biography.* London and Sydney: Angus & Robertson, 1976.

Tuccille, Jerome. *Rupert Murdoch.* New York: Donald I. Fine, 1989.

NISSAN MOTOR COMPANY, LTD.

17–1, Ginza 6–chome, Chuo-ku
Tokyo 104–23
Japan
(03) 3543-5523

1991 revenues: $42.4 billion (year ending March 31)
1991 net income: $347.3 million
Publicly traded company
Employees: 138,326
Founded: 1933

OVERVIEW

Nissan Motor Company, whose ancestors include some of the earliest auto-making operations in Japan, evolved in the postwar period from an obscure producer of rather clunky cars into one of the companies that has revolutionized the driving habits of the developed world, especially the United States. It also has been at the forefront of a transformation of the workplace from a site of labor-management antagonism to one of cooperation, although this has usually been accompanied by a marked intensification of the labor process.

Along with Toyota and, later, Honda, Nissan—which until the early 1980s used the name Datsun in the United States—lured people away from the gas-guzzlers made in Detroit to the attractive and well-produced smaller cars that increasingly dominate American roads. The road for Nissan, however, has not always been smooth. It has fallen farther behind Toyota in its home market and in recent years has been outshined in the United States by that company as well as by Honda.

Nissan, with its production operations in twenty-two countries, has been vying with Volkswagen for fourth place among the world's automakers. Nissan may have lost some of its magic, but it remains a major player in an increasingly globalized industry.

HISTORY

The origin of the name Datsun can be traced back to 1911, when an early Japanese automaker named Masujiro Hashimoto produced his first car, a small, ten-horsepower passenger model. The car was named DAT, the initials of Hashimoto's three backers. Hashimoto's company, Kwaishinsha, later brought out a sports car it called son of DAT, or Datson, which eventually was changed to Datsun. The firm then turned its attention to making trucks, mainly for the military.

Kwaishinsha, which took the name DAT Motors in 1925, merged the following year with another struggling car maker called Jitsuyo Jidosha Seizo. Jitsuyo had been founded in 1919 by Kubota Ironworks in order to develop a motorized alternative to the rickshaw. Jitsuyo's operations were based on the designs of an American engineer named William R. Gorham, who was living in Tokyo. The combined operation spent some years making small quantities of trucks, primarily for the military, but in 1932 it introduced a new Datsun automobile.

The following year the rights to the Datsun line and the Osaka factory that produced the cars were taken over by an engineer and entrepreneur named Yoshisuke Aikawa, who controlled a company called Tobata Casting. In 1933 Aikawa combined the Datsun operations with the auto parts business of Tobata to create a company that in 1934 was given the name Nissan Motor. The term *Nissan*, a shortened form of Nippon Sangyo (Japan Industries), was the name of the *zaibatsu* conglomerate controlled by Aikawa.

Nissan Motor initially made auto components for the Japanese subsidiaries of Ford Motor and General Motors, but Aikawa was convinced that the company could succeed by producing small cars—a product in which the big U.S. automakers had not the slightest interest at the time—as well as trucks. To help in the effort he purchased machinery, truck designs, and technology from the U.S. company Graham-Paige as well as equipment from other American suppliers. Nissan Motor began producing trucks in 1941 and found an eager customer in the military establishment.

During World War II Nissan Motor's activities were expanded to include the manufacture of military aircraft engines. After Japan's defeat Aikawa's conglomerate, which had grown to include the Hitachi group, was dissolved along with the other *zaibatsu*. Nissan Motor resumed operations on its own with new management, most of its previous executives having been purged by U.S. occupation authorities. The presidency fell to Taiichi Minoura, a former reporter with little auto industry experience. He was aided by Katsuji Kawamata, a financial specialist sent in by the Industrial Bank of Japan.

The outbreak of the Korean War was a boon to Nissan, as it was to many Japanese companies. As part of a strategy to make Japan a bulwark against communism in Asia, the U.S. government relied on Japanese manufacturers for much of the materiel used in the war. Once the military orders tailed off, Nissan again turned to a Western company for help in building its auto operations. This time the partner was Britain's Austin Motor, which in 1952 formed a technology-sharing agreement with Nissan and licensed the Japanese company to assemble Austins for the domestic market.

Despite the foreign help, Nissan began to fall behind its rival Toyota, which was far more aggressive in establishing a dealer network. Nonetheless, Nissan began preparing for a resumption of the export activity it had engaged in during the years preceding World War II. In 1960 Nissan Motor Corporation of America was established, although the company's cars were not then powerful enough to sustain high speeds over long distances—a type of driving more common in the United States than in cramped Japan. Over the next few years the company established its first overseas manufacturing operations in Mexico and Peru.

Nissan entered a period of growth in the mid-1960s with the introduction of the Sunny in Japan and the merger in 1966 with Prince Motor Company, the latter leading to the creation of the Nissan Prince Royal, the first domestically produced limousine to be used by Japan's imperial family. At the same time, the company started to become a detectable presence in the U.S. import market. That presence became more significant in the early 1970s as a result of the introduction of the Datsun 510 line, which included four-door sedans and station wagons, and the 240-Z sports car.

These cars and their successor models helped propel Nissan to the top tier of importers in the United States. The company, along with all of the other automakers, initially suffered a sharp drop in sales amid the oil crisis, but after the initial shock, small imported cars like those of Nissan captured a larger share of the market. Toyota moved farther ahead of Nissan in U.S. sales, though by 1979 Nissan was selling more than four hundred thousand cars a year in that country.

Nissan enhanced its position in the American market by following Honda in opening an assembly operation in the United States. The company hired former Ford manufacturing executive Marvin Runyon and spent more than $600 million to build a state-of-the-art factory eighteen miles outside Nashville in Smyrna, Tennessee. The plant, which started making pickup trucks in 1983 and then added cars and, later, engines, was held up as a model of the modern workplace. Yet the expense of starting up the facility made it less profitable than the company had hoped. Costs were also increased by the company's decision to change the name of its products in the U.S. market from Datsun to Nissan.

Nissan, meanwhile, was experiencing problems outside the United States as well. It continued to lose ground to Toyota in the Japanese market, and export sales were depressed by the strong yen. The result was a squeeze on profits. In the first half of its 1987 fiscal year, Nissan reported its first operating loss since 1951.

In the late 1980s Nissan attempted a comeback by redesigning its product line, changing the boxy contours of the Maxima, for instance, to sleek, aerodynamic lines. The company also moved into the luxury segment of the market, creating a new line called Infiniti, which was promoted with a Zen-like advertising campaign that showed scenes of nature rather than the product. After a slow start, the Infiniti began to do well in the U.S. market, but overall Nissan was not able to break out of its slump. The company remains one of the world's leading automakers but cannot seem to make it into the passing lane.

OPERATIONS

Vehicles and Automotive Parts (98 percent of 1991 revenues). Nissan produces a variety of passenger cars, trucks, and other commercial vehicles. In fiscal 1991 it sold 1.2 million cars in Japan and 1.1 million in other countries. That year the company introduced two new models—the Presea sedan and the Figaro compact coupe. The company's vehicles are sold in 150 countries, but by far the largest markets are North America and Europe. Production facilities are located in Japan and twenty-one other countries. The largest volume of foreign production is done in the United States, Mexico, the United Kingdom, and Spain. In 1991 Nissan agreed to form a joint venture with Ford's Lincoln-Mercury division to produce minivans.

Other Operations (2 percent of revenues). Nissan has long played a major role in Japan's space program by producing rocket motors, ignition systems, and other components. The company also makes textile machinery, forklifts, marine engines, and pleasure boats.

TOP EXECUTIVES

- Yutaka Kume, chairman
- Yoshifumi Tsuji, president
- Atsushi Muramatsu, executive vice president
- Nagayuki Marumo, executive vice president
- Yoshikazu Hanawa, executive vice president

FINANCIAL DATA

Revenues (in millions of yen) (years ending March 31)

1991	5,964,912
1990	5,645,169
1989	4,811,691
1988	4,243,770
1987	4,273,389

Net Income (in millions of yen) (years ending March 31)

1991	48,831
1990	116,013
1989	114,625
1988	64,515
1987	20,368

GEOGRAPHICAL BREAKDOWN

Net Sales (in millions of yen)

Year*	Japan		Elsewhere	
1991	3,167,368	(53%)	2,797,544	(47%)
1990	2,991,940	(53%)	2,653,229	(47%)
1989	2,555,008	(53%)	2,256,683	(47%)
1988	2,160,079	(51%)	2,083,691	(49%)

*Fiscal year ends March 31.

LABOR RELATIONS

After Nissan was reorganized following World War II, the new management of the company adopted a tough line with the labor unions that were being created with the encouragement of the U.S. occupation authorities. Then–executive director (and later president) Katsuji Kawamata forced the company's union to accept the dismissals of more than seventeen hundred workers in 1949.

Kawamata demonstrated similar toughness four years later, when the militant All-Japan Automobile Industry Labor Union (known as Zenji) sought substantial wage gains. Toyota and Isuzu settled with the union after a few short strikes, but Nissan, which was determined to reduce Zenji's influence, was less willing to compromise. The result was a strike (which later turned into a lockout) that went on for one hundred days. The company ended up victorious in that dispute by encouraging workers to support a new union—the All-Nissan Motor Workers Union—whose posture toward the company was more cooperative. The new union replaced Zenji at Nissan, and since then there have been no strikes of any significance at the company's Japanese operations.

This is not to say that Nissan's workers are totally satisfied with their lot. The extremely close relationship between the union and management, along with the intense pace of production on the shop floor, has created an oppressive atmosphere for the rank-and-file worker. When a small group of workers openly criticized working conditions and the union in 1979, they were expelled from the union and fired from their jobs.

When the company shut down its Kawaguchi diesel engine plant in 1984 and forced workers to commute to another facility more than sixty miles away or else lose their jobs, the union acquiesced without a protest. By this time, however, a network of dissident groups had developed, including some that formed breakaway unions. The groups launched a campaign to protest both the Kawaguchi shutdown and the poor wage package the established union had accepted. Several of the groups called strikes at their plants, but few workers dared to join in. The company responded by demoting some of the dissidents to janitorial positions.

When Nissan opened its manufacturing facility in Smyrna, Tennessee, in 1983 it sought to obtain the same control over labor without the presence of a union. The company interviewed some 120,000 applicants to find the right 2,000 workers, which meant those with an inclination to be "team players" and presumably a lack of interest in unions. Once production began, there were reports of inhuman treatment as workers were pushed to the limits of endurance, but in 1989 the Smyrna labor force voted overwhelmingly against a bid by the United Auto Workers to represent them.

Nissan also has introduced its brand of labor relations to Britain. The company was one of a group of Japanese firms that signed no-strike contracts with conservative British labor groups like the Amalgamated Engineering Union (AEU). The 1986 agreement between Nissan and the AEU was unusual also in that it was a single-union arrangement, which ran contrary to the traditional British practice. The cozy labor-management arrangement created a peculiar situation: Nissan had to encourage dubious workers to join the AEU for the union to retain some measure of legitimacy.

ENVIRONMENTAL RECORD

When engine emissions and automobile safety became major policy issues in the United States in the mid-1960s, Nissan grumbled about cost-benefit considerations but then set out to modify its vehicles to meet the new requirements. The company spent more than $60 million in this effort.

One result was the Nissan Anti-Pollution System (NAPS-Z), a new type of engine introduced in 1978 that reduced hydrocarbon emissions by improving fuel efficiency and lowered nitrous oxide emissions by increasing the amount of exhaust gas recirculated into the incoming fuel. The engine helped to bring fuel efficiency for Nissan's leading models to more than twenty-seven miles per gallon.

In 1991 Nissan gave a boost to the prospects for electric cars by announcing quick-charging batteries that can be rejuiced to 80 percent of full power in only twelve minutes, compared to the eight hours required for previous batteries.

BIBLIOGRAPHY

Barnett, Steve, ed. *The Nissan Report: An Inside Look at How a World-Class Japanese Company Makes Products that Make a Difference*. Garden City, N.Y.: Doubleday, 1992.

Bassett, Philip. *Strike Free: New Industrial Relations in Britain*. London: Macmillan, 1986.

Cusumano, Michael A. *The Japanese Automobile Industry: Technology and Management at Nissan and Toyota*. Cambridge, Mass.: Harvard University Press, 1985.

Gelsanliter, David. *Jump Start: Japan Comes to the Heartland*. New York: Farrar, Straus & Giroux, 1990.

Halberstam, David. *The Reckoning*. New York: William Morrow, 1986.

Maxcy, George. *The Multinational Automobile Industry*. New York: St. Martin's Press, 1981.

Rae, John B. *Nissan/Datsun: A History of Nissan Motor Corporation in U.S.A.* New York: McGraw-Hill, 1982.

Sobel, Robert. *Car Wars*. New York: E. P. Dutton, 1984.

NOMURA SECURITIES COMPANY, LTD.

1–9–1, Nihonbashi, Chuo-ku
Tokyo 103
Japan
(03) 3211-1811

1991 revenues: $6.9 billion (year ending March 31)
1991 net income: $874.1 million
1991 assets: $43.7 billion
Publicly traded company
Employees: 16,600
Founded: 1925

OVERVIEW

Nomura Securities Company holds a commanding position in what has become the most important capital market in the world. With its affiliates the company accounts for some 20 percent of all stock and bond transactions in Japan. Thanks to its policy of pushing its employees to the limits of human endurance, Nomura leads in underwriting, trading, and all other aspects of the securities business in the country. Nomura Securities is part of the Nomura Group, which includes thirteen other subsidiaries or affiliates engaged in asset management, investment banking, real estate, and management consulting.

Nomura has tried to extend its dominance abroad. The company holds a major position in the Euromarket and has worked hard to become a force in U.S. capital markets, forming alliances with specialized firms in the areas of mergers and acquisitions, real estate, and currency and commodity trading.

Since the Nomura family began trading stock early in the century, there has been a constant attempt to overcome the stigma that has traditionally been attached to the securities business in Japan, although this has been made more difficult by the company's occasional descents into questionable forms of business. In mid-1991, for example, Nomura became an international symbol of the dark side of Japanese business when the company admitted that it had paid $100 million to compensate large clients for losses they suffered during the stock market plunge of 1990 *and* that it had provided an even larger amount to an organized crime figure to carry out a stock manipulation scheme.

Nomura also has had to contend with increasing competition at home from U.S. brokerage houses, which have invaded the Tokyo market with their computerized trading programs, unusual financial instruments, and other innovations that the hidebound Japanese securities business has resisted.

HISTORY

Tokushichi Nomura II, the founder of Nomura Securities, was born in 1878, the son of an Osaka money changer who had gone into the field after being disowned by his samurai father. The younger Nomura had little patience for his father's business of trading gold and silver; he was drawn to what was widely considered the somewhat disreputable business of buying and selling stock. He was apprenticed to a relative who ran a brokerage house but soon was fired for trading securities without permission.

After a stint in the army Nomura returned to the family company and eventually wore down his father's resistance to the securities business. Nomura had insisted on beginning his venture in 1905 with the huge sum of ¥ 20,000, but he soon earned that much by making a killing on a long position he took on the shares of a textile company about which Nomura had what amounted to inside information. Nomura shrewdly hired an investigative reporter with extensive contacts to head his research department.

Nomura prospered during the bull market of 1906, but he prematurely anticipated a downturn in prices and found his short position squeezed when the market continued to rise. He had to borrow heavily and risk all of his assets, but finally the turning point came. The sharp decline in prices in 1907 made Nomura, then twenty-nine, a very rich man and gave him a reputation as a market sage. He used this position to take time out for an extended visit to Europe and the United States, where he carefully studied the Western financial system.

After amassing more wealth during World War I, Nomura yearned to create his own *zaibatsu*, a diversified commercial empire like the ones the Mitsui and Sumitomo families had built. He plunged into banking and bought a rubber plantation in Borneo. His holding company, called the Nomura Partnership, purchased a group of insurance companies that were crippled by the payouts they had to make to victims of the devastating Kanto earthquake of 1923. Two years later the group's brokerage business was formally relaunched as Nomura Securities Company, Ltd.

During World War II Nomura was the only brokerage house to avoid forced consolidation by the government. Tokushichi Nomura died just before the end of the war, however, and his son and designated successor passed away shortly after that. As a result of the American occupation Nomura, like the other *zaibatsu*, found its holdings restructured and the shares of its companies changed from private to public ownership. Cross-holdings among the various entities prevented a complete dissolution of the group, but absolute control by the Nomura family came to an end. The subsidiaries ended up divided into two camps, one aligned with Nomura Securities and the other with Daiwa Bank (the new name of Nomura's commercial banking operation).

According to Albert J. Alletzhauser in his book *The House of Nomura*, the head of Nomura Securities formed an alliance with a leading black-market operator after the war to engage in illicit currency and stock transactions (the country's stock exchange was officially shut down at the time). The black marketer, Minoru Segawa, used a variety of unorthodox schemes to keep the company afloat during the chaotic days of the early postwar period. He was arrested for money laundering but was released after a short time because the police could not understand Nomura's transactions. Segawa was rewarded for his efforts by being named managing director of Nomura Securities in 1948.

After the Tokyo Stock Exchange was reopened in 1949, Nomura became a leading force in the market. The company also played a key role in expanding the ranks of individual investors, in part by encouraging personal savings. In 1953 Nomura launched a campaign in which it distributed thousands of traditional wooden strongboxes and urged people to fill them with coins. When the boxes were filled, the customer was supposed to call a Nomura salesman, who would open the lock and place the money in an investment trust, the Japanese equivalent of a mutual fund.

Nomura prospered during the economic go-go years that began in the late 1950s, and the firm helped industrial development by promoting the stock of newer companies like Sony and Matsushita. Yet this period also was marked by a chaotic and unregulated market in over-the-counter securities. Although the Ministry of Finance tried to bring some order to the mess, the market ballooned and then burst in 1965. Yamaichi Securities, the audacious leader of the industry, collapsed, clearing the way for Nomura to take the number-one spot.

In 1953 Nomura sent a man to New York to reopen the office that had been shut down in 1936. It took some time, but the company finally built up a business selling Japanese securities to Americans. This growth was stemmed, however, after Congress enacted legislation taxing ownership of foreign stock. At that point Nomura, like others in the industry, shifted the focus of its foreign operations to London. In the following years Nomura accelerated its international expansion, opening offices in Hong Kong, Amsterdam, Singapore, Frankfurt, Toronto, and Geneva.

Business was expanded in New York, too, where Nomura built an extensive bond-trading operation; in 1981 it also became the first Japanese firm to obtain a seat on the New York Stock Exchange. In 1986 Nomura was the first foreign institution to be named a primary dealer by the U.S. Federal Reserve Board.

Yet there were also problems in New York. The company pushed its sales force, especially the Americans, so hard that it sparked a revolt. The company, moreover, enjoyed little of the prominence it enjoyed in Japan, and earnings from American operations were (and have continued to be) trivial. To try to remedy this situation, Nomura took the unusual step for a Japanese company of putting an American in charge. He was Max C. Chapman, Jr., former president of Kidder, Peabody.

Shaken by the 1987 stock market crash, Nomura chief executive Yoshihisa Tabuchi (no relation to chairman Setsuya Tabuchi) reshuffled the management of the company, giving directorships to eight men in their forties and shunting seven older directors into less-sensitive positions with affiliates.

The Nomura Group moved into the field of mergers and acquisitions in 1988 by paying $100 million for a 20-percent stake in Wasserstein Perella Group, a mergers and acquisitions "boutique" formed by two prominent defectors from First Boston Corporation. A joint venture of the two firms, Nomura Wasserstein Perella Company, was designed to focus on nonhostile cross-border deals, but so far it has not made a big splash. Another U.S. alliance was formed in 1991, when Nomura joined with Tudor Investment Corporation to create a venture to trade currencies and commodity and financial futures throughout the world.

In June 1991 Nomura was still reeling from the sharp fall in profit—a result of the plunging Japanese stock market—it had reported for the fiscal year that ended in March. Then the company was hit with another serious blow. News reports suddenly appeared alleging that Nomura had paid out some 16 billion yen ($114 million) in 1990 to compensate large investors for losses they suffered in the market.

Nomura initially denied that it had engaged in the practice, which a group of other securities firms had admitted doing the year before. A day later the company's management admitted it had indeed done so. At the same time, it confirmed reports that the company had provided more than $150 million in financing to organized crime figure Susumu Ishii for a stock manipulation scheme assisted by Nomura. The scandal forced the resignation of Nomura president Yoshihisa Tabuchi and, later, chairman Setsuya Tabuchi. The government punished Nomura by ordering it to close more than half of its domestic branches for a month. A criminal investigation was launched as well.

OPERATIONS

Nomura engages in all aspects of the securities business, including underwriting, dealing, and brokerage. Its network consists of 150 domestic and 62 overseas offices. Nomura has subsidiaries in the United States, Canada, England, France, Belgium, Holland, Luxembourg, Germany, Switzerland, Spain, Italy, Hungary, Bahrain, Hong Kong, Singapore, Indonesia, and Australia. In many of its foreign operations the company also engages in commercial banking.

In fiscal 1991 some 33 percent of Nomura's operating revenues came from commissions on securities transactions (a higher figure than at U.S. brokerages, thanks to the Japanese system of fixed commissions), 13 percent from underwriting and distribution, 13 percent from its net gain on trading, and 39 percent from interest and dividends. The latter is derived principally from margin lending to customers, from other lending activities, and from the securities in its inventory.

In the area of equity financing Nomura has served as the lead manager for such major issues as the privatization of Nippon Telegraph and Telephone in 1987 and of Japan Airlines in 1988. During calendar year 1989 Nomura lead-managed 47 of the 127 initial public offerings made by Japanese firms. Nomura has lead-managed issues by foreign companies as well, including British Telecom, Deutsche Bank, Texas Instruments, and Apple Computer.

Nomura is also a leader in the underwriting of corporate and government bonds. The company has held the top spot in lead-managing samurai bonds (yen-denominated foreign issues), and it pioneered the Euroyen market. Overseas Nomura has been number one in Eurobond underwriting, although its business has been mainly with Japanese companies. It is also strong in bond trading, both at home and abroad. In 1988 the company's London subsidiary, Nomura Gilts, gained the status of market maker of U.K. government bonds.

Nomura Securities Investment Trust Management Company is the leader in its field in Japan, with the equivalent of $80 billion in net assets under management at the end of fiscal 1991. This operation has branched out to New York, London, Luxembourg, and Hong Kong.

Nomura Babcock & Brown Company is a joint venture that was formed in 1986 with Babcock & Brown, a San Francisco–based investment bank involved in the field of lease financing. The joint venture has formed an affiliation with Eastdil Realty, a New York investment bank specializing in real estate.

TOP EXECUTIVES

- Hideo Sakamaki, president and chief executive
- Masashi Suzuki, executive vice president
- Yasuhiro Mizuuchi, executive vice president
- Shozo Hashimoto, executive vice president
- Yoshikazu Kitsuda, executive vice president

FINANCIAL DATA

Revenues (in millions of yen)

1991	976,073
1990	1,201,265
1989	584,666*
1988	959,795
1987	1,073,007

*This figure represents a six-month transitional period ending March 31, 1989; the company switched from a fiscal year ending September 30.

Net Income (in millions of yen)

1991	122,899
1990	276,120
1989	137,530*
1988	214,137
1987	268,090

*This figure represents a six-month transitional period ending March 31, 1989; the company switched from a fiscal year ending September 30.

GEOGRAPHICAL BREAKDOWN

Revenues (in millions of yen)

Year	Japan		Americas		Elsewhere	
1991	682,806	(70%)	67,476	(7%)	225,791	(23%)
1990	962,803	(80%)	48,939	(4%)	189,523	(16%)
1989*	500,839	(86%)	12,744	(2%)	71,083	(12%)
1988	842,582	(88%)	24,210	(3%)	93,003	(10%)

*Fiscal year 1989 was a six-month transitional period from a fiscal year ending September 30 to one ending March 31.

Assets (in millions of yen at the end of each fiscal year)

Year	Japan		Americas		Elsewhere	
1991	2,970,358	(48%)	1,426,935	(23%)	1,752,059	(28%)
1990	3,197,762	(52%)	1,187,952	(19%)	1,774,578	(29%)
1989	3,092,773	(67%)	462,893	(10%)	1,045,816	(23%)
1988	2,718,695	(64%)	407,626	(10%)	1,080,270	(27%)

LABOR RELATIONS

Nomura has generally had cooperative relations with the unions representing its employees, but financial workers have responded to the recent scandals in that company and other Japanese brokerage houses with expressions of militancy. In November 1991—during the period Nomura was ordered to suspend much of its business—hundreds of securities industry employees paraded through Tokyo's financial district, protesting the reduction in their annual bonuses. They blamed the questionable practices of top management for the loss of public confidence in the stock market and the consequent drop in brokerage house earnings.

BIBLIOGRAPHY

Alletzhauser, Albert J. *The House of Nomura: The Inside Story of the Legendary Japanese Financial Dynasty*. New York: Arcade/Little, Brown, 1990.

Beyond the Ivied Mountain: The Origin and Growth of a Japanese Securities House. Tokyo: Nomura Securities, 1986.

Fitzgibbon, John E., Jr. *Deceitful Practices: Nomura Securities and the Japanese Invasion of Wall Street*. New York: Carol Publishing Group, 1991.

PHILIP MORRIS
COMPANIES, INC.

120 Park Avenue
New York, New York 10017
(212) 880-5000

1991 revenues: $48.1 billion
1991 net income: $3 billion
Publicly traded company
Employees: 166,000
Founded: 1847

OVERVIEW

Philip Morris Companies, which brags of being the largest consumer packaged goods producer in the world, is a tobacco giant that has gobbled up large portions of the food and beverage industries. The company's Marlboro cigarettes are one of the globe's most famous brands, and the product's cowboy-theme advertising has helped shape the image many people have of the United States.

Seeking to dispel the increasing antagonism toward cigarettes and those who make them, Philip Morris has spent large sums to associate its name with more socially acceptable activities. The company is one of the leading corporate patrons of the arts and has spent many millions on an ad campaign publicizing the bicentennial of the Bill of Rights. One significant sign of change: in 1991 Michael A. Miles, one of the few nonsmokers among the company's top management, was chosen as the new chief executive.

HISTORY

This consumer-products behemoth had its origins in a London tobacco shop opened by a man named Philip Morris in 1847. The operation soon moved into manufacturing, and during the latter years of the century the company prospered under the leadership of William Curtis Thomson. In 1919 the firm was taken over by its American investors, who expanded production and distribution in the United States.

During the 1930s Philip Morris became a formidable low-price competitor to the firms (American Tobacco, R. J. Reynolds, Liggett & Myers, and Lorillard) that had been created as a result of the breakup of the tobacco trust. It achieved this in large measure through a marketing coup. The company ran an enormously successful ad campaign using a midget bellhop singing out "Call for Philip Morris."

The company gained greater stature in 1954 by merging with Benson & Hedges, maker of the Parliament brand of cigarettes. The merger—and especially the "acquisition" of Benson & Hedges executive William Cullman III—stimulated Philip Morris to shoot for the stars in the consumer products world. Led by Cullman, who became president and, later, chief executive, the company carried out one of the greatest feats in marketing history—transforming Marlboro from a filtered brand oriented to women into a macho product that allowed Philip Morris to take over leadership of the cigarette industry at home and to challenge BAT's dominance of the market abroad.

Philip Morris turned its marketing prowess on the beer industry after the purchase of Miller Brewing Company from W. R. Grace in 1969. Miller, founded in 1855, was the somewhat lackluster seventh-largest brewer in the United States. The Philip Morris wizards quickly instilled new life in the operation, changing the ad orientation from the "champagne of bottled beer" pitch to white-collar types to the "Miller time" campaign, which suggested that the brew was a suitable reward for a day of hard manual labor.

Later the company was one of the first to recognize the population's increased calorie consciousness, to which it responded with the introduction of Miller Lite. It also seized a big share of the discriminating-palate market with the introduction of a domestically brewed version of Löwenbräu, a German beer with a six hundred–year history.

These tactics prompted a more aggressive approach by industry leader Anheuser-Busch, which also jumped on the light-beer bandwagon. The two companies fought an intense beer war, but the main victims were their smaller competitors. By the beginning of the 1980s the big two had 50 percent of the U.S. beer market; by the end of the decade that figure had risen to more than 63 percent.

Philip Morris tried to work the same magic with Seven-Up after that company was acquired in 1978. But it was not to be. The lemon-lime drink continued to lose market share, and a caffeine-free cola called Like that Seven-Up introduced in 1982 never received wide acceptance. In 1986, after an attempt to sell Seven-Up to PepsiCo was blocked by federal antitrust regulators, the domestic operations of Seven-Up were sold to Hicks & Haas. Matilda Bay, Philip Morris's late entry into the wine cooler business, was a flop.

The company did not limit its diversification to beverages. In the 1980s it also spent a mind-boggling sum—a total of some $18 billion—to acquire some of the biggest names in the food industry. The first such target was General Foods, which was swallowed in 1985. General Foods, one of the great innovators of the food-processing industry, dates back to the cereal business started by Charles Post after his time at the Battle Creek Sanitarium. Postum Cereal later merged with the Jell-O Company and Clarence Birdseye's frozen food operations. Long a leader in coffee roasting and frozen vegetables, General Foods in the early 1980s sought to reduce its dependence on mature products by acquiring companies like Entenmann's bakers, the Ronzoni pasta company, and hot dog maker Oscar Mayer. General Foods also scored with new products, such as Crystal Light beverage mix and Jell-O Pudding Pops.

In 1988 Philip Morris moved on to the next course—Kraft. The food processor had its origins in the cheese business started by James Kraft in Chicago in 1903. Functioning as a subsidiary of National Dairy Products, Kraft produced such processed favorites as Velveeta cheese spread and Miracle Whip salad dressing. In 1980 the company merged with Dart Industries, maker of Tupperware products, Duracell batteries, and other items. Six years later Dart and Kraft decided to go their separate ways, with Kraft keeping the food businesses and Duracell and Dart holding on to everything else.

Philip Morris took its appetite for food companies abroad in 1990 with the $4.1-billion acquisition of Swiss coffee and confectionery producer Jacobs Suchard. That firm, which had its origins in a candy shop established in 1825, went on to become one of the giants of the chocolate business. It merged with rival Tobler in 1970 and in the late 1980s munched the U.S. candy company E. J. Brach and the Belgian chocolatier Côte d'Or, but rival Nestlé won the battle for the British candy firm Rowntree.

Foreign expansion of the cigarette business, especially in the former Soviet bloc, is also part of the Philip Morris strategy. The company took over a cigarette factory and set up a subsidiary in eastern Germany, acquired an 80-percent interest in a formerly state-owned cigarette maker called Egri Dohangyar in Hungary, and took a majority interest in the Czech company A.S. Tabak.

OPERATIONS

Tobacco (42 percent of 1991 operating revenues). The fact that products in this segment, mainly cigarettes, accounted for 72 percent of operating profit indicates just how profitable the little tubes of tobacco are. The company's commanding position is seen most clearly in the United States, where its 1991 production of 220 billion cigarettes constituted about 43 percent of the market. Aside from Marlboro, the company's leading tobacco brands are Benson & Hedges, Merit, and Virginia Slims. The company also supplies the growing demand for discount smokes with brands like Cambridge. In 1991 the company introduced a low-tar version of its flagship brand called Marlboro Medium. The following year the company sought to shore up its faltering Merit brand by introducing a low-nicotine version called Merit Ultima.

The company's tobacco products are well known in other parts of the world as well; in fact, Marlboro has been the world's best-selling brand since 1972. Philip Morris International, the leading U.S. cigarette exporter, estimated that in 1991 it had an 8.4-percent share of the 5-trillion-unit non-U.S. world cigarette market. The company claimed to have shares of at least 15 percent— in some cases substantially higher—in more than twenty-five countries. Building market share in the third world is made easier by the lack of the kind of advertising restrictions that have become common in the more developed countries.

Another factor has been the crusade by Philip Morris and the other big U.S. producers to get the federal government to pressure foreign countries to reduce trade barriers to cigarette imports. The Reagan and Bush administrations were especially eager to comply, so U.S. exports, especially to Asia, soared in the late 1980s. However, this tobacco invasion has prompted new international efforts by antismoking groups in defense of third world lungs. There is less resistance in what used to be known as the second world. In 1990 the Soviet government asked Philip Morris and RJR Nabisco to supply thirty-four billion cigarettes to alleviate a shortage of smokes that was fomenting civil unrest.

To make its tobacco products the company owns ten manufacturing and processing facilities in the United States—seven in the Richmond, Virginia, area, two in Louisville, Kentucky, and one in Cabarrus County, North Carolina. The company also has cigarette manufacturing facilities in twenty-three other countries.

Food (50 percent of operating revenues). The Kraft General Foods subsidiary calls itself the largest processor and marketer of packaged grocery, coffee, cheese, and processed meat products in the United States. The General Foods unit produces such familiar products as Maxwell House, Yuban, Sanka, and Brim coffees; Jell-O desserts; Post cereals; Log Cabin syrups; Kool-Aid, Tang, Crystal Light, and Country Time beverages; Entenmann's bakery products; Minute rice; Stove Top stuffing; Shake 'n Bake coatings, and Good Seasons salad dressings. By the late 1980s many of the company's products were out of sync with changing tastes, causing the firm to lose ground in markets like breakfast cereal.

The Kraft unit is the king of processed cheese and cheeselike products, including Velveeta, Cheez Whiz, and Philadelphia Brand cream cheese. It also purveys Miracle Whip salad dressing, Seven Seas pourable dressings, Parkay and Chiffon margarines, and Bull's-Eye barbecue sauce. The arrival of Kraft added new zest to the Philip Morris food operations. The company, for instance, has successfully exploited America's concern about cholesterol and fats by introducing fat-free versions of popular products ranging from Sealtest ice cream to Entenmann's baked goodies.

The Oscar Mayer Foods unit is one of the largest producers of processed meat and poultry products in the United States. Its principal brands include Oscar Mayer, Louis Rich, Louis Kemp Seafood surimi products, and Claussen pickles.

The Kraft General Foods Frozen Products unit supplies such familiar products as Birds Eye frozen vegetables, Cool Whip dessert toppings, Light n' Lively ice milk, and Budget Gourmet frozen entrees. Kraft General Foods is also a supermarket stalwart in Canada, Europe, and Asia, a position greatly boosted by the 1990 purchase of Jacobs Suchard. In addition to exporting many of the familiar U.S. products, the company now supplies such international brands as Milka, Tobler, Toblerone, Suchard, and Côte d'Or confections; Carte Noire, Gevalia, Grand'Mère, Hag, Jacobs Café, Jacques Vabre, Kenco, Night & Day, and Saimaza coffees; Negroni and Simmenthal meats; Miracoli pasta dinners; Dairylea processed cheese; Vegemite sandwich spread; and Hollywood chewing gum. The company's food operations have some 152 manufacturing and processing facilities and 469 distribution centers in the United States as well as 86 foreign plants in 21 countries.

Beer (7 percent of operating revenues). The Miller Brewing Company subsidiary's leading products are Miller Lite, Miller High Life, Miller Genuine Draft, Meister Brau, Milwaukee's Best, and Löwenbräu, which is brewed and sold in the U.S. under a license agreement with Löwenbräu München AG. Miller owns and operates eight breweries, located in Milwaukee, Wisconsin; Fulton, New York; Fort Worth, Texas; Eden, North Carolina; Albany, Georgia; Irwindale, California; Chippewa Falls, Wisconsin; and Trenton, Ohio.

Financial Services and Real Estate (1 percent of revenues). The company engages in various financing and investment activities, including third-party-leveraged and direct-finance leasing as well as financing for Philip Morris customers and suppliers.

TOP EXECUTIVES

- Michael A. Miles, chief executive officer
- William Murray, president
- Hans G. Storr, executive vice president

OUTSIDE DIRECTORS

- Elizabeth E. Bailey, professor of public policy and management at the Wharton School
- Harold Brown, chairman of the Foreign Policy Institute, School of Advanced International Studies, Johns Hopkins University
- J. A. Cordido-Freytes, member of the law firm Betancourt, Cordido & Associates (Caracas, Venezuela)
- William H. Donaldson, chairman of the New York Stock Exchange
- Paul W. Douglas, former chief executive of Pittston Company
- Jane Evans, vice president of US West Communications
- Robert E. R. Huntley, counsel at the law firm Hunton & Williams
- T. Justin Moore, Jr., counsel at the law firm Hunton & Williams

- Rupert Murdoch, chief executive of News Corporation
- Richard D. Parsons, chief executive of Dime Savings Bank of New York
- Roger S. Penske, president of Penske Corporation
- John S. Reed, chairman of Citicorp
- John M. Richman, counsel at the law firm Wachtell, Lipton, Rosen & Katz

FINANCIAL DATA

Revenues (in millions of dollars)

1991	48,064
1990	44,323
1989	38,332
1988	25,391
1987	22,234

Net Income (in millions of dollars)

1991	3,006
1990	3,540
1989	2,946
1988	2,337
1987	1,842

GEOGRAPHICAL BREAKDOWN

Operating Revenues (in millions of dollars)

Year	United States		Foreign (incl. exports)	
1991	34,829	(62%)	21,629	(38%)
1990	33,086	(65%)	18,083	(35%)
1989	30,890	(70%)	13,190	(30%)

Operating Profit (in millions of dollars)

Year	United States		Foreign	
1991	7,028	(78%)	1,928	(22%)
1990	6,715	(81%)	1,567	(19%)
1989	6,061	(86%)	980	(14%)

LABOR RELATIONS

Unlike rival RJR Nabisco, whose R. J. Reynolds unit has adamantly opposed unions, Philip Morris made its peace with organized labor back in the 1930s. Some eleven thousand of its tobacco workers are represented by the Bakery, Confectionery and Tobacco Workers (BCTW). Relations have been so harmonious that the company and the union in 1979 signed an unusual nine-year, no-strike agreement whose wage provisions were renegotiated every three years.

The company's food operations also have a union presence, but the attitudes toward unions in some cases are much different. The Kraft operations maintain a hostility toward collective bargaining that was company policy when Kraft was still an independent company. The General Foods part of the company is less antagonistic but not as friendly toward the BCTW as the cigarette operation is. In the brewing area, many Miller workers are represented by the Teamsters and the United Auto Workers.

ENVIRONMENTAL AND HEALTH RECORD

As a leading producer of cigarettes, the main environmental effects of the company are to be found in the lungs of its customers. Like its sister companies in the industry, Philip Morris continues to resist acknowledging the deleterious effects of tobacco. The company's 10-K financial report refers only to "the alleged harmful physical effects of cigarette smoking."

And when Michael Miles, a nonsmoker, was named to the chief executive's job in 1991, succeeding the avid puffer Hamish Maxwell, he said that his avoidance of the habit had nothing to do with health considerations. "I used to smoke, and for some reason that I can't even remember now, I lost my taste for it," he told a reporter, presumably with a straight face. "I used to eat a lot of scallops and now I don't anymore. It's just one of those things."

For years Philip Morris and the rest of the industry have vigorously fought product liability suits brought by smokers claiming that cigarettes had given them lung cancer and other diseases. The industry's legal winning streak was unbroken until 1988, when a federal judge declared that the evidence brought out in a trial showed that the industry had engaged in a "conspiracy vast in its scope, devious in its purpose and devastating in its results" to mislead the country about the dangers of smoking.

The jury in the case did not find the defendants—Liggett, Lorillard, and Philip Morris—guilty of conspiracy, but it did find Liggett liable in the death of Rose Cipollone from lung cancer. The jury found that the company had failed to alert smokers to the health risks of cigarettes in the period before the federal warning label started to be used. The verdict, which involved a modest award of $400,000 to Cipollone's husband, failed to act as an inducement to more lawsuits. In 1990 a federal appeals court overturned the verdict but opened the door to suits covering the period after warning labels began to be used. In 1992 the legal uncertainty was eliminated as the Supreme Court ruled that the existence of warning labels did not bar suits against cigarette companies.

BIBLIOGRAPHY

Ferguson, James L. *General Foods Corporation: A Chronicle of Consumer Satisfaction*. Exton, Pa.: Newcomen Society, 1985.

Finger, William R., ed. *The Tobacco Industry in Transition*. Lexington, Mass.: Lexington Books, 1981.

Sobel, Robert. *They Satisfy: The Cigarette in American Life*. Garden City, N.Y.: Anchor, 1978.

Taylor, Peter. *The Smoke Ring: Tobacco, Money and Multinational Politics*. New York: Pantheon Books, 1984.

White, Larry C. *Merchants of Death: The American Tobacco Industry*. New York: William Morrow, 1988.

PHILIPS ELECTRONICS NV

Groenewoudseweg 1
5621 BA Eindhoven
Netherlands
(40) 786700

1991 revenues: $33.4 billion
1991 net income: $704.2 million
Publicly traded company
Employees: 240,000
Founded: 1891

OVERVIEW

Philips Electronics, known until 1991 as NV Philips' Gloeilampenfabrieken, was one of the pioneers of the light bulb business. The company grew after World War II into a leading producer of electrical goods. Philips ended up focusing on a vast array of consumer products, avoiding the heavy equipment markets pursued by companies like General Electric, Toshiba, and Hitachi in addition to their household items.

Philips has struggled to survive in the consumer electronics business in the face of the Japanese invasion of the field. The company's renowned research and development operation was responsible for such inventions as the VCR and the compact disc player. Today Philips is the world's biggest manufacturer of television sets (with brands like Magnavox and Sylvania as well as Philips), and it is the largest consumer electronics company in the West. It also owns 80 percent of PolyGram, one of the world leaders in the record industry.

Yet all is not well with the Dutch company. It failed to enjoy the full fruits of its inventions as competitors came to dominate the VCR and CD markets. Also unsuccessful has been the effort to become a major force in computers and semiconductors. The company has spent the last decade dismantling much of its huge network of production facilities around the world—and more retrenchment has been planned as Philips management deals with losses that skyrocketed to $2 billion in 1990. The company managed to return to profitability in 1991, but chairman Jan Timmer did not restore the dividend to stockholders, saying that Philips was "still far removed from where we want to be."

In addition to slashing expenses and workers, Philips is basing its comeback in the emerging areas of consumer electronics. The company has received high marks for its digital audiocassette system, scheduled for release in 1992, and Philips is spending heavily on high-definition television as well as on compact disc systems that combine video, audio, text, and graphics.

HISTORY

A dozen years after Thomas Edison created the first practical incandescent light bulb, a young Dutch engineer named Gerard Philips established a light bulb factory in the town of Eindhoven with the financial backing of his father, a wealthy businessman. The firm, called Philips & Company, had a difficult start and nearly went under in the face of intense competition from German producers.

It was only a generalized boom in the industry in the late 1890s and the managerial assistance provided by Gerard's younger brother Anton (who later took control of the firm) that allowed the company to survive. Yet price competition, including what today would be considered dumping by the German producer AEG, remained intense. In 1903 Philips was thus eager to participate in the formation of a cartel of a dozen light bulb producers—led by AEG and Siemens & Halske—in Germany, Holland, and Austria-Hungary. The cartel was an unstable one and in 1913 it finally was abolished.

Yet the group had served to stabilize the industry and establish various technical standards; it also helped Philips become known outside Holland. That reputation was enhanced by the Dutch company's decision in 1907 to form a new entity called NV Philips' Metaalgloeilampenfabriek to sell the recently devised metal-filament bulb. Marketing that product came up against joint ventures formed by the large German company Auer, including one with Britain's General Electric Company.

The entire industry, however, was transformed as a result of the discovery by General Electric in the United States of a new method of producing a filament of pure tungsten. AEG, Auer, and Siemens quickly arranged to license the technology, but Philips decided to import some specialized equipment from the United States to improve its own technique of making tungsten filaments. Philips was hit with patent challenges in Britain and Germany but managed to negotiate relatively advantageous settlements. Meanwhile, it gained a foothold in the United States through the creation of a joint venture with the importing firm Lamont, Corliss & Company.

The company, which in 1912 reorganized itself as NV Philips' Gloeilampenfabrieken, had to adjust again when GE made another innovation: the half-watt bulb, which was filled with nitrogen, had a coiled filament, and was twice as efficient as the standard tungsten variety. Philips devised its own version of the new bulb, and when its supplies of glass were interrupted by the onset of World War I the company established its own glassworks. Holland's neutrality during the war also made it easier for the company to continue doing business.

After the war the company began expanding both its marketing efforts and its production abroad. During the 1920s factories were established in France, Spain, Belgium, Italy, Poland, Sweden, Australia, and other countries. The company also branched into X-ray tubes, electronic components, and radios. Philips's growth slowed down during the depression, but the company found the resources to continue its international expansion. When the Nazis invaded the Netherlands in 1940 most of the top management of Philips went into exile, first in England and then in the United States, where the company's operations had been reorganized as an autonomous firm called North American Philips Corporation.

In the postwar period the first task of the company was to rebuild its Dutch facilities, which had been heavily damaged; in doing so it received extensive financial assistance from the government. Philips also broadened its research activities and entered new fields, such as transistors, integrated circuits, televisions, and home appliances. In 1952 Philips helped Matsushita by entering a technology-sharing arrangement, never imagining that the Japanese company would soon become a major rival. Later in the decade Philips moved into military electronics and communications through the purchase of a majority stake in Hollandse Signaalapparaten NV in 1956.

The creation of the European Economic Community was a boon to Philips, which was already highly internationalized. To take further advantage of the new situation the company opened production facilities in the low-wage parts of the EEC, including Greece. Philips did not enjoy great success, however, in its efforts to enter the computer and office equipment field, yet it did go on to make significant innovations in consumer electronics, including the audiocassette system, the VCR, and the compact disc player. The company refused to back down when Japanese manufacturers began their assault in the market, but it took a beating when, for example, its VCR format was rejected, even by North American Philips, in favor of the VHS standard promoted by JVC and Matsushita. In 1979 Philips purchased a controlling interest in the German consumer electronics company Grundig.

North American Philips, which in 1974 acquired the U.S. semiconductor company Signetics, moved to enhance its position in the American market with the purchases of GTE's Sylvania television business and Westinghouse's lighting operations in the early 1980s. Sylvania was consolidated with the Magnavox television line it already owned. In 1987 Philips, deciding to end the anomaly of having an independent affiliate in the United States, took full control of North American Philips.

After Cornelius van der Klugt took over the company in 1986, he initiated a radical restructuring of the firm. Dozens of plants were shut down, the work force—which had already been slashed in the late 1970s—was further diminished, and an entire layer of management was eliminated. Operations were pared down to four major areas: consumer electronics, lighting, computers, and electronic components.

When all of this failed to bring about a rebound in profitability, van der Klugt was ousted in 1990 and replaced with Jan Timmer, head of the consumer electronics business. That part of the company was the only one showing some signs of progress, while the plan to become a high-tech leader via computers and semiconductors was going nowhere. This problem, along with the cost of restructuring, created a whopping $2.3-billion loss for 1990. Timmer responded by announcing plans to shed tens of thousands of additional jobs, including many in the huge white-collar work force at the headquarters in Eindhoven. Also in the cards were more shutdowns of money-losing operations. "Don't mention the word 'strategic' to me anymore," Timmer was quoted as telling his managers. "We will just look at profit figures. Everything not making a profit, we will cut back." Timmer dubbed this new approach Operation Centurion.

Despite its weakened condition, Philips continued to do battle in the consumer electronics field. In January 1991 it announced its version of a digital audio tape recorder to compete with the DAT system previously introduced by Sony. The Philips system, called digital compact cassette (DCC), had the advantage of being able to play conventional cassettes as well. The company also scored a coup in getting Matsushita to back DCC.

In 1991 Philips made a deal with video game producer Nintendo for Philips technology to be used in a device that would allow optical discs to be connected to Nintendo game players. The announcement came only a day after Nintendo had agreed to cooperate with Sony on a game player that could accommodate both Nintendo cartridges and compact discs.

In other bold moves Timmer sold off his money-losing minicomputer operation to Digital Equipment Corporation for about $300 million and sold out Philips's share of an appliance joint venture to partner Whirlpool Corporation. Philips also continues to invest heavily in research and development on high-definition televisions and on multimedia compact disc systems.

OPERATIONS

Lighting (13 percent of 1991 revenues). This segment, the original business of Philips, includes the production of a wide range of incandescent and halogen light bulbs, automobile headlights, and various other residential, commercial, and industrial lighting products. The company also produces large-scale lighting systems for stadiums and other outdoor applications, such as floodlighting for buildings and monuments. In 1991 the company announced a new industrial bulb that is supposed to last as much as six times as long as fluorescent bulbs.

Consumer Products (47 percent of revenues). This segment consists of three major areas. The most notable is consumer electronics, including television sets (Philips is the world leader), VCRs, camcorders, audio equipment (including the DCC system scheduled for release in 1992), personal computers, fax machines, and CD-ROM players. The domestic appliances and personal care business includes electric shavers, hair dryers, coffee makers, food pro-

---

cessors, fruit presses, blenders, ice-cream makers, toasters, vacuum cleaners, irons, and air-treatment products.

PolyGram, 80-percent owned by Philips, is one of the largest recorded music companies in the world and the biggest outside the United States. Two-thirds of the company's income is derived from popular music by such artists as Dire Straits, Sting, U2, Janet Jackson, and Jon Bon Jovi. Yet PolyGram is also the world leader in classical music, with labels like Deutsche Grammophon, Decca/London, and Philips Classics. Recently PolyGram acquired the Island and A&M labels. PolyGram, which has bought substantial interests in several film companies (including Propaganda Films, which produced Madonna's *Truth or Dare*), announced in 1991 that it would spend $200 million over several years to expand its involvement in movies.

Professional Products and Systems (22 percent of revenues). This segment, too, is made up of a variety of businesses. The information systems area includes office automation systems, document-handling equipment, automatic teller machines, and dictation machines. Communications systems covers telephone equipment, cellular phone networks, paging systems, two-way radio equipment, and fiber-optic cables. Medical systems includes X-ray, computed tomography, magnetic resonance, and ultrasound diagnostic systems.

Components (14 percent of revenues). Philips has invested heavily to remain a player in the intensely competitive semiconductor industry. Although it is the leading European integrated circuit producer, the company ranks only tenth in the world chip market. There have been reports that Philips intends to either sell this operation or merge it, although the company has rebuffed merger overtures from the Italian-French joint venture SGS-Thomson, which has sought to include Siemens in the deal as well. This segment also includes electronic components, such as picture tubes, liquid crystal displays, and advanced ceramics used in sensors and other electronic devices.

Miscellaneous (4 percent of revenues). This catchall grouping, which includes the revenues from several joint ventures and minority holdings, has been reduced by the dissolution of an optical disc joint partnership with Du Pont and the sale of the company's interest in a major-appliance joint venture to its partner, Whirlpool. In 1991 Philips increased its holdings to a majority stake in the Super Club video rental chain, which has some five hundred stores in the United States and one hundred in Belgium. This resulted from an emergency capital infusion for the money-losing operation.

TOP EXECUTIVES

- Jan D. Timmer, chairman of the board of management
- Y. G. Bouwkamp, executive vice president
- F. P. Carrubba, executive vice president
- Wisse Dekker, chairman of the supervisory board

OUTSIDE DIRECTORS

- J. F. Bennett
- Peter Carey, senior adviser to Morgan Grenfell
- Pehr G. Gyllenhammar, chairman of Volvo
- Wolfgang Hilger, chairman of Hoechst
- G. Jeelof
- M. Kuilman
- André Leyeson, chairman of the supervisory board of Agfa-Gevaert
- François-Xavier Ortoli, former chairman of the French company Total
- N. Rodenburg

Philips does not disclose the affiliations of its outside directors. Those given above are the ones that could be obtained from other sources.

FINANCIAL DATA

Revenues (in millions of Dutch guilders)

1991	56,986
1990	55,764
1989	57,224
1988	56,079
1987	52,715

Net Income (in millions of Dutch guilders)

1991	1,202
1990	−4,240 (loss)
1989	1,374
1988	1,056
1987	818

GEOGRAPHICAL BREAKDOWN

Revenues (in millions of Dutch guilders)

Year	Europe		U.S. and Canada		Elsewhere	
1991	33,639	(59%)	12,833	(23%)	10,514	(18%)
1990	33,970	(61%)	11,819	(21%)	9,975	(18%)
1989	32,809	(57%)	13,768	(24%)	10,467	(18%)

Operating Income Excluding Restructuring (in millions of Dutch guilders)

Year	Europe		U.S. and Canada		Elsewhere	
1991	2,378	(76%)	−19	(0%)	751	(24%)
1990	2,246	(78%)	−614	(0%)	628	(22%)
1989	2,040	(69%)	−323	(0%)	917	(31%)

LABOR RELATIONS

Philips was one of a group of employers in Eindhoven that created a network of social service organizations around the turn of the century to provide benefits to their employees. The company also paid high wages (relative to those of other Eindhoven employers) to its production workers, who were primarily young women—in some cases barely in their teens. Nonetheless, workers began to join the Netherlands Association of Factory Workers or the General Netherlands Metalworkers Union. Those two organizations, the latter having a socialist orientation, developed good relations with the company. Yet there was a problem when some Roman Catholic labor organizations appeared on the scene and protested against the company's refusal to shut down production on all of the saints' days.

Soon after that dispute died down, the company found itself in conflict with the metalworkers' union over the terms of a new contract, especially on the issue of piecework. A work stoppage in 1911 angered the company and ended the honeymoon with the union. Philips, however, did not abandon its paternalism entirely. It continued to build housing for workers and it instituted a pension and disability plan in 1913. Five years later the company agreed to shorten the workday to eight hours. There were, nonetheless, strikes in 1919 that led to the creation of militant labor groups that served as a counterbalance to the company-dominated system of works councils.

Over the following decades Philips gained a reputation for paternalism and a tolerance for unions. In the 1960s it was one of the first major companies to negotiate with an international labor organization. Between 1967 and 1972 Philips held a series of meetings with the European Metalworkers Federation (EMF) to discuss conditions in different European countries. The EMF was seeking an international labor agreement, but the company refused to enter into such a formal relationship. What did occur was that links between Philips workers in various countries were strengthened through the efforts of the EMF and those of a Dutch group called SOBE (Center for Research on the Electronics Industry), which organized an international conference of Philips workers in 1982.

One of the conclusions of that gathering was that Philips did not mind unions as long as they were not militant. It was noted that when labor organizations were more aggressive, the company did not hesitate to respond with force. For example, when Philips workers in Spain occupied a plant in

Barcelona in 1975 to protest dismissals of a group of labor activists by the company, Philips asked that riot police be sent in to retake the factory. In another instance more than two thousand workers at the Philips factory in Poona, India, were locked out of their jobs for five months in 1984 after they protested the dismissal of a union activist.

In the late 1980s there were significant labor disputes—often prompted by announcements of plant closings—at Philips facilities in such countries as Brazil, the Philippines, and Belgium. The chance of peaceful labor relations became even more dim at the beginning of the 1990s as the company announced plans for large numbers of additional layoffs.

ENVIRONMENTAL AND HEALTH RECORD

In 1989 a group of four thousand in New Orleans filed a suit against North American Philips and another company charging that toxic releases from a plant (one that Philips no longer owns) had caused extensive health damage.

Philips subsidiary Signetics was one of three companies hit with a class-action environmental lawsuit in 1991. The suit, filed on behalf of residents of Sunnyvale, California, charged that Signetics—along with Advanced Micro Devices and TRW—was responsible for releasing toxic substances into residential areas near semiconductor manufacturing facilities.

In 1990 Philips joined with a subsidiary of Royal Dutch/Shell to create a company to develop photovoltaic solar energy systems for electric lighting and other applications.

BIBLIOGRAPHY

Bouwman, Teo, ed. *Philips: International Reorganisations and Workers' Resistance.* Eindhoven, Netherlands: SOBE, 1982. (SOBE, an independent center studying the electronics industry, merged in 1991 with SOMO—Center for Research on Multinational Corporations. SOMO's address is: Paulus Potterstraat 20, 1071 DA Amsterdam, Netherlands.)

Heerding, A. *The History of N.V. Philips' Gloeilampenfabrieken.* 2 vols. Cambridge: Cambridge University Press, 1986, 1989.

Philips, Frits. *45 Years with Philips: An Industrialist's Life.* Poole, Dorset: Blandford, 1978.

TIE-Europe Bulletin 12 (1982). (Special issue on Philips.)

PROCTER & GAMBLE COMPANY

One Procter & Gamble Plaza
Cincinnati, Ohio 45202
(513) 983-1100

1991 revenues: $27 billion (year ending June 30)
1991 net income: $1.8 billion
Publicly traded company
Employees: 94,000
Founded: 1837

OVERVIEW

Procter & Gamble Company (P&G), known variously as the Power and the Glory and the Colossus of Cincinnati, is one of the behemoths of the packaged goods industry. A pioneer in market research, and famous for the practice of introducing products that compete with its own brands, P&G has evolved from a maker of soap to a purveyor of dozens of items for body and home.

The company was somewhat slow in expanding abroad in its first century of existence, but it has since established a global presence. Its products are now sold in some 140 nations, and P&G is striving to match the international moves of its competitors, especially the Anglo-Dutch Unilever and Japan's Kao Corporation.

Since the early 1980s P&G has spent heavily to establish itself as a leading supplier of over-the-counter drugs and cosmetics. The acquisitions have made P&G into the world leader in the market for personal-care products. In 1991 P&G got a black eye when it pressured police in its headquarters city of Cincinnati to investigate a leak of information to the *Wall Street Journal*.

HISTORY

The Procter & Gamble packaged goods empire had its origin in a partnership formed in 1837 by two young men, William Procter and James Gamble, to make soap in Cincinnati. They were far from alone in the field, so before long they sought to distinguish their soap and candles by shipping them in boxes marked with a unique symbol—a circle containing a man-in-the-moon face and thirteen stars.

The company grew steadily but enjoyed a major boost during the Civil War, when P&G was able to supply large quantities of soap to the Union Army by virtue of having cornered the market on rosin (a key soap-making material that came from the South) before the war began. Growth continued after the war, especially beginning in 1879, when the company introduced Ivory, a white soap meant to offer the appeal of Castile soaps (derived from olive oil) but at a lower price.

Ivory, touted as the soap that floats, was one of the first nationally advertised brands. The description of the product as "99 and 44/100 percent pure" became one of the most famous slogans in U.S. marketing history.

The company's candle business went into decline with the rise of electric lights, but the business had a last hurrah in 1909, when ten thousand pounds of the wax product were sold to the commission in charge of building the Panama Canal.

P&G's soap business also was being challenged—by the introduction of powdered soap for laundering. The company moved to exploit the popularity of the product by purchasing the Schultz Soap Company of Zanesville, Ohio, in 1903 and bringing out a powdered formula called Star Naphtha.

At about the same time, the company bought the U.S. rights to a German engineer's technique for hydrogenating, or hardening, vegetable oils into a solid state. The result, introduced to the world in 1912, was a shortening called Crisco.

The first instance of P&G's practice of introducing directly competing brands came in 1923, when Camay soap was launched with great fanfare as a rival to Ivory. During the 1930s the company began promoting both of these soaps as well as its other products on the radio, which is how the serials they sponsored came to be known as soap operas.

After World War II the company moved its marketing efforts into high gear, beginning with the launch of a new product called Tide in 1946. This synthetic detergent, the result of the discovery that a chemical called tripolyphosphate worked much better on laundry than did existing products, was trumpeted as "the washday miracle." Within a few years P&G was boasting that Tide was the most popular product in the United States. Soon the company introduced its own competing brand of detergent—Cheer.

Up to the 1940s P&G's main foreign activities were in Canada and England, with smaller operations in Cuba, the Philippines, and Indonesia. In the postwar period P&G moved to take on the world. Manufacturing facilities were set up in Mexico and Venezuela and subsidiaries were established in Switzerland, France, and Belgium. Eventually the company would have production facilities in several dozen countries.

The company's next major product milestone came in 1956 with the introduction of Crest, a toothpaste that contained stannous fluoride, a substance that made teeth more resistant to decay. Crest did not make a big splash until P&G successfully lobbied the American Dental Association to give its imprimatur, for the first time, to an oral hygiene product.

During this period, P&G introduced many other products that subsequently have become standard items in many American homes: Head & Shoulders dandruff shampoo, Scope mouthwash, Secret deodorant, and Comet cleanser. In 1963 P&G purchased the company that produced Folger's coffee. P&G suffered a setback when the Federal Trade Commission forced the company to divest itself of the Clorox bleach company, acquired in 1957, because of antitrust considerations. Some of the Folger's assets had to be sold for the same reason.

The company also got into the tree-farming business as a result of its accurate forecast that disposable paper products would become a significant growth area for American business. It was this operation that gave rise to one of the major inventions of modern times—the disposable diaper. Pampers began to be test marketed in 1961 and quickly developed a loyal following among parents. The company owned the market for twenty years, until Kimberly-Clark came out with a superior product called Huggies. P&G responded with a comparable new brand called Luvs as well as improvements in the Pampers product.

P&G spent heavily on acquisitions in the 1980s, beginning with the purchase of Crush International, marketer of Crush and Hires soft drinks. The company then made a major push into the drug business with the purchases of the pharmaceutical operations of Morton-Norwich (led by Pepto-Bismol) in 1982, Richardson-Vicks (maker of cold remedies) in 1985, and, in the same year, the over-the-counter drug business of G. D. Searle (Metamucil and other products).

For a while it appeared that shopping had replaced product innovation at P&G, but the company went on to successfully launch Liquid Tide to challenge Unilever's Wisk, the leader in the field. In the mid-1980s the company enjoyed big boosts in market share for such items as Pampers and Crest through brand extensions (in these cases, Ultra Pampers and Crest Tartar Control), but it was defeated in the soft cookie wars by Nabisco. Another disappointment was the soft drink business, so the Crush and Hires brands were sold off.

P&G has gone even further into the health field by forming joint ventures with drug companies like Upjohn, Syntex, and the Dutch firm Gist-Brocades. The company has entered the fat substitute derby with a substance called olestra (a sucrose polyester), but it faced a long delay in regulatory approval.

In 1990 P&G established a new operating division for Eastern Europe and began installing sales managers in countries like Hungary and Poland. The following year P&G spent $20 million to purchase the leading soap company in Czechoslovakia.

Among the things P&G wants to sell in those countries and elsewhere are beauty products. In 1989 it became the largest cosmetics company in the United States by purchasing Noxell (maker of Cover Girl and Noxema products) for $1.3 billion. P&G injected new life into the Cover Girl line and combined it with other products to create a $3-billion beauty business. In 1991 it became even more of a cosmetics powerhouse by spending more than $1 billion to purchase Revlon's Max Factor line and its German operation, Betrix.

OPERATIONS

Laundry and Cleaning Products (32 percent of 1991 revenues). This segment includes detergents (Cheer, Tide), hard surface cleaners (Comet, Mr. Clean, Spic and Span), and fabric softeners (Downy). P&G is among the companies testing superconcentrated versions of their detergents in the United States; the compact products have been selling well in Europe and Japan since the early 1980s.

Personal-Care Products (49 percent of revenues). This segment includes personal cleansing products (Ivory, Zest), deodorants (Secret), hair-care products (Head & Shoulders, Pert, Vidal Sassoon), skin-care products (Clearasil and Oil of Olay), cosmetics (Cover Girl and Max Factor), oral-care products (Crest toothpaste, Scope mouthwash), paper tissue products (Charmin, White Cloud), disposable diapers (Luvs, Pampers), digestive health products (Pepto-Bismol), cough and cold remedies (Vicks), and other pharmaceuticals.

Foods and Beverages (13 percent of revenues). Among the products in this segment are shortening and oil (Crisco), snacks (Pringle's potato chips), prepared baking mixes (Duncan Hines), peanut butter (Jif), coffee (Folger's), soft drinks (Hawaiian Punch), and citrus products (Citrus Hill orange juice). The latter, introduced in 1983, has had difficulty competing with Coca-Cola's Minute Maid products and the Tropicana line now owned by Seagram. In 1991 the FDA pressured P&G to drop the word *fresh* from its Citrus Hill containers because the juice is made from concentrates.

Because Folger's coffee is made partially from Salvadoran beans, P&G was the subject of a boycott effort by groups opposing U.S. policy in Central America. There have been reports that the company is planning to sell off parts of its food and beverage business.

Pulp and Chemicals (6 percent of revenues). This sector includes the raw material for disposable diapers, toilet tissue, and paper towels.

TOP EXECUTIVES

- Edwin L. Arzt, chairman and chief executive
- John E. Pepper, president
- John G. Smale, chairman of the executive committee
- Gerald V. Dirvin, executive vice president
- Durk I. Jager, executive vice president

OUTSIDE DIRECTORS

- David B. Abshire, president of the Center for Strategic and International Studies
- Norman R. Augustine, chief executive of Martin Marietta
- Theodore F. Brophy, retired chairman of GTE
- Richard J. Ferris, former chief executive of UAL
- Robert A. Hanson, retired chief executive of Deere & Company
- Jerry R. Junkins, chief executive of Texas Instruments
- Joshua Lederberg, president emeritus of Rockefeller University
- Walter F. Light, retired chairman of Northern Telecom
- David M. Roderick, retired chairman of USX
- Robert D. Storey, partner in the law firm of McDonald Hopkins Burke & Haber (Cleveland)
- Marina v. N. Whitman, vice president of General Motors

FINANCIAL DATA

Revenues (in millions of dollars) (years ending June 30)

1991	27,026
1990	24,081
1989	21,398
1988	19,336
1987	17,000

Net Income (in millions of dollars) (years ending June 30)

1991	1,773
1990	1,602
1989	1,206
1988	1,020
1987	327

GEOGRAPHICAL BREAKDOWN

Revenues (in millions of dollars)

Year*	United States		Foreign	
1991	15,276	(55%)	12,327	(45%)
1990	14,962	(61%)	9,618	(39%)
1989	13,312	(61%)	8,529	(39%)
1988	12,423	(63%)	7,294	(37%)

*Fiscal year ends June 30.

Net Income (in millions of dollars)

Year*	United States		Foreign	
1991	1,360	(72%)	527	(28%)
1990	1,304	(74%)	467	(26%)
1989	927	(69%)	417	(31%)
1988	864	(74%)	305	(26%)

*Fiscal year ends June 30.

LABOR RELATIONS

Starting in the 1880s P&G adopted a policy of paternalism toward its employees, taking the unusual step of giving its workers Saturday afternoon off with no cut in pay. The gesture was not adequate to meet all of the desires of the work force, however. Many workers were attracted to the militant posture of the Knights of Labor, and before long P&G found itself the target of frequent strikes.

William Cooper Procter, grandson of one of the founders and the executive in charge of personnel policy, came up with an unorthodox way of dealing with the labor unrest: He proposed that the company share its profits with its employees. Many workers were cynical about the profit-sharing scheme at first, but when the money was distributed, many of them embraced the plan. The company later tied the plan to employee stock purchases and sweetened the arrangement by protecting workers against depreciation in the value of the shares.

In response to labor unrest during World War I the company established "conference committees" to foster two-way communication with the rank and file—a practice that later was outlawed by the National Labor Relations Act of 1935.

After being represented by the Independent Oil and Chemical Workers for forty-three years, workers at P&G's Kansas City, Kansas, facility voted in 1980 to make the United Steelworkers of America (USWA) their new collective-bargaining representative. The company resisted bargaining with the USWA, prompting the union to launch a boycott of P&G products. But the campaign was not strong enough. P&G stood fast, and after several years the workers at the plant voted to decertify the USWA.

In 1990 the International Federation of Chemical, Energy and General Workers Unions announced plans for a multinational organizing drive against P&G.

ENVIRONMENTAL AND HEALTH RECORD

P&G was one of the first companies to be singled out for environmental sins. Following the publication of Rachael Carson's landmark book *Silent Spring* in 1962, the company was criticized for the detergent residues that were showing up in waterways. P&G and other detergent makers sought to get around the problem by employing enzymes as the active ingredient in their products.

There were, however, reports that workers in European plants were developing allergic symptoms as a result of exposure to enzyme dust generated in the manufacturing process. A public panic ensued, prompting P&G and its competitors to abandon enzymes. Yet P&G refused to relent when another controversy arose over the use of phosphates. The company had, however, developed a phosphate substitute, sodium nitrilotriacetate (NTA), that was supposed to improve detergent performance. Yet NTA also became the subject of health concerns, and in 1970 the surgeon general asked the industry to cease using the substance.

Controversy surrounded the company's Rely tampon, which was introduced in the mid-1970s. By 1980 the federal Centers for Disease Control (CDC) were investigating the spread of a new disease called toxic shock syndrome, which appeared to be most common among menstruating women using tampons. The CDC singled out Rely as being most clearly linked to the disease, prompting P&G to suspend sales of the heavily advertised product. Nonetheless, the company was hit with a series of product liability suits.

In recent years P&G has been confronted with demands that it reduce its contribution to the country's solid-waste problem. P&G redesigned some of its packaging to use less plastic and began selling Downy fabric softener in milk carton–type packages to encourage consumers to reuse the larger plastic containers. The company also has increased its use of recycled plastics.

Things have gone less smoothly in the area of disposable diapers. P&G and its competitors have been struggling to counteract rising criticism of the disposables, with P&G taking the lead in arguing that the solution is not to ban the diapers but to develop ways of composting them into fertilizer. Many environmentalists have challenged the notion, questioning the effectiveness of composting diapers and other nonfood items and charging that the proposal serves to deflect attention from the need to cut down on the volume of solid waste being sent to landfills.

A P&G cellulose plant in Florida has been cited as the cause of extensive dioxin contamination in the Fenholloway River. Health officials have warned against eating fish caught in the river, and P&G has been forced to supply bottled drinking water to area residents because of seepage of toxic substances from the plant into nearby wells.

BIBLIOGRAPHY

Editors of Advertising Age. *Procter & Gamble: The House That Ivory Built.* Lincolnwood, Ill.: NTC Business Books, 1988.

Schisgall, Oscar. *Eyes on Tomorrow: The Evolution of Procter & Gamble.* Chicago: J. F. Ferguson/Doubleday, 1981.

REUTERS HOLDINGS PLC

85 Fleet Street
London EC4P 4AJ
United Kingdom
(071) 250-1122

1991 revenues: $2.7 billion
1991 net profit: $429.4 million
Publicly traded company
Employees: 10,335
Founded: 1851

OVERVIEW

No longer simply a news wire service, Reuters is the world's leading supplier of computerized financial information. The company provides systems that allow financial professionals to get up-to-the-second data on a wide variety of markets and enable them to negotiate and carry out transactions in those markets. Reuters is especially strong in the foreign-exchange field, where it has the most-sophisticated system for facilitating trades in some 130 currencies—ranging, as the company likes to note, from the Algerian dinar to the Zimbabwe dollar.

Reuters represents the cutting edge in the move to replace the chaos of trading floors with high-tech systems that automatically link traders in far-flung offices and allow them to conduct transactions worth millions of dollars by tapping a few keys. By accelerating the circulation of information and the movement of money, Reuters is playing an important role in the emergence of an ever-more-globalized economy.

HISTORY

The history of Reuters begins with the biography of its founder, Paul Julius Reuter. He was born in 1816 in the western German town of Cassel with the name Israel Beer Josaphat. Israel, the son of a rabbi, was sent at the age of thirteen to Göttingen to work in a bank where a cousin was employed. According to legend, while in Göttingen Josaphat met Karl Friedrich Gauss, an eminent mathematician and physicist who was conducting experiments in electro-telegraphy. Gauss befriended the young man, and the two supposedly had discussions from which Josaphat's dream of a telegraphic news agency sprang.

By the early 1840s Josaphat had moved to Berlin, where at the age of twenty-eight he converted to Christianity and took the name Paul Julius Reuter. He then married the daughter of a banker and got capital from his father-in-law to buy a share in an established bookselling and publishing business. Reuter began to publish pamphlets that reflected the growing democratic movement of the day. The lack of tolerance for such activity compelled him to move to Paris in 1848. In that city he went to work for an agency that translated and distributed extracts from foreign newspapers and ran a service sending news from Paris to London and Brussels via carrier pigeon.

Reuter and his wife briefly set up their own service, but the tightening of press restrictions in France prompted them to return to Germany, where he established a firm specializing in commercial information, especially stock market prices. To fill a gap in telegraph service between Paris and Berlin, he set up a carrier-pigeon operation between Aachen and Brussels. When the gap was filled and the owners of the telegraph edged Reuter out, he moved (in 1851) to England, where he took advantage of the newly laid cable underneath the English Channel to provide prompt news from the Continent.

Before long Reuter was providing financial news to brokerage houses and other clients in London who had their reports delivered via messenger. At the same time, Reuter was expanding his network of correspondents in all of the commercial centers of Europe. Yet he also wanted acceptance from the press. The *Times* of London, then largely a monopoly, continued to resist using the service, preferring to get its news from the Continent via a special ship that crisscrossed the Channel. When a series of new papers were founded in the 1850s, Reuter moved quickly to win their trade. Eventually the *Times* came around as well.

During the American Civil War Reuter expanded his political reportage and expedited his American coverage, then still dependent on mail ships, by sending steamers to intercept the vessels off the coast of Ireland. The dispatches were then brought to the town of Crookhaven on the extreme southwestern tip of the Irish coast, from which they were transmitted via a special telegraph line built by Reuter. Beating the competition by two days with news of Lincoln's assassination became the agency's most famous scoop.

The completion of the transatlantic cable in 1866 simplified the newsgathering process, but by that time Reuter was preoccupied with establishing a telegraph link to Asia. The ending of the Austro-Prussian War allowed Reuter to make a deal with the Prussian government to lay a cable that connected London with the lines that stretched to the Persian Gulf and India. He also signed agreements with his two main competitors on the Continent—Charles-Louis Havas in Paris and Bernard Wolff in Berlin—dividing up the world into exclusive spheres of influence for each of the agencies. At home Reuter developed an arrangement with the Press Association, a domestic agency, in which Reuter's virtual monopoly on foreign news was accepted as long as he did not presume to cover local news within England.

By the 1870s the Reuter name was respected throughout the world as a source of reliable, impartial news. Reuter himself was rewarded by the Duke of Saxe-Coburg-Gotha with a barony, so that the founder of the news agency became known as Baron Julius de Reuter. Queen Victoria later gave Reuter the same title in Britain.

Reuter's son Herbert, who took over as managing director of the company in 1878, expanded into Egypt, Turkey, and the Balkans. Reuters, as the agency was known, was the primary source of information from South Africa during the Boer War. Yet the news business itself was not very profitable, so Herbert de Reuter experimented with other ways of using the telegraph to make money. A foray into advertising was a disaster, generating heavy losses. More successful was a telegraph remittance business that provided money-cabling services cheaper than those of the banks. In 1910 the company formed a banking department; two years later Reuters moved to raise capital for this department by selling shares to the public. Still, the company was facing increasing instability, especially after the outbreak of World War I severely restricted operations.

The nature of the firm was altered once again in 1915, after Herbert de Reuter committed suicide following the death of his wife. (His father had died in 1899.) He was succeeded by Roderick Jones, who had built the Reuters operation in South Africa. Jones, working with board chairman Mark Napier, decided that the future of the company lay in placing its resources at the disposal of the Allies. To make their plan easier to carry out, Jones and Napier arranged to buy out the public shareholders and replace the Reuter's Telegram Company with a private firm called Reuters Ltd. They then sold off the banking operation. The next step was to form an arrangement with the British government in which Reuters disseminated official communiqués and received a healthy stipend from the state. Jones briefly served as the government's (unpaid) director of propaganda while retaining his position at Reuters.

After the war Reuters embraced the new medium of wireless communication and a new form of ownership. In 1925 Jones offered a majority interest in the company to the British press—half to the Newspaper Proprietors Association (representing the London papers) and half to the Press Association (representing the provincial publications). There were problems in negotiating the arrangements, with the result that the Press Association ended up taking the majority share by itself. It soon became sole owner of the agency—an arrangement that lasted until 1941, when the London papers finally came in as a 50-percent partner.

During this period, Reuters also faced growing competition from the U.S. agency the Associated Press (AP), which refused to accept the spheres of influence established by the European agencies. During World War II Reuters was heavily outnumbered by AP and the other U.S. agencies in its pool of correspondents. Nonetheless, Reuters provided extensive coverage of the fighting, and, unlike its posture during the previous war, it avoided becoming directly involved in the government's propaganda and information activities. During the war the agency also made inroads among U.S. newspapers; the *Chicago Tribune*, for instance, signed up in 1944.

After the war Reuters solidified its role in the Commonwealth countries by taking in newspaper proprietors in Australia, New Zealand, and India as part owners of the agency. It also strengthened its role in the U.K. market as several small competitors fell by the wayside. Despite its strong position in the news business, Reuters was no cash cow.

In 1964 Reuters found a formula for success by returning to its roots—the business of providing rapid stock market quotations. The company helped to usher out the age of the stock ticker by supplying European brokerage houses with computer terminals, providing them with instant stock prices from the United States. In 1973, just as fixed exchange rates were giving way, Reuters introduced a system called Monitor that provided rapid prices and allowed traders to execute their transactions automatically. The Reuters lead in the foreign-exchange transaction business continues today and is the foundation of the company.

By the mid-1980s the financial business had come to dominate Reuters almost completely; revenues from the media accounted for only 5 percent of its sales. To help raise funds for expansion Reuters once again went public in 1984, but the publishers retained a controlling interest. The company wasted no time in using its new capital. In 1985 it spent $57 million to purchase Rich Inc., a Chicago-based supplier of communications systems for financial-trading rooms. That same year, it obtained non-U.S. marketing rights for a system called Instinet, which provides automated trading of equities and options; two years later it took over the company.

Chief executive Glen Renfrew continued to spend heavily in the United States to promote his goal of creating a comprehensive information and transaction system for the financial services industry. Seeking to take on Dow Jones and Citicorp's Quotron unit on their home turf, he set up an impressive array of satellite dishes and other equipment in Hauppauge, a Long Island suburb of New York City. Yet Reuters remained less dependent on the U.S. market than on Europe and the Far East, which worked to the company's advantage during the slump in the securities business following the market crash in 1987.

Reuters, however, is not satisfied with the relatively small portion of its revenues that comes from the United States. This has resulted in intensified competition with its American rivals. Reuters has been pushing its new Dealing 2000 system in the United States, while Dow Jones has been pushing its Trading System product at home and in Europe.

OPERATIONS

Information Products (77 percent of 1991 revenues). The major business of Reuters is the delivery of financial information—through more than 200,000 video terminals and teleprinters. In 1990 three product groups—real-time information, historical information, and trading room systems—were consolidated.

The company packages real-time information covering the world's foreign-exchange, money, commodities, securities, bond, energy, and shipping markets. Data are drawn from more than 160 organized exchanges and over-the-counter markets around the world, as well as from quotations provided by dealers in markets with no physical trading floor. The services are distributed through video terminals, directly into client computers, or, to a limited extent, via teleprinters. The company's fastest real-time products are its Dealing 2000 series, which are carried on the Reuters Integrated Data Network. The foreign-exchange component of this segment is the company's leading source of revenue.

Historical information ranges from data only a few seconds old to material referring to trends over many years. Reuters mixes its own data with textual material from other sources to produce such services as Reuter Country Reports, which provide profiles of some 190 countries and regions, and Reuter Company Newsyear, which provides summaries of news on more than 22,000 companies worldwide. The Textline data base service draws from more than two thousand publications and wires in sixteen different languages. In 1990 Textline added more Eastern European sources and a German-language version.

Reuters designs, installs, and maintains digital and video information systems for trading rooms of all sizes. The systems allow access to Reuters real-time, historical, and transaction products.

Transaction Products (16 percent of revenues). This segment includes services that enable dealers to contact one another through a Reuters network in order to effect trades.

The best-known product here is the Reuter Monitor Dealing Service, which allows dealers to contact one another to negotiate and conclude trades in foreign exchange, bullion, and bonds. A rapid alternative to telex and dial-up telephone communications, the system generates hard-copy confirmations of trades.

In 1989 Reuters introduced the first phase of Dealing 2000, an enhanced service for foreign-exchange transactions. It increases the number of dealing conversations that can be conducted simultaneously and computerizes the production of dealer "tickets," which traditionally have been handwritten. The second phase of Dealing 2000, introduced in 1992, enables all traders to see the best buy or sell price for a currency simultaneously, automatically match bids and offers using central computers, and verify that the parties have sufficient and mutually acceptable credit limits.

In 1988 Reuters began development of GLOBEX, an automated system for trading futures and options contracts outside of normal trading hours. Originally developed for the Chicago Mercantile Exchange, the system also has been adopted by the Chicago Board of Trade.

Through its Instinet subsidiary Reuters operates a computer-based network that allows investment professionals to trade in equities. The system provides two-way computerized transactional capability while supplying continuously updated market information on all major U.S. exchanges and NASDAQ (over-the-counter) market makers and some British information.

Media Products (7 percent of revenues). The wire service business Reuters was built on is still prestigious but accounts for only a small portion of the company's revenues. Using some thirteen hundred staff journalists and photographers based in seventy-four countries, the company provides comprehensive reports on international news for more than three thousand subscribers. Service for the media is provided in English, French, German, Spanish, and Arabic. Third-party vendors also make the Reuters wire available in such languages as Italian, Dutch, Portuguese, Swedish, Norwegian, Japanese, Hebrew, and Turkish.

Reuters antagonized many of its British media clients—and lost some of them to Agence France-Presse—when it sharply increased its rates in 1992.

In 1990 Reuters launched its News Graphics Service, which provides daily computer graphics illustrating world news. The company also owns a majority interest in Visnews Ltd., a service that provides video coverage of international events to more than four hundred television stations and other subscribers in eighty countries.

TOP EXECUTIVES

- Christopher Hogg, chairman
- Peter Job, managing director and chief executive
- David Ure, executive director
- Andre Villeneuve, executive director
- Robert Rowley, finance director
- Mark Wood, editor in chief

OUTSIDE DIRECTORS

- Richard Giordano, deputy chairman of Grand Metropolitan
- Pehr Gyllenhammar, chairman of Volvo

- Andrew Knight, executive chairman of News International
- Ian Park, managing director of Northcliffe Newspapers Group
- David Snedden, chief executive of Trinity International Holdings and former chairman of the Press Association

FINANCIAL DATA

Revenues (in millions of pounds)

1991	1,467
1990	1,369
1989	1,187
1988	1,003
1987	867

Net Profit (in millions of pounds)

1991	230
1990	208
1989	181
1988	134
1987	110

GEOGRAPHICAL BREAKDOWN

Revenues (in millions of pounds)

Year	Europe		Western Hemisphere		Elsewhere	
1991	831	(59%)	228	(16%)	347	(25%)
1990	805	(58%)	234	(17%)	341	(25%)
1989	655	(54%)	235	(19%)	318	(26%)
1988	569	(55%)	198	(19%)	259	(25%)

LABOR RELATIONS

The main labor dispute between the British employees of Reuters—who belong to the National Union of Journalists and several other unions—came in 1980, when the staff went on strike for a week when contract talks broke down. During the same period, Reuters workers in the United States, represented by the Newspaper Guild, walked off the job. Since then there have been frequent tensions between management and the unions in both countries over the company's attempts to convert guaranteed wage increases into discretionary ones—that is, merit raises.

BIBLIOGRAPHY

Boyd-Barrett, Oliver. *The International News Agencies*. London: Constable, 1980.

Lawrenson, John, and Lionel Barber. *The Price of Truth: The Story of the Reuters Millions*. Edinburgh: Mainstream, 1985.

Storey, Graham. *Reuters: The Story of a Century of News-Gathering*. 1951. Reprint. New York: Greenwood, 1969.

RJR NABISCO HOLDINGS CORP.

1301 Sixth Avenue
New York, New York 10019
(212) 258-5600

1991 revenues: $15 billion
1991 net income: $368 million
Publicly traded company
Employees: 56,000
Founded: 1875

OVERVIEW

Like Philip Morris, RJR Nabisco is a tobacco giant that has sought to insulate itself from the problems of the cigarette industry by plunging into the food business. In recent years, however, the company has been more widely known as the object of a dramatic takeover battle. That contest, which became a symbol of the financial excesses of the 1980s, resulted in the largest corporate transaction ever consummated: a $25-billion leveraged buyout.

HISTORY

The origins of RJR can be traced to the arrival of twenty-five-year-old Richard Joshua Reynolds in the town of Winston, North Carolina, in 1875. Winston was the center of the new flue-cured leaf that made the best chewing tobacco. For several decades Reynolds built a prosperous chewing tobacco business, selling the plugs under dozens of brand names.

During the 1890s the company fell prey to the tobacco empire being assembled by James Duke, who controlled the rights to cigarette-rolling machines. After the tobacco trust was broken up by the Supreme Court in 1911, R. J. Reynolds Tobacco took advantage of its regained independence to charge into the cigarette business. Like many advances in the tobacco industry, this initiative took the form of a marketing blitz. Using a massive advertising campaign announcing that "the Camels are coming," the company succeeded in creating the first national cigarette brand.

Camels became so popular during World War I—thanks in large part to the free samples given to American troops—that General John Pershing himself contacted the company to be sure that his doughboys would not run out of smokes. After the war the brand was etched onto the American consciousness with the famous slogan "I'd walk a mile for a Camel." That line was most conspicuous on a billboard (which emitted real smoke rings) that stood in New York's Times Square for many years.

RJR, like its brethren in the tobacco industry, took great pains to resist the growing realization of the hazards of smoking—an awareness that began to be created on a large scale by a 1952 article in *Reader's Digest*. While downplaying the significance of the evidence, RJR hedged its bets in 1954 by introducing a filtered brand called Winston, which went on to become one of the perennially best-selling brands in the United States.

When the pressure on the industry became more intense in the wake of the surgeon general's 1964 report, Reynolds began to diversify its operations. Among its purchases were Chun King foods, Del Monte Foods, and Sea-Land shipping. In 1970 the company took the word *tobacco* out of its name and rechristened itself R. J. Reynolds Industries.

The diversification strategy was accelerated in the 1980s. In 1982 the target was Heublein, a distilled spirits producer founded in 1875. The company sold the first prepared cocktails and survived Prohibition by selling A-1 steak sauce. After World War II the company transformed America's drinking habits by heavily promoting vodka and introducing mixed drinks, such as the Bloody Mary, that used the Russian liquor. In 1971 Heublein acquired the Kentucky Fried Chicken fast-food chain.

Once Heublein was swallowed, Reynolds turned its appetite toward a $5-billion meal—Nabisco Brands, the product of the 1981 merger of Nabisco and Standard Brands. Nabisco itself was born of the merger of two rival baking groups in 1898. Originally known as the National Biscuit Company, it developed the first brand-name cracker (Uneeda) and went on to dominate the cookie and cracker market with such brands as Ritz, Oreo, and Fig Newton. Standard Brands was built on Fleischmann yeast and gin, Royal baking powder, and Chase & Sanborn coffee.

The transformation of Reynolds continued through the rest of the 1980s. In 1986 the Kentucky Fried Chicken operation was sold to PepsiCo, and the following year most of the rest of Heublein was purchased by Britain's Grand Metropolitan for $1.2 billion. The Canada Dry and Sunkist soft drinks businesses, which had been acquired only a few years earlier, were sold to Cadbury Schweppes.

But the real drama came in 1988. A bold proposal by chief executive F. Ross Johnson to take the company private through a leveraged buyout prompted an intense bidding war as well as a great deal of public criticism of the greed and ruthlessness of the parties maneuvering for control. In the end the winner was Kohlberg Kravis Roberts & Company, which acquired the firm for $25 billion—the largest takeover ever.

As part of the effort to service the company's gargantuan debt load, nearly $6 billion in assets have been sold off. These have included several European and Asian food businesses, Chun King, and much of Del Monte Foods. In 1990 and 1991 the company also engaged in an extensive recapitalization, which involved an extensive trade of debt for equity, including the reissuance of common and convertible preferred stock.

The company's 1990 annual report, the first in three years, tried very hard to dispel the idea that the leveraged buyout had stifled investment and prompted short-term thinking. "The impact has been just the opposite at RJR Nabisco," the reports says. "We have a new sense of urgency and entrepreneurial energy." Yet the report puts an inordinate emphasis on generating cash flow, vital to the company's struggle to meet its debt payments.

This quest has made the company obsessive about cutting costs, so today's RJR is a much less flamboyant operation than it was during the days of Ross Johnson, when millions were spent on a fleet of corporate jets. Even so, interest payments continue to depress the company's bottom line, which in 1991 showed a net of only $368 million, despite operating income of nearly $3 billion.

OPERATIONS

Tobacco (57 percent of 1991 net sales). RJR and its subsidiaries and licensees manufacture cigarettes in the United States and thirty other countries. The company's tobacco products are marketed in some 160 nations. In the United States RJR lost its leading position to Philip Morris in 1983. The company's domestic market share in 1991 was 30 percent. Tobacco accounted for 77 percent of what the company calls business unit contribution—that is, operating income before amortization of trademarks and goodwill.

The company's leading cigarette brands are Winston, Salem, Doral, Camel, and Vantage. In 1989 the company withdrew its highly touted "smokeless" Premier brand from the market in the face of unfavorable consumer response. The company began to mount a more aggressive challenge to Philip Morris in late 1990 with the splashy introduction of super-low-tar Camel Ultra Lights. At the same time, RJR has been suffering from a growing defection of smokers from its full-price products to discount brands. Nearly all of the company's domestic tobacco-manufacturing facilities are located in and around Winston-Salem, North Carolina. Among them is the two-million-square-foot Tobaccoville plant that went into full operation in 1987.

Although the international position of Philip Morris is much stronger, RJR's Tobacco International has reasonably good brand presence in much of Europe and some other key foreign markets. In late 1990 RJR and Philip Morris were asked by the Soviet Union to supply thirty-four billion cigarettes to alleviate a severe shortage of smokes there. The company also has moved to take advantage of the transformation of Eastern Europe by acquiring the Club brand, one of the best-selling cigarettes in eastern Germany. In 1991 it also began exploring additional investments in Poland, Hungary, and Czechoslovakia. RJR is the only U.S. cigarette company with a manufacturing facility in China, the world's largest cigarette market.

Food (43 percent of net sales). The foods group is divided into Nabisco and Planters LifeSavers. Nabisco manufactures or markets cookies (such as Oreos and Fig Newtons), crackers (Ritz, Triscuit, and others), other snack foods, hot and ready-to-eat cereals (Cream of Wheat and Shredded Wheat), margarine, pet foods, dessert mixes (Royal), and other grocery products ranging from Grey Poupon mustard to Ortega Mexican foods. The biscuit portion of Nabisco claims to be number one in the U.S. cookie and cracker industry, with the top eight brands. The company is also number one in dog snacks (Milk Bone), but it trails behind Kellogg in the ready-to-eat cereal business and behind Quaker Oats in hot cereals. Nabisco's international operations are centered on Latin America, where it is a leading producer of powdered dessert and drink mixes, biscuits, and baking powder.

Planters LifeSavers manufactures and markets nuts, hard roll candy, chewing gum, and snacks primarily for sale in the United States. Among the leading brands are Planters nuts, Life Savers candy, Breath Savers sugar-free mints, Bubble Yum gum, and Care*Free sugarless gum. The first four of these products are the leaders in their segments.

In the food business Nabisco's products are made in bakeries and other facilities spread throughout the United States, Canada, and Puerto Rico. Among foreign operations the greatest presence is in Brazil, where the company operates eleven plants.

TOP EXECUTIVES

- Louis V. Gerstner, Jr., chairman and chief executive
- Eugene R. Croisant, executive vice president, human resources and administration
- Lawrence R. Ricciardi, executive vice president and general counsel
- Karl M. von der Heyden, chief financial officer
- James W. Johnston, chairman of R. J. Reynolds Tobacco
- H. John Greeniaus, president of Nabisco Foods

OUTSIDE DIRECTORS

- Vernon E. Jordan, Jr., partner in the law firm of Akin, Gump, Hauer & Feld
- John G. Medlin, Jr., chief executive of Wachovia Corporation
- Rozanne L. Ridgway, former assistant secretary of state

Henry R. Kravis, George R. Roberts, and six other executives from Kohlberg Kravis Roberts & Co. are also on the board.

FINANCIAL DATA

Net Sales (in millions of dollars)

1991	14,989
1990	13,879
1989	12,674
1988	12,635
1987	11,765

Net Income (in millions of dollars)

1991	368
1990	− 429 (loss)
1989	− 1,149 (loss)
1988	1,393
1987	1,209

LABOR RELATIONS

R. J. Reynolds has a reputation as one of the most antiunion employers in the country. It has been on the AFL-CIO boycott list for nearly forty years. Unions have organized the company, but they tend to get dislodged as a result of company resistance. This happened after both world wars. Although more recent organizing drives (such as the one in 1974) have been beaten back, in 1989 the Bakery, Confectionery and Tobacco Workers (BCTW) announced plans for a new campaign. Several of the company's tobacco operations overseas are unionized.

The BCTW did succeed in organizing many workers at Nabisco, and the union continued to have a working relationship with the company even after it was taken over by RJR. Since RJR was taken private by Kohlberg Kravis Roberts, relations have been even better. Helped by federal mediators, the company and the union began cooperating on such projects as a $5-million jointly administered fund to help workers learn the higher-tech skills needed in modern bakeries. In recognition of the new labor-management harmony, the company and the BCTW were given an award for "excellence in industrial relations" by the Federal Mediation and Conciliation Service in 1991.

Some rank and file workers, however, are not pleased with the results of this labor-management cooperation. In September 1991 BCTW members at a local union in Portland, Oregon, concerned that seniority and job security were being eroded, voted to abandon the team concept.

ENVIRONMENTAL AND HEALTH RECORD

As with Philip Morris, the main environmental issue for RJR is the health effects of its tobacco products. The company is not quite as outspoken on the issue as Philip Morris, but it does resist acknowledging the deleterious effects of cigarettes. The company's 10-K financial report complains that for twenty-five years cigarettes have been "under attack" by government and health officials in the United States and abroad.

For years RJR and the rest of the industry have vigorously fought product liability suits brought by smokers claiming that cigarettes had given them lung cancer and other diseases. The industry's legal winning streak was unbroken until 1988, but in 1992 the Supreme Court ruled that the existence of federal warning labels did not bar suits against cigarette makers.

In the meantime, RJR has had to contend with increasing criticism of its marketing strategies. In 1990 it was forced to cancel a brand aimed at black smokers amid a wave of protest led by Health and Human Services secretary Louis Sullivan. The company also has come under fire for running ads that critics say are aimed at teenagers. Because of ads featuring a cartoon character named Old Joe Camel, an organization called Stop Teenage Addiction to Tobacco issued a call in 1990 for a boycott of all RJR products. Old Joe also came under attack by the U.S. Surgeon General in 1992, but the company resisted giving up such a successful marketing tool.

In the late 1980s RJR was found to have shipped large quantities of cigarettes to Japan containing tobacco with excessive pesticide residues.

BIBLIOGRAPHY

Burrough, Bryan, and John Helyar. *Barbarians at the Gate: The Fall of RJR Nabisco.* New York: Harper & Row, 1990.

Cahn, William. *Out of the Cracker Barrel: The Nabisco Story From Animal Crackers to Zuzus.* New York: Simon & Schuster, 1969.

Finger, William R., ed. *The Tobacco Industry in Transition.* Lexington, Mass.: Lexington Books, 1981.

Lampert, Hope. *True Greed: What Really Happened in the Battle for RJR Nabisco.* New York: New American Library, 1990.

Reynolds, Patrick, and Tom Shachtman. *The Gilded Leaf: Triumph, Tragedy, and Tobacco.* Boston: Little, Brown, 1989.

Sobel, Robert. *They Satisfy: The Cigarette in American Life.* Garden City, N.Y.: Anchor, 1978.

Sticht, J. Paul. *The RJR Story: The Evolution of a Global Enterprise.* Exton, Pa.: Newcomen Society, 1983.

Taylor, Peter. *The Smoke Ring: Tobacco, Money and Multinational Politics.* New York: Pantheon Books, 1984.

Tilley, Nannie M. *The R.J. Reynolds Tobacco Company.* Chapel Hill: University of North Carolina Press, 1985.

White, Larry C. *Merchants of Death: The American Tobacco Industry.* New York: William Morrow, 1988.

ROCHE HOLDING LTD.

Grenzacherstrasse 124
CH-4002 Basel
Switzerland
(61) 688 11 11

1991 revenues: $8.4 billion
1991 net income: $1.1 billion
Publicly traded company
Employees: 55,134
Founded: 1989 (F. Hoffmann–La Roche was founded in 1894)

OVERVIEW

Roche Holding Ltd. is a holding company that was created in 1989 for the pharmaceutical giant F. Hoffmann–La Roche. With operations in more than fifty countries, research facilities in eight of them, and a research and development budget that now surpasses $1 billion a year, Roche is a major player in the prescription drug business. It is also the leading producer of vitamins and one of the top suppliers of fragrances and flavorings.

In the drug business, however, Roche no longer has the commanding position it held during the 1970s, when its tranquilizers Librium and Valium were among the most widely prescribed (some would say overprescribed) medications on earth.

The problems with those tranquilizers—which included charges of excessive pricing and then the loss of revenues when their patents expired—and bad publicity from a major industrial accident in Italy have prompted Roche to seek its salvation in biotechnology. During the 1980s it formed alliances with a number of firms in the field and in 1990 paid $2.1 billion to acquire 60 percent of the well-known biotech company Genentech.

HISTORY

Fritz Hoffmann, the son of a prosperous silk merchant in Basel, worked briefly for a Belgian drug company after finishing his university education. He then returned to Basel and in 1894 set up a small manufacturing firm with chemist Max Traub. After two years Traub departed, and the venture continued under the name F. Hoffmann–La Roche (La Roche being the maiden name of Hoffmann's wife).

The company focused on three areas: specialized prescription drugs; the extraction of plant alkaloid drugs, such as atropine; and the manufacture of synthetic organic chemicals, such as vanillin and salicylic acid. Of these the most important were a cough remedy called Thiocol and a heart medication made from digitalis leaves, called Digalen.

Hoffmann and his chief chemist, Emil Barell, spent large sums on research—something almost unheard of at the time—and vigorously promoted the principle of drug standardization. On these bases the company was an important influence in the evolution of pharmaceuticals from generic items prepared by druggists or doctors to brand-name products.

In the early years of the twentieth century the company began expanding abroad, but those foreign operations were disrupted by World War I, and a large Russian operation was seized by the government after the Bolshevik revolution. In 1919 the company went public, and a year later, upon the death of Hoffmann, Barell took over the firm and resumed the international expansion, using Roche as its world trademark.

A key part of that expansion took place in the United States. The company had first opened an American sales office (in New York City) in 1905. Barell decided to devote substantial investment to manufacturing and research in the United States (and several other countries). In 1929 the company began to construct such facilities in Nutley, New Jersey (a suburb of New York where the U.S. subsidiary is still based today). The U.S. operation, along with those in South America, the British Commonwealth, southern Africa, Asia, and Australia, were put under the control of a subsidiary called Sapac Corporation, with legal headquarters in Panama.

During the 1930s chemists working with Hoffmann–La Roche managed to synthesize vitamin C and then moved on to vitamins B_2, E, K_1, and A. These developments had a dramatic impact on human health by making essential substances more easily available. The company's daily output of synthetic ascorbic acid, for instance, soon reached the equivalent of the vitamin C in millions of oranges.

Soon after World War II the company developed an anti-infective called Gantrisin, which became one of the most widely prescribed drugs. But Hoffmann–La Roche gained much greater recognition—both positive and negative—in connection with two tranquilizers introduced in the early 1960s. Librium and, to a greater extent, Valium revolutionzied the way people dealt with the pressures and frustrations of modern society. Prompted by Hoffmann–La Roche's heavy promotion of these medications as appropriate treatment for everyday emotional problems, physicians turned Valium into the best-selling drug in the United States.

The company's success was not without its price. In fact, price became a major point of controversy in connection with the tranquilizers. Hoffmann–

La Roche came under attack in numerous countries for the high cost of Librium and Valium, and in some cases the company was pressured to lower its prices. There was also a backlash against the overprescription of these drugs, and in the United States, for instance, Congress enacted limits on the refilling of prescriptions. In 1991 the company was still defending itself in a class action suit brought in Britain by patients who claimed that doctors had not adequately informed them about the risks of addiction from prolonged use of Valium.

During the 1970s the company also got itself in trouble in the vitamin business. An investigation by the European Economic Community found that Hoffmann–La Roche and six other companies had fixed prices for vitamins. Hoffmann–La Roche was fined several hundred thousand dollars.

In recent years the company has had to contend with the loss of revenues stemming from the expiration of its tranquilizer patents and the resulting appearance of low-cost generic substitutes. Also, new tranquilizers were on the market from Upjohn and Bristol-Myers.

To deal with this problem Hoffmann–La Roche formed a joint venture with the British drug house Glaxo in 1982 to market that company's Zantac ulcer medication. In 1988 Hoffmann–La Roche made a bid for the U.S. company Sterling Drug, best known as the producer of Bayer aspirin but was defeated when Eastman Kodak was brought in as a white knight. Hoffmann–La Roche was itself the target of an audacious but unsuccessful takeover bid in 1987 by the U.S. company ICN Pharmaceuticals.

The company plunged into biotechnology, first by forming a marketing agreement with industry pioneer Genentech in 1980 covering the cancer-fighting drug interferon. Hoffmann–La Roche went on to form research or marketing alliances with half a dozen other small biotechnology firms. But its most dramatic move came in 1990, when its newly formed parent company put up more than $2 billion to acquire 60 percent of Genentech.

Founded in 1976 by a leading biochemist and a venture capitalist, Genentech came to epitomize the excitement of biotechnology in the minds of many people. When the company went public in 1980 there was a scramble to buy shares, which on the first day more than doubled in value from the initial price of $35. The company succeeded in synthesizing human insulin and a growth hormone called Protropin and became a leader in the development of interferon. In 1987 Genentech got approval from the U.S. FDA for TPA, a blood clot dissolver for heart attack victims. The company fought off a patent challenge on TPA and captured two-thirds of the market for heart attack drugs but faced intensified competition when SmithKline Beecham introduced Eminase in 1990. It was the resulting uncertainty that helped push Genentech into the arms of Roche. Though the move shored up Genentech's finances, the biotechnology company was later confronted with reports suggesting that its expensive TPA product was no more effective than a much less costly alternative called streptokinase.

Roche has not neglected its own research. It introduced Roferon-A, a form of interferon, in 1986. An antidepressive called Aurorix and an antihypertensive called Inhibace went on the market in 1990. Roche also has developed a drug called dideoxycytidine (DDC) for the treatment of AIDS. Following protests by AIDS activists over restricted access, the FDA approved DDC in 1992 on an accelerated schedule.

In 1991 Roche moved to capture a greater share of the over-the-counter medicine market in Europe by purchasing Holland-based Nicholas Laboratories from the U.S. company Sara Lee Corporation for $821 million.

OPERATIONS

Pharmaceuticals (52 percent of 1991 revenues). The company produces a wide range of prescription drugs, including anti-infectives (among them Rocephin, the world's best-selling injectable antibiotic); cardiovascular preparations (Inhibace); medications for rheumatic and metabolic disorders (such as the anti-inflammatory Tilcotil); medications for oncological and virological applications (Roferon-A, which is used in treating both cancer and hepatitis B, and the AIDS drug DDC); central nervous system drugs (including the antidepressant Aurorix and the Parkinson's disease medication Madopar); and dermatological products (including Roaccutane and Tigason). Also included here are Roche's 60-percent holding in the U.S. biotechnology company Genentech and an over-the-counter drug business.

Vitamins and Fine Chemicals (24 percent of revenues). Roche is the world's leading producer of bulk vitamins for use in food preparation and vitamin tablets sold to consumers. This segment also includes animal nutrition products, such as the feed enzyme Roxazyme.

Diagnostics (12 percent of revenues). Roche is a leader in the field of diagnostic laboratories, especially in the United States. The company also markets diagnostic systems in fields like microbiology, immunology, and hematology.

Fragrances and Flavors (11 percent of revenues). This segment consists of two subsidiaries—the Givaudan Group and the Roure Group—that are among the world's leading suppliers of fragrances to the perfume industry and flavorings to the food industry. Some of the world's most expensive perfumes have originated in Roure's labs.

TOP EXECUTIVES

- Fritz Gerber, chairman and chief executive
- Lukas Hoffmann, vice chairman
- Andres F. Leuenberger, vice chairman
- Armin M. Kessler, chief operating officer

OUTSIDE DIRECTORS

- Beat A. Sarasin, chairman of Bâloise Holding

- Werner Stauffacher
- Charles Weissmann

The company does not disclose the affiliations of its outside directors. The ones listed above were obtained from other sources. The board also includes Paul Sacher, who married the widow of the son of Fritz Hoffmann and now has voting authority over a controlling interest in the company; and Sacher's stepson-in-law Jakob Oeri, a Basel surgeon. Vice chairman Lukas Hoffmann is Sacher's stepson.

FINANCIAL DATA

Revenues (in millions of Swiss francs)

1991	11,451
1990	9,670*
1989	9,814
1988	8,690
1987	7,705

*The company says that the 1990 figure is not comparable with those of earlier years due to changes in group accounting practices.

Net Income (in millions of Swiss francs)

1991	1,482
1990	948*
1989	852
1988	642
1987	482

*The company says that the 1990 figure is not comparable with those of earlier years because of changes in group accounting practices.

GEOGRAPHICAL BREAKDOWN

Revenues (in millions of Swiss francs)

Year	Europe		North America		Elsewhere	
1991	4,482	(39%)	4,353	(38%)	2,616	(23%)
1990	4,054	(42%)	3,443	(36%)	2,173	(22%)
1989	4,037	(41%)	3,550	(36%)	2,227	(23%)
1988	3,872	(45%)	2,834	(33%)	1,984	(23%)

LABOR RELATIONS

Hoffmann-La Roche has generally harmonious relations with the union—Gewerkschaft Textil Chemie Papier—that represents many of its employees in Switzerland.

ENVIRONMENTAL AND HEALTH RECORD

The name Hoffmann–La Roche is still associated by many people with one of the most notorious industrial accidents in recent times. In 1976 an explosion at a company plant in northern Italy sent a dioxin-contaminated cloud over the town of Seveso and nearby villages. The toxic release killed thousands of animals and caused severe skin reactions in many people.

Although initial fears of genetic damage may have been unfounded, the company was widely criticized for its delay in notifying public authorities of the emission and what it contained. Hoffmann–La Roche never provided a complete explanation of what had caused the accident, although it did pay out more than $100 million for the relocation of some seven hundred people and other compensation.

The Seveso controversy heated up again in 1983. While several former company employees were being tried on criminal charges relating to the accident, there were reports that more than six tons of dioxin-contaminated waste from Seveso had secretly been transported across Europe and dumped at an undisclosed location.

Hoffmann–La Roche's Accutane, a potent prescription drug for the treatment of acne, resulted in hundreds of birth defects in the 1980s in children delivered by women who had taken the drug during pregnancy despite clear warnings that Accutane could do great harm to a fetus. Given the dangers, the FDA in 1988 ordered the company to take extraordinary measures to discourage the use of the drug by pregnant women.

In 1991 the *New York Times* revealed that internal company documents showed that Hoffman–La Roche had ignored warnings that its injectable sedative Versed was being marketed in concentrations that could cause life-threatening side effects.

BIBLIOGRAPHY

Braithwaite, John. *Corporate Crime in the Pharmaceutical Industry.* Boston: Routledge & Kegan Paul, 1984.

Chetley, Andrew. *A Healthy Business? World Health and the Pharmaceutical Industry.* London: Zed Books, 1990.

Mahoney, Tom. *The Merchants of Life: An Account of the American Pharmaceutical Industry.* New York: Harper & Brothers, 1959.

Mintz, Morton. *By Prescription Only.* Boston: Beacon, 1967.

ROYAL DUTCH/SHELL GROUP

Royal Dutch Petroleum Company
30 Carel van Bylandtlaan
2596 HR The Hague
Netherlands
(70) 377-4540

"Shell" Transport and Trading Company PLC
Shell Centre
London SE1 7NA
United Kingdom
(71) 934-3856

1991 revenues: $108.6 billion (combined)
1991 net income: $4.5 billion (combined)
Publicly traded companies
Employees: 133,000
Founded: 1907 (Royal Dutch was founded in 1890, Shell in 1897)

OVERVIEW

This peculiar British-Dutch partnership is the second-largest industrial company in the world in terms of revenues and profits. For most of this century it has been one of the most powerful of the oil giants known as the Seven Sisters, having successfully challenged the Rockefeller Standard Oil empire that previously ruled supreme.

Royal Dutch/Shell is one of the most international institutions in the world. It explores for oil in some fifty countries, refines in thirty-four, and markets in more than one hundred. It is so well established in the United States, as Shell Oil Company, that many Americans are unaware that Shell is foreign-owned. The company, in fact, has a tradition of decentralization, giving its subsidiaries a great deal of autonomy.

The central decision making is carried out by a committee of six managing directors. Although there is a chairman's position, which alternates between the head of the Dutch and the head of the British company, the top executives operate by consensus. The company engages in elaborate corporate planning, including devising detailed alternative scenarios for the future of the world. Whichever of the scenarios comes to pass, Royal Dutch/Shell will undoubtedly play a major role in satisfying the energy needs of the human race.

HISTORY

The British side of the company had its origins in a firm set up by Marcus Samuel in the 1830s to import a variety of items—including polished sea shells, tea, and jute—from the Orient and to export manufactured goods from England. The firm prospered, thanks to both its trading skills and its prowess in transportation. After Samuel's death in 1874, his sons Samuel and Marcus took over the business and decided to move into the kerosene trade.

The younger Marcus Samuel looked to Russia as a source of supply. An oil industry was already being developed around Baku on the Caspian Sea by the Swedish Nobel brothers and the French Rothschilds; the latter financed the construction of rail links and a refinery to make the Russian oil available to Europe. The Nobel and Rothschild interests arranged to carve up the European market with the U.S.-based Standard Oil empire.

But Samuel had his eye on Asia, where he intended to challenge Standard's monopoly. He arranged to purchase lamp oil from the Rothschilds on the condition that he sell it east of Suez. He then built a tanker called the *Murex*, which in 1892 carried the first load of kerosene through the Suez Canal and on to Asia. Soon the Samuel firm had a fleet of tankers (each named after a shell) and an elaborate network for transporting bulk kerosene—which was cheaper to distribute than the five-gallon cans in which Standard shipped its products—to seaports in India, Malaya, and China. Samuel managed to withstand the price war launched by Standard to assert its control of the market.

When there were signs that the Russian government would take over the oil trade, Samuel established a new source of supply by purchasing a concession to explore for oil in East Borneo, then controlled by the Netherlands. In 1897, after rejecting a buyout offer from Standard, Samuel reorganized his family's oil operations as the "Shell" Transport and Trading Company, taking its name from the brand of kerosene they were selling.

Another survivor of the price wars in Asia was an oil company that went by the name Royal Dutch. The firm had its origins in the discovery by Aeilco Janz Zijlker, superintendent of a Dutch tobacco plantation on Sumatra, of oil that could be used for lighting. The oil, which seeped out of the ground in various places, had long been used by the people of Sumatra for torches. Zijlker was granted a concession and set out to raise money for drilling. The result was Royal Dutch—so named because King William III lent his moral support to the enterprise—which was formally established in Holland in 1890.

The company soon began drilling on Sumatra, though without Zijlker, who died suddenly in late 1890. Royal Dutch pushed ahead with the building of a market for its Crown brand of oil, but the company's growth became much more rapid after a young man by the name of Hendrik Deterding was hired in 1896. Deterding, who had been working as a representative of the Netherlands Trading Society in Penang, revitalized the company's distribution and marketing operations. He developed a network of exclusive distributors and followed the lead of the Samuels in employing bulk shipping.

Meanwhile, the Samuels had found a new way to challenge the Standard Oil monolith. Right after oil was discovered in Texas in 1901, they made a deal with the pioneering J. M. Guffey Petroleum Company to purchase supplies for use in entering the European market. This prompted Shell to expand its tanker fleet, which by the beginning of the new century consisted of thirty oceangoing vessels.

Despite the growth of both his firm and Shell, Deterding, who became managing director of Royal Dutch in 1901, was increasingly of the mind that the two companies—along with other smaller players in the Far East market—needed to band together if they were to survive the competitive pressures being exerted by the Rockefeller group. The first step in this direction was taken in 1902, when Shell, Royal Dutch, and the Rothschilds formed a marketing joint venture in the Far East called the Asiatic Petroleum Company. This arrangement having worked to the satisfaction of Royal Dutch and Shell, the two companies decided in 1907 to merge their properties.

What became known as the Royal Dutch/Shell Group included Asiatic Petroleum (in which the Rothschilds maintained an interest until the 1930s); a new entity called the Batavian Petroleum Company, which was to own and manage the other oil lands and refineries of the two companies; and the new Anglo-Saxon Petroleum Company, which took over the tankers and other distribution facilities. In each of these Royal Dutch had a 60-percent interest and Shell 40 percent (an arrangement that continues today).

Within a few years Royal Dutch/Shell was ready to confront Standard in its home market. In 1912 a tanker brought a load of more than a million gallons of gasoline from Sumatra to a storage depot in Seattle. Only a few days before, Royal Dutch/Shell had established the American Gasoline Company, and within a year it was drilling for oil in California as well. In 1914 the U.S. operations were renamed Shell Company of California, which within a few years enjoyed some major discoveries in the Los Angeles area. During this period, Royal Dutch/Shell also began investing in Oklahoma production companies, organizing its holdings in that state under the name Roxana Petroleum Company. In 1922 the growing Royal Dutch/Shell interests in the United States were merged with Union Oil Company of Delaware (which had a controlling interest in the Union Oil Company of California) to form Shell Union Oil Corporation. In 1949 the name of this holding company was changed to Shell Oil Company.

While becoming a major production and marketing force in the United States, Royal Dutch/Shell also was developing new sources of supply all over the world. Most important, the company gained a foothold in what would turn out to be the largest oil-producing region of the world—the Middle East. Deterding arranged to participate in a syndicate called the Turkish Petroleum Company that was formed in 1914. After the large American producers muscled into the consortium in the 1920s, a group of the major players endorsed the Red Line Agreement, which obligated them not to compete with one another in a vast area representing the old Ottoman Empire. Then, in 1928, Deterding met secretly at the Achnacarry hunting lodge in Scotland with his counterparts from Standard Oil of New Jersey and Anglo-Persian to carve up world markets.

These arrangements were never completely implemented, and Royal Dutch/ Shell continued to vie with Jersey Standard for leadership of the industry. During the 1930s, however, the behavior of Deterding himself was becoming, as Anthony Sampson puts it in *The Seven Sisters*, "increasingly autocratic with signs of incipient megalomania." He also was becoming openly sympathetic to the Nazis, so in the late 1930s he was eased out of his job. He died in 1939.

After World War II Royal Dutch/Shell expanded its network of refineries around the world and moved into the chemicals business. The company also became a leader in the production of natural gas and its distribution in liquefied form. In 1956 Royal Dutch/Shell gained a 14-percent share in Iranian production as part of a new consortium formed after a CIA-led coup overthrew the government that had expropriated the holdings of Anglo-Iranian Oil Company (later known as British Petroleum).

Because of its traditional emphasis on trading and its greater strength in refining and marketing, Royal Dutch/Shell was less affected than the other Seven Sisters when oil-producing countries like Libya began to take control of the petroleum operations within their borders.

The Shell Oil Company, in which Royal Dutch/Shell increased its ownership from 69 percent to 100 percent in 1985, rose to the top of the gasoline business in the United States. In 1979 the U.S. company spent an astounding $3.7 billion to acquire the Belridge Oil properties in the San Joaquin Valley in California, but the investment paid off handsomely.

During the 1980s Royal Dutch/Shell became the target of a widespread campaign to pressure the company to end its extensive oil, chemical, and coal business in South Africa. The company was accused of violating the United Nations embargo on the import of oil into the white-ruled country and of supplying oil products to the South African military and police.

In 1986 the AFL-CIO and other U.S. labor organizations joined with antiapartheid groups in launching a consumer boycott of Shell products, the first such action against a company because of its South African operations. In 1987 Shell Oil mounted a countercampaign, code-named the Neptune Strategy, to enlist the support of mainstream labor and religious leaders to defuse the boycott. But when the plan came to light, it only served to fuel the efforts against Shell. In 1991 the governor of New Jersey barred Shell service stations from the New Jersey Turnpike because of its South African connection.

Despite this public relations problem Royal Dutch/Shell continued to grow, and by the late 1980s it was poised to overtake Exxon as the world's largest oil company. In 1987 it surpassed the U.S. company in revenues and oil production, but Exxon remained more profitable. Subsequently the two companies have traded the lead, with Shell assuming the top spot in both revenues and profits in 1990. Exxon regained the profit lead in 1991. Exploration efforts also continued to pay off, as in the large strike in Gabon in 1985 and another in the Gulf of Mexico in 1991. Although Royal Dutch/Shell was sitting on a huge pile of cash during the 1980s, it avoided indulging in the acquisitions wave of that period.

OPERATIONS

Oil and Gas (86 percent of 1991 revenues). Royal Dutch/Shell is a fully integrated petroleum company. It engages in exploration and production in dozens of countries, including the U.K. portion of the North Sea, Denmark, Holland, Nigeria, Oman, Syria, Brunei, Australia, Canada, and the United States. Its reserves at the end of 1990 were some 9.7 billion barrels of crude oil and natural gas liquids and 46.5 trillion cubic feet of natural gas.

The company has refinery operations in thirty-four countries, among them the United States, Switzerland, Singapore, and Japan. During 1990 these facilities processed an average of 3.4 million barrels of crude oil and feedstock per day. Royal Dutch/Shell operates a fleet of 114 oil tankers, 4 dry bulk carriers, and 4 gas carriers. It markets petroleum products in more than one hundred countries. In the United States alone there are ninety-four hundred Shell service stations.

Chemicals (10 percent of revenues). The company produces base chemicals, industrial chemicals, polymers, and crop-protection products in such countries as the United States, the United Kingdom, Holland, France, Brazil, Argentina, and Singapore.

Coal, Metals, and Other Products (4 percent of revenues). Royal Dutch/Shell mines coal in South Africa and Australia; in 1990 it announced plans to sell its coal operation in Canada. Coal sales that year were forty-two million tons. The company mines metals, such as bauxite, alumina, lead, zinc, gold, and silver, in such countries as Brazil, Colombia, Ghana, and Indonesia. Other operations include solar energy projects in France and the Netherlands and a forestry project in Chile.

TOP EXECUTIVES

- Peter Holmes, group chairman and chairman of Shell Transport
- Cornelius A. J. Herkströter, group vice chairman and president of Royal Dutch Petroleum
- John S. Jennings, group managing director

- Mark Moody-Stuart, group managing director
- H. de Ruiter, group managing director

OUTSIDE DIRECTORS

Royal Dutch Petroleum
- T. C. Braakman, former chairman of Nationale-Nederlanden NV
- Kaspar V. Cassani, former vice chairman of IBM
- J. D. Hooglandt, former chairman of Koninklijke Nederlandsche Hoogovens en Staalfabrieken NV
- H. F. van den Hoven, former chairman of Unilever NV
- E. von Kuenheim, chairman of the executive board of BMW AG

The board also includes former group chairman and president Lodewijk C. van Wachem.

"Shell" Transport and Trading
- Anthony Acland, former ambassador to the United States
- Lord Armstrong of Ilminster, former secretary of the cabinet
- Robert Clark, vice chairman of SmithKline Beecham
- Edmund Dell, former member of Parliament and former chairman of Channel Four TV Company
- David Orr, former chairman of Unilever PLC
- Michael Palliser, deputy chairman of Midland Montagu (Holdings)
- John Swire, honorary chairman of John Swire & Sons Ltd.

FINANCIAL DATA

Revenues (in million of pounds)

1991	58,089
1990	59,416
1989	52,166
1988	44,003
1987	47,779

Net Income (in millions of pounds)

1991	2,403
1990	3,609
1989	3,954
1988	2,941
1987	2,831

GEOGRAPHICAL BREAKDOWN

Revenues (in millions of pounds)

Year	Europe		United States		Elsewhere	
1991	31,997	(50%)	12,413	(20%)	19,101	(30%)
1990	33,097	(51%)	13,765	(21%)	18,665	(28%)
1989	27,316	(48%)	13,308	(23%)	16,141	(28%)

Operating Income (in millions of pounds)

Year	Europe		United States		Elsewhere	
1991	974	(38%)	−4	(0%)	1,567	(62%)
1990	1,751	(42%)	453	(11%)	1,980	(47%)
1989	1,485	(39%)	752	(20%)	1,579	(41%)

LABOR RELATIONS

Shell Oil was one of the main targets when union organizing among U.S. oil workers began to escalate in the 1920s. The company fought against union recognition but later changed its tack, focusing instead on creating easily controlled employee associations. It was not until the 1940s that these independent unions began to ally themselves with the Oil Workers International Union. Eventually the large majority of Shell in the United States came under the protection of contracts with the Oil, Chemical and Atomic Workers.

During the 1980s Royal Dutch/Shell came under fire from unions around the world because of its involvement in South Africa. Labor organizations in many countries supported a boycott of the company's products, both as a way of opposing apartheid and because they accused Royal Dutch/Shell of engaging in union busting at the Rietspruit coal mine in South Africa. The management of the mine, half owned by a Royal Dutch/Shell subsidiary, suspended four shop stewards affiliated with the National Union of Mineworkers in 1985 because of a memorial service held during working hours for a mineworker who had been killed in an accident at the facility. When eight hundred miners walked off the job in protest they were attacked with rubber bullets and tear gas. More than eighty of the more-militant workers were fired and evicted from their homes; the rest were forced back to work at gunpoint.

Labor groups in the United States were also angry at the company because of the antiunion policies of the A. T. Massey Coal Company, half owned by Royal Dutch/Shell. The UMW struck Massey in 1984 because of the company's refusal to recognize the union in some of its subsidiaries. After a fifteen-month walkout that saw a great deal of violence, Massey agreed to settle National Labor Relations Board charges and the miners went back to work.

ENVIRONMENTAL RECORD

Although the company has made efforts in recent years to adopt more environmentally conscious policies, many of its facilities have been major sources of pollution and the sites of serious accidents. Also, the company was slow to phase out dangerous pesticides, including some that continued to be shipped to countries like Costa Rica (where thousands of banana plantation workers were exposed) after they were banned in the United States.

Some of the company's worst problems have been at the Shell Oil Company refinery in Martinez, California, near San Francisco. During the 1980s there were numerous fires and major spills at the facility. In 1986, for example, forty-eight thousand gallons of toxic waste water spilled into a local waterway. Local authorities fined the company $75,000, saying that Shell had been negligent in not repairing a stuck valve. Two years later some 440,000 gallons of crude oil were spilled at Martinez, contaminating wetlands and eleven miles of shoreline. Shell, which did not report the accident for four weeks, entered into a consent decree with the EPA and California officials in 1989. The settlement included a payment of $19.8 million by the company.

Shell Oil and the U.S. Army were found liable in 1985 for massive environmental contamination at the Rocky Mountain Arsenal near Denver. The army had built the plant during World War II to make nerve gas, and Shell had leased part of the site in the early 1950s to produce pesticides, ceasing operations in 1982. Local residents reported a variety of symptoms, including miscarriages and chronic nausea, which they claimed were linked to the dumping of toxics and carcinogens by Shell and the army. A Colorado official called it "one of the most contaminated sites on the planet." Shell has spent years fighting with the army, its insurance companies, and environmental authorities about financial responsibility for the cleanup.

Shell's Norco Manufacturing Complex in Louisiana ranked second among all industrial facilities in the United States in terms of toxic releases in 1988. The following year there was a huge reduction in such releases because of the adoption of a new process to convert toxics to a marketable product. In May 1988 an explosion at the refinery in Norco killed seven workers. OSHA fined the company $3,000 for safety violations in connection with the accident. Shell has paid out more than $40 million in damages to settle suits brought by injured workers and the families of those killed.

In 1989 there was a major explosion at a North Sea offshore oil platform partly owned by Royal Dutch/Shell. This was only one of a series of explosions at North Sea facilities, which the company blamed on worker carelessness and union officials said were the result of cost-cutting efforts by management.

In the United Kingdom Royal Dutch/Shell has come under fire because of reports that its Permithrin product, used as a mothproofing agent in the carpet- and wool-processing industry, had caused significant water pollution in several rivers. Also in Britain, a problem at a company pipeline led to the spilling of ten thousand gallons of crude oil in the River Mersey. The company was fined a record £1 million.

In 1991 Shell was one of ten major oil companies in the United States cited by the EPA for discharging contaminated fluids from service stations into or directly above underground sources of water. The company paid a fine of $56,000 and agreed to clean up the sites by the end of 1993.

On the positive side, Shell introduced a reformulated gasoline in 1990 in the U.S. cities with the worst air quality. The gas, SU 2000E, is said to cut hydrocarbon emissions by about 18 percent and carbon monoxide emissions by 14 percent.

BIBLIOGRAPHY

Beaton, Kendall. *Enterprise in Oil: A History of Shell in the United States.* New York: Appleton-Century-Crofts, 1957.

Bridges, Harry. *The Americanization of Shell: The Beginnings and Early Years of Shell Oil Company in the United States.* New York: Newcomen Society, 1972.

Davidson, Ray. *Challenging the Giants: A History of the Oil, Chemical and Atomic Workers International Union.* Denver: OCAW, 1988.

Gerretson, Frederick Carel. *History of the Royal Dutch.* Leiden, Netherlands: E. J. Brill, 1953.

O'Connor, Harvey. *History of Oil Workers Intl. Union (CIO).* Denver: Oil Workers International Union, 1950.

Sampson, Anthony. *The Seven Sisters: The Great Oil Companies and the World They Made.* New York: Viking, 1975.

RTZ CORPORATION PLC

6 St. James's Square
London SW1Y 4LD
United Kingdom
(071) 930-2399

1991 revenues: $9.1 billion
1991 net income: $575.8 million
Publicly traded company
Employees: 73,495
Founded: 1873

OVERVIEW

RTZ Corporation, until 1987 known as Rio Tinto–Zinc, is the world's largest mining company and—with operations in forty countries involving almost every major mineral—one of the most global of corporations. It is also one of the most controversial: the company's operations have been clouded by frequent controversies over its involvement in southern Africa, its harsh labor policies, the environmental impact of its activities, and its moves to take over lands belonging to indigenous peoples. A 1991 book by Roger Moody of the British group PARTiZANS provides an exhaustive look at RTZ's confrontations on five continents.

RTZ, which started out mining copper in Spain, has survived the ups and downs of commodity prices because of its diversified operations and its powerful position in such fields as copper, uranium, borates, and industrial diamonds. In the past decade or so the company also has introduced a bit more stability into its life by moving into such businesses as building materials and engineering products.

HISTORY

Rio Tinto–Zinc had its origins in one of the earliest examples of the privatization of government property. In 1873 a consortium of European businessmen, led by London banker Hugh Matheson, arranged to pay the government of Spain—then being racked by civil war and the abdication of its king—some £3.5 million for the celebrated copper mines of Rio Tinto. As soon as the transaction was complete, Matheson and his partners formed the Rio Tinto Company in London. Making ambitious promises about the firm's likely performance, Matheson took the company public in a period when mining shares were popular.

The mines lived up to everyone's expectations. By 1884 Rio Tinto was the greatest mining center in the world, with more than 13,000 tons of copper produced along with 1.4 million tons of pyrite ore, from which sulfur was extracted for the production of sulfuric acid. The company benefited from a plan by Hyacinthe Secrétan, head of the Société Industrielle et Commerciale des Métaux, to corner the market on copper in the late 1880s and drive up the price of the metal. Yet Secrétan overextended himself and his company went bankrupt, leaving Rio Tinto and other producers with substantial losses.

The company, nonetheless, proceeded with its ambitious plans for the mine, including the construction of a rail line to ship out both ore and the copper produced on site. Over the following decades Rio Tinto became one of the largest employers in Spain and found itself the frequent target of labor and political campaigns. Yet the company, with its Spanish work force and British managers, kept on mining copper ore.

After World War I, however, demand for the company's ore declined as some of its major customers, especially in Germany, switched to a new method of making sulfuric acid that did not require pyrites. In 1923, to help cope with the change in market conditions Rio Tinto formed a cartel, called the Pyrites Producers Association, with its major competitors. That arrangement lasted only until 1926, when Rio Tinto decided it could do better by forming a separate alliance with the German company Metallgesellschaft to create the European Pyrites Corporation to market ore.

The company struggled during the depression, especially since the Spanish government initially would not permit layoffs or wage reductions for the miners. Later in the 1930s the rise of worker militancy and civil unrest forced the company to evacuate British managers and their families. The mines fell into the hands of Republican forces, but soon they were retaken by Franco's Nationalist troops, who subsequently executed many of the workers. The company was widely criticized as a supporter of the Fascist seizure of power.

The mines continued to operate during World War II (Spain was a noncombatant),but it was difficult to make deliveries to customers. After the war Rio Tinto struggled to rebuild the operation but was hampered by its outdated equipment and the foreign currency controls of the Spanish government. By the early 1950s there was growing sentiment to return the mines to Spanish control. This was done in 1954, with the sale of the famed copper source to a new entity, Compañía Española de Minas de Rio-Tinto SA, for £7.7 million and a one-third interest in the new company, the remainder of which was held by a group of Spanish banks.

By this time Rio Tinto had expanded its operations beyond the Spanish mines. In the late 1920s Rio Tinto began buying properties in Northern Rhodesia, where a large copper deposit had been discovered. The company became the largest shareholder in Minerals Separation Ltd., which had interests in the area, and also made a substantial investment in the Rhodesian Congo Border Concession Ltd. Auckland Geddes, chairman of Rio Tinto at the time, worked with South Africa's Ernest Oppenheimer to block American investment in the Rhodesian mines. They formed a company called Rhokana Corporation Ltd., with Geddes as the chairman.

In the 1950s the company accelerated its progress toward becoming a global mining giant, widening its reach to Canada, Australia, and South Africa. Yet a much larger step in that process came in 1962, when Rio Tinto merged with Consolidated Zinc to form Rio Tinto–Zinc. Consolidated Zinc started out as Zinc Corporation, which was founded in 1905 to develop Australian zinc and lead deposits at the rich lodes of the Broken Hill area. It later moved into zinc smelting through a merger with Imperial Smelting and made the first discovery of bauxite in Australia.

The combined company of Rio Tinto–Zinc thus had extensive operations Down Under, held through its subsidiary Conzinc Riotinto (later CRA), which on its own remains one of the largest companies in Australia. As a result of pressure from the Australian government RTZ's share in the company has been brought down to 49 percent.

In 1968 RTZ widened its scope once again by purchasing the British firm Borax Holding, the main property of which was United States Borax and Chemical. That company mined sodium borate and produced the borax used in the cleanser 20 Mule Team (once touted by actor Ronald Reagan), glass fibers, and a variety of other industrial applications.

During the 1970s RTZ began mining for copper in Papua New Guinea and Canada, started mining uranium in South-West Africa (much of which ended up in the hands of South Africa), expanded iron ore production in Australia, and moved into oil exploration in the North Sea (an activity it later abandoned). In the following decade the company acquired Pennsylvania Glass Sand and the Potash Company of America, later merging them to form U.S. Silica.

The biggest deal of the 1980s for RTZ was the purchase of the mineral operations of British Petroleum, including Kennecott Copper, for $4.3 billion in 1989. The acquisition made RTZ the largest mining company in the world.

OPERATIONS

Copper and Gold (18 percent of 1991 revenues). This, the largest segment of RTZ's natural resource operations, includes copper mines and smelters in the United States, Canada, Chile (where it owns 30 percent of the huge Escondida project), Portugal, South Africa, Papua New Guinea (where operations have been disrupted by civil war), and Australia. Gold operations are in the United States, Brazil, Indonesia, Australia, and Papua New Guinea.

Aluminum (9 percent of revenues). RTZ has bauxite, alumina, and aluminum operations in Wales, Sardinia, Australia, and New Zealand. It also has a rolling mill in Lewisport, Kentucky.

Lead, Zinc, and Silver (4 percent of revenues). The company produces these metals in the legendary Broken Hill region of Australia and in Alaska. CRA also has discovered zinc deposits in the Lawn Hill area of Queensland, Australia.

Iron Ore (6 percent of revenues). CRA's iron ore operations in Australia have been doing well by selling to Japanese customers, despite the general slump in demand for steel in much of the world. In fact, CRA has generated a controversy by seeking to expand its mining to a national park in western Australia.

Coal and Uranium (8 percent of revenues). CRA has been challenging Broken Hill Proprietary for the leadership of the coal industry in Australia. In 1991 CRA made an unsuccessful bid for a smaller competitor, Coal and Allied Industries. RTZ also is involved in a coal joint venture in Indonesia. Uranium operations include the large Rossing mine in South-West Africa and the Stanleigh mine in Canada, which was saved from being closed by the intervention of the Ontario government. Two other Canadian mines operated by RTZ's Rio Algom subsidiary in the Elliot Lake area were shut down as planned in 1990. Rio Algom, however, has been expanding elsewhere. It acquired U.S. uranium properties from Kerr-McGee in 1989 and in 1991 took over Uranium Resources Inc. RTZ sold its share in Rio Algom in 1992.

Industrial Minerals (19 percent of revenues). This segment includes the borax, silica sands, and talc the company mines in the United States and France; the titanium dioxide feedstock, zircon, rutile, and high-purity iron and steel it produces in South Africa and Canada; and the diamonds it mines in Australia.

Related Industries (35 percent of revenues). This segment includes Pillar Building Products (wood, metal, and other components), Pillar Electrical (fire alarm, cable management, and other products), Pillar Engineering (aviation, automotive, and other products), and Indal (construction products).

TOP EXECUTIVES

- Derek Birkin, chairman
- Robert P. Wilson, chief executive
- Ian C. Strachan, deputy chief executive
- George C. Beals, technical director
- Leon Davis, mining director

OUTSIDE DIRECTORS

- Robert Alexander, chairman of National Westminster Bank
- Robert Armstrong, former secretary of the cabinet
- Denys Henderson, chairman of Imperial Chemical Industries
- Martin Jacomb, deputy chairman of Barclays Bank
- David Orr, former chairman of the British Council

The board also includes Alistair Frame, who retired as chairman of RTZ in 1991.

FINANCIAL DATA

Revenues (in millions of pounds)

1991	4,885
1990	5,078
1989	6,156
1988	4,928
1987	4,527

Net Income (in millions of pounds)

1991	308
1990	507
1989	588
1988	425
1987	284

GEOGRAPHICAL BREAKDOWN

Revenues (in millions of pounds)

Year	United Kingdom		United States		Elsewhere	
1991	995	(20%)	1,218	(25%)	2,672	(55%)
1990	1,091	(21%)	1,317	(25%)	2,774	(54%)
1989	1,180	(21%)	1,382	(24%)	3,131	(55%)

Net Income (in millions of pounds)

Year	United Kingdom		United States		Elsewhere	
1991	-2	(0%)	163	(40%)	246	(60%)
1990	18	(3%)	239	(44%)	291	(53%)
1989	21	(3%)	277	(42%)	369	(55%)

LABOR RELATIONS

Relations were tense between the management of Rio Tinto and the thousands of workers brought to the Spanish mines after 1873. Although the company believed that it was paying fair wages and providing generous social benefits, the miners had to put up with difficult living and working conditions. Short, usually unsuccessful strikes were common occurrences. Militancy also was spurred by the presence of anarchist groups organizing in cooperation with a union known as the Confederación Nacional del Trabajo.

In 1888 workers went on strike in response to changes in the way wages were calculated. Soldiers brought in by local authorities at the insistence of the company fired on a demonstration of strikers, killing thirteen people and wounding scores of others. The area was then, in effect, put under martial law, and the workers soon abandoned their strike and returned to work without extracting any concessions from the company. For the next few decades a combination of repression and company paternalism discouraged job actions, although there were major strikes in 1900 and 1913.

Worker militancy escalated again during World War I. The labor unrest was aggravated by the hard line adopted by Walter Browning, who became general manager of the mines in 1908 and never hesitated to bring in strikebreakers. The unrest reached a pitch in the 1920, fueled in part by the rivalries among the anarchist, Communist, and Catholic unions. A walkout that year, which received widespread attention throughout Spain, ended with a settlement that included the establishment of union-management committees, with government-appointed chairs, to address problems.

Whatever stability this brought about dissolved during the civil unrest in the country during the 1930s. There were frequent strikes (including some sit-ins) and pitched battles with civil guard troops. That ended with the victory of Franco's Nationalist forces, who executed many union leaders at Rio Tinto.

As RTZ expanded internationally after World War II, it gained a reputation for its harsh treatment of unions and workers. In 1974 RTZ's U.S. Borax subsidiary found itself in a battle with the International Longshoremen's & Warehousemen's Union when the collective-bargaining agreement expired at the company's flagship Boron mine in the Mojave Desert. The company kept production going during the violent 132-day dispute by using supervisory and administrative personnel.

Black workers at the company's huge Rossing uranium mine in South-West Africa—which the company continued to operate in defiance of United Nations decrees—were forced to live in a squalid tent camp and were paid wages that barely allowed subsistence. Similar criticisms have followed the company at many of its other operations around the world.

ENVIRONMENTAL RECORD

From the beginning RTZ's operations have been rough on the environment. Aside from the effect of the open-cast mining on the land, the Rio Tinto operations in Spain befouled the air because of the burning of ores on site to burn off the sulfur. The heavy smoke caused damage to vegetation, crops, and the health of local residents. The company's position was that these were the unavoidable side effects of progress. Yet an Anti-Smoke League was formed, and the elimination of the ore burning was one of the demands put forth by the unsuccessful uprising of workers in 1888. After that incident the Spanish government issued a decree limiting the amount of burning. The company managed to have the decree withdrawn, but it was inspired to develop a new process that eliminated the burning.

In the following decades there were frequent controversies over the environmental and health effects of the company's operations. Soon after the construction of RTZ's lead and zinc smelter in Avonmouth, England, in the late 1960s there began to appear reports that workers at the facility were developing greatly elevated levels of lead in their blood. High concentrations of toxic metals were found in nearby waterways as well. Similar problems have arisen at the company's Capper Pass tin smelting plant in Yorkshire (now closed) and other smelters in Wales.

Workers at the Elliot Lake uranium mines operated by an RTZ subsidiary in Canada were being exposed to radiation levels seven times higher than the recommended limit. Pressure from the steelworkers' union got the company in 1981 to agree to a plan in which the union sent its own safety inspectors into the mines.

The company has used political influence to get around environmental regulations. For instance, in the late 1970s it successfully lobbied Congress to ignore the objections of the Carter administration and allow RTZ to open a molybdenum mine in a national park in Alaska.

At times RTZ has come up against some formidable opposition, especially from groups of indigenous people and their supporters. In Panama, for instance, the Guaymi Congress joined with the Catholic church and other groups to block the company's plan for a huge copper mining project because of the planned displacement of thousands of indigenous people and the destruction of their land.

RTZ's Kennecott subsidiary also has faced opposition to its plan for opening an open-pit copper mine in Wisconsin within fishing and hunting lands of Chippewa native Americans. The Chippewa joined with environmental groups, such as Greenpeace and Earth First!, in opposing the project. Although the state government in 1991 gave RTZ approval to proceed with the project, the opposition has kept up the battle, with occupations of the site and other nonviolent protests.

In 1991 the EPA issued a complaint against Kennecott for improper use of PCBs and improper discharge of other hazardous substances at its mining and smelting facilities in Utah. The agency proposed penalties of more than $1.4 million.

BIBLIOGRAPHY

Avery, David. *Not on Queen Victoria's Birthday: The Story of the Rio Tinto Mines.* London: Collins, 1974.

Elliott, Mary, ed. *Ground for Concern: Australia's Uranium and Human Survival.* Harmondsworth, England: Penguin Books, 1977.

Harvey, Charles E. *The Rio Tinto Company: An Economic History of a Leading Mining Concern, 1873–1954.* Penzance, England: Alison Hodge, 1981.

Moody, Roger. *Plunder!* London: PARTiZANS/CAFCA, 1991. (The organization PARTiZANS—short for People Against RTZ and its Subsidiaries—is located at 218 Liverpool Road, London N1. Tel. [071] 609-1852.)

The Rio Tinto–Zinc Corporation Limited Anti-Report. London: Counter Information Services, n.d.

Roberts, Janine. *From Massacres to Mining: The Colonization of Aboriginal Australia.* London: CIMRA, 1978.

West, Richard. *River of Tears: The Rise of the Rio Tinto–Zinc Corporation.* London: Earth Island, 1972.

SAMSUNG GROUP

Major affiliate:

Samsung Electronics
7, Soonwha-dong
Chung-ku Seoul
South Korea
(02) 751-6114

1991 revenues: $6.9 billion
1991 net income: $90.4 million
Publicly traded company
Employees: 45,000
Founded: 1969 (Samsung Group was established in 1938)

OVERVIEW

Samsung Electronics is the most internationally recognized component of the Samsung Group, the largest and best run of the South Korean conglomerates known as *chaebol*. The Samsung Group, with revenues of about $45 billion, consists of several dozen affiliated companies, about half privately held and half public, involved in such industries as food processing, chemicals, aerospace, shipbuilding, insurance, retailing, and newspaper publishing.

Yet it is mostly through the product line of Samsung Electronics that the conglomerate is known to people outside Korea. With devices ranging from cellular telephones to microwave ovens, vacuum cleaners, and VCRs, the Samsung name is beginning to become as familiar to Western consumers as are the ubiquitous products made in Japan.

HISTORY

Samsung (which means "Three Stars" in Korean) was founded by Byung-Chull Lee, the son of a wealthy landowner who had studied briefly in Japan. In 1936, at the age of thirty-five, he moved to the city of Taegu and set up a rice mill, but he ended up spending more time trading a variety of commodities, including dried fish, wool, and textiles. Two years later he incorporated the trading operation as the Samsung Commercial Company, and soon he branched out to Beijing and Manchuria.

Lee managed to go on operating during World War II; in fact, he expanded into transportation, food and beverages, real estate, and other businesses. In 1947 he moved his headquarters to Seoul and established an international trading operation called Samsung Mulsan.

Samsung's operations were devastated during the Korean War, looted by both sides during the conflict. Lee was left with only one business, the Choson Brewery in Pusan, a city that had been spared in the fighting. Using that as a base, he reestablished Samsung in 1951 and resumed rapid growth, thanks in large measure to the company's role in supplying the United Nations forces that remained in the country. He created the Cheil ("Number One") Sugar Company in 1953 and the Cheil Wool Textile Company the following year.

With the success of these operations, Lee moved into the service sector, with the founding of the Dongbang Life Insurance Company and Samsung Construction and the purchase of extensive bank holdings. By the end of the 1950s Samsung had become a true *chaebol*.

After Park Chung Hee seized power in 1961, Lee was accused of tax evasion and other financial crimes. However, he managed to have the politically motivated charges dropped in exchange for an agreement to turn over to the government a huge fertilizer plant he was constructing. Lee later regained control of the plant, but in the mid-1960s he found himself and one of his sons embroiled in another public scandal. Once again Lee managed to escape jail by turning over the fertilizer plant to the government.

These troubles did not slow the company's growth. Samsung diversified into department stores, papermaking, broadcasting, newspaper publishing, and other fields. In 1969 the company established Samsung Electronics with help from Japan's Sanyo. The electronics company first got involved in producing inexpensive black-and-white television sets (designed by disassembling foreign models) that were supplied to customers like Sears, Roebuck and J.C. Penney, which sold them under their own brand names. The company soon expanded to color televisions, VCRs, and microwave ovens.

Meanwhile, the Samsung Group continued to grow, entering—with government encouragement—shipbuilding, aircraft engine maintenance, petrochemicals, and other heavy industry. The government, however, limited automobile production to company rivals Daewoo and Hyundai. In 1980 the company purchased Korea Telecommunications and renamed it Samsung Semiconductor and Telecommunications, which soon became an important producer of memory chips and later was merged into Samsung Electronics.

After Chun Doo Hwan seized power in 1981, the government took over Samsung's television and radio stations.

Samsung Electronics gradually transformed itself from a low-end producer into a manufacturer of more-sophisticated equipment. This went along with an ambitious marketing drive to make the company's name better known to consumers abroad. By the late 1980s Samsung was becoming as familiar as Japanese brands like Toshiba and Hitachi.

Samsung, run by Kun-Hee Lee following his father's death in 1987, has, along with the other *chaebol*, been subject to increasing criticism in South Korea in recent years. The conglomerates have been targets of labor unrest, blamed for causing real estate inflation through their extensive land purchases, and generally resented by much of the population. In 1991 the Korean government instituted a policy that will force the *chaebol* to end their octupuslike operations and specialize in a handful of activities.

Under this plan Samsung is to focus on electronics, chemicals, and heavy industry (including shipbuilding). As for electronics, Samsung aims to move beyond mass-produced memory chips to more specialized semiconductors as well as larger-scale systems, such as the advanced workstations the company announced in mid-1991.

OPERATIONS

Semiconductors. Samsung first entered the chip business in 1974 and made rapid progress developing the business. By 1983 it was producing 64K memory chips, making South Korea the third country (after Japan and the United States) to perfect what was then a great leap forward in semiconductor technology. The company proceeded to introduce a 256K chip and by the early 1990s was one of the largest producers of 1-megabit devices. Samsung has signed cross-licensing agreements with Texas Instruments and Fujitsu.

Computers. In 1983 Samsung introduced the first educational computer designed and built in Korea. The company expanded into a wide range of personal computers, workstations, and peripheral devices. In 1987 it began making laptop computers. Samsung announced in 1992 that it would launch a series of low-cost personal computers based on chip designs from Hewlett-Packard. It also began to sell laser printers.

Information and Telecommunications. Samsung manufactures a variety of telecommunications equipment, ranging from large switching devices for phone companies to pagers, cellular phones, and fax machines. The company won contracts to provide telecommunications equipment at the 1990 Asian Games in Beijing and the 1992 Olympics in Barcelona.

Consumer Electronics. Included here are a variety of televisions, VCRs, camcorders, digital audio tape recorders, laser disc players, refrigerators, microwave ovens, washing machines, vacuum cleaners, and other home appliances.

TOP EXECUTIVES

Samsung Electronics
- Jin-Ku Kang, chairman and chief executive
- Kwang-Ho Kim, president, semiconductors
- Yong-Moon Jung, executive vice president, information systems
- Sun-Doo Hwang, executive vice president, domestic operations
- Young-Soo Kim, executive vice president, computers
- Jong-Yong Yun, executive vice president, consumer electronics

FINANCIAL DATA

Samsung Electronics

Revenues (in millions of Korean won)

1991	5,227,000
1990	4,626,492
1989	4,117,051

Net Income (in millions of Korean won)

1991	68,900
1990	73,019
1989	158,482

GEOGRAPHICAL BREAKDOWN

Revenues (in millions of Korean won)

Year	Domestic Sales		Export Sales	
1990	1,866,247	(41%)	2,645,472	(59%)
1989	1,499,551	(37%)	2,507,256	(63%)

LABOR RELATIONS

Although the Samsung Group, like the other Korean manufacturers, traditionally took advantage of the country's inexpensive labor, it offered somewhat better wages and benefits to its workers. Consequently, when a wave of strikes swept the country in 1987, Samsung's operations (aside from its money-losing shipbuilding business) were unaffected. There has, nonetheless, been discontent over the group's staunch antiunion stance. In 1990 an official of the Samsung branch of the Federation of Korean Metal Unions took his life in protest against the refusal of the company to recognize the union.

ENVIRONMENTAL RECORD

Although environmental considerations are not yet a major issue in Korea, in 1991 Samsung Engineering established an environmental services operation. The company arranged to license a high-tech waste-water treatment system from Britain's Imperial Chemical Industries.

In 1992 the Samsung Group announced that it would cease using coal and ozone-destroying CDCs by 1996.

BIBLIOGRAPHY

Amsden, Alice H. *Asia's Next Giant: South Korea & Late Industrialization.* Oxford: Oxford University Press, 1989.

Kearney, Robert P. *The Warrior Worker: The Challenge of the Korean Way of Working.* New York: Henry Holt, 1991.

Min-Ju No-Jo: South Korea's New Trade Unions. Hong Kong: Asia Monitor Resource Center, 1988.

Steers, Richard M., Yoo Keun Shin, and Gerardo R. Ungson. *The Chaebol: Korea's New Industrial Might.* Cambridge, Mass.: Ballinger, 1989.

SANDOZ LTD.

Lichtstrasse 35
CH-4002 Basel
Switzerland
(061) 24 11 11

1991 revenues: $9.9 billion
1991 net income: $821.2 million
Publicly traded company
Employees: 53,400
Founded: 1886

OVERVIEW

Sandoz is one of the big three Swiss companies that ply the drug and chemical business around the world. After starting out in dyes, Sandoz moved into drugs and made a splash with a medication that controlled bleeding during childbirth. Company chemists later created the hallucinogens LSD and psilocybin for the treatment of mental illness, though they ended up being used more widely for recreational purposes.

In recent years the company has diversified its activities with a rash of acquisitions, especially in the United States (though an attempted takeover of spice maker McCormick was defeated). It also has been in the news less favorably because of a controversy over the high price of its antipsychotic drug Clozaril.

HISTORY

Sandoz emerged out of the synthetic dye industry that grew up in Basel, previously a center of silk and cotton production, in the late nineteenth century. The company was founded in 1886 by businessman Edouard Sandoz and chemist Alfred Kern. After some initial technical and legal setbacks, the

596

products devised by Kern found wide acceptance, and the revenues of the firm, then known as Kern & Sandoz, reached SFr 2 million within five years.

Kern's sudden death in 1893 set the company back. Sandoz tried to run it himself, but ill health soon forced him to go public and bring in others to take over the management. The new executive team developed innovative products, such as sulphur and azo dyes, while also expanding the company's marketing apparatus.

Despite these improvements, the early years of the twentieth century were difficult for Sandoz. Falling prices, more-expensive raw materials, and costly patent litigation were elements of a slump so serious that the company's board considered merger or even liquidation. Sandoz recovered just in time for World War I, which disrupted trade somewhat but also made it possible for the Swiss dye companies (including Ciba and Geigy) to enter markets that previously had been dominated by the big German producers.

After the war Sandoz, Ciba, and Geigy declined an offer to join the German IG Farben cartel and instead formed their own "community of interest." This association was all but a merger, as it involved a pooling of dye production facilities, research, and profits. The companies were better positioned to expand internationally (Sandoz formed a U.S. subsidiary in 1919), but they still suffered during the industry slump of the early 1920s.

Sandoz began a process of diversification in 1917 when it hired a chemist named Arthur Stoll, who had studied under Nobel Prize–winner Richard Willstaetter in Zurich, to establish a pharmaceuticals division. Stoll concentrated on isolating a number of pure active substances from established plant drugs like digitalis, white squill, and ergot. The latter, a fungus that grows on rye, was known to stop bleeding in childbirth. Stoll's work led to a celebrated drug that became a standard medication for women about to give birth.

The company, whose chairman at this time was the cofounder's son, Aurèle Sandoz, also expanded its involvement in chemicals, introducing products for the textile, leather, and paper industries as well as for agriculture. These activities, along with dyes and drugs, allowed Sandoz to prosper both during and after World War II. The dyes division created products for the new plastics, paints, and synthetic fibers that were being adopted. The agricultural chemicals business, outshined by the advances of Geigy with DDT, progressed more slowly.

In the pharmaceutical area, Sandoz ended up concentrating on medications for mental illness and migraine headaches. The former began with the work of a Sandoz chemist named Albert Hofmann in the 1940s with lysergic acid diethylamide. After Hofmann inadvertently ingested some of the compound, he experienced intense hallucinations and thus realized the power of what would become widely known as LSD. Hofmann later worked with mushrooms from Mexico and isolated another hallucinogen, which he called psilocybin. These discoveries lent support to the notion that psychoses are often due to the presence of small quantities of abnormal substances in the brain.

The company's next major diversification came in 1967, when it acquired

Wander Ltd., a Berne-based producer of nutritional products, such as Ovaltine. This resulted in the creation of a nutrition division in Sandoz, to which were later added the U.S. companies Delmark and Chicago Dietetic Supply as well as the Wasa Group, a Swedish producer of crispbreads.

Sandoz also entered the hospital supply business by purchasing several small companies in the field and later putting them in a joint venture with similar operations belonging to Rhône-Poulenc. Another new area was seeds, which Sandoz took on by acquiring the U.S. companies Rogers Bros. and Northrup King in the mid-1970s. The seed business was given a bioengineering dimension through the purchase of the U.S. company Zoecon in 1983. Another U.S. acquisition, that of the Master Builders Group in 1985, put Sandoz in the field of construction chemicals. In 1991 Sandoz spent $392 million to acquire a 60-percent interest in a U.S. biotechnology company called SyStemix.

OPERATIONS

Chemicals (18 percent of 1991 revenues). Along with the company's original product, dyes, this segment includes pigments, additives, master batches for plastics production, and specialty chemicals for such industries as textiles, leather, and paper. In 1990 the company introduced its first biochemical product, Cartapip, an agent for extracting pulp from wood in what Sandoz calls an "environment-friendly" fashion.

Pharmaceuticals (47 percent of revenues). Sandoz's drug business specializes in medications for cardiovascular diseases, diseases of the central nervous system, dysfunction of hormonal regulations and bone metabolism, and asthma and allergies. The company also makes Sandimmun, an immunosuppressant that has significantly aided transplant procedures and that the company is trying to apply to disorders involving the immune system.

The company's antischizophrenia medication Clozaril has been the subject of a controversy in the United States in recent years. One reason was the cost of the drug and a special blood-monitoring system that Sandoz said had to go with it. Since a year's dose originally cost about $9,000, many state mental health and Medicaid programs refused to make the drug available to their clients, and some private insurers resisted reimbursing policyholders for it. Another element of the controversy was the fact that Clozaril sometimes produces fatal side effects.

In late 1990 Sandoz responded to public pressure by ending its practice of requiring users of the drug to buy its licensed monitoring system and thus allowing blood tests to be done in less expensive ways. Nonetheless, a group of state attorneys general brought an antitrust lawsuit against the company. A similar action brought against Sandoz by the Federal Trade Commission was settled in 1991.

In 1990 the FDA approved the company's application to market an antihypertensive calcium antagonist called Dynacirc. In 1991 the company agreed to invest up to $100 million over ten years for research on anticancer drugs at the Dana-Farber Cancer Institute in Boston.

Agricultural Products (9 percent of revenues). This segment consists mainly of a variety of herbicides, fungicides, and insecticides. Other products include the Vet-Kem line of pet-care products and Apistan, which combats the Varroa mite in beehives.

Seeds (7 percent of revenues). As a result of a series of acquisitions in the United States, Holland, and Sweden, Sandoz is now the world's second-largest producer of seeds. The company's products are used for such crops as corn and sorghum, vegetables, flowers, and forestry.

Nutrition (11 percent of revenues). Included here are the Wasa line of crisp-breads and other baked goods; nutritional drinks, such as Ovaltine; and the U.S. weight-reducing program Optifast (which has slowed from its previous rapid growth).

Construction and Environment (8 percent of revenues). Beginning with the purchase of the Master Builders Group, Sandoz has developed a substantial business involving construction chemicals (concrete additives, mortars, coatings, and so on) and environmental engineering.

TOP EXECUTIVES

- Marc Moret, chairman and chief executive
- Hans Letsch, vice chairman
- Pierre Languetin, vice chairman

OUTSIDE DIRECTORS

- Duilio Arigoni, professor of chemistry at the Swiss Federal Technical Institute
- Peter Böckli, professor at the University of Basel
- Louis Dominique de Meuron
- Gian Pietro de Ry
- Fred-Henri Firmenich, chief executive of Firmenich SA
- Robert Louis Genillard, director of Thyssen-Bornemisza Group
- Nicolas Gossweiler
- Pierre Landolt
- Heinz Schöffler
- Jean Wander
- Josef Zumstein

Since Sandoz does not disclose the affiliations of its outside directors, those given above are the ones that could be obtained from other sources.

FINANCIAL DATA

Revenues (in millions of Swiss francs)

1991	13,444
1990	12,367
1989	12,497
1988	10,151
1987	8,879

Net Income (in millions of Swiss francs)

1991	1,114
1990	967
1989	958
1988	761
1987	627

GEOGRAPHICAL BREAKDOWN

Revenues (in millions of Swiss francs)

Year	Europe		United States and Canada		Elsewhere	
1991	6,050	(45%)	4,077	(30%)	3,317	(25%)
1990	5,689	(46%)	3,586	(29%)	3,092	(25%)

LABOR RELATIONS

Like the other Swiss chemical companies, Sandoz has sought to keep the loyalty of its employees through paternalistic practices. As a result, the employees of Sandoz were slow to heed the calls of the labor movement. Around 1917, however, a significant number of chemical workers in Basel began to join the Swiss Confederation of Trade Unions. There was a considerable amount of protest over the fact that the company, then doing quite well, was not sharing enough of its good fortune with its employees. Although the unions staged a general strike in the industry in 1919, the unrest did not lead to union recognition.

During the early 1940s union sentiments were rekindled, led by the left-wing textile workers' union, the Schweizerische Textil- und Fabrikarbeiter-Verband (STFV). In 1943 Sandoz and the other leading chemical companies in Basel recognized the STFV, and two years later the first collective-bargaining agreement in the industry was signed. Relations generally have been friendly since then.

ENVIRONMENTAL AND HEALTH RECORD

On numerous occasions Sandoz has sought to increase the demand for its prescription drugs by promoting them in ways that go beyond their approved usage. The company received a rebuke from the U.S. FDA for an advertisement that suggested to physicians that the drug Serentil, intended for the treatment of schizophrenia, might be used to help patients who were having trouble adjusting to changes, such as moving to a new town. A 1976 U.S. Senate report found that Mellaril, another powerful antipsychotic tranquilizer made by Sandoz, was being promoted in Central America for minor childhood problems like bed-wetting and nail biting.

A 1986 fire at a Sandoz warehouse near Basel led to one of the most serious industrial accidents of recent years. Water from firefighters' hoses swept tons of highly toxic chemicals into the Rhine River. The chemicals, which included mercury and phosphate compounds, were used in the production of potent pesticides.

The company now says that it puts a high priority on environmental protection and worker safety, but its 1990 annual report admitted that during the year there were a number of significant accidents, including one in which two employees were killed while cleaning a tank at a plant in Brazil and another in which four workers were injured by a hydrogen sulfide leak at a German facility.

BIBLIOGRAPHY

Braithwaite, John. *Corporate Crime in the Pharmaceutical Industry.* Boston: Routledge & Kegan Paul, 1984.

Chetley, Andrew. *A Healthy Business? World Health and the Pharmaceutical Industry.* London: Zed Books, 1990.

Mahoney, Tom. *The Merchants of Life: An Account of the American Pharmaceutical Industry.* New York: Harper & Brothers, 1959.

SCANDINAVIAN AIRLINES SYSTEM

S-161 87 Stockholm
Sweden
(8) 797 00 00

1991 revenues: $5.8 billion
1991 pretax income: − $220.9 million (loss)
Consortium of three airlines whose shares are publicly traded
Employees: 38,940
Founded: 1946

OVERVIEW

Scandinavian Airlines System (SAS) is a consortium of the national airlines of Denmark, Norway, and Sweden. The first two carriers each own two-sevenths and Swedish Airlines owns three-sevenths of the consortium. Each parent company is half government owned and half private.

SAS is not one of the very largest airlines in the world (it ranks about eleventh), but it has been the most aggressive at building international alliances. Under the leadership of Jan Carlzon, the company has sought to overcome its inherent disadvantages (the relatively small population of its home countries, high labor costs, and so on) and become a global provider of travel services.

During the 1980s Carlzon, who has been called the Lee Iacocca of northern Europe because of his zeal in reviving SAS, established relationships with carriers in such countries as Austria, Thailand, Japan, Chile, and the United States. The latter involved an extensive relationship with Frank Lorenzo's Texas Air holding company and its Continental Airlines subsidiary. He also bought (and later sold) a large share of the Inter-Continental Hotels chain.

At the beginning of the 1990s SAS, along with much of the rest of the industry, was suffering from a slump in air travel. The company also had to contend with the bankruptcy filing of Continental Airlines. Although these conditions have forced Carlzon to slow down the building of his international empire, he remains committed to the goal of being "one of five in ninety-five"—one of the handful of European carriers expected to survive the shake-out of the 1990s.

HISTORY

SAS had its origins in the 1930s, when the three Scandinavian airlines, inspired by the historic flight of a Swedish-American named Charles Lindbergh in 1927, began exploring cooperative service across the Atlantic. That plan was sidetracked with the advent of World War II, during which Denmark and Norway were occupied by Nazi Germany. But the three companies secretly remained in contact with one another during the hostilities. One of those companies, Swedish Intercontinental Airlines (SILA—now the holder of the private portion of SAS's Swedish parent), placed an order for seven Douglas DC-4s.

As soon as the war in Europe ended, SILA arranged to obtain some B-17 bombers from the U.S. military and quickly began service between Stockholm and New York with those aircraft. A year later the DC-4s were put into service.

SAS was officially established in 1946 as a consortium only for the trans-atlantic service of the three Scandinavian carriers; each continued to operate its domestic and European services for several more years. To overcome some of the rivalry among Sweden, Norway, and Denmark, a Canadian-American, Peter Redpath, was chosen to run the operation, and English was used as a neutral language. In 1951 SAS became the international flag carrier of the three countries.

That international service expanded steadily. In addition to the service to Brazil and Uruguay that was initiated in the late 1940s, SAS began flying to Japan via Bangkok and later via a polar route. The carrier also pioneered such a route to Los Angeles. During the 1950s the company was approached by the government of Thailand for help in extending its airline service internationally. SAS, which provided technical help and money, ended up with a 30-percent share in the new Thai Airways International, which was repurchased by the Thai government in 1977. The deal helped to enhance Bangkok's role as a major stopping-off point between Europe and the Far East, and it gave SAS landing rights in Hong Kong. Despite the end of the ownership relationship, SAS later set up a hub in Bangkok, and the two carriers have maintained an alliance into the present.

SAS took its first step toward diversification in 1960 with the purchase of the Royal Hotel in Copenhagen. This was the beginning of what would become an extensive international hotel network. In 1965 the carrier created the first computerized reservation system for all of Europe. Five years later the company entered into a cooperative arrangement with KLM, Swissair, and the French UTA to pool maintenance and technical services.

SAS modernized and expanded its fleet during the 1970s, but by the end of that decade it was facing increased competition from deregulated U.S. airlines and cut-rate operators like Freddie Laker. In an attempt to get out of this rut, the SAS board named Jan Carlzon to take over the carrier in 1980. He carried out an internal restructuring and made SAS more appealing to the international business traveler through such innovations as linking hotel and rental car bookings with flight reservations. He also made a crusade of punctuality and refurbished the carrier's older planes. Also, Copenhagen's airport was upgraded to meet every need of the flying executive. Carlzon's EuroClass service was a hit, and SAS rebounded.

By the late 1980s Carlzon was saying that there was room for no more than five major carriers in Europe, and he sought to make SAS one of them by forming a series of international alliances. He came close to merging with Belgium's Sabena, but the deal collapsed, reportedly over Carlzon's demands. He also lost to British Airways in a bid for part of British Caledonian, and an attempt to get a piece of Aerolíneas Argentinas also failed.

Yet in 1987 the company succeeded in forming a joint venture with Air France, Iberia, and Lufthansa to operate a common computerized reservations system called AMADEUS. The following year SAS announced a major alliance with Frank Lorenzo's Texas Air holding company, then the biggest air transport enterprise in the United States. The arrangement called for SAS and Texas Air's Continental Airlines subsidiary to combine ground facilities, create a joint training facility, link their reservations systems, and coordinate marketing efforts.

At the same time, SAS injected $50 million into the troubled Texas Air and indicated that it would purchase up to ten percent of the company's shares. In 1990 Frank Lorenzo, hounded by the unions at his strike-bound Eastern Air Lines, bowed out of Texas Air and sold his holdings to SAS, which ended up owning 18.4 percent of the American company. After Continental filed for Chapter 11 bankruptcy in December 1990, SAS wrote off its $106-million total investment in Texas Air (now called Continental Airlines Holdings). This was the main reason the Scandinavian company ended up in the red for the year.

In December 1988 SAS paid £25 million for 24.9 percent of Airlines of Britain Holdings, the parent of several small British carriers. Three months later SAS formed an alliance with Japan's All Nippon Airways that included joint flights. Then, in line with his plan to create a global travel services company, Carlzon spent $500 million to purchase 40 percent of Inter-Continental Hotels Corporation from Japan's Seibu/Saison Group.

Other moves in 1989 included signing a broad cooperative agreement with Swissair, buying an option (later exercised) to acquire up to 35 percent of LAN-Chile, and forming alliances with Finnair, Canadian International Airlines, and Austrian Airlines.

As the 1990s began, Carlzon slowed down his network building somewhat and, amid the slump that was depressing the entire airline industry, turned his attention to the problem of controlling costs. In early 1991 he announced the elimination of thirty-five hundred jobs—16 percent of the work force—

as part of an effort to reduce expenses by some $540 million. The travel slump also has resulted in problems in the company's hotel business.

Carlzon has not given up his networking entirely. In 1991 he signed a deal with Walt Disney giving SAS exclusive Scandinavian rights to market excursions to the theme park and resort Disney was building outside Paris. That same year, he agreed to begin merging SAS's operations with those of three other carriers—Swissair, Austrian Airlines, and British Midland Airways.

OPERATIONS

SAS Airline (64 percent of 1991 operating revenues). SAS operates more than seven hundred flights a day to eighty-two cities in thirty-six countries. In 1991 it flew fourteen million passengers with a load factor of about 60 percent. SAS also owns 16.8 percent of Continental Airlines Holdings in the United States, 37 percent of LAN-Chile, and 25 percent of Airlines of Britain Holdings. SAS was one of the founders of the AMADEUS computerized reservations system, but in 1991 the company announced that it would withdraw from the system.

SAS Service Partner (13 percent of revenues). This segment consists of several dozen flight kitchens and more than one hundred airport restaurants in Europe and Asia. It also does catering for conventions, fairs, hospitals, and commercial events.

SAS Leisure (12 percent of revenues). Included in this segment are several Scandinavian tour operators, a 17-percent stake in Spain's largest operator, and a 32-percent stake in Italy's second largest operator. SAS also owns the fourteen-unit Sunwing hotel chain, the charter carriers Scanair and Spanair, and the Spanish travel agency Viajes Astral.

SAS International Hotels (5 percent of revenues). In 1991, SAS owned 25 hotels with 6,000 rooms and held 40 percent of a joint venture with Japan's Seibu/Saison Group that operated 112 Inter-Continental Hotels in 85 cities. The relationship with Seibu/Saison was not an easy one. The Inter-Continental venture had problems with heavy debt, management instability, and clashes between the partners. SAS announced in 1992 that it had sold its stake in the chain back to its partner, now known as Saison Holdings.

SAS Trading (5 percent of revenues). This segment involves in-flight media, wholesaling, and retailing at forty airport shops in Scandinavia, including the large shopping center at the Copenhagen airport.

SAS Financial Services (1 percent of revenues). SAS owns Diners Club Nordic, a one-third interest in the Polygon airline insurance company, and an interest in an aircraft-leasing operation.

TOP EXECUTIVES

- Jan Carlzon, president and chief executive
- Kjell Fredheim, executive vice president
- Lars Thuesen, senior vice president and chief financial officer
- Steffen Harpøth, senior vice president
- Sven A. Heiding, senior vice president

OUTSIDE DIRECTORS

- Tage Andersen, former chairman of Den Danske Bank
- Curt Nicolin, former cochairman of ABB ASEA Brown Boveri
- Tor Moursund, chairman of Christiana Bank og Kreditkasse
- Bjørn Eidem, senior vice president of Fred. Olsen & Company
- Lars P. Gammelgaard, chairman of the Danish Conservative party
- Krister Wickman, chairman of the Swedish Authors Foundation

The board also includes three employee representatives.

FINANCIAL DATA

Revenues (in millions of Swedish kronor)

1991	32,286
1990	31,883
1989	28,786
1988	27,556
1987	24,288

Pretax Income (in millions of Swedish kronor)

1991	−1,223 (loss)
1990	−763 (loss)
1989	2,206
1988	3,690
1987	1,689

LABOR RELATIONS

Like most large Swedish companies, SAS is heavily unionized, and employees have direct representation on the board of directors. While Carlzon was restructuring the company in the 1980s he put special emphasis on establishing an esprit de corps among the employees. His evangelical zeal has been compared to that of Donald Burr at the now-defunct airline People Express in the United States. When workers at Eastern Air Lines went on strike soon after SAS bought a share of the carrier's parent company, Texas Air, SAS unions provided expressions of solidarity with the U.S. workers. In recent years there has been escalating tension between management and the three pilots' unions at SAS over the company's attempts to alter working conditions as part of its cost-cutting efforts.

BIBLIOGRAPHY

Carlzon, Jan. *Moments of Truth*. New York: Harper Business, 1987.
Sampson, Anthony. *Empires in the Sky*. New York: Random House, 1984.

SEAGRAM COMPANY LTD.

1430 Peel Street
Montreal, Quebec H3A 1S9
Canada
(514) 849-5271

1992 revenues: $5.3 billion (year ending January 31)
1992 net income: $727 million
Publicly traded company
Employees: 16,800
Founded: 1924

OVERVIEW

The Bronfman family of Canada built Seagram Company from a bootlegging operation during the Prohibition era into the largest producer of liquor in the world. The company developed the first national and international liquor brands with the introduction of Seagram's 5 Crown and 7 Crown, blended whiskies that were lighter and smoother than the rye and bourbon North Americans had been drinking. Aside from its commanding position in the wine and spirits world, the company enjoys $276 million in annual dividends from its 24.5-percent ownership of chemical giant Du Pont.

Thanks to family trusts that control more than 38 percent of the company, the Bronfmans enjoy substantial wealth. Chief executive Edgar Bronfman's net worth has been estimated by *Forbes* magazine at $1.9 billion and that of his brother and cochairman Charles at $1.6 billion. That wealth has brought unwelcome attention as well, such as extensive coverage of Edgar's various marriages and a kidnapping scandal involving Edgar's son Samuel II. Edgar (who became a U.S. citizen) also has gotten press coverage for his role in Democratic party politics and in the World Jewish Congress. In 1986 Edgar annointed his son Edgar—who had abandoned a brief career as a film producer to return to the family business—as his successor in the chief executive's position.

Once far and away the leading alcoholic beverages company in the world, Seagram in recent years has faced increasing competition from such companies as Guinness, Grand Metropolitan, and Allied-Lyons.

HISTORY

The Bronfman dynasty had its origins in a mill and tobacco plantation owned by Yechiel Bronfman in the Bessarabia province of the Russian empire. Faced with the pogroms of Czar Alexander III, Yechiel decided to join the exodus of Jews to North America. Taking with him his wife, three children, two servants, and his rabbi and his family, Yechiel moved in 1889 to a pioneer settlement in eastern Saskatchewan. Conditions were harsh on the prairie, so Yechiel (who anglicized his name to Ekiel) took jobs as a railway laborer and then a sawmill worker to support his growing family.

Ekiel began his own operation selling wood scraps from the sawmill as fuel. The wood business, along with whitefish trading and a cartage operation, gave the Bronfmans a measure of financial security. But their ambitions were greater. According to family legend, around the turn of the century young Sam, who had been born en route to Canada, urged his father to move into the hotel business. Soon the Bronfmans controlled a string of such establishments, which prospered along with the development of the Canadian West.

When Prohibition began to be introduced in the Canadian provinces in 1916, the Bronfmans moved into the whiskey trade, exploiting loopholes like the exceptions for mail order sales from Quebec (which was slow to go dry) and alcoholic beverages sold for medicinal purposes.

The opportunities were even greater when the United States officially went dry in 1920. Although family accounts are fuzzy about business activities during the Prohibition era, Peter Newman's book *King of the Castle* documents the Bronfman role in bootlegging. Under the guise of his wholesale drug business, Harry Bronfman set up a distillery in Yorkton, Saskatchewan, to produce whiskey bottled with bogus Scotch labels. Taking advantage of the fact that exporting liquor was not illegal, his brother Sam set up a network of connections with U.S. bootleggers. Political connections and, according to some reports, bribery kept the Bronfmans in business. By this time Ekiel and his wife Minnie had died, leaving operations in the hands of their sons Harry, Sam, Allan, and Abe, along with various in-laws. One of those in-laws, Paul Matoff, husband of Jean Bronfman, was murdered by bootleggers in 1922.

In 1925 the Bronfmans sought greater respectability by opening a large distillery on the outskirts of Montreal under the name of Distillers Corporation—a name quite similar to Distillers Company Ltd., the British and Scottish firm that produced such famous brands as Haig, Black & White, Dewar's, and Johnnie Walker. In fact, the Bronfmans agreed to turn over 51-percent ownership of their operation to Distillers Company in order to gain Canadian licensing rights to those esteemed labels.

The Bronfman firm gained additional pedigree when it merged in 1928 with Joseph E. Seagram & Sons Ltd., a distilling company with a history going back to 1857. The resulting company, Distillers Corporation–Seagram Ltd., was controlled by Distillers Company. After Prohibition was lifted, Distillers Company rebuffed the Bronfmans' proposal for a joint entry into the U.S. market, so the Bronfmans raised the money to buy out the British company's share and ventured south of the border on their own.

The volatile "Mr. Sam," now the clear patriarch of the family business, decided to take the high road in the confusing post-Prohibition environment. He ran an advertising campaign headlined WE WHO MAKE WHISKEY SAY: DRINK MODERATELY that built goodwill among wets and drys alike. Thanks to the inventories it had built up, Seagram was well positioned to take advantage of the new legal environment for its products.

Growth was not limited to North America. The company began buying up some of the most famous names in the wine and spirits world. In France Seagram acquired champagne producers G. H. Mumm and Perrier-Jouët Champagnes, wine producer Barton & Guestier, and cognac makers Chemineaud Frères and Augier Frères. In the 1960s subsidiaries were formed in countries ranging from Brazil to New Zealand.

Although the company initially missed the boat on the growing popularity of vodka, it went on to dominate the spirits industry worldwide—and the Bronfmans were building up one of the largest family fortunes. Sam's son Edgar became president in 1957, but Mr. Sam remained a formidable presence until his death in 1971.

The acquisitions binge heated up again in the 1980s with the purchase of cognac maker Martell SA, port producer Geo. G. Sandeman Sons & Company, Coca-Cola's Wine Spectrum group (Taylor, Great Western, Sterling Vineyards, and the Monterey Vineyard), and other wine and spirits companies. In 1987, however, the company made a major retreat from the wine business by selling off the Taylor labels and Paul Masson (which had been acquired in 1943) to a new company called Vintners International.

Seagram also has dabbled in the energy business. In 1953 it bought Frankfort Oil Company and a decade later it purchased Texas Pacific Coal and Oil. The two companies were merged, and in 1980 the oil and gas properties of the combined firm were sold to the Sun Company for $2.3 billion. An attempt to use those proceeds to acquire St. Joe Minerals was rebuffed.

More dramatic was the company's involvement in one of the first megamergers—the battle for Conoco in 1981. After the Canadian company Dome Petroleum bid for 20 percent of Conoco's shares in an effort to get at its Canadian oil reserves, all of Conoco ended up in play. Seagram made a hostile offer for a larger portion of the company, whose management turned to Du Pont as a white knight. A bidding war ensued, involving Mobil as well; after the dust settled, Du Pont was the winner with what was then an astounding offer of $7.2 billion. Yet Seagram ended up with more than 20 percent of Du Pont after selling its interest in Conoco to the chemical giant.

Faced with a decline in demand for spirits in the United States, its largest market, the company has responded in two ways. First has been to expand into new areas where liquor consumption is still growing—for example, Taiwan, where a wholesale company was formed in 1990. That same year, a sales office in what had been East Berlin was set up to sell the company's products in eastern Germany. The other part of the strategy has been to emphasize nonalcoholic beverages. The most important step in this direction was the purchase of Tropicana Products, a leading juice maker, from Beatrice in 1988.

OPERATIONS

Spirits and Wine Group (78 percent of 1992 revenues). This division produces and markets some 200 brands of distilled spirits and more than 240 brands of wines, champagnes, ports, and sherries, which are sold in over 150 countries. The company maintains distilleries and bottling plants in twenty-one countries in North America, Europe, Latin America, and the Asian Pacific region. The aggregate daily capacity of the distilleries is approximately 300,000 U.S.-proof gallons and of the bottling plants 274,000 standard cases.

Among the leading brands in the spirits area are the whiskies Crown Royal, Seagram's V.O., Seagram's 83, and Seagram's Five Star; the Scotch whiskies Chivas Regal (the world's leading premium Scotch), Royal Salute, and Glenlivet; Martell cognacs (the second-largest cognac company in the world); Janneau Armagnacs; Seagram's Extra Dry Gin; and Captain Morgan and Myers's rums. Mount Royal Light, a lower-alcohol whiskey, was introduced in 1990. Seagram sold seven of its liquor brands—including Lord Calvert Canadian whiskey and Wolfschmidt vodka—to American Brands in 1991.

The company's wines include Barton & Guestier (the leading exporter of quality French wines); the two-hundred-year-old House of Sandeman, which makes ports and sherries; Mumm, Perrier-Jouët, and Heidsieck-Monopole French champagnes; Sterling Vineyards and Monterey Vineyard California wines; Mumm Cuvée and Napa California sparkling wines; Metheus and Mumm German sekt; and Saltram Australian wines. The company's wineries are located in Argentina, Australia, Brazil, Canada, France, Germany, Italy, Portugal, Spain, and the United States.

The Seagram Chateau and Estate Wines Company imports into the United States wines from France, Germany, and Spain. The Seagram Classics Wine Company markets premium California wines, including Sterling Vineyards, Monterey Vineyard, Bandiera Winery, Charles Krug Winery, and C. K. Mondavi.

Fruit Juices, Coolers, and Mixers (22 percent of revenues). The company's Tropicana subsidiary is the leader of the ready-to-serve orange juice market in the United States, with a market share of more than 20 percent. The company also produces and distributes other fruit juices and beverages, including Tropicana Juice Sparkler carbonated juice beverages and Tropicana Twister blended fruit beverages. Tropicana operates two production facilities in Florida and one in California. Tropicana products also are sold in Canada and France and are being introduced in other parts of Europe. In 1990 a joint venture was formed with Kirin Brewery to distribute fruit juices and juice beverages in Japan. The president of Tropicana, Robert Soran, and another top executive were forced to resign in 1991 because of multi-million-dollar cost overruns in a series of construction projects.

Other company beverages include Seagram's Wine Cooler (a leader in a shrinking market), Seagram's Spritzer, and Premium Beverages Inc., which produces and markets mixers (ginger ale, tonic water, club soda, and seltzer) under the Seagram name. A joint venture in China is producing and distributing wine coolers and liquor products in that country. The Soho Natural soft drink business, acquired in 1989, was sold in 1992.

TOP EXECUTIVES

- Edgar M. Bronfman, chairman and chief executive
- Charles R. Bronfman, cochairman of the board
- Edgar Bronfman, Jr., president and chief operating officer
- Stephen E. Herbits, executive vice president, corporate policy
- Edward F. McDonnell, executive vice president and president of the Seagram Spirits and Wine Group
- William G. Pietersen, executive vice president and president of the Seagram Beverage Group
- Stephen E. Banner, senior executive vice president

OUTSIDE DIRECTORS

- David M. Culver, chairman of CAI Capital Corporation
- William G. Davis, counsel to the law firm of Tory Tory DesLauriers & Binnington
- Paul Desmarais, chief executive of Power Corporation of Canada
- Marie-Josée Drouin, executive director of the Hudson Institute of Canada
- A. Jean de Grandpré, chairman emeritus of BCE Inc.
- David L. Johnston, principal and vice chancellor of McGill University
- E. Leo Kolber, member of the Senate of Canada
- C. Edward Medland, former chief executive of Wood Gundy Inc.
- Neil F. Phillips, resident senior counsel of the law firm of Goodman Freeman Phillips & Vineberg
- John L. Weinberg, senior chairman of the Goldman Sachs Group

Also on the board are Alain de Gunzburg, chairman of the company's G. H. Mumm subsidiary; former vice chairman David G. Sacks; Edgar S. Woolard, Jr., chief executive of Du Pont (which is 25-percent owned by Seagram); and Richard E. Heckert, director and former chief executive of Du Pont.

FINANCIAL DATA

Revenues (in millions of U.S. dollars) (years ending January 1)

1992	5,278
1991	5,027
1990	4,482
1989	3,956
1988	2,815

Net Income (in millions of U.S. dollars) (years ending January 1)

1992	727
1991	756
1990	711
1989	589
1988	521

GEOGRAPHICAL BREAKDOWN

Revenues (in millions of U.S. dollars)

Year*	Canada and United States		Europe		Elsewhere	
1992	3,038	(48%)	2,391	(38%)	916	(14%)
1991	2,964	(48%)	2,312	(38%)	851	(14%)
1990	2,947	(53%)	1,863	(33%)	772	(14%)

*Fiscal year ends January 31.

Operating Income (in millions of U.S. dollars)

Year*	Canada and United States		Europe		Elsewhere	
1992	215	(28%)	447	(59%)	98	(13%)
1991	184	(26%)	418	(59%)	106	(15%)
1990	171	(30%)	290	(51%)	113	(20%)

*Fiscal year ends January 31.

LABOR RELATIONS

The company has collective-bargaining agreements with labor unions representing about forty-one hundred of its hourly employees in the United States and Canada. The major collective-bargaining relationship in Canada is with the Canadian Auto Workers, which represents employees at the Seagram plant in Amherstburg, Ontario. In 1987 and 1990 the union came close to striking before the company agreed on new contracts with significant improvements in pay, pensions, and other issues. In the United States Seagram workers are represented mainly by the Distillery, Wine, and Allied Workers and the Teamsters.

ENVIRONMENTAL RECORD

Seagram and its subsidiaries are heavy users of packaging—including relatively wasteful bottling of juice in very small plastic containers—but the company has taken steps to cut down on energy usage at some of its facilities by setting up cogeneration systems.

BIBLIOGRAPHY

Cavanagh, John, and Frederick Clairmonte. *Alcoholic Beverages: Dimensions of Corporate Power.* New York: St. Martin's Press, 1985.

Clairmonte, Frederick, and John Cavanagh. *Merchants of Drink: Transnational Control of World Beverages.* Penang, Malaysia: Third World Network, 1988.

Jacobson, Michael, Robert Atkins, and George Hacker. *The Booze Merchants.* Washington, D.C.: Center for Science in the Public Interest, 1983.

Marrus, Michael R. *Samuel Bronfman: The Life and Times of Seagram's Mr. Sam.* Hanover, N.H.: University Press of New England, 1992.

Newman, Peter C. *King of the Castle: The Making of a Dynasty—Seagram's and the Bronfman Empire.* New York: Atheneum, 1979.

SIEMENS AG

Wittelsbacherplatz 2
D-8000 Munich 2
Germany
(089) 234-0

1991 revenues: $43.9 billion (year ending September 30)
1991 net income: $1.1 billion
Publicly traded company
Employees: 402,000
Founded: 1847

OVERVIEW

Founded by Werner Siemens, the German Thomas Edison, Siemens is one of the powerhouses of the European electrical and electronic equipment industry. Until the 1970s it was a rather lethargic company, depending a great deal on government contracts, especially the Deutsche Bundespost's state-owned telephone system. During that decade it began to compete much more vigorously in world markets and was soon seen by the U.S. company General Electric as its most formidable rival in the global electrical equipment business.

Siemens's new activism was even more dramatic in the 1980s as top management sought to ensure the company's position as a high-tech leader through a dazzling series of acquisitions (including the U.S. telephone equipment maker Rolm) and joint ventures with companies ranging from Philips to BASF. The company also has struggled to stay alive in the chip business by resisting the intense competition from Japan. Most recently the company acquired German computer maker Nixdorf and formed a semiconductor joint venture with IBM.

With its huge product line and two hundred manufacturing facilities in dozens of countries around the world, Siemens remains one of the great industrial empires of Europe.

HISTORY

In the 1840s Werner Siemens, a young officer in the Prussian army with a gift for science (he had developed a new technique for gold plating), was exposed to the developing field of electric telegraphy. Siemens was taken with the technology and soon devised a method of transmitting signals more efficiently. In 1847 he formed a company with mechanic Johann Georg Halske to make the telegraph equipment. The firm of Siemens & Halske got its first major job when the Prussian government commissioned it to construct the first telegraph line between Berlin and Frankfurt.

The government went on purchasing the dial telegraphs of Siemens & Halske even after the appearance of faster devices invented by the American Samuel F. B. Morse. But within a few years, problems with the insulation on the lines laid down by Siemens & Halske upset the cozy relationship the firm had with the government. The company thus turned to new markets, winning a contract from the Russian czar to construct and maintain a line between St. Petersburg and Kronstadt. This led to the establishment of a representative office in St. Petersburg under the direction of Werner's brother Carl.

The company then got involved in the booming business of laying submarine cables. Following a technique created by Siemens for laying the cables more efficiently, the Siemens & Halske firm was retained in 1858 as a consultant by the leading operation of the day, Newall & Company. As a consequence, a company directed by another Siemens brother, Wilhelm, was set up in London. In 1865 the British company took the name Siemens Brothers.

In the late 1860s Siemens took on the project of constructing a line from London to Prussia and on to Persia, where it connected with a line that stretched to India. The massive undertaking involved stringing cable across thousands of miles of desolate terrain, but the Siemens brothers managed to overcome the obstacles. In 1870 the first telegraph message was sent from London to Calcutta—a distance of more than eleven thousand kilometers, or more than a quarter of the earth's circumference—and a reply was received within an hour. Werner Siemens was celebrated throughout the world.

The Siemens company (Halske retired in 1867, but the firm retained his name until 1966) got involved in producing cable and commissioned its own cable-laying ship, named the *Faraday* in honor of the great physicist. In 1875 the *Faraday* laid a cable from Ireland to the United States that proved to be more efficient than the three previous transatlantic connections. Siemens went on to lay cables between Rio de Janeiro and Montevideo as well as a series of additional cables between Europe and North America.

Werner Siemens's contributions were not limited to the extension of the world's telegraph network. In 1867 he announced the discovery of what he called the electrodynamic principle—that is, the creation of an electric current without the use of a permanent magnet by making use of residual magnetism. On this basis Siemens developed power generation machines and electric lighting devices. In 1879 his firm built the world's first electric railway (albeit a small one) at a trade fair in Berlin. Other milestones included the construction in 1880 of one of the first elevators and a trolleybus two years later.

After Thomas Edison's incandescent light bulb reached Europe in the early 1880s, Siemens signed an agreement with the local holder of the Edison patent to manufacture the bulbs. The company, which went public in 1897, went on to obtain the patent for the first X-ray tube and to develop an automatic telephone exchange. Around the turn of the century the company began construction of a manufacturing complex on the outskirts of Berlin that came to be known as Siemens City. Werner Siemens died in 1892, but family members remained in control of the firm.

During World War I the company made a major contribution to the German military effort but lost its subsidiaries in Russia and Britain. After the war the company introduced new products, such as radios and traffic lights, and set up a subsidiary in Japan (which later became Fuji Electric). Siemens also built power stations in Ireland, the Soviet Union, and other countries while entering a light bulb consortium called Osram with two German competitors, AEG and Auer.

The depression cut deeply into the company's business, but in the mid-1930s Siemens shared in the benefits of the Nazi military buildup (although family members later insisted that they had not been supportive of Hitler). Siemens produced an automatic pilot system for the Luftwaffe and the V-2 rockets used in the bombing of London. Some of the work was done by forced labor. The company's plants were heavily bombed during the war, and Soviet occupation forces later dismantled the Siemens City complex.

Hermann von Siemens, the founder's grandson, who had taken over the firm in 1940, was arrested after the war and spent two years in detention. After his release in 1948 he resumed leadership of the company and set about to resurrect its business. Siemens City was rebuilt and the corporate head-quarters were reestablished in Munich. By the mid-1950s the company was hard at work producing electrical, telephone, medical (including the first implantable pacemaker), and other equipment. Siemens introduced its first computer in 1955 and a few years later completed its first nuclear reactor.

During the 1960s the company produced some components for the U.S. space program and manufactured high-speed trains used at home. The following decade saw such milestones as being chosen to serve as the official telecommunications and computer supplier at the 1972 summer Olympics in Munich and entering a joint venture with the American firm Allis-Chalmers to produce turbine generators in the United States. Siemens attempted to enter the semiconductor business in the late 1970s, first by acquiring shares in the U.S. companies Advanced Micro Devices (20 percent—later sold) and Litronix (100 percent) and then by forming a joint venture with its Dutch counterpart, Philips. The collaboration was slow to pay off, so Siemens purchased technology from Toshiba.

In 1981 management of the company was taken over by Bernhard Plettner, the first person from outside the family to run the firm. Over the course of the next decade, Plettner and his successor, Karlheinz Kaske, launched a plan to decentralize Siemens and make it a world leader in high tech. One of the major elements of this strategy was the 1988 acquisition of Rolm from IBM for $844 million. However, Rolm, the third-largest supplier of PBX equipment in the United States, never fit in at the computer giant. IBM, nonetheless, remained until 1992 in a joint venture for marketing and servicing Rolm products.

This was only one of several Siemens forays into the U.S. market. In 1986 the company agreed to become a partner in the telephone equipment business of GTE; in 1988 it formed a joint venture with Intel to make computers; that same year, it bought Bendix Electronics; and in 1990 it purchased the solar energy business of Atlantic Richfield.

Meanwhile, in Europe, Siemens and the U.K.'s General Electric Company together took over the British telecommunications producer Plessey. The German company also acquired the French computer manufacturer IN2 and in 1990 paid an estimated $350 million for the ailing German computer maker Nixdorf. The latter deal put Siemens in minicomputers and prevented rivals like Groupe Bull (France) and Olivetti (Italy) from getting an important foothold in the German market. In 1991 Siemens formed an alliance with IBM to make advanced memory chips and joined with Olivetti and Groupe Bull to design a computer network for all of Europe. Siemens is expanding its activities in Eastern Europe and the former Soviet Union as well.

OPERATIONS

Power Generation (6 percent of 1991 revenues). The company's Kraftwerk Union (KWU) division produces fossil fuel–powered and nuclear power plants. Anticipating a revival in nuclear power, Siemens formed a joint venture called Nuclear Power International with the French firm Framatome SA that has developed a new reactor expected to be available in 1993. This segment also includes the company's involvement in solar energy. KWU has been criticized for being part of a drive to expand nuclear power in Eastern Europe. In 1991 Siemens purchased a 67-percent interest in the power generation business of the Czech company Skoda-Pilsen.

Power Transmission and Distribution (6 percent of revenues). Siemens is a leading producer of electrical equipment for utilities around the world. Recent projects have included a facility for interconnecting the German and Czechoslovakian power grids and a large switching station for the Rabigh power plant in Saudi Arabia. Siemens has acquired several electrical cable factories in the former German Democratic Republic to increase the company's presence in the eastern part of the country.

Industrial and Building Systems (11 percent of revenues). Siemens is one of the world's leading suppliers of electrical engineering systems for office buildings, factories, airports, and other large structures. It also produces highway systems, such as an experimental traffic guidance and information project for drivers in Berlin.

Drives and Standard Products (8 percent of revenues). The company manufactures a full range of constant- and variable-speed drives, along with switches, relays, and other equipment for industrial low-voltage systems.

Automation (7 percent of revenues). This segment includes products for the factory and process automation markets, including the automotive and electronics industries. A new company called Siemens Automatisierungstechnik GmbH was created to form partnerships with machine tool producers in eastern Germany.

Siemens Nixdorf Information Systems (15 percent of revenues). Siemens sells mainframe computers (many of them produced by Fujitsu), personal computers, and peripheral devices. Its Sinix line is the leader in the Western European market for machines using the UNIX operating system. The company is supplying DOS-based PCs for use in the AMADEUS airline reservation system. Starting with the fiscal year 1991 this segment includes the operations of Nixdorf, the computer maker purchased by Siemens in 1990. Siemens also participated until 1991 with the chemical company BASF in a joint venture called Comparex, which sells mainframes and peripheral equipment made by Hitachi.

Private Communications Systems (6 percent of revenues). Siemens is a leading producer of advanced telephone equipment, such as digital PBX systems. Its Rolm subsidiary ranks third in the U.S. PBX market behind AT&T and Northern Telecom. In 1991 Siemens and GPT Ltd. of Britain agreed to merge their British PBX distribution companies.

Public Communications Networks (14 percent of revenues). Siemens is also a major producer of larger switching equipment used by telephone companies. Although this market has been stagnant, Siemens has been pursuing customers in Eastern Europe. In 1990 Siemens's U.S. subsidiary in this segment merged with Stromberg-Carlson Corporation, owned by GPT. Siemens has been trying for some time to consummate plans for a joint venture in the former Soviet Union to produce switching equipment.

Defense Electronics (2 percent of revenues). The most significant military work being done by Siemens involves adapting the Patriot antimissile system, developed by the U.S. company Raytheon, for German defense requirements. The acquisition of Plessey's military electronics operations has given a substantial boost to this segment.

Transportation Systems (3 percent of revenues). Siemens is an important supplier of rail systems, both for urban mass transit and for intercity transportation. In additon to its continuing involvement in Germany's high-speed rail network, the company has supplied subway and light-rail systems in such countries as the United States, Portugal, and Taiwan. In the United States Siemens has a joint venture with General Motors for producing an AC traction motor for diesel-electric locomotives. In early 1991 a consortium led by Siemens won a $1.6-billion contract to extend the Athens subway system.

Automotive Systems (3 percent of revenues). Included in this segment are fuel injectors, antilock brakes, air bags, and many other components for automobile production. This segment has been expanded through the addition of the auto operations of Bendix Electronics and those of MACI Industries Group, a Canadian motor manufacturer acquired by Siemens.

Medical Engineering (9 percent of revenues). Siemens makes a variety of advanced diagnostic equipment, including computer tomography, magnetic resonance, and positron emission tomography devices. The company has a joint venture in Japan with Asahi Chemical Industry Company to produce a magnetic resonance imaging system with permanent magnets.

Semiconductors (2 percent of revenues). Siemens has made a major effort to ensure the survival of a semiconductor industry in Western Europe. It has done this through a joint venture with Philips and by participating in the Joint European Submicron Silicon (JESSI) project, launched in 1989. The company also is collaborating with the U.S. company MIPS Computer System on a new 32-bit RISC processor.

Since the fall of 1990 Siemens has been discussing a merger of its semiconductor operations with those of SGS-Thomson, itself a joint venture of the French firm Thomson SA and Italy's IRI/Finmeccanica. Later the chip operations of Philips were said to be involved as well. While that deal remained uncertain, Siemens announced in July 1991 that it would join with IBM to build a $700-million facility in France to produce the world's most-advanced memory chips, the 16-megabit devices that within a few years will be standard components in electronic devices.

Passive Components and Electron Tubes (2 percent of revenues). Since October 1989 the company's passive components business (capacitors, thermistors, and so on) has been part of a joint venture with the Japanese company Matsushita.

Electromechanical Components (1 percent of revenues). The main products in this segment are relays and connectors. The company's U.S. subsidiary, Potter & Brumfield, is a leading producer of relays and circuit breakers.

Osram (4 percent of revenues). This subsidiary is one of the largest suppliers of advanced lighting systems for commercial, industrial, residential, theatrical, and other markets. Among its products are compact fluorescent lamps, tungsten halogen lamps, and metal halide lamps. In 1991 Siemens completed the purchase of Osram operations in the United Kingdom, which had been expropriated by the British government after World War I.

Other (2 percent of revenues). The most important other operation is the joint venture with Bosch that is one of Europe's largest producers of home appliances.

TOP EXECUTIVES

- Heinrich von Pierer, chief executive
- Heribald Närger, chairman of the supervisory board
- Karl-Hermann Baumann, member of the managing board
- Hans Baur, member of the managing board
- Hermann Franz, member of the managing board
- Claus Kessler, member of the managing board
- Gerhard Kühne, member of the managing board
- Horst Langer, member of the managing board

OUTSIDE DIRECTORS

- Ulrich Cartellieri, member of the board of management of Deutsche Bank
- Rolf Diel, chairman of the supervisory board of Dresdner Bank AG
- Herbert Grünewald, chairman of the supervisory board of Bayer AG
- Maximilian Hackl, chairman of the supervisory board of Bayerische Vereinsbank AG
- Heinz Hawreliuk, head of the shop stewards department on the executive committee of IG Metall
- Reimar Lüst, president of the Alexander von Humboldt Foundation
- Werner Neugebauer, regional manager for Munich of IG Metall
- Wolfgang Schieren, president of the board of management of Allianz AG
- Nikolaus Senn, chairman of the board of administration of Union Bank of Switzerland
- Dieter Spethmann, former chairman of the management board of Thyssen AG
- Horst Wagner, regional manager for Berlin-Brandenburg of IG Metall

The supervisory board also includes seven employee representatives.

FINANCIAL DATA

Revenues (in millions of deutsche marks) (years ending September 30)

1991	73,008
1990	63,185
1989	61,128
1988	59,374
1987	51,431

Net Income (in millions of deutsche marks) (years ending September 30)

1991	1,792
1990	1,668
1989	1,577
1988	1,391
1987	1,275

GEOGRAPHICAL BREAKDOWN

Revenues (in millions of deutsche marks)

Year*	Germany		Rest of Europe		Elsewhere	
1991	51,245	(58%)	23,338	(26%)	13,895	(16%)
1990	44,504	(58%)	19,532	(26%)	12,413	(16%)
1989	43,945	(60%)	17,630	(24%)	11,768	(16%)

*Fiscal year ends September 30.

LABOR RELATIONS

The company generally has orderly relations with its unions, which are represented on the supervisory board. Yet the company has been swept up in the campaigns of the largest of those unions, IG Metall, to bring about reductions in the workweek. In May 1990, for example, Siemens workers walked off the job for several hours to support IG Metall's drive for the thirty-five-hour week.

ENVIRONMENTAL RECORD

To environmentalists, Siemens is both a villain because of its role in making nuclear reactors and a bit of a hero because of its much smaller involvement in solar energy. The company presents as an environment-friendly innovation its new gas turbines, whose fatigue-resistant blades increase fuel efficiency. The hot turbine exhaust can be used in cogeneration of electricity. Siemens says that environmental considerations are now included in all of its activities, noting in particular that the company is rapidly phasing out use of ozone-destroying CFCs.

Siemens was one of several companies named by the EPA as potentially responsible parties in connection with a superfund toxic waste site in Scottsdale, Arizona. In 1991 Siemens and the other companies involved agreed to contribute toward the $17-million clean-up of the site.

BIBLIOGRAPHY

Siemens, Georg. *History of the House of Siemens.* 1957 Reprint. New York: Arno, 1977.

SONY CORPORATION

7-35, Kitashinagawa 6-chome
Shinagawa-ku, Tokyo, 141
Japan
(03) 3448-2111

1991 revenues: $25.7 billion (year ending March 31)
1991 net income: $831.6 million
Publicly traded company
Employees: 112,900
Founded: 1946

OVERVIEW

For more than a quarter of a century Sony Corporation has been one of the world's leaders in consumer electronics. From transistor radios and tape recorders to VCRs and compact disc players, Sony has repeatedly revolutionized the way people are electronically entertained and informed. Its name is among the most readily recognized brands throughout the world—especially in the United States, where the company derives 30 percent of its sales.

In the late 1980s Sony began expanding from the hardware to the software of modern media, purchasing a leading U.S. record company and a major Hollywood studio. This is the most ambitious melding of the artistic and the technological sides of entertainment since the 1920s, when wireless manufacturers began establishing radio stations to expand the demand for their products.

Chairman Akio Morita, the flamboyant international symbol of Sony, has recently become more controversial as the coauthor of a book that was critical of the United States and that urged Japan to be more aggressive about its international status.

HISTORY

Mighty Sony had very humble beginnings. It started out as a radio repair shop that Masuru Ibuka set up in a bomb-damaged department store in Tokyo soon after the end of World War II. Ibuka, a thirty-seven-year-old engineer who had produced electronic devices for the military during the war, had higher ambitions. To help realize them he persuaded Akio Morita, a young physicist from a prominent sake-brewing family, to join the team. In May 1946 Tokyo Tsushin Kogyo Kabushiki Kaisha, or Tokyo Telecommunications Engineering Company Ltd., was incorporated with the equivalent of about $500 in capital.

The company began developing a reputation as a reliable supplier of vacuum-tube voltmeters, telegraph equipment, and broadcasting devices. But it was sound recording that fascinated Ibuka and Morita. They obtained the Japanese rights to a new technology called tape recording (which was replacing wire recorders) and by late 1949 had manufactured their own device as well as a method for producing the magnetic tape.

This original recorder was a cumbersome affair. Ibuka and Morita realized that recorders (and other devices) would be much more appealing if their bulky vacuum tubes could be replaced with the new transistor technology developed by AT&T in the United States. They managed to get Japanese licensing rights for the transistor, and Ibuka collected a substantial amount of technical information during an American visit. By 1957 Tokyo Telecommunications was ready to introduce the world's first pocket-sized, all-transistor radio. The product was marketed under the brand name Sony (taken from *sonus*, the Latin word for "sound"), which in 1958 became the company's name as well.

The company went on to introduce a series of transistor-based televisions, with screens as small as four inches; color TVs called Trinitrons that produced exceptionally sharp images; increasingly smaller audiocassette recorders; and a wide variety of other electronic products. Such goods went a long way toward changing America's perception of the label MADE IN JAPAN.

Sony was the first Japanese company to have its shares traded on the New York Stock Exchange. And in 1972, while American electronics companies were shifting production to Asia, Sony opened a manufacturing plant in San Diego.

In the 1970s the company created a mass market for home video through the introduction of its Betamax videocassette recorder. The new technology allowed consumers to tape broadcast and cable transmissions for later viewing—a practice, dubbed "time shifting," that was especially disturbing to advertisers because of the viewer's tendency to fast-forward through the commercials when playing the tapes. Legal challenges to VCRs went all the way to the U.S. Supreme Court, which upheld the right of home taping.

But Sony's marketing magic could not overcome an onslaught from competitors, such as Matsushita and Victor Company of Japan (JVC), whose VHS standard proved more popular than the Beta system. Sony did, however, go on to introduce a number of other innovative products—such as the Walkman portable stereo cassette player and the Video Walkman—that came to dominate the market.

In recent years Sony has expanded from the hardware to the software side of the entertainment business. In January 1988 it acquired all common shares of CBS Records and its affiliates from CBS Inc. for more than $2 billion. In November 1989 Sony paid the Coca-Cola Company $3.4 billion to acquire Columbia Pictures Entertainment.

CBS Records had its origins in the Columbia Phonograph Record Company, which dated back to the nineteenth century and was an important distributor of jazz and blues. Columbia Phonograph was briefly involved in an effort to establish a radio network to compete with industry leader NBC. But after a complicated series of maneuvers, control of the new radio company, Columbia Broadcasting System (CBS), ended up in the hands of William Paley, the twenty-six-year-old son of a cigar magnate. In 1938 Paley purchased Columbia Phonograph and made it part of CBS.

CBS Records pioneered the LP and became one of the giants of the recorded music industry, distributing the work of such artists as Billie Holiday, Benny Goodman, Barbra Streisand, Bruce Springsteen, and Michael Jackson. Initially CBS resisted Sony's overture, but in the wake of the 1987 stock market crash and Sony's sweetening of its original offer by 60 percent, the broadcast company relented.

Columbia Pictures was founded in the 1920s as a small independent producer by Harry Cohn, his brother Jack, and Joe Brandt. The company, which pioneered the practice of shooting scenes out of sequence in order to keep down production costs, specialized in low-budget features but also prospered from the social-minded films of Frank Capra. Columbia—run by Harry Cohn, the quintessential ruthless studio boss, until his death in 1958—was the first studio to move into television production.

In the late 1970s Columbia was embarrassed when it was revealed that its hotshot film head, David Begelman, had forged more than $60,000 worth of company checks for personal use. The investment house of Allen & Company, which had bought a controlling interest in the studio in the early 1970s, thwarted a takeover by financier Kirk Kerkorian in 1981 by purchasing his shares. But the Allens turned around and sold their interest at a great profit to the Coca-Cola Company in 1982.

Five years later Coke spun off Columbia and combined it with Tri-Star Pictures to form Columbia Pictures Entertainment (49-percent owned by Coke). Tri-Star Pictures had been founded in 1982 as a joint venture of Columbia Pictures, Home Box Office, and CBS. The plan was that Tri-Star would produce films that Columbia would help distribute in theaters, that HBO would show on pay-TV, and that CBS would show on network TV.

By the end of 1985 the three partners were putting increasing amounts of cash into the venture, but only Columbia seemed to be getting anything out of it (mainly from the distribution fees it was receiving). The venture went public in 1985, but CBS bailed out. As a result the company was 43-percent owned by Columbia, 43 percent by the public, and 14 percent by HBO's parent, Time Inc.

In buying the parent of Tri-Star and Columbia Pictures, Sony also acquired the Guber-Peters Entertainment Company for $200 million. The heads of that company, superproducers Peter Guber and Jon Peters (famed for *Batman*), were installed as the cochairmen of Columbia Pictures Entertainment and charged with injecting new life into the film operation. In 1991 Peters announced that he was departing to set up his own film company, leaving Guber in sole charge.

An indication of the reach of the new Sony came in 1991, when the company signed a new contract with superstar Michael Jackson. The deal covered feature films, television programming, theatrical shorts, and a new record label. Jackson's fees were not disclosed, but the company said it could realize some $1 billion from retail sales of the resulting products.

While deals like these raise expectations, there is still limited evidence that Sony's grand synergistic dream in combining hardware and software will pay off enough to justify the large sums that the Japanese company has been sinking into the movie and recording businesses.

OPERATIONS

Video Equipment (25 percent of net sales in fiscal 1991). Sony has been a pioneer of home video since its 1975 introduction of the Betamax VCR. Its Betamax products, which used half-inch tape, initially lost the battle with the VHS standard, prompting the company to bring out a line of VHS videocassette recorders. But Sony made a spectacular comeback in 1989 with the introduction of the ultracompact and lightweight (1.7 pounds) 8-mm Handycam camcorder.

Other consumer products include the Video Walkman, introduced in 1988, which combines a small TV and VCR; the Mavica video camera, also brought out in 1988, which records still images that with an adaptor can be displayed on a standard television; and multidisc players, marketed in Japan since 1987, which can play compact discs, CD videos, and laser discs.

Sony's digital video equipment has long been widely used in television stations and film production companies. Since 1985 it has marketed a high-definition system line of equipment that uses 1,125 scanning lines, about twice the number in conventional television.

Audio Equipment (24 percent of net sales). In 1979 Sony, a tape recorder pioneer, invented a new way of listening to music in public. The company's Walkman, a set of headphones attached to a compact stereo cassette player, soon became standard equipment for joggers, subway riders, and others seeking to replace the noise of modern life with more pleasant sounds.

In cooperation with its Dutch rival, Philips, Sony developed a revolutionary new audio system in which a laser is used to reproduce music recorded digitally on a small plastic disc. Since compact discs, or CDs, were first introduced in 1982 they have surpassed records and cassettes to become the leading medium of music. Sony has brought out an extensive line of products that use CDs, including portable models, car stereo units, and players incorporated into home music systems. A portable CD player called Discman, introduced in 1984, has brought the new technology to headphone users.

While music lovers adored the high-quality sound of CDs, they were frustrated by the fact that one could not record onto the devices. Sony sought to satisfy this demand in 1987 with the introduction of the digital audio tape (DAT) deck, which featured superior sound quality without the noise and distortion of conventional tape recording. DAT players and cassettes were delayed in reaching the United States until 1990 because of legal threats from the recording industry, which feared that the system would encourage piracy of CDs. Sony overcame this obstacle by agreeing to insert a chip that makes duplication more difficult.

DAT products got off to a slow start in the United States, and the reason seems to be that consumers were not prepared to abandon all of their existing cassettes. That drawback was rectified by Philips, which in 1991 announced its own version, called the digital compact cassette (DCC), which will be used with decks that can play traditional cassettes as well. DCC could end up eliminating the mass market potential of DAT. Some of the conflict between the two systems seemed to be resolved in October 1991, when the two companies announced a cross-licensing deal. But the dust has not settled in this affair.

Further complicating the picture was the Mini Disc that Sony introduced in 1991. This 2.5-inch compact disc can play up to seventy-four minutes of music and is meant to be used in the new, Walkman-sized portable players that Sony planned to introduce.

The company also has a line of products for children called My First Sony. Sony's audio equipment, which includes products sold under the Aiwa name, is made in Japan, France, Malaysia, Austria, and the United States.

Televisions (15 percent of net sales). Since 1968, when Sony introduced a new type of color picture tube, the company's TVs have been regarded as among the best available. The Trinitron technology has been employed in a variety of products, including large-screen TVs, professional-use monitors, and computer displays. Sony also makes projection televisions, ranging up to the JumboTron giant display system used in sports arenas and convention halls.

Sony is a major proponent of high-definition television that can reproduce images as sharply as those on a movie screen. Sony's televisions are produced in Japan, the United Kingdom, Germany, Spain, Malaysia, and the United States.

Other Electronic Products (15 percent of net sales). Sony's semiconductor operations focus on metal oxide semiconductor (MOS) devices, such as static random access memory chips, charge-coupled devices, and bipolar integrated circuits for consumer audiovisual equipment. In 1990 the company arranged to obtain a chip-manufacturing plant (in Texas) from Advanced Micro Devices in exchange for $55 million and access to Sony's MOS technology.

In 1989 the company acquired Materials Research Corporation, a leading manufacturer of sputtering equipment for thin metal films, etching equipment, and high-purity metals and ceramic substrates.

Sony's experience in computers has been quite uneven. The company ran into numerous brick walls but finally made a major push in 1986 that resulted in a low-priced and superior workstation. The product, called NEWS (for net work station) was designed for engineering applications, such as software development, but in Japan it also has sparked a boom in desktop publishing. The company's computer reputation got a boost in 1991, when Apple Computer announced a new line of portable Macintoshes, including one that was manufactured by Sony. Apple and Sony also have agreed to work together on the development of a multimedia computer.

Sony also produces CD-ROM memories and other optical disc systems, micro floppy discs, telephone answering machines, and some telecommunications equipment. In 1990 the company introduced the Data Discman, a hand-held device that displays pages of books stored on optical discs. To encourage the development of such devices and their integration with its entertainment assets, the company in 1991 established a unit called Sony Electronic Publishing. This, in turn, is part of Sony Software Corporation, an entity headed by Sony USA chairman Michael Schulof that is supposed to oversee the integration of the company's involvement in film, music, and electronic publishing. In 1991 Sony formed a consortium with Philips and Matsushita for the development of compact discs that combine audio, still images, motion video, computer graphics, and data.

Sony also has moved into the electronic game business by agreeing to produce game players in cooperation with Nintendo. But when Nintendo realized that the devices also would be capable of playing games on compact discs, it made a separate deal with Philips.

Music (13 percent of net sales). Sony's 1988 purchase of CBS records propelled it to the top ranks of the recorded music business. Now known as Sony Music Entertainment, the operation distributes the work of a wide range of artists, from established superstars like the Rolling Stones to more recent successes like New Kids on the Block. Outside the United States, the business has been doing especially well in Europe and Latin America. Sony's recorded-music products are made in Japan, Holland, Austria, the United Kingdom, and the United States.

Filmed entertainment (7 percent of net sales). In 1989 Sony shook up the U.S. entertainment industry with its acquisition of Columbia Pictures Entertainment. But the Japanese company was acquiring problems as part of its investment. During the reign of David Puttnam at the studio, Columbia had a series of expensive flops. The company's television production, however, was much more attractive, as was its library of twenty-seven hundred films and twenty-three thousand TV episodes. Columbia is also in the exhibition end of the business. Through Loews Theatre Management Corporation and its affiliates the company operates about 880 screens in some 185 locations.

The Sony team has high hurdles to jump. In 1991 Tri-Star ranked sixth among the major studios with a domestic market share of 10.9 percent, while Columbia Pictures was seventh with only 9.1 percent. Sony will face increased competition from one of its old rivals, Matsushita, which purchased MCA, the parent company of Universal Studios, in 1990.

TOP EXECUTIVES

- Akio Morita, chairman; he also controls Morita & Company, a family sake business that is the largest holder of Sony stock
- Norio Ohga, president and chief executive
- Nobuo Kanoi, deputy president
- Ken Iwaki, deputy president
- Tsunehiko Ishizuka, senior managing director
- Tsunao Hashimoto, senior managing director
- Koji Adachi, senior managing director
- Kozo Ohsone, senior managing director
- Minoru Morio, senior managing director
- Michael P. Schulhof, vice chairman of Sony Corporation of America and president of Sony Software Corporation.

OUTSIDE DIRECTORS

- Kenichi Kamiya, director and adviser of Sakura Bank
- Peter G. Peterson, chairman of the Blackstone Group

FINANCIAL DATA

Net sales (in millions of yen) (years ending March 31)

1991	3,616,517
1990	2,879,856
1989	2,145,329
1988	1,555,219

Net Income (in millions of yen) (years ending March 31)

1991	116,925
1990	102,808
1989	72,469
1988	37,236

GEOGRAPHICAL BREAKDOWN

Net Sales (in millions of yen)

Year*	Japan		United States		Elsewhere	
1991	952,459	(26%)	1,053,949	(29%)	1,610,109	(45%)
1990	869,478	(30%)	857,812	(30%)	1,152,566	(40%)
1989	731,297	(34%)	586,278	(27%)	827,754	(39%)
1988	537,942	(35%)	434,473	(28%)	582,804	(38%)

*Fiscal year ends March 31.

LABOR RELATIONS

Sony generally has harmonious labor relations in Japan, although in 1961 there was a short strike by militant workers that coincided with the company's fifteenth anniversary celebration. It ended with a face-saving settlement for both sides.

After Sony opened its manufacturing operation in San Diego in 1972, an organizing drive was initiated by the Communications Workers of America. The company worked hard to convince the workers that a union was unnecessary, given the company's enlightened policies. Apparently a majority of the employees were persuaded: the vote was 299 to 100 against the union.

Today Sony estimates that 10 percent of its workers are members of labor unions; the company considers its labor relations to be "excellent."

ENVIRONMENTAL RECORD

Along with many other electronics companies, Sony has announced plans to phase out the use of cleaning solvents containing ozone-destroying CFCs. Sony is supposed to end its CFC use by 1995.

BIBLIOGRAPHY

Katzenstein, Gary. *Funny Business: An Outsider's Year in Japan.* New York: Soho, 1989.

Lyons, Nick. *The Sony Vision.* New York: Crown, 1976.

Morita, Akio, Edwin M. Reingold, and Mitsuko Shimomura. *Made in Japan: Akio Morita and Sony.* New York: E. P. Dutton, 1986.

SUMITOMO GROUP

Major affiliates:

Sumitomo Corporation
5-15, Kitahama 4-chome
Chuo-ku, Osaka 541
Japan
(06) 220-6000

1991 revenues: $142.4 billion (year ending March 31)
1991 net income: $334.7 million
Publicly traded company
Employees: 6,363
Founded: 1919

Sumitomo Bank, Ltd.
6-5, Kitahama 4-chome
Chuo-ku, Osaka 541
Japan
(06) 227-2111

1991 revenues: $35.3 billion (year ending March 31)
1991 net income: $1 billion
1991 assets: $446.5 billion
Publicly traded company
Employees: 16,669
Founded: 1895

Sumitomo Chemical Company, Ltd.
5-33, Kitahama 4-chome
Chuo-ku, Osaka 541

Japan
(06) 220-3272

1991 revenues: $8.7 billion (year ending December 31)
1991 net income: $161.3 million
Publicly traded company
Employees: 14,546
Founded: 1925

Sumitomo Electric Industries, Ltd.
5-33, Kitahama 4-chome
Chuo-ku, Osaka 541
Japan
(06) 220-4141

1991 revenues: $7.9 billion (year ending March 31)
1991 net income: $224.8 million
Publicly traded company
Employees: 14,348
Founded: 1920

Sumitomo Heavy Industries, Ltd.
2-1, Ohtemachi 2-chome
Chiyoda-ku, Tokyo 100
Japan
(03) 3245-4078

1991 revenues: $3.3 billion (year ending March 31)
1991 net income: $43.2 million
Publicly traded company
Employees: 6,500
Founded: 1934

Sumitomo Metal Industries, Ltd.
5-33, Kitahama 4-chome
Chuo-ku, Osaka 541
Japan
(06) 220-5111

1991 revenues: $8.2 billion (year ending March 31)
1991 net income: $338.8 million
Publicly traded company
Employees: 19,817
Founded: 1897

OVERVIEW

Sumitomo is one of Japan's largest *keiretsu* conglomerates, with operations ranging from mining and electric cables to banking and pharmaceuticals. The House of Sumitomo was built over several centuries by revenues from copper mining and smelting. It became one of the powerful *zaibatsu* groups that controlled the Japanese economy from the late nineteenth century through World War II.

Along with the other *zaibatsu*, it was dissolved after the war but gradually coalesced again in somewhat less centralized form. Today the group includes Japan's largest general trading company, which, like its counterparts in groups like Mitsubishi and Mitsui, has huge revenues and tiny profits. Other companies in the Sumitomo constellation include one of Japan's largest and most aggressive banks, whose reputation has been tarnished by some recent scandals. Sumitomo also has a presence in a wide range of industrial activities, including both mature fields like shipbuilding and dynamic new ones like optoelectronics.

HISTORY

The Sumitomo Group dates back to the late sixteenth century, when Riemon Soga was the first in Japan to perfect a technique for extracting silver from copper ore. The innovation revolutionized the Japanese copper industry and brought prosperity to Soga's company, which was known as the Izumiya ("Fountainhead Shop"). It also helped to enrich the Sumitomo family, to which Soga was related by marriage. Masatomo Sumitomo, who ran a medicine and book shop called the Fujiya, had no sons, so he "adopted" his brother-in-law into the family.

Descendants of Soga continued to operate the copper business, which received a major boost in 1690 when it gained control of a massive copper deposit discovered in Besshi on the island of Shikoku. For the next two centuries what was considered the Sumitomo family business thrived as a result of the Besshi operation. The mine was modernized in the late nineteenth century, during which period Sumitomo began to move into other fields.

The financial operations of the family business were formalized as Sumitomo Bank in 1895. Two years later Sumitomo established the Uraga Dock Company shipbuilding operation, and the same year, the family began producing electric cables and wires at a factory near Osaka. The latter operation, which became known as the Sumitomo Copper Rolling Works, got its raw material from the Besshi mine.

Over the following years Sumitomo branched out into many more fields, becoming one of the large family-run conglomerates, known as *zaibatsu*, that took over much of the Japanese economy. Sumitomo Electric was incorporated in 1920 to take over the cable and wire business; Nippon Electric Company also came into the Sumitomo universe. A process for converting sulfur dioxide from a Sumitomo copper smelter into fertilizers led to the creation of Sumitomo Fertilizer Manufacturing, which later expanded its product line and changed its name to Sumitomo Chemical.

Sumitomo's operations were drawn into the militarization of Japan that took place during the 1930s, and the director general of the Sumitomo trading firm later became a minister in the government. The Sumitomo companies made a variety of military products during World War II and consequently were frequent targets of Allied bombers.

After the war Sumitomo was broken up into independent companies that were forbidden to use the group's logo, a stylized form of an ancient well frame. Within a few years, however, the United States decided to make Japan a bulwark against the spread of communism in Asia. The former Sumitomo companies began to reestablish ties with one another through financial relationships and regular meetings of executives to coordinate business strategies. Sumitomo thus reemerged as one of the *keiretsu*, which were less centralized than the *zaibatsu* but still constituted coherent groups that attained similar influence over the Japanese economy.

The group's trading company reestablished itself as Sumitomo Shoji Kaisha in 1952 (and took the name Sumitomo Corporation in 1978). The main financial entity in the group resumed use of the name Sumitomo Bank and once again served a coordinating role among the companies.

Those companies took full advantage of the recovery of the Japanese economy. Sumitomo Electric became a major supplier to Japan's growing automobile industry. Sumitomo Chemical moved into petrochemicals, pharmaceuticals, and aluminum smelting. It also shifted out of the less profitable business of fertilizers (especially during the 1970s) and into the more profitable one of pesticides. Sumitomo Heavy Industries continued its shipbuilding activities—it produced Japan's first supertanker in 1975—and began manufacturing power transmission equipment in the United States in the 1960s. It also got into new fields, such as medical diagnostic equipment, water treatment facilities, data processing, and semiconductor equipment.

During the 1980s Sumitomo Bank increased its already prodigious size by purchasing Switzerland's Banca del Gottardo and, closer to home, the Heiwa Sogo Bank. Sumitomo became one of the most aggressive of the Japanese banks in pursuing foreign business. In 1986 it shook up Wall Street by purchasing 12.5 percent of the prominent investment bank Goldman Sachs. The bank's reputation was tarnished by a 1990 scandal involving loans to a speculator who had been charged with stock market manipulation. The incident prompted Ichiro Isoda, chairman of the bank, to resign. That same year, the bank was embarrassed again by reports of its close relationship with the trading company Itoman & Company, which found itself close to collapse because of risky real estate investments.

In the industrial area, Sumitomo Metal Industries joined with U.S. steel company LTV in an electrogalvanizing venture and invested in other American steel makers like Baker Hughes. Sumitomo Rubber purchased the Dunlop tire business. In 1991 Sumitomo Corporation and Sumitomo Metal Mining Company acquired a 20-percent interest in Phelps Dodge's La Candelaria copper and gold mining project in northern Chile. That same year, Sumitomo Metal Industries announced that it was prepared to make a substantial investment in LTV to help the U.S. steel maker emerge from Chapter 11 bankruptcy. Sumitomo Corporation lost a $121 million contract to supply rail transit cars for Los Angeles amid a burst of "buy American" sentiment in early 1992.

OPERATIONS

Sumitomo Corporation. Sumitomo Corporation is the *sogo shosha*, or general trading company, of the group. Its main areas of activity, conducted through offices in eighty-seven countries, are as follows:

- Metals (38 percent of 1991 sales): crude steel, iron ore, coal, scrap metal, steel products, and titanium products as well as aluminum, nickel, and other nonferrous metals.
- Machinery (29 percent of sales): industrial equipment, air-conditioning systems, medical equipment, office automation equipment, marine equipment, transportation equipment, motor vehicles, and telecommunications systems.
- Chemicals and fuels (17 percent of sales): a wide range of organic and inorganic chemicals, plastics, synthetic rubber, dyestuffs, pharmaceuticals, crude oil, liquefied petroleum gas, and carbon products.
- Foodstuffs (6 percent of sales): grains, fresh fruits and vegetables, meat, seafood, processed foods, and cut flowers.
- Textiles (2 percent of sales): raw cotton, synthetic fibers, woven and knit fabrics, floor coverings, and other household and apparel products.
- Commodities and construction (8 percent of sales): natural rubber, wood, pulp and paper, building materials and other commodities. Construction activities include developing, contracting, and consulting on large-scale commercial and residential projects.

Sumitomo Bank. The second-largest banking company in the world in terms of assets and the most profitable of the big Japanese banks. Sumitomo Bank operates a network of 381 offices in Japan and 65 foreign offices in 33 countries. The bank provides a full range of financial services, including corporate banking, investment banking, retail banking, money market operations, and credit cards. It owns banks in the United States (California), Brazil, Germany, and Switzerland as well as 12.5 percent of investment bank Goldman Sachs. In 1991 the bank formed a joint venture with American Express to issue the American Express Gold Card in Japan.

Sumitomo Chemical Company. As one of the leading chemical producers in Japan, Sumitomo Chemical makes a variety of petrochemical products, including fertilizers, plastics, synthetic rubber, and industrial chemicals. It also produces organic intermediates, polymer additives, organic pigments, dye-stuffs, and pesticides. In recent years the company has moved into pharmaceuticals and biotechnology. In 1988 it joined with Chevron to form a venture called Valent USA to make agricultural chemicals; in 1991 Sumitomo took over Chevron's share in the company.

Sumitomo Electric Industries. Sumitomo Electric Industries has branched out from its traditional business of making electric wire and cable (in which it is still a major supplier to Nippon Telegraph and Telephone) into high-tech areas like fiber optics, semiconductor materials, automotive navigation systems, and hand-held scanners. The company also produces disc brakes, antilock braking systems, wiring harnesses, and other automotive products.

Sumitomo Heavy Industries. Traditionally the shipbuilding arm of the group, with the vagaries of that industry Sumitomo Heavy Industry has moved into a variety of other fields. These include medical diagnostic equipment, injection-molding machines, semiconductor-manufacturing systems, cryogenics and superconductivity technology, biotechnology, and nuclear engineering.

Sumitomo Metal Industries. One of the largest steel producers in the world, Sumitomo Metal Industries also produces titanium and parts for railroad and mass transit cars. Newer businesses include semiconductor components, medical equipment, and asbestos-free building materials. The company also provides plant engineering and systems engineering services.

TOP EXECUTIVES

Sumitomo Corporation
- Tadashi Itoh, chairman
- Tomiichi Akiyama, president
- Akitoshi Oshima, executive vice president
- Eiichi Miyoshi, executive vice president

FINANCIAL DATA

Sumitomo Corporation

Gross Trading Volume (in millions of yen)

1991	20,018,751
1990	18,230,529
1989	14,532,263
1988	13,105,002
1987	12,387,284

Net Income (in millions of yen)

1991	47,063
1990	50,006
1989	35,111
1988	28,924
1987	28,021

LABOR RELATIONS

Sumitomo Corporation of America is one of numerous Japanese companies that have gotten into legal trouble because of their employment practices in the United States. A group of some one hundred Sumitomo employees brought suit against the company, charging that it discriminated against non-Japanese personnel. In 1990 the suit was settled with an agreement that included commitments by the company to raise salaries and establish career-development programs for the Americans.

ENVIRONMENTAL RECORD

The attempt to solve an environmental problem was the basis for the creation of one of the main companies in the Sumitomo Group. In the early years of the twentieth century the Sumitomo copper smelter at Nihama was endangering nearby communities with its high levels of sulfur dioxide emissions. In 1913 a new technique was devised to transform the sulfur dioxide into sulfuric acid and calcium superphosphate, which was used as a fertilizer. This led to the creation of Sumitomo Chemical Company.

In 1990 a Japanese court ordered Sumitomo Metal Mining to pay compensation equal to about $1.5 million to nine people suffering from arsenic poisoning and the families of nine others who had died from the poisoning. The victims claimed that they had been exposed to the arsenic as a result of activities of a mine the company once operated in Miyazaki Prefecture.

Sumitomo Forestry has come under criticism for its harvesting of wood in the rain forests of Papua New Guinea. Sumitomo Heavy Industries has produced double-hulled oil tankers, which significantly reduce the chances of major oil spills.

BIBLIOGRAPHY

Bisson, Thomas Arthur. *Zaibatsu Dissolution in Japan.* 1954. Reprint. Westport, Conn.: Greenwood, 1976.

Kunio, Yoshihara. *Sogo Shosha: The Vanguard of the Japanese Economy.* Tokyo: Oxford University Press, 1982.

Yoshino, M.Y., and Thomas B. Lifson. *The Invisible Link: Japan's Sogo Shosha and the Organization of Trade.* Cambridge, Mass.: MIT Press, 1986.

Young, Alexander. *The Sogo Shosha: Japan's Multinational Trading Companies.* Boulder, Colo.: Westview, 1979.

THOMSON SA

51, Esplanade du Général de Gaulle
92045 Paris La Défense 10
France
(01) 49 07 80 00

1991 revenues: $13.8 billion
1991 net income: −$135.5 million (loss)
State-owned company; subsidiary Thomson-CSF is publicly traded
Employees: 105,460
Founded: 1893

OVERVIEW

Thomson is a company that, after being taken over by the French government in the early 1980s, has undergone a wrenching process of restructuring akin to what usually happens these days after a state-owned firm is privatized.

Under the leadership of Alain Gomez—who in his past was at various points a militant leftist and a paratrooper—the one-time diversified electrical products company has become focused on two major businesses—consumer electronics and military and aerospace electronics. In the former area, Gomez is determined to prevent the Japanese from completely taking over the industry. By moves like the purchase of General Electric's television and VCR business, Gomez has made Thomson into a formidable competitor to the likes of Matsushita and Sony, but the company is still facing a bruising battle.

In the area of military and aerospace electronics, the company's Thomson-CSF subsidiary is the second-largest producer in the world, behind the Hughes division of General Motors—a position that is becoming less desirable as military spending declines. Thomson is also a partner in the SGS-Thomson joint venture, which is struggling to preserve a semiconductor industry in Europe.

In December 1991 the French government announced the latest in a long line of industrial reorganizations involving Thomson. This time the idea was to merge Thomson with the civilian operations of the state-owned Commissariat à l'Énergie Atomique (CEA). As of May 1992 the plan, which would result in the creation of a new government-owned company called Thomson-CEA Industrie, was facing substantial opposition.

HISTORY

Thomson began life in 1893 as the French subsidiary of Thomson-Houston Corporation, an American producer of streetcars and other electric equipment. Called the Compagnie Française Thomson-Houston, it began making electric railway cars and power generation gear and was sold to French investors when Thomson-Houston was taken over by General Electric in the early years of the twentieth century.

For a long time the French company kept the name of its original parent and continued to license technology from GE. It also followed GE's lead and entered the market for consumer goods like radios and household appliances. In the 1920s it formed a light bulb joint venture called Compagnie des Lampes with Compagnie Générale d'Électricité (CGE), France's other major electrical equipment maker. Yet Thomson-Houston did not grow as fast as its American role model. The company was subjected to the vagaries of French industrial policy, and after the Nazi invasion it was forced to reorient its operations to the needs of the German military.

After the war Thomson-Houston was asked by the French government to help rebuild the country's infrastructure. In keeping with the French emphasis on economic autonomy, the company, which shortened its name to Thomson, ended its long-standing relationship with GE in 1953. The government came to depend on Thomson to play a key role in such fields as nuclear power and military systems.

In 1966 the company acquired Hotchkiss-Brandt, a French firm with operations in the automotive and military fields, and renamed itself Thomson-Brandt. Two years later it merged its electronics division with telecommunications equipment maker Compagnie Générale de Télégraphie Sans Fil. The combined operation, called Thomson-CSF, became the leader of French high technology. In another government-induced restructuring, the Alsthom subsidiary of Thomson-Brandt, which manufactured power generation equipment and built power plants, was joined to CGE in 1969. In return CGE left the home appliance and computer markets to Thomson.

During the 1970s Thomson sought to enter new markets by means of joint ventures with the likes of Xerox, but poor financial management kept the company weak. In 1982, after the Socialists took power, the ailing Thomson-Brandt was taken over by the government. Alain Gomez, who was appointed to head the company, carried out a thorough reorganization, including the creation of a new holding company called Thomson SA. He also streamlined operations, focusing on consumer products and military electronics. As part of another industry restructuring, most of Thomson's telecommunications operations were transferred to CGE, which in turn handed over its consumer and military electronics businesses to Thomson.

Gomez tried to purchase the German electronics company Grundig in 1984 but was deterred by antitrust problems and the opposition of the company's founder. Yet Gomez did succeed in taking over another German firm, Telefunken, which gave Thomson a valuable marketing foothold in Germany. He also bought most of the assets of the Mostek semiconductor subsidiary of United Technologies and merged Thomson's chip-making operations with those of the Italian company SGS.

In 1987 Gomez, who was one of only a few chief executives of state-owned companies to survive the change in political climate that brought conservative Jacques Chirac to power, greatly expanded the consumer electronics portion of Thomson through two acquisitions. The first was the television and VCR business of the British company Thorn-EMI. More significant was the deal to take over the consumer electronics business of General Electric in exchange for $800 million and Thomson's medical equipment operation. The move made Thomson the world's second-largest (after Philips) producer of television sets, and number one in the United States, thus slowing down the rising Japanese dominance of the consumer electronics industry.

Gomez has been struggling in recent years to assure that Thomson will be one of the survivors in the shakeout of the European high-tech companies. He put Thomson-CSF in the JESSI chip development project with Siemens and Philips and had it purchase the military operations of the latter company. In 1990 Philips and Thomson also formed a partnership, along with the U.S. television network NBC (owned by General Electric), to develop a high-definition television system.

In 1991 Gomez formed alliances with two other U.S. companies—Control Data Corporation (for joint marketing of computers and related equipment) and Boeing (for joint development of aerospace products). A plan to merge the missile business of Thomson-CSF with that of British Aerospace collapsed, but Thomson did form a joint venture with GEC-Marconi, a subsidiary of Britain's General Electric Company, to develop radar equipment for the next generation of European fighter aircraft. The French company also decided to reenter the European market for residential telephone equipment and arranged to produce video and audio products in Poland.

Despite all of these deals, Thomson remained financially weak because of the decline in military spending and the intense competition in consumer electronics. To give a boost to the firm the French government decided in April 1991 to ignore European Community regulations and give the company a subsidy of FF 1.8 billion. The move caused an uproar in the EC, so the plan was put off.

Instead, in late 1991 the French government announced the planned merger of Thomson with the civilian operations of the state-owned Commissariat à l'Énergie Atomique (CEA). The strategy was to use the profits from the CEA's involvement in building nuclear reactors and processing nuclear fuel to subsidize Thomson's consumer electronics and semiconductor businesses.

As part of the plan, Thomson-CSF would be spun off into a separate state-owned enterprise.

The reorganization ran into criticism from French politicians who criticized what they saw as the haste of the government in attempting to implement the proposal. It was also unclear whether the plan would meet European Commission rules on state aid to industry.

OPERATIONS

Consumer Electronics (44 percent of 1991 revenues). Thomson Consumer Electronics is one of the world's leading producers of televisions, VCRs, and video cameras. It acquired the consumer electronics business of General Electric in 1987 and continues to sell those products under the GE and RCA names, giving it the lead in the U.S. market for color televisions. Other brands include Ferguson, Nordmende, Saba, Thomson, Brandt, and Telefunken.

Thomson, a major proponent of high-definition television, joined with its Dutch rival, Philips, to pressure the European Community to adopt their MAC standard over the HDTV system being pushed by the Japanese. As a stepping stone to the new age of movie theater–quality television reception, Thomson in 1991 introduced its Space System wide-screen TVs in Europe.

Electronics and Defense Systems (49 percent of revenues). The company's 60-percent owned subsidiary Thomson-CSF is the leading military electronics company in Europe. It produces systems for radar, sonar, navigation, communication, and other applications. In 1985 Thomson-CSF, in partnership with the U.S. telephone company GTE, won a \$4.3-billion order to supply the U.S. Army with battlefield communications equipment—the largest contract the Pentagon had ever awarded for non-American technology. Thomson-CSF also has been a major military supplier in the Middle East, where it won a multi-billion-dollar contract from the government of Saudi Arabia. A plan to merge the company's missile operations with those of British Aerospace fell through in 1991. Later that year, however, Thomson-CSF formed an alliance for missile work with France's Aérospatiale and the Daimler-Benz subsidiary Messerschmitt-Bölkow-Blohm. In 1992 Thomson-CSF joined with Hughes Aircraft and the Carlyle Group to purchase the missile business of LTV, but the deal ran into strong political opposition.

This segment also includes civilian activities. In 1989 Thomson-CSF created Sextant Avionique, a joint venture with Aérospatiale that is now the European leader in flight electronics, both civilian and military. Thomson-CSF also makes flight simulators. The company also participates with the Italian state-owned company IRI/Finmeccanica in a joint venture called SGS-Thomson, which is one of the largest semiconductor producers in Europe. Yet it is a troubled operation, and Thomson has sought to merge it with the chip-making businesses of Siemens and Philips. That plan encountered resistance from the other two companies, so SGS-Thomson formed a joint venture with Britain's

General Electric to make semicustom chips. Subsequently, Philips did agree to work with SGS-Thomson in developing advanced chip technology.

Home Appliances (7 percent of revenues). The company's Thomson Electroménager subsidiary is the leading French producer of refrigerators, washing machines, dryers, microwave ovens, and other household appliances.

TOP EXECUTIVES

- Alain Gomez, chairman and chief executive
- Bernard Isautier, executive vice president and chief executive of Thomson Consumer Electronics
- Pierre Cabanes, senior vice president
- Alain Hagelauer, senior vice president, finance
- Erich Spitz, senior vice president, research and technology

OUTSIDE DIRECTORS

- Norbert Ansquer
- Pierre-Yves Cossé, former senior executive vice president of Banque Nationale de Paris
- Jacques Dondoux
- Robert Gros
- Jacques Grossi, head of the Defense Ministry Armaments Directorate
- Paul Hamon
- Jean-Claude Hirel
- Olivier Lecerf, honorary chairman of Lafarge Coppée
- Didier Lombard, director of Crédit Lyonnais
- Luis Manjon
- Bernard Patin
- Jean-Benoît Ramé
- Bruno Roger, managing partner of Lazard Frères & Cie
- Jacques Stern, member of Air France's board of administration
- Didier Thomas
- Jean-Claude Trichet, director of the French Treasury
- Antoine Veil

The board also includes six representatives elected by the employees of the company. Thomson does not disclose the affiliations of its outside directors. Those listed above were obtained from other sources.

FINANCIAL DATA

Revenues (in millions of French francs)

1991	71,277
1990	75,228
1989	76,663
1988	75,100
1987	60,182

Net Income (in millions of French francs)

1991	−702 (loss)
1990	−2,474 (loss)
1989	497
1988	1,197
1987	1,063

GEOGRAPHICAL BREAKDOWN

Revenues (in millions of French francs)

Year	France		Rest of Europe		Elsewhere	
1990	22,318	(30%)	18,861	(25%)	34,039	(45%)
1989	21,547	(28%)	15,915	(21%)	39,201	(51%)
1988	21,823	(28%)	16,641	(22%)	36,636	(49%)
1987	23,232	(39%)	15,047	(25%)	21,903	(36%)

LABOR RELATIONS

The restructuring of Thomson after its takeover by the French government in the early 1980s upset the workers and the unions at the company by eliminating thousands of jobs. To help smooth out relations, in the late 1980s the company adopted a policy of worker consultation, both within the French union structure and on a European-wide basis for the consumer electronics business.

TIME WARNER INC.

Dual headquarters:

1271 Sixth Avenue
New York, New York 10020
(212) 522-1212

75 Rockefeller Plaza
New York, New York 10019
(212) 484-8000

1991 revenues: $12 billion
1991 net income: −$99 million (loss)
Publicly traded company
Employees: 41,000
Founded: 1922

OVERVIEW

Time Warner, the quintessential media octopus and the world's largest publishing and entertainment company, is the result of the 1989 marriage of Time Inc. and Warner Communications. The combined company, though weighed down with debt as a result of the $7-billion merger, is at the top of the magazine business, controls one of the biggest cable television operations in the country, owns two of the leading pay-TV services, operates one of the major Hollywood studios, and owns several leading book-publishing houses. Time Warner's status seems less formidable, however, in light of its decision to sell a $1-billion stake in its TV and film businesses to two Japanese companies: Toshiba and C. Itoh.

HISTORY

Half of this company, the Time Inc. portion, was founded by Henry Luce in the 1920s. Luce, the son of a missionary, used *Time*, *Life*, and *Fortune* to promote his conservative view of the world. Through these publications Luce, who proclaimed this to be the "American century," became one of the most influential men in America. After Luce died in 1967, Time Inc. became a more traditional but also more aggressive corporation.

The company expanded its involvement in book publishing with the 1968 purchase of Little, Brown. It also plunged into the television business. Starting with a fledgling cable company in Manhattan, Time ended up with the second-largest cable system in the country. Time also created Home Box Office, which transformed the pay-cable business, and later added another pay service, Cinemax. In the 1970s video became the fastest-growing part of the company.

There was expansion in the magazine business, too. *Money* was launched in 1972, *People* in 1974, and *Discover* in 1980. The weekly *Life*, shut down in 1972, was revived as a monthly in 1978. While all of these new ventures (with the exception of *Discover*) were successful, the company also had a string of conspicuous failures. The company bought the *Washington Star* in 1978, only to close it down three years later.

In an embarrassing fiasco, Time spent nearly $50 million on a listings publication called *TV-Cable Week*, which was terminated after five months when it became clear that the company was in over its head. A teletext project also was dropped. In the early 1980s, as the cable business declined, Time established a magazine development group to explore possibilities for new publications. The main outcome of the group's work, a magazine called *Picture Week*, was abandoned after about a year of market testing.

Breaking with its tradition of creating rather than buying magazines, Time spent $480 million in 1985 to purchase Southern Progress Corporation, publisher of *Southern Living* and other publications. In 1986 the company purchased and then shut down *Science 86* and *Science Digest* in order to reduce the competition faced by *Discover*, but it ended up selling that magazine a year later.

Time Warner's film business is based on the Warner Brothers studio, which was founded in the 1920s by four sons of a Polish immigrant couple. Warner, which produced the first talking feature film (*The Jazz Singer*, in 1927), gained a reputation for movies with social and political themes, although the studio also did its share of musicals. The company became a major owner of movie theaters while prospering from the work of stars ranging from Rin-Tin-Tin to Ronald Reagan and Bette Davis.

The studio went into decline in the 1950s and 1960s, and in 1969 it was acquired by Kinney National Service Corporation, a conglomerate built by Steven Ross beginning with funeral parlors and parking lots. Under its new parent, which renamed itself Warner Communications in 1971, the studio rebounded with hits like *The Exorcist* and *All the President's Men.*

In the mid-1980s the parent company rode an earnings roller coaster after acquiring video game producer Atari and fighting off a takeover attempt by Rupert Murdoch. Ross became embroiled in a long-running feud with his largest shareholder, Herbert Siegel, who had taken a 19-percent stake in the company (later increased to 29 percent) to fend off Murdoch. As a result of Siegel's pressures to streamline, Ross sold off the company's interests in the MTV and Showtime cable services.

During this time the Warner studio emerged as one of the most stable and best run in the movie industry. It was not known for giant hits but had a good number of successes. In 1989 Warner's film involvement was boosted with the acquisition of TV and movie producer Lorimar-Telepictures, the Hollywood highflier best known for giving the world the TV series "Dallas." During this period Warner enjoyed a rare smash hit with *Batman,* which lifted the studio to first place in market share.

Also in 1989, Time Inc. merged with Warner Communications to form Time Warner. The friendly merger started out as a stock swap, but after a last-minute competing bid was made for Time by Paramount Communications it became a cash deal in which Time had to take on some $10 billion in long-term debt. The company, then led by Ross (despite his sharing the chief executive's title with Time's N. J. Nicholas), insisted that it could manage the debt burden, but many outside observers believed that major asset sales would be necessary. A complex rights offering made by the company in 1991 to convert some of that debt into equity generated more criticism of Ross, who was already under fire for receiving compensation of more than $70 million the previous year.

Yet Time Warner still had ambitious global plans, symbolized by its decision to publish its 1990 annual report in six languages. By 1991 the company was actively pursuing nearly two dozen joint ventures and other relationships with media companies throughout Europe and Asia.

To help subsidize those efforts, Time Warner agreed to sell a 12.5-percent interest in its cable TV, cable programming, and film operations to a pair of Japanese companies—Toshiba and C. Itoh—in 1991.

Soon after the Japanese came in, Time Warner's president, Nicholas J. Nicholas, Jr., went out. Nicholas was supposed to succeed chairman Steven Ross as the supreme leader of the company. Ross, who was undergoing treatment for prostate cancer, decided to anoint a new successor—veteran Time Incer Gerald Levin.

Yet more damage began to occur in May 1992, when it was reported that Time Warner was negotiating with IBM on a plan to join Big Blue's computer technology with Time's entertainment operations. The focus of the plan, which reportedly involved a 12.5 percent investment by IBM in Time Warner's entertainment assets, was to be the creation of new multimedia products and services.

OPERATIONS

Magazine Publishing. Time has long been the most powerful force in the magazine business in the United States. Its *Time, Life,* and *Fortune* titles helped shape modern American reading habits and—especially before the rise of television—were major forces in molding public opinion.

Newsweeklies are no longer as influential as they once were, but *Time* still sells some 4 million copies per issue in the United States and about 1.5 million copies through its foreign editions. The monthly *Life,* also a less important publication than its weekly incarnation some decades ago, sells about 1.7 million copies. *Fortune,* with a rate base of some 780,000, still has prestige value, but it continues to face tough competition from *Business Week, Forbes,* and, indirectly, the wide variety of other business news sources.

Sports Illustrated, which represents the second generation of Time magazines (it was founded in 1954), was a money loser in its early years but has subsequently developed a wide following. It sells about three million copies a week. *People,* the company's popular celebrity publication, has about the same rate base. The personal finance magazine *Money* sells some 1.8 million copies a month. *Entertainment Weekly,* launched with great fanfare in 1990, has reached a rate base of seven hundred fifty thousand.

Time Warner's other magazines include those acquired as part of the purchase of Southern Progress Corporation—*Southern Living, Progressive Farmer, Southern Accents,* and others. In recent years the company also has purchased *Sunset: The Magazine of Western Living, Parenting, Health,* and *Hippocrates.* In addition the company owns the satirical magazine *Mad* and the DC line of comic books.

Time has equity interests in such publications as *American Lawyer, Working Woman,* and *Working Mother* in the United States; *AsiaWeek,* published in Hong Kong; *Elle Japon,* a Japanese edition of the French fashion magazine; *President,* a Japanese business magazine; and *Yazhou Zhoukan,* a news magazine aimed at the Chinese-speaking population of Asia living outside China. The company also owns 37 percent of Whittle Communications, which produces magazines for highly targeted audiences and has been promoting an advertiser-supported news program for distribution in schools.

Book Publishing. Both Time Inc. and Warner brought substantial book-publishing holdings to the merger of the two companies. The combined book operations are the fifth-largest book publisher in the United States, with some $977 million in revenues in 1990, according to the newsletter *BP Report.*

Time's units include Time-Life Books, the largest direct-mail distributor of books sold in a series format. Covering subjects from the Civil War to the occult, the series are heavily promoted on late-night television. Time also owns Little, Brown, a leading publisher of general books that was founded in 1837 and acquired by Time in 1968. Book-of-the-Month Club, established in 1926 by Harry Scherman, was bought by Time in 1978.

Warner Books, an aggressive publisher of mass market paperbacks, has gradually improved its presence in hardcovers. It had a runaway success in 1991 with *Scarlett*, the sequel to *Gone with the Wind*. Time Warner also owns Oxmoor House, the book-publishing arm of Southern Progress Corporation. The Scott, Foresman textbook operation, which Time bought in 1987, was sold to Harper & Row (now HarperCollins) in 1989.

Magazine and book publishing together contributed 24 percent of revenues in 1991.

Music (24 percent of revenues). Time Warner owns some of the leading labels in the recorded music business, including Warner Brothers, Atlantic, and Elektra. The company's music operations, which include music publishing, extend to more than fifty countries throughout the world. Among the artists distributed by the company are Paula Abdul, AC/DC, Tracy Chapman, Phil Collins, Madonna, Motley Crüe, Linda Ronstadt, and Paul Simon.

The company is involved in a fifty-fifty partnership with Sony Music Entertainment that engages in direct marketing of compact discs, cassettes, LPs, and videos in the United States and Canada. The company manufactures its music products in Olyphant, Pennsylvania; Terre Haute, Indiana; and two locations in Germany.

Filmed Entertainment (25 percent of revenues). In the film business Time Warner is represented by the Warner Brothers studio. In 1991 Warner was in first place among film majors, with a domestic box office market share of 13.9 percent. In recent years Warner has released more films per year than any other studio.

In January 1991 the company announced that it had entered into a long-term arrangement with the Dutch-owned Regency International Pictures, the French pay-TV company Canal Plus, and the German production and distribution firm Scriba & Deyhle. The three companies agreed to provide Time Warner with some $600 million to produce at least twenty movies for international distribution.

Warner operates a worldwide theatrical distribution organization, which includes both the company's own films and some produced by others. In 1991 the company announced the formation of a joint venture with Japanese retailer Nichii Company to construct the first multiplex movie theaters in Japan.

Time Warner also operates theaters in the United Kingdom, Australia, and Denmark; is in a joint venture with Paramount Communications that operates some five hundred screens in eight states; and has formed joint ventures for constructing and operating movie theaters in Germany, Portugal, Spain, Italy, and the former Soviet Union.

Time Warner participates in the television production business through both Warner Brothers and Lorimar-Telepictures. During the 1991–92 television season in the United States, Warner produced five network prime-time series and Lorimar produced thirteen.

Warner Home Video distributes prerecorded videocassettes and laser optical videodiscs containing films produced by Warner as well as those of others, including Pathe Communications, which in late 1990 entered into a long-term distribution agreement with Time Warner as part of Pathe's arrangements for purchasing MGM/UA Communications.

TV Programming (11 percent of revenues). Time Warner owns two of the largest pay-television services in the United States—Home Box Office and Cinemax. HBO, with 17.3 million subscribers at the end of 1991, gained enormous influence during the early 1980s when cable TV viewership was rising rapidly. HBO used its muscle to drive down the prices of the exhibition rights it was buying from the movie studios. Yet by the middle of the decade pay-TV growth was leveling off and the hot new area was videocassettes. HBO was no longer the terror of Hollywood. In 1991, as part of an effort to reduce the turnover rate among subscribers, the company announced plans to turn HBO and Cinemax into multichannel services.

Among the other ventures under the Home Box Office umbrella are CTV: The Comedy Network, a joint venture with Viacom International (formed after the two companies realized that their competing comedy channels could not survive); equity interests in the E! and Black Entertainment Television channels; various pay-per-view services; and a planned Spanish-language pay-TV service aimed at Latin America. Time Warner also owns an equity interest of about 22 percent in Turner Broadcasting System, parent company of Cable News Network and other cable services.

In 1991 the company announced plans for an advertiser-supported twenty-four-hour cable channel devoted to news of New York City.

Cable Television (16 percent of revenues). Time Warner not only provides programming for cable TV, but it also owns two of the largest cable-operating companies in the United States. American Television and Communications Corporation (ATV), the country's second-largest cable operator with some 4.6 million subscribers at the end of 1990, was acquired by Time in 1978. Warner Cable, previously a loss-ridden joint venture with American Express, had 1.9 million subscribers at the end of 1990. Time Warner is also in a joint venture to develop cable TV systems in Hungary.

The merger of Time and Warner gave the combined company a commanding—and to many observers, excessive—presence in some cities. In New York, for instance, both of Manhattan's franchises are held by the company, as are numerous others in the outer boroughs. Discontent with the quality of the company's service led to a difficult franchise renewal process in Manhattan in 1990. Yet the following year the company announced plans for upgrading a cable system in Queens to accommodate a record 150 channels and interactive services, such as electronic banking.

Other Interests. Time Warner is a partner in Six Flags Theme Parks, Inc., operator of seven amusement parks in the United States; and owns about 14 percent of the Hasbro toy company and 25 percent of Atari Corporation, maker of home computers and video games.

TOP EXECUTIVES

- Steven J. Ross, chairman and cochief executive
- Gerald M. Levin, president and cochief executive
- J. Richard Munro, chairman of the executive committee
- Martin D. Payson, vice chairman
- Bert W. Wasserman, executive vice president
- Peter R. Haje, executive vice president

OUTSIDE DIRECTORS

- Merv Adelson, chairman of East-West Capital Associates and former head of Lorimar-Telepictures
- Lawrence B. Buttenweiser, partner in the law firm of Rosenman & Colin
- Hugh F. Culverhouse, partner in the law firm of Culverhouse & Botts
- Michael Dingman, chief executive of the Henley Group
- Allan B. Ecker, partner in the law firm of Parker Duryee Rosoff & Haft
- Edward S. Finkelstein, former chairman of R. H. Macy & Company
- Beverly Sills Greenough, former president of the New York City Opera
- Benjamin D. Holloway, director of the Continental Companies
- Matina S. Horner, executive vice president of TIAA-CREF
- John R. Opel, chairman of the executive committee of IBM
- Richard D. Parsons, chief executive of Dime Savings Bank
- Donald S. Perkins, former chairman of Jewel Companies
- Raymond S. Troubh, former senior adviser to Salomon Brothers
- William J. Vanden Heuvel, counsel to Stroock & Stroock & Lavan

FINANCIAL DATA

Revenues (in millions of dollars)

1991	12,021
1990	11,517
1989	7,642

Net Income (in millions of dollars)

1991	−99 (loss)
1990	−227 (loss)
1989	−256 (loss)

Operating Income of Business Segments (in millions of dollars)

1991	1,154
1990	1,114
1989	848

GEOGRAPHICAL BREAKDOWN

Revenues (in millions of dollars)

Year	United States		Foreign	
1991	8,862	(74%)	3,159	(26%)
1990	8,550	(74%)	2,967	(26%)
1989	6,361	(83%)	1,281	(17%)

Operating Income (in millions of dollars)

Year	United States		Foreign	
1991	1,041	(90%)	113	(10%)
1990	1,035	(93%)	79	(7%)
1989	774	(91%)	74	(9%)

LABOR RELATIONS

Time Inc. was affected by the wave of unionization in the 1930s, but founder Henry Luce managed to keep his magazine operation an open shop. Moreover, the union that organized Time, the Newspaper Guild, was for many years content to play a rather passive role in its dealings with the company. As a reward the company allowed the guild's jurisdiction to be extended to Time-Life Books and the new magazines that were created.

The one serious conflict came in 1976, when magazine and book employees went on strike over the demand for guaranteed rather than merit raises. The strike ended in defeat in less than three weeks, after managers and strike-breakers succeeded in putting out the magazines without interruption.

During the 1980s both the company and the guild hardened their positions. Time sought to keep the staff of its *TV-Cable Week* venture outside union jurisdiction, but the magazine folded before the matter was resolved. In 1986, just as negotiations on a new contract were beginning, the company announced a cost-cutting program and took the unusual step of laying off employees. This set the stage for drawn-out contract talks, in which the guild resorted to such unusual tactics as urging employees to pressure management by delaying contributions to a company-sponsored United Way charity drive.

Since the merger with Warner, the guild has had to contend with additional cost cutting and further movement away from the company's traditional paternalism. After a new round of layoffs was announced at the magazines in 1991, guild members attended the company's annual meeting and suggested to chief executive Steven Ross that someone who had earned more than $70 million the previous year was in no position to demand austerity from the work force.

BIBLIOGRAPHY

Behlmer, Rudy, ed. *Inside Warner Brothers (1935–1951)*. New York: Viking, 1985.

Byron, Christopher. *The Fanciest Dive: What Happened When the Media Empire of TIME/LIFE Leaped Without Looking Into the Age of High-Tech*. New York: W. W. Norton, 1986.

Elson, Robert T. *Time Inc.: The Intimate History of a Publishing Enterprise, 1923–1941*. New York: Macmillan, 1968.

———. *The World of Time Inc.: The Intimate History of a Publishing Enterprise, 1941–1960*. New York: Macmillan, 1973.

Freedland, Michael. *The Warner Brothers*. New York: St. Martin's Press, 1983.

Prendergast, Curtis, and Geoffrey Colvin. *The World of Time Inc.: The Intimate History of a Publishing Enterprise, 1960–1980*. New York: Macmillan, 1986.

Swanberg, W. A. *Luce and His Empire*. New York: Charles Scribners' Sons, 1972.

TOSHIBA CORPORATION

1-1, Shibaura 1-chome
Minato-ku, Tokyo 105-01
Japan
(03) 3457-2104

1991 revenues: $33.4 billion (year ending March 31)
1991 net income: $859.5 million
Publicly traded company
Employees: 162,000
Founded: 1875

OVERVIEW

Toshiba Corporation is one of the Japanese, and thus world, giants in the fields of electronics and electrical equipment. Its product line in the latter area—ranging from locomotives and nuclear reactors to light bulbs—is similar to that of General Electric in the United States, with which Toshiba has had a long association. Yet while GE abandoned the computer and semiconductor businesses, Toshiba pushed ahead in both of these areas. The company is one of the leading memory chip producers and the top manufacturer of laptop computers.

Toshiba's reputation—already tarnished by frequent charges of dumping by U.S. competitors—was further blemished in 1987, when it was revealed that one of its subsidiaries had illegally sold sophisticated military-related machinery to the Soviet Union. Toshiba bashing was a popular sport in Washington for awhile, though the company soon recovered from the scandal and resumed selling a wide range of products in the United States, including some that were manufactured in American factories. In 1991 there were reports that Toshiba would follow the path of Sony and Matsushita and buy into Hollywood. But unlike the expensive takeovers by those companies, Toshiba's plan turned out to be more limited. It and trading company C. Itoh each

654

invested $500 million in debt-laden Time Warner, the parent company of movie studio Warner Brothers, *Time* magazine, and many other entertainment and media operations.

HISTORY

Toshiba's roots go back to 1875, when inventor Hisashige Tanaka founded a company to make telegraphs and other electrical gear. The company, later renamed Shibaura Seisaku-sho, began producing steam engines, dynamos, and related equipment, growing into one of Japan's leading producers in the field.

Another branch of the company originated in 1890, when Ichisuke Fujioka and Shoichi Miyoshi began producing light bulbs under the name Hakunetsu-sha (meaning "White Heat"). The operation, incorporated in 1896 and retitled Tokyo Denki (Tokyo Electric Company) in 1899, went on to make such innovations as the first incandescent coiled bulb, the first frosted bulbs, and Japan's first X-ray equipment.

In 1939 Tokyo Denki and Shibaura merged to form Tokyo Shibaura Denki, or Toshiba for short. The combined company emerged as a leader in the production of televisions and equipment for industrial and office automation.

After World War II the company, with backing from the Mitsui Group, rebuilt its operations and entered new fields. During the 1950s and early 1960s Toshiba developed one of the first Japanese computers, the country's first transistor radio, and its first nuclear turbine power plant. Toshiwo Doko, chairman of the large shipbuilding company IHI, was brought in to head Toshiba in 1963, a time when problems in the Japanese economy were depressing the electrical company's profits. Doko retained his chairmanship of IHI and created close links between the shipbuilder and Toshiba.

Doko arranged for a new infusion of capital from the U.S. company General Electric, which had had ties to Toshiba for decades. He also began to orient Toshiba to export markets. In 1965 Toshiba America, for instance, was established in New York, with branches in Chicago, Los Angeles, San Francisco, and Hawaii. It was in the 1970s, however, that the company became a world-class exporter, especially of televisions and microwave ovens. The company also joined the trend among Japanese firms of producing goods in the United States. A manufacturing facility in Lebanon, Tennessee, was opened in 1978 to produce color televisions and later was expanded to make microwave ovens.

Toshiba got involved in more-sophisticated products as well. It was one of the five companies chosen by the Japanese government to make what turned out to be a successful push into the semiconductor market. Toshiba eventually rose past rival Hitachi to take second place among world chip makers, behind NEC. The company's advance in this field has been aided by strategic alliances, such as those formed with LSI Logic and Motorola. Toshiba also has emerged as a producer of advanced medical equipment, especially for the Japanese market.

Another field in which Toshiba has excelled is laptop computers. The processing power and speed, along with the easier-to-read gas plasma screen, of its top models made them into some of the most popular of the lightweight PCs. Their prices, however, were less popular after the Reagan administration imposed substantial tariffs on Japanese laptops in 1987. The move was made in response to what the administration saw as the failure of the Japanese semiconductor companies to adhere to a trade agreement.

Toshiba's progress along the path to marketing success in the West hit another major roadblock in 1987, when it was reported that one of its subsidiaries, Toshiba Machine, had illegally shipped milling tools to the Soviet Union that could be used for making submarine propellers more difficult to detect. The revelation caused a political uproar in the United States, then still in the grips of neo–cold war fever. Politicians called press conferences to smash Toshiba products with sledge hammers and the Senate voted to ban the company's products from the United States for five years.

In the end the sanctions were far less severe, but the scandal did prompt the resignations of Toshiba's president, Sugiichiro Watari, and its chairman, Shoichi Saba. The new president, Joichi Aoi, purged the management of Toshiba Machine and established new review procedures for sensitive exports.

The company rebounded from the scandal and its laptops rose to a strong first-place position in the U.S. market. Toshiba introduced the first portable with a color screen and has been a major user of longer-lasting nickel-hydride batteries. Yet the company's leadership in this field is in question because it has not moved quickly enough into the lighter notebook-type machines that have become so popular. Another blow was a decision by the U.S. International Trade Commission in 1991 to impose penalties against Toshiba and several other Japanese companies for dumping flat-panel display screens used in laptops.

Toshiba has continued its strategy of forming alliances with Western companies. One of the most significant of these arrangements was a new joint venture with General Electric announced in 1991. The pact covered development and marketing of refrigerators, washing machines, dishwashers, and other home appliances. Toshiba also has continued its foreign manufacturing operations, announcing, for instance, in 1991 that it would construct its first plant (to make parts for televisions and VCRs) in China.

OPERATIONS

Information and Communications Systems and Electronic Devices (50 percent of 1991 revenues). This segment actually consists of two subsections and a total of nine divisions within them. Under the rubric of information and communications systems there are:

- information-processing equipment and systems (computers, workstations, word processors, printers, optical character readers, copiers, and fax machines);
- telecommunications equipment (digital PBXs, telephones, packet-

switching systems, broadcasting transmitters, radar systems, and runway lighting);
- space-related products (broadcasting satellites and satellite broadcast receiving stations);
- control and instrumentation systems;
- medical equipment (CT scanners, ultrasound, magnetic resonance imaging, and X-ray equipment); and
- automation equipment (letter- and package-sorting systems, automatic fare collection systems, automatic tellers, and point-of-sale systems).

Toshiba's electronic devices include:

- semiconductors;
- electron tubes; and
- printed circuit boards.

In 1990 Toshiba and Motorola announced that as part of their technology-sharing agreement the companies would jointly produce the next generation of (4-megabit) memory chips. The following year Toshiba entered into an alliance with Siemens to develop and market RISC-type microprocessors.

Heavy Electrical Apparatus (20 percent of revenues). This segment consists of equipment for nuclear, thermal, geothermal, and hydroelectric power plants; industrial control equipment; electric locomotives, mass transit control systems, elevators, and escalators; and machine tools, precision machinery, semiconductor-manufacturing equipment, and plastic-fabricating machines.

Consumer Products and Other Activities (30 percent of revenues). Included in this segment are such products as televisions, VCRs, camcorders, audio equipment, air conditioners, vacuum cleaners, refrigerators, microwave ovens, light bulbs and fixtures, clinical thermometers, prefabricated housing, and a variety of materials (like alloys, ceramics, and resins).

TOP EXECUTIVES

- Joichi Aoi, chairman
- Fumio Sato, president
- Kinichi Kadono, senior executive vice president
- Keiichi Komiya, senior executive vice president
- Tsuyoshi Kawanishi, senior executive vice president

FINANCIAL DATA

Revenues (in millions of yen) (years ending March 31)

1991	4,695,394
1990	4,251,953
1989	3,800,857
1988	3,572,435
1987	3,307,593

Net Income (in millions of yen) (years ending March 31)

1991	120,852
1990	131,836
1989	119,402
1988	60,711
1987	34,178

GEOGRAPHICAL BREAKDOWN

Sales (in millions of yen)

Year*	Domestic		Foreign	
1991	3,240,621	(69%)	1,454,773	(31%)
1990	2,907,634	(68%)	1,344,319	(32%)
1989	2,582,072	(68%)	1,218,785	(32%)

*Fiscal year ends March 31.

LABOR RELATIONS

After World War II three different labor federations arose to represent Toshiba's employees. Resisting a company plan for large-scale layoffs, Toshiba workers staged a strike against the company in 1946. U.S. military police joined with local authorities in dislodging a group of workers who were sitting in at one of the company's facilities. The strike was crushed, but the unions did end up getting some concessions from the company.

Today Toshiba has an orderly relationship with its unions, but there are some workers who feel they are getting less than vigorous representation. During the early 1980s a Toshiba worker named Ueno Hitoshi began to circulate a newsletter that expressed dissatisfaction with the union leadership, with workplace conditions, and with the danger of the nuclear reactors he was helping to build. Management harassed Hitoshi for his dissent, and union leaders supported the company in its efforts to intimidate and isolate him.

When a more aggressive union leadership emerged at the Toshiba-Ampex joint venture operation, the Japanese management moved in 1982 to shut down the magnetic tape plant. A group of fifty-eight workers kept the factory running on their own and brought suit against the company. After five years of legal proceedings, a labor relations board ordered Toshiba to reopen the plant. Instead the two sides reached a settlement in which the company agreed to pay back wages while the workers agreed to resign as Toshiba employees. The worker-run plant went on to produce alternative products, such as a portable loudspeaker system for use in political demonstrations.

Toshiba was a pioneer among the Japanese companies that have pushed British unions into accepting single-union, no-strike agreements. In the United States Toshiba is one of the few Japanese companies to have a collective-bargaining relationship with a union. Since 1980 workers at the company's electrical appliance plant in Lebanon, Tennessee, have been represented by the International Brotherhood of Electrical Workers. In 1989 the union staged a two-week strike at the plant before reaching a settlement on a new three-year contract that included modest pay increases and improvements in pension and medical benefits. Replacement workers hired during the walkout were terminated when the dispute was settled.

ENVIRONMENTAL RECORD

Toshiba gets poor marks from environmentalists because of its involvement in the production of nuclear reactors, even though it also makes equipment for geothermal and hydroelectric power. In 1991, however, the company did its bit for the environment by announcing a new cleaning product for printed circuit boards, developed jointly with Sharp Corporation, that does not contain ozone-destroying CFCs. Toshiba has vowed to cease its own use of CFCs by the end of the 1990s.

BIBLIOGRAPHY

Anchordoguy, Marie. *Computers, Inc.: Japan's Challenge to IBM*. Cambridge, Mass.: Harvard University Press, 1989
Sobel, Robert. *IBM vs. Japan: The Struggle for the Future*. Briarcliff Manor, N.Y.: Stein & Day, 1985.

TOYOTA MOTOR CORPORATION

1, Toyota-cho
Toyota City, Aichi Prefecture 471
Japan
(0565) 28-2121

1991 revenues: $71.6 billion (year ending June 30)
1991 net income: $3.1 billion
Publicly traded company
Employees: 102,423
Founded: 1937

OVERVIEW

If *Fortune* is to be believed, Toyota Motor Corporation is "the best carmaker in the world" and "keeps getting better." Toyota has won such accolades because it has become a seemingly unstoppable force in the world auto industry. After overtaking the likes of Chrysler, Fiat, and Volkswagen in the 1970s, Toyota is expected to zoom past Ford in the mid-1990s and may even threaten the leading position of General Motors.

The reason for this is that Toyota has won the loyalty of millions of drivers around the world, but especially in the all-important U.S. market. Only a few years after being laughed out of that market in the early 1960s, Toyota returned with new cars that began selling by the tens of thousands and later the hundreds of thousands. Some of Toyota's thunder was stolen by Honda in the 1980s, but the company has fought back with a dazzling array of new products, including the well-received Lexus luxury line.

Although traditionally not a technological leader in the auto industry, Toyota has been at the forefront of improvements in production methods. It pioneered the famed *kanban* (just-in-time) system for managing the flow of parts, considered one of the secrets of Japanese industrial success.

<u>HISTORY</u>

Toyota emerged indirectly out of the work of Sakichi Toyoda, a famed Japanese inventor. In 1926 Toyoda established a company to market an automatic loom he had created. Three years later he sold the rights to his machine to Platt Brothers, the British company that was then the leader of the textile machinery industry.

Toyoda gave the proceeds from the sale, ¥ 1 million (the equivalent of around $460,000), to his son Kiichiro, who was also an inventor but who had grown interested in an area other than spinning and weaving. The younger Toyoda, then in his mid-30s, had become enamored of motor cars, and his father encouraged him to explore the business possibilities of the field. Kiichiro used the ¥ 1 million, plus whatever else he could get after his father's death from Toyoda Automatic Loom, then run by his brother-in-law, to develop a prototype for a small passenger car. In 1933 Toyoda was allowed to establish an automotive division within the loom company and set out to improve his car through some reverse engineering from various American models.

The prospects for the car business were substantially improved by the protectionist policy adopted by the Japanese government in 1936. This prompted Toyoda to spin off the auto operation into an independent company called Toyota Motor the following year. There are a variety of stories about why the spelling of the family name was changed, ranging from the claim that Toyota was easier to pronounce to numerological superstitions concerning the number of calligraphic strokes required to write the names.

If the hope was that the new name would be luckier for auto production, that did not immediately turn out to be the case. The government suspended passenger car production in 1939 and Toyota was compelled to devote its attention to trucks, a situation that continued through World War II.

After the war Toyota benefited from the fact that although it had ties to Mitsui, it was not a direct subsidiary of one of the *zaibatsu* conglomerates that U.S. occupation authorities were dismantling. Unlike Nissan, Toyota was able to retain its top executives. Although Nissan had more experience in making automobiles, Toyota was ready with its own product, the Toyopet, when Japan's first postwar cars were introduced in 1947. The company underwent dramatic changes a few years later, including a major labor dispute over job eliminations and the splitting off of the marketing operation into a separate company (Toyota Motor Sales), but Toyota began to move ahead of Nissan as the 1950s began.

That lead grew during the remainder of the decade as Toyota Motor Sales built a formidable dealer network, including different dealers for different product lines. The company also cultivated customers by investing in a string of driver education schools, which, of course, provided instruction in Toyota cars. Toyota Motor Sales was also the first in the Japanese car industry to make installment plans widely available to customers.

Toyota Motor Sales soon began looking abroad for market growth, and in

1957 a small American subsidiary was established in California. However, like the Datsuns of the time, the company's Toyopets were ill suited to U.S. roads, because their small engine and relatively weak chassis could not stand up to prolonged high-speed driving. It was not until the mid-1960s, when Toyota returned with new cars—first the Corona and then the Corolla—that it started to gain a position of any significance in the U.S. market.

Toyota's U.S. sales took off in the late 1960s, and by 1971 the company was selling nearly three hundred thousand cars a year in that country. The rise in demand for compacts following the oil price increases of 1973–74 gave the company an even bigger boost. By the end of the decade its U.S. car sales were more than half a million units. Toyota was growing elsewhere in the world as well. It zoomed past Fiat, Chrysler, and Volkswagen to assume the number-three spot in the world auto industry, trailing only General Motors and Ford.

After reabsorbing the sales company in 1982, Toyota Motor followed the path of other Japanese automakers in deciding to initiate production in the United States. While Honda and Nissan established their own plants, Toyota began by forming a joint venture with General Motors. The plan, announced in 1983, was for the two companies to cooperate on producing a subcompact car at a GM factory in Fremont, California. The car was to be built using Toyota's manufacturing and personnel practices.

While GM received a fair amount of criticism over the joint venture, which took the name New United Motor Manufacturing Inc., Toyota was seen by many as the savior of auto production in the United States. While it had the upper hand, Toyota decided to go a step farther and open its own American assembly operation, in Georgetown, Kentucky. The step was part of Toyota's "Global 10" strategy, a plan to increase its share of world vehicle production from about 8 to 10 percent.

Toyota pursued that goal in part by going upscale. Like Nissan, it created a new line of luxury cars, called Lexus, that began to encroach on the market that traditionally had been dominated by German car makers like Mercedes-Benz and BMW. Toyota's top-of-the-line Lexus LS 400 got off to a good start in the U.S. market, despite some technical problems that led to a recall. Between its pricey vehicles and its less-expensive ones, Toyota sold more than a million cars and trucks in the United States during the 1990 model year.

Another target was the European market. Toyota announced plans to open an assembly plant and an engine factory in Britain as well as a European design center in Belgium. Business, meanwhile, continued to boom in Japan, where the company's biggest problem was finding enough workers to staff its busy factory. In the United States, while American automakers were cutting back, Toyota announced that it would build another assembly plant in Kentucky, at a cost of $800 million. The company also brought out a flashier version of the Camry to compete directly against Honda's Accord and, Toyota hoped, allow it to seize U.S. market leadership away from Honda.

OPERATIONS

Motor Vehicles, Parts, and Components. Toyota, the third-largest car maker in the world, sold some 3.7 million passenger cars and nearly 900,000 trucks and buses in its 1991 fiscal year. Foreign sales accounted for 43 percent of the car sales and 57 percent of the truck and bus sales. By far the company's largest export market is North America, where it sells more than one million vehicles a year. Production facilities are located in Japan (mostly in the Toyota City area in Aichi Prefecture), the United States, Canada, Brazil, New Zealand, Thailand, and more than a dozen other countries where Toyota licenses its technology or else is a minority partner with local interests. In 1992 Toyota formed a design and engineering joint venture with General Motors in Australia.

Industrial Vehicles and Other Operations. The company is one of the world's leading producers of forklifts and is a major supplier of automatically guided vehicles and other equipment for factory automation systems. Also included in this segment, which accounts for less than 10 percent of sales, are a prefabricated-housing business and equity stakes in various telecommunications ventures, including cellular telephone companies in Tokyo and other Japanese cities. Toyota also has minority interests in a group of companies involved in textile machinery, specialty steel, machine tools, auto parts, synthetic resins, and other fields.

TOP EXECUTIVES

- Eiji Toyoda, chairman
- Shoichiro Toyoda, president
- Masamai Iwasaki, executive vice president
- Shiro Sasaski, executive vice president
- Tatsuro Toyoda, executive vice president
- Shohei Kurihara, executive vice president

FINANCIAL DATA

Revenues (in millions of yen) (years ending June 30)

1991	9,855,132
1990	9,192,838
1989	8,021,042
1988	7,215,798
1987	6,675,411

Net Income (in millions of yen) (years ending June 30)

1991	431,450
1990	441,301
1989	346,262
1988	310,952
1987	260,704

GEOGRAPHICAL BREAKDOWN

Net Sales (in millions of yen)

Year*	Japan		Foreign	
1991	5,714,685	(58%)	4,140,447	(42%)
1990	5,400,100	(59%)	3,792,700	(41%)
1989	4,907,100	(61%)	3,113,900	(39%)
1988	4,449,600	(62%)	2,766,200	(38%)

*Fiscal year ends June 30.

LABOR RELATIONS

After the end of World War II the U.S. occupation authorities encouraged the establishment of new trade union organizations in Japan. One of these was the All-Japan Automobile Industry Labor Union, known as Zenji. U.S. officials instituted deflationary measures in 1949 that prompted the major auto companies to eliminate thousands of jobs. Zenji protested these actions, to no avail, but at Toyota the conflict over the issue was serious enough that president Kiichiro Toyoda had to resign to restore labor peace.

In 1953 Zenji was on the offensive again, demanding substantial wage gains in contract negotiations. Toyota and Isuzu reached compromises with the union, but Nissan stood firm, which led to a three-month strike (and later lockout) that ended when Nissan management successfully persuaded many workers to ally themselves with a new, less militant union. In the wake of the defeat, Zenji collapsed, and company-oriented unions took over at all of the major automakers.

Union-management relations at Toyota have been harmonious since then, but that does not necessarily translate into total job satisfaction on the shop floor. In 1972 a journalist named Satoshi Kamata took a job as a temporary worker at a Toyota plant and later published a book that described the workplace as a "factory of despair" because of the punishing pace of the assembly line and the strict regimentation.

When Toyota and General Motors established their New United Motor Manufacturing Inc. (NUMMI) joint venture in 1983, the two companies agreed to accept the United Auto Workers as the collective-bargaining representative of the employees even before anyone had been hired. Deciding that cooperation was called for, the UAW signed a contact with NUMMI that provided a high degree of management control over the workplace. Yet like Toyota's domestic plants, the NUMMI facility has been criticized for overworking its employees. Some critics began to talk of the NUMMI system as "management by stress."

When Toyota decided to set up its own manufacturing operation in Kentucky in the mid-1980s, the company did not extend the welcome mat to the UAW. Toyota was successfully pressured to use union labor in the construction of the plant, but the production work has remained nonunion.

Toyota has been the subject of complaints that it discriminates against Americans in hiring for higher levels in its U.S. operations. In August 1991 a manager who had worked for Toyota's U.S. technical center for ten years testified before a congressional committee that he had been denied a promotion to a top administrative position because he had complained about the preferential treatment given to Japanese employees.

Toyota made it clear that it wanted a cooperative union in the plant it planned to establish in Britain. It obtained such an arrangement from the single-union pact signed with the Amalgamated Engineering Union in 1991. The factory was scheduled to begin production in 1992.

ENVIRONMENTAL RECORD

Toyota has not made the kind of innovations achieved by Honda and Nissan in improving engine design to cut down on polluting emissions. The company has, however, done some research on electric vehicles and engines that run on a combination of methanol and diesel fuel. Its NUMMI joint venture in the United States demonstrated enough sensitivity to environmental issues to win an award from the Bay Area Earth Day Committee.

BIBLIOGRAPHY

Cusumano, Michael A. *The Japanese Automobile Industry: Technology and Management at Nissan and Toyota*. Cambridge, Mass.: Harvard University Press, 1985.

Gelsanliter, David. *Jump Start: Japan Comes to the Heartland*. New York: Farrar, Straus & Giroux, 1990.

Kamata, Satoshi. *Japan in the Passing Lane: An Insider's Account of Life in a Japanese Auto Factory*. New York: Pantheon Books, 1983.

Maxcy, George. *The Multinational Automobile Industry*. New York: St. Martin's Press, 1981.

Sobel, Robert. *Car Wars*. New York: E. P. Dutton, 1984.

Toyoda, Eiji. *Toyota: Fifty Years in Motion*. Tokyo and New York: Kodansha International, 1987.

UNILEVER

Parent companies:

Unilever NV
Burgemeester s'Jacobplein 1
3015 CA Rotterdam
Netherlands
(10) 464-5911

Unilever PLC
Unilever House
Blackfriars
London EC4P 4BQ
United Kingdom
(071) 822-5252

1991 revenues: $40.8 billion
1991 net income: $2 billion
Publicly traded company
Employees: 292,000
Founded: 1885

OVERVIEW

Unilever, one of the leviathans of the global packaged goods industry, is a peculiar English-Dutch hybrid enterprise. The two Unilever companies are supposed to be of roughly equal size, they report consolidated financial results, and they have identical boards of directors. The chairman of one is the vice chairman of the other, and those two men, along with an heir apparent from one of the companies, constitute a ruling body called the Special Committee.

Unilever's roots are in the Lever Brothers soap business in Britain and the leading margarine producers in Holland—two parts of the fats and oils industry that merged in 1929. In the following decades the company expanded into a wide range of foods, cleaning materials, personal products, and, most recently, perfumes and cosmetics. Unilever is a dominant presence in virtually all corners of the world. Its United Africa Company subsidiary, owned since 1929, is itself a large multinational within a multinational.

The United States has been a tough nut for Unilever to crack, especially since its archrival, Procter & Gamble, led the way in the development of synthetic detergents and has ruled the American packaged goods business ever since. Unilever has, however, made some substantial U.S. acquisitions in recent years and has endeavored to become a more important force in the world's largest consumer market.

HISTORY

William Hesketh Lever spent his early adulthood in the 1870s working for his father's wholesale grocery business in Lancashire. In the course of mastering the trade, he became fascinated with soap, which at the time was still in the process of changing from a luxury item to a necessity for a wider portion of the population (largely because of the smoke and grime of industrial society).

Lever commissioned soap makers to produce supplies according to his specifications for resale under a private brand. One of his favorite items was a soap made from oils rather than tallow; he called it Sunlight Self-Washer Soap. Deciding he could do better making the soap himself, Lever and his brother James took over a soap works in 1885. Within a few months they were producing twenty tons of the cleaning material every week. In 1889 the company moved its operations to Port Sunlight, a combination factory and planned community constructed by the Levers in Lancashire across the Mersey River from Liverpool.

The soap business grew rapidly in the following years, and the Lever Brothers company expanded its sales operation to Holland, Belgium, South Africa, Australia, Canada, and the United States; later manufacturing and raw material production were begun overseas as well. In 1894, the year the firm went public, it introduced Lifebuoy, a household soap containing carbolic acid, giving it disinfectant qualities. Five years later it brought out soap flakes, which were slow to catch on but then took off when sold (with heavy advertising) under the name Lux.

In the early years of the new century, Lever Brothers and Britain's other soap makers banded together to divide up markets and fix prices. The cozy arrangement was in existence for only a few years when it was disrupted by an upheaval in the raw materials market brought about by the increasing use of tallow and oils by makers of margarine and lard. The soap companies, led by Lever, responded by considering even closer integration of their operations—that is, the formation of a combine. Yet once the plans were discovered by the press, there was a big public uproar over what were seen as the sinister plans of the soap trust.

The companies decided to abandon the merger plan, but Lever accomplished much the same result by beginning to acquire many of its competitors, both small and large, individually. At the same time, the company took greater control of its supply of raw materials (copra, palm, and others) by establishing plantations and trading posts in Africa and the South Seas. By the eve of World War I Lever Brothers and its subsidiaries were producing more than 60 percent of all soap consumed in the United Kingdom.

The outbreak of war raised concerns in Britain about the cutoff of certain food supplies from the Continent, so in 1914 the government asked Lever Brothers to begin making margarine. The company did so in a joint venture called Planter's Margarine Company with Joseph Watson & Sons (in which Lever owned an interest). After the war Lever Brothers resumed buying up competitors and expanding its raw materials holdings.

The biggest change in the company came in 1929, when D'Arcy Cooper, who became chairman after William Lever's death four years earlier, agreed to merge with a cartel formed by the Dutch companies Jurgens and Van den Bergh. Both of those firms had begun as butter merchants in Holland early in the nineteenth century. During the 1870s the two rivals began dealing with the recently developed butter substitute initially known as butterine and then margarine. The spreadable fat had been invented by French chemist Mège Mouriès in 1869 in response to a call from Napoleon III for a less expensive alternative to butter.

In 1908, amid a period of slumping prices for the Dutch companies, Jurgens and Van den Bergh signed an agreement pooling their profits from the margarine business. The arrangement remained in effect, at least on paper, for nearly two decades, although relations between the partners often were less than friendly. They finally decided that greater consolidation might resolve the differences, so in 1927 they merged into an organization comprised of two holding companies—Margarine Unie NV in Holland and Margarine Union in Britain—that had identical boards and would share profits equally. The dual structure avoided double taxation from the governments of the two countries.

Soon after the Margarine enterprise had been created, its leaders decided to approach Lever Brothers with a plan to reduce competition between the two. The first proposal was that Margarine Unie/Union should buy Lever's margarine business, Planters. To this Lever responded by proposing that it acquire the holding companies' soap interests in Holland and France. This led to negotiations that culminated in a decision in 1929 to merge Lever with Unie/Union while preserving the dual-country structure. Thus were born Unilever Ltd. and Unilever NV.

The depression of the 1930s had a substantial impact on the new companies, necessitating the creation of a special committee to closely coordinate the operations of the two Unilevers. When trade disruptions in Continental Europe began to erode the financial position of Unilever NV, some of the assets of Unilever Ltd. were transferred to it to maintain the goal of nearly equal revenues and profits in the Dutch and British firms.

During the German occupation the Dutch government in exile expropriated, as a protective measure, all Dutch property outside Holland and named Unilever Ltd. as the custodian of the foreign assets of Unilever NV. The latter firm operated, with much difficulty, under Nazi supervision, while in Britain Unilever Ltd. had to convert many of its operations to the production of government-issue commodities.

After the war the Dutch and British Unilevers were reunited and the old arrangement was resumed. Yet the companies faced a severe shortage of fats and oils. To cushion the effect of that problem Unilever began moving further into new lines of business, especially foods, perfumes, and toothpaste. The company hastened to develop its research operations, scrambling in particular to catch up with the new detergents—the first of which was Procter & Gamble's Tide—that were replacing soap for washing clothes.

While Unilever lost ground to Procter & Gamble in the United States, it benefited from the recovery of Europe and the growing demand for personal-care products in many countries of the world. In some of those countries Unilever used its dual nationality to get around political problems—for example, presenting itself as British when the Indonesian government was nationalizing Dutch companies in 1958.

It was not until the 1980s that Unilever began to take steps to confront Procter & Gamble's dominance in the American market. The task was formidable, given that the U.S. subsidiary, Lever Brothers Company, had essentially been drifting for a decade. Many of its primary U.S. products—including All and Wisk detergents, Aim and Pepsodent toothpastes, and Dove and Lifebuoy soaps—had market shares half or less of those of Procter & Gamble's competing products. Unilever ranked first or second in sales of products like shampoos, ice cream, and frozen food in much of the world but was hardly a factor in those markets in the United States.

In addition to reviving the marketing effort and manufacturing process for existing products, Unilever went shopping for new American properties to add to previous acquisitions, such as its purchase of National Starch & Chemical in 1978. It made a takeover bid for cold remedy maker Richardson-Vicks in 1985 but was defeated by Procter & Gamble. But the following year it won a battle for Chesebrough-Pond's Inc.—maker of Vaseline, Q-tips, and Ragú spaghetti sauce—for $3.1 billion. In 1989 Unilever propelled itself to the top tier of the world cosmetics and perfume industry by purchasing the Fabergé and Elizabeth Arden lines from Meshulam Riklis for $1.6 billion as well as the Calvin Klein fragrance operation from Minnetonka for $306 million. Yet its old nemesis Procter & Gamble leaped ahead in 1991 by acquiring the Max Factor line (and its German operation Betrix) from Revlon.

OPERATIONS

Food Products (51 percent of 1991 revenues). Unilever is the world's largest producer of margarine and is the market leader in many countries around the world; it also sells a wide range of cooking fats and table oils. The second major product group here covers frozen foods and ice cream. Unilever produces frozen foods under the Birds Eye brand in the United Kingdom and under the name Iglo in most other European countries. It sells ice cream under the brand name Wall's in Britain, Good Humor in the United States, and Langnese and Ola in Europe.

Under the names Lipton and Brooke Bond, Unilever is also a leading tea producer. Other food products include Cup-a-Soup instant soups, salad dressings, mayonnaise, meat products, and Ragú spaghetti sauce.

Detergents (23 percent of revenues). Unilever manufactures detergents and other cleaning and washing products in some forty countries. It is the largest producer in Europe and the market leader in several other places. Aside from washing powders, this segment includes bathroom soap (in which Unilever is the world leader, with such brands as Lux, Dove, and Shield), other personal washing products, and household cleaners. In 1991 Unilever agreed to buy an 80-percent stake in Polish detergent maker Pollena Bydgoszcz. The company's new Lever 2000 soap—which is supposed to moisturize, deodorize, and kill bacteria—was introduced in the United States with a huge marketing blitz in 1991, and it soon reached the number two spot among deodorant soaps in that market.

Personal products (12 percent of revenues). This segment includes toothpastes (Signal, Aim, Close-up, Pepsodent, and others), deodorants and antiperspirants (for which Unilever is the world leader, with such brands as Rexona and Impulse), skin- and hair-care products (Vaseline lotions and petroleum jelly, Sunsilk shampoo), and cosmetics and fragrances (Fabergé, Elizabeth Arden, and Calvin Klein).

Specialty Chemicals (8 percent of revenues). The company's U.S.-based National Starch & Chemical subsidiary is a leading producer of adhesives, food starches, and industrial starches. It also makes resins and specialty organic chemicals for industrial use. Its customers include paper, packaging, textiles, plastics, electronics, and other industries. In 1992 National Starch entered the intensely competitive market for fat substitutes with a line of six products to be sold under the N-Lite brand.

Other Operations (6 percent of revenues). This segment includes the company's palm oil, tea, rubber, cocoa, and coconut plantations in Africa, India, Southeast Asia, and South America; an animal feed business in Britain; a salmon-farming business in Scotland and Chile; Unipath medical diagnostic products; and fish-processing facilities in Germany.

TOP EXECUTIVES

- Floris A. Maljers, chairman of Unilever NV and vice chairman of Unilever PLC; member of the Special Committee

- Michael Perry, chairman of Unilever PLC and vice chairman of Unilever NV; member of the Special Committee
- Morris Tabaksblat, vice chairman of Unilever NV; member of the Special Committee
- Niall W. A. FitzGerald, detergents coordinator
- Christopher M. Jemmett, agribusiness coordinator
- Antony Burgmans, personal products coordinator
- Iain Anderson, chemicals coordinator

OUTSIDE (ADVISORY) DIRECTORS

- Frits H. Fentener van Vlissingen, member of the supervisory council of Amsterdam-Rotterdam Bank
- Lord Haslam of Bolton, former chairman of British Coal
- Brian Hayes, former permanent secretary of the U.K. Department of Trade and Industry
- François-Xavier Ortoli, former chairman of the French company Total
- Donald E. Petersen, former chief executive of Ford Motor
- Karl Otto Pöhl, former president of Deutsche Bundesbank
- Romano Prodi, professor of economics at the University of Bologna and former president of the IRI Group
- H. Onno Ruding, vice chairman of Citicorp
- Dieter Spethmann, chairman of the executive board of Thyssen Duisburg
- Patrick Wright, former permanent under secretary of state at the U.K. Foreign and Commonwealth Office

FINANCIAL DATA

Revenues (in millions of U.S. dollars)

1991	40,767
1990	39,620
1989	33,444
1988	30,980
1987	30,948

Net Income (in millions of U.S. dollars)

1991	2,030
1990	1,634
1989	1,629
1988	1,510
1987	1,459

GEOGRAPHICAL BREAKDOWN

Revenues (in millions of U.S. dollars)

Year	Europe		North America		Elsewhere	
1991	24,225	(59%)	8,393	(21%)	8,149	(20%)
1990	24,169	(61%)	8,247	(21%)	7,204	(18%)
1989	19,581	(59%)	7,414	(22%)	6,449	(19%)
1988	18,673	(60%)	6,189	(20%)	6,118	(20%)

Operating Profit (in millions of U.S. dollars)

Year	Europe		North America		Elsewhere	
1991	2,185	(62%)	595	(17%)	739	(21%)
1990	2,193	(60%)	647	(18%)	810	(22%)
1989	1,619	(53%)	739	(24%)	719	(23%)
1988	1,603	(58%)	509	(19%)	631	(23%)

LABOR RELATIONS

William Lever considered himself an enlightened capitalist, so the industrial community he constructed in the late 1880s at Port Sunlight was designed to include attractive housing for workers and other amenities. Working conditions in the factory were good, relative to the standards of the time, and the company instituted a profit-sharing plan for its employees. It later added free life insurance and forms of unemployment insurance and disability pay.

Starting in 1909 there were works committees of employees at Port Sunlight and joint works councils on which both labor and management were represented. Yet there were also a variety of unions representing various groups of Lever Brothers workers. Labor relations were fairly harmonious and strikes were few.

In more recent years, however, there have been disputes in Britain over the company's use of subcontractors. A 1990 dispute at a Birds Eye–Wall's frozen foods plant involved a company attempt to impose new work rules. Some twelve hundred workers walked off the job and were quickly replaced by strikebreakers. This prompted the workers to call off the strike after a month and accept the company's conditions.

The record has been mixed in other countries. In the United States Unilever signed a companywide agreement with the International Chemical Workers Union in 1946. Today it has good relations with both that union and the Oil, Chemical and Atomic Workers as well as several other unions.

In the third world, however, the company often has taken an antiunion position. A 1984 gathering in London of Unilever workers from half a dozen countries heard some dismaying reports. In India, for example, there had been "almost constant strife" between labor and management. Among the complaints of the Indian workers were incidents in which union activists had been fired and the practice of keeping a substantial part of the work force in contingent status so that they could be paid less and deprived of benefits.

In 1988 workers at the Hindustan Lever plant in Bombay were locked out by management, which demanded that wages be tied to productivity. Only after a year were the workers allowed to return to their jobs, and this was followed, union officials say, by a period of harassment and intimidation of labor activists.

In 1985 the International Union of Food and Allied Workers (IUF), an umbrella organization for trade unions from around the world, staged a demonstration of some thirty-five hundred Unilever workers from ten countries at the company's annual meeting in Rotterdam. The purpose was to protest a corporate reorganization that management had planned without negotiating with unions on the consequences for workers. The IUF has continued to hold periodic meetings of Unilever workers from around the world.

ENVIRONMENTAL RECORD

Unilever, along with the other producers of detergents, found itself at the center of controversy in the late 1950s over the residues its cleaning products left in waterways. Such pressure prompted Unilever to introduce biodegradable detergents in the mid-1960s.

Thirty years later Unilever was making another alteration in its detergent products to address (in part) environmental concerns. This time the innovation was superconcentrated detergents, which began to appear in U.S. stores at the beginning of the 1990s. The superconcentrates, which require less powder per load of laundry, are thus sold in smaller quantities, meaning that less packaging is used.

Unilever also is promoting conservation by encouraging the U.S. suppliers of its containers to use recycled plastics. In 1990 the company opened a research center in Maryland to develop packaging that is less harmful to the environment.

BIBLIOGRAPHY

Fieldhouse, David K. *Unilever Overseas: The Anatomy of a Multinational.* Stanford, Calif.: Hoover Institution Press, 1979.

Reader, W. J. *Fifty Years of Unilever.* London: Heinemann, 1980.

Social and Labour Practices of Multinational Enterprises in the Food and Drink Industry. Geneva: International Labour Office, 1989.

Wilson, Charles. *The History of Unilever: A Study in Economic Growth and Social Change.* 3 vols. New York: Frederick A. Praeger, 1968.

UNITED TECHNOLOGIES
CORPORATION

United Technologies Building
Hartford, Connecticut 06101
(203) 728-7000

1991 revenues: $20.8 billion
1991 net income: − $1 billion (loss)
Publicly traded company
Employees: 185,100
Founded: 1925

OVERVIEW

One of the last remaining powerful conglomerates in the United States, United Technologies Corporation (UTC) is the parent company of Pratt & Whitney, one of the most famous names in jet engines; Sikorsky Aircraft, a leader in helicopter production; Carrier Corporation, the largest supplier of heating and air-conditioning systems; and Otis Elevator.

UTC, which began with the amalgamation of various aviation companies during the 1920s, has had severe ups and downs over the years, especially at Pratt & Whitney. The engine maker once ruled the industry, then suffered a series of technical mishaps and fell behind competitors like General Electric, and recently has begun to rebound. Sikorsky, the second-most-important part of UTC's large military business, was in a slump until 1991, when it and Boeing were chosen to supply a new combat helicopter for the U.S. Army.

The company's building systems operations have been affected by the recession of the early 1990s, but Otis, for instance, with contracts to service more than half a million elevators and escalators, continues to rake in revenues. Otis also has taken some bold steps to expand in Eastern Europe and the former Soviet Union.

HISTORY

United Technologies began with the commitment of Frederick Rentschler to making better airplane engines. While serving in the Army Signal Corps during World War I, Rentschler ended up inspecting engines at the pioneering Wright-Martin Aircraft Company (later Wright Aeronautical). He stayed on after the war and eventually worked his way up to the presidency. Frustrated with the preoccupation of the company's directors with short-term profitability, in 1924 he resigned and set out to form a company of his own to build powerful air-cooled engines of a type that the U.S. Navy had indicated interest in.

Rentschler was able to achieve his goal with the help of Edward Deeds, a business friend of his father, and George Mead, chief of engineering at Wright. Deeds was chairman of machine tool company Niles Bement Pond, which owned a Connecticut gun company called Pratt & Whitney. Established in 1860, Pratt & Whitney had prospered making arms for the Union army during the Civil War. The two founders, Francis Pratt and Amos Whitney (a cousin of Eli Whitney), went on to become international arms merchants, but by 1901 they were getting old and decided to sell out to Niles.

The new owner pushed Pratt & Whitney to focus on making machine tools for manufacturing weapons rather than the weapons themselves. This strategy paid off, and by World War I Pratt & Whitney was an important military contractor. After the armistice, however, the company lost most of its business and was looking for new ventures. Deeds persuaded his fellow Niles board members (who included Rentschler's brother Gordon, the president of the company) that Rentschler's engine plan made perfect sense for Pratt & Whitney.

Everyone agreed, and in 1925 Pratt & Whitney Aircraft was formed, half owned by Pratt & Whitney, which put up $250,000 for development and turned over its idle machine tool plant in Hartford to Rentschler. After only six months Pratt & Whitney turned out the first Wasp engine for the navy. The admirals were pleased and, encouraged by the recent recommendation of the presidentially appointed Morrow Board that the military make long-term procurement commitments, they ordered two hundred of the engines.

Having established Pratt & Whitney with the military, Rentschler turned to the civilian sector. The aircraft makers and carriers were starting to grow as a result of federal incentives provided by airmail contracts. Rentschler formed an alliance with William Boeing, the son of a lumberman, who had started building planes in 1916. The result was the Boeing 40A, which started out as a fighter but was adapted and became a popular airmail carrier. During this period, Rentschler, who made extensive use of subcontractors to keep up with demand, also began to export engines.

Pratt & Whitney was a thriving operation, making a profit of some $2 million on the sale of nearly one thousand engines. Also prospering were Boeing's operations, which included both building planes (with Pratt Wasp engines) and flying them on various airmail routes. Their mutual success encouraged Rentschler and Boeing to join forces and make even more money. In line with the financial consolidation that was spreading throughout American business at the time, they formed a holding company in 1928, which, under the name United Aircraft and Transport Corporation, soon became the largest aviation company in the world.

It was also one of the most profitable companies in the world, at least for Rentschler and Boeing. They and the principals of the other firms that were brought under the umbrella, including Sikorsky Aviation and the Hamilton propeller company, exchanged stock in their own firms for the rapidly appreciating shares of the holding company and enjoyed massive gains.

United Aircraft, which in 1930 bought some additional carriers and formed United Airlines, became an increasingly dominant force in U.S. aviation, especially after Boeing introduced its 247 in 1933. That lead, however, evaporated after Donald Douglas came out with his remarkable DC-2.

The industry was turned upside down in 1934, when the consolidation that had been encouraged by postmaster Walter Folger Brown came under attack after the Roosevelt administration took office. The result was the passage of the Air Mail Act of 1934, which mandated both a ban (that turned out to be short-lived) on private transport of airmail and a requirement that aircraft producers and air transport companies be separated from one another.

This meant that the United Aircraft behemoth had to be partially dismantled. United Airlines and Boeing's manufacturing operation were spun off, and the United Aircraft Company name was used as the parent firm for what remained, which included Pratt & Whitney, Hamilton Standard, Sikorsky Aviation, and Chance Vought.

United survived a series of embarrassing congressional hearings and controversy over its dealings with Japan to play a major role in the great airplane production push during World War II. Pratt & Whitney expanded its manufacturing facilities enormously in 1939 and began turning out huge numbers of engines, first for the French government and then for the British. The company had more orders than it knew what to do with; still, it was slow in ending its relationships with companies in Germany, Japan, and Italy.

In the United States, President Roosevelt made a bold call in May 1940 for the construction of fifty thousand airplanes a year—at a time when the military's total fleet was under three thousand. United's divisions, like the rest of the aircraft industry, were jolted into high gear (and high profitability). Pratt & Whitney was chosen as the primary engine maker for the navy, Hamilton Standard had a near monopoly on propellers, and a huge contract for observation planes was granted to Vought and Sikorsky. The company was excluded from early work on jet engines, but Sikorsky was given military funding to develop helicopters.

After the end of the war United was faced with the sudden loss of most of its revenues. Yet, unlike other aviation executives, who began diversifying their operations, Rentschler was confident that civilian and military demand would soon rebound. The advent of the cold war (and later the Korean War) and the revival of commercial air transport bore him out. At first United depended mainly on the military, concentrating on the production of the jet engines that were rapidly replacing piston engines in the Pentagon's fleets.

Pratt & Whitney was slow in making the conversion to jets in its civilian business. One problem was that some of its customers were uncomfortable dealing with a company that was tied to a competing airframe maker, namely Chance Vought. So in 1954 Vought was spun off (and later became part of LTV). Pratt & Whitney shot ahead when the J-57 engine it originally had built for the military was enthusiastically accepted by the aircraft makers and the airlines that were entering the age of civilian jet travel. In 1958 United branched into avionics with the purchase of Norden-Ketay Corporation, producer of sophisticated components for most of the Pentagon's missiles.

While continuing to expand its military activities, United also maintained its lead in the civilian engine area, largely through a close association with Boeing. In the early 1960s the Seattle company introduced its 727 jet, which was powered almost exclusively by Pratt & Whitney, and later in the decade, when Boeing was prompted by Pan American to build huge planes that would become known as jumbo jets, it looked to Pratt to supply the power plants (as engines are called in the industry).

The final design of the planes turned out to be considerably heavier than Boeing had intended, and this put much greater demands on the engine Pratt & Whitney was developing. When the 747 began flying it experienced frequent problems with engines overheating, and the jumbos often had to be taken out of service. The repair costs, borne by United, ran to several hundred million dollars. This, along with problems relating to work on the F-111 fighter, caused the company in 1971 to report its first net loss since 1934.

United's board brought in Harry Gray, the number-three man at the Litton Industries conglomerate, to try to fix the damage. Gray's efforts were made more difficult by yet more problems the company was having with an engine, this time the F100, which was being developed for a joint air force–navy program. The power plant was stalling and even exploding during tests, but the military was so eager for the engines that it lowered its standards to allow Pratt & Whitney to pass. When the problems persisted, the navy dropped out of the joint procurement plan, and the company was starting to run up major expenses in fixing the engines supplied to the air force, which gave money to Pratt & Whitney's rival, General Electric, to develop an alternative product.

Meanwhile, Gray was pursuing his goal of turning the company (which he arranged to rename United Technologies in 1975) into a conglomerate like Litton. His first major move in this regard was the 1975 takeover of the venerable Otis Elevator. Gray was outbid for nuclear reactor maker Babcock-Wilcox by J. Ray McDermott & Company, but in 1979 he snared Ambac, a producer of diesel fuel injection systems; Carrier Corporation, a leading supplier of heating and air-conditioning systems; and Mostek, which made semiconductors (this company was shut down in 1985 in the face of intense competition from the Japanese).

While Gray was out shopping, Pratt & Whitney was losing ground in the commercial arena as well as the military arena. Part of the problem was the success of Airbus Industrie in taking business away from the leading U.S. airframe makers, Boeing and Douglas. Airbus, a European consortium, initially decided to get its power plants from General Electric. In 1984 the company suffered another blow when both the air force and the navy turned to GE for major fighter plane engine contracts.

Pratt & Whitney sought to stabilize itself by joining the trend toward international cooperation among engine makers. In 1974 General Electric had created a joint venture with the French Société Nationale d'Étude et Construction de Moteurs d'Aviation (SNECMA). By the mid-1980s such partnerships were the only way new engines were being developed. The biggest combination was International Aero Engines, formed in 1983 by Pratt & Whitney, Rolls Royce, and companies from Japan, Italy, and West Germany.

International Aero stumbled in its development of engines for the Airbus A340, allowing GE-SNECMA (now known as CMF International) to fill the void. GE also shot ahead of Pratt & Whitney in their individual efforts. Starting in the mid-1980s Pratt lost its thirty-year lead in the engine business as a result of poor planning and a deteriorating reputation for quality and service.

Robert Daniell, who took over United Technologies after Harry Gray reluctantly retired, set out to revive the company by cutting costs, including the elimination of thousands of jobs. He also sought to change the corporate culture from the autocratic atmosphere that prevailed under Gray to one that encouraged team building, "worker empowerment," and closer relationships with customers.

Presumably aided by Daniell's reforms, Pratt & Whitney began to regain lost ground in 1989, especially with its powerful PW4000 engine, although the company's market share was still far behind the commanding 90 percent it had held in the 1970s.

That progress was put into question in early 1990, when GE announced plans for the GE90, which at eighty thousand pounds of thrust would be even more powerful than the PW4000. One of GE's partners on the GE90 was supposed to be a Daimler-Benz subsidiary, Motoren- und Turbinen-Union (MTU). But only a few months after the announcement of the GE90, Pratt, which had worked with the German company on a limited basis since the early 1970s, formed a closer alliance with MTU, which then had to end its relationship with GE. Later that year, however, Pratt & Whitney and GE announced plans to work together on a new commercial supersonic engine.

In 1991 Pratt & Whitney, GE, Rolls Royce, and SNECMA were chosen by the Japanese government to work on an engine that could enable a plane to fly five times the speed of sound. That same year, Pratt & Whitney's new F119 engine was chosen by the U.S. Air Force to power the Advanced Tactical Fighter—a contract that over time could be worth $12 billion. United Technologies, hit hard by the recession and the decline in military spending, received another piece of good news: a team headed by Boeing and United's Sikorsky division was chosen to build a new generation of combat helicopters for the army.

All of this suggests that United Technologies, despite its long-running problems, will remain a major player in the world aerospace game. Whether its current chief executive remains part of that activity is not as certain. The *Wall Street Journal* reported in 1991 that Robert Daniell was being investigated as part of an ongoing probe of corruption among Pentagon contractors.

The future is also uncertain for many of the company's production workers. In January 1992 United Technologies announced that, because of reduced military spending, the company would eliminate nearly fourteen thousand jobs by 1995.

OPERATIONS

Power (34 percent of 1991 revenues). This segment consists of Pratt & Whitney's engines and parts. On the commercial side this includes the JT8D-200 used in the Douglas MD-80; the PW2000 used in the Boeing 757; and the PW4000 used in the Boeing 747 and 767, the Douglas MD-11, and the Airbus A300 and A310. The International Aero Engines consortium, of which Pratt & Whitney is a member, produces the IAE V2500, which is used in the Airbus A320.

For the military Pratt & Whitney makes the F100 engine used in the air force's F-15 and F-16. The F117, to be used by the air force C-17, was scheduled to begin operation in 1992.

Flight Systems (19 percent of revenues). Included in this segment are the operations of Sikorsky Aircraft, Hamilton Standard, Norden Systems, and Space Propulsion and Systems. Sikorsky, one of the world's leading producers of helicopters, currently makes the Black Hawk for the U.S. Army and derivatives for foreign governments; the Seahawk for antisubmarine warfare missions for the U.S. Navy and derivatives for overseas sales; the Jayhawk recovery helicopter for the U.S. Coast Guard; and others.

Hamilton Standard makes engine controls, flight controls, and propellers for commercial and civilian aircraft. It also makes the space suits used by astronauts on the space shuttle. Norden makes radars, electronic systems, and antisubmarine warfare systems for the U.S. and foreign governments. The Space Propulsion business involves work on launch systems for Titan missiles and commercial rockets.

Building Systems (38 percent of revenues). The two main units in this segment are Carrier Corporation and Otis Elevator Company. Carrier is the world's leading producer of residential and commercial heating, ventilating, and air-conditioning (HVAC) systems. That position, however, is being eroded by strong competition from Japanese producers of air conditioners and by sagging demand for HVAC systems in the United States.

Otis, the world's leading name in elevators, makes lifts, escalators, and moving sidewalks. It derives a substantial portion of its revenues from the service contracts it holds for more than 700,000 people-moving devices. Otis has been building a presence in the former Soviet bloc. In 1990 the company bought a majority interest in Berliner Aufzugs- und Fahrtreppenbau (BAF), an elevator company in what used to be East Berlin. Otis also has formed joint ventures with Russian elevator makers in Moscow and Leningrad.

Automotive Products (10 percent of revenues). This segment includes automotive wire systems and harnesses, instrument panels, door panels, and electromechanical devices used for automotive ignition, emission control, and lighting. In 1989 the company completed its purchase of Sheller-Globe, a major supplier of steering wheels, instrument panels, and other automotive products.

TOP EXECUTIVES

- Robert F. Daniell, chairman and chief executive
- George A. L. David, president and chief operating officer
- John A. Rolls, executive vice president and chief financial officer
- Irving B. Yoskowitz, executive vice president and general counsel

OUTSIDE DIRECTORS

- Howard H. Baker, Jr., partner in the law firm Baker Worthington Crossley Stansberry & Woolf, former U.S. senator, and former White House chief of staff
- Antonia Handler Chayes, senior consultant to Endispute Inc.
- Robert F. Dee, retired chairman of SmithKline Beckman
- Charles W. Duncan, former U.S. secretary of energy
- Pehr G. Gyllenhammar, executive chairman of Volvo
- Gerald D. Hines, owner of the real estate development firm Gerald D. Hines Interests
- Robert H. Malott, chief executive of FMC Corporation
- Richard S. Smith, retired vice chairman of National Intergroup
- Jacqueline G. Wexler, retired president of the National Conference of Christians and Jews

FINANCIAL DATA

Revenues (in millions of dollars)

1991	20,840
1990	21,442
1989	19,532
1988	18,000
1987	17,170

Net Income (in millions of dollars)

1991	−1,021 (loss)*
1990	751
1989	702
1988	659
1987	592

*Reflects a pretax restructuring charge of $1.275 billion and a $256 million pretax charge to increase environmental reserves.

GEOGRAPHICAL BREAKDOWN

Revenues (in millions of dollars)

Year	United States		Europe		Elsewhere	
1991	14,201	(64%)	4,121	(19%)	3,908	(18%)
1990	15,020	(66%)	3,986	(17%)	3,854	(17%)
1989	14,467	(69%)	3,101	(15%)	3,389	(16%)

Operating Profit (in millions of dollars)

Year	United States		Europe		Elsewhere	
1991	−1,034	(0%)	370	(67%)	184	(33%)
1990	909	(51%)	524	(29%)	349	(20%)
1989	881	(55%)	360	(22%)	375	(23%)

LABOR RELATIONS

The majority of workers at Pratt & Whitney have long been represented by the International Association of Machinists (IAM). Relations between the union and management traditionally were adversarial but peaceful. A major exception came in December 1985, when thousands of workers struck the company to demand improved job security provisions and a better wage package than the company was offering. The two-week walkout ended with an agreement that improved worker protections regarding subcontracting and other job security issues. As a result of a decertification of the IAM and the United Auto Workers in the wake of a 1960 strike, most workers at Sikorsky Aircraft are represented by the Teamsters.

Since 1987 the Sheet Metal Workers International Association has used a variety of in-plant tactics in lieu of striking in support of contract demands at Carrier Corporation. The union attributed the success of the 1988 negotiations to that campaign. Similar solidarity tactics were employed during the 1991 round of talks.

ENVIRONMENTAL RECORD

United Technologies has come under federal scrutiny for its handling of PCBs, which are suspected carcinogens. In 1989 the EPA filed a complaint against the company alleging various violations of PCB regulations; two years later the company agreed to pay $730,000 to settle the charges.

In 1991 United Technologies was the target of the largest criminal fine ever levied for a hazardous waste violation. In response to charges brought by the EPA, the company agreed to plead guilty to six felony violations and pay a fine of $3 million in connection with illegal dumping of toxic wastes at the Sikorsky Aircraft operation in Stratford, Connecticut. The EPA's complaint included the charge that the in-house environmental officer had called attention to the dumping (which involved oil, transmission fluid, and industrial solvents) in 1982, but the company had done nothing to correct the situation.

Responding to pressure to end the use of ozone-destroying CFCs, Carrier Corporation in 1991 announced plans for a cryogenic cooling system. The helium-based technology, first developed by nineteenth-century Scottish inventor Robert Sirling, has recently been rediscovered as part of the campaign to eliminate CFCs. The Carrier product was intended for cooling large computers, medical diagnostic machines, and other devices.

BIBLIOGRAPHY

Adams, Gordon. *The Iron Triangle: The Politics of Defense Contracting*. New York: Council on Economic Priorities, 1981.

Biddle, Wayne. *Barons of the Sky*. New York: Simon & Schuster, 1991.

Bluestone, Barry, Peter Jordan, and Mark Sullivan. *Aircraft Industry Dynamics: An Analysis of Competition, Capital and Labor*. Dover, Mass.: Auburn House, 1981.

Douglas, Donald W. *Wings for the World: The DC Family in Global Service*. New York: Newcomen Society, 1955.

Fernandez, Ronald. *Excess Profits: The Rise of United Technologies*. Reading, Mass.: Addison-Wesley, 1983.

Gansler, Jacques S. *The Defense Industry*. Cambridge, Mass.: MIT Press, 1980.

Horner, H. M. *The United Aircraft Story*. New York: Newcomen Society, 1958.

IMF Guide to World Aerospace Companies and Unions. Geneva: International Metalworkers Federation, 1987.

Newhouse, John. *The Sporty Game*. New York: Alfred A. Knopf, 1982.

Rae, John B. *Climb to Greatness: The American Aircraft Industry, 1920–1960*. Cambridge, Mass.: MIT Press, 1968.

Shaw, Linda, et al. *Stocking the Arsenal: A Guide to the Nation's Top Military Contractors*. Washington, D.C.: Investor Responsibility Research Center, 1985.

VOLKSWAGEN AG

W-3180 Wolfsburg 1
Germany
(5361) 92 44 88

1991 revenues: $50.4 billion
1991 net income: $735.3 million
Publicly traded company
Employees: 260,137
Founded: 1937

OVERVIEW

Volkswagen has gone from being the "people's car" pet project of Adolf Hitler to a symbol of the 1960s counterculture to one of the world's most aggressive automakers. For thirty years after World War II Volkswagen (VW) produced an unchanging compact car that became affectionately known as the Beetle or Bug. Eventually the allure of that functional car wore off, and VW had to scramble to keep its position in the top tier of auto companies.

VW did recover in Europe, where it reached first place in a close race with Italy's Fiat, but the German company has had repeated disappointments in the United States, where it opened the first foreign-owned auto assembly plant in 1978, only to close it a decade later.

VW is determined to remain an industry leader, however, and toward that end it has made a series of bold (though expensive) investments in recent years that have given it important footholds in Spain, Czechoslovakia, China, and what used to be East Germany.

HISTORY

The concept for a "people's car" originated in the mind of Ferdinand Porsche, a pioneering auto designer who worked for the Austrian subsidiary of the

Daimler Motor Company, one of the earliest producers of motor vehicles. Inspired by Henry Ford's success in making cars available to a much wider portion of the population, Porsche fought against the idea that automobiles were a luxury to be enjoyed only by the upper classes.

In 1931 Porsche went into business for himself, setting up a shop in Stuttgart to develop prototypes of small, inexpensive cars. Making such vehicles available to the German masses was one of the promises Adolf Hitler made soon after he got himself named chancellor of the country in 1933.

Porsche, who is said to have had little interest in politics, simply saw Hitler's rise as an opportunity to pursue his dream. He met with Hitler and came away with a subsidy equal to that being given to Daimler-Benz, a larger company formed by the 1926 merger of the operations of two German auto pioneers. Hitler, a car enthusiast, took a personal interest in the development of the *Kleinauto* (small car), to the extent of giving Porsche specifications on its gas mileage, cooling system, and other features.

Porsche struggled to design a car that would meet the designated price of 900 marks (about $360), which was about 40 percent lower than what he had initially considered to be the break-even figure. He also had to contend with the fact that the other German automakers privately thought that the führer's *Kleinauto* plan was mad and had no intention of seeing it succeed. When Porsche finally delivered three prototypes of what was now, in 1936, being called the *Volksauto*, the other companies subjected them to brutal testing, apparently hoping to find them unfit.

By this time Hitler was fed up with the industry's resistance. In 1937 he ordered the creation of the Volkswagen Development Company and put Porsche (along with some Nazi officials) in charge. Porsche quickly modified his prototypes—which had such later-to-be-famous features as the sloping hood and beetlelike shape—so that what was now termed the *Volkswagen* was ready for production.

Porsche had all of the resources of the Nazi government at his disposal, but he needed to travel to the United States for some specialized equipment and to enlist skilled personnel from among the German-American community. Back home, the car was promoted by a Nazi-dominated worker recreational organization called Kraft durch Freude (Strength through Joy). The KdF encouraged all workers to participate in a plan that had everyone paying five marks a week toward the eventual purchase of the *Volkswagen*. Soon tens of thousands of workers were putting aside what in the aggregate was a substantial sum every week for a product that did not yet exist in significant numbers.

The plan was to build the Volkswagen factory in the rather remote region of Lower Saxony, where ten thousand acres of land were commandeered from the local aristocracy to accommodate the production facility and housing for a huge work force. Hitler himself laid the cornerstone for the project on May 26, 1938—in between annexing Austria and invading Czechoslovakia—with a bombastic ceremony involving some seventy thousand people. In his dedication speech Hitler decreed that the car would be called the KdF-Wagen.

Yet as Walter Nelson notes in his book *Small Wonder*, a 1965 history of Volkswagen, "no one, except obdurate Nazis, ever called it that."

The onset of World War II forced Porsche to modify the Volkswagen into a military vehicle called *Kübelwagen* (Bucket car) with an amphibious version called the *Schwimmwagen* (Floatable car). Then, in 1944, the Volkswagen factory was hit by a series of Allied bombings, which did extensive damage. Not a single civilian vehicle had been produced.

After the collapse of the Nazi regime, the heavily damaged Volkswagen plant was put under British supervision; gradually the place was repaired and production resumed. By October 1946 it had turned out ten thousand cars.

Porsche himself was first detained, then released and given an offer by the French to help produce a people's car for sale in France. Then he was arrested again, reportedly at the instigation of the big French auto companies, which were threatened by the plan. He was imprisoned for several years and died in 1951.

Meanwhile, in Wolfsburg (the town created around the Volkswagen plant), new life was brought to the factory with the naming of Heinz Nordhoff, an experienced auto engineer, to head the operation in 1948. Although Henry Ford II had passed up a chance to take over the plant—advisers had told him that it was worthless—Nordhoff saw great potential in the company, and he worked hard to improve the quality of its products. (The issue of who owned the company, however, remained ambiguous until 1960, when it was designated a publicly traded corporation, with 40 percent owned by the federal and local governments.)

Volkswagen grew along with the recovery of the German economy. In the mid-1950s Nordhoff branched out into other vehicles, such as the famous Microbus and, with the help of the coach builder Karmann and Italian designer Ghia, a sporty version of the VW "Bug" called the Karmann-Ghia. Overall during that decade, VW's output leaped from 90,000 to 697,000 vehicles a year. By the early 1960s Volkswagen had become one of the world's largest auto producers; it ranked third when Chrysler had a bad year and otherwise was fourth.

Nordhoff was aggressive in developing new markets. Exports to Denmark, Sweden, Belgium, and other countries began in 1948, and deliveries of knocked-down cars to Ireland and Brazil started two years later. Production facilities would open in Brazil in 1959.

Volkswagen first tried to export to the United States in the late 1940s—with little success, since the big chrome boats of Detroit ruled the roads. Through the early 1950s the company slowly built an American market by selling to nonconformists, and by the latter part of that decade the demand for small cars like the VW Beetle had grown enough to prompt Detroit to introduce its own compact models. Many imports lost ground, but VWs developed a kind of cult following, created in part by a series of unorthodox advertising campaigns with slogans like "Ugly is only skin deep" and "Think small." During the 1960s the now rapidly selling Beetle became a counterculture symbol.

Production of the Beetle peaked in the late 1960s, and soon it was clear to the company, which recently had purchased the Audi operation from Daimler-Benz, that it was time for a change. VW introduced a new generation of cars—Passat in 1973 and Scirocco and Golf in 1974—but intensified international competition, especially from the Japanese, caused the company to lose ground. An attempt to win a bigger market share in the United States, through an assembly plant in Pennsylvania that was opened in 1978, had disappointing results. (It finally was abandoned in 1988.)

It was not until the mid-1980s, with the introduction of the new Golf, which underpriced the Japanese, that VW recovered and jumped to first place among the European auto producers. The Golf, however, like its predecessor, the American-made Rabbit, did not go over big in the United States. VW's strong European position was enhanced in 1986, when it purchased a majority interest in Spain's Sociedad Española de Automóviles de Turismo (SEAT). That same year, VW and Ford Motor agreed to merge their money-losing operations in Brazil and Argentina into a new company called Autolatina Ltd.

In 1987 VW had to contend with a scandal regarding its handling of foreign currency as well as a controversy in the United States over the safety of its luxury Audi 5000S, which was said to have a tendency to accelerate on its own. At the same time, union opposition prevented the company from transferring production of its Polo compact to lower-wage SEAT plants in Spain.

VW has nevertheless continued its international expansion. It was an early entrant into Eastern Europe—in 1984 it struck a deal to use engines made in East Germany in its Polos. By 1990 VW was beginning construction of a $1.9-billion assembly plant in the former German Democratic Republic. In late 1990 the Czech government chose Volkswagen to be a partner with Škoda, the leading Czech automaker, which was being converted from a state-owned to a publicly traded company. The decision was a victory for VW—which committed more than $6 billion over a number of years in exchange for a 70-percent stake—over rival bidder Renault.

In 1991 VW introduced the third generation of its Golf (the best-selling car in Europe), which was used to launch a new effort by the company to improve its market share around the world, including the United States. Also in 1991, VW formed a second Czech joint venture with Bratislavske Automobilove Zavody (BAZ) to make transmissions and assemble a limited number of complete cars. VW signed, along with Ford Motor, a $2.8-billion agreement with the Portuguese government under which the companies will produce a new multiple-purpose vehicle in that country for the European market. All of this is in addition to VW's $1-billion commitment for an auto plant in China.

OPERATIONS

Volkswagen derives virtually all of its revenues from the production and sale of motor vehicles and parts. Its main operating units are Volkswagen AG and

Audi AG in Germany, SEAT in Spain, a joint venture with Ford in Brazil and Argentina called Autolatina, and manufacturing subsidiaries in Belgium, Yugoslavia, Nigeria, South Africa, Mexico, and China.

The company's leading models are the VW Golf, Passat, Polo, and Jetta; the Audi 80/90 and 100/200; and the SEAT Ibiza and Marbella.

TOP EXECUTIVES

- Carl H. Hahn, chairman of the board of management (until the end of 1992)
- Ferdinand Piëch, chairman of the board of management (beginning in 1993)
- Daniel Goeudevert, member of the board of management
- Günter Hartwich, member of the board of management, production
- Werner P. Schmidt, member of the board of management, overseas business and sales strategy

OUTSIDE DIRECTORS

- Rolf Diel, chairman of the supervisory board of Dresdner Bank AG
- Walter Hiller, minister for social affairs of Lower Saxony
- Hans-Günter Hoppe, former member of the Berlin Senate
- Walther Leisler Kiep, general partner in Gradmann & Holler
- Otto Lambsdorff, president of Deutsche Schutzvereinigung für Wertpapierbesitz e. V. (German stockholders' association)
- Klaus Liesen, chairman of the management board of Ruhrgas AG
- Günther Sassmannshausen, member of the supervisory board of Preussag AG
- Friedrich Schiefer, managing director of Robert Bosch GmbH
- Gerhard Schröder, president of the state of Lower Saxony
- Ulrich Weiss, member of the board of management of Deutsche Bank

The supervisory board, which represents shareholders and labor, also includes nine representatives elected by the employees of the company.

FINANCIAL DATA

Revenues (in millions of deutsche marks)

1991	76,315
1990	68,061
1989	65,352
1988	59,221
1987	54,635

Net Income (in millions of deutsche marks)

1991	1,114
1990	1,086
1989	1,038
1988	780
1987	598

GEOGRAPHICAL BREAKDOWN

Revenues (in millions of deutsche marks)

Year	Germany		Rest of Europe		Elsewhere	
1991	36,360	(48%)	26,825	(35%)	13,130	(17%)
1990	26,929	(40%)	26,680	(39%)	14,451	(21%)
1989	23,682	(36%)	26,595	(41%)	15,075	(23%)

LABOR RELATIONS

Since the early 1950s Volkswagen's German operations have followed paternalistic policies, such as profit sharing, extensive benefits, and provisions for transferring older workers to less-strenuous jobs. This, along with legal requirements for union representation on the company's supervisory board, created a relatively cooperative relationship with labor.

VW found a less compliant labor force when it opened its assembly plant in the United States in 1978. Workers were unhappy that they were being paid less than their counterparts at the large American auto producers, and six months after the plant opened, they launched a wildcat strike. Even their union, the United Auto Workers, which had negotiated the wage rates with VW, was caught off guard. Stopping production of the Rabbit, the workers chanted, "No Money, No Bunny."

The workers eventually returned to the job, but labor relations at the plant remained tense as the UAW pressured the company to narrow the wage gap. VW also was confronted with a lawsuit charging that it discriminated against black employees.

Faced with intensified competition and eroding market share in the late 1980s, VW's German operations turned to the powerful union IG Metall and asked for cost savings of more than $1 billion, equal to 13 percent of VW's labor bill. The union resisted the concessions and by 1990 had negotiated a contract with a 6-percent wage increase and a gradual reduction in the work-week.

Along with Germany, there is extensive union presence at VW's operations in such countries as Belgium, Brazil, Mexico, and South Africa. Brazilian employees of VW's Autolatina joint venture staged job actions in 1991 to protest plans by VW and its partner Ford Motor to eliminate thousands of jobs.

ENVIRONMENTAL RECORD

VW prides itself on being concerned about the environment. It introduced the first diesel engine with a catalytic converter and has started a pilot program at one of its facilities for disassembly of abandoned vehicles. In 1991 VW formed a joint venture with the Swiss watch company SMH to produce a low-cost, electric-powered car. VW was already testing a prototype of its Golf model with a hybrid motor that runs on electric power in urban areas and diesel power when higher acceleration is needed for longer journeys.

BIBLIOGRAPHY

Hopfinger, K. B. *Beyond Expectation: The Volkswagen Story*. London: G. T. Foulis, 1954.

Maxcy, George. *The Multinational Automobile Industry*. New York: St. Martin's Press, 1981.

Nelson, Walter Henry. *Small Wonder: The Amazing Story of Volkswagen*. Boston: Little, Brown, 1965.

Nitske, W. Robert. *The Amazing Porsche and Volkswagen Story*. New York: Comet Press Books, 1958.

Sobel, Robert. *Car Wars*. New York: E. P. Dutton, 1984.

The Volkswagen File. Geneva: International Metalworkers Federation, 1986.

WASTE MANAGEMENT, INC.

3003 Butterfield Road
Oak Brook, Illinois 60521
(708) 572-8800

1991 revenues: $7.6 billion
1991 net income: $606.3 million
Publicly traded company
Employees: 64,000
Founded: 1968

OVERVIEW

Waste Management, Inc., which has been called "the king of garbage," is
the largest waste collection and disposal company in the world. Barely a
quarter of a century old, Waste Management has taken an industry that used
to be dominated by small, often Mafia-connected operators and turned it into
a multi-billion-dollar business operating in nearly twenty countries.

Waste Management has achieved a spectacular rate of growth and is far
and away the leader in its field—a field that remains small because most
companies are scared off by the formidable regulatory and political problems
of the business. Waste Management is not afraid of regulators or controversy.
The company has hardly been distracted by the wave of litigation that has
been brought against it. It has been investigated by more than a dozen grand
juries and frequently has found itself indicted, sued, or cited for violations
of environmental rules. Among the most frequent charges are price-fixing,
bribery, and improper handling of hazardous substances.

Yet Waste Management has taken steps to improve its image, including
hiring environmentalists and putting one on its board, making substantial
contributions to some environmental groups, and heavily promoting the company's involvement in recycling. Given the omnipresence of waste and toxic
substances, the company presents itself as a necessary and even environmen-

tally correct service; "Helping the world dispose of its problems" is its motto. Indeed, given the way most of the world makes things and consumes them, it is likely that Waste Management will continue to be one of the leading growth companies of the age.

HISTORY

Waste Management had its origins in a Chicago trash-hauling company called Ace Scavenger Service, a descendant of the first garbage collection company in the city—Huizenga & Sons, founded in the late nineteenth century. In 1956 Dean L. Buntrock, who had married a member of the Huizenga family, was asked to take over the company, which then operated twelve collection trucks and had less than $1 million in annual revenues. Buntrock built up the business and tried to raise the overall image of the industry through the creation of the National Solid Wastes Management Association.

During this same period, another family member, H. Wayne Huizenga, was given a chance to manage a small trash-hauling operation in Pompano Beach, Florida, after dropping out of college. By 1962 he had purchased a garbage-hauling route of his own and was aggressively seeking new customers. Eventually he began to buy out other hauling companies, and by the late 1960s his Southern Sanitation Service operated twenty trucks in Ft. Lauderdale, Miami, Tampa, and Key West.

In 1968 Buntrock, who had a vision of a nationwide sanitation company, brought together Ace, Southern Sanitation, and several other operations to form Waste Management Inc. Buntrock correctly perceived that rising concerns about air quality were making it more difficult for localities and businesses to engage in on-site trash burning, thus creating greater demand for hauling services. Waste Management, which went public in 1971, would satisfy that demand.

To make this possible, the company went on a shopping spree. Huizenga led the effort to acquire scores of hauling companies around the country—a process made more urgent when competitor Browning-Ferris Industries began doing the same thing. (Huizenga left the company in the early 1980s and went on to build the Blockbuster video rental chain.) In addition to amassing more than four hundred trash companies during the 1980s—including one of its largest competitors, SCA—Waste Management also entered specialized services, such as the removal of toxic and radioactive wastes and asbestos abatement, through the creation of Chemical Waste Management Inc.

Starting in the mid-1970s the company turned its sights to foreign garbage. In 1977 Waste Management received a $268-million contract from the government of Saudi Arabia to develop a modern sanitation system for the city of Riyadh. In the following years Waste Management International grew rapidly, winning municipal cleaning contracts in the Middle East, South America, and Australia. Between the new foreign and domestic markets, Waste Management's revenues grew at a torrid rate of some 25 percent a year during the 1980s. It became a billion-dollar company in 1983, only fifteen years after its founding.

Waste Management has long been an ardent proponent of burning trash to create energy. In 1985 it began operating a waste-to-energy facility in Tampa, Florida, and soon was developing similar projects in various parts of the country. In 1988 the company made a deal with the Henley Group in which Waste Management put its waste-to-energy operations in a company called Wheelabrator Technologies, in which Waste Management was given a 22-percent share (since increased to 55 percent). Other significant deals in the 1980s included the acquisition of the Port-O-Let portable sanitation company in 1985, the purchase of the Modulaire Industries mobile structures business in 1987, and the establishment of WMI Medical Services to operate medical waste incinerators.

As Waste Management expanded it collected controversy as well as trash. The company and many of its vast list of subsidiaries have been fined hundreds of times for illegal dumping and other violations of environmental regulations and frequently have been investigated for criminal charges like bribery and price-fixing.

Waste Management has paid out more than $20 million in fines and settlements of civil suits in connection with its Vickery, Ohio, hazardous-waste facility alone. In 1989 its subsidiary California Waste Management pleaded guilty in the largest criminal antitrust case in the state's history and paid a fine of $1 million. A fine of the same amount was paid in connection with price-fixing charges in Florida. Chemical Waste Management paid a $3.8-million penalty for improperly burning PCBs in Chicago, where it operates the largest toxic-waste incinerator in the country. In 1990 Waste Management paid $19.5 million to settle a civil antitrust lawsuit brought against the company and its competitor Browning-Ferris on behalf of some five hundred thousand customers across the country.

Although investors have not been overly concerned about Waste Management's less-than-sterling legal record, these problems have at times affected its business. In 1989 the company lost its contract to collect trash for the city of Chicago because executives of Waste Management subsidiary Ohio Waste Systems had been convicted of bid rigging. In most cases, however, the company manages to get its way by ensnaring its opponents in long, costly legal battles.

Yet Waste Management may have a harder time defending itself against a new kind of legal attack. In 1991 an environmental group in California filed suit against Chemical Waste Management, charging that the company had engaged in racial discrimination by deciding to build the state's first commercial toxic-waste incinerator in a minority area. The suit alleged that this was part of a nationwide practice—which some have dubbed environmental racism—of locating hazardous-waste facilities near communities that are poor and populated predominantly by people of color.

Waste Management has tried to improve its image through substantial contributions to the more conservative environmental organizations. One of these groups, the National Wildlife Federation, invited Waste Management chief executive Dean Buntrock to join its board of directors. The company in turn invited the head of the World Wildlife Fund to become a director. More militant environmental organizations have remained ardent foes of Waste Management. In 1987 Greenpeace dumped half a ton of horse manure outside the building where the company's annual meeting was being held and put up a banner reading WASTE MANAGEMENT STINKS.

Waste Management also has sought to look better by putting more emphasis on its recycling activities. In the late 1980s the company's Recycle America subsidiary became the nation's largest recycling operation. The company also has formed recycling joint ventures with Stone Container and American National Can.

In recent years Waste Management has continued to widen its international reach. A major push was made in Europe, where Waste Management began operations in Denmark, Germany, Italy, Spain, and Sweden. Other foreign activities were initiated in China and New Zealand. In 1990 the company was chosen by the government of Hong Kong to construct and operate a $125-million chemical waste processing and disposal system.

OPERATIONS

Solid Waste (52 percent of 1991 revenues). The company provides solid-waste management and related services to customers in forty-eight states, the District of Columbia, Puerto Rico, and five Canadian provinces. It has nearly one million commercial and industrial customers for its solid-waste collection services, which are provided to more than 12 million homes and apartment units as well, usually through contracts with local governments. The company operates more than seventy transfer stations, where solid waste is received from collection vehicles and compacted in large trailers for transportation to disposal or resource recovery sites.

This segment also includes the company's recycling and resource recovery businesses. Its Recycle America and Recycle Canada programs are the largest recycling operations in North America. In 1991 the company collected about 1.8 million tons of recyclable materials from some 4 million households in 600 communities. For the trash that cannot be recycled, Waste Management operates 130 solid-waste sanitary landfill facilities.

Hazardous Waste (18 percent of revenues). This segment consists of chemical- and radioactive-waste management services and site remediation, as well as asbestos abatement services. These activities are carried out through Chemical Waste Management Inc. (76-percent owned by Waste Management Inc.), which makes use of seven approved hazardous-waste disposal sites. Radio-active-waste services are conducted by its subsidiaries Chem-Nuclear Systems and Chem-Nuclear Environmental Services. The company operates one of the three licensed low-level radioactive waste disposal facilities in the country, located in Barnwell, South Carolina. In 1991 the company announced plans to build a $100-million facility to handle toxic and radioactive materials in order to participate in the $50-billion cleanup of the federal government's Hanford Nuclear Reservation in the state of Washington.

International Environmental Services (14 percent of revenues). Through Waste Management International the company provides solid-waste collection to more than 150,000 commercial and industrial customers in eight European countries as well as in Argentina, Australia, New Zealand, Saudi Arabia, and Venezuela. It also provides recycling services in Europe, Australia, and New Zealand. The company operates about forty solid-waste sanitary landfills in Europe and one each in Australia, Argentina, and Saudi Arabia. Waste Management also provides city cleaning services in Buenos Aires and Jeddah, Saudi Arabia. The company offers hazardous-waste collection, treatment, and disposal services in Italy, Denmark, and the Netherlands; in Sweden and Germany it offers collection and storage services for chemical waste. In 1990 the company received a contract to operate a comprehensive hazardous-waste treatment facility in Hong Kong. Twenty percent of Waste Management International was sold to the public in 1992.

Energy, Environmental, and Industrial Projects (16 percent of revenues). Through Wheelabrator Technologies (58-percent owned by Waste Management) the company is a leading developer and operator of trash-to-energy projects in the United States. It currently burns waste to produce energy at 14 locations, processing garbage from more than 400 communities. The company also develops and operates small power projects, which either cogenerate electricity and thermal energy or generate electricity alone for sale to utilities. Wheelabrator also develops water treatment projects and air pollution control systems.

TOP EXECUTIVES
- Dean L. Buntrock, chairman and chief executive
- Phillip B. Rooney, president and chief operating officer
- Jerry E. Dempsey, chairman of Chemical Waste Management
- David P. Payne, senior vice president
- Harold Gershowitz, senior vice president

OUTSIDE DIRECTORS
- Howard H. Baker, Jr., senior partner with the law firm Baker Worthington Crossley Stansberry & Woolf, former U.S. senator, and former White House chief of staff
- Kathryn S. Fuller, chief executive of the World Wildlife Fund
- Lee L. Morgan, former chairman of Caterpillar Inc.
- Peer Pedersen, chairman of the law firm Pedersen & Houpt
- James R. Peterson, former chief executive of the Parker Pen Company

- Alexander B. Trowbridge, president of the consulting firm Trowbridge Partners and former president of the National Association of Manufacturers

The board also includes Donald F. Flynn, former senior vice president of Waste Management and currently president of Flynn Financial Corporation; and Peter H. Huizenga, former vice president of Waste Management and currently president of Huizenga Capital Management.

FINANCIAL DATA

Revenues (in millions of dollars)

1991	7,551
1990	6,034
1989	4,414
1988	3,528
1987	2,729

Net Income (in millions of dollars)

1991	606
1990	685
1989	562
1988	464
1987	327

GEOGRAPHICAL BREAKDOWN

Revenues (in millions of dollars)

Year	United States		Foreign	
1991	6,251	(83%)	1,300	(17%)
1990	5,078	(84%)	957	(16%)
1989	3,916	(89%)	498	(11%)

LABOR RELATIONS

Of the company's 18,970 nonmanagerial and nonadministrative employees engaged in solid-waste services in North America, some 5,490, or 29 percent, are represented by unions. In Chemical Waste Management's operations the comparable percentage is 14 percent. The main union the company deals with is the Teamsters.

ENVIRONMENTAL RECORD

All of the company's activities have a profound effect on the environment. In addition to the record outlined earlier, Waste Management has had problems involving air and water contamination at many of its facilities. One of the most dangerous of the sites is in Emelle, Alabama, the largest hazardous-waste landfill in the country. The company was fined $600,000 in connection with improper storage of PCBs at Emelle, and aquifers below the site have been found to be contaminated with dioxin and other toxic substances. In 1990 a chemical reaction at the facility caused a cloud of toxic fumes to float over nearby homes. While Waste Management likes to think of the Emelle site, located in a rural area whose residents are mostly poor and black, as the "Cadillac of landfills," a local prosecutor has called it "America's biggest pay toilet."

The company has been named as a potentially responsible party at more than a hundred Superfund sites.

BIBLIOGRAPHY

Crooks, Harold. *Dirty Business: The Inside Story of the New Garbage Agglomerates*. Toronto: James Lorimer, 1983.

Goldman, Benjamin A., James A. Hulme, and Cameron Gordon. *Hazardous Waste Management: Reducing the Risk*. Washington, D.C.: Island, 1986.

Waste Management, Inc.: A Corporate Profile. Falls Church, Va.: Citizens Clearinghouse for Hazardous Wastes, 1988.

Waste Management, Inc.: An Encyclopedia of Environmental Crimes and Other Misdeeds. Chicago: Greenpeace USA, 1991.

WHIRLPOOL CORPORATION

2000 M-63
Benton Harbor, Michigan 49022
(616) 926-5000

1991 revenues: $6.8 billion
1991 net income: $170 million
Publicly traded company
Employees: 37,900
Founded: 1911

OVERVIEW

Whirlpool, which used to content itself making washing machines sold under the store brands in the Sears, Roebuck chain, has developed global ambitions. The company has made a string of acquisitions in Canada and Europe and entered into joint ventures in such countries as India and Mexico. Today Whirlpool products are manufactured in eleven countries and marketed in more than ninety.

This international focus has allowed the company to cushion the impact of the slump in white goods sales in its home country in recent years. The company sees more promise, for example, in the third world, for which it has developed a low-cost washer to try to lure people away from traditional, hand-washing practices. Following the 1991 buyout of its European joint venture partner, Philips, Whirlpool is now the world's leading producer of major appliances.

HISTORY

Whirlpool began with the 1911 founding of the Upton Machine Company in St. Joseph, Michigan. The firm, established by brothers Fred and Lou Upton and their uncle Emory Upton, set out to produce electric motor–drive wringer washing machines. The company struggled until 1916, when Sears, Roebuck began purchasing their washers—which, like all laundry machines of the time, were fairly primitive. By 1924 the company had become the retail giant's sole supplier for the devices.

The Uptons merged in 1929 with the Nineteen Hundred Washer Company of Binghamton, New York. The combined company, by now the leading washing machine manufacturer, took the name Nineteen Hundred Corporation. The ongoing relationship with Sears brought steady growth, although during World War II the company's facilities were converted for military production.

It was in the early postwar years that the company took off. In 1947 it introduced the first automatic washer, nicknamed the "Jeep." A much bigger success was a machine introduced the following year under the Whirlpool brand—so much so that in 1950 the company renamed itself after the product. That same year, Whirlpool Corporation, which was now selling directly to consumers as well as supplying Sears with machines sold under the Kenmore name, added its first automatic dryer.

In 1951 Whirlpool merged with Clyde Porcelain Steel. That firm's Clyde, Ohio, factory was converted to washer production and eventually became the world's largest washing machine plant. Whirlpool took over another company, Motor Products Corporation, and used its facilities in Marion, Ohio, for dryer production. Also in 1955, Whirlpool merged with the Seeger Refrigerator Company of St. Paul, Minnesota, and bought the Estate range and air-conditioning divisions of RCA. A year later the company, now a full-range appliance maker, brought out its first full line of RCA Whirlpool products. The RCA name was used until 1967.

Whirlpool continued to expand its manufacturing capacity, both through the purchase of existing plants (such as the one-million-square-foot Norge factory in Fort Smith, Arkansas) and the construction of its first totally new facility in Findlay, Ohio. The company also began to invest abroad, taking equity positions in appliance firms in Brazil and Canada.

During the late 1980s the company purchased the upscale KitchenAid division of Hobart Corporation from Dart & Kraft, cabinet maker St. Charles Manufacturing Company (later sold), and the dishwasher and trash compactor business of Emerson Electric. As a result of a bidding war with General Electric for range maker Roper Corporation, Whirlpool ended up with the right to use the Roper name. Whirlpool also moved into Italy with the acquisition of cooling compressor manufacturer Aspera and formed joint ventures in India and Mexico. A joint venture also was formed with Japan's Matsushita Electric to produce vacuum cleaners for the North American market. Canadian appliance maker Inglis Ltd., in which Whirlpool first took an equity position in 1969, became a wholly owned subsidiary in 1990.

Most important, in 1989 Whirlpool spent $361 million to purchase 53 percent of a joint venture consisting of the appliance operations of the Dutch electrical giant Philips. This arrangement, which gave Whirlpool such major brands as Bauknecht and Philips, put the company in a strong position in

Europe, although it was still behind Sweden's Electrolux. In 1991 Whirlpool solidified its European position by spending $610 million to buy out Philips. Whirlpool thus made itself the world's largest maker of major appliances and situated itself to challenge Electrolux on a global basis.

Whirlpool is putting special emphasis on the third world, where it is cultivating markets with products like its low-cost "world washer," made in Brazil, Mexico, and India. Overseas markets in general are attractive to Whirlpool, given the slow growth and stiff competition at home.

OPERATIONS

The company sells white goods in the United States under the brand names Whirlpool, KitchenAid, Roper, and Estate. Major foreign brands include Inglis in Canada and Philips, Whirlpool, Bauknecht, and Ignis in the rest of the world. The company has ten manufacturing facilities in the United States, three in Canada, six in Italy, three in Germany, and one each in France, Argentina, Mexico, Spain, and Sweden. Whirlpool has equity interests in several appliance manufacturers in Brazil and one in Mexico. In 1991 Whirlpool formed a joint venture with the Czech company Tatramat AS to manufacture and sell washing machines and other appliances in Czechoslovakia.

Home Laundry Appliances (34 percent of 1991 revenues). In addition to seventy years of supplying laundry appliances to Sears, Roebuck, which are sold under the retailer's brand name, Kenmore, Whirlpool markets washers and dryers under its own brand names.

Home Refrigeration and Room Air-Conditioning Equipment (34 percent of revenues). This segment includes refrigerator-freezers, room air conditioners (for which Whirlpool has been a major supplier to Sears), dehumidifiers, and ice makers.

Other Home Appliances (28 percent of revenues). Included in this segment are dishwashers, ranges, ovens, microwave ovens, trash compactors, and other appliances and components.

Financial Services (3 percent of revenues). This segment consists of inventory financing services for dealers and distributors, end-user financing services for retail sales by dealers, and several other forms of financing.

TOP EXECUTIVES

- David R. Whitwam, chairman, president, and chief executive
- James R. Samartini, executive vice president
- Robert I. Frey, executive vice president
- William D. Marohn, executive vice president
- Michael J. Callahan, executive vice president

OUTSIDE DIRECTORS

- Victor A. Bonomo, former executive vice president of PepsiCo
- Robert A. Burnett, chairman of Meredith Corporation
- Douglas D. Danforth, chief executive of Pittsburgh Pirates Baseball Club
- Allan D. Gilmour, executive vice president of Ford Motor Company
- Miles L. Marsh, president of Pet Inc.
- Philip L. Smith, chairman of Golden Cat Corporation
- Paul G. Stern, chief executive of Northern Telecom
- Janice D. Stoney, executive vice president of US West
- Kenneth J. Whalen, former executive vice president of AT&T

FINANCIAL DATA

Revenues (in millions of dollars)

1991	6,770
1990	6,613
1989	6,274
1988	4,413
1987	4,198

Net Income (in millions of dollars)

1991	170
1990	72
1989	187
1988	94
1987	192

GEOGRAPHICAL BREAKDOWN

Revenues (in millions of dollars)

Year	North America		Elsewhere	
1991	4,236	(63%)	2,540	(37%)
1990	4,165	(63%)	2,456	(37%)
1989	4,116	(65%)	2,169	(35%)

Operating profit (in millions of dollars)

Year	North America		Elsewhere	
1991	326	(80%)	83	(20%)
1990	277	(79%)	73	(21%)
1989	311	(75%)	101	(25%)

LABOR RELATIONS

Whirlpool's U.S. operations are extensively unionized, the major unions being the Allied Industrial Workers, the United Auto Workers, the International Union of Electronic Workers, and the International Association of Machinists. Yet relations between the company and the unions have often been rocky.

In 1990 the Allied Industrial Workers launched a boycott of the company to protest its unilateral implementation of a concessionary contract at its Fort Smith, Arkansas, plant. The union also was unhappy about what it said was a company policy of moving work to nonunion facilities, including *maquiladora* factories on the Mexican border.

The company has pressured other local unions in the United States to accept contract concessions, in one case using strikebreakers to defeat a walkout by one group of workers who resisted the givebacks.

ENVIRONMENTAL RECORD

Whirlpool was cited in 1990 by the Michigan Department of Natural Resources for failure to comply with hazardous-waste regulations. The charge was that the company had not followed procedures for closure of an interim hazardous-waste storage facility.

Along with the rest of the refrigeration industry, Whirlpool is required under federal law and international treaties to begin phasing out the use of CFCs in its products. In order to comply with the requirements, the company invested $55 million in 1989 to begin upgrading its refrigeration facility in Evansville, Indiana, to permit the adoption of alternative substances. The company also has begun to require technicians to capture and contain CFCs during the servicing of machines, a requirement that was extended to independent service operations in 1991. CFCs gathered in this manner are then reprocessed for new use.

APPENDIXES

The following lists provide some key quantitative measures of the companies profiled in *World Class Business*. The rankings are mostly self-explanatory, but a few items do need to be pointed out.

The reason why there are more than one hundred companies in the lists has to do with the Japanese conglomerates Mitsubishi and Sumitomo. In the text they are lumped together under the single headings of Mitsubishi Group and Sumitomo Group. The various companies in these groups are closely allied enough to be analyzed together, but they do report separate financial results, so the main affiliates of the two groups are listed individually here. The trading arms of these groups have enormous revenues and thus end up at the top of the revenues list, even though they do not actually produce anything.

There is also a complication regarding the South Korean *chaebol* conglomerates. The companies in these groups (Daewoo, Hyundai, Lucky-Goldstar, and Samsung) are more closely tied to one another than are those in the Japanese groups. Yet only Daewoo discloses full consolidated results for the group, so those figures are given in the following lists. The others report full results only for individual firms, so their main affiliates are the ones listed.

The final point about groups has to do with what in the text are called the Baby Bells—the offshoots of the breakup of AT&T. Because of their common origin and their similar development since becoming independent, they are profiled in a single chapter. But they definitely are autonomous companies, so their financial results are listed individually here.

Where there were ties in the lists, the ranks were determined by considering more decimal places than those presented. When there was no difference at all, the companies were given the same ranking.

Companies Ranked by Revenues (in millions of dollars)

1.	Sumitomo Corp.	142,381	44. Fujitsu	21,134
2.	Mitsubishi Corp.	140,030	45. Daewoo Group	21,088
3.	General Motors	123,056	46. United Technologies	20,840
4.	Royal Dutch/Shell	108,597	47. Mitsubishi Motors	19,899
5.	Exxon	104,271	48. Eastman Kodak	19,419
6.	Ford Motor	88,286	49. Dow Chemical	18,807
7.	Toyota Motor	71,596	50. McDonnell Douglas	18,448
8.	IBM	64,792	51. Mitsubishi Heavy	18,246
9.	AT&T	63,089	52. BCE	17,208
10.	Daimler-Benz	62,713	53. Ciba-Geigy	15,538
11.	British Petroleum	60,970	54. Grand Metropolitan	15,317
12.	General Electric	60,236	55. RJR Nabisco	14,989
13.	Mobil	56,910	56. Citicorp	14,750
14.	Hitachi	55,028	57. Hewlett-Packard	14,494
15.	Fiat	50,570	58. BellSouth	14,446
16.	Volkswagen	50,373	59. Electrolux	14,276
17.	Philip Morris	48,064	60. Bridgestone	14,134
18.	Matsushita Electric	46,937	61. Thomson	13,760
19.	Siemens	43,901	62. 3M	13,340
20.	Nissan Motor	42,425	63. NYNEX	13,229
21.	Unilever	40,767	64. Michelin	13,059
22.	Elf Aquitaine	38,740	65. AMR	12,887
23.	Du Pont	38,031	66. International Paper	12,703
24.	Chevron	37,386	67. Johnson & Johnson	12,447
25.	Nestlé	37,218	68. Bell Atlantic	12,280
26.	Sumitomo Bank	35,291	69. Time Warner	12,021
27.	Dai-Ichi Kangyo Bank	34,996	70. Broken Hill	11,877
28.	Toshiba	33,395	71. Coca-Cola	11,572
29.	Philips Electronics	33,384	72. Motorola	11,341
30.	Hoechst	31,146	73. Bristol-Myers Squibb	11,159
31.	Alcatel Alsthom	30,907	74. Goodyear Tire	10,907
32.	Mitsubishi Bank	30,879	75. Ameritech	10,818
33.	BASF	30,776	76. US West	10,577
34.	Honda Motor	30,594	77. Sandoz	9,910
35.	Boeing	29,314	78. Pacific Telesis	9,895
36.	ABB	28,883	79. Southwestern Bell	9,332
37.	Deutsche Bank	28,316	80. RTZ	9,133
38.	Bayer	27,987	81. Sumitomo Chemical	8,696
39.	Proctor & Gamble	27,026	82. British Airways	8,632
40.	NEC	26,806	83. Merck	8,603
41.	Sony	25,722	84. Roche Holding	8,442
42.	Mitsubishi Electric	23,586	85. News Corp.	8,409
43.	Imperial Chemical	23,346	86. Sumitomo Metal	8,228

87. Bertelsmann	7,995	99. Seagram	5,278
88. Sumitomo Electric	7,921	100. Levi Strauss	4,903
89. Waste Management	7,551	101. Goldstar	4,854
90. Hyundai Motor	7,388	102. Cable & Wireless	4,534
91. Nomura Securities	6,942	103. Sumitomo Heavy	3,307
92. Samsung Electronics	6,889	104. Kyocera	3,280
93. Whirlpool	6,770	105. Reuters Holdings	2,743
94. McDonald's	6,695	106. Dow Jones	1,725
95. Apple Computer	6,309	107. Fanuc	1,313
96. Colgate-Palmolive	6,060	108. CS Holding	408
97. SAS	5,833		
98. Glaxo Holdings	5,516	TOTAL	2,899,225

Note: Anglo American is not included in the revenue list become it does not disclose its revenues.

Companies Ranked by Net Income (in millions of dollars)

1. Exxon	5,600	26. 3M	1,154
2. Royal Dutch/Shell	4,492	27. BCE	1,150
3. Toyota Motor	3,134	28. Broken Hill	1,115
4. Philip Morris	3,006	29. Roche Holding	1,093
5. General Electric	2,636	30. Siemens	1,078
6. Merck	2,122	31. Southwestern Bell	1,076
7. Bristol-Myers Squibb	2,056	32. Sumitomo Bank	1,028
8. Unilever	2,030	33. Pacific Telesis	1,015
9. Mobil	1,920	34. Imperial Chemical	1,013
10. Elf Aquitaine	1,891	35. Fiat	971
11. Matsushita Electric	1,841	36. Ciba-Geigy	944
12. Nestlé	1,821	37. Dow Chemical	935
13. Procter & Gamble	1,773	38. Deutsche Bank	931
14. Hitachi	1,637	39. Hoechst	896
15. Coca-Cola	1,618	40. Nomura Securities	874
16. Boeing	1,567	41. Cable & Wireless	862
17. Glaxo Holdings	1,481	42. McDonald's	860
18. BellSouth	1,472	43. Toshiba	860
19. Johnson & Johnson	1,461	44. Sony	832
20. Du Pont	1,403	45. Sandoz	821
21. Chevron	1,293	46. Grand Metropolitan	756
22. Daimler-Benz	1,282	47. Hewlett-Packard	755
23. Bayer	1,223	48. Volkswagen	735
24. Alcatel Alsthom	1,193	49. Seagram	727
25. Ameritech	1,166	50. Mitsubishi Bank	725

51.	British Petroleum	716	84.	Whirlpool	170
52.	Philips Electronics	704	85.	British Airways	166
53.	Mitsubishi Heavy	689	86.	Sumitomo Chemical	161
54.	BASF	686	87.	Colgate-Palmolive	125
55.	Dai-Ichi Kangyo Bank	652	88.	Daewoo Group	122
56.	ABB	609	89.	Goodyear Tire	97
57.	Waste Management	606	90.	Samsung Electronics	90
58.	NYNEX	601	91.	Dow Jones	72
59.	Fujitsu	588	92.	Hyundai Motor	71
60.	RTZ	576	93.	Electrolux	68
61.	Mitsubishi Electric	567	94.	Bridgestone	60
62.	US West	553	95.	Sumitomo Heavy	43
63.	Honda Motor	542	96.	Goldstar	25
64.	AT&T	522	97.	Eastman Kodak	17
65.	Anglo American	513			
66.	Mitsubishi Corp.	464		**TOTAL PROFITS**	**90,534**
67.	Motorola	454			
68.	Reuters Holdings	429	98.	Time Warner	−99
69.	McDonnell Douglas	423	99.	Thomson	−136
70.	NEC	387	100.	Michelin	−196
71.	RJR Nabisco	368	101.	SAS	−221
72.	Levi Strauss	357	102.	Bell Atlantic	−223
73.	Nissan Motor	347	103.	AMR	−240
74.	Sumitomo Metal	339	104.	News Corp.	−301
75.	Sumitomo Corp.	335	105.	Citicorp	−457
76.	Apple Computer	310	106.	United Technologies	−1,021
77.	Bertelsmann	298	107.	Ford Motor	−2,258
78.	Fanuc	268	108.	IBM	−2,827
79.	Kyocera	229	109.	General Motors	−4,453
80.	Sumitomo Electric	225			
81.	CS Holding	198		**TOTAL LOSSES**	**12,432**
82.	International Paper	184			
83.	Mitsubishi Motors	184		**TOTAL NET INCOME**	**78,102**

Note: Since SAS does not report net income, the figure given above is for pretax profits.

Companies Ranked by Number of Employees

1.	General Motors	756,300	6.	AT&T	317,000
2.	Siemens	402,000	7.	Hitachi	309,757
3.	Daimler-Benz	379,252	8.	Anglo American	300,000
4.	IBM	344,396	9.	Unilever	292,000
5.	Ford Motor	332,700	10.	Fiat	287,957

11.	General Electric	284,000	57.	NYNEX	83,900
12.	Volkswagen	260,137	58.	Johnson & Johnson	82,700
13.	Philips Electronics	240,000	59.	Bell Atlantic	75,700
14.	ABB	214,399	60.	Ameritech	73,967
15.	Matsushita Electric	210,848	61.	RTZ	73,495
16.	Alcatel Alsthom	205,500	62.	Deutsche Bank	71,400
17.	Nestlé	201,139	63.	International Paper	70,500
18.	United Technologies	185,100	64.	Mobil	67,500
19.	Hoechst	179,332	65.	US West	65,829
20.	McDonald's	168,000	66.	Waste Management	64,000
21.	Philip Morris	166,000	67.	Pacific Telesis	62,236
22.	Bayer	164,200	68.	Dow Chemical	62,200
23.	Toshiba	162,000	69.	Southwestern Bell	61,200
24.	Boeing	159,100	70.	RJR Nabisco	56,000
25.	Fujitsu	145,872	71.	Roche Holding	55,134
26.	Nissan Motor	138,326	72.	Chevron	55,123
27.	Electrolux	134,229	73.	British Airways	54,427
28.	Eastman Kodak	133,200	74.	Bristol-Myers Squibb	53,500
29.	Du Pont	133,000	75.	Sandoz	53,400
30.	Royal Dutch/Shell	133,000	76.	Broken Hill	51,000
31.	Michelin	131,976	77.	Bertelsmann	45,110
32.	BASF	129,434	78.	Samsung Electronics	45,000
33.	Imperial Chemical	128,600	79.	Mitsubishi Heavy	44,272
34.	BCE	124,000	80.	CS Holding	44,153
35.	Grand Metropolitan	122,178	81.	Glaxo Holdings	43,384
36.	NEC	117,994	82.	Hyundai Motor	41,700
37.	AMR	116,300	83.	Time Warner	41,000
38.	British Petroleum	115,250	84.	Cable & Wireless	39,426
39.	Sony	112,900	85.	SAS	38,940
40.	McDonnell Douglas	109,123	86.	News Corp.	38,400
41.	Thomson	105,460	87.	Whirlpool	37,900
42.	Toyota Motor	102,423	88.	Merck	37,700
43.	Motorola	102,000	89.	Levi Strauss	32,100
44.	Exxon	101,000	90.	Goldstar	32,000
45.	Goodyear Tire	99,952	91.	Coca-Cola	28,900
46.	Mitsubishi Electric	97,002	92.	Mitsubishi Motors	25,515
47.	BellSouth	96,084	93.	Colgate-Palmolive	24,900
48.	Bridgestone	95,276	94.	Sumitomo Metal	19,817
49.	Procter & Gamble	94,000	95.	Dai-Ichi Kangyo	18,640
50.	Daewoo Group	92,000	96.	Seagram	16,800
51.	Ciba-Geigy	91,665	97.	Sumitomo Bank	16,669
52.	Hewlett-Packard	89,000	98.	Nomura Securities	16,600
53.	3M	88,477	99.	Sumitomo Chemical	14,546
54.	Elf Aquitaine	86,900	100.	Apple Computer	14,432
55.	Citicorp	86,000	101.	Sumitomo Electric	14,348
56.	Honda Motor	85,500	102.	Kyocera	14,031

103.	Mitsubishi Bank	13,899	108.	Sumitomo Corp.	6,363
104.	Reuters Holdings	10,335	109.	Fanuc	2,041
105.	Dow Jones	9,459			
106.	Mitsubishi Corp.	9,429		TOTAL	12,196,758
107.	Sumitomo Heavy	6,500			

Note: Since Anglo American does not disclose the number of its employees, the figure given above is an estimate.

Companies Listed by Year of Founding

Note: The dates in this list are the earliest year for a major portion or direct descendant of the company.

1.	Ciba-Geigy	1758	30.	Chevron	1879
2.	Du Pont	1802	31.	BCE	1880
3.	Colgate-Palmolive	1806		Eastman Kodak	1880
4.	Citicorp	1812	33.	Daimler-Benz	1882
5.	Bertelsmann	1835		Dow Jones	1882
6.	Procter & Gamble	1837	35.	ABB	1883
7.	Philip Morris	1847	36.	Mitsubishi Heavy	1884
	Siemens	1847	37.	Broken Hill	1885
9.	Reuters Holdings	1851		Unilever	1885
10.	Levi Strauss	1853	39.	Sandoz	1886
11.	CS Holding	1856	40.	Johnson & Johnson	1887
12.	Bristol-Myers Squibb	1858	41.	Royal Dutch/Shell	1890
13.	BASF	1861	42.	Merck	1891
14.	Bayer	1863		Philips Electronics	1891
	Exxon	1863	44.	Coca-Cola	1892
	Hoechst	1863	45.	Thomson	1893
	Michelin	1863	46.	Roche Holding	1894
18.	Mobil	1866	47.	Sumitomo Bank	1895
	Nestlé	1866	48.	Dow Chemical	1897
20.	Deutsche Bank	1870		Sumitomo Metal	1897
	Mitsubishi Corp.	1870	50.	Alcatel Alsthom	1898
22.	Cable & Wireless	1872		Goodyear Tire	1898
23.	Dai-Ichi Kangyo Bank	1873		International Paper	1898
	Glaxo Holdings	1873		NEC	1898
	RTZ	1873	54.	Fiat	1899
26.	RJR Nabisco	1875	55.	Electrolux	1901
	Toshiba	1875	56.	3M	1902
28.	AT&T	1877	57.	Ford Motor	1903
29.	General Electric	1878	58.	General Motors	1908

59.	British Petroleum	1909	85. Fujitsu	1935
60.	Hitachi	1910	86. Toyota Motor	1937
	IBM	1910	Volkswagen	1937
62.	Whirlpool	1911	88. Hewlett-Packard	1939
63.	Boeing	1916	89. Elf Aquitaine	1941
64.	Anglo American	1917	90. Honda Motor	1946
65.	Matsushita Electric	1918	SAS	1946
66.	Mitsubishi Bank	1919	Sony	1946
	Sumitomo Corp.	1919	93. Fanuc	1955
68.	McDonnell Douglas	1920	McDonald's	1955
	Sumitomo Electric	1920	95. Goldstar	1958
70.	Mitsubishi Electric	1921	96. Kyocera	1959
71.	Time Warner	1922	97. Daewoo Group	1967
72.	News Corporation	1923	Hyundai Motor	1967
73.	British Airways	1924	99. Waste Management	1968
	Seagram	1924	100. Samsung Electronics	1969
75.	Nomura Securities	1925	101. Mitsubishi Motors	1970
	Sumitomo Chemical	1925	102. Apple Computer	1976
	United Technologies	1925	103. Ameritech	1984
78.	Imperial Chemical	1926	Bell Atlantic	1984
79.	Motorola	1928	BellSouth	1984
80.	AMR	1930	NYNEX	1984
81.	Bridgestone	1931	Pacific Telesis	1984
82.	Nissan Motor	1933	Southwestern Bell	1984
83.	Grand Metropolitan	1934	US West	1984
	Sumitomo Heavy	1934		

Companies Listed by Headquarters Country

Distribution

Australia	2
Britain	10
Canada	2
France	4
Germany	8
Italy	1
Japan	16
Netherlands	3
South Africa	1
South Korea	4
Sweden	2
Switzerland	6
United States	43
Dual country*	2

*Both Royal Dutch/Shell and Unilever have dual headquarters in Britain and the Netherlands.

Australia

Broken Hill Proprietary
News Corporation

Britain

British Airways
British Petroleum
Cable & Wireless
Glaxo Holdings
Grand Metropolitan
Imperial Chemical
Reuters Holdings
Royal Dutch/Shell Group
RTZ
Unilever

Canada

BCE
Seagram

France

Alcatel Alsthom
Elf Aquitaine
Michelin
Thomson

Germany

BASF
Bayer
Bertelsmann
Daimler-Benz
Deutsche Bank
Hoechst
Siemens
Volkswagen

Italy

Fiat

Japan

Bridgestone
Dai-Ichi Kangyo Bank
Fanuc
Fujitsu
Hitachi
Honda Motor
Kyocera
Matsushita Electric
Mitsubishi Group
NEC
Nissan Motor
Nomura Securities
Sony
Sumitomo Group
Toshiba
Toyota Motor

Netherlands

Philips Electronics
Royal Dutch/Shell Group
Unilever

South Africa

Anglo American

South Korea

Daewoo Group
Hyundai Group
Lucky-Goldstar Group
Samsung Group

Sweden

Electrolux
SAS

Switzerland

ABB
Ciba-Geigy
CS Holding
Nestlé
Roche Holding
Sandoz

United States

AMR
Apple Computer
AT&T
Baby Bells
  Ameritech
  Bell Atlantic
  BellSouth
  NYNEX
  Pacific Telesis
  Southwestern Bell
  US West
Boeing
Bristol-Myers Squibb
Chevron
Citicorp
Coca-Cola
Colgate-Palmolive
Dow Chemical
Dow Jones
Du Pont
Eastman Kodak
Exxon

Ford Motor
General Electric
General Motors
Goodyear Tire & Rubber
Hewlett-Packard
International Business Machines
International Paper
Johnson & Johnson
Levi Strauss
McDonald's
McDonnell Douglas
Merck
Mobil
Motorola
Philip Morris
Procter & Gamble
RJR Nabisco
3M
Time Warner
United Technologies
Waste Management
Whirlpool

Companies Listed by Industry

This list covers the major activities of the *World Class Business* companies. Many of the firms are listed in several categories.

Aerospace and Military

Boeing
Daewoo Group
Daimler-Benz
General Electric
General Motors
McDonnell Douglas
Mitsubishi Group
Nissan Motor
Thomson
United Technologies

Airlines

AMR
British Airways
SAS

Appliances

Electrolux
General Electric
Lucky-Goldstar Group
Matsushita Electric
Philips Electronics
Thomson
Toshiba
Whirlpool

Automobiles

Daewoo Group
Daimler-Benz
Fiat
Ford Motor
General Motors
Honda Motor
Hyundai Group
Mitsubishi Group
Nissan Motor
Toyota Motor
Volkswagen

Broadcasting and Cable Television

General Electric
News Corporation
Time Warner

Chemicals

BASF
Bayer
British Petroleum
Chevron
Ciba-Geigy
Dow Chemical
Du Pont
Eastman Kodak
Elf Aquitaine
Exxon
Hoechst
Imperial Chemical
Lucky-Goldstar Group
Mobil
Royal Dutch/Shell Group
Samsung Group
Sandoz
Sumitomo Group
3M
Unilever

Clothing

Levi Strauss

Computers

Apple Computer
AT&T
Daewoo Group
Fujitsu
Hewlett-Packard
Hitachi
IBM
Lucky-Goldstar Group
Matsushita Electric
NEC
Philips Electronics
Siemens
Sony
Toshiba

Construction

Daewoo Group

Consumer Electronics

Daewoo Group
Hitachi
Lucky-Goldstar Group
Matsushita Electric
Mitsubishi Group
NEC
Philips Electronics
Samsung Group
Sony
Thomson
Toshiba

Data-Processing Services

General Motors
IBM

Electrical Equipment

ABB ASEA Brown
  Boveri
Alcatel Alsthom
Daimler-Benz
General Electric
Hitachi
Mitsubishi Group
Philips Electronics
Siemens
Sumitomo Group
Toshiba
United Technologies

Electronic Components

Fujitsu
General Motors
Hewlett-Packard
Hyundai Group
IBM
Kyocera
Lucky-Goldstar Group
Matsushita Electric
Mitsubishi Group
Motorola
NEC
Philips Electronics
Samsung Group
Siemens
Sony
Sumitomo Group
Toshiba

Factory Automation

ABB
Daimler-Benz
Fanuc
General Electric
McDonnell Douglas
NEC
Siemens
Toyota Motor

Filmed Entertainment

Matsushita Electric
News Corporation
Sony
Time Warner

Financial Services

AT&T
Citicorp
CS Holding
Dai-Ichi Kangyo Bank
Deutsche Bank
Ford Motor
General Electric
General Motors
Mitsubishi Group
Nomura Securities
Sumitomo Group

Food and Beverages

Coca-Cola
Grand Metropolitan
Nestlé
Philip Morris
Procter & Gamble
RJR Nabisco
Seagram
Unilever

Forest Products

International Paper

Information Services

Dow Jones
Reuters Holdings

Medical Equipment and Supplies

Bristol-Myers Squibb
General Electric
Hewlett-Packard
Johnson & Johnson
Philips Electronics
Siemens
Sumitomo Group
3M
Toshiba

Mining

Anglo American
Broken Hill Proprietary
Du Pont
Royal Dutch/Shell Group
RTZ

Oil and Gas

BASF
British Petroleum
Broken Hill Proprietary
Chevron
Du Pont
Elf Aquitaine
Exxon
Lucky-Goldstar Group
Mobil
Royal Dutch/Shell Group
Samsung Group

Personal-Care and Household Products

Bristol-Myers Squibb
Colgate-Palmolive
Eastman Kodak
Johnson & Johnson
Procter & Gamble
Unilever

Pharmaceuticals

BASF
Bayer
Bristol-Myers Squibb
Ciba-Geigy
Eastman Kodak
Elf Aquitaine
Glaxo Holdings
Hoechst
Imperial Chemical
Johnson & Johnson
Lucky-Goldstar Group
Merck
Roche Holding
Sandoz

Photographic Products

Bayer
Eastman Kodak
International Paper
3M

Publishing

Bertelsmann
Dow Jones
Matsushita Electric
News Corporation
Time Warner

Recorded Music

Bertelsmann
Matsushita Electric
Philips Electronics
Sony
Time Warner

Restaurants

Grand Metropolitan
McDonald's

Rubber Products

Bridgestone
Goodyear Tire & Rubber
Michelin

Shipbuilding

Hyundai Group
Samsung Group
Sumitomo Group

Special Materials

Kyocera
3M

Steel

Broken Hill Proprietary
Sumitomo Group

Telecommunications Equipment

Alcatel Alsthom
BCE
Fujitsu
Matsushita Electric
Mitsubishi Group
Motorola
NEC
Philips Electronics
Samsung Group
Siemens
Toshiba

Telecommunications Services

AT&T
Baby Bells
BCE
Cable & Wireless

Textiles

BASF
Du Pont
Hoechst

Tobacco

Philip Morris
RJR Nabisco

Transportation and Construction Equipment

ABB
Fiat
Mitsubishi Group
Siemens

Waste Disposal

Waste Management

Wholesale Trade

Daewoo Group
Hyundai Group
Mitsubishi Group
Sumitomo Group

INDEX

Note: This is an index of names—of companies, individuals, products, unions, and other organizations. The company names appear in shortened form (without Inc., Ltd., etc.), except where a fuller title is necessary for clarity. The index does not cover the bibliographies or the appendixes.

717

732 · Index